Disaggregation

Problems in manufacturing and service organizations

Edited by

LARRY P. RITZMAN
LEE J. KRAJEWSKI
WILLIAM L. BERRY
STEPHEN H. GOODMAN
STANLEY T. HARDY
LAWRENCE D. VITT

Production and Operations Management Area
Faculty of Management Sciences
College of Administrative Science
The Ohio State University

Springer-Science+Business Media, B.V.

Originally published by L. Ritzman, L. Krajewski, W. Berry, S. Goodman, S. Hardy, and L. Vitt 1979
MyCopy version of the original edition 1979

Library of Congress Cataloging in Publication Data

Main entry under title:

Disaggregation, problems in manufacturing and service organizations.
Papers presented at a conference held at Ohio State University in March 1977.
1. Industrial management–Mathematical models–Congresses. 2. Operations research–Congresses. I. Ritzman, Larry P.
HD29.D57 658.4'033 78-31953

DOI 10.1007/978-94-015-7636-9
www.springer.com/mycopy

Foreword

This volume is intended to expand the dialogue and interest among both practitioners and academicians in a problem area worthy of attention by all. The concept of disaggregation admits to our current inability to solve many types of interrelated hierarchical problems simultaneously. It offers instead a sequential, iterative process as a workable and necessary procedure. The papers in this volume are selected from those presented at a Disaggregation Conference held in March, 1977 at The Ohio State University. We heartily applaud all those who participated in the conference and particularly appreciate the cooperation of those authors whose work is published in this collection.

Part A contains four papers which define the various dimensions of disaggregation. The paper by Martin Starr, which was the text of his luncheon address at the conference, provides several interesting perspectives to the problem. Although disaggregation suggests tearing apart, as Professor Starr illustrates with his butterfly example, it also suggests a putting together or a synthesis which recognizes interrelationships and dependencies. The next paper by Lee Krajewski and Larry Ritzman offers a general model of disaggregation for both the manufacturing and service sectors. After reading the papers in this section, as well as the papers in subsequent sections, you will identify other dimensions to hierarchical decision making which go beyond this generalized model. One of the important findings of the conference is that the 'disaggregation problem' exists in a wide variety of organizational settings and no universal definition yet exists which completely captures all of its dimensions.

Part B deals with various facets of disaggregation in the manufacturing sector. Section 3 considers hierarchical production and inventory planning systems. In each paper presented, the total problem is broken down into subproblems which are then solved in such a way as to recognize linkages between them. These procedures are heuristic in nature, even though optimizing techniques are often a part of them. Section 4, on the other hand, consists of papers more appropriately classified as optimization procedures. Decomposition, reflection programming and direct procedures with a column generation technique are proposed. The process of disaggregation in the manufacturing sector usually begins with a development of an overall production plan which is translated into a master production schedule. Section 5 is devoted to this upper level of disaggregation, whereas Section 6 considers the lower levels which must be linked to the master schedule. This section includes such topics as lot sizes for manufactured and purchased parts, safety stocks, priorities for open orders and scheduling procedures.

Part C deals with disaggregation in the service sector. Most of the papers in these sections are grouped by application area rather than methodology. Section 7 examines several levels of disaggregation for telephone, mail and transportation services. Section 8 considers such defense and public areas as Navy manpower planning, energy R and D policies, and blood supply systems. Section 9 deals with the three levels of disaggregation in emergency and health services. Two papers relate to police patrols, one to fire departments, five to nursing staff schedules, and one with hospital bed allocations. Finally, Section 10 concentrates on the second level of disaggregation in the service sector, which is often referred to as 'shift scheduling'. The methodologies proposed have been applied to food service operations on military bases, bank encoders, toll collectors and urban emergency service staffs.

The papers in this collection demonstrate that considerable progress has been made on disaggregation and that multilevel, hierarchical problems are quite prevalent. The search for theories, concepts and methodologies which accommodate more realistic views of managerial problems has intensified. However, the readings also raise questions which have yet to be fully resolved. How can we better address individual components or levels within a system, while assuring satisfactory performance for the system in its totality? What coordinating or linking mechanisms must be developed between subproblems and levels? Can disaggregation principles and techniques be transferred among a wider range of problem settings? We believe that a careful reading of these papers will uncover still other levels of new inquiry.

Co-editors:

Larry P. Ritzman
Lee J. Krajewski
William L. Berry
Stephen H. Goodman
Stanley T. Hardy
Lawrence D. Vitt

The Ohio State University
Columbus, Ohio
March, 1978

Contents

Contributors to the volume

N. R. ADAM, Assistant Professor, Graduate School of Business Administration, Rutgers University, Newark, New Jersey.

J. R. BIGGS, Assistant Professor, Department of Management, Bowling Green State University, Bowling Green, Ohio.

D. A. BIRD, Instructor of Management Sciences, University of Missouri-St. Louis, St. Louis, Missouri.

G. R. BITRAN, Assistant Professor, Sloan School of Management, Massachusetts Institute of Technology, Cambridge, Massachusetts.

J. J. BROWNE, Supervisor of Management Engineering Services, Port Authority of N.Y. and N.J., Jersey City, New Jersey.

J. M. BURNHAM, Professor of Business Administration, Tennessee Technological University, Cookeville, Tennessee.

R. C. CARLSON, Associate Professor of Industrial Engineering and Engineering Management, Stanford University, Stanford, California.

N. W. CHLOSTA, Manager, Operations Statistics Branch, U.S. Postal Service, Washington, D.C.

S. C. CHONG, Assistant Professor of Industrial Engineering and Management, North Dakota State University, Fargo, North Dakota.

D. A. COLLIER, Assistant Professor, Graduate School of Business Administration, Duke University, Durham, North Carolina.

M. J. COSGROVE, Customer Services Administrator, GTE Service Corporation, Stamford, Connecticut.

R. D'ALESSIO, Senior Management Analyst, U.S. Department of Housing and Urban Development, Washington, D.C.

P. P. DARUKHANAVALA, Management Science Specialist, The Standard Oil Company (Ohio), Cleveland, Ohio.

W. S. DEMMY, Assistant Professor, Department of Administrative Science and Finance, Wright State University, Dayton, Ohio.

B. T. DOSHI, Assistant Professor of Statistics, Rutgers University, New Brunswick, New Jersey.

A. R. V. ELLENRIEDER, Professor of Engineering, University of Sao Paulo, Sao Paulo, Brazil.

B. H. ELLIOTT, Systems Engineer, Armco Steel Corporation, Middletown, Ohio.

A. O. ESOGBUE, Professor, School of Industrial and Systems Engineering, Georgia Institute of Technology, Atlanta, Georgia 30332.

H. GABBAY, Citibank, N. A. and New York University, New York, New York.

J. W. GAVETT, Associate Professor, Graduate School of Management, University of Rochester, Rochester, New York.

R. J. GIGLIO, Professor of Industrial Engineering and Operations Research, University of Massachusetts, Amherst, Massachusetts.

B. E. GILLETT, Professor of Computer Science, University of Missouri, Rolla, Missouri.

S. H. GOODMAN, Assistant Professor, Faculty of Management Sciences, The Ohio State University, Columbus, Ohio.

W. L. GORR, Associate Professor of Public Administration and Management Sciences, The Ohio State University, Columbus, Ohio.

J. N. D. GUPTA, General Manager, Information Technology Division, U.S. Postal Service, Washington, D.C.

R. W. HAESSLER, Associate Professor, Graduate School of Business, University of Michigan, Ann Arbor, Michigan.

C. K. HAHN, Professor of Management, Bowling Green State University, Bowling Green, Ohio.

R. W. HALL, Associate Professor of Operations Management, Indiana University, Indianapolis, Indiana.

A. W. HAMMOOD, Consultant in Statistics and Operations Research, Office of the Chief of Naval Operations, Department of the Navy, Washington, D.C.

A. C. HAX, Professor, Sloan School of Management, Massachusetts Institute of Technology, Cambridge, Massachusetts.

J. C. HENDERSON, Assistant Professor, Faculty of Management Sciences, The Ohio State University, Columbus, Ohio.

C. M. JONES, Assistant Professor of Engineering Management, University of Alaska, Juneau, Alaska.

J. G. JOHNSON, Department of Mathematics and Computer Science, Shippensburg State College, Shippensburg, Pennsylvania.

U. S. KARMARKAR, Assistant Professor, Graduate School of Business, University of Chicago, Chicago, Illinois.

K. E. KENDALL, Assistant Professor of Business Administration, University of Wisconsin-Milwaukee, Milwaukee, Wisconsin.

D. F. KOCAOGLU, Associate Professor of Industrial Engineering, University of Pittsburg, Pittsburg, Pennsylvania.

L. J. KRAJEWSKI, Professor of Management Sciences, The Ohio State University, Columbus, Ohio.

G. H. KRAUSS, Research Scientist, Battelle Pacific Northwest Laboratories, Richland, Washington.

D. H. KROPP, Assistant Professor of Decision Sciences, Northwestern University, Evanston, Illinois.

A. W. LAI, Associate Professor, Department of Administrative Science and Finance, Wright State University, Dayton, Ohio.

L. S. LASDON, Professor, Departments of General Business and Mechanical Engineering, University of Texas, Austin, Texas.

R. K. LEHTO, Special Assistant for Enlisted Force Analysis, Bureau of Naval Personnel, Department of the Navy, Washington, D.C.

V. A. MABERT, Associate Professor, Department of Management, Bowling Green State University, Bowling Green, Ohio.

P. M. MANGIAMELI, Assistant Professor, Department of Management Science, University of Rhode Island, Kingston, Rhode Island.

H. E. MILLER, Union Carbide Corporation, Bound Brook, New Jersey.

J. G. MILLER, Associate Professor, Harvard Business School, Boston, Massachusetts.

L. E. MILLER, Department of Computer Science, Bowling Green State University, Bowling Green, Ohio.

S. MORITO, Assistant Professor of Operations Research, Case Western Reserve University, Cleveland, Ohio.

S. M. NAZEM, Associate Professor of Decision Sciences, University of Nebraska at Omaha, Omaha, Nebraska.

C. C. PEGELS, Associate Professor of Management, State University of New York at Buffalo, Buffalo, New York.

L. C. PEPPERS, Associate Professor of Economics, Creighton University, Omaha, Nebraska.

W. P. PIERSKALLA, Professor at Northwestern University, Evanston, Illinois.

L. P. RITZMAN, Professor and Chairman of Management Sciences, The Ohio State University, Columbus, Ohio.

H. M. SALKIN, Associate Professor of Operations Research, Case Western Reserve University, Cleveland, Ohio.

J. P. SEAGLE, Associate Professor, School of Business, State University of New York at Albany, Albany, New York.

S. M. SEWARD, Associate Professor, University of Wyoming, Cheyenne, Wyoming.

M. J. SHOWALTER, Assistant Professor, School of Business, University of Wisconsin – Madison, Madison, Wisconsin.

A. J. SINGH, Chief, Management Sciences Program, Evaluation Service, Veterans Administration Hospital, Los Angeles, California.

L. D. SMITH, Assistant Professor of Management Science, University of Missouri – St. Louis, St. Louis, Missouri.

M. K. STARR, Professor, Graduate School of Business, Columbia University, New York, New York.

J. SURKIS, Associate Professor, Graduate School of Business Administration, Rutgers University, Newark, New Jersey.

A. Z. SZENDROVITS, Professor of Production and Management Science, McMaster University, Hamilton, Ontario, Canada.

J. TALAVAGE, Associate Professor of Industrial Engineering, Purdue University, West Lafayette, Indiana.

R. C. TERJUNG, Section Manager of Systems Research, Department 450B, Goodyear Tire and Rubber Company, 1144 East Market Street, Akron, Ohio 44316.

R. K. TIBREWALA, Associate Professor of Management, New York Institute of Technology, Old Westbury, New York.

L. D. VITT, Associate Professor, Faculty of Management Sciences, The Ohio State University, Columbus, Ohio.

T. E. VOLLMANN, Professor, Graduate School of Business, Indiana University, Bloomington, Indiana.

G. O. WESOLOWSKY, Associate Professor of Management Science, McMaster University, Hamilton, Ontario, Canada.

A. WIGGINS, Assistant Director of Nursing, The Jewish Hospital of St. Louis, St. Louis, Missouri.

H. B. WOLFE, Senior Staff Member, Arthur D. Little, Inc., Cambridge, Massachusetts.

Part A. Introduction

Section 1. General perspectives

1. Perspectives on disaggregation

MARTIN K. STARR

Abstract

While doing research for this paper, I used the standard literature search which consists of looking up 'Aggregate' in the dictionary. My eye wandered to the entry above and I read 'to make worse, to exasperate; annoy'. And thus was born the slogan 'Aggregation is preceded by Aggravation.'

I thought, if that is so, then disaggregation should be preceded by pleasure. When I remarked on this twist of logic to a learned colleague, I was told that Anna Freud had observed that children take pleasure in taking things (e.g., butterflies) apart. She went on to point out that children are criticized for this taking apart, and consequently grow up resisting the powerful learning experience of thoughtful disassembly.

1.1. Planned disaggregation versus hit or miss techniques

Perhaps for this reason, recognition that *planned* disaggregation is an essential part of the architecture of decision making is only recent. Instead, there is a long history of individuals (striving for an acceptable future state of the system) disaggregating their decision systems on a 'hit or miss' basis.

Once, when my secretary went on vacation, the temporary replacement, Helen, was told that I carry a heavy load of work. She obtained two typewriters and started a letter in each, hoping in this way to increase her productivity. Her disaggregation of my work load did not lead to synergism (where the action of two or more components can achieve an effect of which each component is individually incapable). On the contrary, it led to the opposite of synergism, which is called antagonism. Literally, running between typewriters she got very little work done. The next day, she quit in frustration. From this experience, I generalized my Helen of Troy model. The essence of the model is that while you do not know what will come out of the Trojan Horse, it probably will not be anything good. The secretary's Trojan Horse was an emotional, hit-or-miss, plan for disaggregation.

The energy system has always been managed on a hit-or-miss disaggregation basis. The results speak for themselves. Part of the problem of using planned aggregation techniques, in this case, is the fact that such planning produces a dilemma. On the one hand, even well-planned inter-industry activity runs afoul of the anti-trust acts. On the other hand, government regulation is considered anathema by industry which has ample evidence that regulation is seldom based on a well-planned model. Now, there is an opportunity to show that a properly disaggregated system can lead to a sequence of decisions that will insure a sufficient supply of energy for the country's future well-being.

1.2. Principles for disaggregation

The need for intelligent, *planned* disaggregation is great. Unfortunately, it is not easy to achieve. The principles for excellence in disaggregation are not yet well understood. (Perhaps, Anna Freud explained why this is so.) Certainly, there isn't a conspiracy against well-planned disaggregation, but there may be some ingrained blocks that prevent the effectiveness of intuition.

A number of years ago I wrote a book subtitled *Systems and Synthesis* [1]. My aim was to recognize the respective roles of analysis and synthesis. Both proper analysis and adequate synthesis are needed for planned disaggregation. Thus, from the Preface:

'To understand the spirit of this book, it is essential to recognize the relationship of systems analysis to systems synthesis. The distinction between analysis and synthesis is neither esoteric nor academic. Analytic behavior follows what might be called *principles of disassembly*. It exists in terms of operations that involve division, dissection, classification, separation, partitioning and segmentation. Using analysis we take the production system apart. We study the pieces and attempt to improve them. Then we reassemble, hoping for a better system. But, because of interactions and dependencies among the parts, often the reassembled production function will not be improved. It may even be impaired.

Knowledge of the principles of synthesis is required to put things together in a measurably *satisfactory* way. To achieve this objective, it can be necessary to modify analytic results. Synthesizing behavior should be viewed as a set of *conditions for reassembly* involving operations of summation, integration, unification, combination, amalgamation; i.e., in general, the *gestalt* point of view. (Gestalt occurs with the recognition of organized totalities, such as 'man,' rather than the cataloging of distinct parts, such as cells, muscles, heart and brain.)'

Analysis and synthesis opportunities exist for improving both rail and air transportation; also, communication (which is a potential substitute for transportation); education, health care, police and fire protection, consumer product quality assurance, postal services and many other vital to life components that determine the individual's quality of life. The tax bite for that present quality of life is a gross overcharge.

Not to be forgotten is industrial productivity which conditions the cost of living. Within the profit-making sector, much wasteful behavior is charged to the consumer's bill. A good share of this waste can be eliminated. A lot of waiting in lines and being caught in traffic can be eliminated. But this will not happen until there is general recognition of the fact that because problems are too complex or because they are dynamic is not a reason to say there is no solution, or to say we will carve the big problem up into small, tractable problems which we will analyze but never synthesize. The disaggregation concept provides both analysis and synthesis. In the process, some highly creative, counter-intuitive solutions will appear. We have past the point where subsystems can be treated as independent entities. Disaggregation of the problem begins with aggregate, interdependent solutions for the large and complex system.

In the 1300's, William of Occam, a Franciscan friar set down the Principle of Parsimony which called for the simplest explanation that satisfies observations. In the 1970's this was called common sense which as Stuart Chase noted 'tells us that the world is flat.' Occam's Razor (as the Principle of Parsimony was known) was rejected by Henry Adams who wrote in 1913 'simplicity is the most deceitful mistress of all' while studying the complex cathedrals at Mont-Saint-Michel and Chartres [2]. The disaggregation concept is not simple – but it simplifies. I feel certain that Occam (a monk in his monastery) and Adams (an intellectual in his cathedral) would agree that disaggregation is a unifying concept with which they both can agree.

1.3. Disaggregation because of complexity (static)

If a problem has many parts or components, then we disaggregate that problem in order to resolve its complexity. First, we use analysis, which means subdividing the problem, and then we study the subproblems. We provide solutions to the subproblems. Next comes synthesis. We try to put together the new policies and procedures derived from the solutions to the subproblems.

We evaluate our results. Does the new system perform: 1) as well as we had hoped?, 2) better than before?, 3) as best it can? It is not difficult to answer the first question, but it is uncertain how useful that answer is. In a start up situation, we cannot answer the second question. The third question is the critical question. Have we performed an optimal analysis/synthesis? Have we created an optimal disaggregation model?

There are some well known problems that have been solved by optimizing the behavior of the total system subject to constraints. Thus, the multi-item inventory system does not disaggregate the problem into each item's economic order quantity. Instead, it uses the square root of each item's dollar volume divided by the sum of the square roots of all items' dollar volumes. This is used as a critical ratio for determining order quantities subject to constraints on total dollars available for inventory investment. The point to be noted is that the critical parameter of the total system is the sum of the square roots of all subsystems. It is a complex measure that does not lent itself to intuition, either in application or in derivation.

Another disaggregation model of a complex system is involved in the design of the components of a rocket. If we analyze the guidance system, the re-entry nose cone, the propulsion system, etc. and design the optimal component in each case, then the synthesis of the components is not optimal at all. The bird won't fly. So we go back to the drawing board.

This time we start with a rocket that works poorly, and we improve its performance iteratively. We change one component and then another. On every occasion that there is improved performance (overall) we retain the design change in the component and test it in combination with modifications of other components. Ultimately, most (if not all) of the components will be underdesigned, but the total system performance will have been the best found in the series of experiments. This type of improvement algorithm is similar in concept to Craft [3], which is used for obtaining a satisfying layout; or the combinatorial strategy inventor which has been used to improve product and package design [4].

1.4. Disaggregation because of insufficient lead time (dynamic)

There are dynamic decision problems which lead to disaggregation. These have been made a central focus of this conference. The character of such processes is that it takes time to bring about a desired configuration for the system. Consequently, such decisions must be based on forecasts. When all the relevant data are on hand, it is too late to alter the system's configuration.

Thus, when the manager is ready to sequence work on hand or provide a detailed work schedule, decisions concerning kind and amount of facilities, size of workforce and inventory levels cannot be made. These are decisions that must have been made many months before.

We observe that these early decisions are made with the realization that a variety of actual, detailed futures can occur. Thus, in a real sense, the 1st level aggregate decision is a flexible plan which is intended to produce a near optimal result for a great range of 3rd level situations. As in Figure 1, the performance response surface is assumed to be quite flat in the neighborhood of the various demand combinations that are anticipated. We recognize that 1st and 2nd level early decisions reflect many attributes that we often associate with contingency planning. This relationship should be explored.

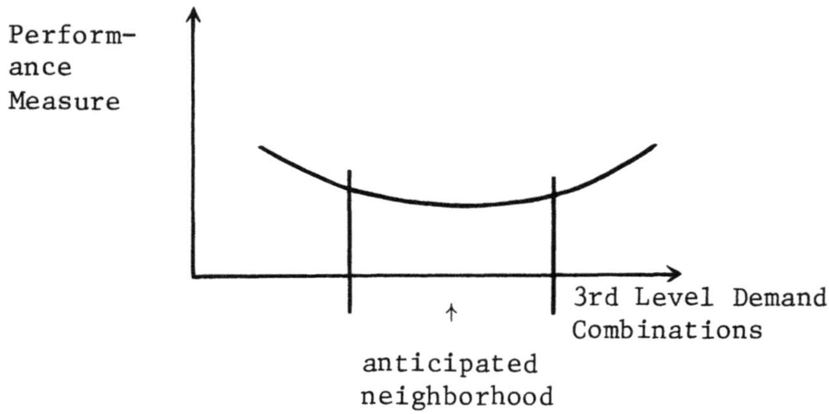

Figure 1

There is a clear hierarchical ordering of the sequential decisions that must be made, which is based on the lead time required to design and achieve the system's configuration at a specific future time. That is the way in which the aggregate production scheduling problem is resolved. That is the way in which the aggregate manpower planning problem is resolved.

But the question remains as to which techniques should be used at the first and second levels, so that performance at the third level is as good as possible. A reasonable approach to this problem is to work backwards. Thus, with all the data *on hand* concerning manufacturing jobs that have been done or services that have been performed, it is possible to compare the forecasts with the actual events. It is also possible to determine what would have been the optimal 1st level and 2nd level decisions. These a posteriori results can then be compared to the aggregate 1st level decisions and shop loading or shift scheduling (2nd level) decisions that might have been arrived at by using alternative disaggregation models.

Two other important questions can be resolved by working backwards. First, how long should the planning horizons be between the temporally disaggregated decisions? Second, how often should the plans be up-dated? Hopefully, by studying what could have been (after the facts are in) we can improve our disaggregation methodology.

1.4.1. System size and specificity

Because of lead time requirements, there is a natural hierarchy for production scheduling and manpower planning decisions. It should be noted that we are working with system's *dimensions* concerning capacity, resources, etc., and details reflecting the actual jobs and work requirements. In Figure 2 below, a relationship between the size of the system (i.e., dimension) and the specificity level of the decision process (i.e., detail) is hypothesized. Essentially it says that if the system is large, then the level of detail tends to be low and vice versa. However, the point ⓧ is considered the ideal level of both dimension and detail for problem resolution. The manager using disaggregation achieves a high order of both dimension and detail by following the natural decision sequence 1 → 2 → 3.

Similar reasoning can be applied to many problems where planned disaggregation would be of great benefit. Thus, if there is a psychological distrust for disaggregated decision processes, the study and generalization of the disaggregation process will help to alleviate the somewhat academic penchant for the purity of overall, simultaneous optimization. This conference goes a long way in that direction.

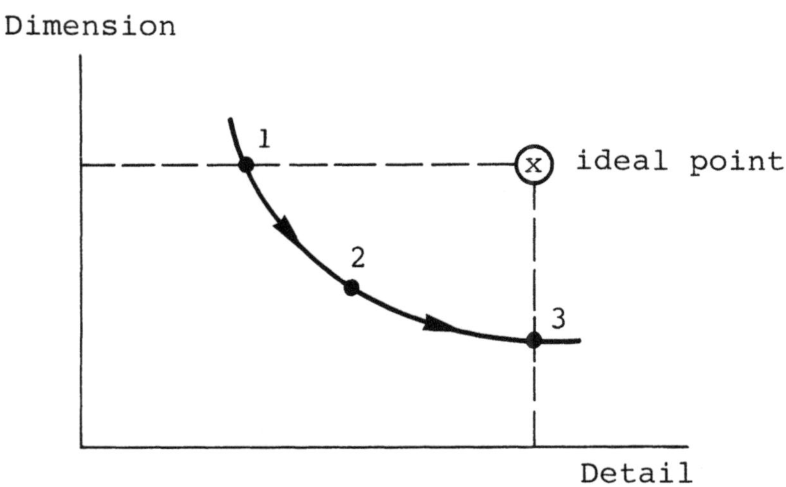

Figure 2

References

1. Starr, Martin K., *Production Management: Systems and Synthesis*, 2nd edn. (Englewood Cliffs, New Jersey: Prentice-Hall, Inc., 1972).
2. Adams, Henry, *Mont-Saint-Michel and Chartres* (New York: Houghton-Mifflin Co., 1905).
3. Developed by G. C. Armour and E. S. Buffa, see Buffa, Elwood S., *Basic Production Management* (New York: John Wiley & Sons, 1971), pp. 289–298.
4. Starr, Martin K. and Greenwood, Leonard H., 'Generation of Decision Alternatives with Multiple Criteria Evaluation' (forthcoming) in *Multiple Criteria Decision Making*, North-Holland/TIMS Studies in the Management Sciences (Amsterdam: North-Holland Publishing Company).

2. Disaggregation in manufacturing and service organizations: survey of problems and research

LEE J. KRAJEWSKI and LARRY P. RITZMAN

Abstract

This paper addresses a class of problems, referred to as 'disaggregation problems,' which lie between aggregate planning at the top level and the more detailed decisions of inventory control and scheduling at the bottom level. Most real-world problems are sufficiently complex to warrant a sequential or top-down approach to problem solving. However, researchers have paid scant attention to disaggregation until very recently. The resulting lack of an interfacing mechanism diminishes the utility of solution procedures for aggregate planning, inventory control, and scheduling. In order to draw attention to this gap, a taxonomy of disaggregation problems is developed for both manufacturing and service organizations. The purpose is to identify and classify problems, describe representative research, and identify unresolved issues.

2.1. Introduction

Considerable research during the last two decades has concentrated on aggregate production planning, inventory control, and scheduling. *Aggregate planning* procedures, which have been proposed for both manufacturing [3] and service organizations [55], [69], help determine monthly (or quarterly) output, inventory and manpower aggregates. *Inventory* and *scheduling* procedures, using the aggregate decisions as input, tend to focus on such short-term decisions as (i) the sizing and timing of production (purchase) orders for specific items, (ii) sequencing of individual jobs (orders), and (iii) short-term allocations of resources to individual activities and operations [5], [16], [21]. The total process of going from aggregate plans to more detailed plans can be called *disaggregation*. This paper attempts to

Reprinted by permission from *Decision Sciences*, vol. 8, no. 1, January 1977.

categorize representative research of specific disaggregation problems to demonstrate that, although much work has been done in the past, additional research in disaggregation is needed.

Disaggregation is an important issue in manufacturing as well as service organizations. Depending upon the nature of the production system, disaggregation decisions in a manufacturing organization may exist on one or more of the following three levels:

1. Given aggregate decisions on output and capacity, determine the timing and sizing of specific final product production quantities over the time horizon (sometimes referred to as a master schedule).
2. Given the timing and sizing of final product production quantities, determine the timing and sizing of manufactured (or purchased) component quantities.
3. Given the timing and sizing of component quantities, determine the short-term sequences and priorities of the jobs (orders) and the resource allocations to individual operations.

The taxonomy shown on the left side of Figure 1 provides the framework with which the three levels of disaggregation in manufacturing organizations are discussed in Section 3.

Disaggregation problems in service organizations possess the complicating characteristics of stringent response time requirements, time dependent demand rates, and no finished goods inventories to smooth production rates. Disaggregation decisions in service organizations also exist at three levels:

1. Given aggregate decisions on output and capacity, allocate man-

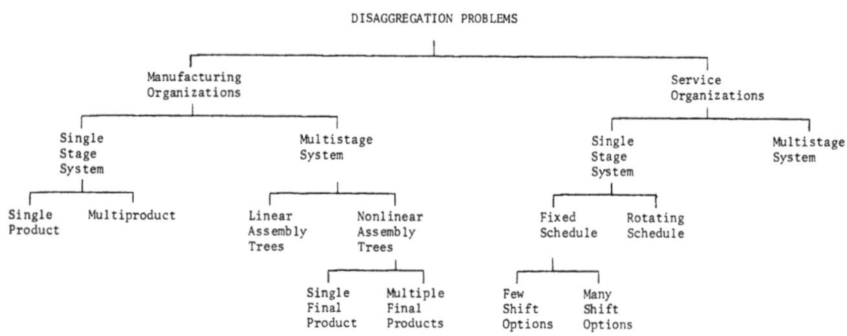

Figure 1. A taxonomy of disaggregation problems.

power and other resources to specific operations over the time horizon (sometimes referred to as the staff sizing problem).

2. Given the allocation of resources to specific operations, determine the shift schedules and crew assignments of employees.
3. Given the shift schedule assignments, determine short-term adaptations, reallocations between operations, and priorities of the service requirements.

The right half of Figure 1 provides a basis for describing disaggregation problems in Section 4. Although there is a certain degree of uniqueness in the structure of service sector disaggregation problems, Section 4 surveys research in a wide variety of organizational settings.

2.2. A general model

The definition of disaggregation in Section 1 for manufacturing and service organizations begs the question of uniqueness in problem structures. Although all levels of disaggregation decisions in a manufacturing organization cannot be made to look exactly like those in a service organization, disaggregation levels 1 and 2 in the manufacturing sector and disaggregation level 1 in the service sector bear remarkable similarity. In this section we present a general mathematical programming model which serves to demonstrate this similarity as well as provides a basic model with which to compare research reported in Sections 3 and 4. To facilitate later reference, the model presented below will be called GDM (General Disaggregate Model).

Optimize:

$$Z = \Psi(X_{it}, S_{it}, I_{it}, B_{it}, H_{jt}, O_{jt}, W_{jt}) \tag{1}$$

Subject to:

$$I_{i,t-1} - I_{it} + X_{i,t} + S_{it} - \sum_{\substack{k \in L \\ i \neq k}} \alpha_{ik} X_{k,t+l_k} + B_{it} - B_{i,t-1} = D_{it}$$

$$i \in L$$
$$t = 1, 2, \ldots, T \tag{2}$$

$$\sum_{m=1}^{l_i} (r_{imj}X_{i,t+m-1} + r'_{imj}\phi_{i,t+m-1}) = P_{ijt} \qquad (3)$$

$$i \in N_j, \quad j \in J, \quad t = 1, 2, \ldots, T$$

$$\sum_{i \in L} P_{ijt} - W_{jt} - O_{jt} \leqq 0 \qquad (4)$$

$$j \in J, \quad t = 1, 2, \ldots, T$$

$$W_{jt} - W_{j,t-1} - H_{jt} + F_{jt} = 0 \qquad (5)$$

$$j \in J, \quad t = 1, 2, \ldots, T$$

$$O_{jt} - \theta W_{jt} \leqq 0 \qquad j \in J, \quad t = 1, 2, \ldots, T \qquad (6)$$

$$\phi_{it} = \begin{cases} 1 \text{ if } X_{it} > 0 \\ 0 \text{ if } X_{it} = 0 \end{cases} \qquad i \in L, \quad t = 1, 2, \ldots, T \qquad (7)$$

where:

X_{it} = output of product (service) i in period t.
I_{it} = on hand inventory level of product i in period t (manufacturing setting only).
S_{it} = subcontracted output of product (service) i in period t.
D_{it} = market requirements for product (service) i in period t.
l_i = production (or procurement) lead time for product (service) i. In service settings l_i would normally equal 1 time period.
α_{ik} = the number of units of product i which are required for one unit of immediate parent product k. For final products the value of α_{ik} is zero for all i, k. (In service settings, the α_{ik} would be zero for all i, k).
B_{it} = amount of product (service) put on backorder in period t.
r_{imj} = number of manhours required per unit of product (service) i at operation j in the mth period since production started on i. (In service settings, r_{imj} is usually 0 or 1 for all i, m, j since output is normally measured in manhours.)
r'_{imj} = total setup time required by product i at operation j in the

m^{th} period since production started on i. (In service settings, r'_{imj} is zero for all i, m, j.)

ϕ_{it} = binary variable which assigns a setup time for product i whenever $X_{it} > 0$.

P_{ijt} = production output of product (service) i at operation j in period t, expressed in manhours.

W_{jt} = regular time manhours assigned to operation j in period t.

O_{jt} = overtime manhours assigned to operation j in period t.

H_{jt} = manhours of labor hired for operation j at the start of period t.

F_{jt} = manhours of labor released from operation j at the start of period t.

θ = proportion of the regular time workforce which can be used on overtime.

L = set of all products (services) to be controlled. In manufacturing settings, each raw material, component, subassembly, and final product has its own identity.

T = length of the planning horizon.

J = set of all operations where we assume there is only one type of skill at each operation.

N_j = set of all products (services) which require resources at operation j.

Although most of the constraints are self-explanatory, several need elaboration. Constraint (2) is the basic inventory identity relationship with the added feature of recognizing the demands placed on the inventory of product i by higher order components and subassemblies. In the service sector (2) merely identifies the amount of service i backordered in period t. Constraint (3) defines the production output of product (service) i at operation j in period t. For any given i and m, there is at most one j for which r_{imj} (or r'_{imj}) is greater than zero. Finally, (4) insures that the work planned for operation j in time period t does not exceed the manpower capacity planned for department j in period t. Although service sector variables such as X_{it}, B_{it}, and S_{it} are expressed in terms of manhours rather than units of product, GDM demonstrates the similarities in the two sectors. The X_{it} values determine the entire planned production schedule, from master schedule through component production, in a manufacturing setting. In a service setting these same values represent the planned output of each service. The W_{jt} values are the staff sizes at each operation. However, there are differences in emphasis between the two sectors. Level 1 disaggregation decisions in manufacturing organizations emphasize final product production schedules with manpower capacities to support these schedules. Level 1 disaggregation decisions in service organizations make the selection of manpower capacities paramount. In the manufacturing setting it is the X_{it} values for final products which are further disaggregated in level 2, whereas in the service sector the W_{jt} values become the inputs to level 2 disaggregation.[1] Sections 3 and 4 review representative research done to date in the manufacturing and service sectors respectively following GDM and the taxonomy in Figure 1.

2.3. Manufacturing organizations

Figure 1 shows that disaggregation problems in manufacturing organizations can be found in single stage as well as multistage production systems. Since single stage systems are really a special case of multistage systems, we begin with them.[2]

2.3.1. Single state systems

A single stage system consists of a single productive phase and stocking point. The complexity of disaggregation in this type of system depends upon the independence of the inventoried products.

Disaggregation in a single product, single stage environment is limited to level 1 and 2 decisions since level 3 decisions are trivial. Essentially, the problem is to determine production (or order) quantities, $X_{i,t-l_i}$, such that the annual costs of setup (ordering), holding inventory, and backorders (or stockouts) are minimized. With reference to GDM, L contains only one product, l_i is usually

1. Level 2 decisions in the service sector, shift scheduling, are not included in GDM because (i) it is not a major problem in most manufacturing settings, and (ii) the complexities imposed by a generalized shift scheduling structure in GDM would detract from its usefulness in relating to both the manufacturing and service-oriented literature.
2. A vast amount of literature has been written on the scheduling aspect of level 3 disaggregation decisions in manufacturing organizations. Because of space limitations we cannot begin to do justice to the topic. As such, we refer the reader to any one of a number of excellent references on this topic, not the least of which is [5].

deterministic, $\alpha_{ik} = 0$ for all i and k, and only constraint (2) is recognized.

Procedures for this problem mainly fall into the category of mathematical inventory theory.[3] Recently much attention has been focused on discrete lot sizing methods such as Wagner-Whitin's [34] dynamic version of the Economic Order Quantity (EOQ) model. A dynamic program is developed for determining discrete $X_{i,t-l_i}$ values where demand, inventory holding charges, and setup costs can vary over the planning horizon of T periods.

Presumed computational difficulties with Wagner-Whiten's model have led to a number of heuristic approaches. Gorham [14] discusses a method called Least Total Cost which steps through the product requirements accumulating a lot size until that future period t where the total cost of carrying the inventory through t equals the setup cost. Orlicky [28] presents the Periodic Order Quantity (POQ) and the Lot-for-Lot approaches. The POQ model is a variant of the EOQ model whereby the economic time interval between replenishment orders, τ, is determined by dividing the EOQ by $\Sigma_{t-1}^{T} D_{it}/T$. The order quantity, $X_{i,t-l_i}$, is the sum of D_{it} over the interval $[t, t + \tau]$. The Lot-for-Lot method simply makes the lot size equal to the demand each period, or $X_{i,t-l_i} = D_{it}$.

The importance of these single product, single stage methods is not that they solve a relatively simplified production planning problem.[4] They can also be applied to the much more complex multi-product, multi-stage level 2 decisions where total optimization is difficult, if not impossible, to achieve in practice.

Multiple products introduce the complexities of resource constraints and nontrivial level 3 disaggregation decisions. Most research on this problem is focused on level 1 decisions. Manne [24] computes economic lot sizes using linear programming. He assumes $l_i = 1$, $\alpha_{ik} = 0$ for all i, $B_{it} = S_{it} = 0$ for all i and t, J contains only one department and W_{jt} is predetermined for all t. A set S_i' of production sequences $s: \{X_{i1}, X_{i2}, \ldots, X_{iT}\}$ is specified *a priori* for each product i. The objective is to determine the fraction of the total

3. 't is not the purpose of this paper to provide yet another review of a topic which is already documented so well. In addition to the references cited below as well as many others, the reader can refer to [16] and [32] for reorder point systems and dynamic inventory models.
4. The lot sizing methods discussed in this section are not all inclusive. Other approaches have been proposed by [13], [29] for example. Berry [1] compares the performance of several of the commonly used lot size methods.

requirements for the i-th product to be supplied by the s-th alternative sequence of inputs, f_{is}, such that overtime expenditures are minimized. This results in a large scale programming model. Dzielinski and Gomory [9] followed by Lasdon and Terjung [23] apply decomposition methods to reduce the computational burden.

Whereas the above methods are optimizing, Winters [35] develops a heuristic procedure for determining specific values for X_{it} given an aggregate production constraint. The lot size for each product is computed and reorder points are determined. A priority function, consisting of the ratio of the reorder point to the expected end-of-period inventory level, is used to select the products to produce. The lot sizes of the high priority items are accumulated until they reach the aggregate production constraint.

A distinguishing feature of the work of Manne and Winters is that aggregate capacities are predetermined. Others, however, include aggregate capacity determination in the level 1 decision. Newson's [25] model is similar to GDM except that $\alpha_{ik} = 0$ for all i and k, $B_{it} = S_{it} = 0$ for all i and t, and $l_i = 1$. Wagner-Whitin's model is used to find X_{it} values that minimize setup, production and holding costs for each product i given (2) and (7). The values of P_{ijt} can now be computed using (3). These values are used in (4) and along with (5) and (6) the aggregate planning problem is solved. The dual prices in (4) are used to modify the Wagner-Whitin solution to further reduce total costs. The procedure iterates in this way until no further improvement is possible. O'Malley et al. [27] outline a procedure similar to Newson's except that the iterative aspect of modifying the X_{it}'s is not pursued. Zoller [37] first solves the aggregate planning problem and then disaggregates it to determine optimal individual sales quantities where the objective function is nonlinear.

Several studies attempt to link level 1 and level 3 decisions. Gelders and Kleindorfer [12] use a branch and bound technique. Given a set of jobs to perform in a one machine system, their due dates, and fixed regular time resources, the objective is to find the production schedule which minimizes total tardy and inventory holding costs as well as aggregate overtime costs. Green [15] and Shwimer [30] extend the system under study to include multiple machines and use heuristics to link aggregate production plans to detailed production schedules. Hax and Meal [19] develop a hierarchical planning system for a process manufacturing firm. Composed of a number of planning subsystems, their procedure disaggregates the aggregate plan to arrive at detailed schedules for each product. For other disaggregation studies in process manufacturing, refer to [10], [11], [20], [26].

Perhaps the most difficult disaggregation decisions in manufacturing occur in the multistage system where there are a number of production phases and stocking points. Production decisions for a given product (any inventoried item) can affect the production decisions of other inventoried products. The nature of this interaction depends upon how the final products are assembled.

A *linear assembly tree* is one in which for all $i \in L$, $\alpha_{ik} > 0$ for one and only $k \neq i$ and $\alpha_{ik} = 0$ for every other $i' \in L$, $i' \neq i$. Thus the objective is to determine the lot sizes X_{it} (level 2 disaggregation) at each of the production stages arranged serially given the final product demand pattern. Zangwill [36] represents this structure as a single source network and applies the theory of concave cost networks.[5] Taha and Skeith [31] allow for delay between production stages and back-orders for the final product. Their procedure assumes that lot sizes at any stage are an integer multiple of the lot sizes at the succeeding stage, an assumption later proved correct by Crowston et al. [8] under certain conditions.

A *nonlinear assembly tree* is more general than the linear assembly tree because $\alpha_{ik} > 0$ for each i and at least one $k \neq i$, and there may exist $i' \in L$, $i' \neq i$ such that $\alpha_{i'k} > 0$. Each inventoried product i can have more than one successor (parent) and each successor can have more than one predecessor. The literature can be categorized according to the number of final products considered.

An implicit assumption in this section is that the individual final products in a manufacturing organization can be analyzed independently of each other. Another assumption is that each product $i \in L$ can have only one parent k. Even with these simplifying assumptions the analysis is complex and often heuristic methods must be used. The work focuses on level 2 decisions.

Crowston et al. [6] discuss a case where the final product is sub-

5. A very complete reference to other studies along these lines can be found in Clark [4]. Even though reference is made to multi-echelon systems, some of the references relate to multistage systems as defined here.

ject to stochastic seasonal demands and demand forecast revisions can be made during the planning horizon. Dynamic programming formulations become unwieldly and heuristics must be used to find the X_{it} values if delivery of the final product must be made during the selling season.

In [8] Crowston et al. propose a dynamic programming model to determine the optimal lot sizes at each stage when demand is constant over an infinite horizon. A sequel to this study by Crowston et al. [7] demonstrates that heuristics models can do just about as well as the dynamic programming model with about one-fourth the computational effort. As evidenced by the introduction of heuristics, the problem can get complex; however, considerations for capacity limitations and multiple products are still absent.

Multiple final products and nonlinear assembly trees probably represent the largest set of practical disaggregation problems in existence. In [17] Haehling von Lanzenauer proposes a model similar to GDM to address the link between level 1 and level 2 decisions. In his model $l_i = 1$ and setup costs are ignored. The objective is to determine integer values for X_{it}, W_{jt} and O_{jt} such that contribution to profit is maximized. In [18] a bivalent linear programming model is presented for level 2 and 3 decisions.

One of the major shortcomings in normative models such as those proposed above is that problems of practical size are not yet computationally feasible. However, a descriptive methodology which has proven to be quite useful in practice for level 2 decisions is Material Requirements Planning (MRP).[6] In essence, MRP is a sophisticated information system and deterministic simulation model which takes the master schedule of final product production quantities from level 1 decisions and translates that schedule into the time-phased net requirements, as well as the planned timing and sizing of production lot releases, of each component required by the schedule over the planning horizon. Many of the single product, single stage lot sizing approaches discussed in Section A.1 can be used to determine the $X_{i,t-l_i}$ values for the components once net requirements are known. MRP has massive data processing capabilities and provides the information to plan material coverage and

6. See Orlicky [28] for an excellent presentation of MRP.

adjust open order priorities; this is a useful input to level 3 disaggregation decisions.[7]

In terms of the taxonomy in Figure 1, all manufacturing problems are special cases of the multiproduct, nonlinear assembly tree case. Many of the procedures and models discussed in the preceding sections can be applied to the more general case. However, there are some areas that need more research. Foremost is the need for a practical procedure for level 1 decisions, i.e., generating master schedules. Man-machine interaction models may be useful here. Another area is the specific timing, sizing and allocation of resources to operations discussed as part of level 3 decisions. In this respect a topic worthy of attention is the determination of the number of shifts to have in a particular manufacturing setting. Other research questions are discussed by Wagner [33].[8] As we shall see in the next section, similar gaps in the research exist for service sector organizations.

2.4. Service organizations

As mentioned in Section 1, disaggregation decisions in the service sector appear on three levels.[9] Level 1 decisions must recognize that manpower planning cannot rely on inventories to buffer operations from demand variability. If backorders are not acceptable, the only economical buffering mechanism is to systematically vary manpower levels over the horizon to meet demand. Although an aggregate plan may stipulate overall levels of manpower hires, overtime, and backorders, it is not sufficiently detailed as to short time periods and individual operations. Therefore level 1 disaggretation decisions must determine staff sizes for smaller time periods at each operation, within the overall constraints imposed by the aggregate plan.

The level 2 decisions assign employees to 2 or more alternate shift schedules, subject to the constraints of desired staff sizes deter-

7. Biggs [2] analyzes the interaction of lot sizing decisions and detailed schedules via simulation using MRP to determine the order releases.

8. See Krajewski [22] for research needs on the interface between level 2 and level 3 disaggregation decisions.

9. Due to space limitations, level 3 decisions are not considered further in this paper.

mined in the first level. A *shift* is the set of time periods during which an employee can be on duty during the day. A *shift schedule*, on the other hand, is the set of on-duty periods assigned to an employee over some total time horizon. A shift schedule always covers a time horizon longer than a shift; it can cover a full day, week, or many weeks, depending on the situation.

By their very nature, service sector disaggregation decisions must be judged in terms of many criteria and constraints. These include: (i) bounds imposed by the aggregate plan, (ii) service standards, (iii) wage costs, (iv) legal constraints (such as the Fair Labor Standards Act and safety regulations), (v) labor contracts, (vi) company policies, (vii) amount of departure from previous plans, (viii) administrative convenience, (ix) attitudinal differentials caused by transfers between operations, and (x) workload imbalances.

Since level 1 decisions on staff sizing are a necessary prelude to lower level disaggregation in any service setting, we treat them first before proceeding with the rest of the taxonomy in Figure 1. With respect to GDM, the best values of W_{jt} must be found where $\alpha_{ik} = 0$ for all i, $l_i = 1$, and $\phi_{it} = I_{it} = 0$ for all i, t.

Staff sizing procedures can be divided into two segments, depending on whether employees must be *permanently* assigned to a particular operation or whether there is flexibility to assign them to more than one operation over the time horizon.

Mathematical programming methods for determining W_{jt} include linear programming [53], [68], integer quadratic programming to minimize the least squares fit of manpower to workload [50], nonlinear programming to minimize the weighted sum of dollar and social costs [39], dynamic programming [54], and mixed integer quadratic programming using the projection technique of decomposition [70]. The time horizon of these models varies. Larson's model for patrol allocation is a 1-period model, whereas Vitt's model has an 84-period horizon so as to plan vacation schedules. Many of the models ignore probabilistic variations in demand,[10] with D_{it} presumably being increased judgmentally beyond its expected value to handle randomness.

10. Larson combines a multiserver queuing model with his dynamic programming algorithm to more adequately cope with randomness.

Since most disaggregation problems involve probabilistic variations[11] in D_{it}, queuing and simulation models can also be used to assess cost-service tradeoffs. Such models help identify W_{jt} values which are sufficiently large so that the probability of a customer being delayed by more than α units of time does not exceed a threshold probability β. Although some single-server queuing models have been proposed, multi-server queuing models are normally more appropriate [44], [49], [54], [63]. When demands for service are spatially disbursed and the server must travel to the customer, supplementary models have been developed to relate service time to staff levels, D_{it} values, and geographical characteristics [56]. Simulation models have also been applied, particularly when mean arrival rates are time dependent, queue disciplines are not first-come-first-served, equipment capacities must be recognized, and multistage systems are encountered [57] [61].

Employee assignments can be systematically varied from one operation to another in some problems. In addition to a basic nursing staff assigned to a hospital floor (operation) Wolfe and Young [71] propose allocating nurses to a 'float pool' operation which in turn is assigned to other operations to handle short-term fluctuations in workloads. This concept has been successfully implemented [59], although the impact on employee attitudes has not been fully ascertained [65]. Ignoring such behavioral considerations, Abernathy et al. [38] apply a simulation model to demonstrate that a sufficiently large float pool can yield significant economies. Other examples of variable assignment staffing, using a variety of solution procedures, can be found in police departments [44], fire departments [56], and banking [58].

Whenever service demands go beyond a 5-day week and 8-hour day, mere specification of staff sizes is not adequate. To develop an operational plan, level 2 disagregation decisions must specify on-duty times for each person over the relevant time horizon. As shown in Figure 1, shift scheduling[12] can be classified as either a single or multistage problem. *Single stage* problems involve one

11. Exceptions are in the transportation industry where the demand for operator crews is determined by the timetable of scheduled trips, which is known under conditions of certainty.
12. Bodin [43] has recently proposed standardized terminology for shift scheduling, although a variety of approximate synonyms (tour, watch trick and rotation) are found in the literature.

operation or several independent operations; the customer must pass through only one phase of service. In a *multistage* problem customers are routed through more than one operation, so that the demand pattern imposed on any one operation is a complex function of (i) customer arrivals to the system, (ii) customer routing patterns, and (iii) the staffing of other operations.

Shift scheduling problems can be further subdivided into fixed and rotating schedules. With *fixed* (as opposed to *rotating*) schedules, each employee works the same days and shifts week after week, over the whole time horizon. The following integer programming model serves to present the basic structure of single stage, fixed schedule problems.

Minimize:

$$\sum_{n=1}^{N} c_n Y_n \tag{8}$$

Subject to:

$$\sum_{n=1}^{N} \underline{a}_n Y_n > \underline{W} \tag{9}$$

$$Y_n > 0, \text{ integer}, n = 1, 2, \ldots, N \tag{10}$$

where:

Y_n = number of employees assigned to shift schedule n,
c_n = cost per person assigned to shift schedule n, possibly adjusted judgmentally to recognize intangible considerations,
$\underline{a}_n$ = column vector with element i equal to 1 if shift schedule n calls for an employee to be on duty at operation $j \in J$ during time period t, 0 otherwise,
$\underline{W}$ = column vector with element i equal to W_{jt}, and
N = number of different shift schedules being considered.

Each column vector $\underline{a}_n$ represents a candidate shift schedule n, with a row element for each possible combination of j and t. The essence of the problem is determining how many employees to assign to each shift schedule, so as to minimize costs and meet desired staff sizes W. This model takes on the dimensionality of a large scale programming model.

Fixed schedules have the advantage of simplicity and ease in implementation. Solution procedures to such problems can be divided into two categories, depending on the number of possible shifts used to construct shift schedules.

In some cases time periods as long as a shift or even a day are used, thereby reducing the number of $\underset{\sim}{a}_n$ vectors. This arises when (i) the start times of acceptable shifts are predetermined, (ii) the demand for service is fairly constant throughout the time period, or (iii) service delays as long as a shift or day can be tolerated.

Rothstein considers a 1-shift, 1-operation problem of minimizing the number of employees not receiving two consecutive days off per week. Due to the problem's unique structure, integral solutions are guaranteed. Tibrewala et al. [66] and Baker [41] consider a variant of this problem whereby 5 consecutive work day constraints must be met, with the objective of minimizing the number of employees required. Their manual procedure can optimally solve this integer programming problem. Finally, Mabert and Raedels [58] consider a problem where shift schedule n is enlarged to handle both time periods and multiple operations. Due to the size of the problem, which allows transfers between operations (variable assignments), two heuristic algorithms are proposed. One of them has been successfully implemented in a bank.

Another class of fixed schedule procedures is designed to cope with hour-by-hour demand variations, overlapping shifts, and relief periods. The number and size of the $\underset{\sim}{a}_n$ vectors is expanded. Time periods can be as short as 15 minutes. Dantzig originally modelled this problem [47] as a linear program. He suggests that most of the optimal Y_n's will be zero and the others can be integerized heuristically with little effect on the objective function. Segal [63] offers an approximate solution with a network-flow model, which is solved with a 2-phase iterative procedure using the out-of-kilter method. In addition to heuristic procedures, Henderson and Berry [51] [52] provide a branch and bound algorithm to find optimal solutions for problems of practical size. They show that low cost solutions are generated even when the number of $\underset{\sim}{a}_n$ vectors is trimmed to a relatively small number (say 50).

Arabyre et al. [40] survey different approaches attempting to optimize the allocation of airline crews to flights.[13] Column vector

13. The higher level plans being disaggregated are flight timetables, rather than an aggregate plan as conventionally defined. However, the problem of allocating airline crews is mathematically identical to shift scheduling.

$\underline{a}_n$ usually implies a round trip consisting of several legs or flight segments. Since each leg is to be covered just once, the problem is reduced to a Boolean programming problem where the Y_n values must be 0 or 1. A variety of methods can be used to reduce the size and number of $\underline{a}_n$ vectors. Methods for solving the resulting model include: heuristic algorithms, branch and bound, implicit enumeration, various integer programming codes, and combinatorial enumeration.

Rotating schedules call for each *bracket* of employees (a set of employees with identical work periods over the time horizon) to rotate each week to the work periods assigned to another bracket during the previous week. By the end of the time horizon, all brackets will work through the same pattern of work and recreation (days off) clusters, thereby providing non-preferential treatment to all employees. Designing rotating schedules is more difficult than fixed schedules, owing to additional constraints forcing rotation. Solution procedures proposed are multiple phased. In the first phase, the day-off pattern is constructed in a fashion similar to the procedures of Sections A.1 and B.1. Subsequent phases then assign shifts to the day-off pattern.

Bennett and Potts [42] attempt to maximize the number of recreation clusters (consecutive days off) consisting of 2 or more days as well as spread the clusters evenly over the time horizon. Maier-Rothe and Wolfe [59] also recognize multiple criteria in their heuristic approach to staffing each of $7W$ days in a W week cyclic graph. Heller et al. [50] provide a computerized package of sequential procedures. Given the W_{jt} values for each shift and day of the week, cyclic graph analysis is applied to one shift at a time to determine recreation clusters. Implicit enumeration is coupled with the notion of a separation matrix to construct feasible schedules, which are then ranked with a lexicographic scheme to recognize the multiplicity of criteria. Given the highest ranking schedule found, a branching procedure enumerates all feasible multi-shift schedules. The most attractive rotating schedules, again measured with a lexicographic scale, are printed out for management's consideration.

Another impressive set of procedures and perspectives is provided by Bodin [43], who structures the problem for sequentially solving 3 submodels. Given appropriate W_{jt} values, a *grouping* model is used to find the best collection of recreation clusters. The *pattern* model is next applied to intersperse recreation clusters, with a *shift* model finally applied to assign shifts to clusters so as to satisfy W_{jt} requirements without resorting to broken clusters.

2.4.1. *Multistage shift schedules*

One of the most difficult, albeit less frequently encountered, disaggregation problems in the service sector is multistage shift scheduling. Such a problem is encountered by a post office where several categories of mail must be sorted sequentially at a series of operations. One major source of complexity is that staff assignments at one stage affect the D_{it} values for other stages. Additional complications are the multiplicity of (i) criteria and constraints, (ii) mail categories (types of services), and (iii) dispatch schedules. A dispatch schedule is the set of times (unique to each mail category) at which sorted mail can be loaded onto trucks and transported to its next destination. With the existence of dispatch schedules, staffing levels providing good service at low cost are not necessarily those which closely match the pattern of mail arriving to the whole system.

Level 1 and 2 disaggregation procedures for solving this problem have been designed for the fixed schedule case, relying on heuristic algorithms coupled with simulation [61], [64]. The objective is to minimize system throughput time while contending with a variety of other criteria and constraints.

2.4.2. *New research directions*

Several new directions can be identified as promising. The first direction is to develop procedures with greater generality, particularly if they are transparent and understandable to management. Current procedures tend to reduce problem dimensionality in one way or another. For example, procedures capable of handling many shift options are limited to single stage problems with permanent assignments required. Procedures to design rotating schedules in a multistage system have yet to be developed. Multiple criteria decision methods [45] have received scant attention in disaggregation.

Other directions are (i) research on how best to revise shift schedules over time (so as to accommodate new hires, temporary employees, or vacations), (ii) comparative work on the relative merit of techniques proposed for similar problems, and (iii) research assessing the impact of alternate staff scheduling policies on employee attitudes and behavior.

2.5. Conclusion

An assumption providing the motivation for this paper is that decisions made at any level in an organization must be compatible with higher level decisions. The process of decomposing high level aggregate plans into more detailed plans is called disaggregation. In trying to provide a useful framework for defining and identifying disaggregation problems, this paper presents a taxonomy of disaggregation problems in the manufacturing and service sectors. It describes a small, but representative, segment of literature to demonstrate today's state of the art. It shows that although much work has been done, much work still remains. Specific recommendations for future research are made at the ends of Sections 3 and 4. In general, more research is needed which (i) recognizes the interface between the various disaggregation decisions and (ii) provides procedures useful for practicing managers.

References

Manufacturing organizations

1. Berry, W. L., 'Lot Sizing Procedures for Requirements Planning Systems: A Framework for Analysis', *Production and Inventory Management*, vol. 13, no. 2 (1972), pp. 19–34.
2. Biggs, J., 'Sequencing and Lot Sizing Heuristic Decision Rules in a Hierarchical Multistage Production and Inventory System', Unpublished doctoral dissertation, The Ohio State University (1975).
3. Buffa, E. S. and Taubert, W. H., *Production-Inventory Systems: Planning and Control.* Homewood, Ill.: Irwin (1972).
4. Clark, A. J., 'An Informal Survey of Multi-Echelon Inventory Theory', *Naval Research Logistics Quarterly*, vol. 18 (1971), pp. 621–650.
5. Conway, R. W., Maxwell, W. L. and Miller, L. W., *Theory of Scheduling*. Reading, Mass.: Addison-Wesley (1967).
6. Crowston, W. B., Hausman, W. H., and Kampe II, W. R., "Multistage Production for Stochastic Seasonal Demand', *Management Science*, vol. 19, no. 8 (April 1973), pp. 924–935.

7. Crowston, W. B., Wagner, M. and Henshaw, A., 'A Comparison of Exact and Heuristic Routines for Lot-Size Determination in Multi-Stage Assembly Systems', *AIIE Transactions*, vol. 4, no. 4 (December 1972), pp. 313–317.
8. Crowston, W. B., Wagner, M. and Williams, J. F., 'Economic Lot Size Determination in Multi-Stage Assembly Systems', *Management Science*, vol. 19, no. 5 (January 1973), pp. 517–527.
9. Dzielinski, B. P. and Gomory, R. E., 'Optimal Programming of Lot Sizes, Inventory and Labor Allocations', *Management Science*, vol. 11, no. 9 (July 1965), pp. 874–890.
10. Fabian, T., 'Blast Furnace Production Planning – a Linear Programming Example.' *Management Science*, vol. 14, no. 2 (October 1967), pp. B1–B27.
11. Garvin, W. W., Crandall, H. B., John, J. B. and Spellman, R. A., 'Applications of Linear Programming in the Oil Industry', *Management Science* (July 1957).
12. Gelders, L. and Kleindorfer, P. R., 'Coordinating Aggregate and Detailed Scheduling Decisions in the One-Machine Job Shop: Part 1. Theory', *Operations Research*, vol. 22, no. 1 (January–February 1974), pp. 46–60.
13. Gleason, J. M., 'A Computational Variation of the Wagner-Whitin Algorithm: An Alternative to the E.O.Q', *Production and Inventory Management*, 1st Quarter (1971), pp. 15–22.
14. Gorham, T., 'Dynamic Order Quantities', *Production and Inventory Management*, 1st Quarter (1968), pp. 75–81.
15. Green, R. S., 'Heuristic Coupling of Aggregate and Detailed Models in Factory Scheduling'. Unpublished doctoral dissertation, Massachusetts Institute of Technology (1971).
16. Hadley, G. and Whitin, T. M., *Analysis of Inventory Systems.* Englewood Cliffs, N.J.: Prentice-Hall, (1963).
17. Haehling von Lanzenauer, C., 'Production and Employment Scheduling in Multistage Production Systems'. Working paper, School of Business Administration, The University of Western Ontario (1969).
18. Haehling von Lanzenhauer, C., 'A Production Scheduling Model by Bivalent Linear Programming'. *Management Science*, vol. 17, no. 1 (September 1970), pp. 105-111.
19. Hax, A. C. and Meal, H. C., 'Hierarchial Integration of Production Planning and Scheduling', in *Studies in the Management Sciences, Volume 1 Logistics*, M. A. Geisler, editor, North Holland-American Elsevier (1975).
20. Hodges, S. D. and Moore, P. G., 'The Product-Mix Problem Under Stochastic Seasonal Demand'. *Management Science*, vol. 17, no. 2 (October 1970), B107-B114.
21. Ignall, E. J., 'A Review of Assembly-Line Balancing', *Journal of Industrial Engineering*, vol. 16, no. 4 (July–August 1965), pp. 244–254.
22. Krajewski, L. J., 'Detailed Planning in Multistage Systems – A Review of the Literature with Recommendations for Future Research', Working paper, The Ohio State University (1975).
23. Lasdon, L. S. and Terjung, R. C., 'An Efficient Algorithm for Multi-Item Scheduling'. *Operations Research*, vol. 19, no. 4 (July–August 1971), pp. 946–969.
24. Manne, A. S., 'Programming of Economic Lot Sizes'. *Management Science*, vol. 4, no. 2 (January 1958), pp. 115–135.
25. Newson, E. F. P., 'Multi-Item Lot Size Scheduling by Heuristic – Part 1: With Fixed Resources and Part 2: With Variable Resources'. *Management Science*, vol. 21, no. 10 (June 1975), pp. 1186–1203.
26. Nicholson, T. A. J., *Optimization in Industry – Volume II Industrial Applications*. Chicago, Ill.: Aldine-Atherton (1971).
27. O'Malley, R. L., Elmaghraby, S. E., and Jeske, J. W., 'An Operational System for Smoothing Batch-Type Production". *Management Science*, vol. 12, no. 10 (June 1966), pp. B433–B449.
28. Orlicky, J., *Material Requirements Planning: The New Way of Life in Production and Inventory Management.* New York: McGraw-Hill (1975).
29. Silver, E. A. and Meal, H. C., 'A Heuristic for Selecting Lot Size Quantities for the Case of a Deterministic Time-Varying Demand Rate and Discrete Opportunities for Replenishment'. *Production and Inventory Management*, 2nd Quarter (1973), pp. 64–74.

30. Shwimer, J., 'Interaction Between Aggregate Planning and Detailed Scheduling in a Job Shop'. Unpublished doctoral dissertation, Massachusetts Institute of Technology (1972).
31. Taha, H. A. and Skeith, R. W., 'The Economic Lot Size in Multistage Production Systems'. *AIIE Transactions*, vol. II, no. 2 (June, 1970), pp. 157–162.
32. Veinott, A. F. Jr., 'The Status of Mathematical Inventory Theory'. *Management Science*, vol. 12, no. 11 (July 1966), pp. 745–777.
33. Wagner, H. M., 'The Design of Production and Inventory Systems for Multifacility and Multiwarehouse Companies'. *Operations Research*, vol. 22. no. 2 (March–April 1974), pp. 278–291.
34. Wagner, H. M. and Whitin, T. M., 'Dynamic Version of the Economic Lot Size Model'. *Management Science* (October 1958), pp. 89–96.
35. Winters, P. R., 'Constrained Inventory Rules for Production Smooting'. *Management Science*, vol. 8, no. 4 (July 1962), pp. 470–481.
36. Zangwill, W. I., 'A Backlogging Model and a Multi-Echelon Model of a Dynamic Economic Lot Size Production System – a Network Approach'. *Management Science*, vol. 15, no. 9 (May 1969), pp. 506–527.
37. Zöller, K., 'Optimal Disaggregation of Aggregate Production Plans'. *Management Science*, vol. 17, no. 8 (April 1971), B533-B549.

Service organizations

38. Abernathy, W. J., Baloff, J., Hershey, J. C., and Wandel, S., 'A Three-Stage Manpower Planning and Scheduling Model: A Service-Sector Example'. *Operations Research*, vol. 21, no. 3 (May–June 1973), pp. 693–711.
39. Altman, S. M., Beltrami, E. J., Rappaport, S., and Shoepfle, G. K., 'Nonlinear Programming Model of Crew Assignments for Household Refuse Collection'. *IEEE Transactions on Systems, Man, and Cybernetics* (July 1971), pp. 289–291.
40. Arabeyre, J. P., Fearnley, J., Steiger, F. C. and Teather, W., 'The Airline Crew Scheduling Problem: A Survey'. *Transportation Science*, vol. 3 (May 1969), pp. 140–163.
41. Baker, K. R., 'Scheduling a Full-Time Workforce to Meet Cyclic Staffing Requirements'. *Management Science*, vol. 20, no. 12 (August 1974), pp. 1561–1568.
42. Bennett, B. T. and Potts, R. B., 'Rotating Roster for a Transit System'. *Transportation Science*, vol. 2, no. 1 (February 1968), pp. 14–34.
43. Bodin, L. D., 'Towards a General Model for Manpower Scheduling: Parts I and II'. Urban and Policy Sciences Program, State University of New York, Stony Brook, New York (September 1972).
44. Chaiken, J. M. and Larson, R. C., 'Methods of Allocating Urban Emergency Units: A Survey'. *Management Science*, vol. 19, no. 4 (December 1972), pp. 110–130.
45. Cochrane, J. and Zeleny, M. (eds.), *Multiple Criteria Decision Making*. Columbia, South Carolina: University of South Carolina Press (1973).
46. Connor, R. J., 'Inpatient Classification System'. Unpublished doctoral dissertation, The Johns Hopkins University (1960).
47. Dantzig, G. B., 'A Comment on Edie's Traffic Delays at Toll Booths', *Operations Research Journal*, vol. 2 (1954), pp. 339–341.
48. Harveston, M. F., Luce, B. J. and Smuczynski, T. A., 'Telephone Operator Management System – TOMS', Joint National Meeting of ORSA/TIMS/AIIE (November 1972).
49. Heller, N. B., "Operations Research at the St. Louis Metropolitan Police Department', 39th National ORSA Meeting (May 1971).
50. Heller, N. B., McEwen, J. T. and Stenzel, W. W., 'Computerized Scheduling of Police Manpower: Methods and Conclusions', Report NI 72 018G, National Institute of Law Enforcement and Criminal Justice, vol. I (March 1973).
51. Henderson, W. B. and Berry, W. L., 'Determining Optimal Shift Schedules for Telephone Traffic Exchange Operators', Working Paper no. 507, Krannert Graduate School of Industrial Administration, Purdue University (April 1975).
52. Henderson, W. B. and Berry, W. L., 'Heuristic Methods for Telephone Operator Shift

Scheduling: An Experimental Analysis', Working Paper no. 20, Center for Business and Economic Research, The University of Tennessee (March 1975).
53. Ignall, E., Kolesar, P. and Walker, W., 'Linear Programming Models of Crew Assignments for Refuse Collections' *IEEE Transactions on Systems, Man, and Cybernetics*, vol. 2, no. 5 (November 1972).
54. Larson, R. C., *Urban Police Patrol Analysis.* MIT Press, Cambridge, Mass. (1972).
55. Krajewski, L. J. and Thompson, H. E., 'Efficient Employment Planning in Public Utilities', *The Bell Journal of Economics*, vol. 6, no. 1 (Spring 1975), pp. 314–326.
56. Kolesar, P. and Walker, W. E., 'An Algorithm for the Dynamic Relocation of Fire Companies', *Operations Research*, vol. 22, no. 2 (March–April 1974), pp. 249–274.
57. Linder, R. W., 'The Development of Manpower and Facilities Planning Methods for Airline Telephone Reservation Offices', *Operational Research Quarterly*, vol. 20, no. 1 (1969), pp. 3–21.
58. Mabert, V. A. and Raedels, A. R., 'The Detail Scheduling of a Part-Time Work Force: A Case Study of Teller Staffing', Working Paper no. 531, Krannert Graduate School of Industrial Administration, Purdue University (September 1975).
59. Maier-Rothe, C. and Wolfe, H. C., 'Cyclical Scheduling and Allocation of Nursing Staff', *Socio-Economic Planning Sciences*, vol. 7, no. 5 (October 1973), pp. 471–487.
60. Rising, E. J. and Kaminsky, F. C., 'Analytical Scheduling of Small Nursing Teams', *International Journal of Production Research*, vol. 9, no. 1 (1971), pp. 169–179.
61. Ritzman, L. P., Krajewski, L. J. and Showalter, M. J., 'The Disaggregation of Aggregate Manpower Plans', *Management Sciences*, vol. 22, no. 11 (July 1976).
62. Rothstein, M., 'Scheduling Manpower by Mathematical Programming', *Industrial Engineering*, (April 1972), pp. 29–33.
63. Segal, M., 'The Operator-Scheduling Problem: A Network-Flow Approach', *Operations Research*, vol. 22, no. 4 (July–August 1974), pp. 808–823.
64. Showalter, M. J., 'A Methodology for Manpower Tour Assignment within a U.S. Postal Service Processing Center Facility', Unpublished doctoral dissertation, The Ohio State University (1976).
65. Stimson, R. H. and Stimson, D. H., 'Operations Research and the Nurse Staffing Problem', *Hospital Administration* (Winter 1972), pp. 61–69.
66. Tibrewala, R., Phillippe, D., and Browne, J., 'Optimal Scheduling of Two Consecutive Idle Periods', *Management Science*, vol. 19, no. 1 (September 1972), pp. 71–75.
67. Trivedi, V. M. and Warner, D. M., 'A Branch and Bound Algorithm for Optimum Allocation of Float Nurses', *Management Science*, vol. 22, no. 9 (May 1976), pp. 972–981.
68. Vitt, L. D., 'Aggregate Programming for Police Patrol', *Proceedings of Midwest AIDS Conference* (April 1975), pp. 36–39.
69. Vitt, L. D. and Krajewski, L. J., 'Employment Planning for a Major U.S. Post Office', *Proceedings of Midwest AIDS Conference*, (April 1971), pp. 1–11.
70. Warner, D. M. and Prawda, J., 'A Mathematical Programming Model for Scheduling Nursing Personnel in a Hospital', *Management Science*, vol. 19, no. 2 (December 1972), pp. 411–422.
71. Wolfe, H. and Young, J. P., 'Staffing the Nursing Unit: Part II', *Nursing Research*, vol. 14, no. 4 (1965), pp. 299–303.

Section 2. Theories

3. Toward a theory of hierarchical coordination and conflict

J. TALAVAGE and B. ELLIOTT

Abstract

Management and control structures for steel-producing firms are widely envisioned as multi-level hierarchies. A system-theoretic framework is developed in this paper for quite general three-level hierarchical structures. A notion of organizational conflict is defined, and it is shown that the additional structure of three-level hierarchies provides more flexibility to *resolve* conflict than do two-level structures. A discussion is given of current and anticipated future developments for this theory.

3.1. Introduction

Hierarchical structures seem to provide a natural way of describing the management and control of steel production processes [7], [8]. This paper presents the initial development of a hierarchical framework suitable for the investigation of several important issues in the steel industry such as: (a) What are the advantages and disadvantages of intra-level communication? (b) What are the relationships between organizational conflict and certain characteristics of management information systems? (c) What are the significant aspects of the so-called 'trade-off' between inventory level and the quality of management information? The approach is that of an axiomatic theory and employs a basic framework that is similar to the combined work of Mesarovic, Macko and Takahara [5] which displays a rigorous model for hierarchies. They have mathematically formalized the structure as follows (refer to Figure 1). The hierarchy consists of a supremal control system C_0, n infimal control systems $C_1, \ldots, C_n$, the controlled process P and the information links γ, w_i, m_i, and z_i. The process is assumed to be a mapping

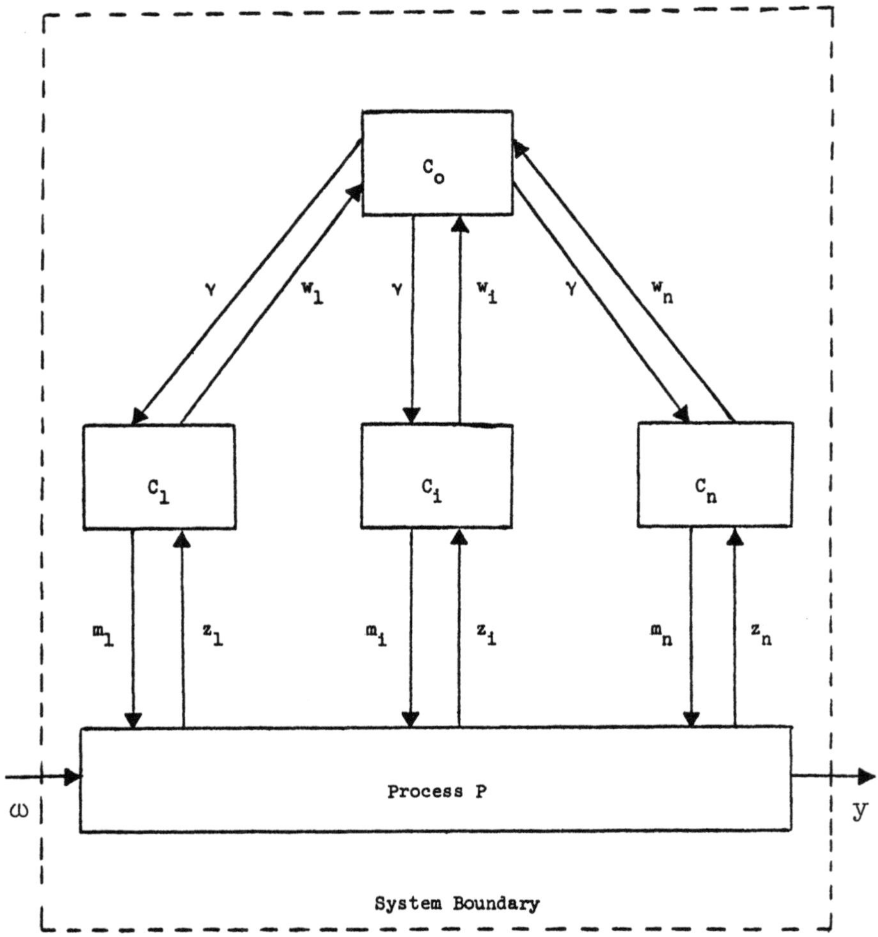

Figure 1

$P:M * \Omega \to Y$ where M is the control object of the process represented as the cartesian product of n components $M = M_1 * \ldots * M_n$ such that $m_i \in M_i$, Ω is the environment input set and Y is the output set such that $\omega \in \Omega$ and $y \in Y$. The infimal control systems are a mapping $C_i: \mathcal{C} * Z_i \to M_i$, where $\mathcal{C}$ is the set of coordination inputs γ provided by the supremal control system and Z_i is the set of feedback information z_i coming from the process. The supremal control system, C_0 is the mapping $C_0: W \to \mathcal{C}$ where W is the set of feedback information inputs w_i. The description is completed by specifying the nature of the feedback information. The feedback information received by an infimal C_i is the mapping $f_i: M * \Omega * Y \to Z_i$. Similarly the mapping f_0: $\mathcal{C} * Z * M \to W$, where $Z = Z_1^* \ldots {}^*Z_n$.

The operation of this structure is such that the supremal control system attempts to coordinate the infimal control systems with respect to a given overall goal of the two-level system. Each control unit in a two-level system is defined in terms of a family of decision problems. Formally, let $\mathbb{P}(x, \mathcal{D})$ be a logical statement defined for all pairs $(x, \mathcal{D})$, where $\mathcal{D}$ is an arbitrary decision problem and the predicate $\mathbb{P}(x, \mathcal{D})$ is true whenever x is a solution of $\mathcal{D}$. Two notions of coordination are developed from this formulation. First there is coordinability relative to the supremal decision problem. It requires that the supremal decision problem have a solution and for some coordination input, γ, from the supremal to the infimals (where γ solves the supremal problem), the set of infimal decision problems, $\bar{D}$, also have a solution. Second there is coordinability relative to the overall decision problem, D. It requires that the supremal control system influence the infimal decision units so that their resulting action satisfies the overall decision problem. These notions of coordination are related by the coordinability and consistency postulate which may be expressed as:

$$[(\mathbb{P}(x, \bar{D}(\gamma, z)) \text{ and } Q(x, \gamma, w)] \to \mathbb{P}(\pi_M(x), D)$$

where,

> $\bar{D}$ is the ordered set of decision problems $\bar{D} = (D_1, \ldots, D_n)$
> X_i is the solution set of x_i for component i $\pi_M: X_1^* \ldots {}^*X_n \to M$
> $Q(x, \gamma, w)$ is a logical statement representing some relationship among system variables

Finally, principles of coordination are derived that are strategies for the interactions between the supremal unit and the infimal units.

Several researchers have been concerned with advancing this development [1], [2], [3], [4]. All of these efforts retain the basic structure of Figure 1. The power of this theory is severely limited by the restrictions on the structures to be modeled. First, the input to the hierarchy can only come from the process. Second, there can be no information exchanged directly between infimals. Third, there can only be one supremal per infimal. Fourth, the coordination schemes have only been developed for a two-level hierarchy. Finally, the theory does not include the concept of time. These shortcomings provide some of the impetus for the work shown in this paper.

3.2. Canonical three-level hierarchy

This theoretical development overcomes the restrictions required by the existing two-level model. That is, the three-level structure will accept input at any level from the environment. It will also allow direct interaction among subinfimals and among infimals. Each subinfimal will be capable of interacting with more than one infimal or the supremal. Each component of the hierarchy will be able to interact with the environment (refer to Figure 2).

The model as represented in Figure 2 clearly exhibits additional structure complexity over the two-level model in Figure 1. The three-level hierarchy $\mathcal{H}$ consists of a supremal C_0, n_1 infimals $C_1, \ldots, C_{n_1}$, n_2 subinfimals $C_{n_1+1}, \ldots, C_{n_1+n_2}$, the process P and the information links γ, w, e, λ, m, z. The process is assumed to be a mapping $P: M * \Omega \to Y * Z$ where M is the control object as represented previously, Ω is the disturbance object, Y is the output of the process and Z is the feedback information object. The subinfimal control systems are represented by a mapping

$$C_i: \mathcal{C}_{k,i} * Z_{l,i} * \mathcal{E}_{.,i} * \Lambda_{j,i} \to M_{i,l} * W_{i,i} * \mathcal{E}_{i,.} * \Lambda_{i,j},$$

$$j \neq i,\ j,\ i = n_1 + 1, \ldots, n_2,\ k = 0, 1, \ldots, n_1,\ l = 1, 2, \ldots, n_2 - n_1$$

where $\mathcal{C}_{k,i}$ is the set of coordination inputs γ, $Z_{l,i}$ is the set of feedback information z from P, $\mathcal{E}_{.,i}$ is the set of information e from the environment, $\Lambda_{j,i}$ is the set of information λ from other subinfimals and $W_{i,k}$ is the set of information returned to the infimals and the supremal, $\mathcal{E}_{i,.}$ is the set of information returned to the environment and $\Lambda_{i,j}$ is the set of information passed on to the other infimals. The infimals are represented by a mapping

$$C_i: \mathcal{C}_{0,i} * \mathcal{E}_{.,i} * \Lambda_{j,i} * W_{k,i} \to \mathcal{C}_{i,k} * \mathcal{E}_{i,.} * \Lambda_{i,j} * W_{i,0},$$

$$i, j = 1, \ldots, n_1,\ k = n_1 + 1, \ldots, n_2.$$

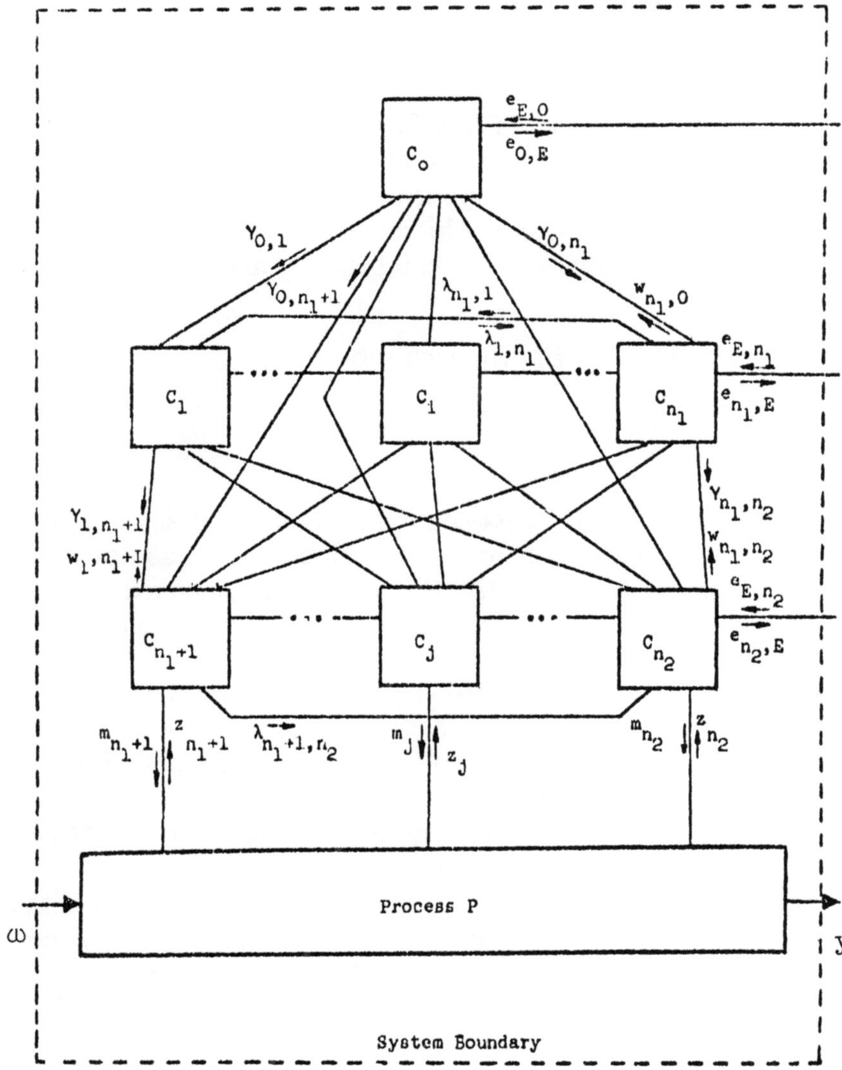

Figure 2

The supremal is also shown as a mapping

$$C_0: W_{i,0} * \mathscr{E}_{.,0} \to \mathscr{C}_{0,i} * \mathscr{E}_{0,.}\, , \; i = 1, \ldots, n_1, n_1 + 1, \ldots, n_2 .$$

The process P is assumed to represent $n_2 - n_1$ subprocesses each of which is under the control of a specific subinfimal control system.

The i-th subprocess is a mapping

$$P_i : M_i * U_i * \Omega \rightarrow Y_i * Z_{i,.}$$

where the set U_i is the set of interface inputs u_i through which the subprocess P_i is coupled with the other subprocesses. These subprocesses along with the components $C_0, C_1, \ldots, C_{n_1+1}, \ldots, C_{n_2}$ are all of the subsystems of the hierarchy.

To couple the subsystems, several coupling maps must be specified including:

(a) $H_i^U : M * Y \rightarrow U_i$ for each subprocess i,

(b) $H_i^\Lambda : \mathcal{C}_{l,i} * \mathcal{E}_{.,i} * \Lambda_{j,i} * W_{j,i} \rightarrow \Lambda_{i,j}$

$l = 0, 1, \ldots, n_1 \qquad i, j = 1, 2, \ldots, n_2$

to express the flow of 'cross-communication' from any component i to any other component j at the same level. In addition, the similarly defined mappings $H_i^{\mathcal{C}}$, $H_i^{\mathcal{E}}$ and H_i^W are associated with the other three types of information transfer for each of the components $\mathcal{C}_i$.

The operation of the three-level structure is similar to the two-level system. Each component C_i, $i = 0, 1, \ldots, n_1, n_1 + 1, \ldots, n_2$ of the hierarchy is assumed to make decisions. The subinfimals solve problems concerning the control of the process. The infimals and the supremals attempt to coordinate the subinfimals with respect to the overall goal of the system. Hence, the decision problems for the components may be the result of the decomposition of the decision problem that represents the overall goal of the system. Thus, the solution of the components' problems must be appropriately related to the solution of the overall decision problem. If they are, then the system is said to be consistent.

The formal expression of these structural characteristics is a postulate for this theory. A given three-level system is consistent and coordinable by the supremal and infimal decision problems if and only if the following proposition is true:

$$\mathbb{P}(x, \overline{D}(\gamma, \lambda, e, z)) \text{ and } \{Q_1(x, \gamma, \lambda, e, w) \text{ or } Q_2(x, \gamma, \lambda, e, w)\}$$
$$\text{and } \{Q_3(x, \gamma, \lambda, e, w) \text{ or } Q_4(x, \gamma, \lambda, e, w)$$
$$\text{or } Q_5(x, \gamma, \lambda, e, w)\}$$

and $Q_6(\gamma, \lambda, e, w)$ or $Q_7(\gamma, \lambda, e, w)$

$$\rightarrow \mathbb{P}(\pi_M(x), D)$$

where $\bar{D}$ is the ordered set of subinfimal decision problems $\bar{D} = (D_{n_1+1}, \ldots, D_{n_2})$

X_i is the solution set for component i

$$\pi_M : X_{n_1+1} * \ldots * X_{n_2} \rightarrow M$$

This will be referred to as the combined consistency and coordinability postulate.

The postulate states that the subinfimal decision problems $\mathbb{P}$ $(x, \bar{D}(\gamma, \lambda, e, z))$ are coordinated with respect to the overall decision problem $\mathbb{P}(\pi_m(x), D)$ whenever they are coordinated with respect to the infimal-associated conditions Q_1, Q_2 or Q_6 and the supremal-associated conditions Q_3, Q_4, Q_5 or Q_7. The conditions Q_1, Q_2, Q_3, Q_4, Q_5, Q_6 and Q_7 are predicates defined over the Cartesian product space $X \times \mathcal{C} \times \Lambda \times \mathcal{C} \times W$. The specific forms of the conditions arise when the coordination principles are considered.

3.3. Coordination principles

The *interaction-prediction* coordination principle is founded on the concept that the supremal and the infimals predict exactly the attributes of the interactions that will occur between process subsystems or between subinfimals. The principle states that the overall system problem is solved whenever the subinfimals solve their problems and the attributes of the interactions are correctly predicted. The formal statement of this principle requires the specification of the seven coordination conditions $Q_1, \ldots Q_7$ found in the combined coordinability and consistency postulate. The mathematical formulation for these conditions may be expressed in terms of the coupling functions as is shown elsewhere [8]. In words, the condition $Q_{1,P}$ states that the attributes of the actual interface inputs in the process equal those predicted by the supremal and infimals. Condition $Q_{2,P}$ states that the attributes of the actual interface inputs in the process equal those communicated among the subinfimals. Condition $Q_{3,P}$ states that the attributes of the actual intra-subinfimal interactions equal those prescribed by the supremal. Condition $Q_{4,P}$ states that the attributes of the actual intra-subinfimal interactions equal those agreed upon by the infimals. Condition $Q_{5,P}$ states that the attributes of the actual intra-subinfimal interactions equal those agreed upon by the subinfimals. Condition $Q_{6,P}$ states that the attributes of the actual intra-infimal interactions equal those agreed upon by the infimals. Condition $Q_{7,P}$ states that the attributes of the actual intra-infimal interactions equal those prescribed by the supremal.

A less demanding form of this principle is embodied as the interaction estimation principle. The specification of the conditions $Q_{1,E}, \ldots, Q_7$ is similar to that of $Q_{1,P}, \ldots, Q_{7,P}$ except that the unit set predictions are replaced by sets of estimations.

The interaction balance principle is founded on the concept that the infimals and subinfimals shall ignore the actual interactions while solving their decision problems. The condition $Q_{1,B}$ states that the attributes of the actual interface inputs in the process equal those desired by the subinfimals. Condition $Q_{3,B}$ states that the attributes of the actual intra-subinfimal interactions equal those desired by the subinfimals. Condition $Q_{6,B}$ states that the attributes of the actual intra-infimal interactions equal those desired by the infimals. Thus the infimals and subinfimals have complete autonomy from the supremal and infimals respectively. ($Q_{2,B}$, $Q_{4,B}$, $Q_{5,B}$, and $Q_{7,B}$ cannot be defined.)

For each of the preceding coordination principles, the supremal and infimals were assumed to coordinate in the same mode. The final class of interaction coordination principle is the one that allows any combination of the preceding principles. Considering all the combinations of the 'pure' coordination principles for $n_1 + 1$ coordinating components would yield

$$3^{(n_1+1)}$$

elements or principles in this class.

3.4. Conflict in hierarchies

In this section the concept of conflict is introduced. The study of conflict in organizations has produced three conceptual models designed to deal with major classes of conflict phenomena [6]. There are three major classes: the bargaining model, the bureaucratic model and the systems model. Each of these models is designed to deal with different circumstances. The bargaining model is designed to deal with conflict among interest groups in competition for scarce resources. The bureaucratic model is applicable to the analysis of superio-subordinate conflicts, i.e., conflicts along the vertical dimension of a hierarchy. The systems model is directed at lateral conflict within a hierarchy. Analysis of the problems of *coordination* is the special province of this last model.

The fundamental source of conflict in hierarchical systems of functional relationships arises out of the pressures toward sub-optimization. Whenever two subunits have differentiated goals and are functionally interdependent, then conditions exist for conflict. Important types of interdependence are: (1) common usage of some service or facility; (2) sequences of work or information flow prescribed by task or hierarchy, and (3) rules of unanimity or consensus about joint activity. Although conflict may be functional as well as dysfunctional for the subunits and the organization, it will be considered dysfunctional for the purposes of this paper.

Conflict is defined here by the following:

hierarchy $\mathcal{H}$ is in *conflict* if

$$\sim (\mathbb{P}(x, \bar{D}(\gamma, \lambda, e, z)) \rightarrow \mathbb{P}(\pi_M(x), D))$$

where $\bar{D}$ and D refer to the collective subinfimal decision problems and the overall decision problem of $\mathcal{H}$, respectively.

One interpretation of this definition is that conflict is present in a hierarchy whenever the result of hierarchical action (i.e., the proposed solutions of the subinfimals) does not engender the achievement of the goal that is stipulated for the entire system. Conflict is then, in some sense, a negative performance indicator for the hierarchy.

Since part of our concern is with the resolution of conflict in a hierarchy by means of coordination, it is interesting to show an intuitively appealing theorem.

Theorem 1. For any three-level hierarchy $\mathcal{H}^3$, $[(Q_1 \text{ or } Q_2) \text{ and } (Q_3 \text{ or } Q_4 \text{ or } Q_5) \text{ and } (Q_6 \text{ or } Q_7)] \rightarrow \mathcal{H}^3$ is not in conflict.

Proof. Assume the left-hand side to be true. Then, by the combined coordinability and consistency postulate, $\mathbb{P}(x, \bar{D}) \rightarrow \mathbb{P}(\pi_M(x), D)$.

Clearly, $\mathcal{H}^3$ is not in conflict.

This result states that satisfaction of at least one coordinating condition at each of the process, subinfimal, and infimal levels guarantees the absence of conflict in the hierarchy.

Comparison of different hierarchical structures with respect to the conflict property can indicate advantages for one structure over another. In particular, an advantage of three-level structure over two-level structure is demonstrated by the following theorems.

Consider, for any three-level hierarchy $\mathcal{H}^3$, a *reduction-morphism* to a two-level hierarchy. That is, consider the following incomplete specification of a function ν such that

$$\nu(M) = M$$

$$\nu(\bar{D}) = \bar{D}$$

$$\nu(D) = D$$

$$\nu(C_{k,i}) = \bigcup_k \bigcup_i C_{k,i} \quad k = 0, \ldots, n_1; i = n_1 + 1, \ldots, n_2$$

$$\nu(W_{i,k}) = \bigcup_i \bigcup_k W_{i,k} \quad i = n_1 + 1, \ldots, n_2 \quad k = 0, \ldots, n_1$$

$$\left.\begin{aligned} \nu(\mathcal{E}_{i,.}) &= \emptyset \\ \nu(\lambda_{i,j}) &= \emptyset \end{aligned}\right\} \quad i, j = 0, \ldots, n_2$$

$$\nu(\mathbb{P}(\pi_M(x), D) = \mathbb{P}(\pi_M(x), D)$$

$$\nu(\mathbb{P}(x, \bar{D}(\gamma, \emptyset, \emptyset, z)) = \mathbb{P}(x, \bar{D}(\gamma, z))$$

$$\nu(Q_1(x, \gamma, \emptyset, \emptyset, w)) = Q(x, \gamma, w)$$

$$\nu(Q_l(x, \gamma, \lambda, e, w)) = \text{False} \quad l = 2, \ldots, 7$$

This rule allows us to consider a class of two-level hierarchies which are structurally and behaviorally 'similar' to $\mathcal{H}^3$. Let $\mathcal{H}^2$ be any representative of this class and denote $\mathcal{H}^2$ as $\nu(\mathcal{H}^3)$.

Theorem 2. For any three-level hierarchy $\mathcal{H}^3$, $\mathcal{H}^3$ is in conflict $\rightarrow$ conflict in $\nu(\mathcal{H}^3)$

Proof. Trivial via substitution of results of ν. Note that each of the two-level hierarchies in $\nu(\mathcal{H}^3)$ may also be a reduction of some other three-level hierarchy, $(\mathcal{H}^3)'$. Denote the collection of these $(\mathcal{H}^3)'$ as $\nu^{-1}(\nu(\mathcal{H}^3))$.

Theorem 3. For any three-level hierarchy $\mathcal{H}^3$, conflict in $\nu(\mathcal{H}^3) \rightarrow (\exists(\mathcal{H}^3)')((\mathcal{H}^3)' \in \nu^{-1}(\nu(\mathcal{H}^3))$ and $(\mathcal{H}^3)'$ is not in conflict).
Proof. Let $\nu(\mathcal{H}^3)$ be in conflict. Then $\sim\mathbb{P}(\pi_M(x), D)$. Consider a member of $\nu^{-1}(\nu(\mathcal{H}^3))$ for which the following is true:

$$[Q_2 \text{ and } (Q_3 \text{ or } Q_4 \text{ or } Q_5) \text{ and } (Q_6 \text{ or } Q_7)]$$

By the combined coordinability and consistency postulate, it must be that $\sim\mathbb{P}(x, \bar{D})$. Thus, this three-level hierarchy is not in conflict.

Theorem 2 indicates that three-level hierarchies as defined here can describe at least as rich a variety of conflict situations as their two-level reductions. More significantly, theorem 3 illustrates that conflict in some two-level structures may be *resolved* via the additional structure of a three-level hierarchy.

3.5. Current and anticipated future work

The immediate objective of our development is to be able to describe certain generalized situations that are observed or are hypothesized by practitioners in the steel industry. Two examples of these situations relate to management information systems and to inventory levels, respectively.

The design of an MIS entails certain decisions about information storage. Data collected from the process or lower levels of the hierarchy obviously cannot be stored forever in an easily accessible form. A number of design criteria may be specified for setting bounds on this storage. A lower bound for such storage from an organizational perspective may be specified via the duration of conflict. That is, the very existence of conflict implies that certain coordinating conditions are not satisfied (this is shown by the contrapositive of theorem 1). In order to even detect and identify conflict (let alone resolve it), information must have been gathered on the coordinating conditions over some minimal period of time. This period of time is clearly dependent on the coordination principle used by the hierarchy since that principle defines the coordinating conditions. This line of reasoning has led to our development of a number of theorems which relate duration of conflict to the coordination principle and to the 'response time' or 'decision interval' for each of the components in the hierarchy.

Another direction now being pursued is regarding the hypothesis that 'a trade-off exists between the level of process inventory and the quality of supervisory management information'. The theoretical framework is proving to be rather parsimonious in this case since it appears that only two new concepts, namely an 'uncertainty set' and a 'search procedure' associated with each of the hierarchy components, are sufficient to describe a relationship between inventory level and management information.

References

1. Benveniste, A. and Chen, G., 'Comparison de Deux Principes de Coordination en Commande Hierarchisee', *Revue Francaise d'Automatique, Informatique et de Recherche Operationelle* (November 1973), pp. 107–119.
2. Gueguen, C. J. and Manich-Mayol, F., 'Dual Decomposition and Effective Coordination of Dynamical Systems', *Information Sciences*, vol. 6 (1973), pp. 235–246.
3. Jennergren, L. P., 'On the Concept of Coordinability in Hierarchical Systems Theory', *International Journal of Systems Science*, vol. 5, no. 5 (1974), pp. 493–497.
4. Matuszewski, J. P. and Lefkowitz, I., 'Coordination for Control in Steel Processing', *IEEE Transactions on Systems, Man, and Cybernetics* (March 1973), pp. 182–184.
5. Mesarovic, M. D., Macko, D., and Takahara, Y., *Theory of Hierarchical, Multilevel, Systems* (New York: Academic Press, 1970).
6. Pondy, L., 'Varieties of Organizational Conflicts', *Administrative Science Quarterly*, vol. 14, pp. 499–505.
7. 'Systems Engineering of Hierarchy Computer Control System for Large Steel Manufacturing Complexes', Purdue Laboratory for Applied Industrial Control, Report 71, Purdue University (December 1975).
8. Talavage, J. and Elliott, B., 'A Theory for Three-Level Hierarchies', *Proceedings of Eighth International Congress for Cybernetics.*

4. An MSA view of disaggregation

JOHN M. BURNHAM

Abstract

Good reaction to change requires cooperative adjustment among all affected elements of the organization – each one understanding the various dependencies. This adjustment is enabled by, but not an automatic consequence of, real-time MIS. It depends on an integration of organizational, informational, and quantitative systems work . . . what is called 'Management Systems Analysis.'

The author uses MSA to discuss and analyze a disaggregative decision situation. Used correctly and fully, MSA enhances decentralized decision-making and overall organizational effectiveness.

4.1. MSA

In a Southeast AIDS workshop just two years ago, representatives of the Coca-Cola Company described the formation under a single 'umbrella'' of a decision support group to do Management Systems Analysis. Group members, chosen for their analytical capability, represented all functional areas [9]. Other antecedents for the term and for its theoretical exposition occur in work by Cleland and King ([6], 1968) and [7], 1972). It seems to be generally agreed that MSA deals with problems by subjecting them to rigorous examination along the lines of the methodologies suggested by the term itself: organizational analysis; information systems analysis; and quantitative analysis.

Writing in a recent (1976) issue of *Operational Research Quarterly*, Keith Tocher [17] points out that mathematical models will not perfectly predict actual behavior, and therefore 'solutions' must be monitored. In practice, a strict mathematical optimization approach has well-documented weaknesses: large size and data validity questions, computation cost, and the potential for unrealism due to mathematical 'tractability' and structure decisions. And people don't trust the complexity of comprehensive models. After citing some of the lacks of routine systems analysis, Tocher provides a number of links between MSA and the disaggregation problem. He calls on Ackoff's proposal [1] that we perceive the system being modeled as a part of yet a larger system, and continues:

> It would be entirely in the spirit of this new mode of thinking if we break a system into parts, describe the properties and behaviour of the parts by (a mathematical programming model) and, having relegated the behaviour of the parts to a fairly mechanical treatment, concentrate on how the parts join together.... The behaviour of the parts, themselves, given an environment determined by the relations, would be automated and an understanding of what they did, because they were smaller and involve less factors, would be easier. *The understanding of the whole would come from concentrating on the relations.* ([17], p. 236. Italics mine).

To deal with the weakness of either top-down (loss of precision) or bottom-up (lack of organizational perspective) planning, he suggests:

> We can now design an adaptive procedure. On an upward pass the most detailed models can be used and the errors calculated. This is evidence to correct the results on a downward pass which will generate similar, but not identical, problems for resolution at each (hierarchical) level ([17], p. 237).

To this might be added the explicit data requirements, timeliness of update, and both sources and destinations for information flows.

In both organizational and MIS work there are ample precedents for this sort of approach. But there exists a significant gap between the individual and 'Systems' theories and their practical application. There are a variety of coordination and control problems with decentralized operating entities. In the Management Information Systems domain it seems a truism that 'Big Systems may mean Big Trouble' [5]. And Tocher is upset about big math models.

MSA use focuses on the management of operations – the 'doing' activities of any organization, is decision-supporting rather than decision-making, and uses its three underlying methodologies in combination. MSA can define the organization's 'natural' activity centers, identify the specifics of the models needed for each activity's decision support, and use the relational linkages and decision interdependencies as inputs for the MIS design for communications, coordination, and control.

The individual techniques and methods have been available for years. Their rigorous use in combination, as one synthesized methodology, can eliminate some of the outlined problems and fulfill the original aspirations for Operations Research as offered twenty years ago by Churchman, Ackoff, and Arnoff: interdisciplinary teams using a broad and systematic approach to deal with executive-level problems of the firm and provide relevant, implementable, and controlled decision guidance [8].

4.2. Component methodologies

4.2.1. Organizational analysis

As a business grows, it evolves an hierarchical structure to cope with specialization, coordination, and control problems. A natural move is to geographical decentralization – with the problem of how to administer such hinterland operations centers. Both the heavy communications burden and good behavioral practice have brought about the profit/cost responsibility concept. Formal planning systems, joint setting of performance goals, and sophisticated management control systems came close behind – to guide divisional performance toward corporate goals.

With decentralization and formal planning came problems which still persist: the 'divisional' or 'departmentalized' response to a company-wide problem; design and implementation difficulties in the policies and procedures area; timeliness of guideline revisions; static decision support (plans + software + data + staff) in a dynamic operational environment; transfer pricing problems between quasi-autonomous profit centers; and so forth.

4.2.2. Information systems analysis

Computer development more or less paralleled that of the hierarchical management structure. Mechanized administrative systems and stand-alone EDP systems providing off-line computational support were all that was possible technically for the early computers – with reliability a major problem. As more power and higher reliability accompanied the move to solid state and disk storage systems, numerous operational activities became computer-supported. As decentralized operations caused increasing management concern, a variety of computer-based information systems was designed. But since those earlier days in which EDP seemed to offer a heaven-sent solution, management has come to realize that a data resource requires management and is, indeed, expensive to acquire, maintain, and use effectively. Most present-generation MIS have centralized data processing, centralized data base, and decentralized data entry and retrieval capabilities – providing for results feedback from below, and revised plans or status information from upper management – and a large EDP budget. Management has also learned that, while the terminals installed in the local plants are inexpensive, the communications network which ties them into the main computer and its data base is not. Further, design of the software which allows a terminal to feed data into the data base with real-time (random) capabilities is costly and there is a variety of administrative problems associated with data base design, protection, and use. These realizations, together with much better training of the non-computer-system managers, has helped to sensitize line management to the user's responsibilities for information system design and implementation. [11, 12, 13].

One of the more intriguing developments in the EDP field has been that of micro-processors and the mini-computer. In his notes on the use of computers in manufacturing, Thorn [16] suggests that:

> ... a natural hierarchy of integrated computers evolves when compared to either the hierarchy of the human organization or the manufacturing system.... A series of micro-processors and mini-computers dedicated to specific functions at the process and flow-control level can be linked to dedicated minicomputers coping with problems and decisions at the production control level which in turn feed into a main-frame machine dedicated to the specific management control level. Naturally this large computer could be tied to (other) machines integrating all organizational areas ... ([16], p. 3).

Far from being a pipe dream, Thorn says there are a number of already-existing systems of this sort – at General Motors and RCA, among others.

4.2.3. Quantitative analysis

The emphasis in application work has been that of executive level problem-solving. Multi-level (as well as multi-stage) mathematical programming models have been used at the strategic level for resolution of competing departmental resource management problems.

As applied to disaggregation, the models involve decomposition, multi-level shadow prices, optimal transfer prices, corporate-wide investment optimization, financing, and so forth [4]. Some such models may be presented at this conference.

Computer codes have been used to solve test problems and, in some instances, actual application situations [2]. However, despite such successful implementation in certain instances, Tocher's expression of dissatisfaction is more generally true than are glowing reports of 'big model' application and use for decision-making. The exceptions at the strategic level seem principally to be simulations which are then used for evaluation of corporate alternatives [10].

4.3. MSA and a situation summary

The application experience seems to indicate that, while the 'big picture' is extremely important, a detailed big picture is incomprehensible, unmanageable, or both – whether in the context of formal planning for a decentralized organization, of a centralized EDP/MIS/DBMS, or of a top-level mathematical model. Pragmatically-oriented problem-solvers like Tocher are suggesting that we build small models that can be used confidently and with user understanding – but that are also relevant to the big picture and consistent with its requirements. One way that I have found to be successful in forcing toward relevant detail is through MSA, in the following steps.

Steps in Management Systems Analysis

1. Assess the complete multi-level organizational framework for: scope; identification of variables; time horizon; resource commitment; responsibility; aggregation.
2. Look for differences between levels: criteria; decision variables; constraints; timing; horizon differences; frequency of action; input sources.
3. Pinpoint effects across levels: sources, magnitude of perturbations, sensitivity to parameter changes; lags, cycle positions, horizons of effecting, affected module(s); nesting.
4. Perform analysis of the dependency-defined organizational framework using math modeling, perhaps with scenarios of possible events, post-optimality analysis, etc.

5. Examine tolerance at this level and module for necessary adjustments by other (action) levels/modules and their impact; rules development for responses and other (action) adjustments.
6. Make adjustment (goals, measurements, constraints, decision variables) toward available data, and decision timing, given the horizons. Achieve corresponding data management system alignment.
7. Define the logical decision domain for each module acting independently; then relate to other horizontal and vertical modules so that matching or interfacing will be achieved.
8. Including all relevant exogenous variables/parameters and data system needs, design small realistic model(s) to support decision(s) at each specific module.
9. Determine and specify the organizationally-effective adjustment in response to anticipated (planning) and observed (feedback) data, through use of relevant interacting activity models.

4.4. MSA and a productive system

The goal is to characterize each level of a generalized productive system. Models, data, and level must be matched and integrated. A stand-alone (disaggregated, decentralized) operating element can then be developed with consistent criteria, relevant inputs and outputs, and foreknowledge of decision impact.

This is a conceptual framework. Amplification will take place as the MSA steps are followed.

4.4.1. Scope, complexity, responsibility, hierarchical differences

Top management's actions are pervasive, as are the indirect influences of the Board of Directors and the Stockholders. Analysis, then, must begin at the (0) or strategic level. MSA suggests two differing perspectives for level (0): shorter-term and inwardly directed, and longer-term and outwardly directed. The internal data (both directions) will carry details of operating policies and details of production planning results. The external data will contain estimates of required capacity/capability/product changes and the costs and benefits of various scale, technological, and locational alternatives. Capital spending proposals will be supported from level (1) by detailed internal cost data, and by level (0) to the Board by estimated return-on-investment results. The investment program decisions to level (1) will provide timing, technology, and other implementation criteria.

Level (0) must determine its measures of effectiveness through interaction with the Board (e.g. What is the meaning of 'maximize long-term shareholder wealth'?) It will then select values for its short-term decision variables (operating policies for Purchasing, Production, Distribution, Marketing, and Credit) as well as its ROI and portfolio variables (investments, financing, dividends). As operating policy criteria are evaluated level (1) will apply these measures of effectiveness to aggregate planning models so that utilization plans are acceptable. The result of these activities is an agreed set of guidelines and weights, and an optimal ((0) to Board and (1) to (0)) program for their respective horizons. Continual revisions respond to change in the environment of both levels.

Level (1) must deal with fixed facilities and known capital additions. Inputs must include consistent products demand and factors cost forecasting, with update frequency dependent on cost and capacity sensitivity. The principal capacity variable is manpower (hire-and-fire, overtime, second or third shift), and the production plan allocates on the basis of lowest average distributed cost per unit. All variable factor prices are included, including working capital (raw materials, in-process, finished goods).

Level (2) makes manpower assignments based on production schedules derived from (1)'s production plan, and manages materials planning to support the schedule. The key variable at level (2) is that of materials conversion to meet delivery priorities. The extension of this perspective horizontally is termed Materials Flow Management (procurement, receipt, in-process, production commitment, finished goods, distribution, and delivery).[1] The schedule established by level (2) is based on materials deliveries timing estimates, and the dispatch efficiencies reported by level (3). Maintenance

1. My progress in using the MSA concept has accelerated greatly due to the comments of Lawrence S. Mannis of the Babcock Graduate School of Management at Wake Forest University. We are jointly preparing a paper in the Materials Flow area.

downtime, vacations, training – all are worked into the schedule, which is based on required distribution rates and current inventory.

Level (3) makes dispatch decisions supporting the schedule. Manpower and materials, and machinery/equipment availability, are known and fixed. The key variable at level (3) is timing – the sequencing decisions which govern the movement of work, and its estimated completion time. Essential inputs to dispatch planning include schedules, materials receipts and condition reports, manpower checkins, machine outages, work status. Level (3) is a turnaround element, where activity planning, performance, and control all take place in real-time. Job shops use sequencing heuristics to maximize throughput, minimize idle time or delay. With assembly lines, a shorter-horizon version of the level (2) schedule is more usual. Outputs from level (3) lead to schedule review and change.

4.4.2. Quantitative analysis and decision domains

The principal issue here is to perceive the entire models structure as being nested – with consistent decision variables directly convertible for use as constraints or reporting values – and with consistent and comparable measures of effectiveness. A capital budgeting variable will be (0, 1) and will have highly aggregated revenue, costs, and timing data during strategic evaluation. The same variable will be represented in terms of time-staged working capital, production capability, manpower budgets, and distribution marketing considerations at level (1). Financing may provide only limited working capital expansion. Both planned and existing facilities must then work within inventory, manpower, training, and receivables restrictions in the aggregate. Such restrictions will show up in all of the departmental budgets in accordance with the operating policy criteria.

As the production plan moves to level (2) each higher variable is converted into a (time-staged) constraint on plant production requirements. The availability of shadow prices and shadow costs throughout these (0, 1, 2) levels allows explicit tradeoff evaluations – as well as a high degree of across-levels understanding – where 'shared' variables are involved. Of particular value is the well

Level and Horizon	Scope	Fin. Reports & Forecasts Inputs (source)	Criteria (0) Outputs (to)
Top (0) 2-5 yrs	Strategic	Criteria (BD) Facilities proposals (1)	Fin. reports (BD) Investment program (BD, 1)
12-18 mo.	Operating policy	Aggregate functional plans (1)	Criteria for op. planning (1)
		Prod. plan results	Policy changes (1, BD)
Dep't (1) 3-18 mo.	Productive system balancing Manpower plan	Op. Policy (0) Scheduling results (2)	Prod. plan results (0) Plan revisions (2)
Plant (2) 1-12 wks.	Scheduling	Prod. plan (1) Dispatch results (3)	Scheduling results (1) Scheduling revisions (3)
Prod. Sup. (3) 1-7 days	Dispatch & control	Schedule (2) Activities (3)	Dispatch results (2) Control revisions (3)

recognized sequence of higher-level decisions to lower-level constraints, and lower-level results to higher-level revision.

The degree of upward dependency and sensitivity can be shown at any level. At level (2), scheduling is actually an implied completion rate which builds on level (3) decisions on time use as they appear in production results. Thus, detailed manpower and materials planning activities are dependent on the quality of level (3) time-use data. At level (1), machine use, materials, and manpower are all implied decision variables when products and their timing are allo-

Level	Criteria	Model Class	Decisions	Output form
Top (0)	ROI, Mkt share, Revenues, Profit (EPS)	Integer LP (maybe NLP) Stochastic	Project choices	Facilities plan and timing
	Contribution, Volume, Cost	LP, NLP + sensitivity Deterministic	Functional op. policies	Working capital, Production, Marketing budget
Dept. (1)	Minimize total relevant cost (incl. capital)	LP (usually) + sensitivity Deterministic	Products, Volumes, Plants, Timing	Prod. plan by location
Plant (2)	Min. plant variable costs	LP (usually) including technology	Volume, Timing	MRP, Schedule, Shift/OT assignments, Shipment plan
Prod. Sup. (3)	Min. idle time, Min. delay, Max. thruput	Heuristic simulation LP (maybe)	Timing of work	Dispatch plan (job, location, next . .)

cated in the aggregate. The effectiveness of scheduling activities at the plants influences direct standard costs data, and the shape of the plant production possibilities curve. Allocations and cost-center managerial rewards will follow. The models manipulation should also indicate the cost penalties associated with non-ideal product mix for any location – a guide for capital expenditure planning.

4.4.3. Data and information flows

Many of the data requirements have been identified in prior steps. If disaggregation and decentralization are necessary, not merely behaviorally desirable, consequences of the firm's characteristics, then decentralized data base and processing capabilities should follow, for the same reasons.

A current trend in data base management is toward distributed systems, with the specifics dependent on the application.

The editor of the *EDP Analyzer*, Richard Canning[5] has reported a number of applications of various aspects of distributed systems both in Europe and in the United States. In essence, data entry takes place at the point where the data is generated, is stored locally, and can be placed into file locally for later retrieval and use. Further, the minicomputers have their own data base capabilities with various query and processing languages already existing and in use and can, of course, communicate with other compatible machines.

Technology indeed exists for such, and the discussion which follows implements the distributed data concept for a production system.

A real-time data processing and information requirement has been shown to exist at level (3). If the complexity and critical nature requires, computers can be used. The needed data relates to the plant and its available factors for production – and to its record of cost and volume results. These data are most readily entered, processed, maintained, and retrieved at the plant. The plant's activities and data needs define it as a natural node for distributed data base. The plant's modeling needs define its required logical decision support programs. The combination of these two specifications define the stand-alone EDP capability needed. As Thorn [16] noted, a minicomputer by today's standards can accommodate rather large-scale demands. The EDP system must also store and retrieve inputs from other parts of the system – notably the schedule from level (2) and probably a portion of the production plan from level (1). Economics and flexibility will determine the best way to accomplish both real-time and batch work.

The characteristics of the other parts of the system are also 'convertible' into a corresponding EDP capability – the models, the data storage volume and logical structure – and the most effective way to retrieve and use them for decision support. In most higher-level cases, real-time EDP is not a requirement, while large-scale batch processing may indeed be needed. Level (2) procurement and follow-up activities may be an exception – and if the same software supports both (2) and (3), then the real-time capability already exists. In each level, the horizon, decisions, criteria, and scope define the necessary organizational, informational, and quantitative arrangements and relationships for effectiveness.

4.5. Conclusion

A holistic yet detailed analysis of the organization and its decision environment is required for planning and control system development. And if the example of the Coca-Cola Company [9] is any indication, our industrial organizations are moving toward the 'aggregated analytic capabilities' idea, with decision support teams *doing* MSA.

We, as decision scientists, are the vital element in uniting modeling methods with management-oriented information system outputs.

References

1. Ackoff, Russel L., A Note on Systems Science', *Interfaces*, vol. 2, no. 4 (August 1972), pp. 40–41.
2. Austin, Larry F. and Hogan, W. W., 'Optimizing the Procurement of Aviation Fuels', *Management Science*, vol. 22, no. 5 (January 1976), pp. 515–527.
3. Burnham, John M., 'Alimentos Latinoamerica, C. A.', *Interfaces*, vol. 6, no. 2 (August 1976), pp. 50–56.
4. ——, 'Accounting and Finance', invited chapter in vol. II in Joseph J. Moder and Salah E. Elmaghraby (eds.) *Handbook of Operations Research* (New York: Van Nostrand-Reinhold, (forthcoming).
5. Canning, Richard G. (ed.), 'Distributed Data Systems', *EDP Analyzer*, vol. 14, no. 6 (June 1976), pp. 1–13.
6. Cleland, David I. and King, William R., *Systems Analysis and Project Management* (New York: McGraw-Hill Book Co., 1968).
7. ——, *Management: A Systems Approach* (New York: McGraw-Hill Book Co., 1972).
8. Churchman, C. W., Ackoff, R. H., and Arnoff, E. L., *Introduction to Operations Research* (New York: John Wiley & Sons, 1957).
9. Copper, J. H. and Underhill, V. D., 'Decision Support: How It Works – One Company's Opinion', presented at the Southeast AIDS Workshop 'How Management Science Can Make a Major Contribution to Business', Atlanta, Georgia (February 1976).
10. Grinyer, Peter H. and Batt, C. D., 'Some Tentative Findings on Corporate Financial

Simulation Models', *Operational Research Quarterly*, vol. 25, no. 1 (March 1974), pp. 149–168.
11. Kanter, Jerome, *Management-Oriented Management Information Systems*, 2nd edn. (Englewood Cliffs, N.J.: Prentice-Hall, Inc., 1976).
12. Kennedy, Miles H. and Mahapatra, S., 'Information Analysis for Effective Planning and Control', *Sloan Management Review*, vol. 16, no. 2 (Winter 1975), pp. 71–78.
13. King, William R. and Cleland, D. I., 'The Design of Management Information Systems: An Information Analysis Approach', *Management Science*, vol. 22, no. 3 (November 1975), pp. 286–296.
14. Sprague, Ralph, H., 'The Functions and Requirements of a Model Base Management System', Proceedings of Seventh Western AIDS Conference, Seattle, Washington (March 1976).
15. Sprague, Ralph H. and Hugh J. Watson, 'Model Management in MIS', Proceedings of Seventh Annual Meeting AIDS, Cincinnati, Ohio (November 1975).
16. Thorn, Ron G., 'Notes to Facilitate Workshop Discussion of Minicomputers in Production Operations', MIS Workshop, Eighth Annual Conference AIDS, San Francisco, California (November 1976).
17. Tocher, K. D., 'Notes for Discussion on "Control"', *Operational Research Quarterly*, vol. 27, no. 1 (March 1976), pp. 231–240.

Part B. Manufacturing

Section 3. Hierarchical production and inventory planning

5. Hierarchical planning systems – a production application[1]

ARNOLDO C. HAX and GABRIEL R. BITRAN

5.1. Introduction

Many authors have attempted to provide definitions to characterize the essence of planning. One definition, which we find particularly suitable for the purposes of this chapter, was presented by Peter Drucker [10] in an old article where he explored the role of management sciences in long range planning. Although his definition was intended to describe primarily long range or strategic planning efforts, we will use it as a vehicle for discussing the most significant element of planning in general. This is what Drucker had to say: 'Planning is the continuous process of making present entrepreneurial (risk-taking) decisions systematically and with the best possible knowledge of their futurity, organizing systematically the efforts needed to carry out these decisions, and measuring the results of these decisions against the expectations through organized, systematic feedback.'

By carefully examining this definition we can identify the following elements in the planning process.

1. Planning is a *continuous* and *systematic* effort, that requires permanent attention on the part of management. It is not an isolated task that can be performed only once or twice a year. On the contrary, it forces managers to consider, in a systematic way, all the opportunities and alternatives available for decision making. Once the appropriate courses of action have been selected and the implementation of these decisions is under

1. This work was partially supported by the Office of Naval Research under contract N00014-75-C-0556.

way, it is necessary to watch closely for the unavoidable differences that will take place between the plan and the actual realization of this plan. This monitoring effort, that leads to the establishment of appropriate measures of performance, the control of the actual observations and the replanning activities, is what makes planning a continuous process.

2. Planning deals with *present* (as opposed to future) decisions, or, as Drucker puts it, planning does not deal with future decisions but rather with *the futurity of present decisions*. These present decisions are obviously affected by uncertain future events, that should be assessed or forecasted in the most appropriate way possible. However, managers have to realize that, no matter how hard they try, it will not be possible to forecast these future events with total accuracy, and today decisions have to be made without these future uncertainties being completely resolved. The planning effort, therefore, attempts to guide managers in making their current decisions.
3. Planning has to be consistent with the policies adopted by the enterprises toward the inherent risks associated with decisions that are conducted under a high level of uncertainty. There are two types of errors managers are exposed to when they decide on a specific course of action:
   i. To make the wrong decision.
   ii. Not to make the right decision.

If a manager is severely penalized when he commits the first type of error, his actions will become extremely conservative and many good, but risky, opportunities will not be seized by the firm. This will result in the realization of a great number of type two errors. The converse is also true. From this point of view planning becomes a complex art of balancing these two conflicting and opposing forces in a way that satisfies the overall objectives of the firm.

As can be inferred from this very brief discussion, planning is an extremely complex activity. Much has been said about the lack of impact management science has had in providing effective support to managers, particularly at the top levels of the organization. To some degree, this is due to the insufficient knowledge on the part of managers to understand the strengths and limitations of mathematical models and computer technology, and the naivete of management scientists to appreciate the complexities of the management process. To some extent this also results from the unstructured nature of some of the planning tasks which do not lend themselves easily to a systematic treatment.

The present paper discusses the general issues associated with the design of hierarchical planning systems to support managerial decisions. It also illustrates the specific development of such a system in the production environment.

We begin by analyzing the managerial decision making process. Section 2 presents Anthony's framework to classify managerial decisions, and Section 3 analyzes the implication of such a framework for the design of planning systems. The role of computers and mathematical models of managerial aids is discussed in Section 4. Sections 5–10, which represent the core of the paper, describe the development of a hierarchical production planning system.

5.2. The decision making process

The major objective of a planning system is to improve the quality of decision making by providing managers with a disciplined way to evaluate the consequences of their actions and to coordinate the managerial process throughout the firm. Therefore, it is important to devote some time to reflect upon the nature of the decision making process, and to evaluate the role that systems and models can play in increasing managerial effectiveness.

Several ways have been suggested to categorize the decisions faced by managers. We would like to discuss the framework proposed by Robert Anthony [2], which has proven to be extremely helpful in generating better insights into the decision making process, and in defining the characteristics that a sound planning system should possess.

Anthony's framework classified decisions into three categories: strategic planning, management control[2], and operational control.

2. Other authors (such as Ackoff [1]) have often designated the intermediate category as tactical planning. We will use management control and tactical planning as equivalent terms throughout the paper.

Let us briefly review the characteristics of each of these categories and comment on their implications for a systems approach to planning.

The examples given to illustrate specific decisions belonging to each category are based primarily on the production and distribution activities of a manufacturing firm. This is done simply for consistency and convenience, as the suggested framework is certainly appropriate to deal with broader kinds of decisions.

5.2.1. Strategic planning

Strategic planning is concerned mainly with establishing managerial policies and with developing the necessary resources the enterprise needs to satisfy its external requirements in a manner consistent with its specific goals. Anthony defines strategic planning as 'the process of deciding on objectives of the organization, on changes in these objectives, on the resources used to attain these objectives, and on the policies that are to govern the acquisition, use, and disposition of these resources'.

In the area of logistics the most important strategic decisions are concerned with the design of the production and distribution facilities, involving major capital investments for the development of new capacity, either through the expansion of existing capacity, or the construction or purchase of new facilities and equipment. These decisions include the determination of location and size of new plants and warehouses, the acquisition of new production equipment, the design of working centers within each plant, and the design of transportation facilities, communication equipment, data processing means, etc. Other decisions of this nature which have significant marketing and financial implications are made-or-buy decisions, product line diversity, quantity versus price trade-offs, divestment of facilities, etc.

These decisions are extremely important because, to a great extent, they are responsible for maintaining the competitive capabilities of the firm, determining its rate of growth, and eventually defining its success or failure. An essential characteristic of these strategic decisions is that they have long lasting effects, thus forcing long planning horizons in their analysis. This, in turn, requires the consideration of uncertainties and risk attitudes in the decision making process. Moreover, strategic decisions are resolved at fairly high managerial levels, and are affected by information which is both external and internal to the firm. Thus, any form of rational analysis of these decisions necessarily has a very broad scope, requiring information to be processed in a very aggregate form to allow all the dimensions of the problem to be included and to prevent top managers from being distracted by unnecessary operational details.

5.2.2. *Management control (tactical planning)*

Anthony defines management control as 'the process by which managers assure that resources are obtained and used effectively and efficiently in the accomplishment of the organization's objective'. The emphasis of management control is on the resource utilization process.

Once the physical facilities have been decided upon the basic problem to be resolved is the effective allocation of resources (e.g., production, storage and distribution capacities, work force availabilities, financial, marketing and managerial resources) to satisfy demand and technological requirements, taking into account the costs and revenues associated with the operation of the resources available to the firm. These decisions are far from simple when we deal with several plants, many distribution centers, many regional and local warehouses, with products requiring complex multistage fabrication and assembly processes, that serve broad market areas affected by strong randomness and seasonalities in their demand patterns. They usually involve the consideration of a medium range time horizon, divided into several periods, and require significant aggregation of the relevant managerial information. Typical decisions to be made within this context are utilization of regular and overtime work force, allocation of aggregate capacity resources to product families, accumulation of seasonal inventories, definition of distribution channels, and selection of transportation and transshipment alternatives. The most common vehicle to communicate the management control decision of the firm is the company's budget.

5.2.3. Operational control

After making an aggregate allocation of the resources of the firm, it is necessary to deal with the day-to-day operational and scheduling decisions. This stage of the decision making process is called operational control. Anthony defines it as 'the process of assuring that specific tasks are carried out effectively and efficiently'. The operational control decisions require the complete disaggregation of the information generated at higher levels into the details consistent with the managerial procedures followed in daily activities. Typical decisions at this level are the assignment of customer orders to individual machines, the sequencing of these orders in the work

Factor	Strategic planning	Management control	Operational control
Purpose	Management of change, resource acquisition	Resource utilization	Execution, evaluation, and control
Implementation instruments	Policies, objectives, capital investments	Budgets	Procedures, reports
Planning horizon	Long	Medium	Short
Scope	Broad, but often affecting a portion of the organization	Broad, corporate wide	Narrow
Level of management involvement	Top	Middle	Low
Frequency of replanning	Low	Medium	High
Source of information	Largely external	External and Internal	Largely internal
Level of aggregation of information	Highly aggregated	Moderately aggregated	Detailed
Required accuracy	Low	Medium	High
Degree of uncertainty	High	Medium	Low
Degree of risk	High	Medium	Low

Figure 1. Differentiating factors of the three decision categories.

shop, inventory accounting and inventory control activities, dispatching, expediting and processing of orders, vehicular scheduling, credit allocation, advertising placement, etc.

These 3 types of decisions – strategic planning, management control, and operational control – differ markedly in various dimensions, the nature of which, expressed in relative terms, is shown in Figure 1.

5.3. Implication of Anthony's framework: a hierarchical integrative approach

There are significant conclusions that can be drawn from Anthony's classification regarding the nature of a decision support system. First, strategic, tactical and operational decisions cannot be made in isolation because they interact strongly with one another. Therefore, an integrated approach is required if one wants to avoid the problems of suboptimization. Second, this approach, although essential, cannot be made without decomposing the elements of the problem in some way, within the context of a hierarchical system that links higher level decisions with lower level ones in an effective manner. Decisions that are made at higher levels provide constraints for lower level decision making; in turn, detailed decisions provide the necessary feedback to evaluate the quality of aggregate decision making.

This hierarchical approach recognizes the distinct characteristics of the type of management participation, the scope of the decision, the level of aggregation of the required information and the time framework in which the decision is to be made. In our opinion, it would be a serious mistake to attempt to deal with all these decisions simultaneously, via a monolithic system or model. Even if computer and methodological capabilities would permit the solution of a large detailed integrated logistics model, which is clearly not the case today, that approach is inappropriate because it is not responsive to the management needs at each level of the organization, and would prevent the interactions between models and managers at each organization echelon.

The basic questions to be resolved when designing a hierarchical system are:

- How to partition the decision process into modules or subproblems which properly represent the various levels of decision making in the organizational structure?
- How to aggregate and disaggregate the information through the various hierarchical levels?
- How to solve each of the subproblems identified by the partitioning procedure?
- What linking mechanisms should be used among the subproblems?, and
- How to evaluate the overall performance of the system, particularly with regard to issues of suboptimization introduced by the hierarchical design?

These questions are not easy to answer. Unfortunately, there is very little theoretical and empirical work that can be used as a practical guide to hierarchical design. Clearly, the questions cannot be addressed in isolation since they strongly interact with one another. Some factors which have to be taken into consideration are:

- The organizational structure of the firm that establishes the hierarchical breakdown of responsibilities, identifies the decision makers the system is intended to support, and provides the basis for a preliminary decomposition of the overall decision process.
- The nature of the resulting subproblems, which suggest the methodology that might be applicable to solve each of the system modules. Naturally, it is preferable to define subproblems which lend themselves to easy and effective solutions.
- The nature of the product structure, which is helpful in identifying ways in which information regarding individual items can be aggregated into families and product types.
- The degree of interaction and transfer of information from each of the hierarchical levels of the system. An effective design should facilitate the specification of the constraints that higher level decisions impose on the lower hierarchical echelons, and the control feedback that is transferred from the lower to the higher level decisions. In addition, the feasibility of disaggregation of information should be guaranteed throughout the process and measures of performance should be available to assess the overall quality of decision making.

Much research needs to be allocated in order to obtain a satisfactory answers to these issues. Meanwhile, the task of hierarchical system design is an art that requires great doses of pragmatism and experience to be accomplished properly. Few practical applications of hierarchical systems have been reported in the literature. From recent work conducted at MIT we can cite publications by Hax [18] dealing with a continuous manufacturing process, Hax and Meal [20], and Bitran and Hax [5] addressing the use of hierarchical systems in a batch processing environment, and Armstrong and Hax [3] describing an application for a job shop activity.

In Section 5 of this paper we provide a brief description of a hierarchical planning system to deal with tactical and operational production decisions.

5.4. The role of management support systems

The next issue to be addressed in the development of a hierarchical planning system is to what extent computers and management science can play an important role in supporting the broad spectrum of managerial decisions. Again, we believe that Anthony's classification provides a useful framework for discussing this issue.

Strategic planning decisions are the most demanding, creative and unstructured decisions managers have to make. They are often triggered by singular opportunities that present themselves at irregular intervals. Obviously, it is impossible to suggest a unique kind of model or approach to deal with these problems. Nonetheless, a significant amount of effort has been spent in the last twenty years oriented toward the improvement of strategic planning effectiveness. We believe there are three major areas of accomplishments in this field:

1. *A process orientation.* As expressed by Vancil and Lorange [33], the theory of corporate strategic planning is simple: 'using a time horizon of several years, top management reassesses its current strategy by looking for opportunities and threats in the environment and by analyzing the company's resources to identify its strengths and weaknesses'. Although this is a fairly straightforward concept, the process of implementing a strategic pro-

gram is far from simple. In a large diversified corporation many executives, occupying different positions in the organizational hierarchy, are called for an active participation, whose coordination has to be handled properly. It is not surprising, therefore, that a lot of attention has been given to the process of strategic planning, attempting to bring some discipline and pragmatism to the overall planning process, to describe the role of the key individuals in charge of planning, and to institutionalize some of the critical phases of planning. Vancil and Lorange [25 and 33] have produced a three cycle approach to planning, particularly useful to diversified, multidivisional companies. The Marketing Science Institute, through project P.I.M.S. (Profit Impact of Marketing Strategy, see references [9] and [29]) has conducted a statistical analysis intended to identify and weigh the various factors that influence the performance of strategic planning, which contains useful guidelines for the selection of strategic courses of action. Also a number of management consulting firms have developed valuable approaches to implement a comprehensive strategic planning process in an organization. Foremost among those approaches are the Stanford Research Institute approach [29], proposing a number of steps leading to the creation of a formal planning system; the Boston Consulting Group approach [37 and 38], using the learning curve concept and portfolio analysis for product diversification; and the Strategy Center's approach recommended by Arthur D. Little, Inc. [35], based on the implications of the product life cycle.

2. *Capital investments analysis.* As we have already indicated, strategic plans normally lead to capital investment decisions, where large amounts of money are allocated with the expectation of generating future revenues in excess of the initial investment costs. These decisions are affected by severe uncertainties and risks, and deserve very careful analysis due to their irreversible nature. Decision analysis, simulation techniques, and utility theory have proven to be very valuable tools in assessing the merits of investment alternatives (see Hax and Wiig [21] for a survey and application of these tools). Many companies are now using routinely more modern approaches to support their capital budgeting decisions.
3. *Corporate models.* A third type of effort aimed at supporting

strategic decisions has been the development of corporate wide models. A good and recent survey of this area is given in Naylor [28]. Corporate models tend to emphasize the financial nature of the business, typically addressing the budgetary implications of a given strategic action. Most of them are simulation models – as opposed to optimization models – constructed to answer 'what if' types of questions.

Strategic planning is regarded very often as a separate activity in the ongoing planning process, that requires a low frequency of updating and is rather opportunistic in nature. By contrast, tactical and operational decisions demand a continuous, repetitive, and structured support. Tactical decisions, dealing with the resource allocation process through a middle range time horizon, call for strong integration and coordination among the choices available to the decision maker. These choices very often are large in number and are affected by complex interactions and constraints. Since they are hard to evaluate on merely intuitive grounds, a decision maker will benefit greatly from a model based support effort. Historically, mathematical programming has been the type of model used more widely in this capacity and has contributed a great deal to improving the quality of decision making at the tactical level.

The role of models in supporting operational decisions is more limited due to the great deal of information required to resolve operational problems. The central issue of the planning process is to allow for consistency between the tactical and operational levels by providing a useful disaggregation scheme of the tactical actions. In the following section, we will explore this issue in detail.

5.5. A hierarchical production planning system

Rather than discussing in the abstract the issues associated with the design and implementation of a hierarchical planning system, we would like to describe in some detail the development of such a system to support tactical and operational decisions in a production environment.

We have decided to conduct our analysis of hierarchical planning systems in the field of production for two primary reasons. First, production decisions involve complex choices among a large number of alternatives. These choices have to be made by trading-off conflicting objectives under the presence of financial, technological, and marketing constraints. Such decisions are not trivial and model based systems have proven to be of great assistance to support managerial actions in this field. In fact, one could argue that, in this respect, production is the most mature field of management. A great many contributions have been made in this field from operations research, system analysis, and computer sciences. We believe it is both significant and feasible to attempt a more comprehensive and integrative approach to production management.

Second, the production environment lends itself ideally to testing the potential strengths and weaknesses of hierarchical planning systems. The optimal planning and scheduling of multiple products has received much attention in the operations research literature. Several attempts (Manne [26], Dzielinski, Baker, and Manne [11], Dzielinski and Gomory [12], Lasdon and Terjung [24]) have been made to formulate the overall problem as a single mixed-integer mathematical programming model to be solved on a rolling horizon basis. However, these approaches require data such as the forecasted demand of every item for a complete seasonal cycle, usually a full year. When the systems involve the scheduling of several thousands of items, these data requirements become overwhelming and the resulting planning process becomes unrealistic due to the magnitude of the forecast errors inherent in such detailed long-term forecasts.

The obvious alternative to a detailed monolithic approach to production planning is a hierarchical approach. As we have indicated, the basic design questions of a hierarchical planning system are the partitioning of the overall planning problem and the linkage of the resulting subproblems. An important input to resolve these questions is the number of levels recognized in the product structure. Hax and Meal [20] identified three different levels:

- *Items* are the final products to be delivered to the customers. They represent the highest degree of specificity regarding the manufactured products. A given product may generate a large number of items differing in terms of characteristics such as color, packaging, labels, accessories, size, etc.

– *Families* are groups of items which share a common manufacturing setup cost. Economies of scale are accomplished by jointly replenishing items belonging to the same family.
– *Types* are groups of families whose production quantities are to be determined by an aggregate production plan. Families belonging to a type normally have similar costs per unit of production time, and similar seasonal demand patterns.

These three levels are required to characterize the product structure in many batch processing manufacturing environments. Obviously, in some practical application more or fewer levels might be needed. In the remainder of this paper we will propose a hierarchical planning system based on these three levels of item aggregation. The system can be extended to different numbers of aggregation levels by defining adequate subproblems.

The first step in the hierarchical planning system is to allocate production capacity among product types by means of an aggregate planning model. The planning horizon of this model covers normally a full year, in order to take into proper consideration the fluctuating demand requirements for the products. We advocate the use of a linear programming model at this level. There are various advantages associated with the use of such a model that will be addressed in the next section. The major drawback is that a linear programming model does not take setup costs into consideration. The implications of this limitation will be examined later.

The second step in the planning process is to allocate the production quantities for each product type among the families belonging to that type. This is done by disaggregating the results of the aggregate planning model only for the first period of the planning horizon, thus reducing quite heavily the required amount of data collection and data processing. The disaggregation is done, assuring consistency and feasibility among the type and family production decisions, attempting to minimize, at the same time, the total setup costs incurred in the production of families. It is only at this stage that setup costs are explicitly considered.

Finally, the family production allocation is divided among the items belonging to each family. The objective of this decision is to maintain all items with inventory levels maximizing the time between family setups. Again, consistency and feasibility are the driving constraints of this disaggregation process.

An extensive justification of this approach is provided in Hax [16]. Figure 2 shows the overall conceptualization of the hierarchical planning effort. A computer based system has been developed

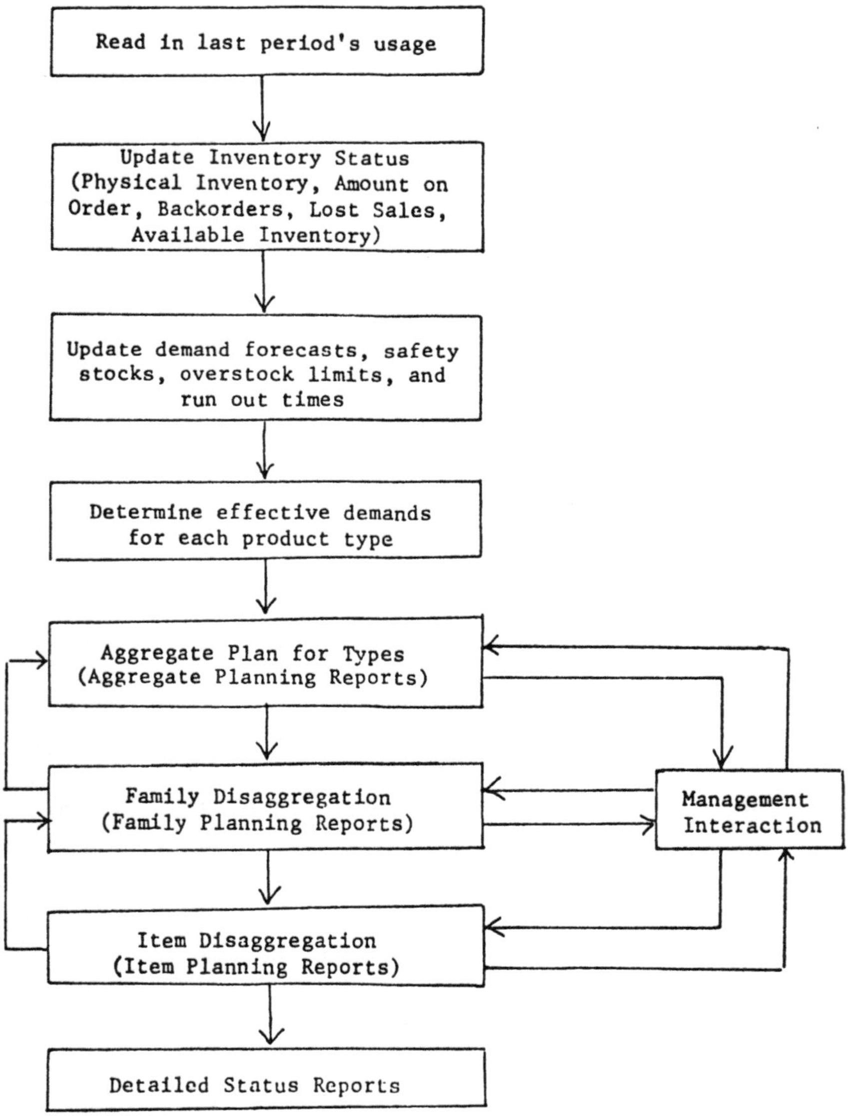

Figure 2. Conceptual overview of hierarchical planning system.

to facilitate its implementation. The details of such a system are reported elsewhere (Hax, Golovin, Bosyj, and Victor [19]). Herein we will concentrate on the methodological issues associated with the system design. This discussion follows closely the paper by Bitran and Hax [5]. The reader interested in further details of the proposed methodology should consult that paper.

5.6. Aggregate production planning for types

This is the highest level of planning in the production system, addressed at the product type level. Essentially any aggregate production planning model can be used as long as it represents adequately the practical problem under consideration. (For extensive discussions of possible aggregate models see Buffa and Taubert [8], Hax [17], and Silver [31]). Without loss of generality and for purposes of presentation in this paper we consider the following simplified linear program at this level:

Problem P

$$\text{Minimize} \sum_{i=1}^{I} \sum_{t=1}^{T} (c_{it}X_{it} + h_{it}I_{it}) + \sum_{t=1}^{T} (r_tR_t + o_tO_t)$$

subject to:

$$\begin{aligned}
& X_{it} + I_{i,t+L} - I_{i,t+L-1} = d_{i,t+L}, && i = 1, \ldots, I;\ t = 1, \ldots, T \\
& \sum_{i=1}^{I} m_i X_{it} \leqq O_t + R_t && , t = 1, \ldots, T \\
& R_t \leqq (rm)_t && , t = 1, \ldots, T \\
& O_t \leqq (om)_t && , t = 1, \ldots, T. \\
& X_{it}, I_{it} \geqq 0 && , i = 1, \ldots, I;\ t = 1, \ldots, T \\
& R_t, O_t \geqq 0 && , t = 1, \ldots, T
\end{aligned}$$

The decision variables of the model are: X_{it}, the number of units to be produced of type i during period t; I_{it}, the number of units of inventory left over at the end of period t; R_t and O_t the regular and overtime hours used during period t, respectively.

The parameters of the model are: T, the length of the planning horizon; L, the length of the production lead time; c_{it}, the unit production cost; h_{it}, the inventory carrying cost per unit, per period; R_t and O_t the cost per manhour of regular and overtime labor, respectively; $(rm)_t$ and $(om)_t$, the total availability of regular and overtime hours in period t, respectively; and m_i, the inverse of the productivity rate for type i, in hours/unit. $d_{i,t+L}$ is the effective demand for type i during period $t + L$. (For a definition of effective demand see next section).

Whenever seasonal variations are present in the demand pattern of product types, the planning horizon has to cover a full seasonal cycle. Normally aggregate planning models have planning horizons of one year divided into equally spaced time intervals. If there is a significant production lead time, say of L time periods, there should be a frozen planning horizon equal to the production lead time. Therefore the decision regarding the amount to be produced at period t, X_{it}, has as primary input the effective demand during period $t + L$, $d_{i,t+L}$. Figure 3 illustrates these timing implications.

Whenever the production costs c_{it} are invariable with time, and the payroll of regular work force is a fixed commitment, terms $c_{it}X_{it}$ and r_tR_t are deleted from the objective function. In that case, the model simply seeks an optimum aggregate plan considering inventory holding costs and overtime costs as the basic trade-offs. It is straightforward to include in the model other cost factors, such as hiring and firing, backorders, subcontracting, lost scales, etc. Also the constraints can represent any number of technological, financial, marketing and other considerations.

Linear programming is a convenient type of model to use at this aggregate level due to the computational efficiency and the wide availability of linear programming codes. In addition, LP permits sensitivity and parametric analyses to be performed quite easily.

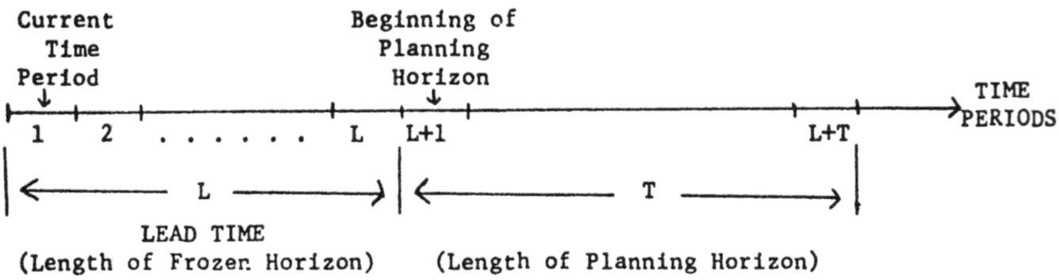

Figure 3. Timing implications in aggregate planning.

The shadow price information that becomes available when solving LP models can be of assistance in identifying opportunities for capacity expansions, market penetrations, introduction of new products, etc.

The most important benefits to be derived from an aggregate approach to production planning (as opposed to a detailed approach) are reduction in computational and data gathering costs, increase in demand forecast accuracy, and easier interaction with and evaluation of model results by managers.

Notice that manufacturing setup costs are purposely ignored in this aggregate model formulation. Normally setup costs have a secondary impact in determining the total production cost (see Section 10 for sensitivity analysis). Moreover, the inclusion of setup costs would force the model to be defined at a family level. This implies a high level of detail which invalidates all the advantages of aggregate planning (i.e. generates high computational costs, forecasts inaccuracies, and difficult managerial interactions). Consequently, setup costs are considered only at the second level of the hierarchical planning process.

Because of the uncertainties present in the planning process, only the first time period results of the aggregate model are implemented. At the end of every time period, new information becomes available that is used to update the model with a rolling planning horizon of length T. Therefore, the data transmitted from the type to the family level are the resulting production and inventory quantities for the first period of the aggregate model. These quantities will be disaggregated among the families belonging to each corresponding type.

5.7. Demand forecasts

Unless care is taken, the use of aggregation may lead to infeasibilities. It is important to realize that inventories and demand only have physical meaning at the item level. The concept of product types is a mere abstraction that makes possible the aggregation process. When calculating product type inventories, it is incorrect to simply add the inventories of all the items belonging to a product type. Implicitly, that practice assumes complete interchangeability of the inventories among all the items in a product type, which is not the case. To illustrate this point, consider a product type consisting of items 1 and 2, whose initial inventories and demand requirements for the next five periods are as follows:

		Demand by period				
	Initial inventory	1	2	3	4	5
Item 1	600	100	100	200	200	400
Item 2	100	200	200	400	400	800
Total	700	300	300	600	600	1200

By simply considering total product type demand and inventory, we would calculate net demands of 0, 0, 500, 600, and 1200. But, in fact, we will run out of item 2 in periods 1 and 2. The problem arose from assuming that we could use product type inventory held in item 1 for item 2. This problem is corrected by defining *effective demands* for each item.

Formally, if $\bar{d}_{k,t}$ is the forecast demand for item k in period t, AI_k is its corresponding available inventory, and SS_k is its safety stock, the effective demand $d_{k,t}$ of item i for period t is given by:

$$\begin{aligned} d_{k,t} &= \max\left(0, \sum_{l=1}^{t} \bar{d}_{k,l} - AI_k + SS_k\right), \quad t = 1, 2, \ldots, t^* \\ d_{k,t} &= \bar{d}_{k,t} \qquad\qquad\qquad\qquad\qquad\quad , t = t^* + 1, \ldots, T \qquad (1) \end{aligned}$$

where t^* is the first time period in which the initial inventory is depleted, i.e.

$$\sum_{l=1}^{t^*-1} \bar{d}_{k,l} - AI_k + SS_k \leq 0, \quad \text{and}$$

$$\sum_{l=1}^{t^*} \bar{d}_{k,l} - AI_k + SS_k > 0$$

The effective demand for a type i is simply given by the sum of the effective demands for all items belonging to a given type, i.e.

$$d_{i,t} = \sum_{k \in K(i)} d_{k,t} \qquad (2)$$

where $K(i)$ is the set of all items k belonging to product type i.

In our previous example, the effective demands are:

	Effective demand by period				
	1	2	3	4	5
Item 1	0	0	0	0	400
Item 2	100	200	400	400	800
Total effective demand for product type	100	200	400	400	1200

The hierarchical forecasting system operates as follows:

1. An aggregate forecast is generated for each product type for each time period in the planning horizon.
2. The type forecasts are disaggregated down to item forecasts. This disaggregation can be done by forecasting the proportion of the total type demand corresponding to each item. These proportions can be updated using exponential smoothing techniques, which are appropriate to apply for a short horizon at a detailed level. Notice that item and family forecasts are only required for a few time periods in the product type disaggregation models we will present.
3. After updating the available inventory for each item, the effective item demand is calculated by applying expression (1) above. Whenever the initial available inventory exceeds the first period's demand, expression (1) requires item forecasts for successive periods in the planning horizon. These forecasts can be obtained by making trend and/or seasonability adjustments to the initial period forecasts, again using exponential smoothing techniques.
4. The effective demand for types is obtained from expression (2). These demands are used in the aggregate model described in Section 6. Computer programs to perform automatically the necessary calculations are discussed in Bitran and Hax [5].

Note that this forecasting system is an example of a top down approach, using aggregate product type forecasts and disaggregating, rather than using detailed forecasts and summing to get the aggregate product type forecasts.

5.8. The family disaggregation model

The central condition to be satisfied at this level for a coherent disaggregation is the equality between the sum of the productions of the families in a product type and the amount dictated by the higher level for this type. This will assure consistency between the aggregate production plan and the family disaggregation process. We want to achieve this consistency by determining run quantities for each family that minimize the total setup cost among families.

We propose the following model to achieve family disaggregation. For every product type i solve:

Problem P_i

$$\text{Minimize} \sum_{j \in J^0} \frac{s_j d_j}{Y_j}$$

subject to:

$$\sum_{j \in J^0} Y_j = X_i^*$$

$$lb_j \leqq Y_j \leqq ub_j, \quad j \in J^0 \tag{3}$$

where Y_j is the number of units to be produced of family j, s_j is the setup cost for family j, d_j is the forecast demand for family j (usually an annual forecast demand), lb_j are lower and upper bounds for the quantity Y_j, and X_i^* is the total amount to be allocated among all the families belonging to type i. X_i^* has been determined by the aggregate planning model, and corresponds to the optimum value of the variable X_{i1} since we only implement the first period result of the aggregate model.

The lower bound lb_j, that defines the minimum production quantity for family j, is given by:

$$lb_j = \max[0, (d_{j,1} + d_{j,2} + \cdots + d_{j,L+1}) - AI_j + SS_j]$$

where $d_{j,1} + \cdots + d_{j,L+1}$ is the total forecast demand for family j during the production lead time plus the review period; AI_j is the current available inventory for family j (equal to the physical inventory, plus the amount on order, minus the backorders), and SS_j is the required safety stock. This lower bound lb_j guarantees that any backorders will be due to forecast errors beyond those absorbed by the safety stock SS_j.

The upper bound ub_j is given by

$$ub_j = OS_j - AI_j$$

where OS_j is the overstock limit of family j. When family j has a terminal demand at the end of its season, OS_j can be calculated by means of a newsboy model (see Zimmermann and Sovereign [36], p. 370).

The objective function of problem P_i assumes that the family run quantities should be proportional to the setup cost and annual demand for a given family. This seems to be a reasonable assumption (which is the basis of the economic order quantity formulation), that has performed satisfactorily when tested. Notice that the total inventory carrying cost has already been established in the aggregate planning model; therefore it does not enter in the current formulation.

The first constraint of problem P_i

$$\sum_{j \in J^0} Y_j = X_i^*$$

assures the equality between the aggregate model input X_i^* and the sum of the family run quantities. It is shown in Bitran and Hax [5, Appendix I-A] that this condition can be substituted by

$$\sum_{j \in J^0} Y_j \leqq X_i^* \tag{4}$$

without changing the optimum solution to problem P_i. In what follows we will relax the equality constraints into inequalities.

$J_0 = \{1, 2, \ldots\}$ denotes the set of indices of the families belonging to the product type under consideration. Initially J^0 contains only those families which trigger during the current planning period, i.e. those families whose current available inventory is such that

$$AI_j < (d_{j,1} + d_{j,2} + \ldots + d_{j,L+1}) + SS_j$$

Equivalently, we can define J^0 as containing all those families whose runout times are less than one time period, i.e.:

$$ROT_j = \frac{AI_j - SS_j}{\sum_{t=1}^{L+1} d_{j,t}} < 1$$

The production for these families has to be started now to avoid future backorders. All other families are put on a secondary list. These families will be scheduled only if extra capacity is available.

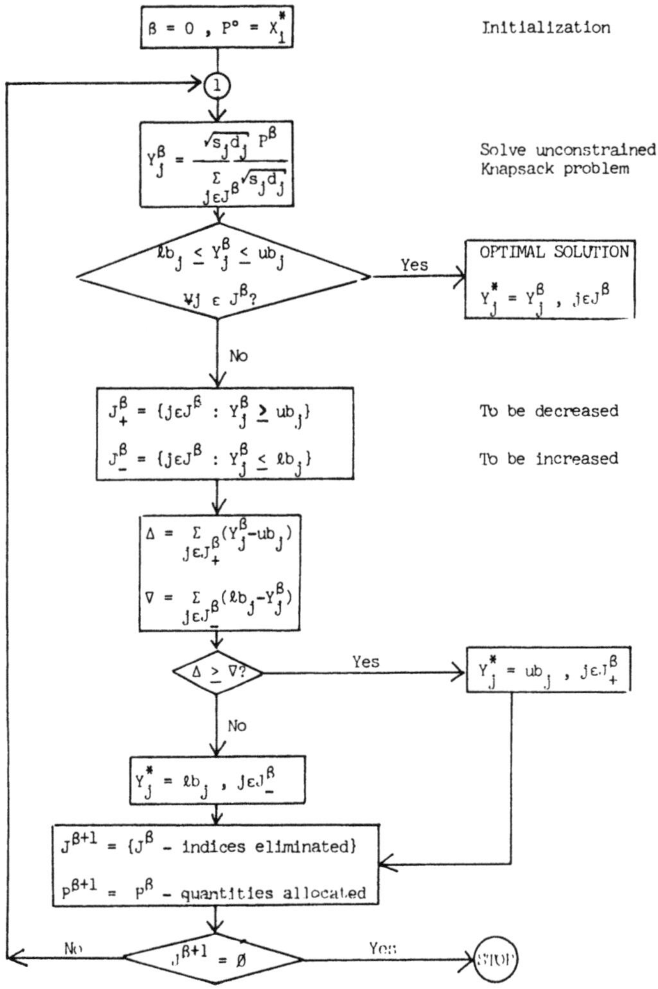

Figure 4. Family disaggregation algorithm.

Figure 4 presents an efficient algorithm to solve problem P_i through a relaxation procedure. Optimality and convergence proofs are given in [5]. The algorithm consists in ignoring initially the bounding constraints (3) and solving the objective function subject to the knapsack restriction (4). Then, a check is made to verify if the optimum values Y_j^* satisfy the bounds (3). If yes, the Y_j^*'s constitute the optimal solution for problem P_i. If no, at least some of the Y_j^*'s are shown to be optimal and a new iteration takes place. The algorithm is finite because at each iteration we determine the run quantity of at least one family.

5.9. The item disaggregation model

For the period in consideration all the costs have been already determined in the former two levels and any feasible disaggregation of a family run quantity has the same total cost. However, the feasible solution chosen will establish initial conditions for the next period and will affect future costs. In order to save setups in future periods it seems reasonable to distribute the family run quantity, among its items, in such a way that the items runout times coincide with the runout time of the family. A direct consequence is that all items of a family will trigger simultaneously. To attain this objective we propose to solve the following strictly convex knapsack problem for each family j:

Problem P_j

$$\text{Minimize}\,\frac{1}{2}\sum_{k\in K}\left[\frac{Y_j^* + \Sigma_{k\in K}(AI_k - SS_k)}{\Sigma_{k\in K}\,\Sigma_{t=1}^{L+1} d_{k,t}} - \frac{Z_k + AI_k - SS_k}{\Sigma_{t=1}^{L+1} d_{k,t}}\right]^2$$

subject to:

$$\sum_{k\in K} Z_k = Y_j^*$$

$$Z_k \leqq OS_k - AI_k$$

$$Z_k \geqq \max\left[O, \sum_{t=1}^{L+1} d_{k,t} - AI_k + SS_k\right]$$

where Z_k is the number of units to be produced of item k; AI_k, SS_k and OS_k are, respectively, the available inventory, safety stock, and overstock limit of item k; $d_{k,t}$ is the forecast demand for item k in period t; $K = \{1, 2, \ldots\}$ is the set of indices of all the items belonging to family j; and Y_j^* is the total amount to be allocated for all items belonging to family j. Y_j^* was determined by the family disaggregation model.

The first constraint of problem P_j requires consistency in the disaggregation from family to items. The last two constraints are the upper and lower bounds for the item run quantities. These bounds are similar to those defined for the family disaggregation model in the previous section.

The two terms inside the square bracket of the objective function represent, respectively, the runout time for family j, and the runout time for an item k belonging to family j. The minimization of the square of the difference of the runout times will make those quantities as close as possible. (The term $\frac{1}{2}$ in front of the objective function is just a computational convenience.)

An algorithm to solve this problem follows very closely the logic presented in the family disaggregation algorithm. Details are given in Bitran and Hax [5] and will not be presented here.

5.10. Computational results

We conducted a series of experiments to examine the performance of the hierarchical system under various conditions concerning size of forecast errors, capacity availability, magnitude of setup costs, and nature of the planning horizon.

The data used for these tests were taken from a manufacturer of rubber tires. The product structure characteristics and other relevant

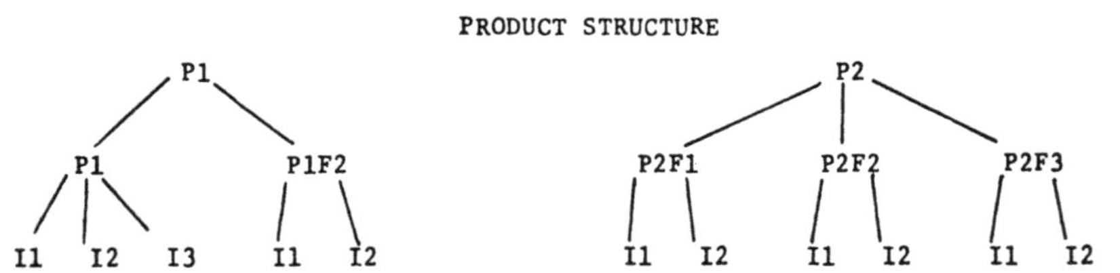

Family setup cost = $90	Family setup cost = $120
Holding cost = $.31/unit a month	Holding cost = $.40/unit a month
Overtime cost = $9.5/hour	Overtime cost = $9.5/hour
Productivity factor = .1 hr/unit	Productivity factor = .2 hrs/unit
Production lead time = 1 month	Production lead time = 1 month

Regular Workforce Costs and Unit Production Costs are considered fixed costs

Total Regular Workforce = 2000 hrs/month

Total Overtime Workforce = 1200 hrs/month

Figure 5. Product structure and other relevant information.

information are given in Figure 5. Figure 6 exhibits the demand pattern for both product types. Product type 1 had a terminal demand season (corresponding to the requirements of snow tires), and consisted of 2 families and 5 items. Demand for product type 2 was highly fluctuating throughout the year. Product type 2 had 3 families and 6 items. Families were groups of items sharing the same molds in the curing presses, and therefore sharing a common setup cost (items were, for instance, white wall and regular wall tires of a given class). Families and items have the same cost characteristics and productivity rates identical to their corresponding types.

The experiments consisted of applying the production planning system to a full year of simulated plant operations. Production decisions were made every four weeks, at which time a report was generated identifying aggregate as well as detailed decisions. The model was then updated, using normally a one year rolling planning horizon, and the process was repeated 13 times. At the end of the simulation total setup costs, inventory holding costs, overtime costs, and backorders were accounted for. A summary of eleven different simulation runs is provided in Figure 7. The simulations were implemented in the Computer Based Operations Management System (COMS) developed at MIT (see Hax, Golovin, Bosyj, and Victor [19]).

TIME PERIOD t	PRODUCT TYPE 1 P1	PRODUCT TYPE 2 P2
1	12,736	6,174
2	7,813	2,855
3	0	4,023
4	0	4,860
5	0	7,131
6	0	9,665
7	1,545	17,603
8	7,895	14,276
9	10,982	11,706
10	15,782	15,056
11	16,870	8,232
12	15,870	7,880
13	9,878	10,762
TOTAL	99,371	120,223

Figure 6. Demand patterns of product types.

Run / Cost components	1	2	3	4	5	6
	Base case No forecast errors	10% Forecast Errors	30% Forecast Errors	High setup cost Case I P1: 5000,50 P2: 400,400,1000 No forecast error	High setup cost Case II P1: 6000,4500 P2: 400,5000,3000 No forecast error	Tight capacity 1600 Reg. hrs. No forecast error
Setup	5,360	5,360	5,250	67,050	104,800	4,480
Holding	72,510	73,611	76,577	72,374	72,597	115,072
Overtime	81,111	81,425	82,365	81,111	81,102	117,439
Total cost	158,981	160,396	164,192	220,535	258,499	236,991
Backorders	2	1,513	6,243	10	4	144

Run / Cost components	7	8	9	10	11
	Loost capacity 2500 Reg. hrs No forecast error	6-month Planning horizon Normal capacity No forecast error	6-month Planning horizon Tight capacity No forecast error	6-month Planning horizon Normal capacity 10% forecast error	1-1-1-1-3-6 Planning horizon Normal capacity No forecast error
Setup	5,910	5,690	5,030	5,690	5,250
Holding	56,002	67,212	83,983	64,971	78,052
Overtime	48,507	88,597	103,332	90,773	75,440
Total cost	110,419	161,499	192,345	161,434	158,742
Backorders	0	0	16,658	2,951	73

Figure 7. Summary of computational results with proposed hierarchical planning system.

Run 1 can be regarded as the *base case*: no forecast errors, planning horizon of one year divided into 13 periods of 4 weeks duration each, normal capacity (defined as 2000 hours of regular time and 1200 hours of overtime per period), normal setup costs ($90 for families belonging to product type 1, and $120 per family belonging to product type 2). All the other runs include some variation with respect to characteristics of Run 1.

5.10.1. Sensitivity to forecast errors

Runs 1, 2, and 3 show the impact of forecast errors in the production planning decisions. As one would have expected, the quality of the decisions deteriorates under increasing forecast errors. Both cost and size of backorders increase when forecast errors begin to escalate. However, the system performs reasonably well even under forecast errors of up to 30 percent, included in run 3. (The 6243 units backordered in run 3 represent a 97 percent service level.) This is an important justification for the hierarchical approach since, obviously, aggregate forecasts can be more accurate than detailed forecasts.

5.10.2. Sensitivity to changes in setup costs

The values imputed to the setup costs in the base case (run 1) were realistic measures of the actual setup costs incurred in the normal manufacturing operations. They included direct setup costs (manpower and materials), as well as opportunity costs for having the machines idle while performing the changeover. We wanted to test the system's performance under extreme setup cost conditions. With this purpose in mind we made two different runs, runs 4 and 5, with the following setup cost characteristics.

	Type 1		Type 2		
	Family 1	Family 2	Family 1	Family 2	Family 3
Run 4	5000	50	400	400	1000
Run 5	6000	4500	400	5000	3000
Base Case – Run 1	90	90	120	120	120

As could be expected, the total cost associated with runs 4 and 5 increases significantly. One could observe that runs 1, 4, and 5 are almost identical in terms of inventory holding costs and overtime costs, which indicates that the overall production strategies for these runs do not change much. This could be a limitation of the hierarchical approach when applied to situations with extremely high set-up costs.

5.10.3. Sensitivity to capacity availability

Runs 6 and 7 evaluate the performance of the system under different capacity conditions. Run 6 makes available only 1600 hours of regular capacity per period; run 7 expands the regular capacity to 2500 hours (as opposed to 2000 hours in the base case). As one could see from the results in Figure 5, the system's performance is quite sensitive to capacity changes. Under tight capacity there is a significant increase in both costs and backorders; the opposite is true under loose capacity. Clearly, the system can be useful in evaluating proposals for capacity expansion.

5.10.4. Sensitivity to changes in planning horizon characteristics

Runs 8, 9, 10, and 11 experiment with various lengths of the planning horizon under different conditions. Shortening the planning horizon from 13 periods to only 6 periods did not affect the system's performance under normal capacity conditions. (Compare runs 1 and 8, and runs 2 and 10). However, as one would have expected, the size of backorders began to increase significantly when the planning horizon is shorter under tight capacity conditions (run 9).

Run 11 deals with an aggregation of time periods in the planning horizon. The length of the planning horizon is still a full year but it is divided into only six time periods of uneven lengths. The first four periods have 4-week duration each, the fifth covers 12 weeks (aggregation of three 4-week periods), and the sixth period covers 24 weeks (aggregation of six 4-week periods). Run 11 shows a performance quite similar to the base case. This result might indicate that this type of aggregation of the planning horizon could be useful in many situations, since it improves the forecasting accuracy in more distant time periods and reduces the computational effort of processing the system, without experiencing a decline in performance.

5.10.5. *Degree of suboptimization*

Although our proposed hierarchical planning system provides optimum solutions to the subproblems that deal with individual decisions at each level, obviously it is not an overall optimum procedure. As we have pointed out, setup costs are ignored at the aggregate planning level, thus introducing suboptimization possibilities. To analyze how serious this suboptimization problem can be, we developed a detailed mixed integer programming (MIP) model at a detailed item level to identify the true optimal solution to our test problem. The MIP model was implemented by means of IBM's MPSX/MIP code, which is a general purpose branch and bound algorithm.

Due to the expensive computational cost of solving MIP models, we limited our comparisons between the hierarchical planning system and the MIP model to situations containing no forecast errors. In those cases, we could solve the MIP model only once, and obtain the optimum yearly cost. (If forecast errors had been introduced we would have had to solve the MIP model 13 times for each run, which was prohibitively expensive).

We computed MIP solutions to three of our previous runs: the base case (run 1′), the first high setup cost run (run 4′), and the tight capacity run (run 6′). The MIP results are given in Figure 8. The existing limits on the node tables of the branch and bound code used

	1′	4′	6′
Run / Cost components	Base case No forecast error	High setup cost Case I P1: 000,50 P2: 400,400,1000	Tight capacity 1600 Reg. hrs.
Setup	4,590	48,050	3,930
Holding	75,953	79,880	115,872
Overtime	77,796	75,430	117,430
Total cost (Best known solution)	158,339	203,360	237,232
Lower bound	153,926	162,783	233,665

Figure 8. Summary of computational results with mixed integer programming models.

did not allow us to determine the true optimum in the MIP runs. Therefore, the solutions reported in Figure 6 might still be improved. Figure 8 also provides the continuous lower bounds obtained at the time at which the computations were interrupted. For all practical purposes, we could consider the solutions corresponding to runs 1′ and 6′ to be optimal. Possibly run 4′ could still be improved.

By comparing the total costs of the three runs:

	Hierarchical system	MIP
Base case	158,981	158,339
High setup cost	220,535	203,360
Tight capacity	236,733	233,665

we see that the hierarchical planning system was extremely efficient. Only under abnormally high setup cost, the system's performance might begin to depart significantly from the overall optimal solution.

References

1. Ackoff, R. L., *A Concept of Corporate Planning*, Wiley Interscience (1970).
2. Anthony, R. N., *Planning and Control Systems: A Framework for Analysis*, Harvard University, Graduate School of Business Administration, Boston (1965).
3. Armstrong, R. J. and Hax, A. C., 'A Hierarchical Approach for a Naval Tender Job Shop Design', in S. P. Bradley, A. C. Hax, and T. L. Magnanti, *Applied Mathematical Programming*, Chapter 10, Addison Wesley (1977).
4. Bitran, G. R., 'Admissable Points and Vector Optimization', unpublished Ph.D. thesis, Operations Research Center, MIT (February 1975).
5. Bitran, G. R. and Hax, A. C., 'On the Design of Hierarchical Production Planning Systems', *Decision Sciences*, vol. 8, no. 1 (January 1977).
6. Bowman, E. H., 'Production Scheduling by the Transportation Method of Linear Programming', *Operations Research*, vol. 4, no. 1 (February 1956).
7. Bowman, E. H., 'Consistency and Optimality in Managerial Decision Making', *Mangement Science* (January 1963).
8. Buffa, E. S. and W. H. Taubert, *Production-Inventory Systems: Planning and Control*, Richard D. Irwin (1972).
9. Buzzell, R. D., Gale, B. T. and Sultan, R. G. M., 'Market Share – A Key to Profitability', *Harvard Business Review* (January–February 1975).
10. Drucker, P. F., 'Long-Range Planning: Challenge to Management Science', *Management Science*, vol. 5, no. 3 (April 1959).
11. Dzielinski, B. P., Baker, C. T. and Manne, A. S., 'Simulation Tests of Lot Size Programming', *Management Science*, vol. 9, no. 2 (January 1963).
12. Dzielinski, B. P. and Gomory, R. E., 'Optimal Programming of Lot Sizes, Inventory and Labor Allocations', *Management Science*, vol. 2, no. 9 (July 1965).
13. Gabbay, H., 'A Hierarchical Approach to Production Planning', unpublished Ph.D. thesis, Operations Research Center, MIT (February 1976).
14. Hanssmann, F. and Hess, S. W., 'A Linear Programming Approach to Production and Employment Scheduling', *Management Technology*, no. 1 (January 1960).

15. Hax, A. C., 'A Comment on the Distribution System Simulator', *Management Science*, vol. 21, no. 2 (October 1974).
16. Hax, A. C., 'The Design of Large Scale Logistics Systems: A Survey and an Approach', in *Modern Trends in Logistics Research*, W. Marlow (ed.), MIT Press (1976).
17. Hax, A. C., 'Aggregate Production Planning', in *Handbook of Operations Research*, Moder J. and Elmaghraby S. E., (ed.), Van Nostrand Reinhold, in press.
18. Hax, A. C., 'Integration of Strategic and Tactical Planning in the Aluminum Industry', in Bradley, S. P., Hax, A. C. and Magnanti, T. L., *Applied Mathematical Programming*, Chapter 6, Addison Wesley (1977).
19. Hax, A. C., Golovin, J. J., Bosyj, M. and Victor, T., 'COMS: A Computer-Based Operations Management System', Technical Report no. 121, Operations Research Center, MIT (January 1976).
20. Hax, A. C. and Meal, H. C., 'Hierarchical Integration of Production Planning and Scheduling', in Studies in Management Sciences, vol. I, *Logistics*, Geisler, M. A., North Holland-American Elsevier (1975).
21. Hax, A. C. and Wiig, K. M., 'The Use of Decision Analysis in Capital Investment Problems', *Sloan Management Review*, vol. 17, no. 2 (Winter 1976).
22. Holt, C. C., Modigliani, F., Muth, J. F., and Simon, H. A., *Planning Production, Inventories and Work Force*, Prentice-Hall (1960).
23. Jones, C. H., 'Parametric Production Planning', *Management Science*, vol. 13, no. 11 (July 1967).
24. Lasdon, L. S. and Terjung, R. C., 'An Efficient Algorithm for Multi-Item Scheduling', *Operations Research*, vol. 19, no. 4 (July–August 1971).
25. Lorange, P. and Vancil, R. F., 'How to Design a Strategic Planning System', *Harvard Business Review* (September–October 1976).
26. Manne, A. S., 'Programming of Economic Lot Sizes', *Management Science*, vol. 4, no. 2 (January 1958).
27. Newson, E. P., 'Multi-Item Lot Size Scheduling by Heuristic, Part I: With Fixed Resources, Part II: With Variable Resources', *Management Science*, vol. 21, no. 10 (July 1975).
28. Naylor, T. H. and Schauland, H., 'A Survey of Users of Corporate Planning Models', *Management Science*, vol. 22, no. 9 (May 1976).
29. Schoeffler, S., Buzzell, R. D. and Heany, D. F., 'Impact of Strategic Planning on Profit Performance', *Harvard Business Review* (March–April 1974).
30. Shwimer, J., 'Interactions Between Aggregate and Detailed Scheduling in a Job Shop', unpublished Ph.D. thesis, Alfred P. Sloan School of Management, MIT (June 1972).
31. Silver, E. A., 'A Tutorial on Production Smoothing and Work Force Balancing', *Operations Research*, vol. 15, no. 6 (November–December 1967).
32. Taubert, W. H., 'A Search Decision Rule for the Aggregate Scheduling Pattern', *Management Science*, vol. 14, no. 6 (February 1968).
33. Vancil, R. F. and Lorange, P., 'Strategic Planning in Diversified Companies', *Harvard Business Review* (January–February 1975).
34. Winters, P. R., 'Constrained Inventory Rules for Production Smoothing', *Management Science*, vol. 8, no. 4 (July 1962).
35. Wright, R. V. L., 'A System for Managing Diversity', Arthur D. Little, Inc. (December 1974).
36. Zimmermann, H. J. and Sovereign, M. G., *Quantitative Models for Production Management*, Prentice-Hall (1974).
37. 'A Note on the the Use of Experience Curves in Competitive Decision Making', Harvard Business School, Note 9-175-174 (1975).
38. 'A Note on the Boston Consulting Group Concept of Competitive Analysis and Corporate Strategy', Harvard Business School, Note 9-175-175 (1975).

6. Optimal aggregation and disaggregation in hierarchical planning

HENRY GABBAY

Abstract

A class of multi-item, single echelon, capacitated production problems are defined which can be solved optimally in a hierarchical procedure. That is, a representative aggregate model is defined over the entire planning horizon which requires aggregate data and can be easily solved. The aggregate production levels can be disaggregated according to certain rules to yield the optimal solution of the original problem.

6.1. Introduction

Production planning is a classic problem in operations research and management science. Researchers have investigated a wide variety of models and various solution procedures both heuristic and optimal. The models and techniques, although at times quite different analytically, seem to share a common philosophy. Decisions at various levels of the organization are all incorporated in one model. For instance, recalling the framework suggested by Anthony [1], we call decisions of a medium time horizon of approximately one year, tactical decisions. A manager is concerned with deciding upon an effective allocation of resources, like capacity, each month over a time horizon of one year. More specifically, the decision may involve not only the total allocation of capacity per month, but also the portions of regular and overtime hours. Once the utilization of capacity is determined, a manager is then concerned with operations control or detailed production scheduling. That is, capacity must be allocated among the various items being produced. This disaggregation of capacity determines monthly, weekly or daily run quantities for each item. Most models do not account for the different levels in the decision-making process. A typical production planning model represents all the decision variables at once. There are of course, several drawbacks to this classical approach. First, the models become very large for multi-item problems and are beyond the scope of present-day computing. Second, the manager is forced, at the outset, to forecast detailed demands over the entire tactical horizon. This commitment in forecasting can cause severe errors in the input data.

It is our intent not to pursue this classical approach, but rather to pursue a hierarchical approach to production planning. Thus the decision process is represented by a model of aggregate or tactical decisions and a model representing operations control or detailed decisions. The time horizon of an aggregate model in a hierarchy typically consists of periods of approximately a one-month duration over a seasonal cycle, while the time horizon of the lower level model is of shorter duration. The aggregate model provides constraints to the lower level model which must behave consistently with respect to the aggregate. Yet it is not at all straightforward to design a hierarchical system. Hax [5] provides an excellent framework for hierarchical planning. We present several important characteristics discussed in this paper. We mentioned a partitioning of the decision process. The definition of different levels of the hierarchy cannot be made arbitrarily. We must be careful in properly representing various levels of decision-making within the organizational structure. In addition, the models that represent these levels must be analytically tractable. Thus, besides organizational issues, we cannot ignore analytic considerations in defining a hierarchy. Once the hierarchy is defined, we must determine linking mechanisms among the subproblems to insure consistency. Lastly, it is imperative to be able to evaluate the overall performance of the system. If a hierarchical scheme does not produce optimal results, some measure of suboptimization should be available.

In this paper we address these issues with respect to a general class of production problems. Many of the results are stated without proof and the reader is referred to Gabbay [3] for a more detailed treatment. The reader is also referred to Holt, Modigliani, Muth, and Simon [7], and Winters [8] for a Lagrangian approach to the disaggregation problem. Hax [4] describes a hierarchical approach to a continuous manufacturing process while Hax and Meal [6] address the use of hierarchical planning in a batch processing environment. We do not claim nor attempt to solve the broadest and most detailed class of production problems. Many detailed issues such as job shop scheduling, dispatching, and expediting are ignored. Nonetheless, our concern is to provide a well-defined framework and methodology to answer the above issues. The hierarchical approach is not only necessary from an implementation point of view, but it is also sound mathematically. Hopefully, this work will provide a firm point of departure for future work in hierarchical production planning.

6.2. The single echelon problem

The basic problem that we address is single echelon, linear, multi-item, and capacitated.

Problem P1:
$$\min \sum_{i=1}^{N} \sum_{t=1}^{T} C_{it} x_{it} + H_{it} I_{it} \tag{1}$$

Subject to,

$$I_{it-1} + x_{it} - I_{it} = d_{it} \quad 1 \leqq i < N,\ 1 \leqq t \leqq T \tag{2}$$

$$\sum_{i=1}^{N} m_i x_{it} \leqq \overline{X}_t \quad 1 \leqq t \leqq T \tag{3}$$

$$x_{it}, I_{it} \geqq 0 \quad 1 \leqq i \leqq N,\ 1 \leqq t \leqq T \tag{4}$$

The variables x_{it} and I_{it} along with the deterministic demands d_{it} are measured in units. The productivity factors m_i are in hours per unit for each item and the total aggregate capacity $\overline{X}_t$ in period t is in hours. Initial inventories are zero unless otherwise mentioned. Equation (2) represents the mass balance for each item in every time period. Equation (3) states that we have some finite capacity in each time period, and (4) is the usual non-negativity requirement. C_{it} represents the cost of producing item i in period t while H_{it} represents the cost of carrying inventory for item i from the end of period t to the beginning of period $t + 1$.

In order to circumvent the issues mentioned in the Introduction, we define a small aggregate problem which is computationally feasible and has reasonable aggregate data requirements. This aggregate model corresponds to a single item problem of the form $P1$. After the aggregate model is solved over the entire horizon we disaggregate the aggregate production among the various items. The data requirements are detailed demands in the period we are in and perhaps several future periods. This procedure continues until we reach the end of the horizon.

Although the approach seems heuristic, we prove that under quite general assumptions this method yields the optimal solution. That is, if we had the computational power and the ability to actually forecast all the detailed data for each period at the beginning of the horizon to solve $P1$ as a linear program, we would obtain the same value of the objective function as the procedure that is proposed. Thus we eliminate the computational infeasibilities and the detailed data requirements at the outset.

6.3. The optimal aggregate production levels

The aggregate variables, x_t and I_t, for $P1$ are defined as $x_t = \Sigma_{i=1}^{N} m_i x_{it}$ and $I_t = \Sigma_{i=1}^{N} m_i I_{it}$, $1 \leqq t \leqq T$. Also, let $D_t = \Sigma_{i=1}^{N} m_i d_{it}$. In addition, we have

Assumption 1:

a) $C_{it} \geqq C_{it+1} \geqq 0,\ 1 \leqq i \leqq N,\ 1 \leqq t \leqq T-1$

b) $H_{it} \geqq 0,\ 1 \leqq i \leqq N,\ 1 \leqq t \leqq T.$

Before stating the optimal aggregate variables for $P1$, we introduce a definition which will be motivated in the next section.

Definition 1: Let $t_0 = T$

$$t_1 = \max(t \mid t \leqq T, \sum_{r=t}^{q} (\overline{X}_r - \sum_{i=1}^{N} m_i d_{ir}) \geqq 0, \forall_q, t \leqq q \leqq T)$$

$$t_p = \max(t \mid t \leqq t_{p-1} - 1, \sum_{r=t}^{q} (\overline{X}_r - \sum_{i=1}^{N} m_i d_{ir}) \geqq 0, \forall q,$$

$$t \leqq q \leqq t_{p-1} - 1); \quad 2 \leqq p \leqq l-1. \quad t_l = 1.$$

So $\quad T = t_0 \geqq t_1 \ldots > t_p > \ldots > t_l = 1.$

The set of points $\{t_p\}$ is such that the aggregate capacity from t_p to T is sufficient to satisfy the demands of every item from t_p to T. So we have

Theorem 1: There is an optimal solution of $P1$ with assumption 1 such that

$$x_t^0 = \overline{X}_t,\ t \neq t_p,\ 1 \leqq p \leqq l$$

$$x_t^0 = \sum_{i=1}^{N} m_i d_{it} + \sum_{n=t_p+1}^{t_{p-1}-1} \left(\sum_{i=1}^{N} m_i d_{in} - \overline{X}_n \right)$$

$$t = t_p,\ 1 \leqq p \leqq l \tag{5}$$

This theorem implies that $I_{t_p-1}^0 = 0,\ 0 \leqq p \leqq l-1$ (where I_{t_0-1} is interpreted as T). So the total production must equal the total demand in the horizon $[t_p, t_{p-1}-1]$. In addition, a nonlinear extension to this theorem can be found in Gabbay [3].

6.4. Consistent disaggregation

Now that we have characterized aggregate production for the problem at hand, it remains to disaggregate this production to run quantities for each of the items. First we address a fundamental problem of any disaggregation scheme. If we disaggregate production in some period, say $\bar{t}$, it may be that at some future period t, $t > \bar{t}$, it is impossible to satisfy item demands without exceeding our allotted optimal production or without backordering. This, of course, is highly undesirable, and an example may be found in Gabbay [3]. So we make the following definition.

Definition 2: Suppose we are given an aggregate production schedule (x_t^0). Any disaggregation which satisfies all future demands of all items without exceeding (x_t^0) and without backordering is said to be a Consistent Disaggregation.

Let us consider this scenario in more detail. We are disaggregating the optimal aggregate production, say $x_{\bar{t}-1}^0$, among all the items yielding the ending inventories in $\bar{t}-1$, $I_{i\bar{t}-1}$, to be carried into period $\bar{t}$. Intuitively, to insure consistency after disaggregating in

$\bar{t} - 1$ we must satisfy the remaining net demand given by

$$\max\left[0, -I_{i\bar{t}-1} + \sum_{n=\bar{t}}^{t} d_{in}\right] \tag{6}$$

for every t, $\bar{t} \leqq t \leqq T$. That is, the cumulative aggregate production must exceed cumulative net demand for the remaining periods. So we must have

$$\sum_{n=\bar{t}}^{t} x_n^0 \geqq \sum_{i=1}^{N} m_i \max\left[0, -I_{i\bar{t}-1} + \sum_{n=\bar{t}}^{t} d_{in}\right] \bar{t} \leqq t \leqq T. \tag{7}$$

Now we are ready to state necessary and sufficient conditions for a Consistent Disaggregation.

Theorem 2: Equation (7) holds if and only if the set of equations

$$I_{it-1} + x_{it} - I_{it} = d_{it} \quad 1 \leqq i \leqq N, \bar{t} \leqq t \leqq T \tag{8}$$

$$\sum_{i=1}^{N} m_i x_{it} = x_t^0 \quad \bar{t} \leqq t \leqq T \tag{9}$$

$$x_{it}, I_{it} \geqq 0 \quad 1 \leqq i \leqq N, \bar{t} \leqq t \leqq T \tag{10}$$

has a feasible solution.

Basically the problem with consistency is that for a disaggregation scheme, future capacity cannot service future demands which leads to inconsistencies. Equation (7) of theorem 2 states that after disaggregation in period $\bar{t} - 1$, the future capacities must satisfy future *net* demands. So the real issue is capacity. First we subdivide the original horizon into subintervals in which the capacity is sufficient to satisfy demands within each subinterval. The set of points $\{t_p\}$ is such that the capacity from t_p to T is sufficient to meet all the demands of every item from time t_p to T. Thus we call the interval of time from $\bar{t}$ to $t_{p_1} - 1$ where $t_{p+1} \leqq \bar{t} \leqq t_p - 1$ for some $p, 0 \leqq p \leqq l - 1$ ($t_0 - 1$ is interpreted as T) a Consistency or Feasibility Horizon. So theorem 2 holds without knowledge of all the detailed demands, since we only need verify the equations of theorem 2 for $t_{p+1} \leqq \bar{t} \leqq t_p - 1$. Extensions of the results presented here can be found in Gabbay [3]. These results also pertain to the hierarchical framework of Hax and Meal [6].

6.5. Optimal disaggregation scheme

So far we have characterized optimal aggregate production for $P1$ under assumption 1. A Consistent Disaggregation has been defined as well as necessary and sufficient conditions to insure consistency.

We make further assumptions on the cost structure in addition to assumption 1. Usually the production cost of an item is proportional to some fixed cost α_i reflecting resources or some measure of work going into the production of that item. In addition, this basic cost can be multiplied by a discount factor C_t, the same for all items. The holding cost is usually determined first by multiplying the basic production cost by a proportionality factor k reflecting the cost of holding the item as a resource per period. Then we can multiply by a discount factor as before. So we finally have

Assumption 2:

a) $C_{it} = \alpha_i C_t,\ C_t \geqq C_{t+1} \geqq 0,\ 1 \leqq i \leqq N,\ 1 \leqq t \leqq T.$

b) $H_{it} = k\alpha_i H_t,\ 1 \leqq i \leqq N,\ 1 \leqq T \leqq T.$

c) $\alpha_i, k, C_t, H_t \geqq 0,\ 1 \leqq i \leqq N,\ 1 \leqq t \leqq T.$

We have already defined the optimal aggregate production and inventory levels (x_t^0, I_t^0). Assume we have a Consistent Disaggregation of $X_{\bar{t}-1}^0$ and we wish to disaggregate $x_{\bar{t}}^0$ optimally. The first step is to define

$$y_{i\bar{t}}^0 = \max[0, d_{i\bar{t}} - I_{i\bar{t}-1}^0] \tag{11}$$

the production in period $\bar{t}$ for item i used to satisfy net demand in period $\bar{t}$. Now we must determine the optimal amount of production for each item i in period $\bar{t}$, $z_{i\bar{t}}^0$, used only as inventory. To do this, order the items by

$$\psi_N \geqq \psi_{N-1} \geqq \cdots \geqq \psi_2 \geqq \psi_1 \tag{12}$$

The constants $\psi_i = \alpha_i / m_i$ are measured in cost per unit of capacity. Suppose we have already determined the optimal quantities $z_{i\bar{t}}^0$, $1 \leqq i \leqq i_0 - 1$. We must find $z_{i_0\bar{t}}^0$ for $i_0 \leqq N - 1$ since $z_{N\bar{t}}^0$ is unique. It can be shown [3] that it is desirable to allocate as much capacity to item i_0 as possible while remaining feasible. This defines $z^0_{i_0\bar{t}}$ as

$$z^0_{i_0\bar{t}} = \max\left\{ z_{i_0\bar{t}} \geqq 0 \,\middle|\, K(i_0, \bar{t}, t) \geqq z_{i_0\bar{t}} + \max\left[0, -z_{i_0\bar{t}} + \right.\right.$$

$$\left.+ \sum_{n=\bar{t}}^{t} \bar{d}_{i_0 n}\right], \bar{t} \leqq t \leqq t_p - 1 \text{ and } z_{i_0\bar{t}} \leqq \left(x^0_{\bar{t}} - \sum_{i=1}^{N} y^0_{i\bar{t}} - \right.$$

$$\left.\left. - \sum_{i=1}^{i_0-1} z^0_{i\bar{t}}\right)\right\} \tag{13}$$

$$\text{where } K(i_0, \bar{t}, t) = \left(x^0_{\bar{t}} - \sum_{i=1}^{N} y^0_{i\bar{t}} - \sum_{i=1}^{i_0-1} z^0_{i\bar{t}}\right) +$$

$$+ \sum_{n=\bar{t}+1}^{t} x^0_n - \sum_{i=1}^{i_0-1} \max\left[0, - z^0_{i\bar{t}} + \sum_{n=\bar{t}}^{t} \bar{d}_{in}\right] - \sum_{i=i_0+1}^{N} \sum_{n=\bar{t}}^{t} \bar{d}_{in};$$

$$\text{and } \sum_{n=\bar{t}}^{t} \bar{d}_{in} = \max\left[0, - I^0_{i\bar{t}-1} + \sum_{n=\bar{t}}^{t} d_{in}\right] - y^0_{i\bar{t}} \tag{14}$$

Finally we define $x^0_{i_0\bar{t}}$ and $I^0_{i_0\bar{t}}$

$$x^0_{i_0\bar{t}} = y^0_{i_0\bar{t}} + z^0_{i_0\bar{t}}$$

$$I^0_{i_0\bar{t}} = I^0_{i_0\bar{t}-1} + x^0_{i_0\bar{t}} - d_{i_0\bar{t}} \tag{15}$$

So by construction $x^0_{i\bar{t}}$ represents the maximum amount we can produce of an item i_0 while maintaining consistency and feasibility. We are now ready to state the algorithm.

Step 1. Define $\{t_p\}$, $0 \leqq p \leqq l$ according to definition 1, (x^0_t) according to theorem 1 and order the items by (12).
Step 2. Let $p = l$.
Step 3. Let $t = t_p$.
Step 4. Define y^0_{it} by (11), $1 \leqq i \leqq N$.
Step 5. Let $i = 1$.
Step 6. Define z^0_{it}, x^0_{it}, I^0_{it} according to (13) and (15).
Step 7. If $i < N$, let $i = i + 1$ and go to 6.
Step 8. If $t = T$, stop.
Step 9. If $t < t_p - 1$, let $t = t + 1$ and go to 4.
Step 10. Let $p = p - 1$ and go to 3.

This procedure has an interesting interpretation. Any disaggregation scheme should consist of three components. The first is to satisfy current demands in the period you are disaggregating. This condition provides lower bounds to the individual item run quantities. The second is not to have the run quantity of any item too large. This can cause excess inventory in the item leading to consistency problems. The last essential component is to determine optimal run quantities while satisfying the first two conditions.

In our procedure the values $y^0_{i\bar{t}}$ serve as the lower bounds to satisfy present demands. In order to find the optimal run quantities we determine a priority list of all items defined by (12). Starting with items having the smallest cost per unit of capacity, the optimal run quantities are determined by the maximum amount of an item that can be produced as inventory without violating consistency. This quantity is, of course, defined by (13). Optimality of the resulting solution is due to the cost structure we have assumed. So the first items, those with the smallest cost per unit of capacity, are given the highest priority to the aggregate production available.

Some comments are in order concerning the sensitivity of the optimal solution with respect to changes in demand. Suppose some demand $d_{i_0\bar{t}}$ is altered. There is no change in the optimal production values for $t > \bar{t}$ over all the items. For period $\bar{t}$, there is no change in items i, $i_0 < i < N$. Analytically, the sensitivity of the optimal solution with respect to demands is determined by the definition of $\{t_p\}$ and equations (11) and (13). In addition the relative ranking of item costs is important, not the absolute values. A complete sensitivity analysis is not presented here.

One natural extension to this problem is requiring an integral solution. By examining this constructive solution procedure, it should be apparent that if $m_i d_{it}$ is an integer, then so is the optimal solution.

6.6. Extensions

In this section we discuss several extensions to $P1$. We may add regular, W_t, and overtime, O_t, to our planning by adding $\Sigma_{t=1}^{T} A_t W_t + B_t O_t$ to (1), replacing (3) by

$$\sum_{i=1}^{N} m_i x_{it} = W_t + O_t \qquad 1 \leqq t \leqq T \tag{16}$$

and adding constraints

$$0 \leqq W_t < \overline{W}_t \qquad 1 \leqq t \leqq T \tag{17}$$

$$0 \leqq O_t \leqq \overline{O}_t \qquad 1 \leqq t \leqq T \tag{18}$$

Call this new problem $P2$. In addition, replace assumption 1 by

Assumption 3:

a) $A_t \geqq A_{t+1} \geqq 0, B_t \geqq B_{t+1} \geqq 0. \quad 1 \leqq t \leqq T - 1.$

b) $B_t \geqq A_t. \quad 1 \leqq t \leqq T.$

c) $1/m_i(C_{it} + H_{it}) + A_t \geqq 1/m_i C_{it+1} + B_{t+1}.$
$1 \leqq i \leqq N, 1 \leqq t \leqq T - 1.$

d) $C_{it}, H_{it}, m_i \geqq 0. \quad 1 \leqq i \leqq N, 1 \leqq t \leqq T$

Some comment is in order about part (c). The left hand side of part (c) is the least costly way of satisfying one hour of demand in period $t + 1$ by production in period t, while the right hand side represents the most costly means of satisfying this demand by production in period $t + 1$. Thus it is always least costly to satisfy demand in period t by production in period t, rather than by production in some earlier period. It can be shown [3] that the aggregate production levels (x_t^0) defined by theorem 1 are optimal to $P2$ with $\overline{X}_t = \overline{W}_t + \overline{O}_t$. It is simple to determine the optimal regular and overtime hours per period once we know the optimal production levels. By (a) and (b) of assumption 3 we first use as many regular hours as available and then use additional overtime hours to satisfy (16). In calculating the optimal production levels, our assumptions in effect permit us to ignore the addition of regular and overtime to the formulation $P1$. Thus we may use the disaggregation scheme with assumption 2 in addition to the allocation of capacity mentioned above to solve $P2$.

Now we are ready to consider $P2$ with setup costs. Again add $\delta_{it} S_{it}$ to the objective function and

$$x_{it} \leqq \delta_{it} U_{it} \quad 1 \leqq i \leqq N, 1 \leqq t \leqq T \tag{19}$$

to the constraints, where the constant U_{it} is an upper bound of the variable x_{it} and δ_{it} is binary. Call this new problem $P3$. Recalling the lower bound procedure of Balinsky [2], we can allow $0 \leqq \delta_{it} \leqq 1$ and solve a relaxation to $P3$. It can be shown that $x_{it} = \delta_{it} U_{it}$ in the optimal solution of the relaxation of $P3$. Thus we can substitute $\delta_{it} = x_{it}/U_{it}$ in the objective function and eliminate constraints (19) in the relaxation. This relaxation only affects the coefficient of x_{it}, which becomes $E_{it} = C_{it} + S_{it}/U_{it}$. Although the cost coefficients are different, this problem has the same form as $P2$. Therefore under the appropriate cost assumptions, we can solve this problem optimally in a hierarchical manner. That is, we have assumption 3 with E_{it} replacing C_{it}. Thus (x_t^0) is optimal to $P3$ and it only remains to optimally disaggregate (x_t^0). Again we merely need to replace C_{it} by E_{it} in assumption 2 and the disaggregation scheme is identical to the one provided. The item ranking depends on the ratio $\psi_i = \alpha_i/m_i$. Since the disaggregation scheme depends only upon the relative ranking of ψ_i, a manager need not necessarily estimate the constants E_{it} and ψ_i. He may provide a detailed priority ranking relating his own item preference on the aggregate capacity available.

Thus we have handled a fixed charge production problem with regular and overtime by considering a relaxation to the integer program. Computational experience with respect to the relaxation of some random fixed charge problems is given in Balinski [2]. We then introduce cost assumptions enabling us to characterize the resulting problem as one without regular and overtime. Further restrictions on the costs enable us to disaggregate the aggregate levels optimally. The resulting values (x_{it}^0) are the optimal decision variables to the relaxed integer program. In addition, the resulting objective function is a lower bound to $P3$. Lastly we may similarly treat a multi-echelon system. The reader is referred to Gabbay [3] for the details to the above procedures and the multi-echelon problem.

References

1. Anthony, Robert N., *Planning and Control Systems: A Framework for Analysis* (Cambridge, Massachusetts: Harvard University Press, 1965).
2. Balinski, Michael L., 'Fixed Cost Transportation Problem', *Naval Research Logistics Quarterly*, vol. 8 (January 1961), pp. 41–54.
3. Gabbay, Henry, 'A Hierarchical Approach to Production Planning', Technical Report no. 120, Operations Research Center, MIT (December 1975).
4. Hax, Arnoldo L., 'Interpretation of Strategic and Tactical Planning in the Aluminum Industry', Technical Report no. 86, Operations Research Center, MIT (September 1973).

5. Hax, Arnoldo L., 'The Design of Large Scale Logistics Systems: A Survey and an Approach', in Logistics Research Conference (Cambridge, Massachusetts: MIT Press, 1975).
6. Hax, Arnoldo, L. and Meal, Harlan, 'Hierarchical Interpretation of Production Planning and Scheduling', *Studies in Management Science*, vol. I, *Logistics* (1975), pp. 53–69.
7. Holt, Charles L., Modigliani, Franco, Muth, John F., and Simon, Herbert A., *Planning Production, Inventories, and Work Force* (Englewood Cliffs, New Jersey: Prentice-Hall, Inc., 1960).
8. Winters, P., 'Constrained Inventory Rules for Production Smoothing', *Management Science*, vol. 8, no. 4 (July 1962), pp. 470–481.

7. A hierarchical approach for the planning of a complex production system

GABRIEL R. BITRAN and ALBERTO R. VON ELLENRIEDER

Abstract

This paper presents a production planning model for a large foundry, producing more than a thousand items, mainly for the automobile and construction industries. The large number of variables and their complex, structural interrelationship suggested the use of a hierarchical model. Initially, an aggregate problem is solved and subsequently, its solution is disaggregated through optimal sub programs. Numberical results are presented.

7.1. The problem to be solved

The solution of production planning problems usually requires large and complicated mathematical models. This paper presents an example of an especially complex situation, regarding a firm that produces and sells about 1,200 different items. The firm, whose name will be omitted, is presently maintaining a substantial share of the Brazilian market for automobile casting parts and for nipples used in the construction industry. Most of its production is sent directly to the customers, and the firm maintains very reduced inventories of finished products.

The foundry can melt three different ferrous alloys, and the total process also includes the thermal treatment of the casted parts, and tooling and zinc plating of some of the items.

The sequence of steps involved in the production process is schematically presented in Figure 1. Basically, it has 8 integrated stages. From the raw material inventory, stage 1, 2, and 3 are fed. The 1st stage consists in the preparation of cores, in two parallel facilities. These cores are stocked, sometimes for a significant time, and used for assembling the casts, which are prepared in the 2nd stage in three parallel facilities and are sent to the 3rd stage, the melting of one of three different ferrous alloys. The melted metal is prepared in three batteries of electric furnaces. The 3rd stage includes some additional operations like cooling the casts, destroying the molds and cleaning the parts. Three inventories of melted items (one for each battery of furnaces) are created.

In the 4th stage each item is processed through a furnace for stress recovery and grain adjustment (thermal treatment). A cleaning operation, after the thermal treatment, is also included in this stage. The thermal treatment is one of the stages that makes this problem a difficult one, given that differences in type and size of items are irrelevant for the processing in this stage, the only criterium for differentation being the alloy used. In special containers (called baskets) different sizes and types of items are put together on a basis of 'filling up the basket' from the inventories. The practical impossibility of optimizing the filling of such baskets is due to the ill-structured nature of the problem and to a large number of possible solutions. In this paper an attempt to obtain sub optimal solutions was made by introducing the concept of 'ficticious items' (see problem TP in section 5.2 of this paper).

The 5th stage is composed of finishing operations (cleaning, grinding, etc.) creating the last significant intermediate inventory.

The subsequent stages are not necessarily in sequence: the items can be dispatched to the customers directly from the above mentioned inventory, or can be submitted to some additional processes. The alternatives, shown in Figure 1, are: zinc plating, machining (tooling and screwing) and assembly of unions (nipples).

A complete description of the problem must also include an exposition of the number of alternative facilities in each stage, and the existence of strong restrictions on the possibility of scheduling the electric furnaces imposed by the Maintenance Department's plans.

7.2. The model

According to the description of the problem and the existence of fixed costs, it seems natural to choose a mixed integer programming model.

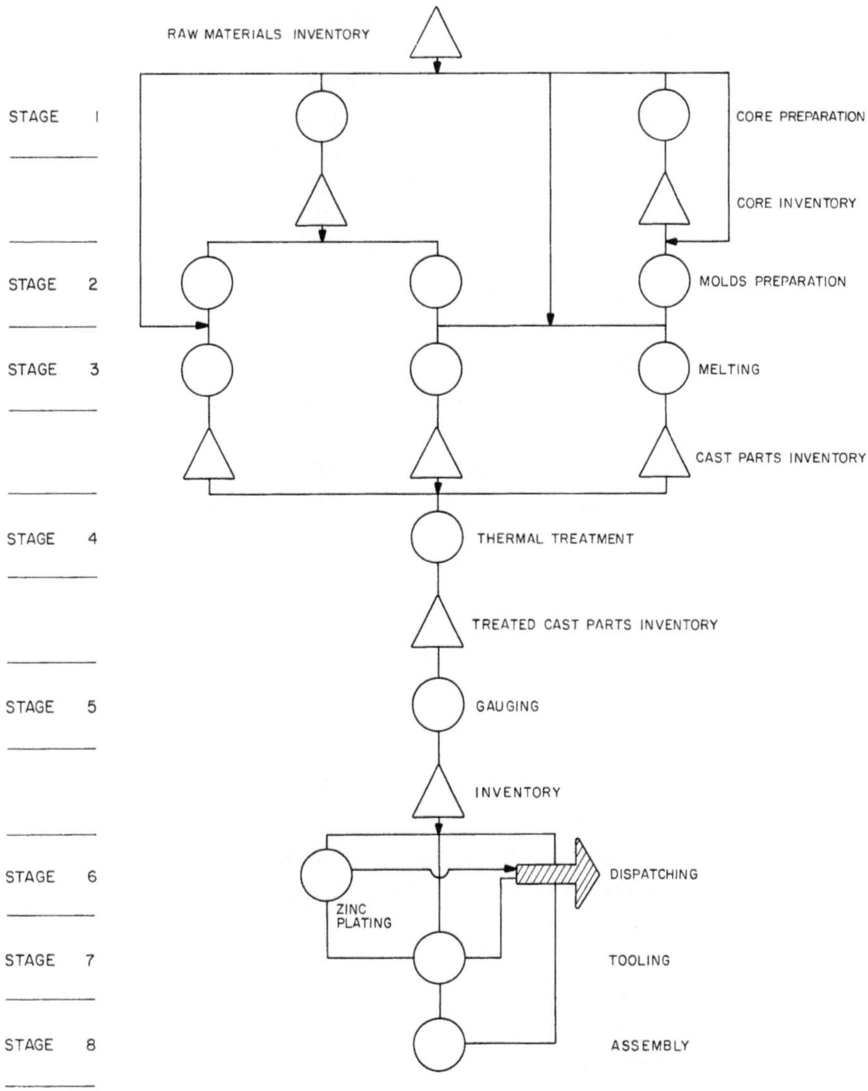

Figure 1. Flowchart of production process.

Nevertheless, the large number of variables implied by the concomitant large number of final products and the significant interrelationship between these variables, make it practically infeasible to use this kind of model.

To overcome this difficulty, it was decided to use a hierarchical approach, (1), (2), (3), (4), (5), that proved to be adequate in similar situations.

Basically, the hierarchical planning process consists in initially solving an aggregate problem, and subsequently disaggregating the solution obtained. Even though it is not possible to guarantee that the disaggregated solution is optimal, the literature has shown that, under certain conditions, satisfactory solutions can be obtained. In fact, if the aggregation level involves a substantial proportion of the total costs and if the disaggregation is processed through well chosen subproblems, good approximations will be obtained. See Figure 2 for a vision of this kind of planning process. For additional details the reader is referred to the bibliography at the end of this paper.

For the problem described, it was considered convenient to divide the production process into the three following sections:

- *Foundry*, including the three first stages in Figure 1 (core preparation, molds preparation and melting).
- *Thermal treatment* (the 4th stage of Figure 1).
- *Factory*, including all the other stages described in Figure 1.

In the first section (Foundry), the costs of cooling the casts, breaking the molds and cleaning the parts (3rd stage of Figure 1) are negligible and the corresponding operations cannot be considered bottlenecks in the process.

The electric furnaces all have the same capacity no matter which alloy is being melted. The cost of energy to operate the furnaces is linear, with a setup, fixed cost.

The thermal treatment is a function of the alloy being treated, and its duration and corresponding cost is fixed. Small variations in this cost, motivated by oscillations in the tonnage included in each batch, can be neglected.

7.2.1. Classification

At this moment, it would be useful to classify all the different final products according to the following criteria:

1. *Alloy*: three different alloys are being used, the set of alloys being indicated by $A = (a)$

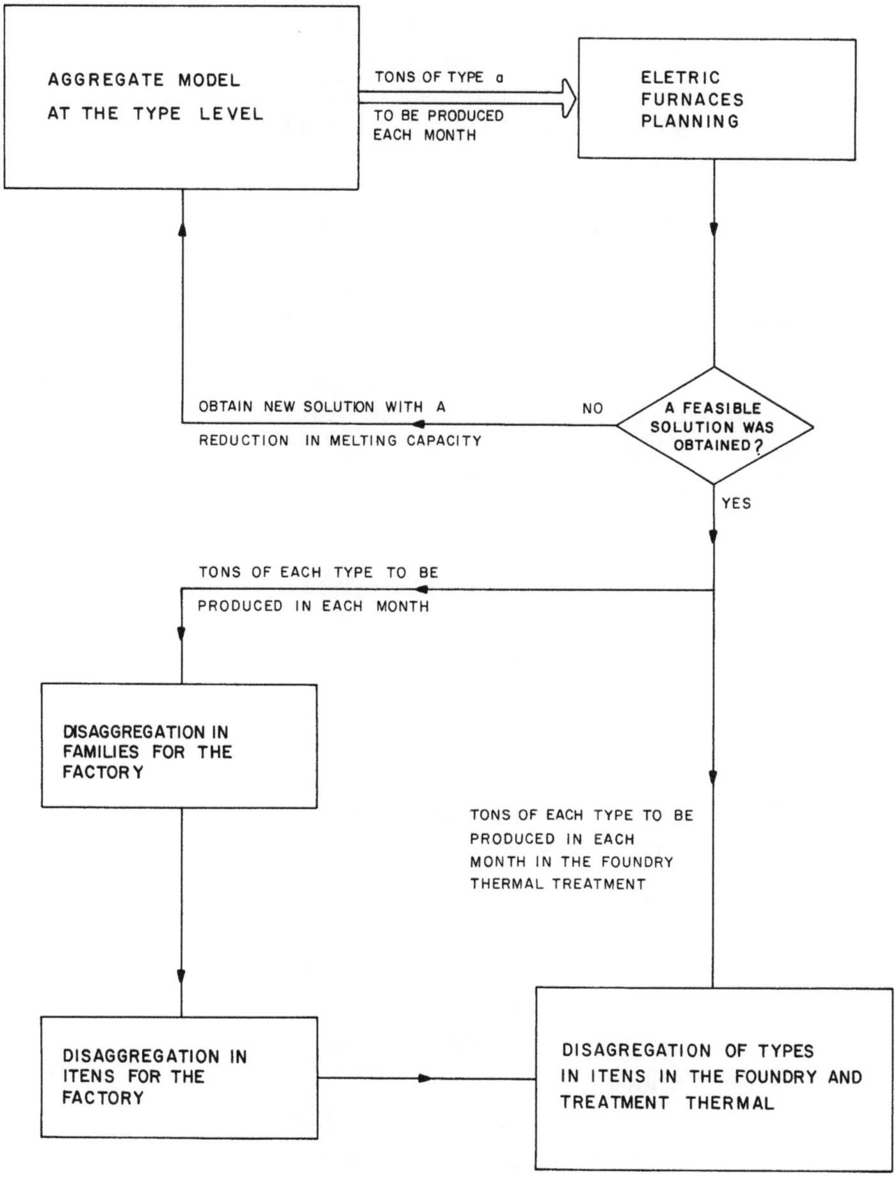

Figure 2. The hierarchical approach for production planning.

2. *Size and form*: products in the same class have similar dimensions, about the same area, approximately the same weight, same cost of melting, molding and manual operation. Each class in this group will be indicated by an index $r \in \{R\}$.

3. *Routing*: items following the same route through the Factory section require the same sequence of operations, with similar costs. Let $p = \{p\}$ denote the set of all possible routings, and $\Phi(p)$ the set of operations included in route p. For example $\Phi(p) = \{1\}$ = zinc plating.

As a consequence of this classification, each item is represented by a vector (a, r, p). Each different vector (a, r, p) constitutes a *Type* at the most aggregate level of the model. Consequently, the following classifications were adopted for the hierarchical model:

Type is each set (a, r, p) resulting from the partition of the items and corresponds to the most aggregate level of the model. As a consequence of the criteria that were used, items of the same type have about the same costs relating to raw materials, manpower, inventories and backorders in the thermal treatment and factory sections.
Family are sets of items of the same type having the same setup costs in the factory section.
Items are all the final products to be delivered to the customers.

7.2.2. Notation

To facilitate understanding the presentation models, the notation to be used is presented below:

$A = \{a\}$ set of the alloys
$R = \{r\}$ set of the size and form classes
$P = \{p\}$ set of the routes
$F = \{f\}$ set of the electric furnaces
$K = \{k\}$ set of the thermal treatment furnaces
$T = \{t\}$ time periods
$C(f, t)$ = capacity of the electric furnace f in period t, in tons,
$C(f)$ = capacity of the electric furnace f, in tons/day,
f_{at} = cost of energy to melt one ton of alloy a, in period t,
$\bar{C}(k, a)$ = nominal capacity (tons) of the basket in the thermal treatment furnace k for alloy a,
$C(k)$ = capacity in m^3 of the basket in the thermal treatment furnace k,

$T(k, a)$ = duration in hours, of thermal treatment of alloy a in furnace k,

$T(k, t)$ = availability in hours of the thermal treatment of furnace k in period t,

$K(k^0, t)$ = total capacity, in hours, of the furnaces for thermal treatment during period t, using as referencial furnace k^0,

α_{at} = cost of raw material during period t, to produce one tone of alloy a,

α_a = density (m^3/ton) of alloy a,

β_{va} = volume in m^3 of a ficticious item (v, a).

δ_i = weight (tons) of one unit of item i,

k^0 = the furnace for thermal treatment whose basket presents the smallest capacity in m^3,

$\overline{x}_{arpt}$, $\overline{z}_{arpt}$, $\overline{w}_{arpt}$ = number of tons of type (a, r, p) that are respectively melted, thermically treated and produced, in period t,

h^1_{arpt}, h^{2+}_{arpt}, h^{3+}_{arpt} = inventory holding costs during period t for each ton of type (a, r, p) respectively melted, thermically treated and produced,

$\overline{I}^1_{arpt}$, $\overline{I}^{2+(-)}_{arpt}$, $\overline{I}^{3+(-)}_{arpt}$ = tons of type (a, r, p) that are stocked (backordered) in sections foundry, thermal treatment and factory, respectively during period t,

h^{2-}_{arpt}, h^{3-}_{arpt} = backorder cost for each ton of type (a, r, p) thermically treated or produced in period t,

C_{arpt} = cost in the factory, excluding setup and workload, of one ton of type (a, r, p) during period t,

x_{it}, z_{it}, w_{it} = number of units of item i that are respectively melted, thermically treated and processed in the factory during period t,

m^1_r, m^4_r = number of man/hours necessary to melt and mold one ton of any type of class r,

$m^3_{r,\Phi(p)}$ = number of man/hours necessary for one ton of any class r in each operation of $\Phi(p)$,

R^1_t, R^4_t, $R^3{}_{r,\Phi(p),t}$ = (for every $\Phi(p)$) number of regular man/hours necessary to melt, prepare the molds and operate the factory section, respectively,

O_t^4, $O_{r,\Phi(p),t}^3$ = (for every $\Phi(p)$) number of overtime man/hours necessary to prepare the molds and operate the factory section, respectively.

UR_t^1, UR_t^4, $UR_{\Phi(p),t}^3$ = (for every $\Phi(p)$) upper limits for the numbers of man/hours,

s_{fat} = setup cost for each operation of furnace f with alloy a in period t,

s_{kat} = setup cost for each operation of furnace k with alloy a in period t,

$e(a, r, p)$ = a real number greater than one, to correct x_{arpt} for including the weight of the channels,

n_{fat}^l = a variable indicating the number of days that furnace f will be used to produce the alloy a in the period t,

$\bar{\bar{a}}_{arpt}$ = effective demand of type (a, r, p) during period t, that are only thermically treated,

d_{it} = effective demand in number of units of item i processed in the section factory during time t,

$\hat{d}_{it}$ = effective demand in number of units of item i, that are only thermically treated during period t.

7.3. The aggregate model (at the level type)

At this level it was decided to use a linear programming model for two reasons. First, because the costs and constraints involved are reasonably linear, and second because of the large amount of information that can be obtained from the simplex multipliers and sensitivity analysis. It was assumed that this second consideration would compensate for eventual discrepancies in the linearity hypothesis, mainly because the hierarchical approach was chosen in order to obtain a good solution, and not an optimal one.

The objective function of this model represents almost 85 percent of the total production costs. These costs correspond to raw materials, inventory and backorders in the three sections, manpower (except in the thermal treatment section) and energy for the melting furnaces. To operate these there are no overtime costs because they work on the basis of a continuous regime.

At this level, the decision variables are the following:

- tons of types (a, r, p) to be casted, thermically treated and processed in the factory each period;
- the corresponding inventories, backorders and regular and overtime manpower.

In the thermal treatment section, manpower is used only in filling up and emptying the baskets. Consequently it will be considered as a constant cost. The setup costs represent a secondary portion of the total cost and will not be considered at this level. These setup costs will be used, in the disaggregation process, to obtain the optimal solutions for the corresponding subproblems.

The model for the aggregated problem (AP) is described below. This model is solved at the beginning of each period, taking into consideration the entire planning horizon, on a 'rolling-horizon' basis. Only the solution corresponding to the first period is disaggregated for the subsequent levels. In this example, the production lead time is considered to be zero. Each type (a, r, p) may have two demands, one after the thermal treatment, and the other at the end of the factory operations.

7.3.1. (AP): Aggregate model (type level)

$$\min \sum_{arpt} (\alpha_{at} + f_{at})\bar{x}_{arpt} + \sum_{arpt} (h^1_{arpt} I^1_{arpt} +$$

$$+ h^2_{arpt} + I^2_{arpt} + h^{3+}_{arpt}\bar{I}^{3+}_{arpt}) +$$

$$+ \sum_{arpt} (h^{2-}_{arpt} I^{2-}_{arpt} + h^{3-}_{arpt}\bar{I}^{3-}_{arpt}) +$$

$$+ \sum_{arpt} C_{arpt}\,\bar{w}_{arpt} + \sum_t r^1_t R^1_t + \sum_{\Phi(p)} r^3_{t\,\Phi(p)t} +$$

$$+ \sum_r R^3_{r\Phi(p)t} + \sum_{\Phi(p)t} O^3_{\Phi(p)t} + \sum_r O^3_{r\Phi(p)t} +$$

$$+ \sum_t r^4_t R^4_t + \sum_t \delta^4_t O^4_t$$

Subject to:

$$\sum_{arp} e(arp)\,\bar{x}_{arpt} \leqq \sum_f C(f, t);\ t \in T \tag{1}$$

$$\overline{I}^1_{arp,t-1} + \overline{x}_{arpt} - \overline{I}^1_{arpt} = \overline{z}_{arpt};\ a \in A,\ r \in R,\ p \in P,\ t \in T \qquad (2)$$

$$\overline{I}^2_{arpt} - \overline{I}^{2+}_{arp,t-1} - \overline{I}^{2-}_{arp,t-1} + z_{arpt} - \overline{I}^{2+}_{arpt} =$$
$$= \overline{w}_{arpt} + \overline{d}_{arpt};\ a \in A,\ r \in R,\ p \in P,\ t \in T \qquad (3)$$

$$\overline{I}^{3+}_{arp,t-1} - \overline{I}^{3-}_{arp,t-1} + \overline{w}_{arpt} - \overline{I}^{3+}_{arpt} - \overline{I}^{3+}_{arpt} + \overline{I}^{3-}_{arpt} =$$
$$= \overline{d}_{arpt};\ a \in A,\ r \in R,\ p \in P,\ t \in T \qquad (4)$$

$$\sum_a \frac{T(k^0, a)}{\overline{C}(k^0, a)} \sum_{rp} \overline{Z}_{arpt} \leqq K(k^0, t);\ t \in T \qquad (5)$$

$$\sum m^1_r \cdot \sum_{ap} \overline{x}_{arpt} = R^1_t,\ t \in T \qquad (6)$$

$$m^3_{r\Phi(p)} \sum_a \overline{w}_{arpt} = R^3_{r\Phi(p)t} + O^3_{r\Phi(p)t}\ ; \qquad (7)$$

$r \in R$, $p \in P$ and all $\Phi(p)$, $t \in T$

$$\sum_r m^4_r \sum_{ap} \overline{x}_{arpt} = R^4_t + O^4_t;\ t \in T \qquad (8)$$

$$\sum_r O^3_{r\Phi(p)t} \leqq q^3_{\Phi(p)t} \cdot \sum_r R^3_{r\Phi(p)t};$$

$p \in P$ and all $\Phi(p)$ $t \in T$ (9)

$$O^4_t \leqq q^4_t R^4_t;\ t \in T \qquad (10)$$

$$\sum_r R^3_{r\Phi(p)t} \leqq UR^3_{\Phi(p)t};\ p \in P \text{ and all } \Phi(p),\ t \in T, \qquad (11)$$

$$R^4_t \leqq UR^4_t;\ t \in T \qquad (12)$$

$$R^1_t \leqq UR^1_t;\ t \in T \qquad (13)$$

$$\overline{I}^{2-}_{arpt} \leqq \overline{d}_{arpt};\ a \in A,\ r \in R,\ p \in P,\ t \in T \qquad (14)$$

All variables are nonnegatives

The constraint equations in the AP model, can be interpreted as follows:

Constraints (1) – Indicate that the tons melted (including cast excess) for all types, in period t, cannot exceed the capacity of the capacity of the furnaces during the same period.

Constraints (2), (3) and (4) – Are the mass balance equations corresponding to the foundry, thermal treatment and factory sections respectively. Note that in equations (3), the demands are the tons of each type to be processed in the factory sections plus the demands of types just after thermal treatment section.

Constraints (5) – Indicate that the number of hours necessary to thermically treat all types, measured in terms of furnace K^0, cannot exceed the available time (also measured in terms of the furnace k^0). $C(k, a)$ is the apparent capacity, in tons, of furnace k for alloy a. These values can be obtained from historical data (using the average *os* past values) and can be recomputed after the present system starts to operate. Since k^0 is the furnace whose basket has minimal volume, it is known that $\overline{C}(k^0, a) \leqq \overline{C}(k, a)$ for all $a \in A$ all $k \in K$. Let (x) be the smallest integer greater than x. For each Q tons of alloy a^0 to be treated thermically, the relation between the required times for furnaces k^0 and k is:

$$\frac{\left\lceil \dfrac{Q}{\overline{C}(k^0, a^0)} \right\rceil T(k^0, a^0)}{\left\lceil \dfrac{Q}{\overline{C}(k, a^0)} \right\rceil T(k, a^0)}$$

This function is illustrated in Figure 3.

The capacity of the thermal treatment section is presently a limiting factor in the production process and the furnaces are used at full capacity most of the time. Thus the Q to be employed to relate k^0 and k is Q_k such that:

$$\left\lceil \frac{Q_k}{\overline{C}(k, a^0)} \right\rceil T(k, a) \cong T(k, t)$$

which is the amount of tons that maintain furnace k working all the time. These considerations imply that:

$$K(k^{0'}, t) = \sum_{k \in K} \frac{\left\lceil \dfrac{Q_k}{\overline{C}(k^0, a^0)} \right\rceil T(k^0, a^0)}{\left\lceil \dfrac{Q_k}{\overline{C}(k, a^0)} \right\rceil T(k, a^0)} T(k^0, t)$$

Note that it was implicitly assumed that $K(k^0, t)$ does not vary significantly if another alloy is chosen as a reference, instead of a^0. This assumption seems reasonable because the differences among furnaces should reflect equally among all alloys.

Constraints (6)–(13) – Express the number of regular and overtime man/hours required in each section (except thermal treatment)

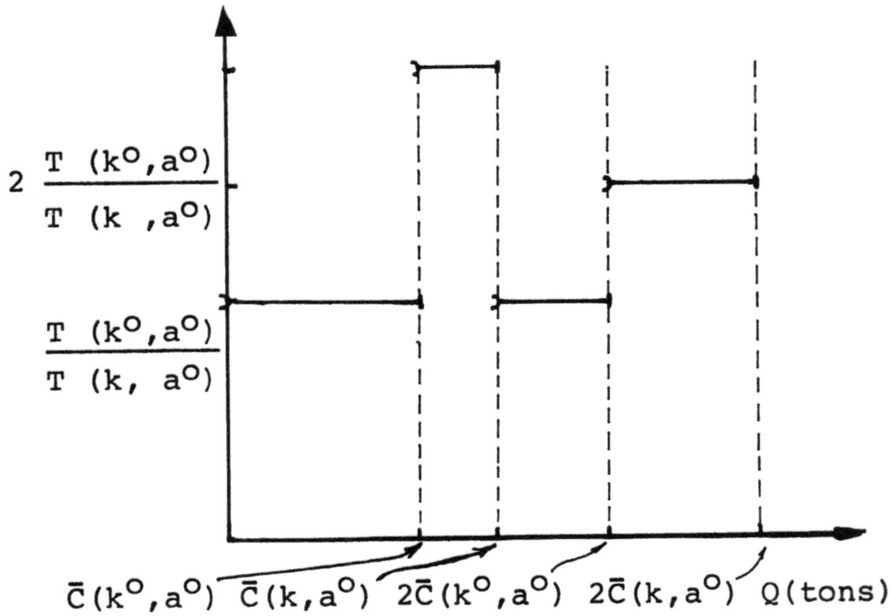

Figure 3.

and their upper bounds. Particularly in the factory section the manpower is determined for each operation $\Phi(p)$ of all production routings $\Phi \in P$.

Constraints (14) – Establish that backorders cannot exceed the demand, after thermal treatment, for every type in each period t.

The following mixed integer program (MP) is attached to the problem (AP) in order to determine the foundry furnaces schedule:

$$\text{(MP): min} \sum_{fatl} \sigma\,(n^l_{fat})\, s_{fat} +$$

$$+ \sum_{ft} M\bar{v}_{ft} \text{ where } M \gg 0$$

Subject to:

$$\sum_{r,p} e(a, r, p)\, \bar{x}_{arpt} \leqq \sum_{l,f} C(f) n^l_{fat} \tag{16}$$

$a \in A, t \in s$

$$\sum_{a,l} n^l_{fat} + \delta(n^l_{fat}) + v_{ft} - \bar{v}_{ft} = 28 \tag{17}$$

$f \in F, t \in S$

$$n^l_{fat} \text{ integer and } 0 < n^l_{fat} < 6, \tag{18}$$

$$f \in F, l \in L, a \in A, t \in S$$

$$v_{ft}, \overline{v}_{ft} > 0 \qquad f \in F, t \in S$$

$$\sigma(n^l_{fat}) = \begin{cases} 1 & \text{if } n^l_{fat} > 0 \\ 0 & \text{otherwise} \end{cases}$$

(MP) is solved after (AP) for the horizon $S < T$.

In this case $S = t_0$ was adopted where t_0 is the current month, since the furnaces' capacity is not presently critical.

(MP) is a mixed integer programming problem whose objective function is composed of the setup costs resulting from the reconditioning of the furnaces and the energy necessary to melt the first charge, plus a penalty that will be positive if the capacity of the furnaces is violated.

The furnaces are subject to the following limitations:

- None of the furnaces can be used continually for more than six days without being reconditioned.
- The reconditioning of a furnace takes approximately one day.
- Whenever an alloy is changed the furnace has to be reconditioned.

Because of these limitations, it is not difficult to see that four variables are necessary just to represent the production schedule of a fixed alloy in a given furnace (i.e., it is sufficient that $L = 1, 2, 3, 4$). Constraints (17) and (18) quantify these limitations. Specifically, constraint (17) states that the utilization of a furnace in a given month, considering the reconditioning time plus slack and surplus variables, must be equal to 28 days (one month). The penalty terms in the objective function will imply that the best solution be chosen among those that have $\overline{v}_{ft} = 0$, if any exists. If such a solution exists, the program will pass to the next levels. Otherwise, (MP) is solved with a smaller capacity for the furnaces. This new capacity is

$$\sum_f C(f, t) = \sum_{arp} e(a, r, p)\, \overline{x}_{arpt} - \sum_f \overline{v}_{ft} + \sigma(\overline{v}_{ft})$$

The process is repeated until a solution is obtained from (MP), with $\overline{v}_{ft} = 0$ for $f \in F, t \in S$.

7.4. Disaggregation of types in families

The quantities of each type which have to be produced in the factory section are subsequently disaggregated in families. To attain this objective the knapsacks $KP(a, r, p)$ below, are solved for each type (a, r, p) at the beginning of period t_0 (the present month), after obtaining the solutions to (AP) and (MP).

$$KP(a, r, p)\text{: min} \sum_{j \in J^0} \frac{sj\, Dj}{\overline{y}_{jt_0}}$$

Subject to:

$$\sum_{j \in J^0} \overline{Y}_{jt_0} = w_{arpt_0}$$

$$1b_{jt_0} \leqq Y_{jt_0}; j\, J^0$$

where J^0 is the set of families in (a, r, p) that trigger during t_0, i.e., those families j such that

$$AI_{jt_0} < \overline{d}_{jt_0} + SS_j$$

Here AI_{jt_0}, d_{jt_0} and SS_j are respectively: the available inventory (physical inventory plus amount on order minus backorders) of family j at the beginning of period t_0, its demand in tons in period t_0 and its safety stock (these quantities are obtained by adding up corresponding items quantities).

S_j is the sum of set up costs, in the factory section, for family j and Dj is the corresponding annual demand. The lower limits are defined in such a way to assure that the demand of each family will be satisfied, i.e.,

$$1b_j = \max(\overline{d}_{jt_0} - AI_{jt_0} + SS_j; O)\, j \in J^0$$

Knapsack problems of the type described above were used previous by Bitran and Hax [1]. An efficient method to solve them is described in [2].

Whenever there are backorders in (AP) $I^{-3}_{arpt_0} > 0$, i.e., the knapsack $KP(a, r, p)$ is infeasible because

$$\overline{w}_{arpt_0} < \sum_{j \in J_0} 1b_{jt_0}$$

In this case the backorders are distributed proportionally among families to the lower limits:

$$\bar{y}_{jt_0} = 1b_{jt_0} + \frac{(\bar{w}_{arpt_0} - \Sigma_{j\in J^0} 1b_j)}{\Sigma_{j\in J^0} 1b_{jt_0}} 1b_{jt_0}; j \in J^0$$

7.5. Disaggregation in number of items

7.5.1. Factory section

The amount of each item to be produced in the factory section is obtained by solving for each family of each type, the following problem:

$$FP(j)\text{: } \min \tfrac{1}{2} i\, I(j) \frac{\bar{Y}_{jt_0+iI(j)}\,(AI_{it_0} - SS_i)}{\bar{d}_{jt_0}} -$$

$$- \frac{it_0 + AI_{it_0} - SS_i}{d_{it_0}} 2$$

Subject to:

$$\sum_{i\in I(j)} \bar{w}_{it_0} = \bar{y}_{jt_0}$$

$$1b_{it_0} \leqq \bar{w}_{it_0}\ i \in I(j)$$

where $I(j)$ is the set of items of family j and $1b_{it_0} = \max(\bar{d}_{it_0} + SS_i; \text{O}) \geqq 0$. In case of backorders, $FP(J)$ is infeasible and similarly to what was done before these are distributed proportionally among the items to their lower bounds. The reader should note that if there are no forecast errors, then the objective function in $FP(j)$ equalizes the run-out time of the items with the run-out time of the family.

The types (a, r, p) which are simply zinc plated in the factory section do not present setup costs and are considered to be a unique family, and thus no problem of the type $K(a, r, p)$ is solved. The quantities of these items are obtained directly through $FP(j)$.

7.5.2. Foundry and thermal treatment sections

For these two sections the items' quantities are obtained directly from types, without having to initially disaggregate them into families. The problem solved is the mixed integer program (TP) below. The objective function expresses the setup costs corresponding to the energy required in each operation of the furnaces.

This cost is constant for each operation of thermal treatment, for a given alloy.

The decision variables in (TP) are the number of units of each item to be produced in the foundry and thermal treatment sections, their inventories and backorders.

$$\text{(TP): } \min \sum_{ka} s_{kat_0} n_{kat_0}$$

Subject to:

$$\sum_{v \in V(a)} \beta_{va}\, y_{vat_0} \leqq \sum_k C(k) n_{kat_0 j'}\ a \in A \tag{20}$$

$$\sum_a n_{kat_0} T(k, a) \leqq T(k, t_0), k \in K \tag{21}$$

$$z_{it_0} = \sum_{v \in V(a)} \alpha_{iva}\, y_{vat_0} \tag{22}$$

for all $i \in (arp)$ all (arp)

$$I^1_{i,t_0-1} + x_{it_0} - I^1_{it_0} = z_{it_0} \tag{23}$$

for all $i \in (arp)$ all (arp)

$$I^{2+}_{it_0-1} - I^{2-}_{i,\ t_0-1} + z_{it_0} - I^{2+}_{it_0} + I^{2-}_{it_0} =$$

$$= w_{it_0} + d_{it_0}, \text{ for all } i \in (arp) \text{ all } (arp) \tag{24}$$

$$\sum_{i \in (arp)} \delta_i I^1_{it_0} = \bar{I}^1_{arpt_0}; \text{ for all } (arp) \tag{25}$$

$$\sum_{i \in (arp)} \delta_i I^{2+}_{it_0} = \bar{I}^{2+}_{arpt_0}; \text{ for all } (arp) \tag{26}$$

$$\sum_{(arp)} \delta_i I^{2-}_{it_0} = \bar{I}^{2-}_{arpt_0}; \text{ for all } (arp) \tag{27}$$

$$\sum_{i \in (arp)} \delta_{i\ it_0} = \bar{x}_{arpt_0}; \text{ for all } (arp) \tag{28}$$

$$n_{kat_0} = 0, 1, 2 \ldots k \in K, \alpha \in A \tag{29}$$

$$I^1_{it_0} \geqq \frac{\bar{I}^1_{arpt_0}}{\delta_i} \frac{d_{i,t_0+1}}{\Sigma_i d_{i,t_0+1}}$$

all variables are nonnegative.

The variables y_{vat_0} represent ficticious items defined for each alloy in the following way: consider an item from the class 'large' and fill it up with smaller items of the same alloy.

Each possible composition generates a ficticious item. Constraint (20) indicates that the volume of the baskets used in the thermal treatment furnaces must be larger than the volume of the ficticious items to be treated thermically. Constraint (1) expresses the fact that the total time for thermal treatment is limited by the furnaces available time.

The number of items to be treated thermically is related to the number of ficticious items in constraint (22).

Finally, the mass balance of each item is established in (23) and (24) while (25) to (29) guarantee coherence with the aggregate problem (ARP).

7.6. Computational advantages of the hierarchical approach

When compared with the direct approach in modelling the program, the hierarchical approach shows the fundamental advantage of actually solving the described problem. In fact, over a planning horizon of 13 months of 4 weeks each (1 year) the direct approach requires such a large mixed integer model, that it is practically impossible to be numerically solved.

The following Table 1 presents the approximate size of the models in both approaches. As an additional advantage of the hierarchical approach, it can be mentioned that the volume of data

Table 1. Comparison between direct and hierarchical approaches.

Approach	Number of restrictions	Number of continuous variables	Number of integer variables
Direct	~95,000	~50,000	~1,000
Hierarchical			
Problem AP	≅2,500	~5,000	none
Problem MP	~90	~15	~70
Problem TP	~3,700	~1,500	~20

necessary to implement the model is far less than for the direct approach. This reduces the burden and cost of implementing a practical solution significantly.

7.7. Computational results

Up to the time of the writing of this paper the authors conducted a limited series of three experiments to examine the performance of the system. A sample of the forty five most important items was selected. The product structure characteristics are given below.

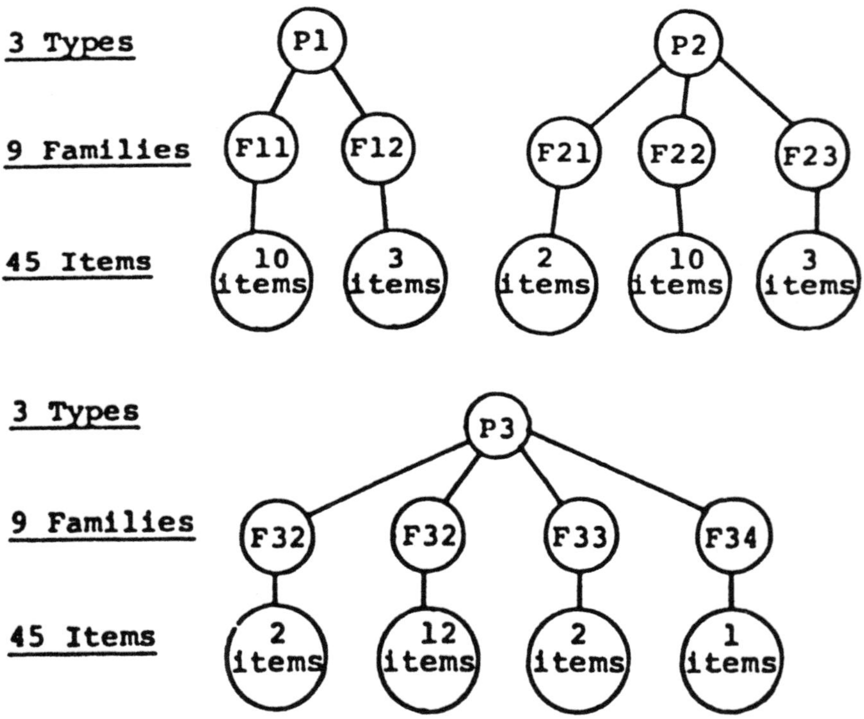

The model was run for an horizon of 4 months. The data used for the first test was taken from the manufacturer. For the second and third tests the data was obtained from the original set by adding a random error uniformly distributed in the interval [10%, + 10%]. For each of these experiments a global mixed integer model was run, in parallel, for comparison purposes. The results obtained are shown in the take below:

First experiment	Global mixed integer model	Hierarchical model
Total cost (Cr$)	3,189,407	3,416,904
Setup costs (Cr$)	344,890	497,093
Backorders	Zero	Zero

Second experiment	Global mixed integer model	Hierarchical model
Total cost (Cr$)	3,355,579	3,605,982
Setup Cost (Cr$)	346,890	503,386
Backorders	25%	4%

Third experiment	Global mixed integer model	Hierarchical model
Total cost (Cr$)	3,249,484	3,489,950
Setup cost (Cr$)	345,479	498,306
Backorders	zero	1,5%

References

1. Bitran, G. R. and Hax A. C., 'On the Design of Hierarchical Production Planning Systems'. To appear in November 1976 special issue of *Decision Sciences* edited by E. S. Buffa.
2. Bitran, G. R. and Hax A. C., 'On the Solution of Convex Knapsack Problems with Bounded Variables', Technical Report 121, Operations Research Center, MIT (June 1976).
3. Hax, A. C., 'Aggregate Production Planning', in *Handbook of Operations Research*, J. Moder and S. E. Elmaghraby (ed.), Van Nostrand Reinhold, to appear.
4. Hax, A. C. and Meal, H. C., 'Hierarchical Integration of Production Planning and Scheduling', in *Studies in Management Sciences*, vol. I, *Logistics*, M. A. Geisler (ed.), North Holland – American Elsevier 1975.
5. Winters, P. R., 'Constrained Inventory Rules for Production Smoothing', *Management Science*, vol. 8, no. 4 (July 1962).

8. A hierarchical approach to multilocation inventory systems

UDAY S. KARMARKAR

Abstract

A hierarchical approach is proposed for the management of multilocation inventory systems. The problem is partitioned into subproblems to reduce complexity. Interactions between subproblems are identified, and the hierarchy of decisions to be made is described in managerial terms. Possible ways of grouping the decisions into planning and scheduling levels are discussed and suitable modeling approaches are suggested. Technical issues are avoided in the interests of accessibility.

8.1. Introduction

This paper outlines a design proposal for the management of multilocation inventory systems. The emphasis is on planning decisions and their interaction with other management functions. Facilities design and detailed scheduling decisions are thus of interest chiefly insofar as they interact with the planning decision. Furthermore, the implementation of the type of planning and control system discussed here presupposes computerization of the methods suggested although technical details are avoided here.

We begin by discussing some properties that might be desirable for an idealized computer-based distribution management system. An obvious desideratum is cost effectiveness in the sense of maximizing the utility of the user within the constraints of the situation. This involves a tradeoff between the cost of the system and its adjuncts on one hand, and the benefits accruing from the system on the other. The costs of the system include fixed charges due to setup, investment and hiring and training of personnel and variable charges of operating the system. The possible benefits are decreased inventory investment, holding and transportation costs, reduced risks and uncertainty, and the improvement of customer service.

Hax [2] and Wagner [9] suggest that a distribution management system ideally ought to support management decision making not only in the area of logistics but also in the functional areas that interact with the distribution system. Conversely the system should allow for and react appropriately to decisions made in other functional areas. The control system should also be *robust* in the sense of being able to function reasonably well even when the assumptions made in system design do not hold exactly. Thus for example, changes in the demand distribution of an item, extreme or outlying observations, or changes in cost structure, should not cause the system to make catastrophic errors. Next, the system should be *stable* in the way it reacts to external changes. Short term changes should not cause drastic oscillations in system behavior. The system should have some tracking capability so that it can detect apparent errors in data or output and produce exception reports when the situation calls for them.

Finally, the system should be compatible with the firm's organization. The organizational resources required in terms of trained personnel and organizational structure should be available so that implementation of the system is feasible. As far as possible the structure of the system should align itself with the existing structure of the organization, and the decisions to be made should correspond to specific responsibility centers within the organization. Apart from the behavioral desirability of such a matching, it also enables the subjective evaluation of the outputs of the system by experts with good local information, and provides a method for allowing subjective inputs to the system. This also implies that the system's outputs and decisions should be in managerial terms that are familiar to the personnel involved.

8.2. The hierarchical approach

The complexity of the problem and the computational difficulties associated with optimal solutions suggest that heuristic methods although suboptimal might prove more cost-effective. The hierarchical approach to complex problems (Hax and Meal [3]) is a systematic procedure that, although heuristic, is based on formal models of the decision problem. The approach consists of trying to partition the problem into subproblems that isolate different aspects of the problem with different degrees of importance and often with different qualitative characteristics. As with formal decomposition the subproblems are not completely decoupled and the interaction between them is recognized. Unlike decomposition, however, a hierarchy of problems is developed and the direction of information flow is only downward in the hierarchy.

While the method is suboptimal, the heuristic approach allows a great deal of flexibility in casting the subproblems so that they are tractable and correspond to conventional ways of viewing the problem. This greatly improves the credibility of the method and permits subjective managerial interaction in the decision process.

8.2.1. A hierarchy of planning and scheduling decisions

It is assumed in the following paragraphs that no capital budgeting or capacity design and location decisions are being considered. The decisions to be made in approximate hierarchical order are:

1. Assign product (type) to plant/vendor: It may be necessary to make long term commitments about the source of a particular product (type). This decision may involve a fixed charge cost structure or a choice between a finite number of alternatives.
2. Set aggregate production and manpower levels: Long term production planning sets production levels so as to meet requirements while manpower levels are smoothed to minimize costs of hiring, firing, and training of personnel. A tradeoff is also made between production, inventory holding, backorder and transportation costs. Long production lead times, shipment lags and constraints on production or shipment capacities are also accounted for.
3. Allocate production/purchases to marketing districts: If the total volume of product (type) in a period is insufficient to meet projected requirements, it must be allocated amongst the marketing districts.
4. Build up stocks for peak seasonal demand: If the product (type) exhibits seasonal behavior, it may be necessary to start ac-

cumulation of stocks early in the season so as to ensure sufficient stock availability in peak periods when production capacity might fall short. This also helps to smooth production over the seasonal cycle.

5. Choose transportation modes: This decision does not refer to the design of transportation systems but rather to the possibility of using slower but cheaper modes of transportation by planning ahead. For example, seasonal stocks built up early in the season could be transported to their destinations by a slow transportation mode.
6. Set service levels for demand locations: Each location has a different replenishment cost associated with it. Thus for each product (type) different locations should, in general, provide different levels of service. A tradeoff has to be made between the cost of providing a given level of service and the implicit costs of failure to provide this level. Service levels are associated with 'demand' locations; that is, locations which receive orders and ship to customers. However, if orders can be transferred to other locations or if a delay in filling the order is permissible then service levels must be set for other locations in the system.
7. Setting safety stocks: Based on the demand characteristics, service policy (excess/shortage cost tradeoffs) review period and replenishment time, safety stocks must be determined for each (item, demand location) combination. In general if orders must be filled immediately, safety stocks should be held at demand locations only. However, if delays are permissible, they may be held at 'higher' locations in the system.
8. Position stock in the system: Given the desired service levels and available stock in the system, the total stock has to be positioned in the system taking transportation and redistribution costs into consideration. The total stock available includes seasonal stock accumulations and safety stocks.
9. Set aggregate shipment schedules: Shipment capacities required for shipments within market districts and shipment quantities are determined on an aggregate basis.
10. Redistribution of excess stocks: Stock imbalances of a product (type) may occur in the form of excess stocks that accumulate at some location over a period of time. These stocks should be

redistributed in the system taking transportation costs into account.

These decision areas summarize the important issues of long term and intermediate term planning. The scheduling decisions remain.

11. Setting shipment quantities: When goods are to be shipped between locations, the size of the shipment must be determined. If economies of scale are involved in making the shipment, small shipments may not be worth making when the incremental benefit from shipping does not justify the fixed costs incurred. If certain items can be shipped together there may be cost commonalities that favor joint scheduling. The shipments made must be consistent with the aggregate schedules.
12. Review period: Stocks of an item will in general be reviewed at different frequencies. Given the centralized management approach, the review period should be some integer multiple of the smallest control cycle which might be a week. The review period will also correspond to the timing of shipments.
13. Vehicular scheduling: Given master shipment schedules, detailed scheduling of shipments may involve vehicular scheduling problems.

Finally, the day-to-day operation of the inventory system involves several functional tasks. These include:

14. Order entry and order filling.
15. Inventory status reporting.
16. Scheduling shipments to customers.
17. Scheduling shipments between locations.
18. Demand forecasting.
19. Generating replenishment orders.

8.3. A design proposal

This section outlines a scheme for planning and control of multi-location distribution systems. The description of the approach is necessarily somewhat sketchy, since many details are problem-specific and will vary from case to case. The analysis of items and their aggregation for planning purposes are discussed. Possible models and computational methods for implementing the hierarchical approach are suggested.

8.3.1. Item analysis

Certain characteristics of stock items affect the approach used to control the items. Thus an analysis and classification of such characteristics is important in designing management systems:

1. Demand characteristics: The case of deterministic demands is not of interest here; the problem reduces in that case to one of deterministic allocation of resources and scheduling. Stochastic demands may be stationary in each period, or non-stationary. In the non-stationary case, several types of behavior may be encountered. Demand may increase (i.e., the location parameter of the demand distribution may increase) in successive periods due to prolonged growth of the market for the product or in the company's market share. Alternatively, decreased demand may be experienced for products subject to vogue changes and obsolescence. An important case is that of seasonal goods where the demand exhibits an annually repeated cyclical variation. In all these non-stationary cases, the problem of dynamically positioning stock in the distribution system is important. For example, it has been suggested (Wagner [9]) that for the seasonal case as stocks are built up they should be carried at lower echelons while in the declining phase at the end of a season they should be carried at higher echelons.

   Another important property of the demand distribution is the degree of uncertainty involved in predicting the demand. If the coefficient of variation of the demand distribution is small, the problem can sometimes be satisfactorily treated as a deterministic one. The effect of high uncertainties is quite complex. Cost tradeoffs become more complex and successive time periods are linked together by the interactions caused by excess or shortage in stock levels. The volume of demand also affects the methodology selected to control an item. Forecasting methods and order size computations vary for slow-moving and fast-moving items.
2. Economic characteristics: Products vary in their contribution to

company profits and hence in their economic significance. The so-called 'ABC analysis' is usually employed to isolate those products that constitute a major share of the dollar sales of the company. The ABC analysis is a relative approach and it could be argued that since the tradeoff to be made involves cost of control versus benefits of control, some sort of absolute analysis of each product's contribution or profit is warranted. Furthermore, within the ABC grouping, there may be considerable variations in sales volumes and unit costs which could imply different methodological approaches. Particularly in the multilocation situation, a type of 'stock or order-on-demand' decision has to be made for each product-location pair that is analogous to the 'stock or make-to-order' decision. For example, a slow moving, high unit cost item may have stocks held at higher echelons in the system and only be transferred to demand locations when demand actually occurs. All this suggests that in the multilocation situation a more detailed analysis of contribution, costs and service requirements may be appropriate.

8.3.2. Aggregation of items

Decisions which are 'higher' in the hierarchy are not made at the same level of detail as those at the lower, functional levels. For example, seasonal planning cannot be realistically done in terms of individual items. On the other hand, replenishment orders are necessarily on a stock item basis. The higher level decisions must employ an aggregated definition of decision variables.

Since the inventory system must interact with a production system, the aggregated variables in these two areas must be compatible. Hax and Meal [3] suggest a two-level aggregation of items in a production context: Product Type/Item Family/Item. The product types are the most aggregated variables defined for seasonal planning purposes. This definition should correspond exactly with that used in the distribution area, since seasonal planning encompasses both production and distribution. The number of distinct product types should be small enough to make the planning model of manageable size.

The intermediate aggregation of items into item families was used in [3] to take into account the joint scheduling of items due to shared setup costs. This classification has no relevance to the distribution side. If there are significant cost commonalities amongst items in shipment, it may be useful to define analogous item-families for distribution purposes. If not, one level of aggregation should suffice: product type/items.

Items falling into the same product-type classification should have approximately similar patterns of seasonal demand and similar excess to shortage cost ratios. This is because the planning decisions deal with the pattern of production and distribution over the year and with tradeoffs between inventory holding costs and customer service. Often, the aggregation into product types will suggest itself quite naturally according to product lines.

8.3.3. Service considerations

Determination of service requirements depends on the structure of the inventory system. In most cases it can be argued that the structure will be multiechelon; this implies that there is a unique supply path from source to customer (group) for each product (type). In this case the service level tradeoff should be made for each (product type, demand location) pair taking into account differing customer service requirements and differing costs of supply. If backorder costs can be estimated [7], a 'newsboy' type of calculation may be used. Costs of excess should be adjusted by a credit allowed for stock carried into the next period.

If the system structure is more complicated due to multiple sources or capacity constraints, the multiechelon assumption may not be valid. In this case a stochastic programming approach may be appropriate in determining optimal service policies. Such an approach is described in Karmarkar [4], [5], and Karmarkar and Patel [6]. The latter paper includes numerical examples of two-location and five-location problems. Such an approach is also appropriate for price redistribution problems.

Where demand is highly seasonal, service levels will vary over the seasonal cycle. Service levels will be higher in the increasing demand phase of the cycle but will drop in the declining phase. It may thus be necessary to assign distinct service requirements for increasing and decreasing demand phases. In this case, the seasonal planning approach described next would have to be augmented by a 'current planning' phase.

8.3.4. Planning decisions

The seasonal planning model covers a decision horizon of one to two years – sufficient to account for seasonal variations. The plan includes decisions (1) through (5) in the scheme of the preceding section. The problems are interrelated and characterized by many interdependent constrained activities and a high degree of intertemporal dependence due to inventory holding, shipping lags and seasonal stock build-up requirements. The only computational methods that appear to be realistic for this type of problem are linear and quadratic programming. Given the wide experience with and the commercial availability of LP codes, the former is thought to be the preferred technique. If decisions such as (1) – the assignment of product to plant/vendor – involve non-linearities due to say a fixed charge cost structure, they must be solved exogenous to the seasonal plan, at a 'higher' level in the hierarchy. Furthermore, the stochasticities inherent in the problem must be removed by replacing random variables with fixed quantities such as expected values or other approximate 'certainty equivalents.' However, for planning purposes, this procedure is not unreasonable, since what is desired is a broad understanding of the major cost tradeoffs and allocation of resources.

We note that it is not necessary in the seasonal plan to consider the detailed structure of regional distribution networks. A multi-echelon structure may be assumed, or, simpler still, all requirements may be stated as time-phased requirements for the whole region projected at the supply point for the region. From the point of view of the distribution problem, the major outputs of the seasonal plan are available production and purchase quantities, pattern of seasonal stock accumulation and transportation and the allocation of available stock to marketing regions.

If necessary, a 'current planning' process then attempts to sharpen the aggregate plan for the current period by taking into account stochastic factors, current distribution of stock and the detailed structure of the distribution network. The problem is formulated as a one-period stochastic program with some allowance made heuristically for the succeeding period as credit for excess stock carried over. The credit allowed could be the average cost of supply for the location or the cost of supply from the preferred supplier. The current plan would try to consider decisions (6) through (10) of the previous section. Its major outputs are target stock levels by location and a current shipments schedule which gives the appropriate levels of service and positioning of stock. The plan does not try to change that part of production capacity assigned to the accumulation of seasonal stocks. Technical issues are discussed in [4], [5], and [6].

8.3.5. Scheduling decisions

The motivation for order-sizing in distribution systems arises from fixed costs of ordering and economies of scale in shipment. Some cases of sizing in multiechelon systems have been discussed by Schwarz [8], and Graves and Schwarz [1]. While the exact solution of sizing problems may not be realistic, these studies indicate that treating locations as though they were independent does not result in severe distortions. Furthermore, if seasonality is involved, the shipment sizes have to be adjusted heuristically to allow for variations in demand rate. In addition, planning guidelines at the product-type level have to be followed. It is suggested that minimum shipment sizes be determined for each item-route combination, and these be proportioned suitably to meet plan guidelines as in [3].

If there are joint economies of scale in shipment, a shipment size has to be determined on some intermediate basis. For example, it may be necessary to batch shipments to fill a truckload on a given route. On the other hand, if there are no economies of scale or fixed charges, aggregate plans may be disaggregated to the item level simply on the basis of runout times.

In a centralized system of control, a periodic review approach seems natural. The shipment timing will presumably be coordinated with the minimum review period. The review period need not be the same for all items and locations but will be a multiple of the minimum. It may be desirable to adjust the review period downward for higher frequency in high demand phases if the added sophistication can be justified.

8.3.6. Information requirements

A considerable amount of data about the problem is required. Apart from specification of the physical structure of the system and listing of products and product types, all cost factors are required to be known. The greatest difficulty is with the estimation of back-order costs. These should be approximately estimated for entire product classes rather than by individual product.

A major input to the planning decisions is demand forecasts by product and product type for each period. The seasonal plan requires point forecasts of demand but for the current plan estimates of the mean and variance of the demand distribution are the minimal requirements. Regression models may be used to provide aggregate seasonal forecasts and smoothing methods for monthly forecasts of demand on a product-wise basis. Both these require a record of past demand history at least for initial parameter estimation purposes. It is apparent that the information collection and generation requirements are quite vast.

8.4. Summary

This paper has briefly outlined a hierarchical approach to the multilocation inventory problem. There is no definitive specification of a solution possible with such a complex problem because of the many particular cases that can occur. While different strategies for modeling the decisions may be followed, the hierarchical structure provides a framework for coordinating these decisions.

References

1. Graves, S. C. and Schwarz, L. B., 'Single Cycle Continuous Review Policies for Arborescent Production/Inventory Systems', forthcoming in *Management Science.*
2. Hax, A. C., 'Comment on the Distribution System Simulator', *Management Science*, vol. 21, no. 2 (October 1974).
3. Hax, A. C. and Meal, H., 'Hierarchical Integration of Production Planning and Scheduling', in *Studies in Management Sciences*, vol. 1, *Logistics*, M. A. Geisler (ed.), North Holland-American Elsevier (1975).
4. Karmarkar, U. S., 'Multilocation Distribution Systems', unpublished Ph.D. thesis, MIT (1975).
5. Karmarkar, U. S., 'Convex/Stochastic Programming and Multilocation Inventory Problems', submitted for publication.

6. Karmarkar, U. S. and Patel, N., 'The One-Period, N-Location Distribution Problem', forthcoming in *Naval Research Logistics Quarterly*.
7. Oral, M., Salvador, M. S., Reisman, A. and Dean, B. V., 'On the Evaluation of Shortage Costs for Inventory Control of Finished Goods', *Management Science*, vol. 18, B344–351 (1972).
8. Schwarz, L. B., 'A Simple Continuous Review, Deterministic, One-Warehouse, N-Retailer Inventory Problem', *Management Science*, vol 19, no. 5 (1973).
9. Wagner, H. M., 'The Design of Production and Inventory Systems for Multifacility, Multiwarehouse Companies', *Operations Research*, vol. 22 (1974).

9. A disaggregation problem and a search enumeration algorithm for a multiplant, multiproduct scheduling application

SUSUMU MORITO and HARVEY M. SALKIN

Abstract

A disaggregation of the production planning in an injection molding industry is considered. The production is completely determined by orders, rather than sales forecast, and an enormous number of different products are involved. A disaggregation problem is identified with emphasis on levels II and III decisions. A simulation approach is considered for level II planning, which plays a major role in disaggregation. We show that disaggregation is the result of various logistical, technological, and computational considerations. The concept of search enumeration in integer programming is applied for level III scheduling. All work discussed here relates to part of an actual case study for a medium size Ohio corporation and resulted in the development of a computer system for order processing, production planning and scheduling, and inventory control.

9.1. Introduction

Recently, the disaggregation problem in aggregate planning started to draw attention of both researchers and practitioners of management science (e.g., [1], [2], [3]). The typical scenario where disaggregation is applicable is in production management, where an aggregate production plan must eventually be transformed into an actual daily schedule (e.g., [2], [3]). The disaggregation approach is especially useful in this area because:

1. In actual planning, disaggregation of the aggregate plan is normally inevitable. In fact, planning is nothing but the process of disaggregation itself.
2. There are normally mathematical techniques which are particularly useful for disaggregated problems.
3. Computational limitations, both in time and memory require-

ment, often associated with mathematical algorithms require a large problem to be disaggregated, so that it can be solved within a reasonable amount of time.

Our discussion will suggest that the disaggregation of the aggregate plan results from the major factors listed below.

1. *Logical considerations*: The aggregate plan does not automatically suggest level III decisions such as daily scheduling. Therefore, the process of disaggregation is essential in order to translate the aggregate plan into a more detailed daily plan. The logical factors can be further classified as logistical considerations, organizational considerations, and technological considerations.
2. *Considerations of particular models and available algorithms and software*: In order to have a viable disaggregation scheme, models must be developed so that efficient algorithms and computer software are available.

In this article, we describe how the complete production scheduling problem is 'disaggregated' into several independent 'sub-problems'; the subproblems are solved by an optimization algorithm. It will be shown that the disaggregation of the complete scheduling is necessitated by computational limitations, and results mostly from logical considerations such as technological, logistical, and logical considerations.

In the next section, we describe the overall production system. The following section identifies the disaggregation problem. This section includes a discussion of level II planning and level III scheduling.

The next two sections give detailed discussions of the techniques adopted for the level II planning and the level III scheduling. A simulation approach is considered for level II planning, whereas an optimization technique, more specifically, a search enumeration algorithm, is used for level III scheduling.

The efforts described here are based on an actual case study for a medium size Ohio corporation. The entire study resulted in the development of a sophisticated computer system for production scheduling as well as for due date assignment, inventory control, machine allocation, and extensive data processing.

9.2. A brief description of the order processing and production scheduling system

9.2.1. Order processing

As previously noted, the production process is initiated by an order, which is a reasonable policy because of the huge number of products (i.e., tens of thousands). A customer, when placing an order, specifies: 1) the exact specification of the part to be produced, 2) the order quantity, and 3) a 'requested' shipment due date. As the parts are relatively small, the order quantity could be in the millions. In order to specify the part to be produced, we must know its: 1) material, 2) die, 3) secondary assembly characteristics, and 4) color. This information is completely specified in a part number code.

Subsequent to receiving an order, a 'promised' shipment due date must be given. This is accomplished by considering:

1. the order quantity and inventory
2. the current status of 'open' orders (i.e., other orders received but not yet shipped because they are being produced or waiting for production
3. the molding and secondary assembly machine schedules
4. customer priority

Also, some orders are of the 'multiple shipment' type, which requires several shipments over the time horizon. As production is based on orders, a substantial amount of inventory is not expected. However, due to such reasons as cancellations, overproduction, etc., there may be inventory, and thus the inventory level has to be checked prior to determining the production quantity. The number of open orders is normally large, and the average delivery lead time is several weeks. Once a promised due date is acknowledged to the customer, a 'new' order will become an open order which is added to the production queue.

9.2.2. Plants, production processes, and molding machines

The production processes consist of 1) molding, 2) a secondary assembly stage, and 3) dying. Depending on the parts requested, the production process varies, and can (e.g.) be 1) molding only, 2) molding and a secondary assembly stage, 3) molding and dying, and 4) molding, a secondary assembly stage and dying. In all cases, molding is required. Moreover, the secondary assembly stage and the dying processes do not cause difficulties in the context of technology, and thus in scheduling. Therefore, we will focus our attention on the molding process.

It is also worth mentioning that the company owns 5 plants in Ohio, which can be segregated into 3 groups. The first group consists of just one plant (a 'base' plant), which also provides a main office and a data processing department. All new orders, as well as order change information, is processed here. The remaining 4 plants are divided into 2 groups of 2 plants. These two 'sister' plants are close to each other, and there is frequent transportation between them. However, there is only minimal transportation between the 2 groups.

The company has several dozen molding machines, which can be further segregated into different machine types. One and only one material can be used on a molding machine at a time. A molding machine accomodates a certain mold, which allows for several dies, each of which corresponds to a specific part. Given a part (i.e., a part number) to be produced, the particular molding machine type to be used and the required material are known. Due to various technological constraints, certain parts must be produced at a slow speed. Typically, two production rates, fast and slow, are prescribed for each machine, and the rate with each associated part (or die) is known. During actual production, these rates vary somewhat to allow for quality control and machine age. A die specified as 'fast' can be run at either a fast or a slow speed.

9.2.3. Plant assignment and molding scheduling

Eventually an order for a particular part has to be assigned to a plant for production. If the molding machine type and the speed constraints specify just one eligible machine, there is no choice and this machine, and the associated plant, have to be assigned. If there is more than one machine available located at more than one plant, a plant has to be assigned. An important consideration for the plant assignment is the plant where the secondary stage assembly is performed, if requested. Once a plant assignment is made, a die, which usually is kept at the base plant, will be sent to the assigned plant.

There are other important technological restrictions. These are die position constraints, and die length constraints. Due to their geometric characteristics and ease of removal from the die, certain parts must be produced by dies located in a mold position near the machine operator. These dies are said to require a 'front position' in the mold, and are labeled 'front runners'. In contrast, the remaining dies can have either a front or rear position, where a rear position is at a farther distance from the operator. In addition to front or rear die positions, quality control dictates that some dies must be located closer to the center of the mold. Also, to avoid part breakage, the difference of lengths of adjacent dies can be no more than a specified amount.

It is undesirable and costly to stop the molding machine during a production run. Thus the molding operation is basically a continuous production process. New jobs to be processed correspond to orders for distinct parts. Based on an order quantity, the number of production days required is obtained. At the end of production for a certain job, a die must be pulled out of a cavity in the molding machine and a new die required for the next job is inserted. During this setup, the whole molding machine must be stopped, which means that production is lost. Although a setup can be completed fairly quickly, say in 30 minutes, it could take several hours until production stabilizes and acceptable parts are molded. Therefore, in order to maximize production, it is desired to minimize the number of setups.

9.3. A disaggregation problem

9.3.1. Designing a computerized production planning and scheduling system

Before identifying the disaggregation problem, a computerized production planning and scheduling, and an order processing system is described. The entire system can be divided into three major master programs, together with supporting programs such as for data processing and statistical analysis. The three areas are described below.

1. *Due date assignment and molding machine mix analysis*: Promised due dates are assigned to all new and change orders. This is done by considering the current molding machine mix and status of the molding machines (i.e. which parts are being produced currently in each cavity of each machine), all old orders yet to be produced, etc. An appropriate molding machine mix is also suggested by this program. This master program includes an Order Change Model, Production Size Model,[1] and a Due Date and Molding Machine Mix Model.
2. *Scheduling molding operation*: The final molding machine schedule is generated using an optimization algorithm considering dies currently in machines, production quantity, etc. Given a set of orders, the algorithm finds a schedule which minimizes the number of molding machine setups, while satisfying all technological and logistical constraints. Included here are an Order Selection Model (to select orders which will be considered in the final schedule) and a Molding Machine Scheduling Model (which contains the algorithm).
3. *Scheduling the secondary assembly operation*: The Secondary Assembly Scheduling Model creates a final assembly schedule based on the promised due dates of orders requiring the secondary assembly operation. The secondary assembly schedule is also based on logistical and technological constraints for the secondary assembly machines.

Figure 1 gives the general structure of the entire computer system.

9.3.2. Disaggregating the molding machine scheduling problem

Let us now observe the production scheduling system with particular emphasis on various levels of aggregation. As the production is based on actual orders and not on forecasted demand, the level I master production schedule corresponds to the following questions:

1. Which plants should be open?
2. Which types of molding machines and the number of each, should each plant have?
3. What should be long-term manpower planning?, etc.

1. This model decides the production quantity as there is flexibility in order quantities. It also considers orders which require several shipments of the same parts and for several orders for the same part.

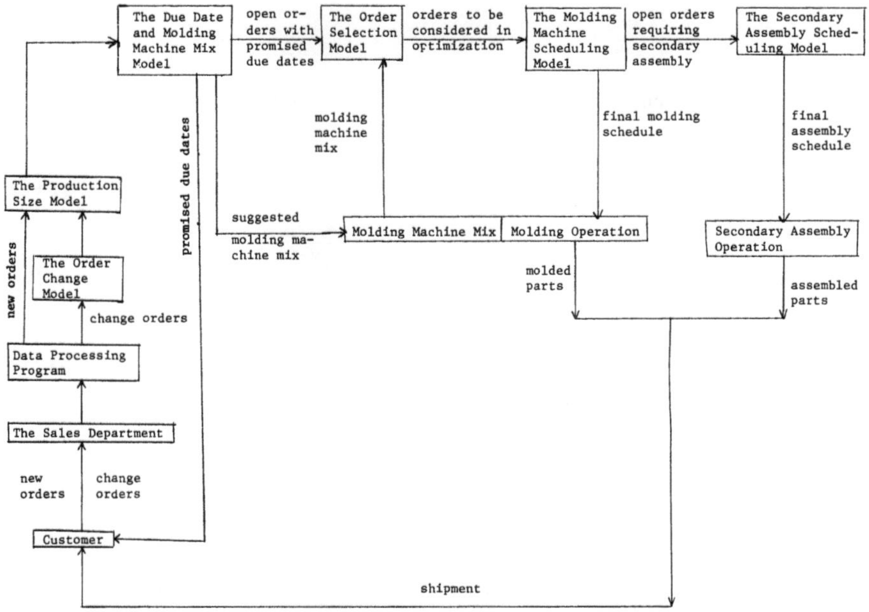

Figure 1. The entire computer system.

The system assumes that these level I decisions are previously specified by management, and thus, the system deals with levels II and III decisions.

The level II decisions deal with the molding machine 'mix'; that is:

1. Which mold is to be used for a particular molding machine? (Molds can be exchanged for certain machines).
2. Which material is to be used?
3. With which speed (i.e. either fast or slow) should the machine be run?

Speed and/or material change is quite common. Therefore, for each molding machine with a certain mold/material/speed configuration, the starting and ending dates have to be specified. An example of the molding machine mix appears in Figure 2. As described in the next section, the molding machine mix has to be decided so that it will reflect the current status of open orders, i.e., the distribution of open orders among various mold/material types. In general, the molding machine mix is fixed several weeks in advance.

CURRENT STATUS OF MOLDING MACHINES

	MACH NO.	MOLD TYPE	MATERIAL	SPEED	PLANT	START	END
1	14	1	3	3500	1	11777	63078
2	14	1	5	3500	1	10577	11477
3	15	31	1	4000	1	122976	10777
4	15	31	2	4000	1	11077	63078
5	16	1	2	4000	1	122876	10777
6	16	1	1	4000	1	11077	63078
7	401	1	1	7500	4	122076	63078
8	403	4	1	4500	4	122076	63078
9	404	1	6	7500	4	10377	11477
10	404	1	1	7500	4	11777	63078
11	405	1	1	4500	4	122076	63078
12	407	31	1	4500	4	122076	63078
13	500	1	2	4000	2	122076	63078
14	501	1	2	7000	2	122076	63078
15	511	1	7	3600	2	122076	63078
16	600	3	1	4500	6	122076	63078
17	601	1	1	8500	6	122076	63078
18	602	2	1	4000	6	122076	63078
19	605	1	2	7500	6	122076	10777
20	605	1	1	7500	6	11077	63078
21	606	31	2	3600	6	122076	63078
22	800	1	8	4500	3	122176	20777
23	801	1	2	4500	3	122076	63078
24	802	1	1	4500	3	122076	63078
25	803	41	2	4000	3	122076	63078
26	804	1	1	7500	3	122076	63078
27	806	2	2	3000	3	122076	63078

Figure 2. A molding machine mix.

Fixing the future molding machine mix answers the first-stage disaggregation decision of the scheduling problem. This disaggregation is achieved mainly from technological reasons. For example, a part specified as a mold type 1/material 5 cannot be processed by any machine other than the ones with the same mold/material configuration, and under the machine mix of Figure 2 the only eligible machine for this part will be machine no. 14. In other words, once a molding machine mix is specified, the molding machine scheduling problem is disaggregated into several subproblems for each mold/material type. The selection of the appropriate molding machine mix is vital, as it limits the performance of level III decisions, i.e., the final molding machine scheduling.

Given the results of the level II decisions, and also based on the open order queue, the final molding machine schedule is developed. However, before applying an optimization algorithm to find the 'best' schedule, the problem is further disaggregated, because of logistical and logical reasons, and also because of computational limitations associated with the optimization algorithm discussed later. The second-stage disaggregation decision is concerned with the plant assignment for each order, and also with the selection of orders to be considered in the final schedule. As noted earlier, dies

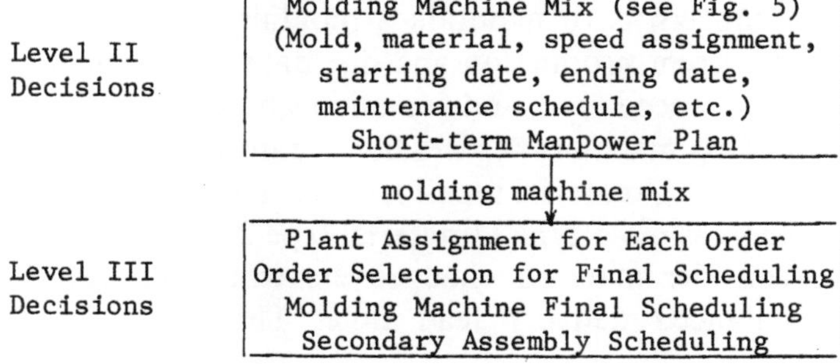

Figure 3. The disaggregation problem.

are normally kept at the base plant and are shipped to other plants when needed. To allow for the transportation lead time, dies are shipped to the plant a week or more prior to the start of production. This means that, when the 'optimal' final schedule is considered, the plant assignment is already fixed and cannot be changed except for changes within sister plants. It is also natural to consider in the final schedule only those orders which have to be started during the final schedule planning horizon (e.g., a week). The above discussion suggests that the scheduling problem can be segregated logically into subproblems for each mold/material/plant group type. If this disaggregation process still yields subproblems which are too large from a computational point of view (for the optimization algorithm), they can be further decomposed by molding machine speed. The preceding discussion is summarized in Figure 3.

9.4. Level II planning – a simulation approach

The major decision on the level II planning is the molding machine mix (Figure 2). This is accomplished by a combination of a simulation and human (i.e. production planner's) judgment approach. Note that the system in steady state does not normally anticipate, nor in fact, allow sudden substantial changes in the molding machine mix. As a result, molding machine mix strategies are (1) to change a mold type,[2] 2) to change a material type, and 3) to change a machine speed. The most common option is the material changeover. Mold changeover requires a day or two of setup time, but dies can be changed within an hour. However, quality control problems may arise whenever a machine is tampered with.

A main concern is to maintain a molding machine mix which reflects the current production and due date requirements of each mold/material/speed type, and reasonably balances the production load of molding machines. Generally, we do not want a situation where mold type 1/material type 1 has average delivery lead time of 3 weeks, whereas mold type 1/material type 2, 6 weeks, etc. Therefore, we consider material changeovers whenever necessary, to avoid unbalanced delivery lead time. Therefore, the average

2. For some machines, a mold type is fixed and inexchangeable. There are, however, some machines for which a mold can be replaced and a mold type can be changed.

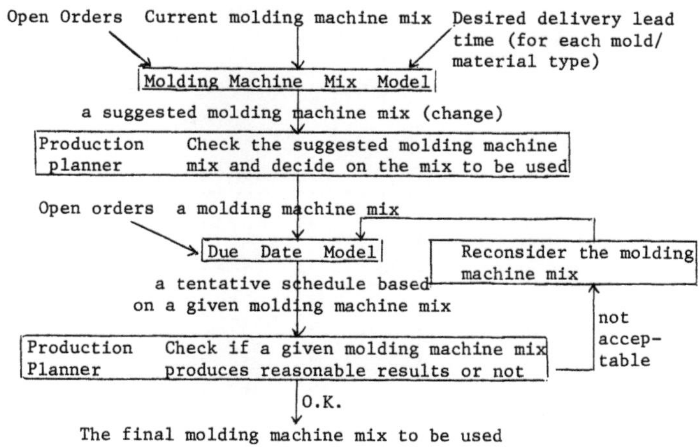

Figure 4. Level II planning.

delivery lead time is estimated for each mold/material/speed type, and it is compared with due dates of open orders to see if they can normally be satisfied. As in Figure 4, the computer system contains two simulation models which first suggest a molding machine mix and then simulate the production environment if a certain mix is adopted. These simulation models interact with a production planner, which results in the molding machine mix that is finally adopted.

The Molding Machine Mix Model detects unreasonably unbalanced delivery schedules among various mold/material/speed types and suggests mix changes, based on the current molding machine mix, the current work load and the desired delivery lead time for each mold/material/speed type. This is accomplished via the construction of a rough preliminary schedule. A suggested mix is then examined by a production planner who decides the mix to be used. Based on this molding machine mix, the Due Date Model constructs a tentative schedule which takes into account most of the logistical and technological constraints. This tentative schedule is not normally the final schedule obtained by an optimization algorithm, but it usually reasonably reflects what will happen. If the production planner believes this results in an acceptable performance, the current mix is adopted. Otherwise, the planner modifies the mix and reruns the Due Date Model with a new, modified mix. Figure 5 represents a tentative schedule printout.

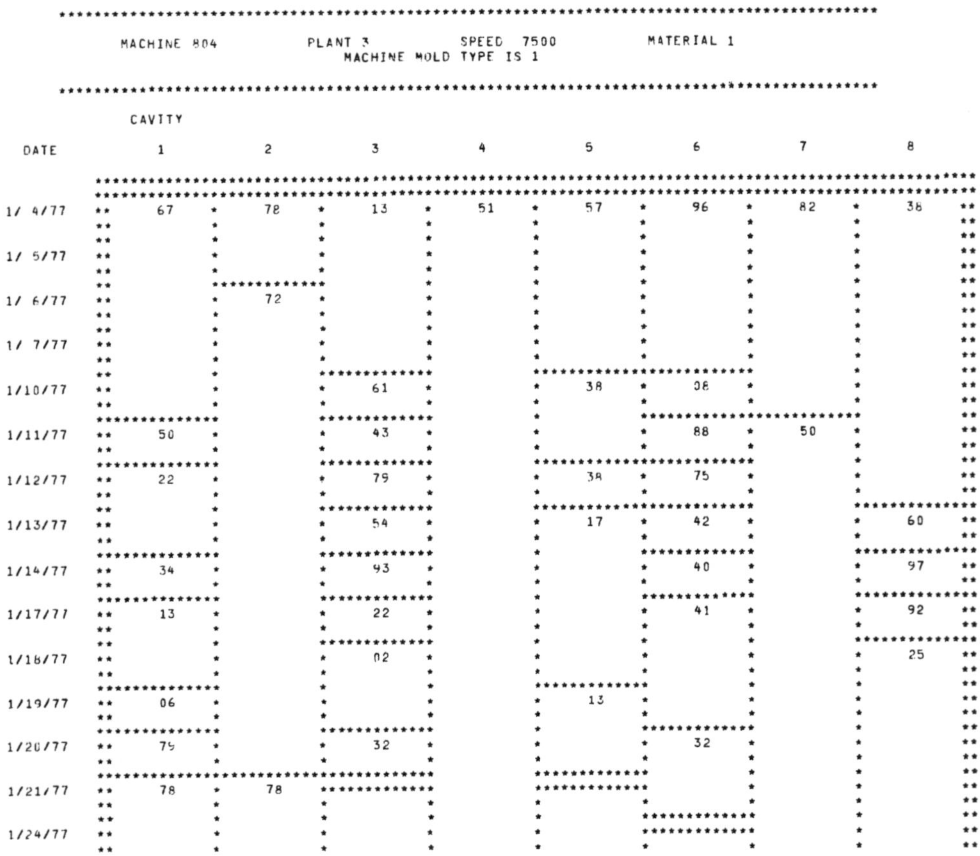

Figure 5. Tentative molding machine schedule.

9.5. Level III scheduling – a search enumeration algorithm

Before an otpimization algorithm is applied to generate a final schedule, orders must be selected to be included in the final schedule. Closely associated with this is a plant assignment for each order, since lead time must be allowed for the shipment of dies to plants for production. Therefore, once an order is selected for final scheduling, a plant is assigned and subsequently, a die is forwarded to the plant. Order selection and plan assignment are done by the Order Selection Model. Note that the molding machine mix is fixed here and is given from level II planning.

The procedure for order selection corresponds to a second stage disaggregation, since once a die is sent to one plant, it cannot be shipped to the other plant unless they are sister plants. Natural criterion used for the order selection is the promised due date.[3] In particular, those orders with earliest promised due dates are selected first. Also, orders requiring small production quantities may be selected regardless of their promised due date, as they sometimes help to produce a better schedule (i.e., with a smaller number of setups).

An optimization algorithm is now applied to produce a final schedule to be used at each plant. Before describing the algorithm, it is convenient to repeat all logistical and technological constraints considered.

For each order,
1. mold type
2. material type
3. plant assignment
4. die speed
5. die position
6. die length

For each molding machine,
a. mold type
b. material type
c. plant location
d. machine speed

A mold/material type requirement is fixed for each order.[4] Also, as there is little interaction among machines with different mold/material types, an algorithm may be applied separately for each mold/material type. Finally, since plant assignments cannot vary, except within sister plants, the problem can be further decomposed by plant groups. Thus, an optimization algorithm is applied for each mold/material/plant group type. The algorithm's objective is to minimize the number of die setups while satisfying all technological and logistical constraints. Minimizing the number of die setups allows for increased production while maintaining the best quality control procedures.

The optimization algorithm is of the search enumeration type in integer programming (e.g., see Salkin [4]), and is similar to a branch

3. Actually we use the 'latest starting date' which is the promised due date minus the number of production days (i.e., production quantity divided by the production norm) minus possibly some buffer.

4. Actually, this is not exactly true as there are exceptions, such as material X can be, if necessary, substituted with material Y.

and bound approach used in scheduling theory (e.g., see Baker [5]). The proposed search enumeration algorithm is described in detail elsewhere [6], and will not be repeated here.

Unfortunately, the algorithm performs exponentially and, in the worst case, it will check $n!$ different schedules, where n is the number of orders to be considered. Computational performance greatly depends on how fast the algorithm finds a good solution; that is, one with a small number of setups. Therefore, a heuristic scheduling rule is first applied to find a 'good' feasible schedule, and hence, a good ceiling on the minimum number of setups. However, the algorithm may still not terminate in a reasonable amount of computer time, if the number of orders is large (say 20 or more). Thus, it may be necessary to decompose the problem further. A decomposition technique based on considering fewer molding machines at one time, is displayed in Figure 6. A final schedule is given in Figure 5.

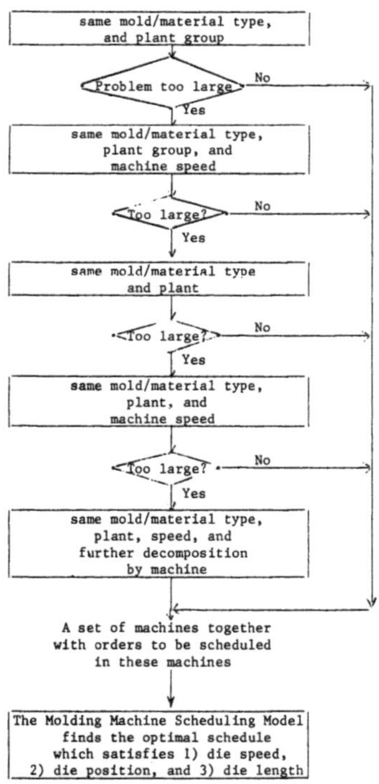

Figure 6. Decomposing a large problem.

9.6. Conclusion

This paper described how an aggregate production plan, representing an actual case study in an injection molding industry, could be disaggregated. The disaggregation resulted in a set of problems which were solved sequentially. Decomposition arose due to technological, logistical, and heuristic factors. Solution techniques varied from heuristic to optimization procedures. The overall computer system is being used on a continuous basis by a Northeast Ohio firm to provide schedules which maximize total production while maintaining high quality control standards and increased customer goodwill.

References

1. Ritzman, Larry P., Krajewski, Leroy, J., and Showalter, Michael J., 'The Disaggregation of Aggregate Manpower Plans', *Management Science*, vol. 22, no. 11 (July 1976), pp. 1204–1214.
2. Krajewski, Leroy, J., Mabert, V. A., and Thompson, H. E., 'Quadratic Inventory Cost Appropriations and the Aggregation of Individual Products', *Management Science*, vol. 19, no. 11 (July 1973), pp. 1229–1240.
3. Zoller, K., 'Optimal Disaggregation of Aggregate Plans', *Management Science*, vol. 17, no. 8 (April 1971), pp. 533–549.
4. Salkin, Harvey M., *Integer Programming*, Addison-Wesley, Reading, Mass. (1975).
5. Baker, Kenneth, R., *Introduction to Sequencing and Scheduling*, John Wiley, New York (1974).
6. Morito, Susumu, and Salkin, Harvey M., 'A Search Enumeration Algorithm for a Multi-plant, Multiproduct Scheduling Problem', *Proceeding of the Bicentennial Conference on Mathematical Programming*, (Spring 1977) (to appear).

Section 4. Large scale optimization

10. An efficient algorithm for multi-item scheduling

L. S. LASDON and R. C. TERJUNG

Abstract

A number of resource-allocation problems, including that of multi-item scheduling, may be solved approximately as large linear programs, as in Manne [*Management Science*, vol. 4, 115–135 (1958)] Dzielinski and Gomory [*Management Science*, vol. 11, 874–890 (1965)] applied the Dantzig-Wolfe decomposition principle to this problem. Here, the problem is attacked directly, using a column generation technique and Dantzig and van Slyke's generalized upper-bounding method [*J. Comp. and System Science*, vol. 1, 213–226 (1967)]. For problems involving I items and T time periods, one need deal with a basis matrix of dimension only T by T. A lower bound on the optimal cost may be developed and intermediate solutions all have Manne's integer property (*loc. cit.*). Computational experiments, including an option for pricing out subproblem solutions until none is useful, show a number of iterations to optimality of from one-half to one-ninth the number required by the decomposition principle with work per iteration remaining approximately the same. Extensions of the basic model are also described. These form the core of an automated production-scheduling and inventory-control system, currently being used by a major U.S. manufacturer. Computational experience with this extended model is presented.

10.1. Introduction

The problem of scheduling the production of many items over time has been studied via linear programming by A. S. Manne [5]. Additional work along these lines has been done by Dzielinski, Baker, and Manne [1] and, most recently, by Dzielinski and Gomory [2]. The latter authors applied the Dantzig-Wolfe decomposition prin-

Reprinted by permission from L. S. Lasdon and R. C. Terjung, 'An Efficient Algorithm for Multi-Item Scheduling', *Operations Research*, vol. 19, no. 4, pp. 946–969, copyright 1971, Operations Research Society of America. No further reproduction permitted without the consent of the copyright owner.

ciple to a problem very similar to that formulated in reference 5. The linear program being decomposed has a very large number of variables and possibly many constraints. Application of the decomposition principle yields an equivalent linear program, called the master program, with fewer constraints and even more variables. These, however, may be dealt with by a column-generation technique, using subproblems. For the problem studied in reference 1, these subproblems are of the Wagner-Whitin [6] type, and may thus be solved efficiently.

Although the decomposition algorithm of Dzielinski and Gomory is an attractive approach, some difficulties still remain. Perhaps the most serious of these stems from the fact that the linear program being decomposed is only an approximation to an integer program whose solution is actually desired, and only a good approximation when the number of items is much greater than the number of time periods. Under these conditions, basic solutions of the linear program have the property that most of the variables will have integral values. This property is not shared by the master program of the decomposition principle. Thus, the approach of reference 2 cannot guarantee a majority of integer-valued variables until optimality. Intermediate solutions may then not be meaningful, and any lower bound on the minimal cost that may be developed has limited value. Since, as mentioned in reference 2, programs with very many columns often have a tremendous number of near-optimal solutions prior to optimality, these limitations can be serious.

This paper proposes an alternate approach to the linear program formulated by Manne. This program is attacked directly, in that it has no equivalent 'master program' handled by column generation via subproblems. The multiplicity of constraints is dealt with by using the generalized upper bounding procedure of reference 4. The subproblems reduce to those of reference 2 for the problem studied there; the size of the basis matrix that must be manipulated is one less than that of the master program (however, the operations performed using this matrix are somewhat more complex). Since only basic solutions of the original problem occur, a majority of integer values is always present. A lower bound may be derived to aid in terminating computations, and a number of additional degrees of freedom inherent in this new approach permits further computational refinement. Computational results suggest that these refinements are among the most attractive features of the method. Comparison with the approach of reference 2 shows an improvement by at least a factor of two in the number of iterations required for all problems studied, with work per iteration approximately the same. The procedure is currently being used to solve problems with over 300 items. Computational results for such problems are discussed.

10.2. Capacity-constrained resource allocation

The multi-item scheduling problems formulated in references 1, 2, and 5 may be imbedded in the following class of resource allocation problems. Let there be I activities, indexed by i, and a single resource to be allocated to these activities in each of T time periods, indexed by t. Let x_{it} be the level of activity i in time period t and define

$$X_i = (x_{i1}, \ldots, x_{i1}) \cdot (i = 1, \ldots, I) \tag{1}$$

Associated with each vector X_i is a cost $c_i(X_i)$. Activity i uses an amount $y_{it}(X_i)$ of the resource in period t, the resource availability in that time period being b_t. Define

$$Y_i(X_i) = [y_{i1}(X_i), \ldots, y_{iT}(X_i)] \tag{2}$$

and

$$b = (b_i, \ldots, b_T). \tag{3}$$

Each activity has its own technological constraints, symbolized by

$$X_i \in S_i \qquad (i = 1, \ldots, I) \tag{4}$$

The problem of optimal allocation is: minimize

$$\sum_{i=I}^{i=I} c_i(X_i), \tag{5}$$

subject to

$$\sum_{i=I}^{i=I} Y_i(X_i) \leqq b \tag{6}$$

and

$$X_i \in S_i. \qquad (i = 1, \ldots, I) \quad (7)$$

In the problems of references 1, 2, and 5, x_{it} is the quantity of item i produced in time period t (i.e., the lot size), S_i is the set of nonnegative production schedules for item i, which, for given demands, yield nonnegative inventory levels, $c_i(X_i)$ is the sum of setup plus inventory costs over time for item i, and the resource is labor. In references 1, 2, and 5, there may be a number of different resources, e.g., labor classes, and their availabilities are decision variables, with associated costs of hiring and firing. For simplicity, these alternatives are not considered here, although their incorporation poses no real difficulty.

Assume, now, that for each i the set of elements of S_i that need be considered as candidates for optimality in (5)–(7) is finite, with the jth candidate denoted by X_{ij}. The set of all such candidates is denoted by V_i. This assumption is valid in reference 2 by virtue of Manne's dominance theorem [5]. In a problem to be examined later, the S_i are finite to begin with. Assume further that $I > T$. Under these assumptions, an approximate solution to (5)–(7) may be obtained by solving the following linear program:

$$\text{minimize} \qquad \left(\sum_{i,j} c_{ij}\theta_{ij}\right), \qquad (8)$$

subject to

$$\sum_j \theta_{ij} = 1, \qquad (9)$$

$$\sum_{i,j} Y_{ij}\theta_{ij} \leqq b, \qquad (10)$$

and

$$\theta_{ij} \geqq 0, \quad \text{all } i, j, \qquad (11)$$

where

$$c_{ij} \equiv c_i(X_{ij}), \quad Y_{ij} \equiv Y_i(X_{ij}). \qquad (12)$$

If the θ_{ij} are restricted to be integers, then, as explained in references 1, 2, and 5, the optimal solution of (5)–(7) results. For the problem (8)–(11), all basic feasible solutions have the following property [1], [2], [5]: the number of indices i for which eactly one θ_{ij} is positive (and hence 1) is at least $I-T$. Thus, (8)–(11) provide a good approximate solution to (5)–(7) when the number of items I is substantially greater than the number of time periods T. We assume that this is the case in what follows.

10.3. Problem solution

The linear program (8)–(11) has, for realistic problems, a tremendous number of columns, and may have many rows if I is large, e.g., in the hundreds or thousands. The columns are easily dealt with. Let B be a basis matrix for (8)–(11) and let $\pi = (\pi_1, \pi_2)$ be the set of simplex multipliers corresponding to this basis, with π_1 associated with the constraints (9) and π_2 with (10). Pricing out a nonbasic column, the reduced cost coefficient is

$$\bar{c}_{ij} = c_{ij} - \pi_2^T Y_{ij} - \pi_i . \tag{13}$$

To choose a column to enter the basis, we must find

$$\min_{i,j} \bar{c}_{ij} = \min_i \min_j \bar{c}_{ij} . \tag{14}$$

The inner minimization in (14) may be accomplished by solving the subproblem: minimize

$$j[c_{ij} - \pi_2^T Y_{ij}], \tag{15}$$

or, since all X_{ij} are elements of V_i, minimize

$$[c_i(X_i) - \pi_2^T Y_i(X_i)] \tag{16}$$

subject to

$$X_i \in V_i \tag{17}$$

Note that these subproblems are single-activity problems with a penalty term $\pi_2^T Y_i$ for use of the resource. Since V_i is assumed finite and the functions c_i and Y_i are assumed to be bounded below on V_i, the subproblems have finite optimal solutions for all values of π_2. To decide on which column is to enter the basis, subtract π_{1i} from the optimal objective value in (16)–(17) and find the minimum of these quantities over i.

The problem of many constraints in (8)–(11) still remains. The solution lies in the special form of the constraints (9). In their work on generalized upper bounding techniques, [4] Dantzig and Van Slyke show that any linear program including constraints like those in (9) can be solved while maintaining a working basis whose dimension is the number of remaining constraints (10), in our case $(T \times T)$. For any basis B of (9)–(11), the simplex multipliers, values for the basic variables, and the product of B^{-1} with the column entering the basis can all be easily derived from the corresponding quantities associated with the working basis. Although the computations involved are somewhat more complex than in the revised simplex method, the procedure appears much more efficient than applying the simplex method directly [4], especially if I is much greater than T. Thus its use greatly reduces computational problems caused by many rows in (9).

10.4. Lower Bounds

A lower bound on the optimal cost, similar to that obtained with the decomposition principle, may be developed here. Let $= (\pi_1, \pi_2)$ again be a vector of simplex multipliers for some basis B of (8)–(11), rewritten here as
minimize

$$\sum_{i,j} c_{ij}\theta_{ij} = z, \tag{18}$$

subject to

$$\sum_{j} \theta_{ij} = 1, \quad (i = 1, \ldots, I) \tag{19}$$

$$\sum_{i,j} Y_{ij}\theta_{ij} + S = b; \tag{20}$$

$$\theta_{ij} \geqq 0, \text{ all } i, j; \; s_t \geqq 0, \quad (t = 1, \ldots, T) \tag{21}$$

where the s_t are slack variables. Multiply (19) by π_1, and (20) by π_2 and subtract from (18), yielding

$$\sum_{i,j} (c_{ij} - \pi_2^T Y_{ij} - \pi_{1i})\, \theta_{ij} - \pi_2^T S = z - \pi_2^T b - \sum_i \pi_{1i}. \tag{22}$$

The bracketed quantity in (22) is, by (13), the reduced-cost coefficient $\bar{c}_{ij}$. Replacing $\bar{c}_{ij}$ by $\min_j \bar{c}_{ij}$ yields

$$\sum_i (\min_j \bar{c}_{ij}) \sum_j \theta_{ij} - \pi_2^T S \leqq z - \pi_2^T b - \sum_i \pi_{1i}. \tag{23}$$

Using (19) in (23), we obtain

$$z \geqq \sum_i (\min_j \bar{c}_{ij}) - \pi_2^T S + \left[\pi_2^T b + \sum_i \pi_{1i}\right]. \tag{24}$$

Let c_B be the ordered vector of cost coefficients corresponding to the columns of B, x_B be the vector of basic variables, and z_B be the cost of this basic feasible solution. Let 1 be an I-component vector of ones. Since

$$(\pi_1, \pi_2) = c_B^T B^{-1} \tag{25}$$

and

$$z_B = c_B^T x_B = c_B^T B^{-1} \left[\frac{1}{b}\right] = (\pi_1, \pi_2) \left[\frac{1}{b}\right], \tag{26}$$

then

$$z_B = \pi_2^T b + \sum_i \pi_{1i}, \tag{27}$$

and, since (24) holds for all values of z obtainable from (18)–(21)

$$\min z \geqq z_B + \sum_i (\min_j \bar{c}_{ij}) - \pi_2^T S, \tag{28}$$

which is the desired lower bound. The behavior of this bound in computations is illustrated in the later section on computational results.

10.5. Multiple pricing

In applying the Dantzig-Wolfe decomposition principle to (8)–(11), master programs having anywhere from one to I convexity constraints (summing subsets of the variables to unity) may be formed. Each corresponds to a partitioning of the constraints (9) into a corresponding number of subsets, then writing any solution of each subset as a convex combination of its extreme points. The approach of reference 2 uses one convexity constraint, while the direct approach described here has I of them, thus reproducing the original program. The same subproblems are solved in each case (although with different multipliers π), yielding solutions $X_i(\pi)$, $i = 1, \ldots, I$. If a master program with p convexity constraints is formed, $1 \leqq p \leqq I$, then, at each iteration, p new columns are formed from these subproblem solutions, with the one with the lowest value of $(\min_j \bar{c}_{ij})$ entering the basis. A pivot operation is then performed, yielding new multipliers π'. Often π and π' will not differ radically, so that some of the columns corresponding to the $X_i(\pi)$ may again price out negative, with the most negative entering the basis. This cycle may be repeated until all reduced costs for these columns are nonnegative. Such a procedure corresponds to a partial solution of Dantzig's restricted master program [3], in which columns leaving the basis are dropped, and makes fullest use of the candidates proposed by the subproblems.

Since pricing out a single column, i.e., forming the scalar product of two vectors, may be expected to involve orders of magnitude less computation than solving a subproblem of the form (16)–(17), this option is quite attractive. As more convexity constraints are used, more new columns are formed at each cycle, and large decreases in the objective become more likely. For the problems considered in the computational results section, the cycle described above is used an average of three times for each set of subproblem solutions, leading to very large reductions in computing time. Of course, the greater number of convexity constraints is a computational disadvantage if a revised simplex code is used. This difficulty is greatly reduced, however, if the generalized upper bounding method is employed.

It should be noted that this multiple pricing option is available even if a master program with only one convexity constraint is used. One simply generates those columns with the k most negative reduced costs, $k \geqq 1$, and forms a restricted master program with these. The experience cited here may suggest that doing this would improve the rate of convergence in this case, although this remains to be demonstrated. Of course, only a direct application of the simplex method, as proposed here, works with basic solutions of the original program. As noted earlier, this is of special importance when solving the program (8)–(11).

The excellent computational experience with this option has

some implications for general use of the Dantzig-Wolfe decomposition principle. For a constraint matrix of the form

$$\begin{matrix} A_1 & A_2 & \dots & A_n \\ B_1 & & & \\ & B_2 & & \\ & & \ddots & \\ & & & B_n \end{matrix}$$

one may form master programs having $1 \leqq p \leqq n$ convexity rows. The computational experience cited later indicates that choosing $p = n$ and solving a restricted master program at each cycle with n non-basic columns may lead to the most rapid convergence.

10.6 Lot-size problems with 'continuous' setups

To test the efficiency of the proposed approach, consider a number of machines available to produce these items. Demands for each item in each time period are assumed known. The costs are (a) inventory holding and shortage costs and (b) setup costs. Setups occur when a given machine is changed from the production of one item to the production of another. We assume that any machine can, if suitably set up, produce any of the items, and that the setup cost is independent of which two items are involved in the changeover. A machine is set up to produce an item by installing in the machine a piece of equipment particular to the item. These pieces of equipment will be called dies. The problem is to allocate the machines to the items so that the sum of inventory and setup costs over all items is minimized.

This problem can be placed in the form of the resource allocation problem (5)–(7). Define:

m_{it} = number of machines used to produce item i in time period t.

$M_i = (m_{i1}, m_{i2}, \dots, m_{iT})$.

b_t = number of machines available in time period t.

$b = (b_1, \dots, b_T)$.

d_{it} = demand for item i in time period t, assumed known.

k_i = production rate of a machine producing item i.

y_{it} = inventory of item i at the end of time period t.

$y_{it} = y_{i,t-1} + k_i m_{it} - d_{it}, t = 1, \ldots, T$

y_{i0} given.

= cost of one setup.

$(y_{it})\max$, $(y_{it})\min$ = given upper and lower bounds on y_{it}.

n_i = number of dies available for item i.

Since the setup cost is assumed independent of the items involved, the total setup cost may be written

$$c_s = p_s \sum_{i=1}^{i=I} s_i(M_i), \tag{29}$$

where

$$s_i(M_i) = \sum_{t=1}^{t=T} (m_{it} - m_{i,t-1})_+, \ m_{i0} \text{ given}, \tag{30}$$

and where

$$(x)_+ = \begin{cases} x, & x \geqq 0, \\ 0, & x < 0. \end{cases} \tag{31}$$

The inventory cost for item i is written

$$\gamma_i(M_i) = \sum_{t=1}^{t=T} \gamma_{it}(y_{it}), \tag{32}$$

where the γ_{it} represent holding costs for $y_{it} > 0$ and shortage costs for $y_{it} > 0$, and may have any convenient functional form. Let

$$c_i(M_i) = p_s \cdot s_i(M_i) + \gamma_i(M_i). \tag{33}$$

Then the problem is to choose $M_1 \ldots M_I$ to minimize

$$c = \sum_{i=1}^{I} c_i(M_i) \tag{34}$$

subject to

$$(y_{it})_{\min} \leqq y_{it} \leqq (y_{it})_{\max}, \quad \text{all } i, t; \tag{35}$$

$$m_{it} \leqq n_i, \quad \text{all } i, t; \tag{36}$$

$$m_{it} = \text{nonnegative integer, all } i, t; \tag{37}$$

and

$$\sum_{i=1}^{I} m_{it} \leqq b_t, \quad t = 1, \ldots, T. \tag{38}$$

Let

$$V_j = \{M_j \mid M_j \text{ satisfies (35)–(37) for } i = j\}. \tag{39}$$

Since the n_i are finite, V_j is finite and is assumed nonempty. Let the elements of V_i be indexed by j, with M_{ij} the jth element. By defining

$$c_i(M_{ij}) \equiv c_{ij}, \tag{40}$$

the linear program (8)–(11) assumes the form

minimize

$$\sum_{i,j} c_{ij}\theta_{ij} \tag{41}$$

subject to

$$\sum_j \theta_{ij} = 1, \quad i = 1, \ldots, I; \tag{42}$$

$$\sum_{i,j} M_{ij}\theta_{ij} \leqq b \tag{43}$$

and

$$\sum_{ij} \geqq 0, \quad \text{all } i, j. \tag{44}$$

The ith subproblem is:

$$\text{minimize } p_s S_i(M_i) + \gamma_i(M_i) = \pi^T M_i, \tag{45}$$

subject to

$$(y_{it})_{\min} \leqq y_{it})_{\max}, \ (t = 1, t \ldots, V) \tag{46}$$

$$m_{it} \leqq n_i, \tag{47}$$

$$m_{it} = \text{nonnegative integer, all } t. \tag{48}$$

Each subproblem may be solved by dynamic programming with two state variables, M_{it}, and y_{it}. Since the initial states m_{i0} and y_{i0} are given, a forward recursion is used.

10.7. Computational results

To test the efficiency of the proposed approach, a number of test problems of the form presented in the previous section were solved. It was found early in the research that use of a full set of artificial variables in phase I led to very poor starting points for phase II. To avoid this, the single-item subproblems (45)–(48) were first solved with $\pi_2 = 0$. If these solutions satisfy (38), they are optimal. If not, an initial basic feasible solution is constructed using a single θ_{ij} for each of subproblem solutions, plus T slack and artificial variables. The inverse of a basis so formed is easily found without numerical inversion, and the procedure has led to much better initial points for phase II.

Four test problems were solved by each of three methods; (1) the decomposition principle, (2) the new approach proposed here, and (3) the new approach with subproblem solutions priced out many times, until none price out negative. These problems had six time periods and 6, 10, 10, and 15 items, respectively. Problems 2 and 3 have, respectively, 22 and 24 machines available in each time period. Other parameters, e.g., demands for each item, machine availabilities, etc., were chosen to approximate reality in the production environment under consideration and to yield nontrivial subproblems. Note that, even though the number of items is small, the number of columns in the program (8)–(11) can be very large. If the upper and lower bounds in (46) are absent, then each item generates $(n_i + 1)T$ different columns, which is 262, 124 if $T = 6$ and $n_i = 7$. Each problem had at least one such item, with problem four having two items with $n_i = 7$, one with $n_i = 5$, and two with $n_i = 4$. Upper and lower bounds were included to reduce the time required to solve the subproblems, but these were 'loose,' i.e., never binding in any cycle. Thus the problems solved here are of substantial size.

Figures 1 through 4 show the behavior of cost versus the number of iterations in phase II. Although the initial cost values differ somewhat because of the different solutions found in phase I, this difference is approximately equalized after the first phase II iteration. The decomposition principle exhibits the expected 'tail,' a characteristic shown to a lesser degree by the proposed method, probably because of the smaller number of columns involved. Continued

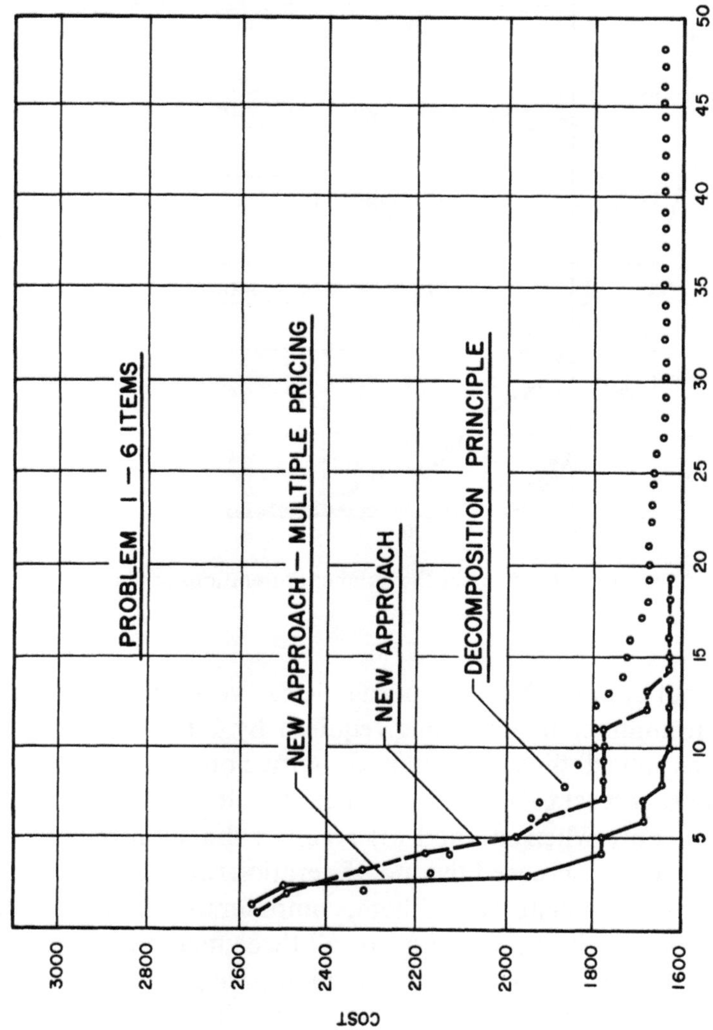

Figure 1. Cost versus the number of iterations in phase 2.

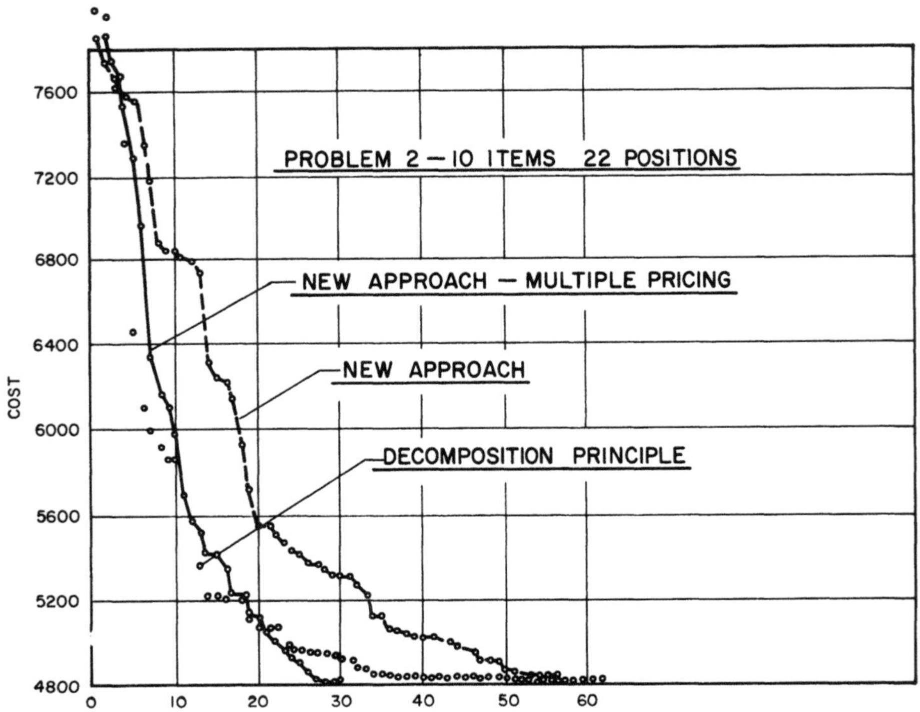

Figure 2. Cost versus the number of iterations in phase 2.

pricing out of subproblem proposals yields a very significant decrease over the number of iterations required by 2 to 9. Since, for the problems solved, the time required to price out a given subproblem solution is at least two orders of magnitude less than to solve a subproblem, only when method (3) resolves the subproblems is the iteration count increased by one. If iterations are tallied in this way, then, for the problems solved here, computer time is approximately proportional to iteration count for all three methods.

Tables 1 and 2 show that, with the multiple pricing option, many of the subproblem solutions are generated in any cycle. Figures 5 and 6 show the behavior of the lower bound of the fourth section using method 2. If one is willing to terminate computations when the predicted improvement in cost is less than 5 percent of current costs, problems 1 through 4, using method 3, could have been terminated in 16, 16, 36, and 26 iterations, respectively, rather than

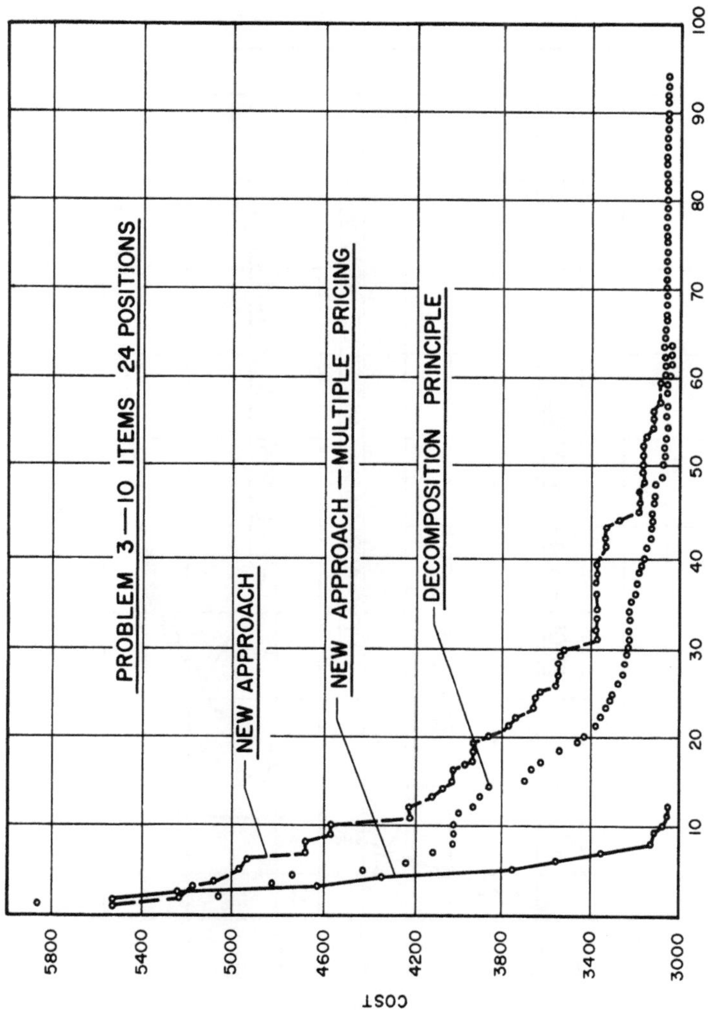

Figure 3. Cost versus the number of iterations in phase 2.

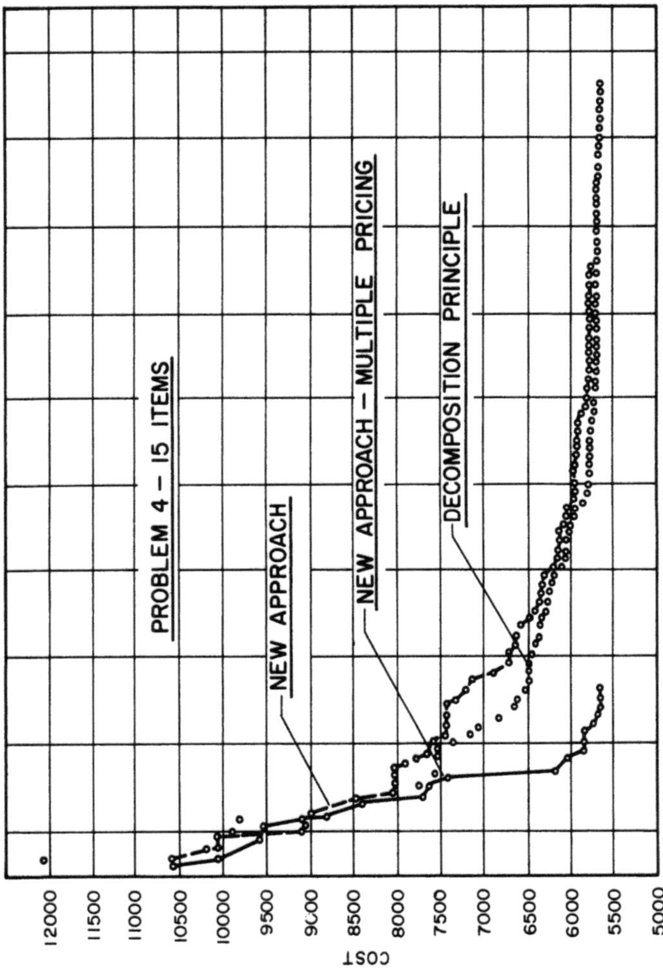

Figure 4. Cost versus the number of iterations in phase 2.

Table 1. Multiple pricing, problem 3

Subproblem solutions, phase II	Cumulative number of multiple pricings
1	7
2	10
3	12
4	15
5	19
6	24
7	25
8	26
9	28
10	30
11	30

Table 2. Multiple pricing, problem 4.

Subprogram solutions, phase II	Cumulative number of multiple pricings
2	5
4	11
6	18
8	21
10	33
12	40
14	44
16	47
18	47

the 20, 18, 43, and 31 iterations required to meet the optimality test.

A number of other ideas to shorten computations were also tested. One of these involves solving the subproblems by a dynamic programming algorithm with only one state variable, the other (the variable m_{it}) being fixed at its initial value m_{i0}. This is faster by factors of from two on up, and often yields either optimal solutions or good approximations to these. As long as this, or any other technique, yields columns with negative reduced cost, it is useful. In three test problems, using this option until it met the optimality test, then switching to the correct, two-state variable algorithm has led to reductions in running time of about one-half.

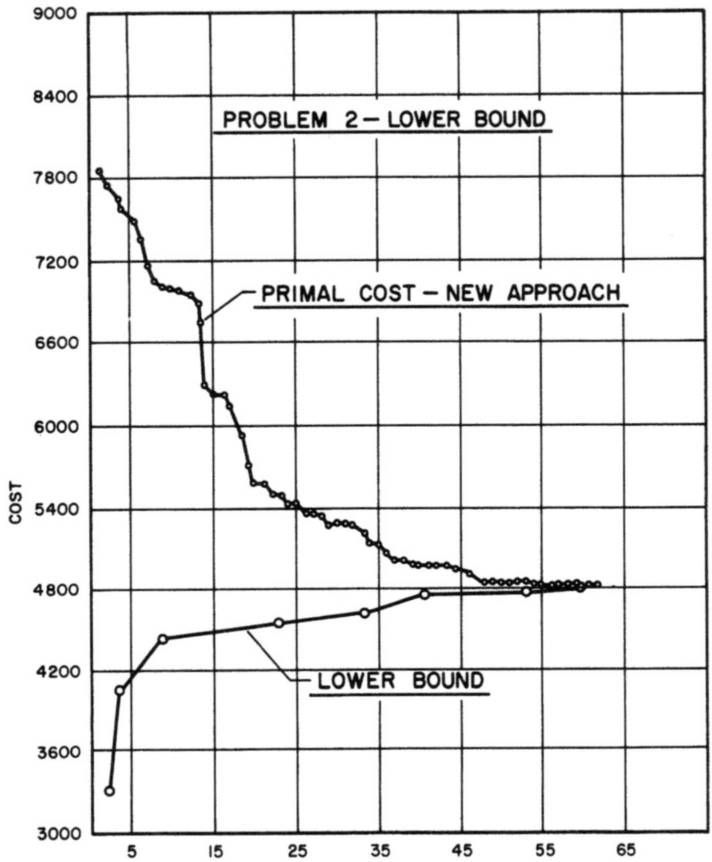

Figure 5. Cost versus the number of iterations in phase 2–behavior of the lower bound.

10.8. Extensions and applications

The last model described above has been significantly extended. It forms the core of a production scheduling and inventory control system currently being used by a major U.S. manufacturer in four of its plants. In this section, we discuss the extensions to the model and give some computational experience.

One major extension of the model is the addition of $3T$ new coupling constraints to the original T given in (38). The first T of these are due to the fact that manpower and equipment are required

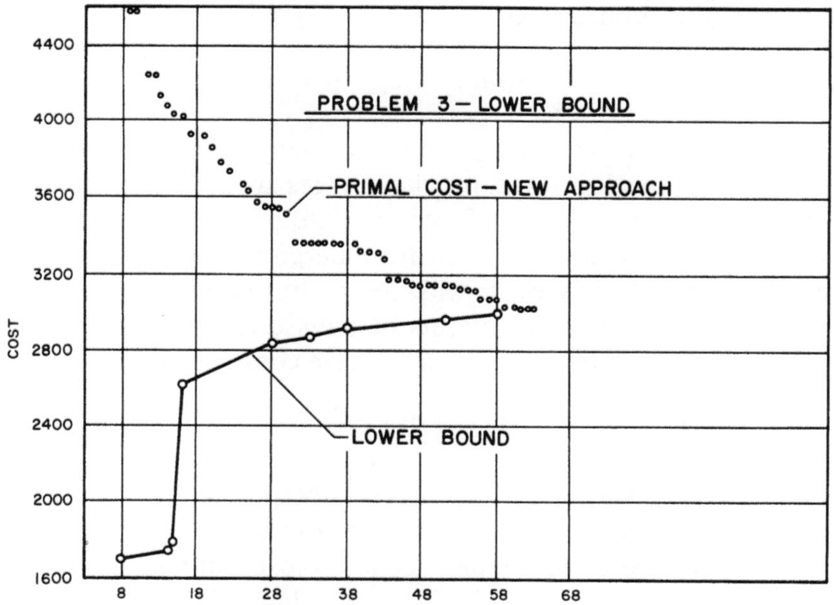

Figure 6. Cost versus the number of iterations in phase 2 – behavior of the lower bound.

both to take an item off a machine and to put a new item on. The total number of changes in production level is limited by requiring that the constraints

$$\sum_{i=1}^{i=I} |m_{it} - m_{i,t-1}| \leqq c_t, \quad (t = 1, \ldots, T) \tag{49}$$

be satisfied, where the c_t are given constants. The second set of constraints arises from the fact that the production process being controlled directly is only the last of a sequence of processing stages, each feeding the next. If, in this last stage, many items go from positive to zero production in a time period, this implies that large quantities of material may have to be scrapped or reworked in previous stages. Limitations on the total number of items making a transition from positive to zero production may be incorporated by using the fixed charge function.

$$\delta(x) = \begin{cases} 1, & x > 0, \\ 0, & x \leqq 0 \end{cases} \tag{50}$$

and writing the constraints

$$\sum_{i=1}^{i=I} \delta(m_{i,t-1})\,[1 - \delta(m_{it})] \leqq e_t. \quad (t = 1, \ldots, T) \tag{51}$$

Finally, if, in a given time period, too many items have positive production in this last stage, previous stages are adversely affected. Too many different kinds of intermediate products are required from these stages, forcing them to undergo many setups of their own. This problem is dealt with by incorporating, in each time period, a limit on the total number of items having positive production. If the limit in time period is f_t, these constraints are

$$\sum_{i=1}^{i=I} \delta(m_{it})\, f_t. \quad (t = 1, \ldots T) \tag{52}$$

The constraints (49) and (51)–(52) are incorporated into the linear program (41)–(44) by extending the vectors b and M_{ij} in (43). The new b is obtained by appending vectors whose components are the c_t, e_t, and f_t to the original b. The new column M_{ij} is obtained by appending vectors whose components are the functions $|m_{it}{}^j - m_{i,t-1}^j|$, $\delta(m_{i,t-1}^j)\,[1 - \delta(m_{it}^j)]$, and $\delta(m_{it}^j)$ to the original M_{ij}.

Inclusion of these additional constraints changes the subproblem of objective (45). Pricing out the new components of a column yields the sum

$$\sum_{t=1}^{t=T} \{\pi_{3t}|m_{it} - m_{i,t-1}| + \pi_{4t}\delta(m_{i,t-1})[1 - \delta(m_{it})] + \pi_{5t}\delta(m_{it})\} \tag{53}$$

Here, the quantities π_{jt} are the simplex multipliers corresponding to the new constraints. The sum (53) is added to (45) to form a new subproblem objective. These new subproblems can still be solved by dynamic programming by using two state variables. Generalizing, any constraints of the form

$$\sum_{i=1}^{i=I} g_{it}(M_i) \leqq \alpha_t \tag{54}$$

may be incorporated in this way with the subproblem having at most two state variables, providing that each function g_{it} depends on at most m_{it} and $m_{i,t-1}$.

To aid understanding of the computational results, some modifications of the phase I procedure will be discussed. With $(Y_{it})_{\min} = 0$ in (46) (i.e., no backlogging of unsatisfied demand) and with realistic values for the demands d_{it} and the various right-hand-side values b_t, c_t, f_t, the linear program (41)–(44) is often infeasible. To achieve feasibility, some of the (y_{it}) are decreased. The items are partitioned into a number of disjoint subsets, each set having a priority level. Backlogging of demands in high-priority sets is less desirable than in sets with lower priority. Increasing the backlog for any group is permitted only if the problem, as it stands, is infeasible. For the problems solved thus far, this procedure generally results in a feasible program. Backlogging is often allowed initially in some groups, based on prior knowledge of the system. This can reduce phase I computations significantly.

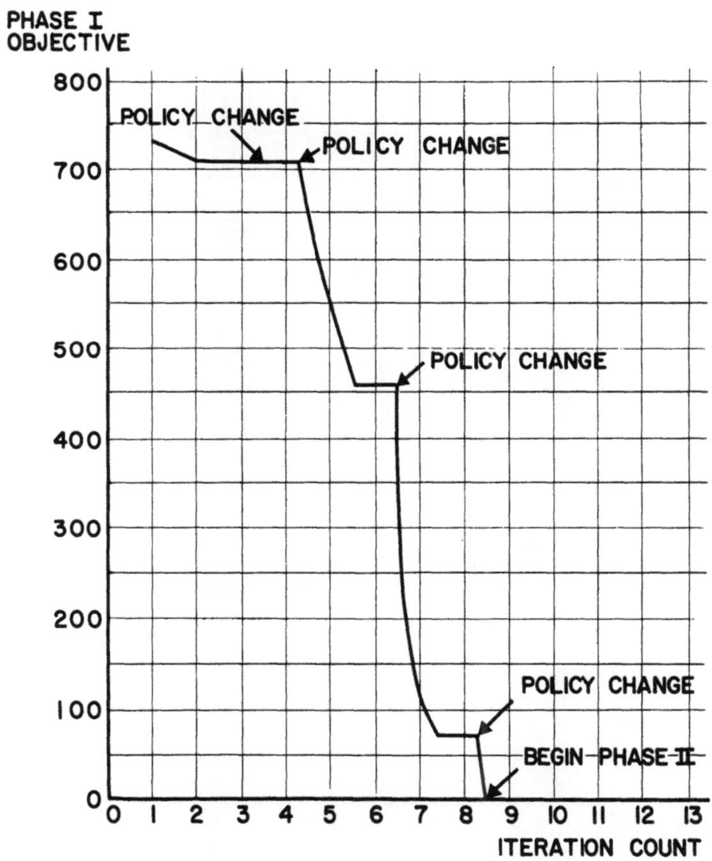

Figure 7. Data for phase 1 of a 364-item problem.

The time periods chosen are one week in length and $T = 6$, so, at the beginning of each week, a scheduling problem of the form (41)–(44), with 24 coupling rows, is solved in each of the four plants. These typically include between 200 and 400 items. Data for a 364-item and a 393-item problem are given in Figures 7–10. As in Figures 1–4, an iteration includes I subproblem solutions (using the current simplex multipliers), plus the pivots needed to introduce all plans that are profitable into the current basis. In a problem of this size hundreds of columns may enter the basis during a single iteration; in iteration one of Figure 7, between 150 and 200 columns entered. Of course, all pivots are done in what is essentially a 24-row program.

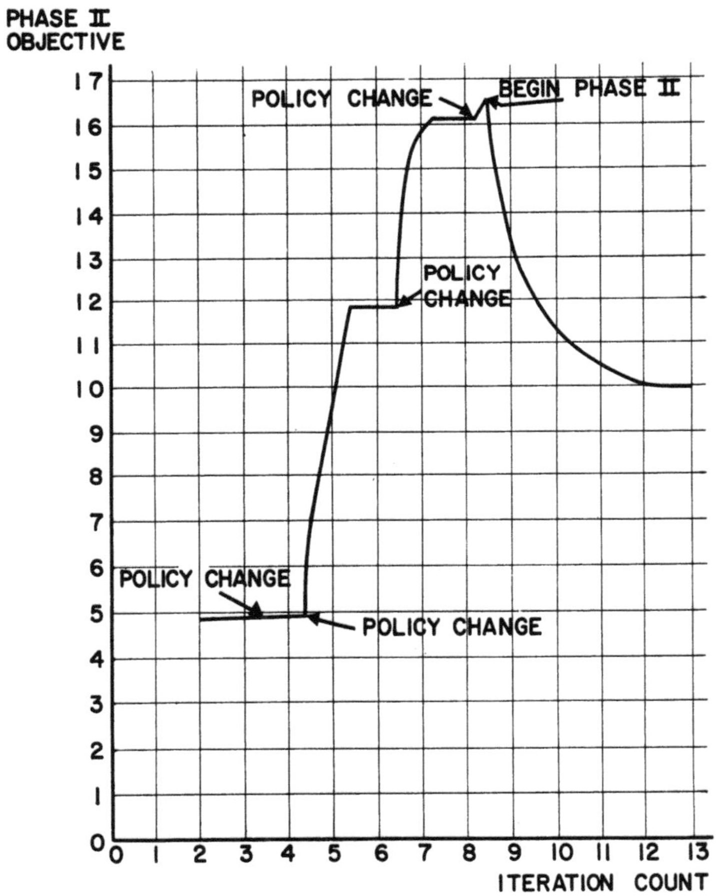

Figure 8. Data for phase 2 of a 364-item problem.

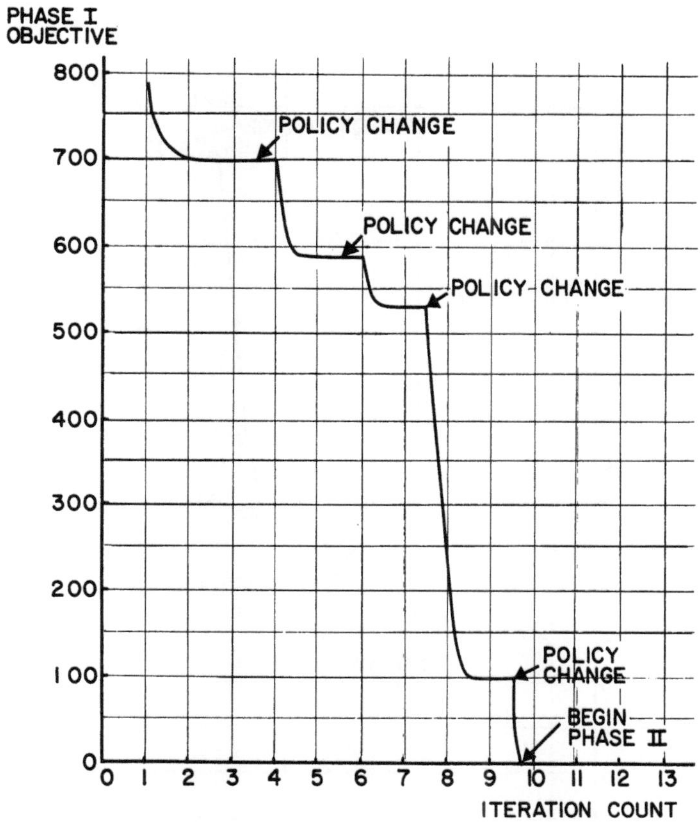

Figure 9. Data for phase 1 of a 393-item problem.

As a consequence, time during an iteration is divided about evenly between subproblem solutions and linear programming operations. The basis is reinverted every 50 pivots to maintain numerical implemented on an IBM system 360 model 50 computer.

Figure 7 shows the progress of phase I for the 364-item problem. The bounds $(y_{it})_{\min}$ are changed at the iterations marked 'policy change,' four times in all. Immediately prior to each change, the phase I objective was minimized and its value was positive. Figure 8 shows the behavior of the phase II objective in phases I and II. The lower bound described earlier was used to terminate phase II, when the difference between the current objective value and its lower bound was less than 5 percent of the objective value. Figures 9 and 10 show similar results for a problem having 393 items, in which the

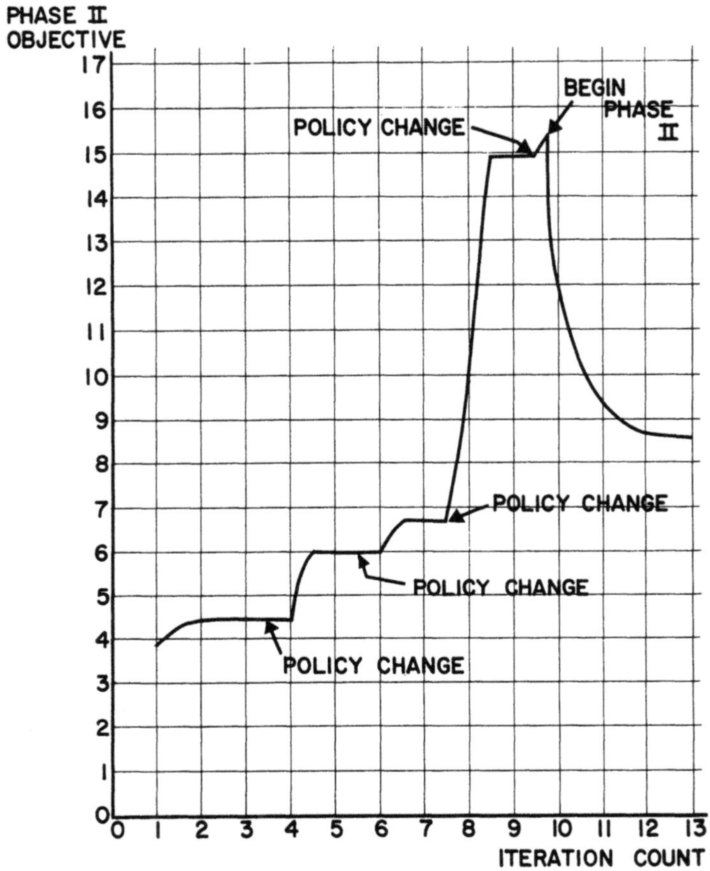

Figure 10. Data for phase 2 of a 393-item problem.

same termination criterion was used. Computation times for these problems are shown in Table 3.

In obtaining these solutions, a number of computational options have been found useful. One of these uses the unconstrained sub-

Table 3. Computation times for problems in figures 7–10

Problem	Phase 1 time	Phase 2 time	Total
364 items	6 min 28 sec	7 min 13 sec	13 min 41 sec
393 items	6 min 37 sec	6 min 41 sec	13 min 18 sec

problem solutions, i.e., the solutions of (45)–(48) with 2 = 0. For each i, the maximum inventory level generated by this solution is calculated, an empirically chosen value is added to it, and the resulting number is used as $(y_{it})_{\max}$ in (46) for all t. This reduces both computation time and computer core memory required for the dynamic programming solutions. Another option reduces the number of indices i with nonintegral θ_{ij}. As explained in the second section, with the current set of $4T$ coupling constraints, as many as $4T$ items can have more than one θ_{ij} positive. However, only the coupling constraints on machine availability need be satisfied exactly. The remaining $3T$ are 'soft', i.e., small violations are permissible. Thus at the end of phase II, the right-hand sides of these 'soft' constraints are increased, and the resulting problem is re-solved over a restricted set of columns. These are the $4T$ slack columns, plus those columns in the final phase II basis. The amounts by which the right-hand sides are increased are chosen to be sufficiently large so that the optimal basis of this revised problem contains at least $3T$ slack columns. This implies that at most T items have more than one θ_{ij} positive. Operating experience has shown that the violations of the original 'soft' constraints introduced by this procedure are not serious.

Acknowledgement

This paper was prepared as part of the activities of the Department of Operations Research, School of Management, Case Western Reserve University, sponsored in part by the Army Research Office, Durham, North Carolina.

References

1. Dzielinski, B. P., Baker, C. T., and Manne, A. S., 'Simulation Tests of Lot Size Programming', *Management Science*, vol. 9 (1963), pp. 229–258.
2. ——and Gomory, R. E., 'Optimal Programming of Lot Sizes, Inventory and Labor Allocations', *Management Science*, vol. 11 (1965), pp. 874–890.
3. Dantzig, G. B., *Linear Programming and Extensions*, Chapter 23, Princeton University Press, Princeton (1963).
4. ——and Van Slyke, R. M., 'Generalized Upper Bounding Techniques', *J. Comp. and Sys. Sci.* vol. 1 (1967), pp. 213–226.

5. Manne, A. S., 'Programming of Economic Lot Sizes', *Management Science*, vol. 4 (1958), pp. 115–135.
6. Wagner, H. M. and Whitin, T. M., 'A Dynamic Version of the Economic Lot Size Model', *Management Science*, vol. 5 (1959), pp. 89–96.

11. Large scale optimization for master production scheduling

PAUL M. MANGIAMELI

Abstract

This paper describes the methodology to be used in solving a disaggregation problem in a multistage, multi-product production system. As defined in the paper, the disaggregation problem is to develop a feasible and economic master production schedule. The solution methodology utilizes a generalized form of Benders decomposition. An example problem is provided.

11.1. Introduction

Planning in a multistage, multi-product production system is an extremely complex process where long-term and short-term decisions are highly interrelated. Aggregate plans, in terms of output, inventory and manpower aggregates, must be disaggregated to arrive at short-term allocations of resources to individual activities and operations. An important link in this process of disaggregation is the determination of a master production schedule. The master schedule, recognizing the constraints imposed by the output, inventory, and manpower aggregates, specifies the timing and sizing of end item production lots. These in turn become inputs to the shop loading and scheduling sub-systems. This sequential planning process is depicted in Figure 1.

11.2. Master schedule development

In order to evaluate how changes in the master schedule affect aggregate costs it is first necessary to develop a procedure for master

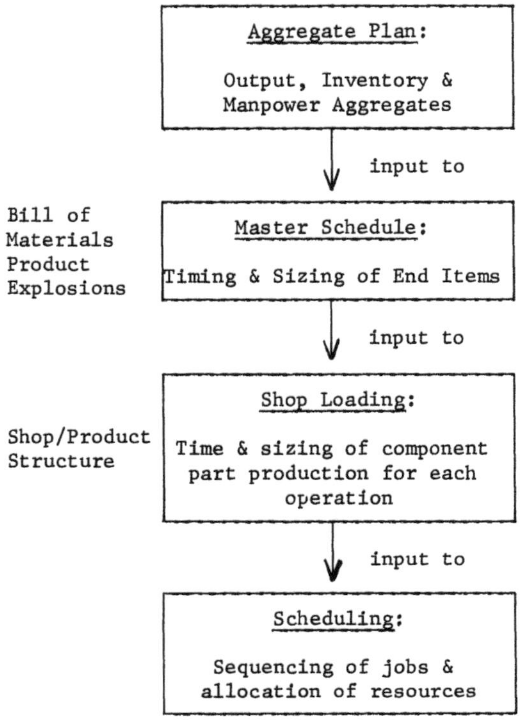

Figure 1. Sequential planning process in a multistage multi-product production system.

schedule creation. This procedure, summarized in Figure 2, starts with a statement of aggregate resource availability and desired output rate. Then a prospective master schedule is developed given the compiled schedule of factory requirements, current backlogs and inventory levels. This prospective schedule implies a certain resource absorption in each period of the planning horizon. This resource absorption can then be translated into aggregate costs for output, inventory, and manpower. The implied resource usage is checked against actual or expected resource availabilities as specified by the aggregate plan and if the master schedule is feasible it becomes authorized. If not, modifications are usually made to the master schedule until feasibility occurs. Each modification indicates a change in aggregate costs, yet this relationship is not clearly understood. As shall be discussed later, in order to gain a better understanding of the economic relationships between master

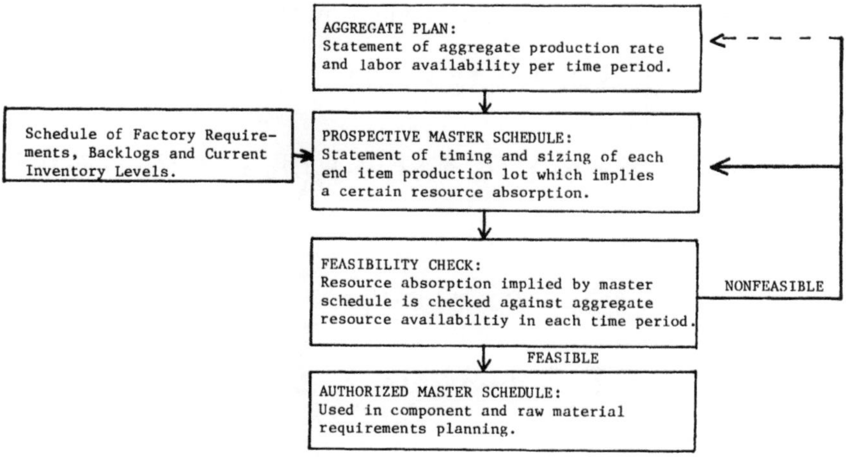

Figure 2. Master schedule development in a multistage system.

schedule changes and resource availabilities, it will be useful to consider modifications to the aggregate plan as indicated by the dashed lines in Figure 2. Although its importance in the planning process is obvious, little research has been done on the economic impact of master schedule changes. This paper utilizes a mathematical model of a manufacturing division of a firm to judge the effects of master schedule changes on the total cost to the firm. The use of the model allows management to draw economic implications for each of the following types of analysis [3]:

- probationary exercises
- optimization with fixed or static resources
- optimization with unlimited resources
- 'what if . . . ?'
- sensitivity analysis
- continuity analysis
- tradeoff analysis
- priority analysis

11.3. Mathematical formulation

Within this framework the following model, which is an adaptation of the one found in [4], can be specified for analyzing the disaggregation problem in a multistage production system.

$$\min \sum_{t=1}^{T} \sum_{i \in N} (s_{it}\phi_{it} + v_{it}X_{it} + c_{it}I_{it})$$

$$+ \sum_{t=1}^{T} (h_t H_t + o_t \sum_{j \in J} O_{jt} + f_t F_t + w_t\left(W_0 + \sum_{k=1}^{t} (H_k - F_k)\right) \quad (1)$$

Subject to:

$$X_{it} + I_{it-1} - I_{it} = D_{it} \quad \forall\, i \in N, t \quad (2)$$

$$W_{jt} + O_{jt} - \sum_{i \in N} \sum_{m=1}^{l_i} (r_{ijm} X_{it+m}) \geqq \sum_{i \in N} \sum_{m=1}^{l_i} (r'_{ijm} \phi_{it+m}) \quad (3)$$

$$- \sum_{k=1}^{t} (H_k - F_k) + \sum_{j \in J} W_{jt} \leqq W_0 \quad \forall\, t \quad (4)$$

$$- \theta \sum_{k=1}^{t} (H_k - F_k) + \sum_{j \in J} O_{jt} \leqq \theta W_0 \quad \forall\, t \quad (5)$$

$$\sum_{t=1}^{T} \phi_{it} \geqq 1 \quad \forall\, i \in N \quad (6)$$

$$X_{it} \leqq \phi_{it} \sum_{q=t}^{T} D_{it} \quad \forall\, i \in N, t \quad (7)$$

$$X_{it} \geqq \phi_{it} D_{it} \quad \forall\, i \in N, t \quad (8)$$

$$\phi_{it} = 0, 1 \text{ interger} \quad \forall\, i \in N, t \quad (9)$$

where

x_{it} = lot size order for end item i to be completed by the beginning of period t

I_{it} = on hand inventory level of end item i at the beginning of period t

D_{it} = factory requirements of end item i for period t which consists of such things as demand forecasts, firm orders, interplant shipments and service requirements

l_i = cumulative production and procurement lead time to make end item i

r_{ijm} = resource requirements for processing a unit of end item i in operation j in the m-th period since production started on i

r'_{ijm} = resources required for set up of product i in operation j in the m-th period since production started on i

ϕ_{it} = binary variable which assigns a setup time for end item i whenever $X_{it} > 0$

W_0 = beginning workforce level in period 0 expressed in manhours

s_{it} = cost of setup for product i in time period t

V_{it} = variable cost of processing product i in time period t

c_{it} = cost of carrying one unit of product i in inventory during time period t

h_t = cost of hiring one manhour of labour in time period t

o_t = cost of one manhour of overtime in time period t

f_t = cost of firing one manhour of labor in time period t

u_t = cost of one manhour of regular time for time period t

W_{jt} = regular time manhours assigned to operation j in period t

H_t = manhours of labor hired at the start of period t

F_t = manhours of labor fired at the start of period t

O_{jt} = overtime manhours assigned to operation j in period t

θ = proportion of the regular time workforce capacity which can be used on overtime

N = set of all end items

T = planning horizon

J = set of all production operations

The cost parameters in equation (1) taken on the usual interpretations with the possible exception of the setup costs for end item i in period t, s_{it}. These will be the total setup costs for the end item plus all components. This is necessary so that there is some consideration in the model for the costs of setup for all the components of product i. However, because of the simplifications necessary for aggregate planning these are assumed to occur in the period in which the production lot of the end item is to be completed. Also, expression (1), with the coefficient C_{wt}, is merely a way of expressing the cost of the regular time workforce in period t.

While constraint set (2) is self-explanatory, set (3) is not. This set guarantees that each operation in each time period has enough resources to perform the work scheduled for it in time period t. Constraint sets (4) and (5) guarantee the manhour availability for regular time and overtime respectively. Constraint set (6) guarantees that a feasible solution relating setups to processing always exists. Constraint sets (7), (8), and (9) are a convenient notational form of insuring that ϕ_{it} is one whenever $X_{it} > 0$ and is zero otherwise.

11.4. Solution methodology

The solution of (1)–(9) is a formidable task whenever the number of binary variables becomes large as would be the case for any realistic problem. This size would far exceed the capabilities of the largest mixed integer package. Fortunately, there are other solution methods available. Clearly, if the binary variables could be fixed at either zero or one, the problem is one of just solving a large linear programming. Benders' decomposition, the methodology chosen in this paper, does exactly that [1]. Geoffrion and Gravis solved an actual problem on warehouse location for Hunt-Wesson Foods, Inc. with 11,854 rows, 727 binary variables, and 23,513 continuous variables [3:827] by using a specialized form of Benders' decomposition.

All the variant forms of Benders decomposition follow the same basic pattern. The problem is split into a master problem which decides on values for the binary variable and one or more subproblems which determine the values of the continuous variables. By constraining the master problem with a function of the extremal values of the linear program (these functions employ duality theory to generate a natural family of cuts, usually the deepest cuts) a cutting plane approach is developed which leads to increasingly higher lower bounds for the problem. This is the generalized form of Benders decomposition developed by Geoffrion [2].

By parametizing the values of the binary variables (found in the solution of the master problem) in the subproblems, an upper bound is obtained. When the lowest of the upper bounds is less than or equal to the lower bound plus some value, ϵ, the procedure terminates. Although not given in this paper, proof that this procedure will terminate in a finite number of steps with the ϵ-optimal answer, or with a conclusion that no solution to the original problem was feasible can be found in [1], [2], [5].

For the problem in this paper, the generalized Benders decomposition can be summarized in the following steps.

Step 1. Set the iteration counter $p = 0$ and set the value for t. Let the upper bound, $UB = \infty$ and the lower bound $LB = -\infty$. Solve the following master problem.

$$\min Z$$

Subject to constraint sets (6), (9) and:

$$Z \geqq s_{it}\phi_{it}$$

To arrive at an initial feasible solution, set $\phi_{i1} = 1\ \forall_i$ and all other $\phi_{it}(t \neq 1) = 0$. Let $Z = LB$.

Step 2. Increment p by 1. Note that in the following linear subproblem, some of the terms appear with the superscript $p - 1$. These terms are the parametized values obtained from the $p - 1$ solution to the master problem. As such they are known values and not variables.

$$\min \quad \sum_t \sum_i (v_{it}X_{it} + c_{it}I_{it})$$

$$+\sum_t \left(h_t H_t + o_t \sum_j O_{jt} + f_t F_t + w_t\Big(W_0 + \sum_{k=1}^{t} (H_k - F_k)\Big)\right)$$

Subject to:

$$X_{it} + I_{it-1} - I_{it} = D_{it} \qquad \forall i, t$$

$$W_{jt} + O_{jt} - \sum_i \sum_m r_{ijm} X_{it+m} \geqq \sum_i \sum_m r'_{ijm} \phi_{it+m}^{p-1} \qquad \forall j, t$$

$$-\sum_k (H_k - F_k) + \sum_j w_{jt} \leqq W_0 \qquad \forall t$$

$$-\Theta \sum_k (H_k - F_k) + \sum_j O_{jt} \leqq \Theta W_0 \qquad \forall t$$

$$X_{it} \leqq \phi_{it}^{p-1} \sum_{q=t}^{T} D_{iq} \qquad \forall i, t$$

$$X_{it} \geqq \phi_{it}^{p-1} D_{it} \qquad \forall i, t$$

The optimal value of this subproblem is denoted as $T(\underline{\phi}^P)$ thus the quantity $\Sigma_t \Sigma_i s_{it} \phi_{it}^{p-1} + T(\phi^P)$ is a potential upper bound on the original problem (1)–(9). If this quantity is less than the previous upper bound, this potential upper bound becomes the incumbent upper bound and the incumbent solution is $(\underline{X}^P, \underline{I}^P, \underline{H}^P, \underline{O}^P, \underline{F}^P, \underline{W}^P)$.

Step 3. As stated previously, duality theory will be used to generate the Benders' cut, thus the optimal value of the dual solution to step 2 is

$$\max \left(\sum_t \sum_i D_{it}\right) \sigma_t^P + \left(\sum_t \sum_j \sum_i \sum_m r'_{ijm} \sigma_{it+m}^{p-1}\right) {}_{jt}^{P} + (W_0)\, \alpha_t^P$$

$$+ (\Theta W_0)\, \beta_t^P + \sum_i \sum_i \left(\phi_{it}^{p-1} \sum_{q=t}^{T} D_{iq}\right) \mu_{it}^P$$

$$+ \sum_t \sum_i (\phi_{it}^{p-1} D_{it})\, \delta_{it}^P$$

Step 4. The dual values are now passed to the master problem where ϕ_{it} is no longer fixed; that is, it is free to assume a value of zero or one. After combining terms the master problem is now:

$$\min Z$$

Subject to (6), (9) and:

$$Z + \sum_t \left(\sum_i D_{it} \sigma_{it}^P + W_0 \alpha_t + \Theta W_0 \beta_t^P\right)$$

$$\sum_t \sum_i \left[\left(s_{it} + D_{it} \delta_{it}^P - \mu_{it}^P \sum_q D_{iq}\right) \phi_{it}\right.$$

$$\left. + \left(\sum_j \sum_m r'_{ijm} \pi_{jt}^P\right) \phi_{it-m}\right] \quad i, t$$

The optimal value for Z becomes the LB. The check for optimality is $UB \leqq LB + \epsilon$. If this is true, the procedure terminates, otherwise it returns to step 2.

Example problem

It would prove instructive to use the methodology in the previous section in a simplified example problem. Assume a company has

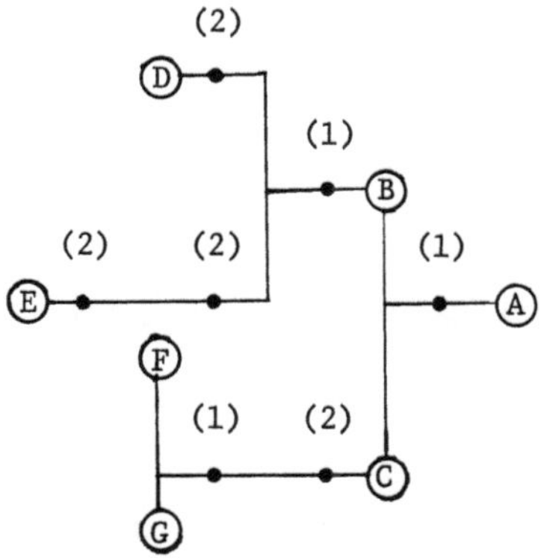

Manhours Needed \ M	4	3	2	1	
Workcenter 2:					
Processing	10	20	10	0	
Setup	15	30	15	0	
Workcenter 1:					
Processing	0	4	5	6	
Setup	0	6	5	4	

Figure 3. Production profile for an example product.

one family of end items and a planning horizon of 8 periods. Referring to Figure 3, the columns are weekly time buckets, the black dots represent work completed at a work center, the figure contained in brackets is the work center number (of which there are two), and the letters in the clear circles represent stockable parts. For each operation, there is a set up and processing time which is expressed in manhours in the chart in Figure 3. As there is only one family of parent items, the subscript i is dropped; thus the costs are for all t:

$$S_t = 10,\ V_t = 5,\ C_t = 2,\ C_{ht} = 4,\ h_t = 6,\ O_t = 5,\ W = 3$$

The demands are, $t_1 = t_2 = t_3 = t_4 = 0$, $t_5 = 15$, $t_6 = 10$, $t_T = 5$, $t_8 = 15$ and the starting workforce is 10 manhours and the maximum overtime allowable is 10 percent of the regular time manhours available.

The master problem can be stated as

$$\min Z$$

Subject to:

$$Z \geqq \sum_t 10\phi_t$$

$$\sum_t \phi_t \geqq 1$$

For an initial feasible solution, let $\phi_5 = 1$ and all other $\phi_t = 0$. $Z = 10 = LB$.

Setting $p = 1$, the linear subproblem is

$$\min \sum \Bigg[5X_t + 2I_t + 4H_t + 5O_t + 6F_t +$$

$$+ 3\left(10 + \sum_{k=1}^{t} H_k - F_k\right)\Bigg]$$

Subject to:

$$(x_t - I_t + I_{t-1} = D_t$$

$$W_{jt} + O_{jt} - \sum_m r_{jm}X_{t+m} \geqq \sum_m r'_{jm}\phi_{t+m}^{p-1}$$

$$- \sum_{k=1}^{t} (H_k - F_k) + \sum_j W_{jt} \leqq 10$$

$$- .1\sum_k (H_k - F_k) + \sum_j O_{jt} \leqq 1$$

$$X_t \leqq \phi_t^{p-1} \sum_{q=t}^{t} D_q$$

$$X_t \geqq \phi_t^{p-1} D_t$$

The optimal solution to the above linear subproblem is 18073.36364. Thus the upper bound is $\Sigma_t\ 10\Phi_t^0 + T(\phi^1) = 18083.36364$.

The optimal dual prices generated are:

σ_5^1	=	-392.54545	α_5	=	3.0
σ_6^1	=	-394.54545	α_6	=	0.0
σ_7^1	=	-396.54545	α_7	=	3.0
σ_8^1	–	-398.54545	α_8	=	0.0
π_{21}^1	=	3.0	β_1^1	=	0.0
π_{12}^1	=	12.27273	β_2^1	=	7.27273

$\pi_{22}^1 = 12.27273$	$\beta_3^1 = 0.0$
$\pi_{13}^1 = 3.0$	$\beta_4^1 = 0.0$
$\pi_{23}^1 = 3.0$	$\beta_5^1 = 0.0$
$\pi_{14}^1 = 3.0$	$\beta_6^1 = 0.0$
$\pi_{24}^1 = 3.0$	$\beta_7^1 = 0.0$
$\pi_{15}^1 = 3.0$	$\beta_8^1 = 0.0$
$\pi_{25}^1 = 0$	$\mu_5^1 = 0.0$
$\pi_{16}^1 = 0$	$\mu_6^1 = -131.81818$
$\pi_{26}^1 = 3.0$	$\mu_7^1 = -244.54545$
$\pi_{17} = 0.0$	$\mu_8^1 = -273.54545$
$\alpha_1 = 3.0$	$\delta_5^1 = 0.0$
$\alpha_2 = 3.0$	$\delta_6^1 = 0.0$
$\alpha_3 = 12.27273$	$\delta_7^1 = 0.0$
$\alpha_4 = 3.0$	$\delta_8^1 = 0.0$

Combining terms, the master problem can now be stated as

$$\min Z$$

Subject to:

$$Z = 18073 \geqq 10\phi_5 - 3580.45448\phi_6 - 466m909\phi_7 - \\ - 3928.18175\phi_8$$

The solution to this problem is $Z = 5906.81841$ which is the value of the lower bound. Obviously, $\phi_5 = \phi_6 = \phi_7 = \phi_8 = 1$. Checking for optimality ($UB = LB$) the upper bound 18083.36364 does not equal that of the lower bound of 5906.81841, thus p is set to two and the process is repeated. Table 1 summarizes the situations where at $p = 5$ the process was terminated at optimality. The optimal solution was $X_5 = 15$, $X_6 = 10$, $X_7 = 5$, $X_8 = 15$, $\phi_5 = \phi_6 = \phi_7 = \phi_8 = 1$ and the optimal value was 13055.90909.

Table 1. Summary of solution methodology for example problem.

Value of p	Potential UB	Incumbent UB	ϕ_6	ϕ_7	ϕ_8	Z = LB
0	∞	∞	0	0	0	10
1	18083.36364	18083.36364	-3580.45448	-4667.909	-3938.18175	5906.81841
2	13055.90909	13055.90909	1273.18169	498.6363	277.0	11782.72707
3	13202.45455	13055.90909	-3840.4545	254.0	337.0	12547.27246
4	13121.35178	13055.90909	499.8115	-2447.6323	175.0	12778.90876
5	14824.06719	13055.90909	1358.08314	428.06731	1813.71545	13055.90876

It should be noted that each line of Table 1 represents a constraint in the master problem when *p* equaled five. Of course, when *p* was less than five, there were correspondingly fewer constraints in the problem.

11.5. Conclusion

In further research using this model, the relationship between changes in the parameters, master schedule, and aggregate costs will be explored. Some examples of master schedule changes and their effects on aggregate costs are:

- Changes in demand patterns and the consequent redistribution of resources
- Engineering changes (i.e., changes in the product structure and routing)
- Maximum ceilings and minimum floors on end item lot sizes
- Changes in manufacturing and vendor lead times

In exploring the above relationships, the following questions can be answered:

- How do changes in the master schedule affect aggregate costs?
- How should changes in the master schedule be made so as to reduce aggregate costs?

Given this information, management can gain a greater understanding about the economic relationship in its master schedule. Thus any changes that occur can be evaluated in terms of the economic impact on the firm.

References

1. Benders, J. F., 'Partitioning Procedures for Solving Mixed Variable Programming Problems', *Numerische Mathematik*, vol. 4 (1962), pp. 238–252.
2. Geoffrion, A. M., 'Generalized Benders Decomposition', *Journal of Optimization Theory and Applications*, vol. 10, no. 4 (1972), pp. 237–260.
3. Geoffrion, A. M. and Graves, G. W., 'Multicommodity Distribution System Design by Benders Decomposition', *Management Science*, vol. 20, no. 5 (January 1971), pp. 822–844.
4. Krajewski, L. J. and Mangiameli, P. M., 'Disaggregation in Multistage Production Systems: An Iterative Approach', Proceedings of the Seventh Annual Midwest Conference of the American Institute of Decision Sciences, Detroit, Michigan (May 1976), pp. 327–330.
5. Lasdon, L. S., *Optimization Theory for Large Systems* (New York: MacMillan Co., 1970).

12. Multi-item scheduling with reflection programming

W. STEVEN DEMMY and ANDREW W. LAI

Abstract

Conceptually, many manufacturing scheduling problems may be modeled as very large mixed integer, multi-period product mix problems with 'soft' constraints. Unfortunately, the very large size of these problems precludes calculation of exact optimum solutions to such models.

This paper presents computational results for solving such problems using reflection programming. This technique is a heuristic integer optimization method which solves a series of single item scheduling problems in such a way that the variables always satisfy integer restrictions, a minimum of computer memory is required, and solutions are obtained much more quickly than when using the Dantzig-Wolfe technique. Computational experience with this method is presented.

12.1. Introduction

Conceptually, many manufacturing scheduling problems may be modeled as a large-scale mixed-integer, multi-period product mix problem with 'soft' constraints. A typical formulation of this problem is as follows:

Let

d_{ij} = demand for units of item j during period i

w_{1j} = number of units of item j on hand at the beginning of period 1

h_{ij} = cost of holding a unit of item j in inventory at the beginning of period i

a_{kj} = amount of resource k required to 'set-up' and begin production of item j

b_{kj} = amount of resource k required to produce one unit of item j, given the job has already been set-up

b_{ik} = amount of resource k available during period i

b_{ik}^{o} = maximum additional units of resource k that can be made available by working overtime

R_{ik}^{s} = cost per unit slack of resource k in period i; i.e. the opportunity cost associated with each unit of resource k that is available but not utilized in period i

R_{ik}^{o} = cost per unit of addition a resource k capability that is obtained by subcontracting or other source external to the production organization.

The above data is assumed known for all items j and resources k in the production system.

Decision variables in the model are:

q_{ij} = number of units of item j to be produced in period i

O_{ik} = number of units of resource k made available in period i by working overtime

A_{ik} = number of units of resource k made available in period i by subcontracting or other auxiliary sources.

The decision variables fix the values of the following status variables.

w_{ij} = number of units of item j and in inventory at the beginning of period i

s_{ik} = amount of unutilized (slack) capacity of resource k in period i.

The scheduling problem is to determine values for q_{ij}, O_{ik}, and A_{ik} that minimize Z,

$$Z = \sum_{ij} [a_{oj}\delta(_{qij}) + b_{oj}\delta(_{qij}) + h_{ij} W_{ij}] +$$

$$\sum_{ik} [R_{ik}^{s} S_{ik} + R_{ik}^{o} O_{ik} + R_{ik}^{A} A_{ik}] \tag{1}$$

subject to

$$\sum_{j} [a_{kj}\delta(_{qij}) + b_{kj} q_{ij}] + S_{ik} - O_{ik} - A_{ik} = b_{ik} \quad \text{all } ik \tag{2}$$

$$O_{ik} \leqq b_{ik}^{o} \tag{3}$$

$$W_{i+1,j} = W_{ij} + q_{ij} - d_{ij} \tag{4}$$

$$W_{ij},\ q_{ij},\ S_{ik},\ O_{ik},\ A_{ik} \geqq 0 \tag{5}$$

$$W_{ij},\ q_{ij} \text{ integer} \tag{6}$$

where $\delta(.)$ denotes the Dirac delta function.

We shall refer to the vector of scheduling variables $Q_j = (q_{1j}, q_{2j}, \ldots, q_{ij})$ as the *production schedule* for item j.

The objective is to minimize the total cost of operating the inventory system for the I-period planning horizon. The terms $a_{oj}\delta(q_{ij}) + b_{oj}(q_{ij})$ denote costs of materials used in the production process; $h_{ij}W_{ij}$ is the cost of carrying inventory, and the remaining terms in (1) represent costs of adjusting resource levels to match scheduled production. Equation (2) states that resources required by the production schedule must equal the adjusted available resources. Relation (3) is the limit on overtime, while (4) is the familiar material balance equation. Conditions (5) and (6) result from the discrete nature of the production process.

The above model is known as the capacitated lot size problem. Conceptually, the problem might be solved using general mixed-integer programming techniques; unfortunately, the general methods are practical for only very small problems.

Several authors have studied methods for obtaining approximate solutions to capacitated lot size problems using linear programming. This includes the work of Manne (1958), Dzielinski, Baker, and Manne (1962), Dzielinski and Gomory (1965), Gornstein (1970), and Lasdon and Terjung (1971).

Manne observed that problems such as (1)–(6) might be restated as follows: Suppose we were to enumerate all production schedules for item j that satisfy conditions (4)–(6), and let $Q_j^t = (q_{1j}^t, q_{2j}^t, \ldots, q_{Ij}^t)$ denote the tth such schedule for item j. Further, let $X_j t = 1$ if schedule t is to be adopted, and $x_j^t = 0$ otherwise. In addition, we define

$$p_j^t = a_{oj}\delta(q_{ij}^t) + b_{oj}q_{ij}^t + h_{ij}W_{ij}^t \tag{7}$$

$$g_{ijk}^t = a_{kj}\delta(q_{ij}^t) + b_{kj}q_{ij} \tag{8}$$

where W_{ij}^t is determined by substituting values for q_{ij}^t into (3). Then the problem (1)–(5) is equivalent to the problem:

$$\min Z = \sum_{jt} P_j^t N_j^t + \sum_{ik} [R_{ik}^s S_{ik} + R_{ik}^o O_{ik} + R_{ik}^A A_{ik}] \tag{9}$$

subject to

$$\sum_{jt} g^t_{ijk} X^t_j + S_{ik} - O_{ik} - A_{ik} = b_{ik} \tag{10}$$

$$O_{ik} \leqq B^o_{ik} \tag{11}$$

$$\sum_t X^t_j = 1 \tag{12}$$

$$X^t_j, S_{ik}, O_{ik}, A_{ik} \geqq 0 \tag{13}$$

where X^t_j is integer. Suppose that integer requirement on X^t_j is replaced by the requirement that

$$X^t_j \geqq 0 \tag{14}$$

The resulting problem (9)–(14) is a linear programming (LP) problem, and may be considered an application of the Dantzig-Wolfe decomposition principle to the LP-equivalent of (1)–(6).

Manne observed that if J is large relative to IK, a majority of the X^t_j variables will have integer values. Specifically, it may be shown that for the above problem, at least $(J - 2IK)$ of the constraints (12) will have exactly one non-zero X^t_j (which must equal 1). In this case, it is hypothesized that good solutions to the original integer problem might be obtained by applying simple rounding rules to non-integer values of X^t_j in the optimum LP solution to (9)–(14).

For most real world situations, the linear programming problem (9)–(14) is still very large, and solution using the standard simplex calculations would be extremely costly. Because of the special structure of (9)–(14), however, computations and computer memory requirements may be reduced substantially by using generalized upper bounding (GUB) and delayed column generation techniques.

Using GUB techniques, dual variables associated with a given solution may be computed from an IK by IK working basis. This is compared with the $(2IK + J)$-square matrix associated with the inverse of a given basis to (9)–(14). Delayed column generation technique makes it unnecessary to explicitly determine the p^t_j and g^t_{ijk} values until the associated column is to enter the basis; at that time, a single-item scheduling problem is solved to determine the best candidate for basis entry. For details on these procedures, see Lasdon and Terjung (1971).

12.2. Reflection programming

In this paper we present results from applying reflection programming to the integer optimization problem (9)–(13). Reflection programming is a heuristic integer optimization procedure based on a variant of Dantzig-Wolfe decomposition. The technique was first reported by Agin and Cullen (1975) in the context of a vehicle scheduling problem. Basically, reflection programming works by requiring that any given time there is one and only one non-zero X_j^t associated with each item j. Once an initial solution is established, the algorithm proceeds by considering each item in succession. When a given item is considered, shadow prices associated with each resource are used to determine a trial schedule Q_j^* that represents a marginal improvement over the existing schedule Q_j for the current item, the same as in Dantzig-Wolfe decomposition, however, reflection programming requires that an entering schedule must completely replace the previous schedule. This one-for-one replacement will generally require adjustments in the basis variables associated with constraints (10).

These adjustments are referred to as the reflection pivot, since the impact of the schedule change is being 'reflected' into its corresponding resource adjustments. In general, exchanging the current schedule for the trial schedule will decrease production and inventory costs, but the resource adjustments will increase resource costs. If the total of these cost changes represents a net improvement in the objective function, the new schedule is adopted. If there is no net improvement, the next item is considered. This process is continued until each of the items has been considered without adopting a new schedule; when this happens, the algorithm stops.

There are a number of computational advantages that reflection programming has over linear programming approaches to the problem (9)–(13). These include:

1. *Integer-valued solutions*. The scheduling variables q_{ij} have integer values at all times, no rounding is necessary when the algorithm terminates.
2. *Rapid Solution*. The reflection programming algorithm appears to terminate with much less computation than required by linear programming methods.

3. *Computer Memory Savings*. When reflection programming is applied to (9)–(13), dual variables associated with each constraint may be computed without reference to the inverse of the basis matrix. Hence, the inverse need not be stored or updated, a significant savings in both computations and memory requirements over LP-methods.

The big disadvantage of reflection programming is, of course, that there is no guarantee that the algorithm will terminate with a near-optimum solution, or even a good solution for that matter. Hence, the primary objective of this research has been to answer the question: How good are the schedules produced by reflection programming?

Unfortunately, even very small scheduling problems of practical interest involve 50 plus constraints and thousands of variables. We have found no algorithms that can guarantee optimum integer solutions to problems of this size at a reasonable cost. Hence, we have approached the evaluation of reflection programming from three basic directions.

1. By derivation of lower bounds on the optimum objective function value.
2. By comparing reductions in the objective function value compared to reasonable initial schedules.
3. By comparisons of reflection programming solutions with solutions obtained by linear programming.

This paper reports progress in the first two areas; work with the linear programming comparisons is in progress.

12.3. A lower bound

A lower bound on the optimum objective value (9) may be derived as follows:

Suppose we have a basic feasible solution to (9)–(14) and let (π, γ, α) be a vector of dual variables associated with the current basis B. Multiply (10) by π, (11) by γ, and (12) by α, and subtract the resulting equations from (9). The result is

$$\sum_{jt}(P_j^t - \sum_{ik} g_{ijk}^t \pi_{ik} - \alpha_j)X_j^t +$$
$$+ \sum_{ik}[(R_{ik}^s - \pi_{ik}) \cdot S_{ik} + (R_{ik}^o - \pi_{ik} - \gamma_{ik})O_{ik} +$$
$$+ (R_{ik}^A - \pi_{ik})A_{ik}]$$
$$= Z - \sum_{ik}[\pi_{ik} b_{ik} + \gamma_{ik} b_{ik}^o] - \sum_{j\alpha j} \tag{15}$$

Let

$$\bar{C}_j^t = P_j^t - \sum_{ik} g_{ijk}^t \pi_{ik} - \alpha_j \tag{16}$$

Replacing $\bar{C}_j^t$ by $\min_t \bar{C}_j^t$ in (15) yields

$$\sum_j (\min_t \bar{C}_j^t) \cdot \sum_t x_j^t + \sum_{ik}[R_{ik}^o - \pi_{ik} - \gamma_{ik})O_{ik}$$
$$+ (R_{ik}^s - \pi_{ik})S_{ik} + (R_{ik}^A - T_{ik})A_{ik}]$$
$$\leqq Z - \sum_{ik}[\pi_{ik} b_{ik} + \gamma_{ik} b_{ik}^o] - \sum_j \alpha_j \tag{17}$$

Hence, substituting (12) into (17), we obtain

$$\sum_j (\min_t \bar{C}_j^t) +$$
$$\sum_{ik}[(R_{ik}^o - \pi_{ik} - \gamma_{ik})O_{ik} + (R_{ik}^s - \pi_{ik})S_{ik} + (R_{ik}^A - \pi_{ik})A_{ik}]$$
$$+ \sum_{ik}(\pi_{ik} b_{ik} + \gamma_{ik} b_{ik}^o) + \sum_j \alpha_j \leqq Z \tag{18}$$

Now let us evaluate the dual variables (π, γ, α) associated with the basis B. Since by definition

$$(\pi, \gamma, \alpha) = c_B B^{-1}, \tag{19}$$

and if e_j is the J-dimensional sum vector,

$$Z_B = c_B X_B = c_{BB}{}^{-1} \begin{matrix} b \\ b^o \\ e_j \end{matrix} = (\pi, \gamma, \alpha) \begin{matrix} b \\ b^0 \\ e_j \end{matrix} \tag{20}$$

Hence,

$$Z_B = \sum_{ik} \pi_{ik} b_{ik} + \sum_{ik} X_{ik} b_{ik}^o + \sum_j \alpha_j \tag{21}$$

Where Z_B denotes the criterion value associated with the basis B and c_B denotes the corresponding vector of cost coefficients. Since (18) holds for all values of Z obtainable from (9)–(14), it also holds for the minimum value of Z. Hence substituting (21) into (18), we obtain

$$\min Z \geqq Z_B + \sum_j (\min_t \bar{C}_j^t) + \sum_k [(R_{ik}^o - \pi_k - \gamma) O_{ik} + (R_{ik}^s - \pi_k) S_{ik} + (R_{ik}^A - \pi_k) A_{ik}] \tag{22}$$

Since the vector of simplex multipliers (π, γ, α) associated with the basis B 'price out' to be zero (Lasdon, 1970, p. 42), i.e.,

$$P_j - \sum_{ik} g_{ijk}^t \pi_{ik} - \alpha_j = 0, \text{ if } X_j \text{ basic} \tag{23}$$

$$R_{ik}^o - \pi_{ik} - \gamma_{ik} = 0, \text{ if } O_{ik} \text{ basic} \tag{24}$$

$$R_{ik}^s - \pi_{ik} = 0, \text{ if } S_{ik} \text{ basic} \tag{25}$$

$$R_{ik}^A - \pi_{ik} = 0, \text{ if } A_{ik} \text{ basic} \tag{26}$$

Hence the right most term in (22) vanishes, yielding

$$\min Z \geqq Z_B + \sum_j (\min_t \bar{C}_j^t)$$

Hence

$$\min Z \geqq Z_B + \sum_j \min (O, \bar{C}_j)$$

where $C_j = \min_t \bar{C}_j^t$

12.4. Experiments with reflection programming

To test the characteristics of reflection programming, we formulated a senario involving 4 resources, 12 planning periods, and 170 items for the Warmdot Company, a hypothetical manufacturing firm studied extensively by Brown (1967). When stated as an integer optimization problem in the form of (9)–(14), the resulting problem has 266 constraints and over 340,000 columns – an optimization problem with substantial dimensions. The data for this senario was constructed by a Monte Carlo Process to have the same statis-

Table 1. Four types of demand rate.

Demand Rate	Distribution
Constant Rate	Monthly demand is normally distributed at a constant rate through the year
Mild Seasonal	Maximum monthly demand = 20% of annual demand
	Minimum monthly demand = 2% of annual demand
Highly Seasonal	Maximum monthly demand = 30% of annual demand
	Minimum monthly demand = 1% of annual demand
Extreme Seasonal	Range from 3 months of "0" demand up to 25% per month of the annual demand

tical characteristics as the top 170 items in the Warmdot inventory. Four basic data sets were generated, each with differing degrees of seasonality as outlined in Table 1.

Reflection programming was applied to each of the data sets under two different cost structures; hence a total of eight runs was performed. In the first cost structure, it was assumed that:

Cost per hour slack = \$4.00
Cost per hour overtime = \$6.00
Cost per hour subcontracted = \$60.00
Cost per period for holding inventory = 2 percent of unit cost.
Setup cost = \$1.00.

The second cost structure was identical to the above, with the exception that the cost of slack was set to zero.

In all tests, an initial schedule was obtained by applying the Wagner-Whitin algorithm to each item independently. Reflection programming was then applied in an attempt to improve the

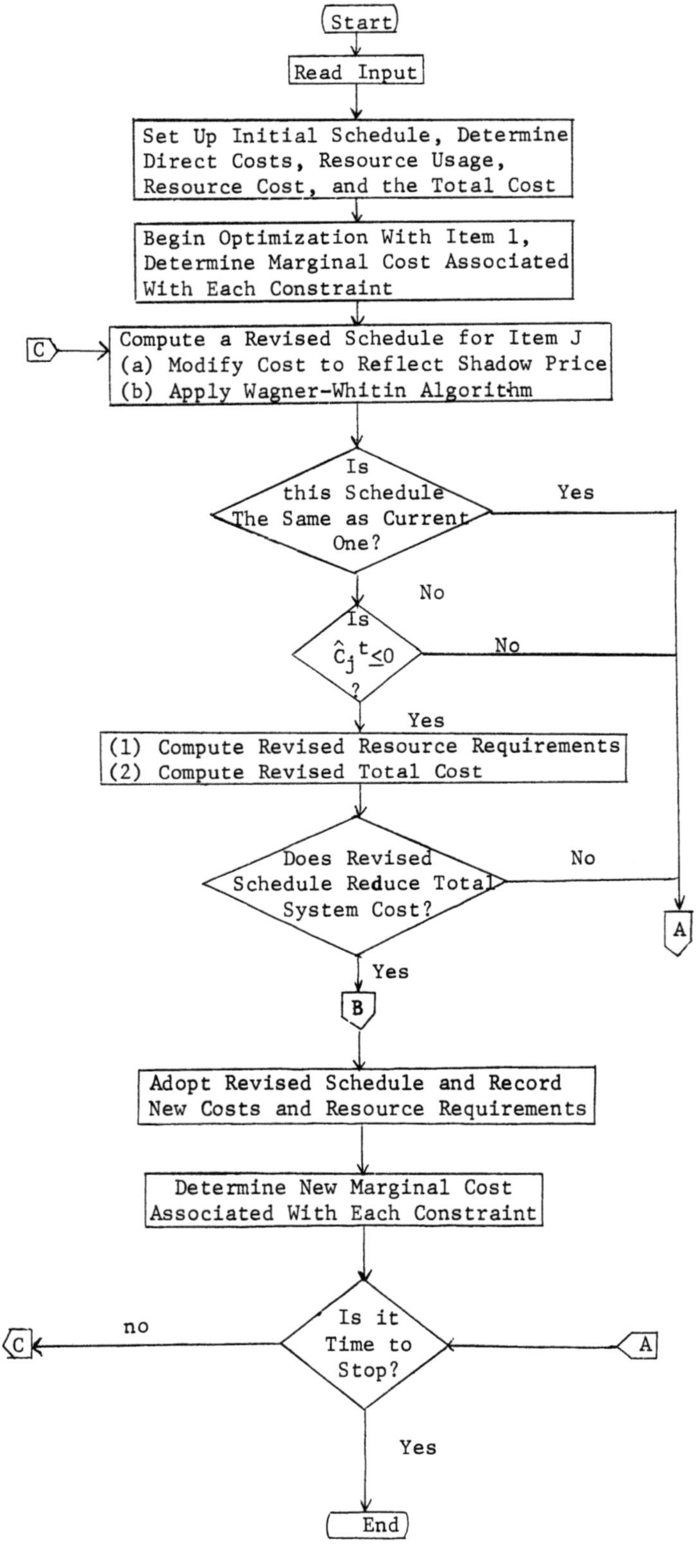

Figure 1. Flow diagram of reflection programming.

Table 2. Summary of experimental runs.

Statistics	Constant Demand Rate		Mild Seasonal Rate		Highly Seasonal Rate		Extremely Seasonal	
	Cost of Slack		Cost of Slack		Cost of Slack		Cost of Slack	
	$4.00	Not Cost	$4.00	No Cost	$4.00	Not Cost	$4.00	Not Cost
Initial Solution	$131,352	$ 5,085	$3,867,611	$2,507,409	$6,298,966	$5,562,524	$3,738,943	$2,911,761
Final Solution	129,689	4,120	358,505	84,141	697,868	288,630	677,430	76,598
Number of Passes Through Each Item	7	5	146	140	144	139	92	92
Total CPU Time (in seconds)	46	30	56	90	57	52	43	72
Percent of Cost Reduction from Initial Solution to Final Solution	1.3%	19%	91%	97%	89%	95%	82%	97%

initial schedules. An outline of the computer program used to implement the algorithm is shown in Figure 1.

Results of our experimental runs are shown in Table 2. These runs demonstrate the speed of the reflection programming. In all eight runs, it took 90 seconds or less of CPU time of IBM 360/65 to reach a heuristic solution. When the demand rate is constant, the cost reductions from the initial solution to the final solution were either moderate (19 percent) or insignificant (1.3 percent). However, when seasonality is present, the cost reduction was substantial, ranging from 82 percent to 97 percent. These results are quite encouraging, since significant cost reductions were obtained for very modest expenditures of computer time.

Results of lower bound calculations

In each of the above runs, we computed the lower bound on the optimum objective value as defined in equation (27) above. In almost all cases, the lower bound was a very poor approximation to the final reflection programming objective function value. Hence, we still do not know if the final solution is 'close' to an optimal one.

12.5. Summary

This paper describes the application of reflection programming to multi-item scheduling problems, and presents limited computational experience with the method. The method appears to produce significantly improved schedules at a modest computing cost relative to schedules derived using traditional 'independent-item' assumptions. Unfortunately, how good the final schedules are relative to the optimal solution is still to be answered.

References

1. Agin, N. I. and Cullen, D. E., 'An Algorithm for Transportation Routing and Vehicle Loading', *Studies in Management Sciences*, vol. I, *Logistics*, M. A. Geisler (ed.), North Holland (1971), pp. 1–20.
2. Brown, Robert G., *Decision Rules for Inventory Management*, Englewood Cliffs, N. J.: Prentice-Hall, Inc. (1967).
3. Dzielinski, B. P. and Gomory, R. E., 'Optimum Programming of Lot Sizes, Inventories, and Labor Allocations', *Management Science*, vol. 11, no. 9 (July 1965), pp. 874–890.
4. Dzielinski, B. P., Baker, C. T., and Manne, A. S., 'Simulation Tests of Lot Size Programming', *Management Science*, vol. 9, no. 2 (January 1963), pp. 229–258.
5. Gorenstein, S., 'Planning Tire Production', *Management Science*, vol. 17, no. 2 (October 1970), pp. B72–B82.
6. Manne, A. S., 'Programming of Economic Lot Sizes', *Management Science*, vol. 4 (1958), pp. 115–135.
7. Lasdon, L. S. and Terjung, R. C., 'An Efficient Algorithm for Multi-Item Scheduling', *Operations Research*, vol. 19, no. 4 (August 1971), pp. 946–969.
8. Wagner, H. M. and Whitin, T. M., 'A Dynamic Version of the Economic Lot Size Model', *Management Science*, vol. 5 (1958), pp. 89–96.

13. An approach to the analysis of integrated production-distribution systems

G. H. KRAUSS

Abstract

This paper develops a framework for coupling warehouse location, distribution and production decision processes. The motivation for this paper is based on the work by Geoffrion and Graves (*Management Science*, vol. 20, 1974) in their paper 'Multicommodity Distribution System Design by Benders Decomposition'. This work has been extended to allow for simultaneous determination of supply levels for each product class at the various plants when raw material levels are determined. The model provides a production schedule for each product class, by production process at particular plants. An efficient procedure to solve the large scale mathematical programming model via two levels of Benders Decomposition is given.

13.1. Introduction

Many firms, in the general business setting, produce goods at spatially separated plants and meet spatially separated demands. These firms frequently have a volume such that intermediate distribution points are necessary. The location of these distribution points is a nontrivial problem. The firm needs to locate these points consistent with its production, demand and transportation facilities. The fundamental problem is to establish a tradeoff between facility, transportation and production costs.

Geoffrion and Graves have recently presented a model which handles a class of distribution problems. However, their formulation assumes that production of each commodity at each plant is fixed and invariant. This paper argues that production is a controllable variable and that the location of production should be considered simultaneously with the location of distribution points. The paper proceeds to first present and discuss the

Geoffrion and Graves formulation. Specific algorithmic advantages of their formulation will be discussed along with a brief discussion of the shortcomings of their model. From here the paper moves on to present a revised formulation which maintains many of the computational features of the Geoffrion and Graves approach. A computational, decomposition approach to this problem is presented followed by a formal algorithm statement.

13.2. Geoffrion and Graves

Geoffrion and Graves present a formulation of the warehouse location problem which is:

$$\underset{\substack{X \geqq 0 \\ Y,\, Z \in (0,1)}}{\text{Min}} \sum_{ijKL} C_{ijKL} X_{ijKL} + \sum_{K} \left[F_K Z_K + V_K \sum_{iL} D_{iL} Y_{KL} \right] \tag{1}$$

Subject to

$$\sum_{KL} X_{ijKL} \leqq S_{ij} \quad \text{for all } ij \tag{2}$$

$$\sum_{j} X_{ijKL} = D_{iL} Y_{KL} \quad \text{for all } iKL \tag{3}$$

$$\sum_{K} Y_{KL} = 1 \quad \text{for all } L \tag{4}$$

$$\underline{V}_K Z_K \leqq \sum_{iL} D_{iL} Y_{KL} \leqq \overline{V}_K Z_K \quad \text{for all } K \tag{5}$$

where

- i denotes commodity
- j denotes production plant
- K denotes possible distribution points
- L denotes demand zones
- C_{ijKL} is the cost of shipping one unit of commodity i from plant j through distribution point K to demand zone L
- X_{ijKL} is the quantity of commodity i shipped from plant j via distribution point K to demand zone L
- f_K is the fixed cost of establishing (or closing) distribution point K

Z_K is a zero one variable indicating whether distribution point K is open or closed

V_K is the variable cost of shipping one unit through distribution point K

D_{iL} is the demand for commodity i at demand zone L

Y_{KL} tells whether distribution point K serves demand zone L

S_{ij} is the supply of commodity i available at plant j

$\underline{V}_K$ is the lower bound on shipments through distribution point K

$\overline{V}_K$ is the upper bound on shipments through distribution point K

In addition to the formal mathematical formulation (1)–(5) configuration constraints may be entered on the distribution points.

Geoffrion and Graves point out several advantages to their formulation which are:

1. Transportation variables are quadruply subscribed retaining the complete identity of the shipping pattern throughout the network. Thus certain transportation features (i.e., storage in transit) may be portrayed.
2. Constraint (4) requires that each demand zone be served by one and only one distribution point. If the restriction is unrealistic Geoffrion has developed a commodity bounding concept.[1]
3. Bounds are placed on distribution point throughput. Thereby economies of scale in distribution may be introduced through the creation of alternative distribution facilities at a site with different throughput restrictions.

The Geoffrion and Graves formulation is structured in such a way that the application of Benders Decomposition yields a series of problems which are of reduced computational complexity. Specifically the problem breaks into an integer problem in Y and Z and a continuous problem in X. Further the continuous problem (due to constraint (4)) is in the form of independent transportation prob-

1. Geoffrion's commodity bundling concept involves the separation of demand zones into demand zones for each commodity bundle. Thus when a group of commodities requires special distribution facilities the group can be formed into a bundle and the bundles can go through special distribution facilities.

lems for each commodity. Finally these transportation problems contain several rows with zero demands ($D_{IL}\,Y_{KL}$ where $Y_{KL} = 0$) which can be dropped and the information implicit in these rows can be recovered through an application of duality theory (Geoffrion and Graves, pp. 820–830).

13.3. Firms control of production

The Geoffrion and Graves Model assumes production at a plant (S_{ij}) is fixed and invariant. This restricts the firm to distribution planning in a distribution context only. However, in a long run planning exercise spatial adjustments frequently occur in production consistent with demand and distribution. Thus when considering distribution, the firm may wish to consider changes in the location of production.

The underlying factors for spatial production adjustments lie in spatial resource availability, product resource requirements, production costs, demands and transportation costs. The firm does have direct input into all of these factors and thus distribution planning can be done with simultaneous consideration of production. The following model is an integrated production-distribution model based upon the Geoffrion and Graves formulation.

$$\text{Min} \sum_{jm} e_{jm} W_{jm} + \sum_{ijKL} C_{ijKL} X_{ijKL} + \sum_{K} \left[F_K Z_K + V_K \sum_{iL} D_{iL} Y_{KL} \right] \tag{6}$$

Subject to

$$-\sum_{m} f_{jm} W_{jm} + S_{ij} \leqq 0 \quad \text{for all } im \tag{7}$$

$$\sum_{m} a_{jmn} W_{jm} \leqq b_{jn} \quad \text{for all } jn \tag{8}$$

$$\sum_{KL} X_{ijKL} S_{ij} \leqq 0 \quad \text{for all } ij \tag{9}$$

$$\sum_{j} X_{ijKL} = D_{iL} Y_{KL} \quad \text{for all } iKL \tag{10}$$

$$\sum_{K} Y_{KL} = 1 \quad \text{for all } L \tag{11}$$

$$V_K Z_K \leqq \sum_{iL} D_{iL} Y_{KL} \leqq \overline{V}_K Z_K \tag{12}$$

$$S, W, X, \geqq 0 \; Y, Z \in \{0, 1\}$$

where in addition to earlier definitions

- m stands for production processes available
- n stands for limits on production
- e_{jm} is the cost of operating one unit of production process m at production plant j
- W_{jm} is the number of units of production process m operated at plant j
- f_{ijm} is the yield of commodity i from one unit of production process m operated at plant j (Note this allows joint products.)
- a_{ijmn} is the use of production limit n by one unit of production process m at plant j
- b_{jn} is the total available of production limit n at plant j
- S_{ij} is an endogenous variable telling how much of commodity i is produced at plant j

This model minimizes production plus distribution cost (6) subject to constraints which related commodity output to supply (7), constraints which impose limits on production's use of resources (8), and the constraints from the Geoffrion and Graves model (9)–(12).

13.4. Decomposition

The above model, like the Geoffrion and Graves model, is a candidate for Benders Decomposition. Further, under decomposition the problem does have desirable computational features. The following discussion does assume knowledge of Benders Decomposition. Background references are Benders, Hu, McCarl and Harling, Geoffrion and Zionts.

The problem may be decomposed into two problems as follows:

Master Problem I

$$\text{Min} \sum_{jm} C_{jm} W_{jm} + \sum_{K} \left[F_K Z_K + V_K \sum_{iL} D_{iL} Y_{KL} \right] + z_0 \tag{13}$$

$$-\sum_m f_{ijm} W_{jm} + S_{ij} \leqq 0 \quad \text{for all } ij \tag{14}$$

$$\sum_m a_{ijmn} W_{ijn} \leqq b_{jn} \quad \text{for all } jn \tag{15}$$

$$\sum_K Y_{KL} = 1 \quad \text{for all } L \tag{16}$$

$$\underline{V}_K Z_K \leqq \sum_{iL} D_{iL} Y_{KL} \leqq \overline{V}_K Z_K \quad \text{for all } K \tag{17}$$

$$Z_0 \geqq \sum_{ij} U_{ij}^h S_{ij} + \sum_{iKL} \Pi_{iKL}^h D_{iL} Y_{KL} \quad \text{for all } h \tag{18}$$

$$Y, Z \in (0, 1)$$

$$W \geqq 0$$

$$Z_0 \; arb$$

Subproblem I

$$\text{Min} \sum_{ijKL} D_{ijKL} X_{ijKL} \tag{19}$$

$$\sum_{KL} X_{ijKL} \leqq S_{ij} \quad \text{for all } ij \tag{20}$$

$$\sum_j X_{ijKL} = D_{iL} Y_{KL} \quad \text{for all } iKL \tag{21}$$

$$X_{ijKL} \geqq 0$$

where the variables are defined as before and

- Z_0 is the predicted value of (19) derived through linear programming theory
- Π_{iKL}^h is the dual variable associated with (20) in solution h
- U_{ij}^h is the dual variable associated with (19) in solution h

The master problem minimizes (1) production plus distribution point plus *predicted* transportation costs (Z_0); subject to constraints on output (14), resource use (15), distribution centers (16), (17); and a Benders type constraint which controls the predicted value of the transportation cost (18). The subproblem is of the transportation type and decomposes into classical single commodity problems when the fact is considered that for each L there is a unique K. For discussion of this problem see Geoffrion and Graves.

13.5. Further decomposition

Master problem I is a mixed integer programming problem which contains distribution and production characteristics. These problems are largely disjoint with the exception of the Benders constraint (18). This problem is a candidate for further decomposition. Specifically we get two new problems.

Master problem II

$$\text{Min} \sum_{K} \left[F_K Z_K + V_K \sum_{iL} D_{iL} Y_{KL} \right] + Z_{00} \tag{22}$$

Subject to

$$\sum_{K} Y_{KL} = 1 \quad \text{for all } L \tag{23}$$

$$\underline{V}_K Z_K \leqq \sum_{iL} D_{iL} Y_{KL} \leqq \overline{V}_K Z_K \quad \text{for all } K \tag{24}$$

$$Z_{00} \geqq \sum_{h} \psi_h^p \left(- \sum_{iKL} \Pi_{iKL}^h D_{iL} Y_{KL} \right) + \sum_{jn} \S_{jn}^p \text{ for all } p \tag{25}$$

$$Y_{KL}, Z \epsilon \text{ integer}$$

$$Z_{00} \; arb$$

Subproblem II

$$\text{Min} \sum_{jm} C_{jm} W_{jm} + Z_0 \tag{26}$$

$$-\sum f_{ijm} W_{jm} + S_i \leqq 0 \quad \text{for all } i, j \tag{27}$$

$$-\sum_{m} a_{ijm} W_{jm} \leqq b_{jn} \quad \text{for all } jn \tag{28}$$

$$\sum_{ij} U_{ij}^h S_{ij} - Z_0 \leqq \sum_{iKL} \Pi_{iKL}^h D_{iL} Y_{KL} \quad \text{for all } h \tag{29}$$

where the new variables are

- Z_{00} is the predicted rate of (26) obtained through duality theory
- ψ_h^p is the dual variable associated with constraint (29) in master problem I decomposition iteration p
- $\S_{ij}$ is the dual variable associated with constraint (28) in iteration p.

The master problem II minimizes distribution facility costs plus the predicted objective function for the rest of the problem subject to the distribution facility constraints (23), (24); and a constraint which reflects the prediction of subproblem II objective function. Subproblem II minimizes the cost of production plus the predicted cost of distribution, subject to constraints on output (27), resource usage (28) and a constraint which reflects the prediction of the distribution cost objective (29) from subproblem I.

13.6. Formal algorithm

The above decomposition leads to the following algorithm which we have implemented in a preliminary version.

Step 0. Establish 0 feasible distribution point ($\bar{Z}$, $\bar{Y}$) and supply (W, S) – solutions choose a convergence parameter ϵ, set the solution upper bound (UB) to ∞, lower bound (LB) to $-\infty$.

Step 1. Solve subproblem I as a set of independent transportation problems. Obtain $-\Pi$ and U if the original objective function value (6) evaluated at the optimal point to this problem $\bar{X}$ and $\bar{Z}$, $\bar{Y}$, $\bar{W}$, $\bar{S}$ is less than or equal to the current lower bound plus ϵ, stop. Otherwise compare this objective value with incumbent upper bound and reset if it is lower.

Step 2. Set master problem bounds $USB = \infty$, $SLB = -\infty$ and set $h = h + 1, p = 0$.

Step 3. Set up subproblem II given Π, U, $\bar{Y}$ and $\bar{Z}$. Solve. If the objective function value from (26) plus $\Sigma_K \left[f_K Z_K + V_K \Sigma_{iL} D_{il} Y_{KL}\right]$ is greater than current global upper bound, stop. Otherwise $p = p + 1$. If (26) plus integer part of the objective function is less than SUB reset SUB.

Step 4. Set up master problem II. Given Π^L, U^L, ψ^{P}, $\S^P$. Solve. If the objective function value is greater than UB-ϵ, stop. If the objective function value (22) is less than $SLB + \epsilon$ then return to (1) with $\bar{Y}$, $\bar{Z}$, $\bar{W}$, $\bar{B}$. Otherwise if (22) is greater than SLB reset SLB. Go to (3).

The algorithm has worked well in trials. Convergence is guaranteed through the Benders convergence proofs and convergence does appear to be rapid.

13.7. Conclusions

This paper has demonstrated a modeling and solution strategy to remove the stringent assumption that supplies are fixed at a plant. The formulation is currently undergoing large scale implementation.

With respect to the solution methodology several questions yet remain to be studied. First, is the two level Benders Decomposition worth the trouble? Second, as Geoffrion and Graves infer would suboptimization of the master problem I (and thus MPII, SPII) be desirable? These questions are currently under study and we hope we know more about their answers in the future.

References

1. Benders, J. F., 'Partitioning Procedures for Solving Mixed-Variables Programming Problems', *Numerische Mathematick*, vol. 4 (1962), pp. 238–252.
2. Geoffrion, A. M., *Programming*, Mathematics Research Center, University of Wisconsin, Madison (May 4–6, 1970).
3. Geoffrion, A. M. and Graves, G. W., 'Multicommodity Distribution System Design by Benders Decomposition', *Management Science*, vol. 20, no. 5 (January 1974) pp. 822–844. pp. 822–844.
4. Hu, T. C., *Integer Programming and Network Flows*, Addison-Wesley Publishing Co., Reading, Mass.
5. McCarl, B. A. and Harling, K. F., 'Multicommodity Distribution Considering Demand Responsiveness', *Proceedings*, Midwest AIDS Conference, Detroit (May 6–8, 1976).
6. Zionts, Stanley, *Linear and Integer Programming*, Englewood Cliffs, N.J., Prentice-Hall (1974).

Section 5. Master production scheduling

14. Empirical relationships among budgets, other financially-oriented aggregate plans and the master production schedule (MPS)

ROBERT W. HALL and THOMAS E. VOLLMANN

Abstract

This paper is primarily concerned with what we call 'the front end' of an MRP-oriented system. In one sense, the front end is the master production schedule, but in a larger sense the master schedule may be thought of as the end product of the disaggregation process where marketing and financial inputs are translated into a schedule of specific end items. After the master production schedule has been established, MRP is the 'engine' which does a much more detailed disaggregation of this schedule into plans for detailed component parts and subassemblies. Execution systems (shop floor control and vendor follow up) are what we call the 'black end' of the MRP-oriented system. The overall MRP system involves not only disaggregation, but the ability to accurately anticipate aggregate results based on detailed actualities.

In this paper, we will concentrate on the front end portion of MRP-oriented systems. We start with a model for front end disaggregation, and thereafter illustrate front end practice based upon an in-depth study of eight companies presently in the process of implementing/using MRP-oriented systems. We conclude with a short section relating to the barriers to execution: When all is said and done, the front end is only a plan and the successful MRP company must be able to execute that plan and replan as required.

14.1. Front end disaggregation: a model

A model for front end disaggregation is presently being implemented in one of the eight companies. We feel that this model clearly shows the activities which result in the establishment of a detailed master production schedule.

14.1.1. The MRP-oriented system

Before we can adequately describe front end disaggregation, it is necessary to define a few terms and to see the relationship of the front end systems to execution. Figure 1 is a schematic of the total MRP-oriented system in place at one of the eight companies.

Figure 1 incorporates what Oliver Wight refers to as 'closed loop MRP'. Shop floor control and vendor follow-up systems routinely update relative priority data on open shop orders and purchase orders, as MRP replans component part requirements on a regenerative or net change basis. We refer to this part of an MRP-oriented system as 'the back end'. The top half of Figure 1 is the development of the day-to-day master schedule, and MRP is the time-phased gross-to-net explosion process which connects the front end and back end.

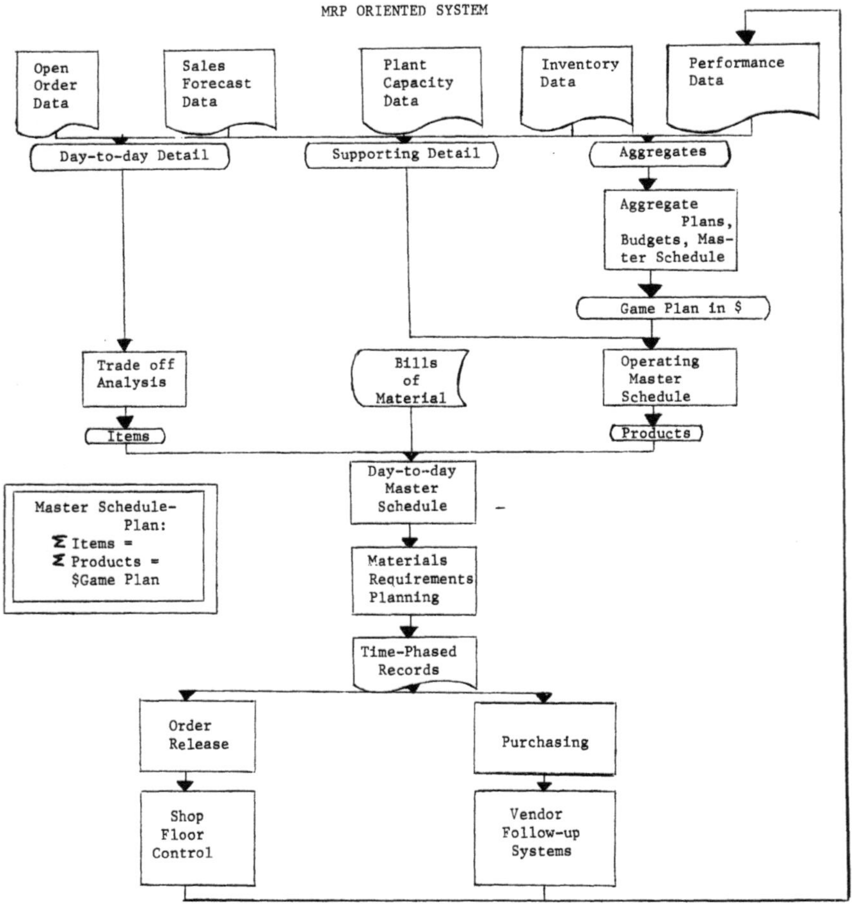

Figure 1. MRP-oriented system.

The front end of this system involves a three-tiered disaggregation process. At the first level, the executive committee determines a basic game plan for company operations. This game plan is reviewed monthly. The second level of disaggregation is done on a weekly basis by the operating master schedule committee. This group disaggregates the game plan into major product groupings and adjusts the major product mix in light of actual results. The final disaggregation involves day-to-day tradeoff analyses of specific customer orders with manufacturing capabilities.

In this three-tiered approach, the sum of the items must equal the sum of the products which must equal the game plan and corresponding production budgets. The process is not only top down. If, for example, a large customer order cannot be incorporated within a specified product plan, *and* the basic product plan itself cannot be altered within budgetary constraints, *then* the executive committee must decide if rebudgeting is desirable.

14.1.2. Level I: The executive committee

In this company, top management has made a commitment to establishing overall direction for company operations. The executive committee meets monthly for this purpose, and is responsible for providing basic input data for further disaggregation. The basic input is expressed in terms of realistic overall dollar shipment goals/expectations for each quarter for the next six quarters, and a statement of overall philosophy in terms of capacity utilization, leveling out sales peaks with inventory build-ups, the use of overtime, hiring and firing, customer delivery service, etc.

The output of the executive committee meeting is a company game plan defined in aggregate output levels for the next six quarters (18 months). This game plan is not specified in terms of individual products or product groupings, but is deliberately constrained to aggregate outputs such as sales dollars, direct labor hours, purchased material budgets, and inventory levels. The final game plan represents a top management commitment to operations: a plan which is reviewed monthly both in terms of necessary changes and evaluation of actual performance.

The monthly game plan meeting necessarily must be supported with completed staff work and performance reporting on an exception basis. Included are:

1. The vice-president of sales will have updated sales and acknowledged order information (aggregate).
2. The vice-president of manufacturing will have cost information on various levels of output, direct costs for changes in output levels, and timing data for when change decisions will be reflected in final outputs.
3. The vice-president of finance will have data on current cash position, and analyze cash flow projections under differing output-sales interaction levels.
4. Performance reporting will be available on dollar outputs vs. manufacturing plans, shipments vs. forecasts, and actual inventories vs. target inventories.
5. An analysis of significant deviations in (4) will attempt to pinpoint root causes.

The establishment of a game plan becomes the 'marching order' to subordinate functions in the company. All budgets are based upon the game plan, and performance is measured in terms of meeting the plan. It is expected that revisions in the game plan will only be warranted by significant deviations in marketing forecasts or operating results; any changes necessitate budgetary adjustments. The budgeting process is tied directly to operating results.

The monthly meeting of the executive committee is deliberately constrained to aggregates; maintenance of disaggregated plans requires full time attention, and top level management should not be concerned with individual customer orders, products, etc. On the other hand, if the executive committee is more comfortable with sales being broken down into five or ten product groupings rather than one aggregate number, the level of aggregation should be consistent with perceived or historical bases. One of our observations in the eight company study is that the higher up one goes in a company, the more people talk like accountants. It is, therefore, extremely desirable to express operating plans in financial terms, and to be able to aggregate and disaggregate on a consistent basis. The executive committee is also a good place for resolution of any significant road blocks to achievement of the company game plan. Examples include new product design status, sales campaigns, or major production problems.

14.1.3. Level 2: the operating master production schedule committee

An operating master scheduling committee is composed of representatives from manufacturing, marketing, finance, customer service, and purchasing. This group meets weekly, and has as its fundamental objective the disaggregation of the company game plan into a workable master schedule by major product line on a weekly basis for at least one year. The marketing representatives are concerned with forecasting, the booking of actual customer orders, and the firming up of that week in the master schedule which will pass over a firm time fence next. Manufacturing (including production control) is concerned with the planning and control of assembly line capacities, the establishment of materials flow to support those capacities, and the day to day maintenance of the master production schedule. Financial representatives are primarily concerned with day to day operating results and the way in which those results track overall company expectations.

The group insures that adequate support systems and information are available for the detailed decision making at the third level in the master scheduling process. Any conflicts which cannot be resolved at that level are resolved (if possible) at this level. Finally, if in preparation for the monthly executive committee meeting it seems to the operating master scheduling group that a different game plan is required, the group takes the initiative to suggest an alternative plan (or plans) for executive committee review.

14.1.4. Level 3: daily tradeoffs

The approved company game plan, now expressed in product groupings, is turned over to production control and order entry-customer service personnel. These two groups are charged with day to day disaggregation into specific end items over a 12 month planning horizon, to support actual customer orders. The day to day plan is considered 'frozen' in the short run, 'liquid' in the long run, and 'slushy' in between. The major objective of this group is to make the inevitable changes that must occur, primarily to satisfy customer delivery requirements. The principle is that while changes are inevitable, they should be done in a way that is consistent with the overall management philosophy and under a set of controlling guidelines. Example tradeoffs are:

1. Tradeoff occurs within a product line in time. Master schedule can sometimes be beefed up in the short range for a particular product if another product in the same product line (or made on the same final assembly line) can be pushed back in master schedule.
2. Tradeoffs among products in the master schedule can occur within production budget constraints, such as fully utilizing the assembly hours in a time period.
3. On a broader fiscal year basis, more substantive tradeoffs should be able to occur as long as they support the overall company game plan for the following four to six quarters as expressed in dollars and production resources.

The basic tradeoff concept is that the master schedule detailed by-product always supports an overall production plan which always supports the company game plan. Within this framework a significant increase in any one product would necessarily be offset by selected decreases in another product or products. If management modifies the dollar goal parameters, it is then necessary to replan (and re-budget) so that production, sales, and detailed product build schedules support the new aggregate goal.

14.1.5. Order entry

This company is largely a build to stock company, but myriad end product configurations forces order entry into detailed co-ordination with master scheduling so that delivery promises do not become a 'wish list'. A specific customer order needs to be analyzed in terms of each end item, first on a finished goods basis, and thereafter on a build schedule. When we reach the end of the first time fence (the frozen period), a customer order must be analyzed in terms of the product modules that will be assembled into the final item. If, on the other hand, the delivery date is beyond the sluchy period, then it can usually be immediately acknowledged and routine planning systems will insure its execution.

As can be seen, a common data base and finished goods data integrity are essential. Moreover, ongoing analysis of actual customer orders is an important part of the replanning cycle. The monitoring is done at various levels, including overall dollar sales, product groupings, and product options.

14.1.6. Capacity utilization

Once the production budgets have been set, aggregate or total capacity has been determined. That is, the establishment of the company game plan leads to exact specifications of capacity. Once the capacity has been established, production *must* work at that capacity level; not above and not below. In order to utilize that capacity completely, seasonal inventories are built and depleted (as set by the game plan). Deviations outside of some magnitude will be cause for executive committee review. Inventories are no longer viewed as something to be minimized, but as something to be planned and to be evaluated in terms of those plans.

The established plan at the operating master schedule level is used for evaluating capacity needs at both the assembly level and the work center level. That is, the overall product plans result in output levels on assembly lines; these plans must be evaluated in terms of feasibility. Similarly, the provision of component parts to satisfy those plans establishes loads on work centers. Major shifts in capacity requirements obviously call for capital expenditures and/or replanning.

14.2. Front end practice

With our model for front end disaggregation behind us, let us now turn to an overview of the eight companies, concentrating on front end disaggregation.

14.2.1. Environmental vs. managerial factors

In any comparison of MRP systems, it is useful to separate those factors that are environmental or part of the business from those that are capable of being changed. In our study of eight companies, we found three fundamental environmental factors:

1. Control over the market-distribution channel.

2. Control over the product structure.
3. Control over the production process.

The last one of these factors concerns the amount of quality failure that must be lived with, and primarily relates to problems in execution. However, master scheduling problems do result, particularly when an entire batch of some product has to be rescheduled because of quality loss. In one of the eight companies, the master schedule was onsistently overstated by a constant percentage hopefully to allow for the quality losses. The result was an overstated master schedule, poor operating results, overstocks on low quality loss components, and shortages on high quality loss components.

Control over the product structure relates to the degree in which the parent company has control over the design specification. For the company that builds to stock or at least controls design to a large extent, bills of material can be more standardized, data base maintenance is eased, and customer orders can more quickly be converted into detailed plans. The pure make to order company, with design residing in the hands of the customer, has both front end and execution difficulties.

Control over the marketing channel has distinct advantages. Companies who control distribution inventories can use them to level demand on their production facilities. The key result is far greater ability to smooth master scheduling requirements, and to generate plans which are more efficient in terms of capacity utilization. Companies who have a large number of customers also have advantages. Those who serve a small group of customers tend to attempt scheduling handsprings to keep customers pleased. Companies who deal with a stable marketplace and are able to adjust prices and advertising to accelerate and decelerate specific product sales similarly have important advantages.

Environmental factors must be lived with. On the other hand, managerial factors can be changed; the key question is how well is one playing the hand he has been dealt? Our study identified eleven factors over which management has some degree of control:

1. Master scheduling
2. Order entry
3. Shop floor control
4. Purchasing systems

5. Data integrity
6. Engineering change
7. Common data base
8. Materials management organization
9. Working capital management
10. Managerial leadership
11. Managing the environment

Each of the eight companies maintained some schedule for end items, but significant differences existed in the formality and integration with other subsystems. In our model shown in Figure 1, we saw that it is important to integrate the master scheduling process with overall company planning activities. Companies using the master schedule to drive MRP usually achieve a renewed understanding of the necessary level of detail required in planning and the need to close the loop. Budgets and other aggregate plans must be unambiguously translated into end item catalog numbers or product features (modules) that are consistent with bill of material data. The problem is *any* consistent or feasible disaggregation – not finding the optimum.

The entry of actual customer orders must be closely integrated with other parts of the materials flow system for all but the pure make to stock company. Even for the companies that control the distribution channel, coordinated decisions are required for order entry. For the custom make to order company, the bill of material may well not be specified until the order is received – sometimes the detailed bill requirements are not even complete at that point. This condition causes serious front end and back end problems. Establishment of delivery dates is often guided by standard quotation dates, but competitive pressures and production realities make these times approximate at best. It is our observation that those companies doing the best job have mechanisms for systematic feedback from production operations to the sales staff and customer service.

Shop floor control systems and purchasing follow-up systems are concerned with execution, a matter to be considered in a subsequent section. Similarly, data integrity and engineering change systems act primarily to support execution. The remaining five factors affect both front end planning and back end execution.

The first of these, the common data base, is in many ways the ultimate objective of the MRP based system. In order for proper disaggregation of planning functions to take place and for the execution to be consistent with plans, it is essential for everyone to be 'singing from the same hymn book'. Achievement of this commonality is never easy, and many companies who are supposedly implementing MRP lack the intestinal fortitude to carry through on this issue.

The materials management organization represents grouping together under a single command the functions of purchasing, production planning, shop floor control, store-rooms, shipping, receiving, and data base maintenance (to include engineering change). In the course of our study whenever we found one of these activities organizationally separate, some price was paid in effectiveness.

Those companies with more pieces of an integrated MRP system in a place seem to feel less direct financial pressure than the run of the mill company. Inventory target levels (and other working capital targets) are based more on what appears necessary to run the business than on arbitrary ratios and pressure to wring cash out of inventory. The top management view of inventory is important. Successful companies view inventory as something for use in the business, not as something static, fixed in storerooms, and a sinkhole for working capital. In part, this is a matter of confidence in the operating system, and integration of financial plans with operations. Actual inventory levels are the detailed residual of what happened, reflecting poor forecasts, errors made, and future plans. Management must avoid the adjustment of operating plans with non-consistent aggregate financial tools.

As far as managerial leadership is concerned the key observation we found in our study is that each successful MRP implementation (two) was led by a senior manager, backed up by a well selected team of key users, not computer whiz kids. Managers who know how and why operating systems work, and how those systems need to be integrated, must put systems revisions into affect. At locations where computer-oriented personnel are the key movers for a revised system, progress is slow or stymied.

Finally, the environment is not something that one must necessarily take as a given. Improved technology may reduce variability in the process, cooperative engineering ventures may improve control over product structure, and sales/marketing efforts may overcome some of the ill effects resulting from lack of control in the marketing channel. The integration potential of MRP oriented systems clearly points out the payoffs in changing our destiny.

14.2.2. Detailed observations

Let us now turn to the study of the eight companies, which cover a spectrum from a very successful user of MRP to companies in various stages of MRP implementation, to one company which is just becoming aware of the need to better control the flow of materials. Detailed reporting of each company is clearly beyond the scope of this paper, and it is also beyond our present scope to go very deeply into execution systems. We will, therefore, concentrate on front end issues.

14.2.2.1. Company A. Company A is the only one of the eight companies which can claim to have a completely implemented MRP-based production/inventory control system. The company is a Fortune 500 company with a primarily product line of consumer electronics. The complex products are nationally advertised under the company brand name through a dominated network of dealers and distributors. Company A is essentially a make to stock company, although finished goods are immediately pushed into the distribution system. The production process is almost exclusively assembly of purchased components. Production/inventory control is strongly guided by two committees, one for the front end (finished product scheduling) and one for the back end (production, purchasing, and inventory control to support the finished product plan). MRP connects these two committees.

Company A schedules all eleven domestic plants from the home office. Great stability is provided to the master schedule by the commitments of Company A's distributors, who each quarter sign firm agreements to accept inventory. Weekly reports from the distributors and retailers provide quick feedback on what models are or are not selling. This information is used to make final adjustments in the master schedule, and is very important early in each model year. Fast feedback through the front end of the production system is very important to market share and profitability.

Almost all production schedule changes are in timing, not quantity. Most changes are negotiated with sales to prevent distributors from running low on popular models. The production front end system is supported with a well integrated data base, including reliable component stock records at all company locations.

Company A's marketing plan, not the financial plan, directs operations. According to the treasurer, 'We do not let the financial impact of the demand for cash run our business. We would be in deep trouble if we did. We plan carefully what we will market, how we will market it, and then what inventory we will need to support that plan. It is necessary to come up with the financing to support that plan.'

Company A's domination of the marketing channel allows them to control the timing of shipments; they are not subjected to violent order changes to support customer crises. We believe that Company A's ability to implement their advanced system is partially due to the more stable environment they face. It is also facilitated by their control of the product structure, by limited work in process inventories (subassemblies), and by integrating the front end of their production system with marketing and financial planning.

14.2.2.2. Company B. Company B is the largest operating division of a medium-sized corporation, and has been actively working on MRP-oriented systems for three years. The ability to produce basic time-phased gross-to-net explosions was accomplished in one year, with subsequent efforts directed to front end and back end systems. The front end has had more extensive work than the back end, and in fact the most serious weakness at Company B is its lack of execution systems. The master schedule covers one year, based on a forecast, modified by the accumulation of actual orders. The first three months are frozen in an attempt to insulate the shop from schedule changes, but the freeze period turns out to be 'truth by proclamation,' and is frequently violated by customer order changes. In fact, about twenty-five percent of all orders are changed after the order is already started in production. Many orders have to be discussed between Company B's engineers and customer engineers, and committing to a specific order can be complex. Frequently not all specification issues are settled when the order is scheduled.

Most of Company B's sales go to OEM customers, and in some

instances the decision point for exact product specification is with the *customer* of the OEM. As a result, Company B lacks complete control over the product structure. Moreover, they are frequently whipsawed on delivery dates to make up for problems in OEM schedules. An interesting feature of Company B's operation is that some of their worst customers are MRP users. These customers tend to pass all their planning changes onto B without buffering. In contrast, the easiest OEM account provides no forecast at all. They give orders with a long enough lead time to cover B's production planning process; they rarely change their mind, and Company B rarely misses on time delivery. Partially because of their instabilities in the front end, it has not been possible to integrate financial planning with materials flow systems. On the other hand, these problems may well have become a crutch to support poor managerial practices. There is always an end of month rush to get out shipments, so that plant operations show black instead of red. This rush results in a vicious cycle, since the early part of the following month faces a dry pipeline. Worse, the objective becomes shipments rather than master schedule; the expenditors find *something* – anything – that can be pulled into assembly to get dollars. Shipments thus determined, *become* the aggregate – based not on any plan – but on what is possible. No one at the company has given serious thought to changing this environment or considering its effect on subsequent schedule changes.

14.2.2.3. Company C. Company C represents a small company with very limited formal systems, where growing pains are making the need for such systems more and more apparent. The company is privately held and operated, with annual sales of approximately $15 million. The product line is specialty drilling equipment; a typical drilling rig is installed on a truck or tractor as specified by the customer. The company does not dominate their marketing channel, but neither are they clearly dominated by others in it. They are an original equipment manufacturer, and have the ability to suggest design features to their customers. The aggregate plan (if one exists) is book all the orders possible, then make them. When capacity gets clogged up – get some more.

The front end of Company C's system is informal, features good communications, and is more stable than at Company B. Few orders are cancelled or changed; the exact specification of what is to be built is greatly helped by engineering, sales, and production personnel all reporting to the same location. Every Monday there is a scheduling meeting at which order status and customer priorities are reviewed. All managers stated the meeting was essential to good communications; they had tried other approaches and confusion resulted.

In a small company like C, the clear distinction between the front end and back end of the production/inventory control system is blurred. The production manager does all production control, knows many of the customers himself, and sometimes second guesses the sales priorities. He sees his job as keeping the front end and the back end of production system tied together.

Company C has just entered a new phase. Product growth and increased spare parts demand are putting pressure on the company; it is being increasingly recognized that the company cannot afford to carry as much inventory as everyone might like. Financial controls and inventory procedures are being tightened, but getting control of the inventory is proving difficult. Obsolescence and stockouts are both increasing and on-hand balances are inaccurate. Clerical inaccuracies often preclude proper transaction reporting, and procedures tend to be overridden by people who get the product out the door. The company lacks a coherent plan for new products and spare parts. The result is day-to-day decision making on a crisis-to-crisis basis, and overall production becoming the summation of chaos instead of the game plan for disaggregation.

14.2.2.4. Company D. Company D is a large canning company which packs under their own label as well as for labels of major retailers. They operate canning factories, some year around and some only in season, and schedule all production from one centralized location. The centralization of scheduling was accomplished within one year, and is integrated with financial and marketing plans. Their system is facilitated by a strong position in the marketing channel, and the company also has control of production design, within reason. There are few execution problems, since there are no job shop operations. Centralized scheduling has provided the company much greater control over operations and the ability to tie operating decisions to overall company objectives.

14.2.2.5. Company E. Company E makes components for heavy equipment drive train and braking systems; they have a very severe problem with production process control since the production process is still somewhat in the art stage. This lack of control results in many execution system problems. The company has just realized that there are also front end problems that result as well. With sales reporting to a location eight hundred miles away, order entry is particularly difficult.

14.2.2.6. Company F. Company F is one division of a Fortune 500 company which produces components primarily sold to the automotive and machine tool industries. This company has had MRP running for four years, but is not achieving significant benefits. Symptoms of the problem can be found in execution systems, but the basic problem is managerial. The company has an environment of power politics with a very poor degree of integration between marketing, finance, and production. In particular, 'customer crises' occasionally become so desperate that sales representatives directly intervene on the production floor, countermanding the orders given by schedulers. None of the managers believed enough in the companies record system to use it for planning. The company is run by financial people who emphasize inventory turnover targets. Their goal is to make turnover improve just a little bit, but there is no method by which to make this happen. The company has tried all the get-well-quick cures of EOQ, MRP, and others. They did not affect the basic sickness. Top management simply must get marketing, production, and finance to submit to the discipline of working together, using one system, and a common data base, before there is any hope for progress.

14.2.2.7. Company G. This company manufactures equipment used in hospitals and nursing homes; the products are largely built to stock. The company has been in an MRP implementation for two years, with the ability to produce time-phased records in eight months. Subsequent efforts resulted in implementation of shop floor control and data record accuracy systems. Present efforts are devoted to master scheduling and order entry. The company maintains control over the product structure and its ability to stock fast selling items also gives it an advantage over companies such as 'B'. The integration or order entry with master scheduling is a strong point in its favor. The managerial commitment exists all the way up the management structure to the top of the company, and computer support exists for establishment of a common data base.

14.2.2.8. Company H. This was the smallest company surveyed, a foundry serving a local area. The company is run on a very informal basis, with no computer touching any part of its operations. Management thinks in terms of a three week lead time, and this serves for both order promising and order scheduling. The actual orders involve many changes on the part of customers, and the president quipped, 'If they don't scream, they don't get it.' No unit inventory records are kept, and a physical inventory is taken once a month to make up financial statements. The company is just beginning to think of formal systems. Managers are no longer able to survey the foundry floor and apprise themselves of order status. As one manager said, 'Up until now we could run the place by coming every morning, seeing how many showed up and how many went fishing, and figuring out what to do for the day. As soon as a customer needed special attention we gave it to him.' An interesting situation: no problems with communicating over long distances, everyone looking at the same data base on the foundry floor, and an informal system that works; but how long can it stay that way?

14.3. Barriers to execution

In the remaining space available in this paper, we would like to point out briefly some of the barriers to execution of the front end plans we saw in the eight company sample.

14.3.1. Back end

Shop floor control systems were primitive in some of the companies and non-existent in others. In particular, Company B had no formal system of shop floor control, and really did not know what was happening on the shop floor. The informal systems broke down, with expediting and pulling of component parts as required by assembly schedules. In fact, the company has just regained the right to know shop status after negotiation with the union. Other job shop companies (with the exception of 'G') had shop floor control problems, but not as severely as Company B. In all cases, these represent severe obstacles to the achievement of planning objectives.

A similar lack of closing the loop was found in many purchasing environments. Instead of treating vendor capacities as if they were part of the same system, many companies used the 'lie and scream' approach. Fifty cents of each sales dollar for the eight companies went out as purchased parts. This represents a great deal of inter-company flow, but we saw no one seriously considering how to best treat the resultant larger systems. In fact, we saw good evidence that many companies with sophisticated systems were amplifying the effects on their suppliers.

14.3.2. Support systems

The most basic problem that we saw in many MRP implementations was the lack of abililty to believe the paper. Without data integrity almost any system is certainly going to fail. Almost every company recognized this, but it is only those who have gone far enough into MRP to realize the essential role of data believability that have undertaken the effort to achieve integrity in on-hand balances and other inventory records.

A related effort involves engineering change. Almost every company recognized the need for engineering change control, but few of them were taking the organizational steps necessary to provide one focal point in the company where authorization, notification, and implementation procedures could be centralized. Company A, on the other hand, had a well thought out and implemented engineering change control system with one focal point in the organization. The results are dramatic, especially for a company that goes through an annual model changeover.

The final support system has already been mentioned: the need for a common data base. It is amazing how very few companies can ask more than three people to give them the number for sales for some prior month and come up with the same result. Serious efforts have to be devoted to getting everyone to sing from the same hymn book. Most companies recognize this need, but don't follow it through with the managerial direction to support the long term systems efforts required.

14.3.3. Managerial factors

The last set of barriers to execution we would like to mention include organizational kinds of issues. We have mentioned already that we must have managerial leadership for both the front end and the back end. We also found that in every case where a materials management type of organization did not exist, some price was paid in effectiveness. In the last analysis, the MRP-oriented company is substantially different from its predecessor. It can only be the top management of a company who can direct this change process. Without their active involvement and support, the effort will only be half-hearted.

15. Hedging the master schedule

JEFFREY G. MILLER

Abstract

Hedging is a master scheduling tactic which allows variations in the level of uncertainty and cost commitments over time to be taken into consideration in ordering decisions. It results in 'pipeline safety stocks' rather than finished goods safety stocks. Because of the value added structure of most firms, pipeline safety stocks require a lower investment in inventory than the latter approach. In this paper, hedging as it occurs in industry is described. In addition, examples are used to show its advantages, and as vehicles for illustrating some fundamental concepts. The paper concludes with a description of the management decisions involved in controlling hedging, and an overview of the research needs in the area.

15.1. Hedging the master schedule

Finished goods safety stocks have been historically viewed as the most appropriate method of protecting against uncertainties in demand when immediate delivery is important. Most of the theory that supports this usage of the safety stock strategy focuses on the uncertainty in demand over the entire lead time required to produce or procure a finished product [9]. A powerful alternative to finished goods safety stocks however, is the utilization of a 'pipeline' safety stock strategy which exploits the dependent demand relationships between final products and intermediate stages in the production-procurement cycle. This strategy can be employed when the master schedule of finished goods output is manipulated by hedging on estimates of future output. The purpose of this paper is to define and explore the utility of hedging ('pipeline' safety stock) strategies.

15.1.1. The master schedule hedge

The master schedule hedge should be distinguished at the outset from its close conceptual relative, the materials hedge. The latter is employed to protect against fluctuations in materials prices. The master schedule hedge is used to pull 'pipeline safety stocks' through a production inventory system to protect against stock-outs or undesirable backlogs. Hedging to create pipeline safety stocks has a long history of usage going back to the first time that a manufacturer 'bet on the come', by placing an order for some materials that would be used in producing a single product if a bid was awarded, while hoping that the order could be cancelled if the bid for the business did not come through. The advent of material requirements planning (MRP) systems however has firmly placed this strategy within the reach of producers of the most complex products, and has extended its applicability beyond bid businesses to consumer goods producers who face a steady, albeit fluctuating stream of demand. This is not surprising, since the hedging concept can only be implemented when the different parts and components in a finished item's product structure are tied together with 'depend demand' logic. Thus, before hedging is defined and illustrated, it is necessary to review some important concepts related to the use of MRP.

Exhibit 1 illustrates a typical 'dependent' manufacturing product structure. The end or finished product, item 0,1, is assembled from two subassemblies, items 1,1 and 1,2. These are in turn assembled from components 2,1 2,2, and 2,3 respectively. The 'dependent demand' logic of MRP ties these items together by successively deriving demand for items at lower levels in the product structure from higher level successor items, while netting out intermediate inventories at all stages in the structure. This approach can be contrasted to other types of systems which 'decouple 'the inventories and management of the various parts and components in the product structure by *assuming* that they are technologically independent of one another.

Recognition of the dependent relationship implied by a product structure has allowed manufacturers who have adopted MRP systems to distinguish clearly and understand the impact of two well-known phenomena on their operations and decisions, that in

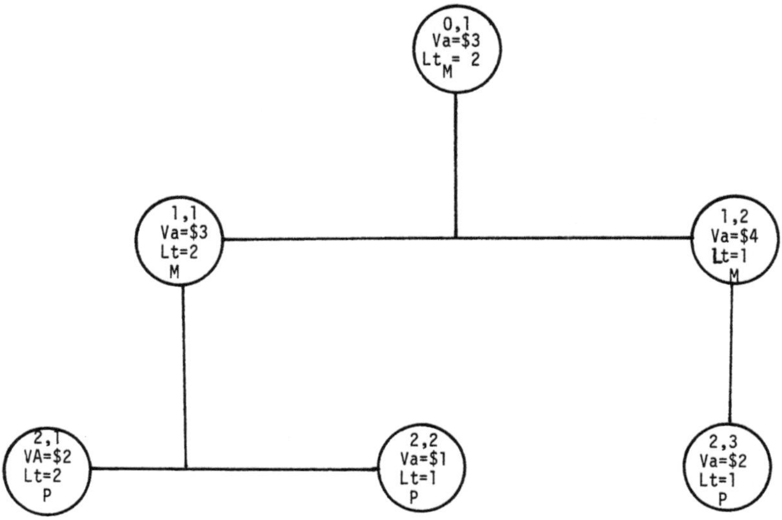

The first set of numbers denotes the item number, e.g., level 0, item 1, level 1, item 1, etc.

Va = Value added at each stage of manufacture or purchase (denoted by M or P). Thus, level two items are all purchased, level 1 items are subassemblies, and level 0 is the finished end product.

Lt = the procurement or manufacturing lead time.

Exhibit 1. Example product structure.

turn have led to the concept of hedging. The first phenomenon is that forecasts of demand in the distant future are less reliable than those made for the near term. This generalization has not only been empirically deduced by a number of experienced practitioners [7, 10] but it also can be shown to exist with statistical theory. Exhibit 2, for example, illustrates the increasing standard deviation of forecast error that applies when cumulative demand is forecast over longer periods. It was derived by applying fundamental concepts relating to the variance of sums of random variables.[1]

When one examines these facts while considering a product structure such as the one shown in Exhibit 1, a rather obvious conclusion results: specifically, that there is more uncertainty associated with

1. Namely, the standard deviation of forecast error for cumulative demand over N periods is equal to the square root of the sum of the variances that apply to each of the N periods individually [1].

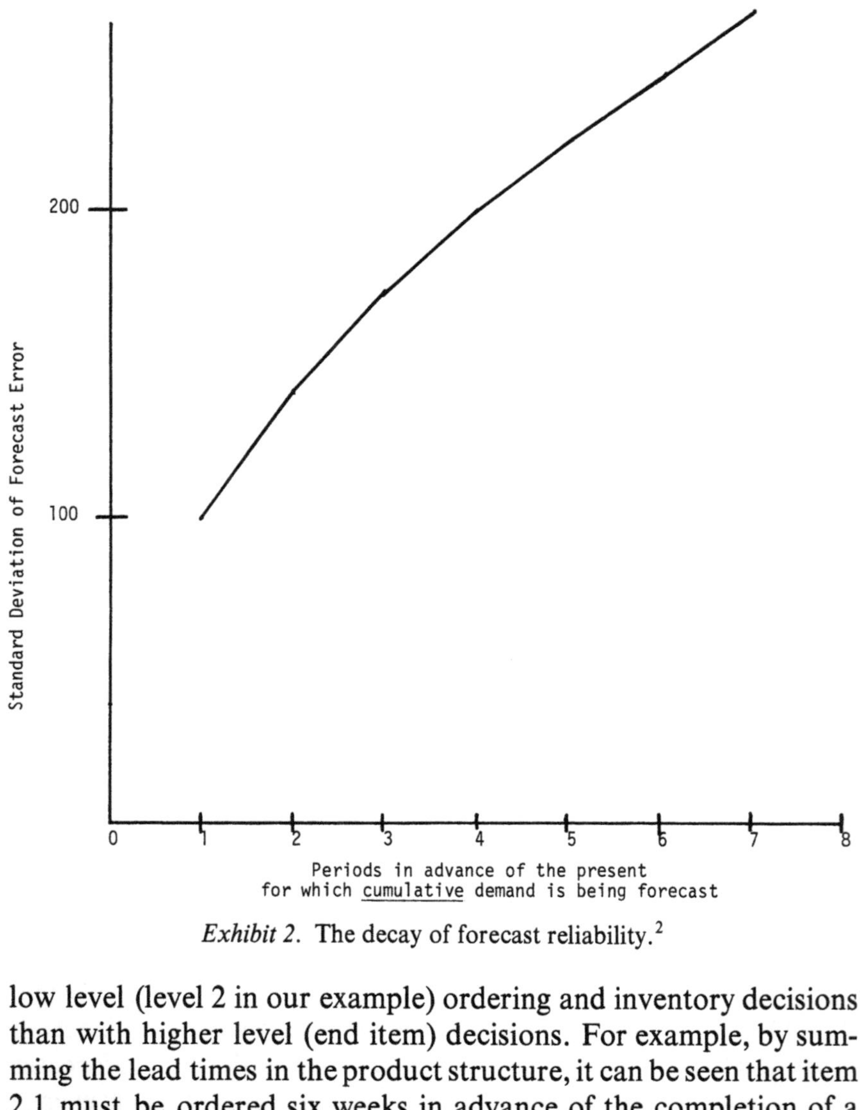

Exhibit 2. The decay of forecast reliability.[2]

low level (level 2 in our example) ordering and inventory decisions than with higher level (end item) decisions. For example, by summing the lead times in the product structure, it can be seen that item 2,1 must be ordered six weeks in advance of the completion of a finished product, when forecast error is high, but that a decision to assemble the end item (assuming subassemblies are available) must be made only two weeks in advance of completion. Obviously, the

2. Assuming a single period standard-deviation of forecast error of 100, and that forecast error for each period is an independent random variable. Thus the standard deviation of forecast error for a two period cumulative forecast is, for example, equal to $\sqrt{100^2 + 100^2} = 141$.

latter decision can be made with more certain estimates of demand, relative to a particular period in which a demand is supposed to exist, than the former.

The second important fact, which also flows directly from the concepts of product structure and dependent demand, is that manufacturing costs and commitments to expenditures are time phased. Exhibit 3 illustrates this graphically. It shows a 'commitment profile,' which portrays the cumulation of value or cost commitments in the course of manufacturing a product which is due for completion at a specific point in time. This graph was constructed by cumulating the value added associated with each item in Exhibit 1, over the corresponding cumulative lead time required to 'commit' to the procurement of components, receive them, and then to manufacture the subassemblies and the end product. Of course, every manufacturing firm will exhibit a different and presumably unique commitment profile as shown in Exhibit 4. The way value is added over time will depend upon such factors as the degree of vertical integration, the process technolgy employed, and vendor lead times. However, the mere fact that manufacturing value in any case is added over time, coupled with the forecast decay phenomenon, leads one to a rather obvious but fundamental conclusion. This is that while there may be more uncertainty associated with ordering and inventorying low level items than high level (finished) items in a product structure, the costs (penalties) associated with these uncertainties will vary depending on the way value is added to a product over time. This generalization forms the basis for hedging.

To be more specific, hedging refers to a master scheduling tactic which results in order quantities for parts, components and end products that vary in accordance with the differentials over time between relative uncertainties (from forecast decay) and costs (from adding value). The result of hedging is a 'paper' or 'pipeline' safety stock, rather than a large safety stock of end product in the physical sense. The following example illustrates the way a hedging tactic is implemented in a 'static' situation.

Assume that a firm produces a non-standard product for a particular customer with the product structure, costs, lead times, and subsequent commitment profile shown in Exhibits 1 and 3. Further assume that the customer is expected to require 1000 units (±300) for immediate delivery six weeks in the future, and that market

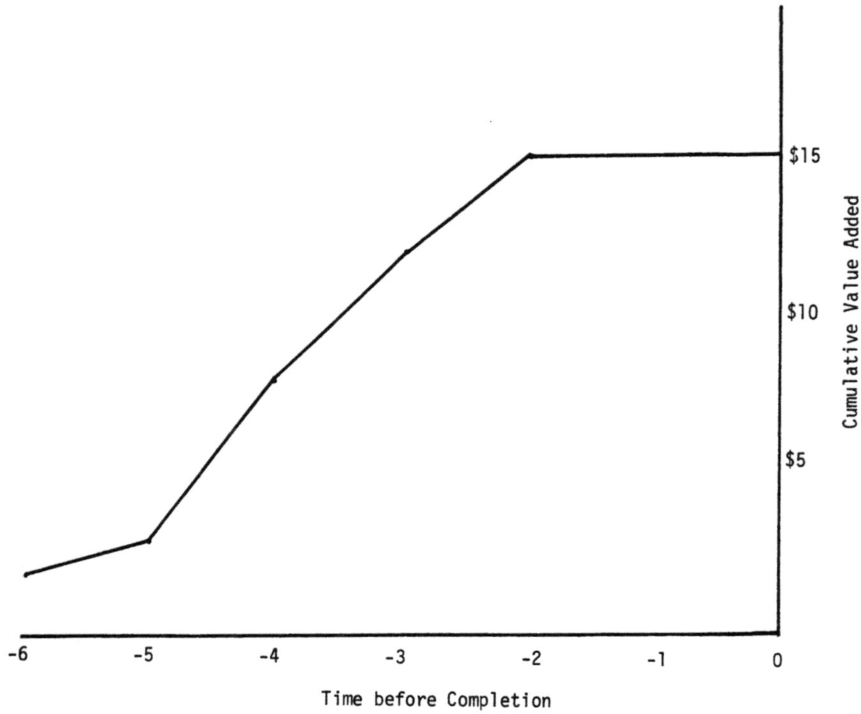

Exhibit 3. Commitment profile.

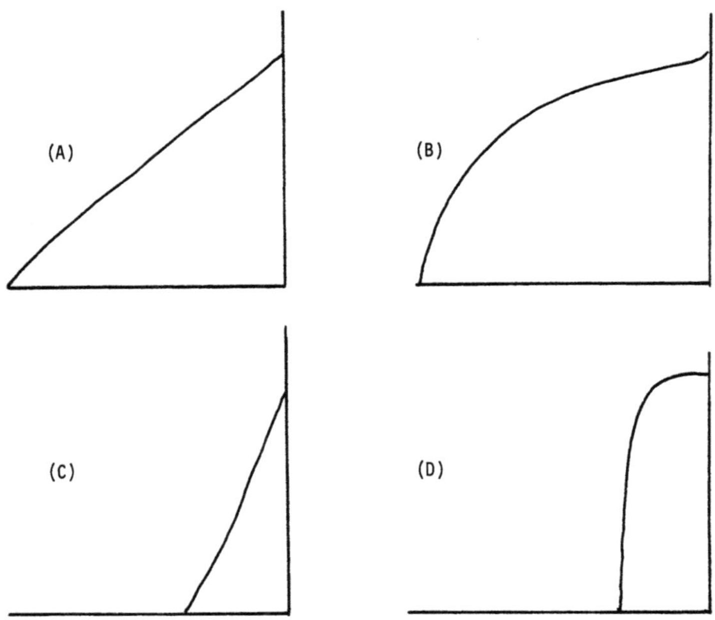

Exhibit 4. Types of commitment profiles.

forces dictate a $10/unit penalty if the firm is unable to meet any of that customer's order at that time. If there are no inventories of any of the parts and components in the product structure on hand, and none are on order, than the company must place orders for item 2,1 now, if it is to satisfy the anticipated order. Given an MRP system, this is equivalent to requiring that a quantity for the product in question must be placed in the master schedule six weeks from the present. The master schedule will then be exploded and a notice to purchase part 2,1 will automatically be generated.

The problem that this example company faces at this point in time is determining the quantity to place in the master schedule. If it decides on scheduling 1000 units, the expected order, there is a good chance that the customer will require more than that, and that penalty costs will be incurred. On the other hand, if the company 'hedges' by specifying 1000 (the expected order) plus say 300 (the hedge) to protect against the stockout, that portion of the quantity produced that is not taken by the customer will have to be declared obsolete inventory and discarded, or, in other instances, held as excess inventory.

Clearly, this problem is similar to the classical 'newsboy' problem [8], with one exception. Only a portion of the total costs of production must be commited to now, namely, those associated with item 2,1. With a six week manufacturing and procurement lead time, revised hedging decisions can be made on the basis of new information before additional commitments are made.

To make the initial decision on the amount to place in the master schedule, the methodology of the newsboy problem can be applied. This involves calculating a critical fractile [8], which yields the probability at which the costs of stocking out and the costs of obsolescence are equalized, and in conjunction with a distribution of demand, can be used to determine the 'optimal' order quantity:

$$\text{Critical fractile} = \frac{Cu}{Cu + Co} = \frac{\$10}{\$10 + \$2} = .833$$

Where:

Cu = the cost per unit of not having enough to satisfy the customer's needs

Co = the cost per unit of having more than the customer

requires, namely, the cost of discarding the product or materials involved.

The critical fractile here is .833, indicating that it would be prudent to select a master schedule quantity such that there were about 83 chances out of a hundred that the customer's order would be met. Thus, presuming the prerequisite distribution of demand, the firm would select a relatively high hedge, say 200 units, and place a total of 1200 units in the master schedule. An MRP system would then translate this master scheduling decision, via the explosion process, into an order for 1200 of item 2,1. Note that at this point, the company is protected with a hedge, or a 'safety stock' against the uncertainties of future demand. Note also, however, that at this point protection costs nothing, since the 'safety stock' is on paper (a purchase order) rather than in the stockroom.

Stepping through time, the example firm might find itself in a different situation after two weeks (four weeks from the date of the anticipated order). At this point, presuming no intermediate changes in the master schedule, it would find that (1) the 1200 units of 2,1 have arrived from the vendor (now there is inventory), and (2) that it would have ordered and received 1200 units of 2,2 in the interim, and (3) it might have new forcast information on the customer's anticipated order. The firm may determine, for example, that the new demand estimate is 1100, plus or minus 50 units. This is certainly a relevant piece of information, since an order for items 2,3 and 1,1 must be placed now if the schedule is to be maintained. While the firm cannot at this point avoid the consequences of its first hedge, since the costs for 2,1 and 2,2 are sunk, it may want to revise the hedge in light of this new information.

Calculation of the critical fractile using the value added figures for 2,3 and 1,1 from Exhibit 1 results in a new optimal risk level of .66. That is, from the firm's current vantage point in time, and considering the value added structure of the company, it is now only worthwhile to schedule production such that there are 66 chances out of 100 of meeting the customer's requirements. Thus, after considering the new distribution of demand, the firm may decide to change the master schedule quantity of 1125 units. This change will mean that the company has 'given up' on 75 units of item 2,1 and 2,2, since there is no way that they will be utilized in constructing the quantity of end product that will eventually be used to satisfy the customer. However, that is the risk that was taken initially, and there is no going back on it.

Exhibit 5 contains an analysis of the situation, decisions, and results that might apply were the firm to continue stepping through time with this example problem. However, by now, the example should have illustrated several important points about hedging:

1. Hedging the master schedule is designed to keep safety stocks in the supply pipeline, rather than in the stockroom in finished product form.
2. Even where physical stocks of inventory do result, they are maintained at the lower end of the product structure, where cumulative value added loss is minimized. Thus hedging is less costly than finished goods safety stocks.
3. Hedging is only effective when one is willing to change or modify the hedge with the passage of time and the acquisition of new information.
4. Hedge decisions are amenable to analysis with statistical tools, but judgement is an important input in gauging the penalties, costs, and subjective probabilities required to perform a statistical analysis.

The simplified example problem that has just been explored is similar in principle to the situations faced by many industrial firms who must produce at least a part of their non-standard products in anticipation of particular customer orders, but not to a finished goods inventory. In two such cases, Perkin Elmer [4], and Granger Transmission [5] (name disguised) hedging of the type described has been employed as a competitive weapon. In both of these cases, hedges are administered on a judgemental basis with a special master schedule authorization called a 'management stock order.' Management stock orders are issued from the general management level to ensure that, in their words, 'the major risks of the company are considered at the highest levels.' Since both of these firms exhibit commitment profiles similar to (b) in Exhibit 4, it is not surprising that hedging decisions for them do represent 'major risks.'

TIME PERIODS

0	1	2	3	4	5	6
<u>Situation</u> Expect customer to order 1000 ± 300 units for delivery at end of period 6	<u>Situation</u> Unchanged	<u>Situation</u> New forecast information indicates customer will order 1100 ± 50 for delivery at the end of period 6. Orders for 1200 of items 2,1 and 2,2 have arrived and are in inventory	<u>Situation</u> 1125 units of item 2,3 arrive in inventory	<u>Situation</u> New forecast indicates customer will order 1100 ± 10, 1125 units of 1,1 arrive in inventory	<u>Situation</u> No change	<u>Situation</u> 1110 units of 0,1 (final product) arrive in inventory Customer takes 1100 units, relieving inventory of 1100 units
<u>Decison</u> Place 1200 units in time bucket t+6 in the master schedule. This will generate an order for 1200 item 2,1.	<u>Decision</u> Explosion of the master schedule will automatically generate an order for 1200 of item 2,2.	<u>Decision</u> Change Master schedule to 1125 units, this will generate an order for 1125 of items 2,3 and 1,1.	<u>Decision</u> Explosion of master schedule will generate an order for 1125 of item 1,2.	<u>Decision</u> Change master schedule to 1100 units. This will generate an order for 1110 units of item 0,1.	<u>Decision</u> None	<u>Decision</u> None
<u>Result</u> Expected Order =1000 Hedge = 200 Inventory = 0 Value of commitments made = $1200x2=$2400	<u>Result</u> Expected Order = 1000 Hedge = 200 Inventory = 0 Value of commitments made = 1200 x 1 = $1200	<u>Result</u> Expected Order = 1100 Hedge = 25 Inventory=$3600 Value of commitments made = 1125x($3 + $1) = $4500	<u>Result</u> Expected Order = 1100 Hedge = 25 Inventory=$4725 Value of commitments made = 1125 x$4 =4500	<u>Result</u> Expected Order = 1100 Hedge = 10 Inventory=$9225 Value of commit ments made = $3x1100=$3300	<u>Result</u> No Change	<u>Result</u> Final Inventory 75(2,1) = $150 75(2,2) = $ 75 0(2,3) = $ 0 15(1,1) = $ 45 15(1,2) = $ 60 10(0,1) = $150 $780
Cum. Value = = $2400	Cum. = $3600	Cum. = $8100	Cum. = $12,600	Cum. = $15930		

Exhibit 5. Hedging through time.

15.1.2. Dynamic hedging

Most of the hedging activity that has been observed in practice has been in response to situations similar to that illustrated by the previous example problem. This type of hedging is called 'static' hedging, since each hedge is oriented toward a particular customer or new product introduction on a one time basis. A different variation of the hedging tactic must be applied where the products of the firm are standardized, produced on a near continuous basis, and distributed to a broad customer base. In such situations, hedge tactics must be continually applied and reapplied, hence, the term dynamic hedging.

To illustrate the concept of dynamic hedging, and some of the tools which may be useful in administering it, we again turn to an example problem. In this case, again suppose that the hypothetical firm is producing the product whose features are characterized in Exhibit 1. Moreover, assume:

1. That the finished product must be immediately available to any customer, and that management has set a service standard of 95 percent. That is, that 95 percent of customer requests on a unit basis must be satisfied immediately. If they are not, the sale is lost.
2. A forecasting procedure is used to predict future demand. This procedure has predicted sales of 1000 units for each of the next 12 periods (say 12 weeks). The standard deviation of forecast error for a single period forecast is 100 units.
3. The forecast is revised each period, but, for the sake of this illustration, continues to be 1000 units.
4. A lot for lot order quantity rule is used. This means that the lot size for each item at each level is equal to the new requirements for the period in question.
5. An MRP system is in use.
6. The beginning inventory and scheduled receipts for each item[3] are as follows:

   0,1, Beginning inventory = 200, 100 due in period 1, 1083 units due in period 2

3. For the sake of simplicity in illustrating the dynamic hedge, the inventory behavior of only the following three items in the product structure will be tracked.

1,1, Beginning inventory = 63, 1000 due in period 1, 1054 units due in period 2
2,1, Beginning inventory = 47, 1000 due in period 1, 1043 units due in period 2

In this example, the firm has two clear alternative strategies. The first strategy involves employing finished goods safety stock to protect against the uncertainties in demand. Using classical inventory control methods, the amount of safety stock that would be required to protect against stockouts over the entire manufacturing and procurement lead time would be 529 units. This can be calculated by using the single period estimate of the standard deviation of forecast error to estimate the standard deviation of forecast error over seven[4] periods (e.g., $\sigma_7 = \sqrt{7 \times \sigma_1^2} = 264.5$). Assuming normality then, 95 percent protection can be ensured by using a safety stock of $2 \times 264.5 = 529$ units. The uppermost inventory planning form in Exhibit 6 shows how a master schedule (that portion denoted by the 'planned orders' row) can be derived while assuming this level of safety stock protection. Safety stock is ensured in this procedure by *planning* so that the on-hand balance will be maintained at the 529 units level.[5] Naturally, the low initial inventory prevents this in the first two periods.

The second alternative for the example company is to recognize that uncertainty varies with the time span over which plans are being laid. In other words, the second alternative is to hedge. Dynamic hedging requires that one recognize that 529 units is really more protection than is required for much of the future. It is true that seven weeks into the future, the uncertainty is great, and that 529 units will be needed then (from the perspective of the present) to maintain a 95 percent service level. Thus, decisions that must be made now for such future periods (the ordering of item 2,1) should reflect this. But, by the same token there is much less uncertainty related to the present decision on how much of item 0,1 to begin assembling for use two periods hence. In this case, the standard

4. Note that the manufacturing and procurement lead time for the longest sequence in the product structure is six weeks, but that inventory and forecasts are reviewed weekly. Therefore, an extra 'review' period must be added to the lead time.
5. A safety stock strategy of this sort is usually accompanied by a 'freeze' of the master schedule over the production/procurement lead time. Naturally, if uncertainty does indeed exist, the *planned* on hand balance will not actually materialize.

deviation of cumulative forecast error is only $\sqrt{3\sigma^2} = 173$, and $2 \times 173 = 246$ units are all that are needed in finished goods safety stock to protect against demand uncertainties. The second inventory planning schedule in Exhibit 6 shows how these differences in the level of uncertainty over time can be taken into account. Here, a 'hedge' which is equal to the level of safety stock required for *each* time period is added to the projected gross requirements for the item. This, clearly, results in a far lower expected level of one-hand inventory over time than the safety stock strategy.

The safety stock approach involves maintaining a constant 529 units at the end item level. The hedge strategy will result in some safety stock at the end item level, with the rest of the 'safety

Exhibit 6. Master schedule with safety stock (529 units).

Item 0,1

Period	1	2	3	4	5	6	7	8
Requirements	1000	1000	1000	1000	1000	1000	1000	1000
Sched. rec'ts	(1000)	(1083)	1246	1000	1000	1000	1000	1000
On hand/200	200	283	529	529	529	529	529	529
Planned orders	1246	1000	1000	1000	1000	1000		

Hedged master schedule

Item 0,1

Period	1	2	3	4	5	6	7	8
Requirements	1000	1000	1000	1000	1000	1000	1000	1000
Hedge	200	283	346	400	447	490	529	566
Sched. rec'ts	(1000)	(1083)	1063	1054	1047	1043	1039	1037
On hand/200	200	283	346	400	447	490	529	566
Planned orders	1063	1054	1047	1043	1039	1037		

( ) Circled scheduled receipts indicate orders actually placed in prior periods, as opposed to planned receipts.

stock' being dispersed through the pipeline of items 1,1, 2,1, etc. Exhibit 7, shows the 'steady state' inventory balances for one serial sequence from the product structure in our example problem. The 'steady state' was reached by moving the example through time, period by period, while 'rolling over' the hedge. Rolling the hedge

Exhibit 7. 'Steady state' conditions.
Hedged master schedule

Item 0,1 – Lead time = 2 periods, Value added = $3

Period	5	6	7	8	9	10	11	12
Requirements	1000	1000	1000	1000	1000	1000	1000	1000
Hedge	200	283	346	400	447	490	529	566
Sched. rec'ts	1000	1000	1000	1054	1047	1043	1039	1037
On hand/346	346	346	346	400	447	490	529	566
Planned orders	1000	1054	1047	1043	1039	1037		

Item 1,1 – Lead time = 2 periods, Value added = $3

Period	5	6	7	8	9	10	11	12
Requirements	1000	1054	1047	1043	1039	1037		
Sched. rec'ts.	1000	1000	1000	1043	1039	1037		
On hand/101	101	47	0					
Planned orders	1000	1043	1039	1037				

Irem 2,1 – Lead time = 2 periods, Value added = $2

Period	5	6	7	8	9	10	11	12
Requirements	1000	1043	1039	1037				
Sched. rec'ts	1000	1000	1000	1037				
On hand/82	82	39	0	0				
Planned orders	1000	1037						

means that the hedge amounts in the hedge row in Exhibit 6 are all moved one period to the right, every time one period of time passes. An examination of the on-hand balances in Exhibit 7 shows that there are 529 units of safety stock in the 'system,' but that only 346 units are at the end item level, 101 units are at the item 1,1 level, and 82 units are at the item 2,1 level. Thus, much of our safety stock is being held where inventory is less costly. An analysis of the complete problem will show that the inventory associated with the safety stock strategy will total \$7935, while the inventory associated with the hedge strategy will only total \$6421.

In general, it can be shown that the safety stock associated with each item in a product structure at steady state can be calculated in the following way:[6]

$$S_{z,j} = k\sqrt{\left(\sum_{i=0,z} L_{ij} + 1\right)\sigma^2} - \sqrt{\left(\sum_{i=0,z-1} L_{ij} + 1\right)\sigma^2}$$

Where:

S_{zj} = safety stock (in units) associated with the *j*th item at level z.

k = the factor associated with the normal distribution that guarantees a certain service level.

L_{ij} = the lead time associated with the *i*th level and *j*th item that is a predecessor of item z, j.

σ = the single period forecast error standard deviation.

It should be noted that the term 'steady state' should be used guardedly with respect to hedging. The restrictive assumptions in our example regarding a constant forecast (and actual withdrawal of 1000 units in each period in the example) yielded the 'steady state' conditions shown in Exhibit 7. Perturbations of demand or of the standard error of the forecast, will mean that the term steady state can only be used in the expected value sense, if at all. The dynamics of hedging when different lot size procedures and assumptions about the stability of demand and forecast error distributions are used, are little understood.

At least one large consumer electronics manufacturer has been observed using a dynamic hedge. In this case, hedges are made

6. This result is similar to that obtained by Hanssmann [2] in treating a related problem.

on a judgmental basis, and are authorized by management in terms of capacity equivalents. Thus, a planner may be authorized to hedge an amount equal to $\frac{1}{2}$ shift's capacity for six to ten weeks in the future, one shift's capacity for ten to 20 weeks in the future, and so on. This practice shows one way of linking capacity considerations to what, up to this point, has been an uncapacitated approach.

15.1.3. Management considerations

The power of hedging as a master scheduling tactic derives from its ability to take advantage of differentials in uncertainty and value added over time. It is thus, a very simple, logical, and straightforward tactic. However, hedging is considerably more complex to administer than safety stocks because it requires more information, requires constant supervision so that hedges can be modified, and because the implementation of a hedging strategy may require changes or adaptations to systems, and to management philosophies. Thus, there are a number of issues that must be considered before a decision to use hedging can be made. Among those that are most important to consider are: (1) How does hedging affect priority control? (2) Does hedging lead to excessive de-expediting? (3) How should hedge decisions be interfaced with capacity decisions, and (4) How does management control hedging?

Priority control

There can be no doubt that heding takes the edge off an MRP system's ability to control priorities at all levels in product structure. This will be a consequence of the fact that an order for a component will reflect the end item demands for two different kinds of needs. The first is for the quantity of parts that are needed to satisfy the base level of demand at the end item level. The second need is generated by the desire to keep or maintain a safety stock in the pipeline. In most cases, the marginal value of the first type of need is higher than the latter. The effect of this is that machine scheduling or lot splitting decisions are more difficult to make, especially if it is difficult to ascertain how much of a particular lot, or which lot, is destined to fill a firm order and how much is to be used to maintain a hedge.

While this problem of priority control is a real disadvantage, one way to overcome this is to separate the hedge from base level requirements at the master schedule level. This can be implemented by assigning an extra 'phantom' product number to each real product which can then be used to identify hedge quantities, or by other coding devices. Such identifiers can then be used to indicate at the shop floor level which lots are hedges, and which have firm orders placed against them. Granger Transmission [5] uses a variation on this approach.

Excessive de-expediting

The fact that hedges must be constantly changed, or rolled over, to be effective can easily lead to excessive rescheduling for lower level components in a product structure. To illustrate this, consider the way that the hedge will change relative to time period 7 in the second master schedule in Exhibit 6. Three periods in advance of period 7, the hedge quantity is 400 units. These 400 units may be partially responsible for generating a purchase order at time zero for a lower level component. After one week passes and the hedge is rolled over, however, the hedge for that period relative to time period 7 will change to 346. In most MRP systems, this will generate a reschedule message indicating that 400-346 = 54 units of the incoming order should be rescheduled to a future period. One might expect a similar message for every component in the product structure each period as the system passes through time. Given that such rescheduling will occur at all product levels for the hedged product, this indicates that the advantages of the hedge in terms of reduced inventory levels must be offset against increased administrative costs. This in turn suggests that hedging as a practical tool should only be used for high value long lead time products.

Capacity requirements planning

A third consideration is that hedging as described thus far applies to materials ordering decisions, and not capacity decisions. The problem is that if a master schedule that contains hedges is also used to derive capacity requirements, the derived need for capacity can be grossly overstated. To illustrate, suppose that a master schedule contains three products that all use the same facility and workforce, and that all three presume a base level of demand of 1000 plus a hedge of 529 units seven periods in the future. The capacity requirements for assembly to meet these demands then would be 3000 units (base level) plus $3 \times 529 = 1587$ units of hedge, or 4587 units. It would be futile to have the material on hand to supply this hedge if the capacity were not also available to implement it. But, should the firm take steps now to ensure that 4587 units of capacity are available? The answer is probably no. A hedge is added to gross requirements to protect against demand uncertainties for a *single product*, and it is statistically unlikely that a number of products will all need to use the hedge (assuming demands across product lines are not correlated) at the same time. A more likely occurrence, for example, is that 1529 units of capacity will be needed for one product, and that the others will need only 1000 units or less. Thus, to make the translation from a hedged master schedule for materials purposes, to a master schedule for capacity requirements planning purposes, the upward bias of the materials hedges must be moderated.

Adapting the master schedule for capacity requirements planning should not present any substantive problems. In fact, the same statistical theory relating the sums of random variables could be used to hedge capacity as well. For example, if the standard deviation for forecast error for all three products that led to the hedge of 529 was 264.5 units, then the standard error of forecast capacity needs will be $\sqrt{3(264.5)^2} = 458$ units. Then, to protect against stockouts with a 95 percent level of assurance, the hedged capacity amount need only be $2 \times 458 = 916$ units. Thus, the total hedged capacity requirement will be 3916, not 4587 units.

Hedging control

The last and most important consideration to take into account before implementing a hedging strategy is how to control it administratively. This issue is important because: (1) hedges, as in the case of Perkin Elmer and Granger Transmission, often reflect the 'major risks of a company,' (2) because managing a hedge requires close attention and good judgement in order that they can be modified on a timely basis and (3) because hedging can get out of control (picture an 'MRP-wise' sales force that begins to progressively factor up forecasts with time more than they already do). Certainly administrative tools such as 'management stock orders' and authorizations to hedge up to certain capacity limits can be effective devices for controlling hedging. One can also envision management reports indicating the amount of inventory tied up in hedges at various stages of manufacture. However, at this point, one can only speculate that the single most important control for hedging is the same control that applies to the proper functioning of any manufacturing system. Namely, close and persistent interfunctional involvement in the master scheduling process by the highest levels of management.

15.2. Conclusion

The purpose of this paper has been to: (1) define master schedule hedging, (2) illustrate the types of industrial situations in which it applies, (3) document the use of hedging in practice, (4) speculate on some of the management considerations that will accompany the increased use of hedging, and (5) illustrate the ways in which some fundamental statistical concepts and decision making tools can be applied to improve the quality of hedging decisions. However, at this early stage in the development and use of the master schedule hedge, there are still far more questions than answers, demonstrating the need for more empirical and theoretical research.

Among the areas where further research efforts might bear fruit of real practical as well as theoretical value are the following:

1. *Forecast decay.* Most forecasting research emphasizes the stationary properties of the various forecasting approaches. There has been little work on the phenomenon for forecast decay. The importance of forecast decay in hedging, and in fact, many other manufacturing control decisions, suggests that our old forecasting tools should be evaluated with a new criterion.
2. *When is hedging most effective?* One can speculate that the shape of a product's/firm's commitment profile is a good indicator of the effectiveness of organized hedging. But, there are undoubtedly numerous other considerations that should be taken into account in making the decision to hedge or not. What are they? Can they be generalized?
3. *Systems design.* In the section on management considerations a number of problems relating to the use of hedging with 'standard' MRP systems were anticipated. What changes in

systems are necessary to use and control hedges most effectively?

4. *Analytical tools.* The simple statistical notions applied to hedging problems here may be of some use in making hedging decisions. However, it seems clear that there are a host of analytical tools that could be developed to improve hedging decision making. For example, the structure of both the static and the dynamic hedging problems suggests that Baysian notions may be very useful.
5. *Hedging dynamics.* The dynamic effects of hedging when different lot sizing rules or varying forecasting or demand perturbations apply are little understood. Such an understanding is crucial to the further development and use of the concept.

References

1. Freund, J. E., *Mathematical Statistics*, Prentice-Hall, Inc., Englewood Cliffs, N. J. (1962).
2. Hanssman, F., 'Optimal Inventory Location and Control in Production and Distribution Networks', *Operations Research*, vol. 7, no. 4 (1959).
3. Miller, J. G. and Sprague, L., 'Behind the Growth in Material Requirements Planning', *Harvard Business Review* (September/October 1975).
4. Miller, J. G., 'Perkin Elmer: The Instrument Division', Harvard Business School Case Study, ICH no. 9-677-150.
5. Miller, J. G., 'Granger Transmission (A)', Harvard Business School Case Study, ICH no. 9-675-201.
6. Orlicky, J., *Material Requirements Planning*, McGraw-Hill Book Company, New York (b) (1975).
7. Plossl, G. W., *Manufacturing Control, the Last Frontier for Profits*, Reston Publishing Company, Reston, Va. (1973).
8. Wagner, H. M., *Principles of Operations Research*, Prentice-Hall, Inc., Englewood Cliffs, N. J. (1969).
9. Whybark, D. C. and Williams, J. G., 'Material Requirements Planning under Uncertainty', *Decision Sciences* (October 1976).
10. Wright, O. W., *Production and Inventory Management in the Computer Age*, Cahner Books, Boston, Mass. (1974).

16. The disaggregation problem in the paper industry

ROBERT W. HAESSLER

Abstract

This paper describes the disaggregation problem in the production setting of a paper mill. The starting point is a machine loading which specifies the quantity of each product grouping to be made on each paper machine during each period of the planning horizon. The first level of disaggregation is discussed in the context of the development of a master schedule for each machine. In a paper mill this involves sequencing and cycling the product groups allocated to each machine. This is complicated by the fact that some customer requirements must be made to order, while others can be satisfied from inventory.

The master schedule is the basis for promising available dates for both customer and inventory replenishment orders. As the time for a production run draws near, the customer and stock replenishment orders to be made in that run are sorted into groups of items that have identical specifications except for width in the case of rolls or width and length in the case of sheets. These groupings represent items that can be made side by side across the width of the paper machine and as such define the requirements for a cutting stock or trim problem. The objective at this point is to minimize all controllable costs of production. The most obvious is the trim loss that is generated as a result of the way the sizes are combined. However, in most mills there are other considerations such as utilization of finishing equipment and material handling costs that make the trim problem a complex combinatorial problem that can be solved only by heuristic procedures. The last issue dealt with in the paper is the information required to make the detailed sequencing decisions on the finishing equipment consistent with order priority.

16.1. Introduction

In recent years, product proliferation, the trend toward larger facilities serving more markets, dramatic increases in the cost of labor and of plant and equipment, and customers requiring faster and more dependable deliveries of smaller quantities have greatly increased management's awareness of the need for improved production planning, scheduling, and control. During the same interval significant improvements in computer software and hardware have made it possible to get a 'handle' on some of the complex problems that must be solved. From an academic viewpoint, the objective might be to plan and schedule production so as to minimize total operating costs consistent with customer service requirements. However, the problems are too complex and there is too much uncertainty to be able to deal with production planning and scheduling problems from a total systems viewpoint. Instead, it is necessary to disaggregate the overall problem into a hierarchy of problems that can be dealt with sequentially going from the broadest questions of facility loading to the most detailed issues of production scheduling.

The purpose of this paper is to view this problem of disaggregation in the context of a particular production setting. The first section describes the essentials of the production process and the types of orders placed on it. The second section develops the hierarchy of problems that must be solved to plan and schedule production. The available problem solving techniques are discussed along with their shortcomings, and an attempt is made to show how the problems at various levels of hierarchy interact. The third section discusses how this approach to production planning and scheduling might be implemented within an organization to attain the majority of the benefits available from its use.

For purposes of this paper, it is assumed that the strategic decisions regarding facilities, product line, pricing and customer service are given. This is also a disaggregation of the total business management problem, but one that usually involves a different time horizon from the issue of facility utilization being considered here.

16.2. The production system

The disaggregation problem is discussed in the context of a paper producer. It is assumed that

- there is more than one mill and there is a certain amount of overlap of production capability among the mills;
- some of the items are sold from inventory and some are made to order;

- each mill has the necessary finishing equipment such as roll slitters and sheet cutters and trimmers to produce rolls and sheets in the sizes ordered;
- one measure of the capacity of each paper machine or piece of finishing equipment is the maximum width roll or sheet that can be produced or processed.

The product ordered by the customer is identified by

- grade of paper (for this purpose this includes basis weight, color, and finish)
- size (width and diameter for rolls, width and length for sheets)
- quantity (number of rolls or sheets).

Because paper is a solid material that is produced in a continuous web on machines whose maximum widths are much greater than required by their users, most of the finishing operations in the mill are performed to change the physical dimensions of the paper. As such, there is a continual concern with what is called the trim problem. This is the problem of combining ordered sizes across the width of an operation to utilize as much of the width capacity as possible without exceeding the upper limit. If a paper machine that can make a roll 200 inches wide is used to make an 180 inch roll, only 90 percent of its capacity is being used.

16.3. Hierarchy of production planning and scheduling problems

The overall production planning and scheduling problem for a paper producer can be disaggregated into three major problem areas:

1. Facility loading – determining in aggregate terms how much of each grade is to be produced on each machine in each period.
2. Master scheduling – determining how often and in what sequence the grades loaded on each machine are to be run.
3. Trimming and scheduling – determining the quantities and sizes of the rolls to be produced on the paper machine and how each is to be cut to fill the orders included in the production run and determining the order in which these production rolls are to be produced on the paper machine and processed through the finishing equipment.

Each of these problems and the manner in which they interact is described below.

16.3.1. Facility loading

An aggregate plan for facility utilization can be done on a produce grade or grade group basis. The large number of similar grades with relatively low volumes usually requires that machine loadings be done on the basis of grade groups. The following linear programming model provides the simplest possible formulation of the problem. (For a more detailed discussion of this problem see [3].)

$$\max \sum_i \sum_j P_{ij} x_{ij}$$

subject to

$$\sum_i A_{ij} X_{ij} \leqq H_j \quad \text{all } j \text{ (machines)}$$

$$\sum_j X_{ij} \leqq D_i \quad \text{all } i \text{ (grades)}$$

$$\sum_j X_{ij} \geqq L_i$$

$$\sum_i \sum_j F_{ijr} X_{ij} = F_r \quad \text{all } r \text{ (special restrictions)}$$

where

- x_{ij} is the tons of grade i to be produced on machine j
- P_{ij} is the contribution to profit and overhead per ton of grade i produced on machine j
- D_i is the upper limit on the amount of grade i that can be sold
- L_i is the lower limit on the amount of grade i that must be produced
- A_{ij} is the hours required to produce one ton of grade i on machine j
- H_j is the total hours of production time available on machine j
- F_{ijr} is the coefficient of a special restriction depending on the particular situation. For example, the above model disregards the non-linearities in the system

such as setup costs and the downstream finishing limitations. In most cases appropriate use of special forcing equations can permit sufficient realism to be included for the linear programming model to be useful.

This model omits two important factors that generally should be considered. The first concerns the impact of transportation costs on the facility assignment decision. The above model does not explicitly consider the possibility that the same product could be made at different facilites to serve customers in different geographic regions. Transportation costs can be included in the above model only to the extent of using weighted freight rates from each location to all shipping points. Under this formulation transportation costs are treated as variable costs depending only on production location. To include cost differentials based on destination, it is necessary to extend the decision variable to x_{ijd}, where X_{ijd} represents the tons of product i to be produced on machine j and shipped to destination d. This requires that the forecasts by grade group be done on a regional basis and may greatly increase the size of the model.

The second factor involves the timing of production and sales for each grade. If the demand for each grade is uniform over time, then a single period model will be satisfactory. However, if there are seasonal fluctuations, it will be necessary to develop a multi-period model to explicitly consider production smoothing alternatives. This involves producing in quantities greater than currently needed while production time is available to build inventories to meet demand at some future time when production capacity is insufficient. A multi-period model can be developed by defining the decision variable to be X_{ijps}, where X_{ijps} represents the tons of grade i to be produced on machine j in period p for sale in period s. With this formulation the demand forecasts must be done by period and once again the size of the problem may be greatly increased. The cost of holding inventory is taken into account by adjusting C_{ijps} based on the differences between p and s.

Although the facility loading problem is the first one in the hierarchy, it is not independent of the master scheduling and trimming problems. There are two important interactions that should be noted.

1. The variable cost and production rates used to load the grade groups on the paper machines are based on assumptions about run length, since the setup cost and time must be built into them. These assumptions must be based on historical experience since the master schedule has not yet been established.
2. The variable cost and production rates for each grade group are based on assumptions about yield which is not known until after the orders have been received and the production run has been trimmed. The yield on any trim problem is determined by the sizes and quantities ordered and the width of the paper machine. Once again the values used must be based on historical experience. This can be very troublesome because substantial shifts can take place in the size-quantity mix over time.

16.3.2. Master scheduling

The output of the aggregate production planning model is simply a listing of the grades and quantities that are to be produced in each time period on each paper machine. Once the machine loading has been done, the next step is to cycle and sequence the grades assigned. This is a plan over time for each paper machine that specifies how often and in what order each grade is to be run. The total quantity scheduled for each grade should, of course, correspond with the aggregate plan for each machine.

There are six factors that affect this decision:

1. The holding cost of the operating inventory. The inventory of stocking items must be sufficient to satisfy a specified percentage of the demand for an item between production runs. The more frequently the grade is produced, the lower the required inventory will be.
2. The customer service requirements. For making orders, the more frequently a grade is produced the better the service will be.
3. Overall mill balance. In any paper mill making both rolls and sheets, care must be taken to have a reasonable balance of these two types of products over any given period of time. Otherwise, there may be severe congestion problems and delays in some parts of the plant and nothing to do in others.
4. The costs associated with changing over the paper machine from

one grade to another. The more frequently the product is produced the greater the number of changeovers. The changeover cost may also be sequence dependent.

5. The costs associated with setting up the finishing equipment to produce the sizes required. More frequent runs will again require more setups.
6. The yield of a production run. The yield of a run depends on the mix of sizes ordered. Less frequent runs will provide a greater variety of sizes to be trimmed together which should improve the yield.

The first three factors favor more frequent runs, while the last three favor less frequent runs. The development of a mathematical model to explicitly deal with these factors appears to be impractical. It is, however, generally possible to manually develop reasonably good schedules based on the types of information discussed above. The procedure would involve first determining a reasonable cycle for each product based on yield, service requirements, economic lot size considerations, and simplicity (every 3 weeks would be preferable to every 18 days so customers can plan their ordering activities). Given production cycles, there generally are natural sequences which should be followed, such as progressively going from lighter to darker colors. The resulting schedules for all paper machines in a mill must then be reviewed in total to determine the overall impact on mill balance.

Of prime significance here is that a fixed master schedule should be established and adhered to wherever possible. A schedule, where each grade is run on a periodic basis, permits the greatest degree of planning for inventory replenishment and equipment utilization. The alternative is to produce next whatever is in greatest demand either from customers or for inventory replenishment. Jamming orders in the schedule may have some short term sales advantages but eventually leads to a breakdown in the ability of the organization to meet its commitments to the majority of its customers which may, in turn, have very severe long term marketing consequences. With a fixed master schedule, making orders are dated for availability based on the next scheduled run of that grade that has open time. Time in a production run must also be reserved for inventory replenishment. This requires a monitoring of the inventory to project replenishment requirements from upcoming runs. Replenishment quantities are determined using periodic review models. Sufficient stock must be produced to meet the demand until some future scheduled run. Open time in a run can be used to produce production smoothing orders if that is appropriate.

The term fixed should not be interpreted as being completely inflexible with regard to length of run. There obviously will have to be some adjustments from run to run to keep things in balance.

16.3.3. Trimming and scheduling

As the time for a production run draws near, the making and stock replenishment orders that have been promised from that run define the items that must be trimmed and scheduled through the finishing equipment. The first step is the development of a solution for the trim problem. This consists of the specification of the number, width and diameter of rolls to be produced and the way these production rolls are to be processed to obtain the sizes ordered. The object is to do this in such a way as to minimize total controllable costs consisting of both trim loss and the downstream processing costs. A trim problem is made up of those orders having similar enough specifications that they can be run side-by-side on a paper machine. In the simplest case assume that there are orders for rolls of the same diameter where the quantity is R_i and the width is W_i for $i = i, \ldots, n$. The trim problem can be formulated as followsB

$$\min C_i \sum_j T_j X_j + C_2 \sum_j \delta(X_j)$$

subject to

$$RL_i \leqq \sum_j A_{ij} X_j \leqq RU_i \text{ for } i = i, \ldots, n$$

$$x_j \geqq 0, \text{ integer}$$

where

A_{ij} is the number of rolls of width W_i to be slit from each production roll that is processed using pattern j. A feasible cutting pattern is one for which

$$\sum_i A_{ij} W_i \leqq W$$

$$A_{ij} \geqq 0, \text{ integer},$$

X_j is the number of production rolls to be processed according to pattern j,

T_j is the number of inches of trim loss incurred by pattern j, (if W is the maximum usable width, then $T_j = W - \sum_i A_{ij} W_{ij}$)

C_1 is the dollar value of trim loss per inch,

C_2 is the cost of changing patterns in dollars,

RL_i and RU_i are lower and upper bounds on order i, reflecting general industry practice to allow limited overruns or underruns,

and

$$\delta(X_j) = 1 \text{ for } X_j \geqq 0 \text{ and } 0 \text{ otherwise.}$$

The mathematical programming problem formulated above is clearly far beyond the capability of existing integer programming codes. However, it is possible to develop heuristic problem solving procedures that work very well in these problems and give better solutions than can be obtained manually. There are two approaches that can be used individually or in combination to solve these problems.

1. Sequentially generate patterns until all the requirements are satisfied.
2. Solve the trim loss minimization problem using a linear programming algorithm to obtain an initial solution that can be rounded to meet the integer requirements.

Both the sequential and linear programming approaches can be used on any type of trim problem. The issue is to find the approach that will be most effective in any given situation. The pivotal consideration in most cases is the difficulty of controlling trim loss using a sequential procedure. In those problems where there are a large number of ways to combine sizes to obtain low trim loss patterns, a sequential procedure is most likely to be preferred.

This usually occurs when there is a large number of sizes ordered that are small relative to the width of the production roll. Conversely, a sequential procedure will not be as successful on problems where there are only a few sizes, or the ordered sizes are large relative to the width of the production roll. In these problems there may be only a few ways to combine sizes into patterns to obtain low trim loss solutions. If this is the case, the total systems capability of linear programming will be needed to determine the proper combination of patterns to find a low trim loss solution. For a more complete discussion of trim problems see [1], [2], [4], and [5].

The solution to the trim problem identifies what must be made on the paper machine and designs the set of tasks to be loaded onto the finishing operations. The question still remains as to how to sequence the patterns on the paper machine and the jobs through the finishing operations. There are a number of ways in which the patterns can be sequenced on the paper machine. The choice of methods depends on the individual situation. Two possibilities are:

1. Sequence based on material handling considerations. Attempt to keep orders together to permit direct loading of shipments. This can be done by prioritizing orders based on urgency of shipments and selecting next that pattern that provides the greatest number of rolls for the highest priority orders.
2. Sequence based on slitter change considerations. Identify patterns with common sizes and run them sequentially to reduce the number of slitter changes that must be made.

The sequencing of jobs through the finishing operations is largely controlled by the sequencing of runs and patterns on the paper machine. To the extent that there are choices to be made, local job shop dispatching rules based on due date will generally work satisfactorily.

16.4. Organizing for production planning and scheduling

The preceding discussion provides a static view of the hierarchy of problems involved in planning and scheduling production in a paper company. The actual problem environment that must be dealt with is dynamic, not static. There are a large number of choices that must be made over time that define the way the productive resources are to be used to satisfy the orders placed upon it. As such, what is needed is an organizational unit that can:

- Identify and evaluate economically from a total systems standpoint the major alternatives available over time at each stage in the planning and scheduling process.
- Analyze its own performance over time and learn more about the cause-effect relationships that affect system performance so that this information can be used to correct problems and take advantage of opportunities that may not otherwise be readily apparent.

The basic requirement to accomplish this is that all activities relating to production planning and scheduling should be brought together into a single organizational unit. The head of this unit can be described as the Resource Utilization Manager. The unconventional title is used to indicate wider responsibilities than those usually associated with production planning or materials management and more detailed than those associated with marketing. This unit should be on the same organizational level as sales and production. The primary responsibility of this unit would be to act as an interface between production and sales and to provide a capability for making economic evaluations of alternative actions available from a general management viewpoint.

Under this approach, the sales unit would be responsible for forecasting customer demand and obtaining the orders to meet those forecasts. It would also be their duty to indicate the level of service required in those situations that are nonstandard.

The Resource Utilization Unit would be responsible for translating the forecasted market opportunities into production plans and ultimately schedules. Their performance could be evaluated based on budgets or standards for:

- inventory
- customer service
- planned production yields
- standard production hours required per ton of scheduled production.

The production unit would be responsible for producing at

standard the manufacturing orders generated by the Resource Utilization Unit.

Clearly it is necessary to make all the units as a whole responsible for meeting some organizational profit goal. In the event that this goal is not met, the reasons for the shortfall should be identified in a detailed fashion so that action can be taken. This must be done in the spirit of a team working together to achieve an objective to avoid a 'finger-pointing' exercise that will polarize the units and inhibit future cooperation.

In order to do its job the Resource Utilization Unit must have the necessary information systems and problem solving tools for determining and evaluating the planning and scheduling alternatives available. The planning requirements are:

- Sales forecasts and service requirements.
- Production capabilities such as maximum sizes and speeds and setup times.
- Costs of setup, production storage and shipping.
- Procedures for loading grades on machines and sequencing and cycling runs.

The operating requirements center around three major files that must be maintained.

1. Open order file – This file contains a listing of the complete specifications including a planned shipment date for each order entered into the system but not yet billed. This information should be stored in such a way that it can be obtained by order number, by customer or by product grade.

   This file should be updated to reflect the completion of major steps in the process of completing the orders. For a making order, these would include the following:
   - quantity scheduled
   - quantity packed
   - warehouse location
   - quantity shipped.
2. Inventory file – The inventory file has two main purposes. The first is to provide information on product availability in response to a customer availability. The second is to provide the basic information for the inventory control system to determine when

and how much should be ordered for replenishment purposes.

3. Manufacturing order file – The original manufacturing order schedules the paper machines and specifies the way in which the output in the form of the production rolls is to be processed to meet customer size specifications. In order to insure that the proper quantity of an order is ready at the proper time it is necessary to keep track of each order as it moves from operation to operation. This can be done most easily by posting to the original manufacturing order the quantity that is output at each of the required operations from the paper machine through the packing line.

The primary problem solving capability required is the ability to solve trim problems. The most obvious reason for developing and using a computerized trimming procedure is the possibility of getting better answers. Another important reason is the speed with which the solutions can be generated and the manufacturing orders prepared. A computerized procedure allows the scheduler to wait for last-minute orders as well as resolve problems quickly in the event of an order change. The ability to solve problems quickly may be very important: For example, in some cases a customer may specify a range of parameters, such as diameters, which is acceptable. It is then up to the scheduler to decide at which diameter to make the order. A very obvious way to make this decision is to solve the appropriate problems with the order included and excluded and decide on this basis where it fits best. Under a manual approach this may be impractical from the standpoint of workload, but a computer procedure may accomplish this with very little increase in effort and at a potentially substantial savings in production costs.

16.5. Conclusion

Perhaps the major problem that stands in the way of doing a more effective job of production planning and scheduling is the fragmentation of responsibility for the various activities required in the process. All too often, the activities such as production and inventory planning, trimming, production scheduling and control and shipment planning are divided haphazardly between manufacturing and sales. This frequently makes the process of change very slow and difficult. An opportunity to save $100 in one area by spending $10 in another area may be foregone because the savings will accrue to one manager and the costs will be incurred by another. There is a great need to integrate the informational activities associated with production planning and scheduling so that they can be carried out in the most effective and efficient manner. This can best be done by giving authority and responsibility for all production planning and scheduling activities to a single manager, and providing strong top managerial support for this concept.

References

1. Gilmore, P. C. and Gomory, R. E., 'A Linear Programming Approach to the Cutting-Stock Problem', *Operations Research*, vol. 9, no. 6 (November 1961), pp. 849–859.
2. Gilmore, P. C. and Gomory, R. E., 'A Linear Programming Approach to the Cutting-Stock Problem – Part II', *Operations Research*, vol. 11, no. 6 (November 1963), pp. 863–888.
3. Godfrey, J. T., Spivey, W. A., and Stillwagon, G. B., 'Production and Market Planning with Parametric Programming', *Industrial Management Review* (Fall 1967).
4. Haessler, R. W., 'Controlling Cutting Pattern Changes in One-Dimensional Trim Problems', *Operations Research*, vol. 23, no. 3 (May 1975), pp. 483–493.
5. Haessler, R. W., 'Single-machine Roll Trim Problems and Solution Procedures', *TAPPI*, vol. 59, no. 2 (February 1976), pp. 145–149.

Section 6. Lot sizing and scheduling procedures

17. An economic lot size algorithm for multi-level inventory systems with acyclic network structures

PHIROZ P. DARUKHANAVALA

Abstract

The research presented in this paper is oriented toward a company organized as a multi-level, production-inventory system with an acyclic network structure. We develop and test an algorithm which specifically derives the dependent stochastic demand distributions in a multi-level system and then computes optimal order quantities based on a trade-off between set-up, holding and safety-stock costs at all levels.

A 7 percent reduction in inventory-related costs (as compared to existing ordering policies) was achieved, when the algorithm was used with 206 manufactured and purchased parts, based on data obtained from a company, which manufactures heating and air conditioning systems, located in the Midwest of the United States. Trade-off curves between service-level policies and inventory-related costs are also developed.

This paper was awarded the first prize in a competition sponsored by the Northern Ohio Chapter of TIMS.

17.1. Introduction

The research presented in this paper, originated in a materials management study for a company located in the Midwest and engaged in manufacturing residential and light-commercial heating and air-conditioning systems. The company is organized as a multi-level production-inventory system; its manufacturing facility is divided into 13 departments or cost centers according to specific functions such as shearing, fabrication, welding, painting and assembly. Each manufacturing level, within the system, *derives its demand* from the next higher level, through a sophisticated, computer-aided material requirements planning (MRP) system. At the time of the study, the effectiveness of the sophisticated MRP system was restricted by the use of lot-to-lot replenishment policies exclusively. The company's objective was to develop methods for generating improved ordering policies based on economic considerations, and using these methods, to establish trade-off curves between service-levels and inventory-related costs.

A look at the literature revealed that very few inventory models addressed the multi-level situation. Discrete linear programming models developed by Dantzig [3], Manne [9], Heahling von Lauzenauer [6] and Gorenstein [5] either did not address the same objective, or could not be applied to practical problems of realistic size. Taha and Skeith [11], Jensen and Khan [7], Young [12] and Love [8] present solutions for serial structures, but their results could not be generalized to non-serial systems. Schussel [10], Crowston, Wagner, and Williams [2] and Zangwill [13] have developed more general models or heuristic decision rules, but they did not consider stochastic dependent demand and the effect of safety-stocks.

The algorithm presented here takes into consideration dependent demand distributions existing at different levels of a multi-level, production-inventory system and then computes order quantities which are optimal for the entire system, based on a trade-off between set-up, holding and safety-stock costs at all levels. The algorithm, when tested with real data from the company, produced very favorable results as compared to other ordering policies. We summarize here some of the important results from this study; a more detailed analysis of results can be found in [4].

17.2. Assumptions used in the model

The following assumptions are used in defining the n-level production-inventory system.

1. The production-inventory system is characterized by an acyclic network structure with *n*-levels ($n \geqq 1$). The levels are numbered in successively increasing order starting with finished goods which are assigned to level 1. All items directly 'going into' the finished goods are assigned level number 2 and so on. In an acyclic structure, each level can have any number of predecessors and

successors, but a level numbered j can only be predecessor of any level p for $p < j$. Under this assumption, whenever an item occurs at several levels, for the purpose of the algorithm, it is assigned to the *largest* of these level numbers.

2. *Demand for finished goods* is stochastic with mean r_{1j} and standard deviation σ_{1j}.
3. *Demand at any other level* is dependent on, and derived from the ordering policies at higher levels.
4. *Ordering Cost*. Every order of size Q has a fixed component K and a variable component v per unit i.e., ordering cost per order = $K + vQ$. Therefore, the total ordering cost per unit $(K/Q + v)$ is a convex function of batch size.
5. *Inventory Carrying Cost* has two components:
   Holding Cost
   Assumed to be a linear function of the average inventory level due to batch ordering.
   Safety-Stock Cost
   Shortages are permitted at all levels and the probability of shortages during lead time is a function of the service level, which is parametrically set by management, based on enlightened trade-offs between costs and desired service-levels. The level of safety-stock carried is a function of the shortage probability, the standard deviation of the demand distribution and the replenishment lead time.
6. *Fractional items* are permitted for the purpose of analysis i.e., the order quantity Q is considered to be a continuous variable.
7. *Lead-times*. Each item has a constant, positive manufacturing or purchasing lead-time.

17.2.1. Notation

n_{aibj} = number of units of item i at level a which go into one unit of item j at level b.
Since items always go into higher level[1] parts, $a > b$. Subscripts i and j identify the parts within each level.

1. The smaller the level number, the higher is the level: i.e., finished goods are at the highest level.

r_{ai} = total demand 'incident' on item i, at level a.
$\bar{r}_{ai}$ = mean value of $r_{ai} = E(r_{ai})$
X_{ai} = demand generated by the ordering policy of item i at level a and transferred to the lower level
Q_{ai} = order quantity of item i at level a
λ_{ai} = lead time for item i at level a
p_{ai} = probability that an order for item i (at level a) will be placed in a given time-period
Z_{ai} = standardized deviation for item i, at level a, corresponding to the service level of that item
$\sigma_{ai}^{(I)}$ = standard deviation of demand for item i, at level a, based on the assumption of uncorrelated demand
$\sigma_{ai}^{(D)}$ = standard deviation of demand for item i, at level a, based on the assumption of totally correlated demand
N_a = total number of items at level a
$N_{a'}$ = total number of manufactured parts at level a
n = total number of levels in the system
K_{ai} = cost per set-up for item i, at level a
h_{ai} = inventory carrying cost/unit/time period, for item i, at level a
C_{ai} = safety stock factor = $Z_{ai}\sqrt{\lambda_{ai}}$
W = weight assigned to the uncorrelated component of demand standard deviation
PCT = iteration stopping percentage

17.2.2. Dependent demand distributions

For a fixed-order-quantity ordering policy, the steady-state probability density for X_{ai} can be expressed as a generalized Bernoulli distribution such that,

$$p(X_{ai}) = \begin{cases} p_{ai} & \text{if } X_{ai} = Q_{ai} \\ 1 - p_{ai} & \text{if } X_{ai} = 0 \\ 0 & \text{otherwise} \end{cases} \tag{1}$$

Therefore,

$$E(X_{ai}) = Q_{ai} \cdot p_{ai} \tag{2}$$

and

$$\mathrm{Var}(X_{ai}) = Q_{ai}^2 p_{ai}(1 - p_{ai}) \tag{3}$$

Moreover, since r_{ai} is the sum of serveral random variables $n_{aibj}X_{bj}$, the distribution of r_{ai} will tend to be normal according to the Central Limit Theorem.

Since the demand for several items at any level (except finished goods) is often dependent on the same item at a higher level, there will be some correlation between the X_{bj} values. The assumption of independent X_{1j} values permits us to add variances at level 2. However, from the third level downwards, this assumption fails (some variables are independent and some are dependent) and therefore, we consider two extreme cases. In case (1), we compute variances under the assumption of totally *uncorrelated* demand X_{bj}. This can be done by addition of variances. In case (2), we consider the assumption of totally *correlated* demand X_{bj}. In this case, standard deviations are additive. The actual standard deviation is then estimated as a weighted average between these extreme cases.

Using these arguments, the expected value and standard deviations of the dependent demand distributions are computed as follows:

For any level b

$$\bar{r}_{bj} = Q_{bj} \cdot P_{bj} = E(X_{bj}) \tag{4}$$

For any level a > b

$$r_{ai} = \sum_{b=1}^{a-1} \sum_{j=1}^{N'_b} (n_{aibj}) \cdot (X_{bj})$$

$$\bar{r}_{ai} = E(r_{ai}) = E\left[\sum_{b=1}^{a-1} \sum_{j=1}^{N_b} (n_{aibj})(X_{bj})\right]$$

$$= \sum_{b=1}^{a-1} \sum_{j=1}^{N'_b} (n_{aibj})\, E(X_{bj})$$

$$= \sum_{b=1}^{a-1} \sum_{j=1}^{N'_b} (n_{aibj})(\bar{r}_{bj}) \tag{5}$$

Since r_{1j} is known, equation (5) can be used recursively to obtain values for all $\bar{r}_{ai}$.

$$r_{ai} = \sum_{b=1}^{a-1} \sum_{j=1}^{N'_b} (n_{aibj})(X_{bj})$$

Case 1

Totally Uncorrelated demand – $\sigma_{ai}^{(I)}$

$$\mathrm{Var}(r_{ai}) = \sum_{b=1}^{a-1} \sum_{j=1}^{N'_b} (n_{aibj})^2 \,\mathrm{Var}(X_{bj}) \qquad \left[\text{The variances are additive}\right]$$

$$= \sum_{b=1}^{a-1} \sum_{j=1}^{N'_b} n_{aibj}^2 Q_{bj}^2 p_{bj}(1 - p_{bj})$$

$$= \sum_{b=1}^{a-1} \sum_{j=1}^{N'_b} n_{aibj}^2 \bar{r}_{bj}(Q_{bj} - \bar{r}_{bj}) \qquad \text{From (4)}$$

$$\sigma_{ai}^{(I)} = \sqrt{\sum_{b=1}^{a-1} \sum_{j=1}^{N'_b} n_{aibj}^2 \bar{r}_{bj}(Q_{bj} - \bar{r}_{bj})} \qquad (6)$$

Case 2

Totally correlated demand – $\sigma_{ai}^{(D)}$

$$\sigma_{ai}^{(D)} = \sum_{b=1}^{a-1} \sum_{j=1}^{N'_b} n_{aibj} \cdot \text{standard deviation } [X_{bj}] \qquad \left[\text{Standard deviation are additive}\right]$$

$$= \sum_{b=1}^{a-1} \sum_{j=1}^{N'_b} n_{aibj} \sqrt{\bar{r}_{bj}(Q_{bj} - r_{bj})} \qquad (7)$$

The total standard deviation of r_{ai} is given by

$$\sigma_{ai} = \begin{cases} W\sigma_{ai}^{(I)} + (1 - W)\sigma_{ai}^{(D)} & \text{for } a \geqq 3 \\ \sigma_{2i}^{(I)} & \text{for } a = 2 \\ s_{1i} \text{ (known)} & \text{for } a = 1 \end{cases}$$

17.2.3. Safety-stocks

Safety-stocks are defined in terms of the service level according to the following relationship.

Prob [Demand during lead-time $\leqq$ Mean lead-time demand + S. Stock] = (Service level percent)/100.

Service level is defined as the probability of not running out of stock during lead-time.

Based on this relationship, it can be shown that, Safety-stock for item i at level a

$$\begin{aligned} a &= Z_{ai}\sqrt{\lambda_{ai}}\sigma_{ai} \\ &= C_{ai}\sigma_{ai} \end{aligned} \tag{8}$$

17.2.4. *The cost function*

The Total Inventory-Related Cost (TIRC) is composed of three components viz. ordering costs, holding costs, and safety-stock costs. The following cost function is formulated.

Total Inventory-Related Cost, TIRC

$$= \sum_{a=1}^{n}\sum_{j=1}^{N_a}\left[\frac{K_{aj}\bar{r}_{aj}}{Q_{aj}} + \frac{h_{aj}Q_{aj}}{2} + h_{aj}C_{aj}\sigma_{aj}\right]$$

$$= \sum_{j=1}^{N_1}\left[\frac{K_{1j}\bar{r}_{1j}}{Q_{1j}} + \frac{h_{1j}Q_{1j}}{2} + h_{1j}C_{1j}\sigma_{1j}\right]$$

Finished goods (Level 1)

$$+ \sum_{i=1}^{N_2}\left[\frac{K_{2i}\bar{r}_{2i}}{Q_{2i}} + \frac{h_{2i}Q_{2i}}{2} + h_{2i}C_{2i}\sqrt{\sum_{j=1}^{N'_1} n_{2i1j}^2 r_{1j}(Q_{1j} - \bar{r}_{1j})}\right]$$

(Level 2)

$$+ \sum_{a=3}^{n}\sum_{k=1}^{N_a}\left[\frac{K_{ak}\bar{r}_{ak}}{Q_{ak}} + \frac{h_{ak}Q_{ak}}{2} + \right.$$

$$+ h_{ak}C_{ak}\left\{W\sqrt{\sum_{b=1}^{a-1}\sum_{j=1}^{N'_b} n_{akbj}^2\bar{r}_{bj}(Q_{bj} - \bar{r}_{bj})} + \right.$$

$$\left.\left. + (1 - W)\left(\sum_{b=1}^{a-1}\sum_{j=1}^{N'_b} n_{akbj}\sqrt{\bar{r}_{bj}(Q_{bj} - \bar{r}_{bj})}\right)\right\}\right] \tag{9}$$

(Levels 3 to n)

Taking derivatives of the cost function w.r.t. Q and setting them equal to zero we get

$(n-1) \geqq a \geqq 2$

$$Q_{ak} = \left[\frac{2K_{ak}\bar{r}_{ak}}{h_{ak} + \sum_{l=a+1}^{n} \left[\sum_{m=1}^{N_l} h_{lm} C_{lm} \left\{ \frac{W \cdot n_{lmak}^2 \bar{r}_{ak}}{\sqrt{\sum_{b=1}^{l-1} \sum_{j=1}^{N'_b} n_{lmbj}^2 \bar{r}_{bj} (Q_{bj} - \bar{r}_{bj})}} + \frac{(1-W) n_{lmak} \sqrt{\bar{r}_{ak}}}{\sqrt{(Q_{ak} - \bar{r}_{ak})}} \right\} \right]} \right]^{1/2} \tag{10}$$

$a = 1$

$$Q_{1k} = \left[\frac{2K_{1k}\bar{r}_{1k}}{h_{1k} + \sum_{m=1}^{N_2} \left\{ h_{2m} C_{2m} \frac{n_{2m1k}^2 \bar{r}_{1k}}{\sqrt{\sum_{j=1}^{N'_1} n_{2m1j}^2 \bar{r}_{1j} (Q_{1j} - \bar{r}_{1j})}} + \sum_{l=a+2}^{n} \left[\sum_{m=1}^{N_l} h_{lm} C_{lm} \{\text{Same as equation (10)}\} \right] \right.} \right]^{1/2} \tag{11}$$

By letting the Q-values on the RHS of these equations tend to ∞, we get

$$\text{Upper bounds } Q_{ak}^{(u)} = \sqrt{\frac{2K_{ak}\bar{r}_{ak}}{h_{ak}}} \quad \forall \; a, k \tag{12}$$

17.2.5. The n-level algorithm

The following algorithm has been developed to obtain order quantities Q_{ak}.

Step 1: Compute upper bounds on all Q_{ak} using equation (12)

Step 2: Set ITR = 1. Set Q_{ak} = upper bound values $\forall \; a, k$.

Step 3: Let $a = (n-1)$

Step 4: Compute $Q_{ak} = f[Q_{ak} \; \forall \; a, k]$, equation (10)
If $Q_{ak} < \bar{r}_{ak}$, set $Q_{ak} = \bar{r}_{ak}$

Step 5: Set $a = (a-1)$
If $a = 1$, go to step 6, else go to step 4.

Step 6: Compute $Q_{1k} = f[Q_{ak} \; \forall \; a, k]$ equation (11)
If $Q_{1k} < \bar{r}_{1k}$ set $Q_{1k} = \bar{r}_{1k}$.

Step 7: Compute $(\text{TIRC})^{\text{ITR}}$ using equation (9)

Step 8: $\left[\text{Is } \frac{\text{TIRC}^{(\text{ITR}-1)} - \text{TIRC}^{(\text{ITR})}}{\text{TIRC}^{(\text{ITR}-1)}} \right] \cdot 100 > \text{PCT?}$

If *Yes*, set ITR = ITR + 1, go to step 3.
If *No*, STOP.

17.2.6. Convergence

It can be shown that the Q_{ak} values obtained on successive iterations, form a monotonically decreasing sequence. Therefore, by the Monotone Convergence Theorem [1], the sequence of values will converge to a solution.

17.2.7. Data base for testing the algorithm

In order to validate the algorithm and then test its performance against other ordering policies, real data from the company's cooling line were used to develop a data base. The data base consisted of two major components.

1. A parts master by levels:

   This parts master contained a list of all parts included in 10 outdoor condensing units, which together comprised about 85–90 percent of the company's condensing unit line. Items whose net usage (standard cost × number of units going into one unit at higher levels) was less than $0.20 were eliminated from the list. This criterion eliminated items such as labels, tags, manuals, small nuts and bolts. Within each level, parts were identified as manufactured or purchased. Table 1 gives the distribution of parts by level.

Table 1. Distribution of parts by level

Level No.	Manufactured	Purchased	Total
1	10 (Finished goods)	-	10
2	50	47	97
3	36	27	63
4	15	10	25
5	-	11	11
Total	111	95	206

Set-up times (from the company's Shop Order File) and lead-times (from the Lead-time file and MRP reports) for each item were also included in the data base as part of each item's record. An average ordering cost of $5.60/order was used based on the company's documents.

2. The Bill of Materials structure:

   Based on individual Bills of Material for the 10 items, a composite Bill of Materials structure was synthesized. This Bill of Materials indicates the n_{aibj} values i.e., the number of units of item i at level a that go into *one unit* of item j at level b.

17.2.8. Computations and results

A set of computer programs was developed to validate the model and compare the results from various ordering policies. The set of programs was used to test three ordering policies: (a) Ordering based on the algorithm (b) Independent EOQ and (c) Lot-to-Lot ordering.

At the end of the computations, a report-writer produced summary cost reports at each iteration of the algorithm. Final Cost reports were broken down by level, by type of part (manufactured or purchased) and by type of cost (set-up, holding, and safety-stock). A profile of the average dollars in inventory by level and by type of part is also printed. In addition, the report-writer prints out a detailed Inventory-Control Report showing the part number, part description, order quantity, safety-stock, and re-order point for each of the items in the system.

For each run of the computer programs, a set of input parameters were entered separately through parameter cards. These parameters included i) the weekly demand distribution for finished goods, ii) ordering policy to be used, iii) holding costs as a percentage of standard costs, iv) job setter's wage v) service-levels for all the system levels, vi) weight W and vii) iteration-stopping percentage.

17.2.9. Validation of the computer models

The computer models were validated before any comparison of alternative ordering policies was attempted. Values from the sample

Table 2. Validation of the computer models

Comparison of projected and actual inventories using the lot-to-lot ordering policy.

CRITERION	Computed Value using 10 finished goods	Projected over all finished goods	Actual** for the company
Total $ in Inventory (fin. goods + W in Process + R.M./PP)	$706,010	$14,120,000	$14,990,000*
$ in Inventory for Manufactured Parts	369,007	7,380,000	7,530,000*
$ in Inventory for Purchased Parts	337,002	6,740,000	7,460,000
Inventory Ratio: (Manufactured Parts / Purchased Parts)	1.09	1.09	1.01
$ in Finished Goods Inventory	273,000 -45,000 S.Stock $228,000	4,560,000	4,880,000*

*Excludes inventory at branches
**Based on May 1974 inventory report

Table 3. Comparison of 3 ordering policies summary table.

Total Inventory Related Costs

	5-level algorithm (W = 0.5)	Independent EOQ	Lot-to-Lot
Total Inventory Related Costs	$122,489.28	$130,637.35	$133,029.13
% Reduction in costs as compared to lot-to-lot	7.92%	1.80%	-
AVERAGE DOLLARS IN INVENTORY			
Average $ in Inventory	785,776.57	911,612.98	706,010.13
% Increase in Inventory $ as compared to lot-to-lot	11.30%	29.12%	-

of 10 finished goods were projected to all items in the company and the projections were compared with the actuals for that time period. Table 2 shows a comparison of projected values with actuals.

17.2.10. Comparison of ordering policies

As stated before, three ordering policies were compared with respect to inventory-related-costs and dollars in inventory. Table 3 gives a summary of the relative performance of the three ordering policies. The first two policies are compared with Lot-to-Lot ordering in order to estimate the change that would result if the company switched to either of them. A more detailed comparison by level is given in [4].

17.2.11. Service-level policies

Five different service-level policies were compared, each policy being defined in terms of individual system levels.

These service-level policies are arranged such that policy I has the highest service-levels and policy V has the lowest. Within each policy, service-levels increase as we go down the system levels. This

Table 4. Definition of service-level policies.

(Service-levels (percent) by systems levels).

Service-Level Policies	System Levels				
	1	2	3	4	5
I	99	99	99	99	99
II	90	90	95	99	99
III (Base case)	85	90	90	95	99
IV	80	85	90	90	95
V	70	75	80	85	90

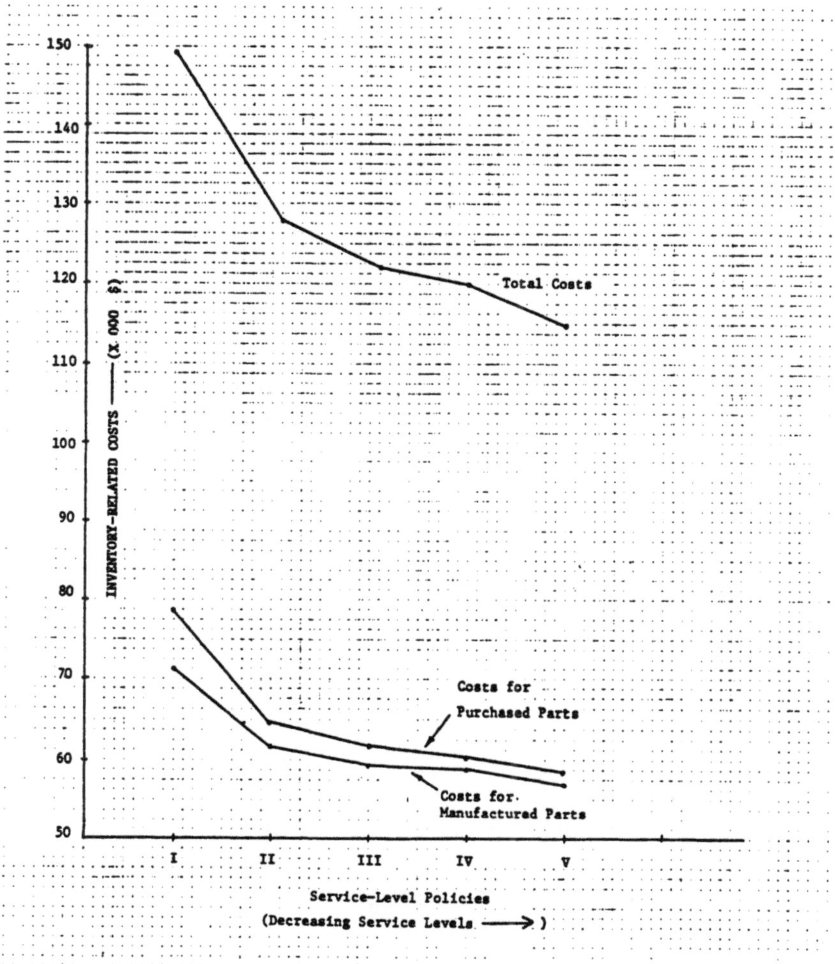

Figure 1. Effect of service levels on inventory-related cost.

is in keeping with the suggestion of company personnel that higher service-levels be assigned to lower level items, since a shortage at lower levels holds up production at all highėr levels. Table 4 lists the 5 service-level policies and Figure 1 presents the effect of these service-level policies on inventory-related-costs. It is celar that inventory-related-costs fall sharply as service-level declines from high values (policy I to III) but there is a much lesser reduction in costs from policy III to V, even though service-levels continue to fall.

17.3. Summary of results

17.3.1. 5-level algorithm properties

1. The algorithm converges in 3 iterations.
2. Cost reduction is high in the first iteration and then it slows down as the point of convergence is reached. Total cost reduction from upper bounds is 6.24 percent.
3. Set-up costs increase, whereas holding, safety-stock, and total costs decrease at each iteration.
4. A total of 38 CRU's were required for each run on the UNIVAC 1108. Each iteration was completed in about 4–6 seconds.

17.3.2. Effect of W

5. There is no significant effect of W on the final costs or the number of iterations to convergence. A value of $W = 0.5$ can be accepted without undue concern.

17.3.3. Ordering policies

6. The 5-level-algorithm gives the lowest inventory-related-costs amongst the three ordering policies tested. Specifically, it results in a 7.92 percent reduction in costs as compared to the currently used Lot-to-Lot policy.
7. Independent EOQing gives a 1.80 percent cost reduction over Lot-to-Lot.
8. The algorithm is most successful where set-up/ordering costs are high.
9. Independent EOQing produces slightly lower costs for level 2, at the expense of much higher costs at lower levels. The effect of this is felt most significantly by purchased parts, for which safety-stocks rise sharply.
10. Lot-to-Lot results in the lowest dollars in inventory. The algorithm results in a 11.3 percent higher inventory, whereas independent EOQ increases inventory by 29.12 percent.

17.3.4. Service-level policies

11. Inventory-related-costs decline sharply as service-levels are decreased from very high values, but cost reduction tends to level off as we move towards lower service levels.
12. Cost reduction is primarily due to a decline in safety-stock with service levels.
13. Policy III (base case) appears to be the best choice of service level if inventory-related-costs is a major criterion for the decision.

References

1. Bartle, R. G., 'The Elements of Real Analysis', Wiley, N.Y. (1964).
2. Crowston, W., Wagner, M., and Williams, Jr., 'Economic Lot Size Determination in Multi-State Assembly Systems', *Management Science*, vol. 19, no. 5 (January 1973), pp. 517–527.
3. Dantzig, G. B., 'Optimal Solution to a Dynamic Leontief Model with Substitution', *Econometrica*, vol. 23 (1955), pp. 295–302.
4. Darukhanavala, P. P., 'Economic Lot Size Determination in Multi-item, Multi-level Production-inventory Systems with Acyclic Network Structures', *Ph.D. Dissertation*, Case Western Reserve University (July 1975).
5. Gorenstein, S., 'Planning Tire Production', *Management Science*, vol. 17, no. 2 (October 1970), pp. B-72, B-82.
6. Heahling von Lanzenauer, C., 'A Production Scheduling Model by Bivalent Linear Programming', *Management Science*, vol. 17, no. 1 (September 1970), pp. 105–111.
7. Jensen P. A. and Khan M. A., 'Scheduling in a Multi-Stage Production System with Set-up and Inventory Costs', *AIIE Transactions*, vol. 4, no. 2 (1972), pp. 126–133.
8. Love, S., 'A Facilities in Series Inventory Model with Nested Schedules', *Management Science*, vol. 18, no. 5 (January 1972), pp. 327–338.
9. Manne, A. S., 'Programming of Economic Lot Sizes', *Management Science*, vol. 4, no. 2 (January 1958), pp. 115–135.
10. Schussel G., 'Job-Shop Lot Release Sizes', *Management Science*, vol. 14, no. 8 (April 1968), pp. B449–472.
11. Taha, H. A. and Sheith, R. W., 'The Economic Lot Size in Multi-Stage Production Systems', *AIIE Transactions*, vol. 2, no. 2 (June 1970), pp. 157–162.
12. Young, H. H., 'Optimization Methods for Production Lines', *Journal of Industrial Engineering*, vol. 18 (1967), pp. 70–78.
13. Zangwill, W. I., 'A Back-logging model and a Multi-Echelon Model of a Dynamic Economic Lot Size Production System – A Network Approach', *Management Science*, vol. 15, no. 9 (May 1969), pp. 506–527.

18. Impact of a product structure measure on the effectiveness of lot sizing techniques

STEPHEN H. GOODMAN

Abstract

Within multi-stage, multi-product manufacturing systems a variety of decision making areas exist, each relating to a specific level of disaggregation in the overall scheme of hierarchical decision making. Appropriate decisions are required in each decision area if the manufacturing system is to perform effectively. Much effort has been exerted in trying to determine the best ways of making these various decisions. However, the best way of making the decisions for a particular manufacturing system can often be a function of the physical characteristics of the system. After describing the types of hierarchical decisions in multi-stage manufacturing systems and the different types of physical characteristics for such systems, this paper will describe experimental efforts to determine the impact of one of these physical characteristics on one of the second level disaggregation decisions.

18.1. Hierarchical decisions in multi-stage systems

In most manufacturing firms production proceeds in stages extending from the acquisition of raw materials to the completion of the finished product. Such multi-stage production systems possess a hierarchical arrangement of inventory items in which the raw materials assume the lowest position in the hierarchy, and finished goods the uppermost. Between these two extremes would lie a continuum of inventory items, such as parts, components, and subassemblies, which have progressed through some subset of the production stages.

It is generally acknowledged that material requirements planning (MRP) can provide a highly effective means for controlling inventories at all levels of production in systems of this type. However, it can be argued that MRP is nothing more than a massive data hand-

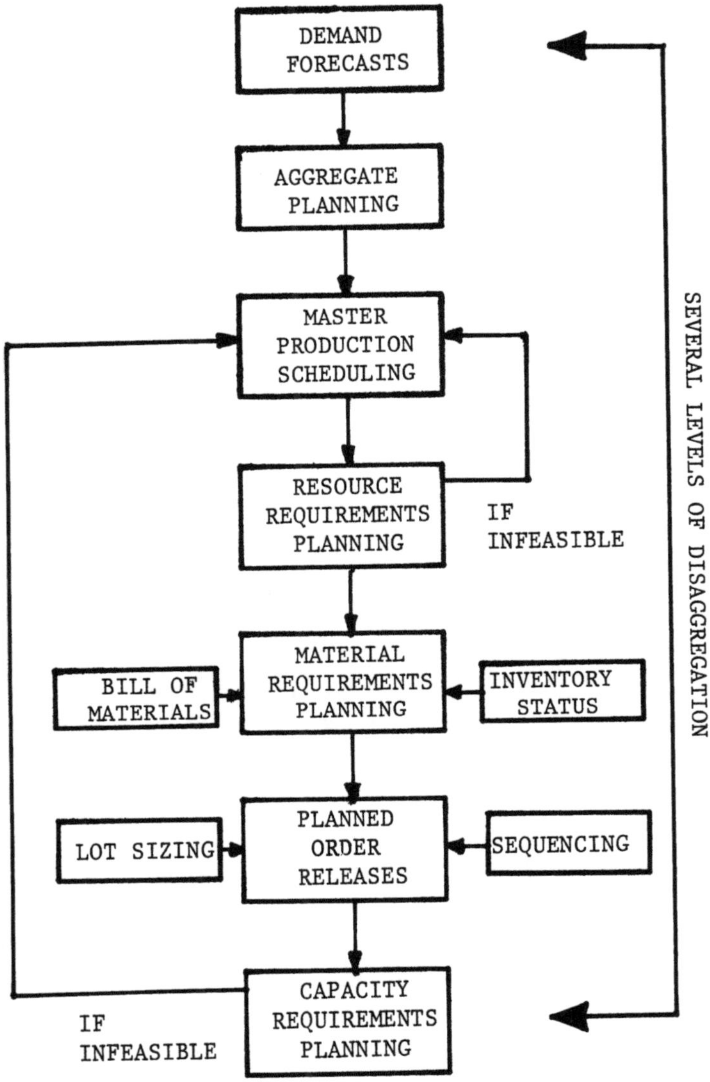

Figure 1. Hierarchical decisions in multi-stage systems.

ling and manipulating routine upon which a multitude of supporting decisions impinge. These decision areas are depicted in Figure 1.

Briefly, these decisions require first that demand forecasts be made and used as input to the aggregate planning process, wherein aggregate levels of production and employment decisions are made. These must be converted into a master production schedule, which will eventually drive the manufacturing operations. However, a process of resource requirements planning should first be employed to determine whether sufficient aggregate levels of all resources (e.g., worker capacity, machine capacity, warehouse space, materials, capital, etc.) will be available to support the master production schedule. If the schedule violates any resource constraints, it must be revised if the production system is to have any hope of making what the master production schedule has asked it to produce.

The master schedule, together with the bill of materials and inventory status, can now serve as input to the MRP system. These inputs alone are not sufficient to determine planned order releases, for MRP will not automatically generate information on the timing and sizing of production lots unless lot sizing and sequencing routines are established. Finally, the output of planned order releases must be put through a capacity requirements planning phase to determine whether sufficient plant capacity will be available during each time period to support the master production schedule. If capacity is not sufficient, revisions must be made to the master production schedule. This brief discussion of the total manufacturing decision making process is intended to illustrate the high degree of interrelationship that exists between several decision areas in multi-stage manufacturing systems. It also serves to illustrate that several levels of disaggregation are encountered in attempting to convert demand forecasts into detailed production schedules.

18.2. System objectives

A simple statement of the basic control problem in systems of the type being considered here might propose that one wishes to 'do what must be done to match supply and demand at the output points of the system in the most economical way.' This simple statement unleashes a multitude of concerns, for 'the most economical way' requires that many decisions be made at all organizational levels. Each of these decision areas will have its own unique set of problems and associated costs. For example, such considerations as worker hiring, layoff, overtime, idle time, inventory accumulation and depletion, stockouts, backorders, subcontracting, expediting, lot sizing, lot timing, lot splitting, lot sequencing, lot aggregating, and capacity adjusting must be taken into account, and decisions made with regard to each. Since each has its own particular set of cost parameters, and since many of these factors are interrelated, it becomes a rather difficult chore to determine what must be done to match supply with demand in the most economical way. In fact, for systems of any appreciable size, the complexities of the interactions are such that optimal solutions to these problems are virtually impossible to achieve analytically.

Because of these barriers to an analytical optimal solution, simulation has quite often been used to examine the effects of various decision alternatives on the performance of multi-stage systems. Such an approach has its limitations in that any results obtained using the simulation approach are applicable only to systems that reflect the characteristics of the simulation model. Although the simulated system may be described as a multi-stage, multi-product system, there are many further dimensions that characterize such systems. These individual dimensions can be said to determine the shop/product structure of the system, for they are generally related to characteristics of the shop and/or the products made in the shop. To obtain generality of results, results that might be applied to a wider variety of real situations, one must contend with the issue of shop/product structure, or system configuration.

18.3. System configuration measures

Among the various dimensions that define a specific system, most can be classified as being either shop related or product related, and either economic or noneconomic in nature. These two dichotomous categories are used in constructing the four way classification scheme for shop/product dimensions that follows.

18.3.1. Noneconomic shop related dimensions

In general, these dimensions define the physical characteristics of a particular multi-stage, multi-product production system. These dimensions include such factors as the number of hierarchical levels (or stages of production), and the ratio of total work content by stage. The resource constraint (machine limited, labor limited, or machine and labor limited) forms another dimension. Each of these resources may have its own characteristics. For example, labor might be highly skilled specialists, unskilled generalists, or some combination of both. Systems might differ in the number of machines or the number of workers. Machines might be single purpose or multi-purpose. Machine and worker output rates might also vary from system to system, thereby defining another dimension. Systems might also vary in their capacities to hold inventories at all stages of production. These are some of the prime examples of noneconomic, shop related dimensions that define characteristics of different multi-stage, multi-product production systems.

18.3.2. Noneconomic product related dimensions

Within this category, the factors which help define the product profile are related predominantly to the product. The work flows and resulting product structures are dimensions to be considered. Systems might vary between convergent systems and divergent systems. With convergent product structures, lower level products tend to be unique to specific higher level products, whereas with divergent product structures, lower level products have more universal use in higher level products. Product structures may differ in their degree of wideness, or their degree of depth. Products may also differ with regard to their demand patterns.

Trend and seasonality may or may not be present, and where seasonality exists on more than one item, the seasonal periods may or may not be in phase. In forecasting these demands, systems and products may differ in the amount of uncertainty associated with the forecasts. Additional dimensions relate to the number of products at each stage of production, ratios of the numbers of products at various stages, and production ordering lead times for various products at various stages of production.

18.3.3. Economic shop related dimensions

The economic dimensions are generally related to the cost of exercising the various shop related decision options. These include such factors as the costs of hiring workers, firing or laying off workers, overtime premiums, subcontracting costs, and most capacity related costs. These cost factors are critical to the objective function, for as was previously stated, one attempts to select alternatives for all the potential decision areas in the most economical way.

18.3.4. Economic product related dimensions

Included in this category are cost items that can be directly associated with individual products. For example, item setup costs, item ordering costs, inventory carrying costs, and item expediting costs can be included. Additional economic factors to be considered in this category include item material and labor costs, and selling prices. This set of economic dimensions would complement the previous set and provide the information needed in the construction of an objective function.

18.4. Objectives of this study

Of particular interest in this paper is the question of the sizing and timing of production lots. Many lot sizing approaches exist, consequently, the choice of an appropriate one for a particular situation should be of concern to anyone responsible for the effective operation of a multi-stage, multi-product production system. Of specific concern is the impact upon lot sizing of one of the system configuration measures noted above. This system configuration measure relates to the degree of depth (flatness or tallness) in the structure of the product.

18.5. Research model description

The vehicle for conducting these experiments is Factory V, a computer simulation model of a multi-stage, multi-product manufacturing system. The program is a highly flexible and powerful model designed to provide the user with the capability of performing exploratory analyses in such areas as sales forecasting, master scheduling, aggregate planning, production lot sizing, priority scheduling and inventory control. Model inputs include the costs of materials, hiring, firing, expediting, carrying inventories, and overtime as well as such parameters as setup times, beginning inventories, product compositions, and demand forecasts.

Production is simulated using specifications submitted by the user in the decision areas noted above. The user has the option of altering the manner of making these decisions by simply rewriting program subroutines. In addition, the user has the capability of altering many of the determinants of the system characteristics by simply changing input cards, or by performing minor programming changes. The output of the system includes inventory information, production information, labor and machine utilization data, stockout and shortage reports, and a variety of production and inventory related cost information.

18.6. Independent variables of the study

It was noted above that this study was concerned with the effects of various lot sizing techniques on the performance of a multi-stage, multi-product production system. Furthermore, it was pointed out that the lot sizing techniques would be examined under differing degrees of depth in the structure of the products being manufactured. These two parameters, lot sizing and degree of depth form the two independent variables of this study.

18.6.1. Lot sizing

Five lot sizing techniques were selected for examination in this study. These techniques are:

1. Lot for Lot (LFL)
2. Economic order quantity (EOQ)
3. Periodic order quantity (POQ)
4. Least total cost (LTC)
5. Wagner-Whitin algorithm (WW)

With the exception of the last technique, these are all commonly applied lot sizing methods in actual practice. The last technique, somewhat sophisticated in its methodology, is included because it

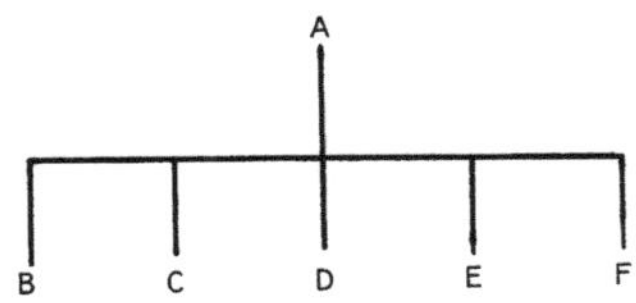

Figure 2. Flat product structure.

is an optimization technique and is often used as a benchmark for comparison. With the exception of the EOQ rule, all of the techniques examined here are discrete lot sizing techniques, i.e., they order the requirements for a discrete number of successive planning periods.

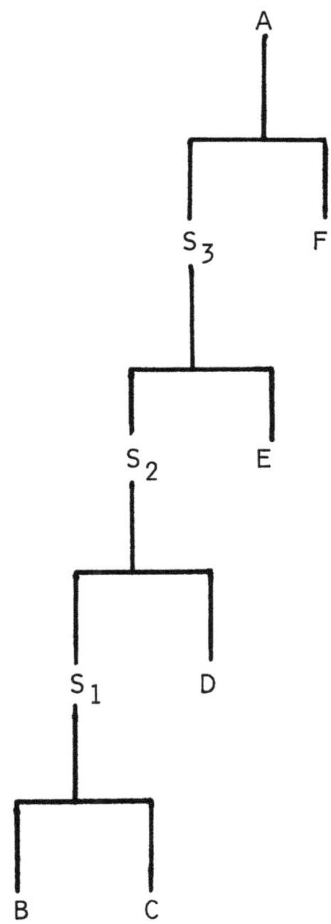

Figure 3. Tall product structure.

18.6.2. Degree of depth

In the simulated production environment, ten finished products are to be manufactured. In alternate experimental runs, structures will be either tall or flat. However, in either case the composition of a particular product is unaltered. The same materials are required for a particular product whether the structure is tall or flat. For example, consider the bill of materials presented in Figure 2.

Figure 2 represents a flat product structure for a finished product, *A*. Figure 3, on the other hand, represents a tall structure for the same product. Close examination of these figures reveals that in each case the finished product is composed of the same materials, i.e., each *A* requires a unit of *B*, *C*, *D*, *E*, and *F*. However, the difference lies in the manner in which these materials are put together. In Figure 2, the flat structure, the *B*, *C*, *D*, *E*, and *F* are all assembled together at the same planning level. In the tall structure of Figure 3, the assembly is quite different. First *B* and *C* are combined to yield a subassembly, S_1, which must be combined with *D* to yield another subassembly, S_2. S_2 is in turn combined with *E* to yield a third subassembly, S_3, which is finally combined with *F* to yield the finished product *A*. The number of planning levels is quite different in each of these figures.

18.7. Dependent variables

The dependent variables of this study reflect a variety of system performance measures. These measures include such information as average inventory levels, backorders, late arrivals of materials, time spent waiting for materials, setup times, run times, machine utilizations, and worker utilizations. Examining several performance measures enhances the possibility of greater applicability of results to real operating systems. Space limitations preclude the possibility of a thorough listing and examination of the output data, i.e., the effects of lot sizing and degree of depth on the system performance measures. However, the results will be provided upon request to any interested reader.

References

1. Berry, W. L., 'Lot Sizing Procedures for Requirements Planning Systems: A Framework for Analysis', *Production and Inventory Management*, 2nd Quarter (1972).
2. Orlicky, J. A., *Material Requirements Planning* (New York, McGraw-Hill Book Company, 1975).
3. Orlicky, J. A., Plossl, G. W., and Wight, O. W., 'Structuring the Bill of Material for MRP', *Production and Inventory Management*, 4th Quarter (1972).
4. Wight, O. W., *Production and Inventory Management in the Computer Age* (Boston, Cahners Books, 1974).

19. The effects of joint lot size strategies on capacity related performance in a multi-stage production-inventory system

DAVID A. COLLIER

Abstract

The introduction of Material Requirements Planning has focused attention on the problems of multi-stage production-inventory systems. Although considerable research has focused on lot sizing much of this research is of little use to the MRP user in selecting appropriate lot size strategies. This paper presents a research methodology that evaluates multi-level lot sizing in an MRP system as a function of capacity, service, and computation time performance measures.

19.1. Introduction

Material Requirements Planning (MRP) has been introduced to industry as a planning methodology for a hierarchical multi-product, multi-period, and multi-stage production-inventory system. A multi-stage production-inventory system begins with raw materials and proceeds through a series of production stages until the final product is produced. Inventory items are arranged in a hierarchical fashion and upon completion of each stage go into and out of an identifiable inventory. Work-in-process inventories of component parts and sub-assemblies serve as input to higher level stages. MRP recognizes this relationship between product structure and the production process.

A review of the articles written by MRP users [5, 7, 10] indicates that existing literature is of little use in selecting appropriate lot size models or in assessing their impact on total system performance. When one compares this literature with existing lot size research one can readily identify the disparity between the needs of the practicing MRP manager and the nature and focus of past research.

Utilizing the results of past lot size research is difficult in an MRP system because of the following reasons:

1. The primary focus of past research has been on single-stage systems. The results of these studies are difficult to extend to multi-stage systems.
2. The interactions between lot size models at different levels of the product structure have not been evaluated in an MRP system. Would the Wagner-Whitin lot size model applied at the end-item level in conjunction with the Lot-for-Lot model at the intermediate levels perform better than other lot size strategies?
3. Useful experimental design factors for selecting appropriate lot size strategies for a given operating environment have not been incorporated into past research. For example, demand variability, demand uncertainty, and product structure characteristics would appear to be useful experimental design factors.
4. Lot size models have not been adequately tested under realistic conditions. For example, lot size strategies should be tested under stochastic conditions and with common component parts at different levels among many end-items.
5. Lot size models have been evaluated in terms of only three variables – setup cost, inventory carrying cost, and computation time. Other performance factors include damping system nervousness and the effects on aggregate load patterns at the work center level. Fixed order quantity models that result in remnant inventories may be advantageous in terms of damping system nervousness.

Although much research has concentrated on lot sizing, these five reasons help explain the disparity between the theoretical and practicing state of the art. This paper outlines a research methodology for analyzing these issues.

19.2. Simulation model

A simulation model called Factory V will serve as the basic simulation model for this research. It was developed jointly by Stanley Hardy of The Ohio State University and David Dukes of Texas Tech University. In general, Factory V is a Fortran based simulation model built around the concept of material requirements planning.

For this research, a Capacity Planning sub-routine will be added to assess the impacts of joint lot size strategies on work center loads.

The simulation model consists of three phases and utilizes the Gasp IV Simulation Language to schedule events, maintain files, and collect most of the performance data. The general content of each of the three phases of Factory V is as follows:

Initialization phase:	Demand function Planning horizon Product structures and related information Routing alternatives Shop configuration Labour productivities Number of machines Capacity available
Planning phase (weekly):	Forecast Demand Aggregate planning Master scheduling Material requirements planning Lot sizing Priority planning Capacity planning Order release
Execution phase (daily):	Operates the factory

The modular design of Factory V allows the user to insert his own sub-routines and to input different decision rules and system parameters and test the performance of the planned decisions via the execution phase of the model.

19.3. End-item demand

The demand for each end-item in Factory V is determined by a sinusoidal function with a trend component plus an error term. The functional form is shown by equation 1 below.

$$D(i, t) = Y_i[1 + X_i t + \sin(\Pi t/W_i)] + e(i, t) \qquad (1)$$

where:

Y_i the Y intercept when $t = 0$ (base demand for product i)
X_i the slope of the trend component divided by Y_i
W_i a coefficient indicating one half a seasonal period

The sine or cosine function can be used to depict periodicity. The trend factor represents the degree of growth or decay in the product demand pattern. The error term is assumed to be normally distributed with zero expectation.

The forcast for product i in period t is given by equation 2 below.

$$F(i, t) = Y_i[1 + X_i t + \sin(\Pi t / W_i)] \quad (2)$$

All of the terms are defined as in equation (1). Thus, the demand for product i in period t is simply the forecast for product i in period t plus the error term.

Demand uncertainty must be distinguished from demand variability. Demand uncertainty is associated with the probability distribution of forecast errors in any single period t. The error term in equation (1) represents the degree of demand uncertainty. If the error term equals zero the demand is described as being deterministic. That is, the demand for product i in period t will equal the forecast for product i in period t. If the error term does not equal zero the demand is described as being stochastic.

Demand variability is associated with the degree of variability in the entire forecast pattern. Demand variability is usually described as being continuous or discontinuous and whether the demand pattern has a trend and/or seasonal component.

19.4. Joint lot size strategies

Lot size models can be categorized into two general classes as suggested by Krajewski [4]. One class of models does not specifically recognize dependencies between assemblies and components at various production levels. This is called the 'independent lot'. Independent lot models include: Lot-for-Lot, Periodic Order Quantity, Economic Order Quantity, Modified Economic Order Quantity, Least Unit Cost. Least Total Cost, and Wagner-Whitin models.

Each of these models can be applied to a single demand pattern like the net requirements for an item in an MRP system.

The second class of models are called 'dependent lot' models. These techniques directly derive a lot size at one level (stage) whose sizing and timing decisions are dependent upon the sizing and timing decisions of other lots at different levels (stages). Dependent lot models include: Crowston, Wagner, and William's model [1], McLaren and Whybark's Adusted Order Moment model [6], and Schussel's ELRS model [9]. These models at their present stage of development cannot handle many of the complexities found in actual MRP systems such as multiple parents, multiple successors, and common components among end-items.

System nervousness and computation time may also be limiting factors with regard to dependent lot models. A nervous MRP system is defined as one that generates excessive changes to lower-level requirements when there are only minor changes in higher-level parameters such as the master schedule, on-hand inventories, lead times, and premature order releases.

A joint lot size strategy is defined as any lot size algorithm or combination of lot size algorithms that is applied to more than one level (stage) of the product structure (production process). Thus, all dependent lot models or combinations of independent lot models represent alternative joint lot size strategies. For example, Figure 1 depicts a joint lot size strategy for two end-items from the same product line. The Wagner-Whitin lot size model is employed at the end-item level and the Lot-for-Lot model for components 3 through 8.

A dynamic lot size model is any lot size technique in which a

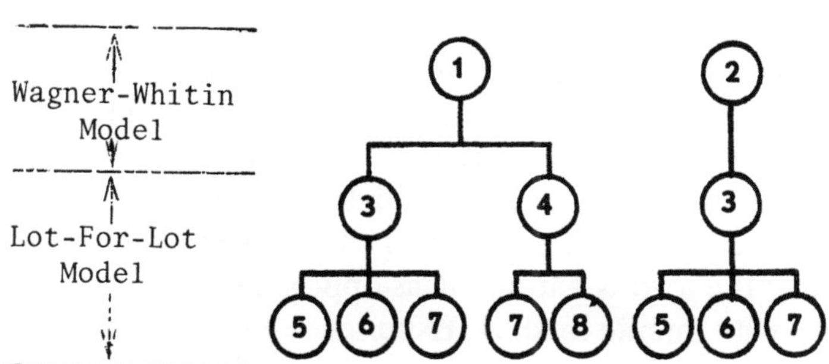

Figure 1. A joint lot size strategy for two end-items.

transaction triggers the recomputation of the lot size and possibly changes the timing and/or quantity of the previous lot size. This is opposed to a fixed lot size model in which transactions can trigger only a change in the timing and not the quantity of the lot size. Such changes in the timing and quantity effect all lower level component parts. The fixed lot size models can result in remnant inventories and thus have a damping effect on system nervousness. In practice, fixed lot sizes normally represent a price break quantity, a full pallet quantity, or restrictions on available storage space.

19.5. Capacity related performance

Three general approaches to resource loading and smoothing at the work center level are: (1) Infinite Loading, (2) Finite Loading, and (3) Input/Output Planning. All three of these approaches have considered the effects of component inventories, product structure, planning lead times, replacement parts, open orders, and lot sizing.

Infinite loading

Infinite loading is a system of loading manufacturing orders usually expressed in terms of man or machine hours in the time periods in which they are required regardless of whether or not capacity is available to produce these jobs in that specific time period. As suggested by IBM [2] and others, if actual capacity is not adequate management must simulate alternative production plans by more or less a trial and error approach.

Finite loading

Finite loading is a system of loading manufacturing orders usually expressed in terms of man or machine hours only in the time periods where adequate capacity is available to produce a certain group of jobs in that specific time period. Such a system requires an order priority system as a basis for loading and rescheduling orders. Thus, smoothing the load is automatic as opposed to direct management decisions with infinite loading. Experience with this approach indicates that it has not been very successful and is considered obsolete by most authorities [8].

Input/Output planning

Input/Output Planning begins with the infinite load report and attempts to stabilize work center backlogs based on maintaining a constant backlog equivalent to a fixed planning lead time in terms of weeks of output. It recognizes that if input is higher than output, the backlog and actual lead times will increase. If output is higher than input the backlog and actual lead times will decrease. If the output rates cannot be adjusted then adjusting the input rate is the remaining course of action. To change the input rate changes must be made in the timing and/or quantity of end-item and component lots.

19.5.1. Effects of joint lot size strategies on load

With infinite loading or input/output planning management replanning decisions are based on the static aggregate load profiles. The implicit assumption during this process is that the static load is equivalent to the dynamic load that will be experienced by the shop. The dynamic load can be measured in terms of utilization per day. Under the assumption of zero planning lead times the static and dynamic load profiles are equivalent.

Figure 2 describes the nature of static aggregate load profiles. Figure 2a depicts a highly irregular load pattern while Figure 2b depicts a more stable load profile. Suppose both load profiles were based on the same group of end-items, end-item demands, amount of component inventories, and planning lead times but differed in joint lot size strategy employed.

Management confronted with a schedule as in Figure 2a would have to make replanning decisions in attempting to stablize the work flow. Typical courses of action include delaying orders, pull-up orders, increasing the planning lead times and thus work-in-process inventories, and adjusting capacity available. A joint lot size strategy which performed favorably with regard to stabilizing aggregate load patterns would reduce the number of potential reschedules required and still meet end-item due dates. For example, for a seasonal demand pattern the Wagner-Whitin lot size model may tend to group lot sizes closely together by following the seasonal pattern. From a capacity viewpoint this could be undesirable.

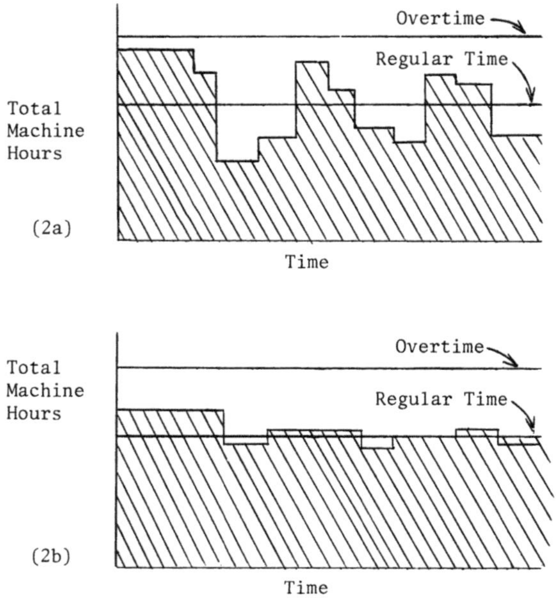

Figure 2. Static effects of two different joint lot size strategies on the load pattern for resource group J.

The evaluation of the effects of joint lot size strategies on aggregate load profiles requires a new measure. It should measure the degree of aggregate load variability at the work center level. Equation (3) below defines Ω_j, the 'Coefficient of Aggregate Load Variation'.

$$\Omega_j = \frac{\sigma_j}{\overline{L}_j} \qquad j = 1, 1, \ldots, J$$

where:

- σ_j the standard deviation of weekly aggregate load in machine hours for resource j
- $\overline{L}_j$ the average weekly aggregate load for resource j

A relative comparison can be made between Ω_j values for alternate joint lot size strategies. The lower the Ω_j value the more stable and even the resulting aggregate load profile.

19.5.2. Cost surrogates

In addition to measuring the degree of aggregate load variability (Ω_j), a second capacity related performance measure is total machine hours. The relationship between regular time costs, overtime costs, setup costs, and inventory carrying costs are company specific. Furthermore, typical cost structures consist of smaller ratios of setup costs to inventory carrying costs at the upper (assembly) levels of the product structure and higher ratios at the lower manufactured component levels. In order to reduce the effects the cost structure may have on the selection of joint lot size strategies, total machine hours are employed as one of the primary performance measures.

Since inventory can be thought of as stored machine hours, inventory carrying costs can be converted into equivalent machine hours (I_t) as shown in equations (4) through (7). Regular time and overtime machine hours include setup and run times. One overtime hour will be equivalent to 1.5 regular time hours. Total machine hours (T_t) used over time t is simply the sum of regular time (R_t), overtime ($\emptyset_t$), and equivalent inventory (I_t) as shown by equation (8).

$$V_t = S_t + F + U \tag{4}$$

$$M_t = R_t + 1.5\emptyset_t \tag{5}$$

$$\beta = V_t / M_t \tag{6}$$

$$I_t = C[X_t + Y_t]/\beta \tag{7}$$

$$T_t = M_t + I_t \tag{8}$$

where:

- V_t the value of total manufactured goods over time t
- S_t the value of finished goods sold over time t
- F the value of finished goods ending inventory
- U the value of work-in-process ending inventory
- M_t the total regular time and overtime machine hours used over time t
- R_t the regular time machine hours used over time t
- $\emptyset_t$ the overtime machine hours used over time t

- I_t the inventory carrying cost expressed as equivalent machine hours over time t
- C the inventory carrying charge expressed as a percentage of inventory value over time t
- X_t the average value of finished goods inventory over time t
- Y_t the average value of work-in-process inventory over time t
- β the average value of goods produced per machine hour
- T_t the total machine hours used over time t
- t the data collection period from $m + 1$ to $l - m$ weeks
- m the longest cumulative manufacturing lead time of all end-items
- l the total number of weeks in the planning horizon

The data collection period 't' will avoid any effects caused by initial on-hand inventories and decreasing capacity requirements at the end of the planning horizon.

19.6. Experimental design

This research is divided into two distinct phases. Demand will be deterministic in Phase One and stochastic in Phase Two. A total of 144 deterministic simulation runs will be made in Phase One. In Phase Two null hypotheses will be evaluated via analysis of variance and nonparametric statistics.

The major problem in testing joint lot size strategies is a combinatorial problem. For example, to test all combinations of four independent lot size models at only three product structure levels would require 64 combinations. There are two bases for reducing the potential number of combinations.

First, product structures are normally viewed as composed of three general levels. The 'top' level is usually the end-item level only; the 'intermediate' level consists of all manufactured subassembly and component parts; and the 'lower' level consists of all raw materials. Since this research is concerned with shop performance and assumes that purchased parts are always available, the lower levels can be ignored. The second factor that allows one to reduce the potential number of combinations relates to the characteristics of each lot size model and the needs of an actual MRP system. Excessive computation time, poor performance, and enhancing system nervousness are major characteristics that are detrimental to the efficient operation of an MRP system.

Combination Number	Top Level	Intermediate Levels
1	WW	LFL
2	WW	LTC
3	WW	FEOQ
4	LTC	LFL
5	LTC	LTC
6	LTC	FEOQ
7	FEOQ	LFL
8	FEOQ	LTC
9	FEOQ	FEOQ

Therefore, the following joint lot size strategies evaluated in this research should provide enough diversity to satisfy theoretical as well as practical considerations. Note that the Wagner-Whitin (WW), Lot-for-Lot (LFL), and Least Total Cost (LTC) models are all dynamic lot size algorithms. The Fixed Economic Order Quantity (FEOQ) model is computed once based on end-item demand and does not change upon each MRP regeneration. Intermediate FEOQ's equal end-item FEOQ's.

In addition to the factors of demand variability, demand uncertainty, and alternate lot size strategies, product structure characteristics are incorporated into the experimental design. Due to space limitations these measures will not be presented. However, the analytically defined product structure characteristics relate to the degree of component commonality, the degree of wideness, and the degree of flatness. Two levels are defined for each of these three factors. These product structure measures are defined over a set of end-items. That is, the measures can be for all end-items or a family (product line) of end-items or just one end-item. Such a measure is useful for real world multi-product environments.

The factors and number of levels for each factor in this research are as follows:

Factor	Number of Levels
Joint Lot Size Strategies	9
Demand Variability	2
Demand Uncertainty	2
Degree of Commonality	2
Degree of Wideness	2
Degree of Flatness	2

For the factor of demand variability two levels will be defined employing Kaimann's [3] Coefficient of Demand Variation. Two levels will be statistically defined for the factor of demand uncertainty.

19.7. Performance measures

The measures of effectiveness in this research are as follows:

1. Capacity Related Statistics
   - *Total Machine Hours (T_t)
   - Regular Time
   - Overtime
   - Equivalent Inventory
     - Finished Goods
     - Work-in-Process
   - * Ω_j Values By Resource Group
   - Static Load Profiles By Resource Group
   - Dynamic Load Profiles By Resource Group
     (Utilization By Day, Week, and Total)
   - Number of Jobs Processed
     - By Resource Group
     - Total

2. Service (Order Processing) Statistics
   * Average, Minimum, and Maximum Number of Weeks Late per End-Item
   Average, Minimum, and Maximum Number of Weeks Late per Component Order
   Total Time in System per Order
3. * Computation Time for each Joint Lot Size Strategy
4. Queue Statistics (Total and by Resource Group)
   Average, Minimum, and Maximum Number of Jobs in Queue
   Average Wait Time per Job

19.8 Conclusion

This research addresses the discrepancies between the theoretical and practicing state of the art that were outlined in the introduction of this paper. Compared to past lot size research, the conditions in this study under which alternate joint lot size strategies are tested more closely resembles an actual operating environment.

The results of this study will provide the MRP user with general guidelines for selecting joint lot size strategies and in assessing their impact on total system performance. Performance is measured as a function of capacity, service, and computation time measures of effectiveness. The ultimate use of the Factory V simulation model would be to model a firm's shop, product, and cost structure and input actual factory data (forecasts, on-hand inventories, etc.). Then alternative production plans and decision rules could be tested prior to implementation.

References

1. Crowston, W. B., Wagner, M., and Williams, J. F., 'Economic Lot Size Determination in Multi-Stage Assembly Systems', *Management Science*, vol. 19 no. 5 (January 1973), pp. 517–527.

* Although all of the above performance measures will be useful in the analysis, the primary performance measures are asterisk (*).

2. IBM, Communications Oriented Production Information and Control System (COPICS Manuals), Form No. G320-1977, Technical Publications Department, White Plains, New York (1972).
3. Kaimann, R. A., 'EOQ vs. Dynamic Programming – Which One to Use for Inventory Ordering', *Production and Inventory Management*, vol. 10, no. 4 (1969), pp. 66–74.
4. Krajewski, L. J., 'Detailed Planning in Multi-Stage Systems – A Review of the Literature with Recommendations for Future Research', Presented at the Annual Midwest AIDS Meeting, Indiannapolis, Indiana (1975).
5. Lowerre, W. M., 'Lot Size Rules a One Act Play', *Production and Inventory Management*, vol. 16, no. 2 (1975), pp. 41–50.
6. McLaren, B. J. and Whybark, D. C., 'A Dynamic Simulation of Joint Lot Sizing Procedures for MRP Systems', Proceedings of the Eight Annual AIDS Meeting, San Francisco, California (November 1976).
7. New, C. C., 'Lot-Sizing in Multi-Levels Requirements Planning Systems', *Production and Inventory Management*, vol. 15, no. 4 (1974), pp. 57–72.
8. Plossl, G. W. and Wight, O. W., 'Capacity Planning and Control', *Production and Inventory Management*, vol. 14, no. 3 (1973), pp. 31–67.
9. Schussel, G., 'Job Shop Lot Release Sizes', *Management Science*, vol. 14, no. 8 (April 1968).
10. Steele, D. C., 'The Nervous MRP System: How to Do Battle', *Production and Inventory Management*, vol. 16 no. 4 (1975), pp. 83–88.

20. The impact of capacity on lot sizing decisions

JOSEPH R. BIGGS and CHAN K. HAHN

Abstract

This paper reports on the results of research intended to examine the impact of capacity level on the performances of different lot sizing rules in a multiproduct, multistage system using Material Requirements Planning. The results are measured on the basis of frequency of stockouts, number of setups and average dollar inventory level, and total inventory cost. Although the impact of capacity level on the relative performance of different lot sizing rules is not as significant as originally suspected, it is an important factor along with other factors to be considered in choosing an appropriate decision rule. Our findings also brought out several points which do not confirm many previous studies.

20.1. Introduction

Although there have been many scientific and mathematical algorithms developed in relation to manufacturing lot sizing decisions, continuing concerns have been expressed by practicing managers regarding selection of an appropriate lot sizing rule to be used in a 'real' world situation. This has been particularly true, in recent years, under the more complex multistage, multiproduct manufacturing environment using Material Requirements Planning.

Some authors suggest that the choice of a lot sizing rule has relatively little impact upon the total manufacturing system [10]. Other authors have tried to answer this question by comparing different lot sizing rules under multistage manufacturing environments [1, 3, 6]. For example, Berry suggested a framework for comparing different lot sizing decision rules with respect to inventory related costs and computing time [1]. Kaimann's studies also suggest relative efficiency of different lot sizing rules under varying operating conditions [5, 6, 7].

There are, however, many major shortcomings related to previous studies. First, most of the previous studies assume the condition of sufficient capacity, and capacity level is treated as a constant. There are some indications that the capacity level of a manufacturing environment might have an impact on scheduling or lot sizing decisions. Vergin [11] argued that the status of capacity (production, employment, and inventory level) at the time of change – the 'point of departure' might have a great impact on production scheduling decisions. Biggs [2] also reported that capacity level might be an influencing factor in determining relative efficiency of different lot sizing decision rules.

Second, most of the previous studies also used unique sets of operating parameters to determine the relative efficiency of different lot sizing rules, thus, the results could vary greatly under the different sets of operating parameters. Berry [1], therefore, suggests further study under a wide range of costs and demand parameters. Lowerre [9] also demonstrated a potential problem of misrepresentation of previous studies.

The purposes of this paper, then are (1) to examine the possible impact and magnitude of capacity level on relative performance of lot sizing rules with regard to several different performance criteria, and (2) to analyze the implications of the findings.

20.2. Research methodology

20.2.1. Simulation

The system simulation model is an adaptation of 'Factory-2', [8] a multistage production inventory model.[1] There are four inventory levels: raw materials, parts, subassemblies, and finished goods. There are eight raw materials, fifteen parts, seven subassemblies, and ten final products (see Figure 1).

This model embodies the capacity to forecast sales, make aggregate and detailed planning decisions, and accumulate data for report generation on timely bases. The model utilizes discrete time

1. A copy of this adaptation is available on request from the following: Biggs, J. R. or Hahn, C. K., Management Department, Bowling Green State University, Bowling Green, Ohio 43403.

periods of one week for updating or making decisions. For a detailed description of this model, the reader is referred to the publication [8] (Kriebel).

To evaluate the effects on system performance of various lot sizing rules, it is necessary to incorporate many simplifying assumptions concerning the system. These assumptions are necessary, for example, in terms of the product demand, shop structure, product lead times, informational capabilities, labor force decisions, and possible interactions among these.

The basic simplifying assumption for this system is that demand is deterministic. The production system consists of three stages of production with each stage being treated as a single machine that never breaks down. Further, it is assumed that manpower is of uniform ability. When the system is constrained, the constraints are imposed by limiting the available manpower.

In the interaction of demand and shop structure it is assumed that no production stage can perform more than one operation at any one time. Each lot size, once started, must be completed if component parts or raw material is available. That is, machine time availability, while a constraint on total production, will not limit a production lot but can cause part of that lot to be shifted to the following week. No preemption of production lots is allowed. These

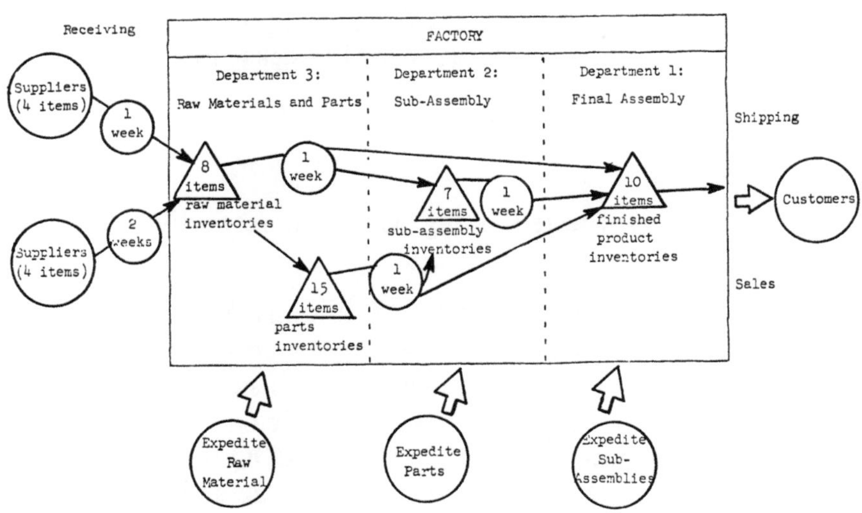

Figure 1. Schematic of factory organization and work flow: a simulation: 'factory-2', p. 9, [8].

assumptions, however, do not rule out the cancellation of orders that have not started production. The machine setup and operation time for each product is finite and known. Finally, it is assumed that these times are independent of any sequencing of other jobs through the system. The priority scheduling rule used throughout the study was an adaptation of the Critical Ratio Rule.

20.2.2. Experimental design and sample size

Of necessity, the experimental design has to be a complete factorial design. It would be difficult to determine possible key interaction of factors with anything less than this complete factorial design. Five runs or replications per combination amounts to 5 replications $\times$ 5 lot sizing rules $\times$ 5 labor force levels = 125 runs of the simulation model.

The difference between replications within each cell is in the demand of the final ten products. A random number generating routine is used to change this demand between replications. A small change is necessary to avoid the possibility of over- or under-loading the simulated system. This small change is achieved by causing demand between replications to be changed by an amount ranging from 0 percent to 10 percent normally distributed, randomly selected by a computer subroutine. Prior to a simulation run, the program is given starting values from an input data deck, after which it is further initialized by a run for 12 weeks prior to a 48-week simulation run.

20.2.3. Rules tested

The lot sizing rules tested, along with their respective abbreviations, are as follows:

1. *Economic Order Quantity* (EOQ). Traditional Wilson Lot Sizing Model which balances inventory carrying cost and order costs.
2. *Lot For Lot* (L4L). Order exactly what is needed in the next production period or 'time bucket', usually one week.
3. *Periodic Order Quantity* (POQ). Use the EOQ to determine the reorder time cycle, and then order what is actually forecast for that time cycle, again attempting to balance order cost and inventory carrying cost.

4. *Part Period Balancing* (PPB). Once again attempting to balance order cost and carrying cost. Using forecast demand keep increasing the size of the order until carrying cost is equal to or less than ordering cost.
5. *Wagner-Whitin* (W-W). Looking ahead for the total planning horizon and working *backwards* to the present, develop lot sizes for each period that achieve the 'best' or optimum order schedule, once more by comparing order costs and inventory carrying costs.

All of the above rules except the L4L rule will tend to combine the net requirements for more than one time period or 'bucket'. All except the EOQ rule will order requirements for integer multiples of time periods. That is, no fraction of a time period's requirement will be split into two different lots except by the EOQ.

20.2.4. Capacity levels

The 'ideal' labor force level of 247 men was determined by using the 'EOQ' model for multiple products from Buffa and Taubert [3] and summing required operation and setup times. This 'ideal' labor force was then increased/decreased to achieve the following constrained situations.

Constrained Capacity Levels

Level 1 = $.90 \times 247 = 222$ workers
Level 2 = $.95 \times 247 = 234$ workers
Level 3 = $1.00 \times 247 = 247$ workers
Level 4 = $1.05 \times 247 = 259$ workers
Level 5 = $1.10 \times 247 = 271$ workers

20.2.5. System performance

The performance of the system was analyzed using the following representative three criteria:

1. Total number of stockouts, final products
2. Total number of setups, total system
3. Average dollar value of inventory, total system

The effect of the various lot sizing rules on each of these individual criteria was measured.

20.3. Review of findings

One of the primary objectives of the study was to examine the impact of capacity level on efficiency of the different lot sizing rules. It has been suggested that relative performance levels of lot sizing rules are subject to the different cost parameters used. It has also been suggested that an accurate estimate of such cost parameters is difficult to obtain and such cost parameters vary widely depending on the characteristics of different operating situations. Therefore, any comparative analysis based on a single set of cost parameters will be difficult to generalize. In order to analyze the operating efficiencies of each lot sizing rule without introducing influences of cost parameters, performances of different lot sizing rules are first analyzed on the basis of a single criterion. The results are later combined into a total inventory cost for overall performance measure.

Table 1. Average number of stockouts by different lot sizing rules under different capacity levels.

	Lot Sizing Rule				
Capacity Level	EOQ	L4L	POQ	PPB	W-W
1	135.0	213.4	218.8	210.6	199.8
2	18.2	14.0	124.4	108.0	121.6
3	10.8	0.2	101.6	73.0	96.0
4	4.6	0	76.6	23.4	83.4
5	3.2	0	81.0	9.4	83.2

20.3.1. Capacity levels and stockouts

Table 1 and Figure 2 show the performance levels of five different lot sizing rules under five different capacity levels on the basis of frequency of stockouts. As the initial limited capacity situation (Capacity level 1), EOQ outperformed all other lots sizing rules. However, as the capacity situation improves, L4L performed equally well, and PPB joins with them at the sufficient capacity situation (Capacity level 5). All three lot sizing rules outperformed POQ and W-W under the sufficient capacity situation. It should be noted that the performance levels of all lot sizing rules improved greatly as the capacity level is changed gradually. The most significant improvement took place when the capacity level is changed from level 1 to level 2.

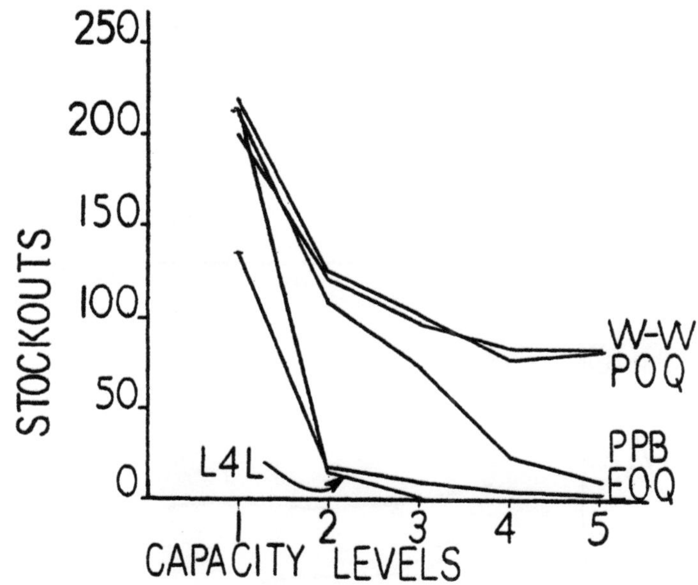

Figure 2

20.3.2. Capacity level and setups

Table 2 and Figure 3 summarize the performance of each lot sizing rule under different capacity situations on the basis of the average number of setups. Under the limited capacity situation (levels 1 and

Table 2. Average number of setups by different lot sizing rules under different capacity levels.

Capacity Level	Lot Sizing Rule EOQ	L4L	POQ	PPB	W-W
1	1565	1917	1653	1651	1684
2	1521	1920	1591	1562	1664
3	1502	1920	1589	1516	1660
4	1492	1920	1572	1469	1666
5	1490	1920	1565	1452	1652

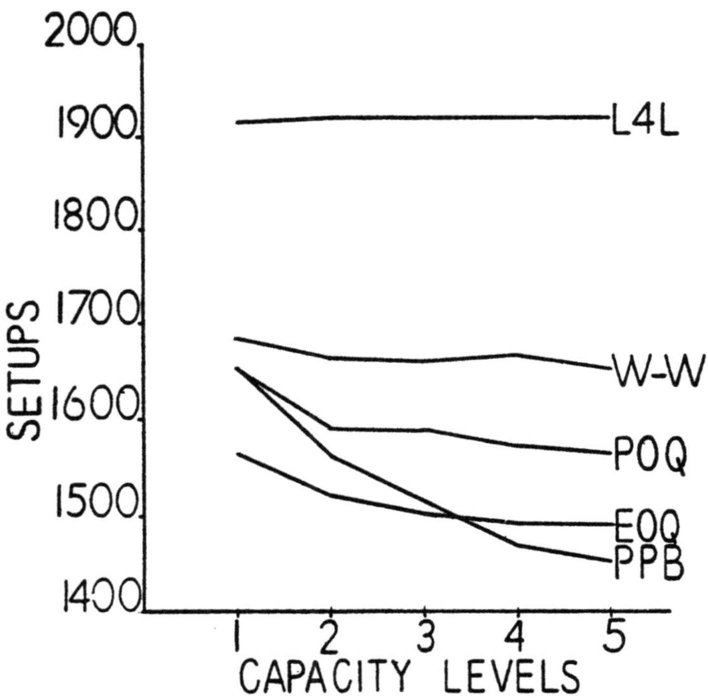

Figure 3

2), EOQ minimizes the average number of setups, and L4L rule requires the most number of setups. When the capacity level is increased to sufficient capacity situation (levels 4 and 5), PPB performed equally as well as, or even better than EOQ, and these two rules outperformed the other three lot sizing rules. In terms of an average number of setups required, all lot sizing rules except the L4L rule improved as the capacity is changed from level 1 through level 5. However, the magnitude of change was not as great as in the cases of stockouts or inventory level. For example, the number of setups needed under Capacity level 2 is not that much different than that of Capacity level 1. But when the performance at Capacity level 5 is compared with the performance at level 1, they were statistically different. The result indicates that the number of setups required are not capacity level sensitive.

20.3.3. Capacity levels and inventory level

Table 3 and Figure 4 show performance levels of each lot sizing rule in terms of average dollar amount of inventory level in the system under the varying capacity situations. Under this criterion, the L4L rule outperforms all other lot sizing rules at all capacity levels, and the EOQ rule required the greatest amount of inventories. As

Table 3. Average dollar amount of total inventories by lot sizing rules and capacity level.

	Lot Sizing Rule				
Capacity Level	EOQ	L4L	POQ	PPB	W-W
1	747700	473512	670984	590191	592810
2	679871	368536	614239	502064	531634
3	662231	367031	590843	474639	521873
4	649481	370238	5731417	425905	517368
5	632276	371074	582669	416924	518631

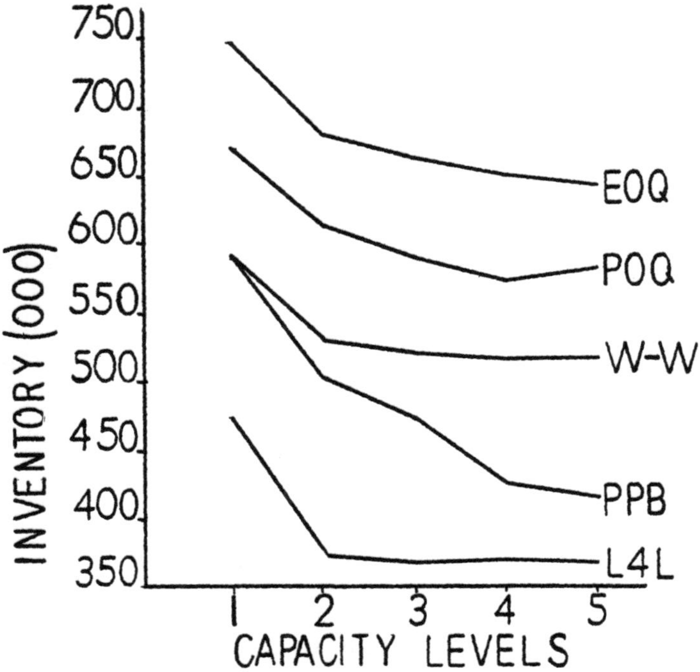

Figure 4

expected, the inventory level for all lot sizing rules decreased as the capacity levels are increased from level 1 through level 5. This result is consistent with the traditional notion that inventory is an alternative to increased capacity level. However, the magnitude of change slows down considerably after the capacity level reaches level 3 with the exception of the PPB rule.

20.3.4. Capacity level and total inventory costs

Table 4 shows the total inventory cost performance for different lot sizing rules under different capacity levels. Although the result is valid only at a given set of cost parameters, it was calculated for the purpose of comparison with previous studies.[2] When capacity level is limited (levels 1 and 2), the L4L rule resulted in the minimum total cost, and PPB closely follows the L4L rule. But when the capacity is raised to sufficient condition (levels 3, 4 and 5), PPB replaced L4L

2. An inventory holding cost of 20 percent of the value of items and an average of $75/setup were used to calculate total inventory cost.

Table 4. Total inventory cost ranking of different lot sizing rules under different capacity levels.

Capacity Level	Rank 1	2	3	4	5
1	L4L	PPB	W-W	POQ	EOQ
2	L4L	PPB	W-W	POQ	EOQ
3	PPB	L4L	W-W	POQ	EOQ
4	PPB	L4L	W-W	POQ	EOQ
5	PPB	L4L	W-W	POQ	EOQ

as the best performer. It is interesting to note that the result does not conform with the previous study results [1]. In previous studies, the W-W rule has been identified as the least total inventory cost rule. In this study, the W-W rule maintained third position behind PPB and L4L under all capacity situations.

The EOQ rule performs poorly throughout all capacity levels. However, it is expected that as the ratio between setup cost and inventory holding cost changes (relatively higher setup cost), the EOQ performance will improve. This result indicates to us the possibility that the relative performance of different lot sizing rules is dependent upon many different factors, and cannot be approached as a single universal optimizing rule.

It must also be noted here that the results of Table 4 should be weighted with respect to the frequency of stockouts. It could be argued that the impact of a stockout is already reflected in the higher inventory level, but the qualitive aspect of stockout should be carefully considered in determining the best lot sizing rule to be used.

20.4. Discussion

From a review of the results of this study, it is apparent that the impact of capacity level on the relative performance of different lot sizing rules is not as significant as originally suspected. However, the study brought out some interesting aspects which do not entirely conform to the conventional wisdom.

First, the expected direct relationship between the stockout frequency and number of setups was not observed. Since the causes of stockouts were thought to be a high demand rate during the lead time and/or longer than expected lead time, and the lead time variation, it was expected that the frequency of stockouts would increase as the number of setups (or orders) was increased. However, the study results indicate that there is no clear-cut relationship between the frequency of stockouts and number of setups. Comparing Tables 1 and 2, there is a strong indication that the frequency of stockouts is largely a function of capacity level (levels 1 and 2), the frequency of stockouts is very high, and as the capacity level is changed to a sufficient level (levels 4 and 5), the stockout frequency decreases greatly.

Second, the expected inverse relationship between the frequency of stockouts and inventory level also did not occur. Here again, the traditional solution to the stockout problem was increased inventory levels (safety stock). As depicted in Tables 1 and 3, inventory level has a high positive correlation with stockout frequency. A possible explanation is that under the multistage manufacturing environment, as more stockouts occur at lower level parts or subassembly items the more work-in-process inventory items keep accumulating. Thus, higher inventory levels will result from higher stockouts. This means simply that in a multistage manufacturing environment, total inventory level, which includes work-in-process inventory, is in a large part a function of the frequency of stockouts. These general cause and effect relationships can be compared in the following fashion:

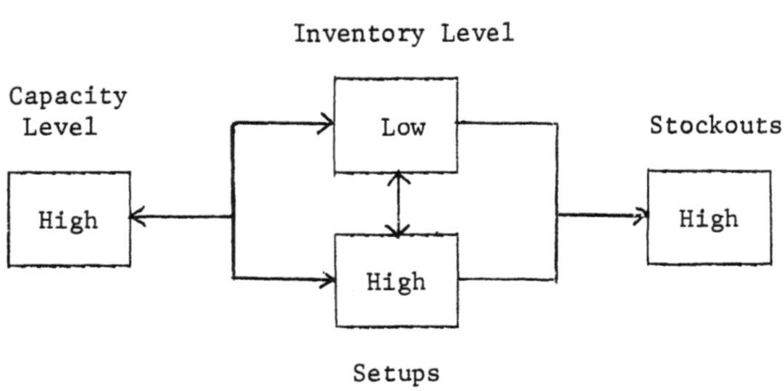

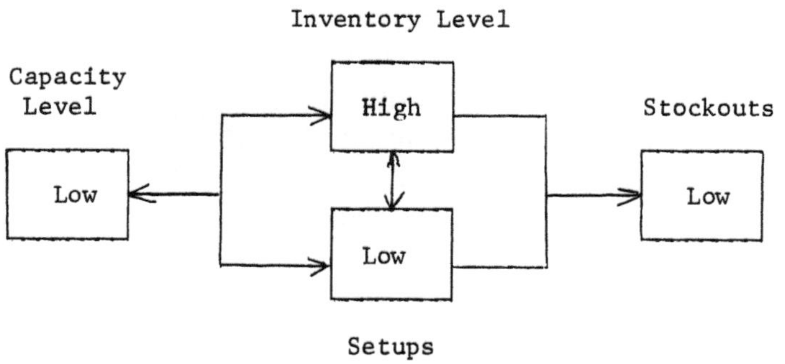

MRP Relationship

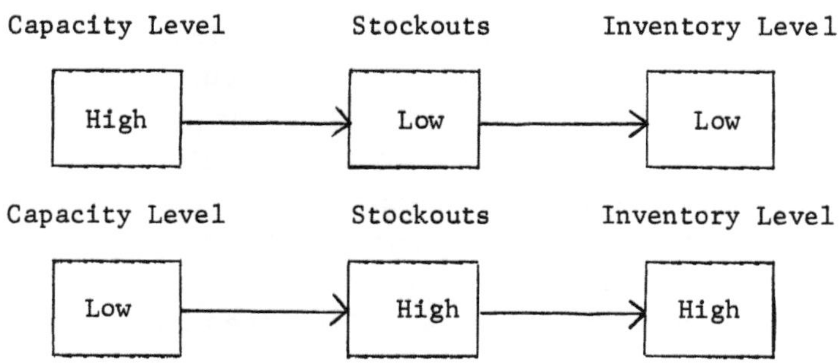

Under the traditional relationship, inventory level was treated as an alternative to capacity level. A high level capacity tends to result in decisions for lower inventory levels and a higher number of setups and thus higher frequency of stockouts. On the other hand, when the capacity level is low, the inventory level must be raised to offset the capacity (at least in the short run) and a lower number of setups, and consequently, lower frequency of stockouts would result.

Under the MRP setting, the relationship would be different. A high capacity level tends to reduce the frequency of stockouts, and would result in a lower total inventory level. On the other hand, the low capacity level would increase the frequency of stockouts, and cause a high level of inventories due to high work-in-process inventory.

Finally, the demand pattern for the products produced in the plant has a major influence on inventory levels and frequency of stockouts.[3] When the demand pattern is changed from the constant demand over the period with random fluctuation, the average

3. A different set of simulations was conducted, but the results are not reported here.

number of stockouts and inventory level increased greatly at all capacity levels. However, the number of setups required under these different demand patterns did not change significantly. This result also supports our previous finding that the frequency of stockouts is largely a function of capacity level, and that inventory level is in large part a function of the frequency of stockouts.

20.5. Conclusion

In selecting an appropriate lot sizing rule for his operating environment, a practicing manager must consider many important factors – cost parameters, demand pattern, capacity situation, and implementation aspects of a particular rule. The current study mainly dealt with impact of capacity on lot sizing rule performances. Our study findings did not confirm many previous study results. However, before many definitive conclusions can be drawn, further expansion and refinement of the current study is necessary.

We are currently engaged in a simulation study with different sets of cost parameters. It is expected that the new research which combines capacity level with different sets of cost parameters will provide us with a further refinement of our current results.

References

1. Berry, William L., 'Lot Sizing Procedures for Requirements Planning Systems: A Framework for Analysis', *Production and Inventory Management* (2nd Quarter, 1972), pp. 19–34.
2. Biggs, Joseph R., *An Analysis of Heuristic Lot Sizing and Sequencing Rules on the Performance of a Hierarchical Multiproduct, Multistage Production-Inventory System Utilizing Material Requirements Planning Techniques*, Unpublished Ph.D.Dissertation, The Ohio State University, Columbus, Ohio (1975).
3. Buffa, Elwoods S. and Taubert, William H., *Production-Inventory Systems: Planning and Control* (Homewood, Illinois: Richard D. Irwin, Inc., 1972), p. 88.
4. Gorenstein, S., 'Some Remarks on EOQ vs. Wagner-Whitin, Production and Inventory Ordering', *Production and Inventory Management* (4th Quarter, 1969).
5. Kaimann, R. A., 'Revisiting a Fallacy of EOQing', *Production and Inventory Management* (4th Quarter, 1968), pp. 12–19.
6. Kaimann, R. A., 'EOQ vs. Dynamic Programming – Which One to Use for Inventory Ordering?', *Production and Inventory Management* (4th Quarter, 1969), pp. 66–74.
7. Kaimann, R. A., 'A Comparison of the EOQ and Dynamics Programming Inventory Models with Safety Stock Considerations', *Production and Inventory Management* (3rd Quarter, 1972), pp. 72–91.
8. Kriebel, Charles H., *A Production Management Operating System Simulation: 'Factory-2'*, Pittsburgh, Pennsylvania: Graduate School of Industrial Administration, Carnegie-Mellon, University (March 1971).

9. Lowerre, William, J., Jr., 'Lot Size Rules a One-Act Play', *Production and Inventory Management* (2nd Quarter, 1975), pp. 41–49.
10. Orlicky, Joseph A., *Material Requirements Planning* (New York: McGraw-Hill Book Company, 1975).
11. Vergin, Robert C., 'Production Planning Under Seasonal Demand', *Journal of Industrial Engineering* (May 1966), pp. 260–266.

21. Variations in optimizing serial multi-stage production/inventory systems

ANDREW Z. SZENDROVITS and GEORGE O. WESOLOWSKY

Abstract

This paper presents two basic, deterministic, infinite horizon models for a serial multi-stage production/inventory system. One model assumes that the lot size is maintained through all production stages while transportation of equal sized sub-batches is allowed between stages. Consequently, only one set-up cost is incurred for each stage; however, the transportation cost of sub-batches must also be considered. An optimal solution is presented for this first model. The other model has varying lot sizes with lot-sized intershipments assuming certain integrality restrictions on the splitting of lots and monotonically increasing stage inventory holding costs. A good approximation to the optimal solution is given for this second model. Comparison of the two models provides an insight into the characteristics of multi-stage production systems. The efficiency of the computational procedures described is demonstrated with extensive computational experience.

21.1. Introduction

Deterministic, infinite horizon models for serial multi-stage production/inventory systems are well known in the literature; a general survey is given by Clark [1]. The continuous production case, but with continuous intershipment, has been treated previously by Jensen and Khan [3]. Lot size intershipment as well as back-logging were built into the model by Taha and Skeith [8] who used complete enumeration and some limiting assumptions to arrive at a solution. Schwarz and Schrage [4] presented a similar model, but with 'echelon' inventory holding costs, the definition of which involves some difficulties in applying the proper holding costs, and may lead to certain anomalies as shown by Szendrovits [7]. Crowston, Wagner and Williams [2] offered a dynamic programming procedure to optimize a model for multi-stage assembly systems where production at each stage occurs instantaneously. Most of these models assume that the lot size at each facility is a positive integer multiple of the lot size at its successor facility. They also assume unconstrained capacity at all stages and do not allow the inventory unit holding cost to be less at a following stage. Transshipment costs are implied to be sunk cost or are built into the fixed cost per lot. Optimization procedures are illustrated by examples for cases with a small number of stages ($n < 10$).

An alternative to lot-splitting is to maintain the lot size through all production stages while allowing transshipment of equal-sized sub-batches between stages. A model for such a system, where the number of sub-batches is predetermined, is offered by Szendrovits [5]. It assumes a uniform (average) unit holding cost for the process inventory at all stages. It also assumes a single production facility at each stage and sunk transportation costs. When the transportation cost for the sub-batches is known, the possibility of optimizing sub-batch sizes is discussed in [6].

The two basic production/inventory models presented in this paper have n manufacturing stages in sequence. These stages are numbered in reverse; that is, the final stage, the one which meets the demand for the finished product is stage 1. Deterministic demand rates over an infinite horizon and unconstrained capacity at all stages are assumed in both models. It is further assumed that at a given stage, the inventory holding cost per unit (the holding cost of units with that stage completed) as well as the set-up cost (of single or multiple facilities), and the production rate are all constant.

Apart from these common characteristics the two models are distinctly different.

Model I incorporates the following assumptions:

- the lot size is uniform at all stages and set-up cost is incurred only once at each stage;
- equal sized sub-batches can be transported from a given stage to the next production stage before the production of the lot is finished;
- the transportation cost of sub-batches between stages is known and constant;

- the stage holding cost per unit at any stage may be greater than that at the next stage;
- both the number of sub-batches per lot and the sub-batch size must be an integer.

Model II encompasses the following assumptions:

- the lot size of a stage is an integer multiple of the lot size of the stage that follows it (this is done for the conventional reason of making the problem analytically tractable);
- the product is transferred between stages in lots; therefore, when the lot size is split at a stage, multiple set-up costs are incurred at that stage and at subsequent stages (reflection on the model will show that the case where the following stage has a larger lot size cannot be optimal);
- the transportation cost of lots is regarded as a sunk cost or, alternatively, it is included in the fixed cost per lot (this assumes that the transportation cost is independent from the lot size);
- the stage holding cost per unit for a stage is never lower than that for a preceding stage (this assumption is to simplify the problem; however, it is also justified in practice when the inventory holding cost is proportional to the value of the product);
- the lot size at a given stage is not restricted to be an integer number (however, the optimization methods proposed could be modified to accommodate this restriction).

The objective for both models is to minimize the sum of the fixed costs and the inventory holding costs of the system. An optimal solution is given for model I and a close approximation to the optimal solution is found for model II. Both optimization procedures are computationally efficient, (in contrast to other known methods) for a large number of stages. This is demonstrated by extensive computational experience.

Symbols common to both model I and model II are as follows:

D = demand rate of the final product (at stage 1);
P_i = production rate at stage i; note that $P_i > D$;
F_i = set-up cost per lot at stage i; note that $F_1 > 0$;
G_i = fixed transportation cost for a lot or for a sub-batch at stage i;
c_i = inventory holding cost per unit at stage i;
Q_i = lot size at stage i.

21.2. Model I – uniform lot size with sub-batches

21.2.1. The model and the objective function

In this model the lot size is the same at every stage and equal sized sub-batches can be transported from a given stage to the next production stage before the lot is finished. At all stages the entire lot is produced continuously, hence with a single set-up cost for each stage. Therefore, when the production rate of a given stage is greater than or equal to that of the following stage, (a shorter operation time followed by a longer), production at the following stage starts as soon as a sub-batch is available; subsequent sub-batches will be available to maintain the continuity of production at the following stage. On the other hand, when the production rate of a given stage is smaller than that of the following stage, production at the following stage must start with an appropriate delay. The inventory model (for the latter case) is illustrated in Figure 1, where the areas represent the time-weighted inventory for each stage. In this model the following additional symbols are used:

Q = uniform lot size at all stages; note that $Q = Q_1 = Q_2 = \ldots = Q_n$;

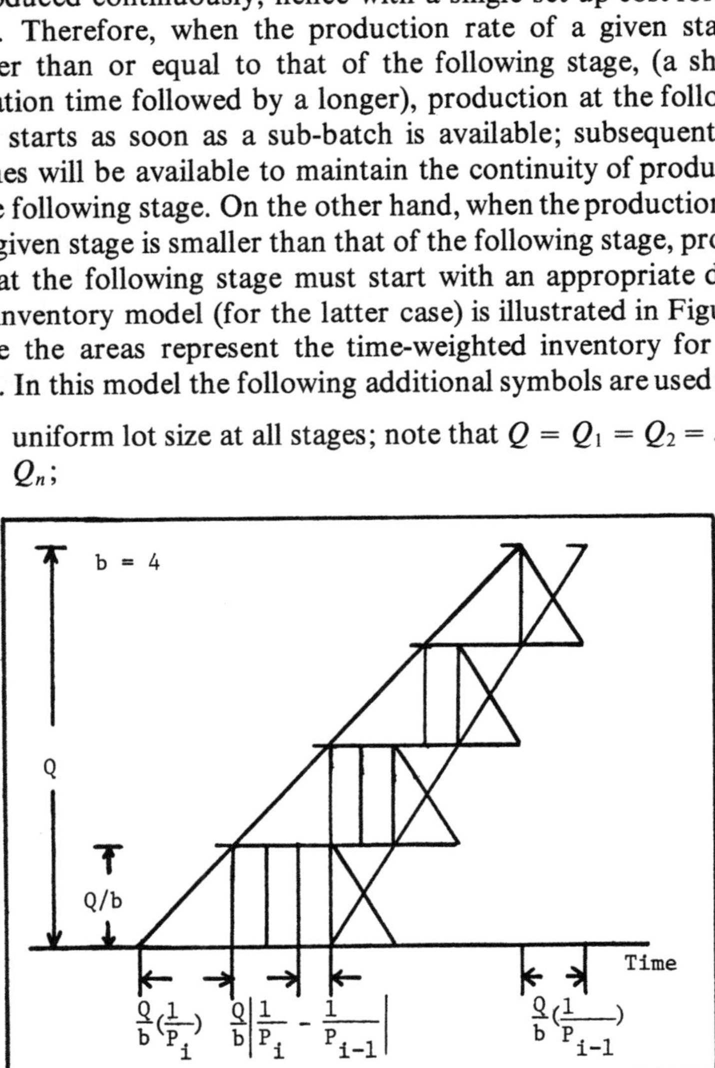

Figure 1. Time-weighted inventory at stage i with $b = 4$.

b = the number of equal sized sub-batches;
F = $\Sigma_{i=1}^{n} F_i$, the total set-up cost of the system;
G = $\Sigma_{i=1}^{n} G_i$, the total transportation cost of one sub-batch through all stages;
x = the number of units in one sub-batch; note that $x = Q/b$.

The inventory holding cost per unit time at stage i can be expressed as follows:

$$C_i = \frac{Q^2}{2b} c_i \left[\left(\frac{1}{P_i} + \frac{1}{P_{i-1}} \right) + \left| \frac{1}{P_i} - \frac{1}{P_{i-1}} \right| (b-1) \right] \frac{D}{Q} \qquad (1)$$

The inventory holding cost of the system is obtained by the summation of (1). Adding to this the total set-up costs and the transportation costs (per unit time) of the sub-batches, we obtain the average total cost of the system:

$$C = \frac{D}{Q}(F + bG) + \frac{QD}{2b} \sum_{i=1}^{n} c_i \left[\left(\frac{1}{P_i} + \frac{1}{P_{i-1}} \right) + \left| \frac{1}{P_i} - \frac{1}{P_{i-1}} \right| (b-1) \right] \qquad (2)$$

where: $P_0 = D$

The objective is to minimize the total cost of the system. To simplify notation the objective function can be written:

$$\text{Minimize } C(Q, b) = \frac{D}{Q}(F + bG) + Q(M + N/b) \qquad (3)$$

subject to: $1 \leqq b \leqq Q$

where: $M = \sum_{i=1}^{n} \frac{c_i}{2} \left| \frac{D}{P_i} - \frac{D}{P_{i-1}} \right|$

$$N = \sum_{i=1}^{n} \frac{c_i}{2} \left[\left(\frac{D}{P_i} + \frac{D}{P_{i-1}} \right) - \left| \frac{D}{P_i} - \frac{D}{P_{i-1}} \right| \right]$$

$P_0 = D$

It is obvious that the larger b becomes, the smaller will be the sub-batch size, $x = Q/b$, and vice-versa. Thus, the rounding of small b or x values would make the result inaccurate. Therefore, the task is to minimize the cost function (3) subject to the integralities of b and x (of course, this also yields an integer optimal lot size).

We substitute $x = Q/b$ in (3) and the objective function becomes:

$$\text{Minimize } C(x, b) = D(F/b + G)/x + x(Mb + N) \tag{4}$$

subject to: b and x integers; $1 \leqq b \leqq Q$ and $1 \leqq x \leqq Q$.

21.2.2. *Optimization without integrality constraints*

We first ignore integrality restrictions. By partially differentiating (4) with respect to x and b, and by solving separately the extremal equations $\partial C(x, b)/\partial x = 0$ and $\partial C(x, b)/\partial b = 0$ we obtain:

$$x = \sqrt{\frac{D(F/b + G)}{Mb + N}} \tag{5}$$

$$b = \sqrt{\frac{DF}{Mx_2}} \tag{6}$$

Solving (5) and (6) we obtain the optimal values:

$$x^* = \sqrt{\frac{DG}{N}} \tag{7}$$

$$b^* = \sqrt{\frac{FN}{GM}} \tag{8}$$

It also will be useful to have:

$$C(x) = \min_b C(x, b) = DG/x + Nx + 2\sqrt{MDF} \tag{9}$$

which is obtained by substituting (6) in (4), and

$$C(b) = \min_x C(x, b) = 2\sqrt{D(F/b + G)(Mb + N)} \tag{10}$$

which is obtained by substituting (5) in (4). It could be shown that both $C(x)$ and $C(b)$ are unimodal. This also will be useful in the next section.

21.2.3. Algorithm for finding integer b and x values

In subsequent expressions, square brackets around a variable indicate that only integer values of that variable are considered, e.g. the integer values of x are denoted $[x]$; $x_{\downarrow}$ denotes x rounded down and $x_{\uparrow}$ denotes x rounded up.

Before showing the algorithm for determining $[x]^*$ and $[b]^*$, we describe the logic of the optimization. First, we determine the continuous optimal values for x^* from (7) and for b^* from (8). Then, we initiate the search on either of the axes. If $x^* \leqq b^*$ we search integers on the x axis, otherwise we search integers on the b axis. Let us illustrate searching on the x axis. We select $x_* = [x^*_{\downarrow}]$ as the initial integer value of x and compute b in (6) at this x_*. We also compute the cost $C(x, b)$ in (4) with two integer values of $[b_{\downarrow}]$ and $[b_{\uparrow}]$ and retain $C_{\min}$, the smaller of the costs. Then we continue searching for a better cost on both sides of x_* simultaneously, i.e., we repeat calculating b and $C(x, b)$ at $x_* - 1, x_* + 1, x_* - 2, x_* + 2, \ldots$, etc., and retain the lowest of the $C_{\min}$ costs obtained at integer b's. Equation $C(x)$ in (9) is the cost which is the lower bound for all b values at a given x value; therefore, we compute $C(x)$ at each integer x value and end the search on the particular side of x_* whenever a $C(x)$ value is higher than the lowest $C_{\min}$ value already obtained. Since $C(x)$ is unimodal, this procedure guarantees an optimal integer solution.

The algorithm for finding $[x]^*$ and $[b]^*$ is illustrated for an initial search on the x axis:

1. Find x^* in (7) and b^* in (8). Since $x^* \leqq b^*$, set $x_* = [x^*_{\downarrow}]$. If $x_* < 1$, set $x_* = 1$. Retain x_*. Set $L = 1$; set $FLAG1 = 0$, set $FLAG2 = 0$, $C_{\min} = \infty$. Set $x' = x_*$ and call Subroutine *CXB*.
2. If $FLAG1 = 1$, go to 4.
3. Check optimality and/or search for a better $C_{\min}$ on the lower side of x_*. Set $x' = x_* - L$ and compute $C(x')$ in (9). If $x' \leqq 1$ or $C(x') \geqq C_{\min}$, set $FLAG1 = 1$ indicating that the search ended on the lower side of x_*. If $C(x') < C_{\min}$, call Subroutine *CXB*.
4. If $FLAG2 = 2$, go to 6.
5. Check optimality and/or search for a better $C_{\min}$ on the upper side of x_*. Set $x' = x_* + L$ and compute $C(x')$ in (9). If $C(x') \geqq C_{\min}$, set $FLAG2 = 2$ indicating that the search ended on the upper side of x_*. If $C(x') < C_{\min}$, call Subroutine *CXB*.

6. If $FLAG1 = 1$ and $FLAG2 = 2$, stop. The optimum solution is: $[x]^* = x_{min}$, $[b]^* = b_{min}$, $C([x]^*, [b]^*) = C_{min}$ and $[Q]^* = [x]^*[b]^*$. Otherwise, set $L = L + 1$ and go to 2.
7. Subroutine *CXB*
   Compute b in (6) at x'; if $b < 1$, set $b = 1$. Compute by (4) $C(x'[b_\uparrow])$ and $C(x'_,[b_\downarrow])$, or only $C(x'_, b)$ when $b = 1$. Select b' $\{[b_\downarrow], [b\ ]\}$ to minimize the cost, C_{min}. Retain the best C_{min} obtained thus far, and the minimizing x_{min} and b_{min} values. Return.

Had we found that $b^* < x^*$ in step 1 of the algorithm, the search would have been initiated on the b axis instead of the x axis. However, equations (5) and (10) would have been used in lieu of (6) and (9). The following example will illustrate the algorithm for such a case.

Example 1

Table 1. Problem parameters for example 1.

i	F_i	G_i	c_i	P_i
1	5.0	5.0	2.0	1000
2	35.0	5.0	1.7	1600
3	395.0	5.0	1.3	400
4	220.0	5.0	0.8	2500
n = 4		D = 300		

From the problem parameters we calculate by (3):

$$M = 1.41325,\ N = 1.25850,\ F = \sum_{i=1}^{n} F_i = 655.0,$$

$$G = \sum_{i=1}^{n} G_i = 20.0$$

We now use the algorithm to find $[x]^*$ and $[b]^*$:

1. In (7), $x^* = 69.05$; in (8), $b^* = 5.40$. Since $b^* < x^*$, we initiate the search on the b axis: $b_* = 5$, $b' = b_* = 5$. We set $L = 1$, $FLAG1 = 0$, $FLAG2 = 0$, $C_{min} = \infty$. Call Subroutine *CXB*. In (5), $x = 73.77$.

By (4), $C(b'[x_\downarrow]) = C(5, 73) = 1228.26$ and $C(b'[x_\uparrow]) = C(5, 74) = 1228.19$. $C_{min} = 1228.19$ at $b_{min} = 5$ and $x_{min} = 74$.
2. $FLAG1 = 0$, continue.
3. $b' = b_* - L = 5 - 1 = 4$. In (10), $C(b') = C(4) = 1234.50$. $C(b') > C_{min}$, hence $FLAG1 = 1$; search ended on the lower side of b_*.
4. $FLAG2 = 0$, continue.
5. $b' = b_* + L = 5 + 1 = 6$. In (10), $C(b') = C(6) = 1228.57$. $C(b') > C_{min}$, hence $FLAG2 = 2$, search ended on the upper side of b_*.
6. $FLAG1 = 1$ and $FLAG2 = 2$, stop. Optimal solution obtained: $[b]^* = b_{min} = 5$, $[x]^* = x_{min} = 74$, $C([x]^*, [b]^*) = C_{min} = 1228.19$, $[Q]^* = [x]^*[b]^* = 370$.

21.2.4. 'Sunk' transportation costs

Transportation costs in a plant are often regarded as sunk costs because the transportation system must handle a whole spectrum of products and it is difficult to allocate the costs of the system to particular product lots. In such cases the sub-batch size is usually predetermined to suit the load capacity, or the best utilization, of the transportation equipment. Undoubtedly, such a choice of sub-batch size yields only a sub-optimal solution, but it still results in a better cost than transporting whole lots.

If the sub-batch size is a fixed integer, $[x^s]$, the sub-optimal number of sub-batches, $[b^s]$, can be found by setting $G = 0$ in the cost function (4) and applying only the subroutine of the algorithm.

21.2.5. Computational experience and conclusions

Numerous randomly selected examples were solved for different numbers of stages ($n = 5$, $n = 10$, $n = 20$, $n = 30$) on a CDC 6400 computer. No significant difference was found in the execution times for smaller and larger number of stages; the small differences appeared to be rather data dependent. Generally, the execution time was between 0.025 and 0.035 seconds per case for $n \leqq 30$.

It is also interesting to note that optimum solutions for all cases were obtained with no more than two iterations. In some contrived cases there could be more than two iterations; nevertheless the computational procedure will always yield an optimum solution.

21.3. Model II – varying lot sizes

21.3.1. The model and the objective function

In this model the lot size may be different at various stages; reflection on the model will show that the case where a following stage has a larger lot size cannot be optimal. The lot size is an integer multiple of the lot size at the stage that follows it, and only lot-sized intershipments are allowed between stages (including the final stage). This inventory model is illustrated by Figure 2 in which the triangular and rectangular areas (distinguished with different lines) represent the time-weighted inventory for each of four stages.

The following additional symbols are used:

$S_{i-1} = Q_i/Q_{i-1}$ for $i = 2, 3, \ldots, n$; note that S_{i-1} is an integer;

$\Pi_{i-1} = \Pi_{j=1}^{j=i-1} S_j$; for later notational convenience we set

$$\Pi_0 = \Pi_{-1} = 1.$$

$$c_i \leqq c_{i-1} \text{ for } i = 2, 3, \ldots, n.$$

To simplify certain expressions, we define for stages

$i = 1, 2, \ldots, n$:

$b_i = c_i(D/P_i + 1)/2$

$d_i = c_i(D/P_{i-1} - 1)/2$, where $P_0 = D$

$e_i = F_iD$

The inventory holding cost per unit time at stage i can be determined from the triangular and rectangular areas in Figure 2. For

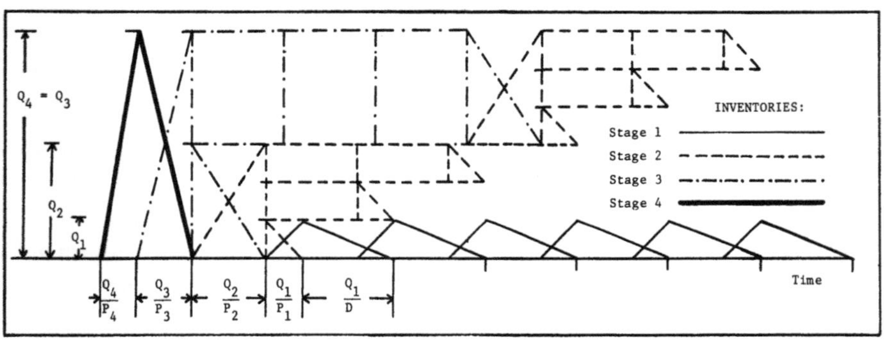

Figure 2. Time-weighted inventory with $S_1 = 3$, $S_2 = 2$, $S_1 = 1$.

the triangular areas we obtain:

$$c_i\left(\frac{Q_i^2}{2P_i}+\frac{Q_{i-1}^2}{2P_{i-1}}\right)\frac{D}{Q_i}=Q_i\Pi_{i-2}c_i\left(S_{i-1}\frac{D}{P_i}+\frac{1}{P_{i-1}}\right)\Big/2$$

for the rectangular areas it is:

$$c_i Q_{i-1}\left(\frac{Q_1}{D}\right)\frac{S_{i-1}(S_{i-1}-1)}{2}(S_1S_2\ldots S_{i-2})\frac{D}{Q_i}$$
$$=Q_1\Pi_{i-2}c_i(S_{i-1}-1)/2$$

The set-up cost per unit time at stage i is:

$$F_iD/Q_i=F_iD/Q_1\Pi_{i-2}S_{i-1}$$

Consequently, the total of inventory holding costs and set-up costs per unit time for stage i is:

$$C_i=Q_1\Pi_{i-2}\left[S_{i-1}c_i\left(\frac{D}{P_i}+1\right)\Big/2+c_i\left(\frac{D}{P_{i-1}}-1\right)\Big/2\right]$$
$$+\frac{F_iD}{Q_1\Pi_{i-2}S_{i-1}} \tag{11}$$

where: $P_0=D$

Thus, C_i is a simultaneous function of Q_1, S_{i-1} and Π_{i-2}. The expression for C_i can be simplified to:

$$C_i=Q_1\Pi_{i-2}(S_{i-1}b_i+d_i)+\frac{e_i}{Q_1\Pi_{i-2}S_{i-1}}$$

The objective is to minimize the total cost of the system. The objective function is obtained by summation of (12) over all stages:

$$\text{Minimize } TC(Q_1\zeta)=Q_1\sum_{i=1}^{n}\Pi_{i-2}(S_{i-1}b_i+d_i)$$
$$+(1/Q_1)\sum_{i=1}^{n}e_i/\Pi_{i-2}S_{i-1} \tag{13}$$

where ζ is the set $\{S_1, S_2, \ldots, S_{n-1}\}$

We partially differentiate (13) with respect to Q_1, set the derivative to zero and solve to obtain the minimizing Q_1, which we designate

$Q_{1\min}$:

$$Q_{1\min} = \sqrt{\frac{\sum_{i=1}^{n} e_i/(\Pi_{i-2} S_{i-1})}{\sum_{i=1}^{n} \Pi_{i-2}(S_{i-1} b_i + d_i)}}$$

For a given Q_1 the cost at any ith stage is defined by Π_{i-2} and S_{i-1}. A dynamic programming approach, using Π_{i-2} as a stage variable and S_{i-1} as a decision variable, will be used to minimize the total cost (13).

21.3.2. Optimization without integrality restrictions

It will be handy, for several reasons, to have a solution to the minimization of (13) but with no integrality restrictions on the S_i's. There are a number of ways of solving a problem of this type. However, the convenient and efficient 'collapsing' method used by Schwarz and Schrage [4] will be employed. A brief outline is given in this section.

To distinguish this case we use q_i's instead of Q_i's and s_i's instead of S_i's. We define

$s_{i-1} = \dfrac{q_i}{q_{i-1}}$ for $i = 2, \ldots, n$, and δ to be the set $\{S_1, S_2, \ldots, S_{n-1}\}$.

Thus, the total cost in (13) can be rewritten:

$$TC_c(\Phi) = \sum_{i=1}^{n} q_i(b_i + d_{i+1}) + \sum_{i=1}^{n} \frac{e_i}{q_i}$$

subject to: $q_1 < q_2 < q_3 < \ldots < q_n$,

where: $\Phi = \{q_1, q_2, \ldots, q_n\}$.

This can be converted to the expression

$$TC_c(\Phi) = \sum_{i=1}^{n} (K_i q_i + M_i/q_i) \tag{17}$$

where: $K_i = b_i + d_{i+1}$ for $i = 1, \ldots, n$, and we set

$d_{n+1} = 0; \qquad M_i = e_i$

Let us now define: q_i^N as the optimal lot size computed independently for stage i:

$$q_i^N = \sqrt{\frac{M_i}{K_i}} \tag{18}$$

It is evident that in the absence of constraints, (18) would give the optimum q values. Since (17) is a convex objective function and constraints are convex, the Kuhn-Tucker conditions are necessary and sufficient for optimality. The problem can be written:

$$\text{Minimize } \sum_{i=1}^{n} (K_i q_i + M_i/q_i) \tag{19}$$

subject to: $q_i - q_{i+1} \leqq 0$ for $i = 1, \ldots, n - 1$

The Kuhn-Tucker conditions (somewhat simplified because we know that the q_i's are always positive for non-trivial cases) are:

$$K_1 - M_1/q_1^{*2} + u_1 = 0 \tag{20}$$

$$K_i - M_i/q_i^{*2} - u_{i-1} + u_i = 0 \quad \text{for } i = 2, \ldots, n - 1$$

$$K_n - M_n/q_n^{*2} - u_{n-1} = 0$$

where: $q_1^*, \ldots, q_n^*$ are the optimal q values.

The u_i's are positive or zero; also, $u_i > 0$ only when constraint i in (20) is tight and holds as an equality.

We can now show (this proof is similar to one in Schwarz and Schrage [4]) that:

$$\text{If } q_i^N < q_{i-1}^N \text{ then } q_i^* = q_{i-1}^*. \tag{21}$$

To prove this we assume the contrary conditions, i.e., $q_i^N < q_{i-1}^N$ and $q_i^* > q_{i-1}^*$ and show that they are not possible. Since, using (20),

$$q_i^* = \sqrt{\frac{M_i}{K_i - u_{i-1} + u_i}}$$

and because $q_i^* > q_{i-1}^*$ means that $u_{i-1} = 0$, the consequence is that $q_i^* \leqq q_i^N$. Using the given conditions, we now have:

$$q_i^* < q_{i-1}^N \tag{22}$$

Further, since

$$q_{i-1}^* = \sqrt{\frac{M_{i-1}}{K_{i-1} - u_{i-2} + u_{i-1}}}$$

the consequence is that $q_{i-1}^* \geqq q_{i-1}^N$. From the given conditions we now have:

$$q_i^* > q_{i-1}^N \tag{23}$$

The inequalities (22) and (23) are contradictory and the proof is complete.

To find the optimum solution to (19), we first find the quantities q_i^N from (18). Suppose that there is an i such that $q_i^N < q_{i-1}^N$ (if there isn't, then $q_i^* = q_i^N$ for all i). Since $q_i = q_{i-1}$ at optimality, we can combine the two stages so that $K_i' = K_i + K_{i-1}$ and $M_i' = M_i + M_{i-1}$. We now have a new problem of the type (17), but with one less stage. This collapsing continues until it can proceed no further and hence the set of optimal q_i values has been found:

$\Phi^* = \{q_1^*, q_2^*, \ldots, q_n^*\}$, and the set of optimal s_i's from (15) is: $\delta^* = \{s_1^*, s_2^*, \ldots, s_{n-1}^*\}$.

Example 2 illustrates the computational procedure.

Example 2

Here we use the same data as in example 1. However, it is assumed that the set-up cost F_i includes G_i, the transportation cost of the lot (which is independent of the lot size) at stage i; i.e. $F_i = F_i + G_i$. Consequently the only change in the problem parameters in Table 1 is that:

$F_1 = 10.0$, $F_2 = 40$, $F_3 = 400$, $F_4 = 225$, and $G_i = 0$ at each stage.

From the problem parameters we can calculate q_i^N using (18) as it is illustrated in Table 2. Since $q_1^N < q_2^N < q_3^N < q_4^N$ no collapsing is necessary. We have obtained a solution to (19) and, consequently, to (16): $q_1^* = 65.23$, $q_2^* = 157.91$, $q_3^* = 340.09$, $q_4^* = 388.16$ or $\Phi^* = \{65.23, 157.91, 304.09, 388.16\}$ and $TC_c(\Phi^*) = TC^*(q_1^*) = 1297.45$. From (15), $s_1^* = 2.42$, $s_2^* = 2.15$, $s_3^* = 1.14$ or $\delta^* = \{2.42, 2.15, 1.14\}$.

Table 2. Calculation of q_i^N values.

i	b_i	d_i	$e_i=M_i$	K_i	q_i^N
1	1.300	0.000	3000.	0.705	65.23
2	1.009	-0.595	12000.	0.481	157.91
3	1.138	-0.528	120000.	1.038	340.09
4	0.448	-0.100	67500.	0.448	388.16

21.3.3. The 'Rounded solution'

The solution to (16) is important for two reasons. First, since (16) is merely the minimization of (13), but with relaxed constraints, the solution to (16) gives a lower bound on the minimum of (13). Secondly, we can obtain an approximate minimum of (13) by 'rounding'.

Let $S_i^R = [s_i^*]$, where the brackets indicate conventional rounding to an integer. If we usę S_i^R for S_i in (14) we obtain q_{1R}^*, and the minimum total cost of this 'rounded solution' can be computed. The value of q_{1R}^* must yield a cost equal to or less than if q_1^* were used with S_i^R's.

From example 2, we have $S_1^R = 2$, $S_2^R = 2$, $S_3^R = 1$ or $\zeta_R = \{2, 2, 1\}$. Using (14) we obtain $q_{1R}^* = 85.69$. The cost of the rounded solution, by substitution in (13), $TC(q_{1R}^*, \zeta_R) = TC_*(\zeta_R) = 1304.12$.

The approximate rounded solution, as shown by computational experience, quite often could be the same as the optimal solution.

21.3.4. Dynamic programming to find integer S_i's at a given Q_1

In this section, we will discuss the problem of minimizing (13) for the case where a set of permissible values for S_i is given.

Let $SI = \{G_1, \ldots, G_{n-1}\}$, where G_i is the set of permissible values for S_i. Given SI, we can construct $PI = \{H_1, \ldots, H_{n-2}\}$, where H_i is the set of permissible values for Π_i. In practice, such limitations on S_i or Π_i could actually exist as a result of storage limitations or transportation convenience; however, they can be eliminated by extending the search region.

Let us assume for the moment that Q_i is known in (13) and that the best S_i's must be selected from SI for that Q_1. The problem of minimizing (13) can be solved by a standard dynamic programming approach.

At any stage i, let Π_{i-2} be the state variable, and S_{i-1} be the decision variable. As seen from (12) the cost C_i of any stage, at a given Q_1, is defined by these two variables. We can now write the recursive relationship.

$$f_i^*(\Pi_{i-2}) = \min_{S_{i-1} \in G_{i-1}} (C_i(S_{i-1}, \Pi_{i-2}) + f_{i+1}^*(\Pi_{i-2} S_{i-1})) \tag{24}$$

where: $\Pi_{i-2} \in H_{i-2}$, $S_{i-1} \Pi_{i-2} = \Pi_{i-1}$, and we set

$$f_{n-1}^*(\Pi_{n-2} S_{n-1}) = 0.$$

This recursive relationship can be used in the conventional way; moving backward from stage n to stage 1 and finding the optimal policy S_{i-1} for each stage Π_{i-2} of stage i. After this is finished, at stage 1 the optimum S_1 will be found; tracing forward through the stages will give the rest of the S_i's. Thus, having found the set $\zeta = \{S_1, S_2, \ldots, S_{n-1}\}$, by using (4) we can find

$$TC^*(Q_1) = \min_{\zeta} TC(Q_1, \zeta) \tag{25}$$

21.3.5. The 'likely optimum solution'

We now describe the finding of a solution that we call (in high hopes) the 'likely optimum solution.' We first define

$$TC_*(\zeta) = \min_{Q_1} TC(Q_1 \zeta) \tag{26}$$

and we denote the Q_1 that minimizes $TC(Q_1, \zeta)$ with $Q_{1\zeta}^*$.

First, the collapsing method is used to find q_1^* as described before. Then, we find the best ζ at q_1^* by dynamic programming described in (24). Once the best ζ is found, a $Q_{1\zeta}^*$ can be determined by (14) and $TC_*(\zeta)$ can be computed. Using the $Q_{1\zeta}^*$, the cycle of dynamic programming and application of (14) is continued iteratively until no further improvement in cost can be found. The result will be the likely optimum solution, $TC(Q_{1L}, \zeta_L) = TC_*(\zeta_L)$. Example 3 illustrates the procedure and notation.

Example 3

We continue with the problem of example 1. Assume that

$SI = \{\{1, 2, 3, 4\}, \{1, 2, 3, 4, 5, 6, 7\}, \{1, 2, 3, 4, 5, 6, 7\}$, hence $PI = \{\{1, 2, 3, 4, 5\}, \{1, 2, 3, 4, 5, 6\}\}$.

To find the likely optimum solution we first determined, by dynamic programming, ζ_1 at $q_1^* = 65.23$ (note that q_1^* was calculated in example 2). The result was $S_1 = 2$, $S_2 = 3$, $S_3 = 1$ (or $\zeta_1 = \{2, 3, 1\}$). Using ζ_1 we calculated by (14) $Q_{1\zeta_1}^* = 61.8$, and the corresponding

Table 3. Dynamic programming.

$f_4(\Pi_2) = C_4(S_3, \Pi_2)$

Π_2 \ S_3	1	2	3	4	5	6	7
1	1115.9	596.3	441.5	378.0	350.8	342.0	343.6
2	590.1	371.8	335.9	345.5			
3	429.2	329.7	351.8				
4	359.5	333.2	398.1				
5	326.2	354.9					
6	311.2	385.8					

$f_3(\Pi_1) = C_3(S_2 \Pi_1) + f_4^*(\Pi_2)$

Π_1 \ S_2	1	2	3	4	5	6	7
1	2325.2	1416.4	1156.1	1067.7	1033.5	1023.8	1043.1
2	1383.8	1035.1	991.3	1047.8			
3	1091.0	958.7	1064.7				
4	969.9	982.7					
5	903.2	1057.4					

$f_2(\Pi_0) = C_2(S_1, \Pi_0) + f_3^*(\Pi_1)$

Π_0 \ S_1	1	2	3	4
1	1243.9	1176.4	1173.6	1230.9

cost by (13) was $TC_*(\zeta_1) = 1305.18$. We now illustrate the dynamic programming procedure by finding ζ_2 at the new Q_1 (which is $Q^*_{1\zeta_1}$).

Table 3 illustrates the calculations according to (24). It can be seen in Table 3 that $f^*_2(\Pi_0) = 1173.60$ occurs at $S_1 = 3$; consequently $\Pi_1 = 3$. At $\Pi_1 = 3$ the best cost is $f^*_3(\Pi_1) = 958.68$ which occurs at $S_2 = 2$, consequently $\Pi_2 = 6$. At $\Pi_2 = 6$ the best cost is $f^*_4(\Pi_2) = 311.18$ which occurs at $S_3 = 1$. Hence $\zeta_2 = \{3, 2, 1\}$. Now using ζ_2 in (14) we calculate $Q^*_{1\zeta_2} = 58.80$, and using (13) we find the cost to be $TC_*(\zeta_2) = 1300.94$.

Since the application of dynamic programming at $Q^*_{1\zeta_2} = 58.80$ does not change ζ_2 (i.e. ζ is stabilized), we have obtained the likely optimum solution:

$$Q^*_{1\zeta_2} = Q_{1L} = 58.80;\ S^L_1 = 3,\ S^L_2 = 2 \text{ and } S^L_3 = 1$$

$$\text{or } \zeta_L = \{3, 2, 1\};\ TC(Q_{1L}, \zeta_L) = TC_*(\zeta_L) = 1300.94.$$

The likely optimum solution, as shown by computational experience, very frequently could be the same as the optimal solution.

21.3.6. The approximate optimum solution

Figure 3 illustrates the cost curves obtained by the solution procedures applied to the example. The minimum cost with continuous s_i's, $TC^*(q^*_1)$, is the lower bound to the solution with integer S_i's. The minimum cost obtained by the likely optimum solution, $TC_*(\zeta_L)$, is smaller than that computed by the rounded solution,

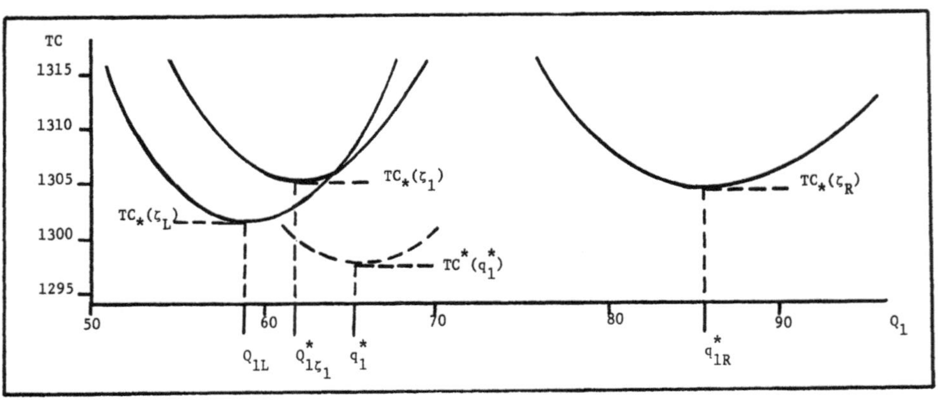

Figure 3. Illustration of the problem and examples.

$TC_*(\zeta_R)$. Hence, in our example the likely optimum solution is chosen for the approximate optimum solution (in fact this is the optimum solution). Of course, the smaller of the two costs will always indicate the approximate optimum solution. Computational experience has shown that the approximate solution is overwhelmingly close (or often identical) to the optimum.

The optimum solution can be computed with an elaborate search procedure somewhat similar to that applied for the likely optimum solution. The achievement of optimality depends on the width of search regions in the dynamic programming procedure. The widths adapted in our computations were such that, for practical purposes, we were assured of optimality.

21.3.7. Computational results and conclusions

The algorithm was tested on a large number of problems (with integer S_i's). Test problems were generated in the following manner. Ranges were chosen for the problem parameters: Range$(D) = [5000, 50000]$; Range $(P) = [60000, 625000]$; Range$(c) = [0.1, 2.5]$; Range $(F_1) = [1,500]$; Range $(F_{i>1}) = [0,500]$.

For D, P and c, in each test problem, values were simply chosen by using a uniform probability distribution within each range. Since values of c_i must decrease with increasing stage number ($c_i < c_{i-1}$), the values generated were ordered accordingly. In practice, zero set-up costs can occur at certain stages, thus, for one half of the cases, F's were chosen so that one sixth of them took up at random a zero value. On the other hand, when $F_1 = 0$ was generated, it was adjusted to $F_1 = 1$; otherwise the model breaks down (if $F_1 = 0$, $Q_1 = 0$). The remaining values were sampled uniformly within the range. Of course, Q_1 is actually an integer and a continuous value is used only as an approximation; if Q_1 is not very small the resulting error is negligible. The parameters were thought to be 'reasonable and representative' of what might be encountered in practice. Some contrived problems were also computed, but no discernible difference in performance was found. Tables 4 and 5 give comparisons of the performance and execution times (on a CDC 6400 computer) of rounded and likely optimum solutions.

Some rather obvious generalizations can be made from the computational results in Table 4. The rounded solution is extremely

Table 4. Accuracy of solutions and CPU times per case.

No. of Stages	No. of Cases	Rounded Solution		Likely Solution	
		% Optimal	Seconds	% Optimal	Seconds
5	400	79.50	0.004	92.75	0.033
10	400	65.50	0.008	85.50	0.077
20	400	33.50	0.018	74.50	0.210
30	400	28.75	0.037	71.75	0.404

Table 5. Cost ratios of approximate and optimum solutions.

No. of Stages	Percent of Cases at Cost Ratios or Below					Highest Ratio
	1.000	1.005	1.010	1.020	1.030	
5	96.75	98.75	99.75	100.00	-	1.011
10	92.75	97.75	99.75	100.00	-	1.018
20	86.25	97.00	99.50	99.75	100.00	1.023
30	81.00	93.50	98.25	99.75	100.00	1.025

fast even for large n, but it is optimal in a large percent of cases only for small n values (79.50 percent for $n = 5$). The likely optimum solution is somewhat slower, but is optimal in a large percent of cases even for large n values (71.75 percent for $n = 30$). Note that in computing the likely optimum solution, it takes a trivially small extra time to obtain the rounded solution. Both solutions can be obtained with virtually the same amount of time that is needed for the likely optimum solution. As shown in Table 5, the approximate optimum, the better of the two solutions for the same case is, in fact, optimal in a large percent of cases even for large n values (81.00 percent for $n = 30$). Further, the costs obtained by the approximate solution do not exceed the optimum costs by more than 1 percent in 99.50 percent of the cases if $n \leq 20$, and the excess cost is hardly more than 2 percent in any case.

21.4. Comparison of the two models and conclusions

21.4.1. Quantitative considerations

Each of the two models implies and identifies a particular organization of the production process and is based on defined assumptions.

There can be variations in process organization for which neither model would fit; nevertheless, our models can be regarded as two basic models for a multi-stage serial system. It can be shown that the cost function of each model reduces to the same expression, when the lot size is the same at each stage and only lot-sized inter-shipments are allowed.

When the stage inventory unit holding costs are not increasing monotonically, the cost function for model II does not identify the best process organization. However, model I still can be applied to such cases. When the conditions of both models are satisfied (the unit holding costs are monotonically increasing and sub-batching is feasible) the choice would be determined by least cost. We have used the same problem parameters for both models in our examples. Model I (example 1) yielded a cost of 1228.19, and the cost computed for model II (example 3) was 1300.94. Thus, in our particular problem, model II resulted in a 6 percent higher cost. Of course, this could be different for another problem; for example, if the transportation cost of a sub-batch had been greater.

21.4.2. Qualitative considerations

The application of the models in the case of 'sunk' transportation costs needs special attention. Sub-batch size (the optimal inter-shipment quantity) and, therefore, the optimal number of sub-batches is often determined by technical feasibility (for example, the sub-batch size may be chosen so that it fully utilizes the load capacity of the transportation equipment). Model I can be applied appropriately for such a case. One must remember, however, that in model II the intershipment cost is incorporated in the fixed costs per lot at each stage (as in example 3) and is assumed to be the same for any lot size. Consequently, if lot sizes at different stages are multiples of the optimal intershipment size, some additional and unaccounted transportation costs exist. Such considerations may warrant adjustment to the calculated cost.

In both models we distinguish between finished product inventory (inventory at the final stage) and process inventory (inventory at all other stages). It can be shown graphically that when the initial lot size, Q_n, as well as b in model I and Π_{n-1} in model II are about the same (as in our examples), the basic difference between the two models is that a relatively larger proportion of the average inventory is shifted to the final stage (stage 1) in model I than in model II. Although this occurrence is problem parameter dependent and is accounted for in the calculated minimum costs for the models, we must be careful because stage inventory unit holding costs derived from cost accounting data may be more unreliable for process inventories. Since they are difficult to measure, many intangible cost factors (e.g. relatively more expensive storage and handling costs in the plant than in stores, record keeping of process inventories, scheduling costs, etc.) are usually ignored in process inventory costs which, therefore, can easily be underestimated.

It is realistic to assume that the more variety of stage inventory exists at a time, the more expensive it is to hold the process inventory. A measure of this variety can be expressed by comparing the manufacturing cycle time (the maximum time span during which any unit from an initial lot is in process inventory), and the demand cycle time (the maximum time span during which any unit from an initial lot is in finished product inventory). The determination of the manufacturing cycle time is discussed in [5]. Accordingly, for model I the manufacturing cycle time is:

$$T_1^m = \frac{Q_n}{b}\left[\sum_{i=1}^{n}\frac{1}{P_i} + (b-1)\sum_{i=1}^{n}\left(\frac{1}{P_i} - \frac{1}{P_{i+1}}\right)I_i\right] \tag{27}$$

where:

$$\frac{1}{P_{n+1}} = 0;\ I_i = 0,\ \text{if}\ \frac{1}{P_i} \leqq P_{i+1};\ I_i = 1,\ \text{if}\ \frac{1}{P_i} > \frac{1}{P_{i+1}}$$

For model II the manufacturing cycle time, derived from Figure 2, is as follows:

$$T_2^m = Q_1 \sum_{i=1}^{n}\frac{\Pi_{i-1}}{P_i} + \frac{Q_1}{D}(\Pi_{n-1} - 1) \tag{28}$$

The demand (usage) cycle time of the initial lot size in each model is:

$$T_j^d = Q_{nj}/D,\ \text{for}\ j = 1, 2 \tag{29}$$

where: Q_{nj} is the lot size at stage n in model j.

The ratio between the holding time of process inventory and that of final product inventory of one initial lot indicates the average number of initial lots in process:

$$r_j = T_j^m / T_j^d \tag{30}$$

The meaning of this is that: if $r_j \leqq 1$, there is only one initial lot in process at a time; if $r_j > 1$, then more than one initial lot could be found in process at some time.

Table 6 contains the cycle time data derived from the problem parameters and the results of our examples. We can see from Table 6 that the average number of initial lots in process is 0.97 for model I, and 1.84 for model II. This implies that in our particular problem one must keep track of a larger variety of stage inventories in model II than in model I.

Again, this result is problem parameter dependent. Nevertheless, the analysis shown is useful because the effect of a larger variety of stage inventories on holding costs is extremely difficult to evaluate and to incorporate in stage inventory unit holding costs. Therefore, in effect, the stage inventory unit holding costs may not be the same for both models. The cycle time analysis presented here could induce further adjustments to the calculated cost.

Table 6. Cycle time data for the two models.

Symbols	Model I	Model II
Q_{nj}	370.00	352.00
D	300.00	300.00
T_j^m	1.19	2.17
T_j^d	1.23	1.18
r_j	0.97	1.84

21.5. Conclusions

Comparison of the two models has revealed the effects of various basic assumptions in multi-stage inventory systems. One must remember that each model fits a particular process organization. The results derived from the model are only valid if the process organization implied by the model is followed. Several models may be feasible under certain conditions. The selection of the 'best' is problem parameter dependent; therefore, the results of different models must be compared. It was shown that inventory unit holding costs incorporated into the models may not account for subtle (but important) effects generated by differing process organizations. Consequently, beyond the quantitative comparisons of results derived from alternative models, a careful qualitative scrutiny of models and data is very much desirable.

References

1. Clark, A. J., 'An Informal Survey of Multi-Echelon Inventory Theory', *Naval Research Logistics Quarterly*, vol. 19 (December 1972), pp. 621–650.
2. Crowston, W. B., Wagner, M., and Williams, J. F., 'Economic Lot Size Determination in Multi-Stage Assembly System', *Management Science*, vol. 19, no. 5 (January 1973), pp. 517–527.
3. Jensen, P. A. and Kahn, H. A., 'Scheduling in a Multi-Stage Production System with Set-Up and Inventory Costs', *AIIE Transactions*, vol. 4, no. 2 (June 1972), pp. 126–133.
4. Schwarz, L. B. and Schrage, L., 'Optimal and System Myopic Policies for Multi-Echelon Production/Inventory Assembly Systems', *Management Science*, vol. 21, no. 11 (July 1975), pp. 1285–1294.
5. Szendrovits, Andrew Z., 'Manufacturing Cycle Time Determination for a Multi-Stage Economic Production Quantity Model', *Management Science*, vol. 22, no. 3 (November 1975), pp. 298–308.
6. ——, 'On the Optimality of Sub-Batch Sizes for a Multi-Stage EPQ Model – A Rejoinder', *Management Science*, vol. 23, no. 3 (November 1976), pp. 334–338.
7. ——, 'A Comment on Optimal and Systems Myopic Policies for Multi-Echelon Production/Inventory Assembly Systems', Research and Working Paper Series, no. 118, *Faculty of Business, McMaster University* (May 1976), p. 5.
8. Taha, Hamdy A., and Skeith Ronald W., 'The Economic Lot Sizes in Multi-Stage Production Systems', *AIIE Transactions*, vol. 2, no. 2 (June 1970), pp. 157–162.

22. Priority updating procedures in dynamic job shop simulation studies: the impact on measures of performance under different due date assignment rules

JULIUS SURKIS and NABIL R. ADAM

Abstract

In job shop simulation studies the effects of local priority dispatching rules have been studied extensively. Among these, due-date oriented priority rules (such as slack, slack/remaining operation, critical ratio) have been found to be effective and useful in practice. These priority dispatching rules are dynamic in nature, that is, the state of the priority entity changes continuously over time. Therefore, one should theoretically update the priorities of jobs waiting in a queue every time a machine at a work center becomes available. This is an extremely costly procedure even in experimental simulation studies.

Some researchers have tried a static version of these rules: the priority is calculated only when an operation arrives at a work center and joins the queue.

In this paper we study a slightly more dynamic version of this rule: in addition to calculating the priority when an operations arrives at a work center, update all job priorities at constant time intervals.

A comparative study between these two versions of handling a dynamic priority rule is presented utilizing three different due date assignment procedures used in practice.

22.1. Introduction

The literature that is concerned with experimental investigations of job shops is extensive. Some representative studies are given in [1]–[18].

These experimental studies have concentrated on the effect of different priority or dispatching rules on the performance of job shops. Among the priority rules those that consider information regarding the due dates of jobs such as 'Slack' or 'Critical Ratio', have been shown to be effective in reducing the lateness of jobs, variance of lateness, and flow time of jobs. The interrelationship between priority rules that rely on due-date information and the assignment of due dates has been studied to some extent in [7], [8], [9], [17], [18]. When utilizing priority rules that are dependent on the flow of time (such as 'Slack' or 'Critical Ratio'), it is clear that the priority changes continuously over time.

To treat these dynamic priority rules properly in the context of job shop computer simulation experiments requires an update of the priorities of jobs in queue every time a machine becomes available at a work center. This is an extremely costly procedure even in experimental simulation studies.

Carroll in [5], Bulkin, et al. in [4], Rivera-Garza in [15] and the authors in [17], among others, chose to use a static version of this priority with respect to an operation: the job priority is calculated when an operation of a job arrives at a work center and joins the queue (procedure 1).

In this paper we explore a more dynamic version of this rule: in addition to calculating the priority when an operation arrives at a work center, update all the job priorities at constant time intervals (procedure 2). We will use a time interval of 4 periods to update all job priorities.

Consider the following 'snapshot' (Table 1) taken at a work center where the priorities are determined under procedures 1 and 2. We

Table 1.

Time Now: 20.0 (Days)
Priority update Time: 20.0 (Days)

Job Number	Job Priority	Position in Queue
10007	-141.96	1
10003	-138.23	2
10036	-137.42	3
10050	-131.45	4
10029	-130.24	5
10065	-128.77	6
10052	-125.03	7
10088	-116.15	8
10094	-106.68	9
10096	-106.19	10

Table 1. (cont.)

Time Now: 20.0 (Days)
Priority calculated at the time of job arrival at the work center.

Job Number	Job Priority	Position in Queue
10007	0.66	32
10003	4.65	50
10036	1.82	41
10050	2.55	45
10029	0.87	36
10065	0.27	25
10052	-2.24	14
10088	-1.88	15
10094	2.18	43
10096	2.34	44

note that the sequence of jobs is significantly different, therefore one would expect interesting differences between these two procedures.

We present experimental results that exhibit the behavior of these procedures using the dynamic slack priority rule on various job shop performance measures under three due date assignment methods that are used in job shop control systems in practice. In the next section, we will review the operational decision rules such as the exact definition of the priority rule and the due date assignment methods. Then we summarize the simulation model design.

22.2. Operational decision rules

22.2.1. Priority dispatching rule

The priority dispatching rule to be used is the 'Dynamic Slack', where dynamic slack is defined as:

Time remaining to due date – remaining expected flow time

22.2.2. Assignment of due dates

The due date assignment methods used in the simulation experiments to be reported in this paper are described in [1], [17]. We will briefly describe them here.

1. Finite capacity loading

This approach requires that the capacity of each work center at each period be specified in advance. Using this technique jobs can be loaded either forward or backward. In the case of forward loading, starting with the job's release date to the shop and working forward through its routing and hence forward through time, its completion time, or due date would be estimated. As an operation of a job arrives at a work center, one has to check that the addition of the processing time of the operation will not cause the total load at that work center for that time period to exceed the available capacity for that time period. If the capacity is not exceeded, then the operation is 'loaded'. Otherwise, the operation is moved forward to the first available period in which the addition of the processing time of the operation does not exceed the available capacity. To find the arrival time of a job at the next work center, one has to add, to the arrival time of the job at the current work center, the set-up, processing and transport times of the operation being performed as well as the existing load at the work center (version 1). In some interpretations of finite capacity planning approaches the existing load at the work center is not added on (version 2).

2. Infinite capacity loading

This approach assumes that the available capacity is infinite. As in the finite capacity planning approach jobs can be loaded either forward or backward. Loading is done in the same way as in the case of the finite capacity planning approach to obtain the due date of the job with the exception that no consideration is given to overloads that may develop.

3. Dynamic capacity loading

Reiter [14] and Holstein [11] proposed an alternate capacity loading method to obtain job due dates. This approach views the job shop as an environment that is constantly changing. It takes into account the congestion that the job entering the shop is going to encounter at every work center at the time it arrives at that center.

In this approach jobs are loaded forward. To find the arrival time of a job at the next work center, one has to add, to the arrival time of the job at the current work center, the estimated delay or waiting time resulting from the congestion at the work center in that time period as well as the set-up, processing and transport time for the operation. The significant departure from the other approaches is the introduction of the periodic delay concept. The delays are calculated for each work center for a specific number of future periods. In order to obtain and update these estimated delays for each work center at each successive time period, a forecast of the number of jobs and their processing times are required.

22.3. Simulation model design

In order to study the interaction between due date assignment procedures and the priority dispatching rules, two sets of computer simulation models were developed. The first set models the three job loading techniques described earlier. The second model is a job shop simulator that performs the actual processing of the jobs through the shop using the appropriate priority dispatching rule. It also collects various statistics related to jobs and average work in process inventory in hours. All programs are written in 'Simscript II.5'.

In the model, the job shop on which the experiments were performed consists of six work centers. The work centers may have a single machine or may contain several identical machines to process incoming jobs. Once work is started on a machine, it is completed on that machine. (The number of work centers was a compromise to keep the simulation runs, especially the job shop simulator model, to a reasonable amount of actual computer time and memory requirements.) The job arrival pattern was chosen to be poisson with a mean interarrival time of .5 hrs. (Again, this was dictated by core limitations.)

The service time was assumed to be exponentially distributed. The mean service time was taken from a random variable uniformly distributed between 1 and 6 hours, depending on the work center and job type. The number of operations on a job was taken to be a random variable uniformly distributed between 2 and 8. Each work center was assumed equally likely to handle the first operation of the job. The job then was assumed equally likely to move to any of the other work centers for its next operation. Return to a work center already visited was permitted but not in consecutive operations.

It is assumed that there is only one queue at a work center. In all the simulation experiments the capacity of the job shop is fixed: single shift no subcontracting or overtime. Each run assumes 200 days of operation with a warm up period of 20 days. Each experiment was replicated 5 times.

22.4. Results

The results of the simulation experiments are displayed in Tables 2, 3, and 4.

Table 2. Due date assignment method: infinite capacity loading priority rule: dynamic slack.

Measures of Performance	Procedure 1	Procedure 2
Number of Jobs Arriving	2904	2904
Number of Jobs Completed Total	1314	1497
Number of First 800 Jobs Completed	391	799
Average Work in Process	2515.2	3231.3
Average Flow Time of Jobs	65.04	357.72
Variance of Flow Time of Jobs	99.65	310.49
Average Lateness of Jobs	6.72	46.81
Variance of Lateness of Jobs	12.80	37.40
% of Jobs Late	86.57	90.68
Average Earliness of Jobs	.33	.31
Variance of Earliness of Jobs	.22	.22
% of Jobs Early or On Time	13.43	9.32

Table 3. Due date assignment method: finite capacity loading (Version 2).

Priority rule: dynamic slack

Measures of Performance	Procedure 1	Procedure 2
Number of Jobs Arriving	2904	2904
Number of Jobs Completed Total	1462	1465
Number of First 800 Jobs Completed	775	798
Average Work In Process	2988.4	3240.2
Average Flow Time of Jobs	348.59	350.96
Variance of Flow Time of Jobs	313.66	310.16
Average Lateness of Jobs	7.74	2.84
Variance of Lateness of Jobs	9.31	1.78
% of Jobs Late	34.45	28.76
Average Earliness of Jobs	19.16	14.20
Variance of Earliness of Jobs	12.13	9.00
% of Jobs Early or On Time	65.55	71.24

Table 4. Due data assignment method: dynamic capacity loading.
Priority rule: dynamic slack.

Measures of Performance	Procedure 1	Procedure 2
Number of Jobs Arriving	2904	2904
Number of Jobs Completed Total	1589	1602
Number of First 800 Jobs Completed	707	715
Average Work in Process	4263.0	3958.7
Average Flow Time of Jobs	251.60	284.42
Variance of Flow Time of Jobs	311.80	299.32
Average Lateness of Jobs	6.80	1.29
Variance of Lateness of Jobs	7.37	.82
% of Jobs Late	5.77	0.02
Average Earliness of Jobs	25.10	21.57
Variance of Earliness of Jobs	21.76	13.10
% of Jobs Early or On Time	94.23	99.08

22.5. Discussion of results

We compare the performance of the two priority update procedures within a due date assignment method and then across due date assignment procedures.

22.5.1. Comparison of priority update procedures within due date assignment methods

– Infinite capacity
The use of procedure 2 increases the throughput by 14 percent and most of the first 800 jobs introduced into the job shop are completed by the end of 200 days of simulation. Under procedure 1 only half of the first 800 jobs are completed at the end of 200 days of operation. With procedure 2 the average flow time of jobs is 5.5 times and the average lateness is 7 times the magnitude of these measures as compared to procedure 1.
– Finite capacity (version 2)
The throughput improves slightly under procedure 2 and a few more of the jobs entering the shop at early stages are completed. The average lateness is reduced by about 2.7 times and the variance of lateness is also reduced significantly. The earliness of the jobs is reduced as well. The average flow time and the average work in process are not affected significantly.

– Dynamic capacity
  Procedure 1 results in fewer of the first 800 jobs being completed, the average work in process is higher by about 10 percent, the average lateness of jobs is about 5 times as large and the variance of earliness is overstated by a magnitude of 1.5 times.

22.5.2. Comparison of priority update procedures across due date assignment methods

The use of procedure 2 emphasizes the completion of a greater percentage of jobs introduced into the shop at earlier periods. This phenomenon is most pronounced in the infinite capacity method. For due date assignments methods that are more 'realistic' in obtaining the due dates, such as finite and dynamic capacity, the average lateness and the variance of lateness are also reduced significantly. For 'realistic' due date assignment procedures, the average flow time and the variance of flow time do not appear to be influenced by varying the priority update procedure. Again for the 'realistic' due date assignment methods, the use of procedure 2 reduces the average lateness and earliness thus attempting to bring the job completions closer to the calculated due dates.

22.6. Conclusion

From the discussion of the results, it is clear that procedure 1 and procedure 2 do produce a significantly different behavior pattern in the performance measures being considered with the dynamic slack priority under three different due date assignment methods.

Procedure 2 does provide definite improvements in the throughput, average lateness, variance of lateness, percentage of late jobs and the measures pertaining to earliness.

In terms of CPU time of performing a single replication of a simulation experiment procedure 2 requires 1.5 to 1.9 times that of procedure 1.

We are currently studying the sensitivity of the update interval of procedure 2. It is apparent that the smaller the update interval, the closer we get to the true state of a dynamic priority rule. However, it remains to be seen whether the improvements in the performance measures can justify the added cost in terms of CPU time.

References

1. Adam, N. and Surkis, J., 'A Comparison of Capacity Planning Techniques in a Job Shop Control System', *Management Science*, vol. 23, no. 5 (January 1977).
2. Baker, C. T. and Dzielinski, B. P., 'Simulation of Simplified Job Shop', *Management Science*, vol. 6, no. 3 (April 1960), pp. 311–323.
3. Berry, W. L. and Rao, V., 'Critical Ratio Scheduling: An Experimental Analysis', *Management Science*, vol. 22, no. 2 (October 1975), pp. 192–201.
4. Bulkin, M. H., Colley, J. L., and Steinhoff, H. W., 'Load Forecasting, Priority Sequencing, and Simulation in a Job-Shop Control System', *Management Science*, vol. 13, no. 2 (October 1966), pp. 29–51.
5. Carroll, D. C., 'Heuristic Sequencing of Single and Multiple Component Jobs', Ph.D. Dissertation Sloan School of Management, MIT (1965).
6. Conway, R. W., Johnson, B. M., and Maxwell, W. L., 'An Experimental Investigation of Priority Dispatching', *Journal of Industrial Engineering*, vol. XI, no. 3 (May–June 1960), pp. 221–229.
7. Conway, R. W., Maxwell, W. L., and Miller, L. W., *Theory of Scheduling*, Addison Wesley Publishing Co. (1967).
8. Eilon, S. and Hodgson, R. M., 'Job Shop Scheduling with Due-Dates', *The International Journal of Production Research*, vol. 6, no. 1 (1967), pp. 1–13.
9. Elvers, D. A., 'A Simulation of Job Dispatching Rules Using Various Delivery Date Criteria', *Proceedings of the Fourth Annual Meeting of the American Institute for Decision Sciences* (1972), pp. 479–486.
10. Gere, W. S., Jr., 'Heuristics in Job Shop Scheduling', *Management Science*, vol. 13, no. 3 (November 1966), pp. 167–190.
11. Holstein, William K., 'Production Planning and Control Integrated', *Harvard Business Review* (May–June 1968), pp. 121–140.
12. LeGrande, Earl, 'The Development of a Factory Simulation System Using Actual Operating Data', *Management Technology*, vol. III, no. 1 (May 1963).
13. Nanot, Y. R. 'An Experimental Investigation and Comparative Evaluation of Priority Disciplines in Job Shop Like Queueing Networks', Ph.D. Dissertation UCLA (1963).
14. Reiter, S., 'A System for Managing Job-Shop Production', *The Journal of Business of the University of Chicago*, vol. XXXIX (July 1966), pp. 371–393.
15. Rivera-Garza, M., 'Labor and Machine Constrained Job Shops: A Simulation Investigation of Dispatching Rules', Ph.D. Dissertation, Stanford University (1974).
16. Rowe, A. J., 'Application of Computer Simulation to Sequential Decision Rules in Production Scheduling', *Proceedings Eleventh Annual Industrial Engineering Institute*, University of California, Berkeley, Los Angeles (February 1959).
17. Surkis, J. and Adam, N., 'Interaction of Priority Dispatching Rules and Due Date Assignment Procedures in Continuous Job Shops', *Proceedings of the Eighth Annual Meeting of the American Institute for Decision Sciences*,
18. Weeks, J. K. and Fryer, J. S., 'A Simulation Study of Operating Policies in a Hypothetical Dual-Constrained Job Shop', *Management Science*, vol. 22, no. 12 (August 1976), pp. 1362–1371.

23. A review of flowshop scheduling research

JATINDER N. D. GUPTA

Abstract

The problem of scheduling n jobs on M machines in a flowshop has received considerable research attention over the last twenty-five years. As a result, several optimization and heuristic solution procedures are available to solve a variety of flowshop scheduling problems. This paper reviews the flowshop scheduling problem formulation, solution approaches, and analyzes the contributions of each approach to solve practical problems. Subsequently, directions for future research are outlined.

23.1. Introduction

A frequently occurring operational problem is one of processing a given number of jobs (commodities) on a specified number of machines (facilities) – referred to by various investigators as scheduling, dispatching, sequencing, or combinations thereof [28, 34]. The first of these terms will be used here since this, in deterministic cases, encompasses dispatching and sequencing [14, 29, 47]. The desire to process the jobs in a special order to achieve some objective function is what creates a problem that remains largely unsolved.

The actual situations that give rise to scheduling problems are wide and varied [28]. Thus, for example, we have single machine scheduling problem, multiple machine scheduling problem, manpower scheduling problem, etc. In this paper, we will consider a special class of multiple machine scheduling problems, called the flowshop scheduling problem. Further, we will restrict our discussion to the deterministic phase of the operational problem.

A flowshop is characterized by more or less continuous and uninterrupted flow of jobs through multiple machines in series. In such a shop, the flow of work is unidirectional since all jobs follow the same technological routing through the machines. Although this description of flowshop resembles an assembly-line operation, there are several differences. First: a flowshop is equipped to handle a variety of jobs as opposed to a standard product manufactured by an assembly-line. Secondly: the jobs in a flowshop do not have to be processed on all machines; that is, a job may skip some operations according to its technological requirements. However, in an assembly-line, all jobs have to move from one station to another without skipping any work-station. Thirdly: in a flowshop, each machine is independent of other machines and can be loaded independently; whereas in assembly-line operations, each work station depends on the preceding one. And finally, each job has its own processing time at each machine in a flowshop; however, all units of a product have a standard time at each work station in an assembly-line [7].

The restrictive assumption of unidirectional flow pattern of jobs in a flowshop, though more general than that of an assembly-line, limits the variety of output of the shop. Indeed the flowshop is very restrictive. Nevertheless, progress in scheduling theory is not appreciable even to solve this very restrictive class of scheduling problems. As a result, the already restrictive case of flowshop must have several additional simplifying assumptions imposed on it. The past twenty-five years of research efforts in scheduling theory have resulted in many solution procedures for the solution of the idealized versions of flowshop scheduling problems. Some of these techniques are relatively more practical than others. However, in spite of all the developments over the last two decades, the general flowship scheduling problem still remains largely unsolved.

This paper reviews the developments in the mathematical theory of flowshop scheduling. The problem assumptions, problem formulation, and solution approaches used in solving the flowshop scheduling problem are described and critically analyzed. Subsequently, several plausible extensions of basic flowshop scheduling algorithms are described and directions for future research are outlined.

23.2. Problem definition and assumptions

23.2.1. Problem definition

As stated earlier, the work-flow in a flowshop is unidirectional. This means that the order in which jobs are processed on various machines is the same for all jobs and is specified. Since the nomenclature of the machines is arbitrary, the machines may be numbered such that each job is processed on machine 1 first, machine 2 second, . . ., and machine M last. With this numbering of machines and the abstract terminology of jobs and machines, the flowshop scheduling problem considered here may be defined as follows:

Given n jobs to be processed on M machines in the same technological order; the processing time of job a on machine m being $t(a, m)$; $(\forall a \leqq n; \forall m \leqq M)$; it is desired to find the order (schedule) in which these n jobs should be processed on each of the M machines to minimize a well defined measure of production cost.

The above problem, when considered in the general case, gives $(n!)^M$ possible schedules. Even for problems as small as $n = M = 5$, the number of possible schedules is so large that a direct enumeration is economically impossible. A simplified version of the above problem, applicable to many situations in reliability, computer centers, and production shops, exists in which it is assumed that the order (sequence) in which these jobs are processed on each machine is the same. For this simplified version, the number of feasible schedules reduces to $n!$

The foregoing simplified version of the flowshop scheduling problem can be solved to seek an optimal schedule for the general flowshop problem described earlier if certain conditions regarding the number of machines (M) and the measure of production cost are satisfied. We state the following two theorems to describe these conditions.

Theorem 1: For the M-machine flowshop scheduling problem with all jobs simultaneously available and the objective of minimizing a non-decreasing function of completion times of jobs, it is sufficient to consider only those schedules in which the same job sequence occurs on the first two machines.

Theorem 2: For the M-machine flowshop scheduling problem with the objective of minimizing make-span, it is sufficient to consider only those schedules in which the same job sequence occurs on the last two machines.

For proof of theorems 1 and 2, see Conway et al. [28] and Roy [104].

Now, if the number of machines, $M = 2$, then the simplified version will in fact find global optimal solution. Similarly, if the objective is minimization of *make-span* (defined as the total throughput time in which all jobs complete processing on all machines) and the number of machines $M \leqq 3$, then the simplified version will lead to global optimal solution. Further, for the general M-machine case, it is not necessary to consider all $(n!)^M$ schedules. By employing theorems 1 and 2, the total number of schedules decreases to $(n!)^{M-1}$ for any objective that is a non-decreasing function of completion times of jobs and to $(n!)^{M-2}$ for make-span problems.

Even when it is sufficient to solve the simplified version to obtain global optima, it may be difficult to identify the optimal schedule. For this reason, the assumption that the same job sequence is followed at each machine is active in practically every research effort in flowshop scheduling.

The above assumption is only one of several assumptions imposed on the flowshop scheduling problem. Scheduling problems in general and flowshop cases in particular are structured rather restrictively from a practical viewpoint. Implicitly, and without specific statement, the formulations of these problems overlook several important factors that are encountered in operational situations. For example, Ashour [7] cites several factors that may interrupt the flow of work in a shop and hence cause unexpected delays. Some of the delay causing factors are: (1) unpredictable breakdown of machines; (2) the variability in the performance and absenteeism of operators; (3) delay in supply of materials, fixtures, or tools; (4) the variability of processing times; (5) changes in job specifications; (6) rejection and changes in job identity due to defective production; and (7) customer pressures that may cause rush orders for early completion of jobs.

The scheduling formulations and models that have been developed are based on several simplifying assumptions. Though these assumptions increase the generality of models thus developed and the possibility of finding an optimal schedule; they do, however, divorce these models from realistic situations. These assumptions include the characteristics of jobs and machines and the operating policies of the shop. The following list describes the assumptions for the flowshop scheduling problems [7, 29, 31, 55, 57].

23.2.2. Assumptions concerning jobs

J1. Each job is released to the shop at the beginning of the scheduling period.
J2. Each job may have its own due date which is fixed and is not subject to change.
J3. Each job is independent of each other.
J4. Each job consists of specified operations, each of which is performed by only one machine.
J5. Each job has a prescribed technological order which is the same for all jobs and is fixed.
J6. Each job (operation) requires a known and finite processing time to be processed by various machines. This processing time includes transportation and set-up times, if any, and is independent of preceding and succeeding jobs.
J7. Each job is processed no more than once on any machine.
J8. Each job may have to wait between machines and thus in-process inventory is allowed.

23.2.3. Assumptions concerning machines

M1. Each machine center consists of only one machine; that is, the shop has only one machine of each type.
M2. Each machine is initially idle at the beginning of the scheduling period.
M3. Each machine in the shop operates independently of other machines and thus is capable of operating at its own maximum output rate.
M4. Each machine can process at most one job at a time. This eliminates those machines that are designed to process several jobs simultaneously like multi-spindle drill.
M5. Each machine is continuously available for processing jobs throughout the scheduling period and there are no interruptions due to breakdowns, maintenance or other such causes.

23.2.4. Assumptions concerning operating policies

P1. Each job is processed as early as possible.
P2. Each job is considered an indivisible entity even though it may be composed of a number of individual units.
P3. Each job, once accepted, is processed to completion; that is, no cancellation of jobs is permitted.
P4. Each job (operation), once started on a machine, is completed to its completion before another job can start on that machine, that is, no preemptive priorities are assigned.
P5. Each job is processed on no more than one machine at a time. (This is a result of assumptions J5 and P2.)
P6. Each machine is provided with adequate waiting space for allowing jobs to wait before starting their processing.
P7. Each machine if fully allocated to the jobs under consideration for the entire scheduling period; that is, machines are not used for any other purpose throughout the scheduling period.
P8. Each machine processes jobs in the same sequence. That is, no passing or overtaking of jobs is permitted.

The above list of assumptions indicates how explicitly practical situations have to be analyzed before conceptual scheduling models can be used. Relaxation of one or more of these assumptions yields various scheduling models, both for the flowshop and other more general shops. For example, Gupta [53], Johnson [69], Mitten [82, 83], and Nabeshima [84–89] relax assumption P5 and allow the presence of start and stop lags. Similarly, Gupta [58], Piehler [98], Reddi and Ramamoorthy [102], and Wismer [123] eliminate assumptions J8 and P6 to develop a traveling salesman model of the flowshop scheduling problem. Except as noted, we will assume that all of the above assumptions are satisfied by a flowshop scheduling problem.

23.3. Problem formulations and solution approaches

The past twenty-five years of research in flowshop scheduling has provided three basic formulations and solution approaches: mathematical programming, curtailed enumeration, and heuristic procedures. Each of these three approaches is briefly discussed below.

23.3.1. Mathematical programming approach

Conceptually, a flowshop scheduling problem can be described as an integer programming or a dynamic programming problem. Without assumption P8 ('no passing allowed' condition), a flowshop scheduling problem follows all the rules of the job-shop. Therefore, formulations by Balas [15], Bowman [21], Conway, et al. [28], Gupta [49], Manne [79], Pritsker et al. [99], Von-Lanzenaur and Himes [121], and Wagner [122] can be used to solve a flowshop scheduling problem through linear integer programming techniques. Additionally, use of Lagrangian multipliers in reducing the computational effort is found in Fisher [35, 36]. With 'no passing' condition, Bellman's [17, 18] dynamic programming formulation or Baker's [11] integer-programming formulation can be employed to reduce the number of variables and constraints in the resulting mathematical programming problem. However, the problem size of the corresponding mathematical programming problem is so large that, except for problems with few jobs and few machines, it is practically impossible to find an optimal schedule. Indeed, the computational experience of Ashour [57], Gifler et al. [40], and Story and Wagner [113] confirms the inadequate nature of this approach to solve scheduling problems.

An alternative method of solving the flowshop problem via mathematical programming is to treat the resultant integer-programming problem as one of determining the minimal-maximum path in a directed network with disjunctive arcs [16]. Thus far, the solution procedures to identify the minimal-maximum path have been of the branch and bound type. The computational experience with the network based algorithms by Ashour and Parker [8] and Florian et al. [37] indicates the inapplicability of the network analysis approach to problems except very small ones. The detailed algorithm descriptions may be found in Balas [16], Florian et al. [37] and Spencer and Dudek [112].

23.3.2. Curtailed enumeration approach

The curtailed enumeration approach to flowshop scheduling consists of improving an existing solution until an optimal schedule is identified. Alternatively, the curtailed enumeration approach may incorporate certain dominance checks which may directly reduce the subset of partial schedules to be examined. In either case, the attempt is to identify an optimal schedule without excessive search. Consider a partial schedule σa obtained by the augmentation of job a to an already available partial schedule σ. Let $T(\sigma a, m)$ be the completion time of partial schedule σa on machine m. Then, from the assumptions of the problems (non-interference of jobs, non-interference of machines, and earliest possible processing of jobs), $T(\sigma a, m)$ may be obtained by the following recursive relation:

$$T(\sigma a, m) = \max[T(\sigma a, m - 1); T(\sigma, m)] + t(a, m) \tag{1}$$

where $T(\sigma a, 0) = T(\emptyset, m) = 0\ \forall \sigma a$ and m and $\emptyset$ is a null (empty) schedule.

Let the total cost of partial schedule σ be $C(\sigma)$ and the additional cost of augmenting job a to partial schedule σ be $f(\sigma, a)$. Then $C(\sigma a)$ can be obtained as:

$$C(\sigma a) = C(\sigma) + f(\sigma, a), \text{ where } C(\emptyset) = 0 \tag{2}$$

With these relations, the flowshop scheduling problem considered here is one of finding the order of jobs so as to minimize $C(\sigma a)$ where σ ranges over all possible permutations of $(n - 1)$ jobs not containing job a and a ranges from 1 through n.

The measure of cost, $C(\sigma a)$ can be given various interpretations. Depending on the desired objective, suitable relations of the form (2) can be developed. Thus, for example, if the desired objective is the minimization of the weighted sum of throughput time at each machine, then equation (2) can be rewritten as:

$$C(\sigma a) = \sum_{m=1}^{M} w_m T(\sigma a, m) \tag{3}$$

where w_m is the weight assigned to machine m. Similarly, if the objective is the minimization of total penalty cost, the equation (2) becomes:

$$C(\sigma a) = C(\sigma) + p_a \max(T(\sigma a, M) - D_a, 0) \tag{4}$$

where p_a is the unit penalty cost of job a and D_a is its due date.

For a discussion of the objective functions for the flowshop scheduling problem, see Gupta [48] and Gupta and Dudek [60].

The above formulation of the flowshop scheduling problem also reveals certain structural characteristics of flowshop schedules. We will state one of these characteristics as it has proved useful in solving several special cases of the general problem.

$$\text{Let: } t'(a, m) = t(a, M - m + 1) \ \forall\, m \leqq M \tag{5}$$

Theorem 3: If the schedule $S = (a_1\ a_2, \ldots, a_n)$ minimizes make-span for a flowshop scheduling problem with processing times $t(a, m)$, then the reverse schedule $S' = (a_n, \ldots, a_1)$ minimizes the make-span of the flowshop scheduling problem with processing times $t'(a, m)$ given by equation (5).

The theorem 3 was intuitively introduced by McMahon and Burton [78] and formally proved by Gupta [55]. The significance of theorem 3 is the fact that it provides two alternatives to solving the same problem by the same method of solution. Computationally, one alternative may require less effort than the other [77, 78].

Now, utilizing the above combinatorial search formulation of the flowshop scheduling problem, two types of curtailed enumeration approaches can be employed to generate an optimal schedule: branch and bound procedures and elimination methods.

The branch and bound procedures treat the flowshop scheduling problem as one of scanning the branches of a tree to generate a minimal length path that retains the feasibility. In order to expedite the search, lower bounds on the objective function are employed and a known trial solution value is considered as upper bound. The existing branch and bound procedures are discussed by Ashour [4], Ashour and Hiremath [9], Bestwick and Hastings [19], Brooks and White [22], Brown and Lomnicki [23], Gupta [44, 45], Ignall and Scharge [66], McMahon and Burton [77, 78], Nabeshima [88], and Van-Deman and Baker [120]. A recent comparative evaluation and comprehensive framework of various branch and bound procedures is described by Lageweg et al. [74].

The combinatorial (or elimination) method attempts to identify the necessary and sufficient conditions for an optimal schedule so that an optimal schedule can be generated. However, to date, no necessary conditions have been developed and the existing sufficient conditions do not in general generate only one schedule. Except for two-machine and some special cases of M-machine problems, the combinatorial analysis approach provides only a reduced set of active schedules that are candidates for an optimal schedule. Within this set of active schedules, the identification of an optimal schedule is essentially one of curtailed enumeration.

Consider two mutually exclusive subsets of the n-jobs (possibly empty) σ and π such that $\sigma \cap \pi = \phi$. Further assume that the sequential order of processing the jobs in σ has been determined, but not in π. The following theorem establishes one possible set of conditions for optimality for the cost measures gives by equation (3).

Theorem 4: Consider two partial schedules σ and σ' that contain the same subset of jobs. If:

$$T(\sigma, m) \leqq T(\sigma', m), \quad \forall\ m \leqq M \tag{6}$$

then:

$$C(\sigma\pi) \leqq C(\sigma'\Pi), \quad \forall\ \pi \notin \sigma. \tag{7}$$

Theorem 4 was originally stated by Smith and Dudek [110] and subsequent proofs are provided by Gupta [50, 53, 56] McMahon [76, 77] and Szwarc [115]. An algorithm that utilizes theorem 4 to solve the flowshop problem is described by Gupta [53].

The theorem 4 above utilized sequence dominance conditions that considered schedules containing the same subset of jobs. It is possible to derive dominance conditions which, if satisfied, can determine the job to be augmented to a partial schedule σ. For this purpose, consider two schedules $\sigma a b \pi' \pi''$ and $\sigma b \pi' a \pi''$ where $\sigma_\epsilon a, b, \pi' \cup \pi'' : \pi' \cap \pi'' = \phi$(null), $a \neq b$, and $\notin \pi' \cup \pi''$. The following theorem develops sufficient conditions for schedule σab to dominate schedule σb with respect to the cost objective of equation (3).

Theorem 5: Consider two schedules σab and σb. If:

$$T(\sigma ab, m) - T(\sigma b, m) \leqq t(a, r) \quad \forall\ 1 \leqq m \leqq r \leqq M \tag{8}$$

then:

$$C(\sigma ab\pi'\pi'', m) \leqq C(\sigma b\pi' a\pi'', m) \tag{9}$$

The theorem 5 is proved by Gupta [50, 56] McMahon [76, 77], and Szwarc [115] in various forms and is an improvement over the original results of Smith and Dudek [110]. Utilizing conditions (8), an optimal schedule can be obtained.

The computational effort required to solve a problem through theorem 5 is quite excessive as is evident from the probabilistic analysis of Baker [13] and Gupta [56]. This is due to the strict conditions (8). When $m = 1$, conditions (8) reduce to:

$$t(a, 1) \leqq t(a, r) \quad \forall\, r \leqq M \tag{10}$$

The probability of job a satisfying condition (10) is very small and decreases with an increase in M.

Recently, Szwarc [116] presented another method of eliminating the schedule σb. His conditions are given by the following theorem. Let

$$\delta_m = T(\sigma ab, m) - T(\sigma b, m) \ \forall\, m \leqq M.$$

Theorem 6: Consider two schedules σab and σb. If:

$$\max(\delta_1, \delta_2, \ldots, \delta_M) \leqq t(a, M) \tag{11}$$

then:

$$T(\sigma ab\pi, M) \leqq T(\sigma b\pi a, M) \tag{12}$$

The advantage of conditions (11) is that only $t(a, 1) \leqq t(a, M)$ is necessary for job a to be a potentially dominant job. However, a direct application of theorem 6 is not feasible since it will either require an examination of too many schedules or would fail to assure optimality, as in the case of Dudek and Teuton's [31] and algorithm [72]. Of necessity, the dominance conditions should either be independent of the job characteristics in σ and π or should ensure that $T(\sigma ab\pi'\pi'', M) \leqq T(\sigma b\pi' a\pi'', M)$. Szwarc's conditions (11) do not satisfy any one of these characteristics. Therefore, it is unlikely that the use of conditions (11) will yield an operational algorithm.

Now, it is possible to use the theorems 4 and 5 iteratively to obtain another combinatorial algorithm. Observe that the partial schedules obtained by employing theorem 5 may be different permutations of the same outset of jobs. Using theorem 4, some of those partial schedules can be eliminated from further search. This blended approach provides computer memory savings more than the reduction in computational effort savings [50]. Another approach is to augment the elimination method with the branch and bound procedures [12, 74, 95] to increase the size of the problem than can be solved through curtailed enumeration approach.

Szwarc's results (theorem 6) can be extended to generate an optimal schedule for the three-machine problems. Let:

$$\Delta = \max(\delta_1, \delta_2) + MC(\pi, 2, 3) - MC(\pi, 3, 3) - t(a, 2) \tag{13}$$

where $MC(\pi, 2, 3) - MC(\pi, 3, 3)$ is the maximum idle time on machine 3 considering the two-machine problem with machine 2 and machine 3 only and the jobs contained in π. The following theorem states dominance conditions due to Gupta and Reddi [63]:

Theorem 7: Consider two schedules σab and σb. If:

$$\max(\delta_1, \delta_2, \delta_3, \Delta) \leqq t(a, 3) \tag{14}$$

then:

$$T(\sigma ab\pi'\pi'', 3) \leqq T(\sigma b\pi' a\pi'', 3) \tag{15}$$

For proof, see Gupta and Reddi [63].

The dominance condition (14) does reduce the computational effort for the three-machine problem considerably.

The above developments cover only the deterministic flowshop scheduling research. The efforts in solving the stochastic problems are reflected in the papers by Makino [80], Parsons [97], and Talwar [119].

23.3.3. Context-free dominance conditions

The elimination methods described above utilize dominance conditions to reduce the set of active schedules. Ideally, it would be advantageous to utilize conditions that do not depend on σ or π. Such conditions are called context-free Dominance conditions since they establish the precedence of jobs without regard to their sequence position. Let $f(a) = f[t(a, 1), \ldots, t(a, M)]$ be a functional value for job a. Then, the following simplified version of Smith's [111] theorem provides a simple way of solving several flowshop scheduling problems.

Theorem 8: If $\forall a \leqq n$, there exists a function $f(a)$ such that $f(a) \leqq (b)$ implies that $T(\sigma ab\pi, M) \leqq T(\sigma ba\pi, M)$, then the schedule obtained by arranging the jobs in ascending order of $f(a)$ values minimizes make-span.

For proof of theorem 8, see Gupta [55]. Observe that if the condition of theorem 8 is applicable, a flowshop scheduling problem reduces to a simple sorting problem. Let:

$$f(a) = \text{sign}(t(a, 1) - t(a, 2))/\min(t(a, 1); t(a, 2)) \quad (16)$$

where sign $(t(a, 1) - t(a, 2))$ equals 1 if $t(a, 1) \geqq t(a, 2)$ and -1 if $t(a, 1) < t(a, 2)$.

The following theorem provides Johnson's [68] two-machine results.

Theorem 9: For the two-machine flowshop scheduling problem, a schedule obtained by arranging jobs in ascending order of $f(a)$ values given by equation (16) minimizes make-span.

The proof of theorem 9 is obtained by combining the developments of Gupta [55] and Johnson [68].

The proof of theorem 9 is obtained by combining the developments of Gupta [55] and Johnson [68].

The theorem 9 above can be extended to the M-machine case. Let:

$$f(a, u, v) = \text{sign}(t(a, u) - t(a, V))/\min(t(a, u); t(a, u)) \quad \forall\ 1 \leqq u < V \leqq M \quad (17)$$

Theorem 10: *Consider two schedules* $\sigma ab\pi$ and $\sigma ba\pi$. If

$$f(a, u, v) \leqq f(b, u, v)\ \forall\ 1 \leqq u < v \leqq M, \text{ then } T(\sigma ab\pi, m) \leqq T(\sigma ba\pi, m),\ \forall\ m \leqq M.$$

For proof of theorem 10, see Nabeshima [89] and Yueh [124], and in its three machine version, see Eilon and Chowdhury [32], and Ellman and Townsend [33]. The general application of theorem 10 is not useful. However, several special structure flowshops can be solved by the application of theorem 10 or its variant. For example, Burns and Rooker [24, 25], Johnson [68], and Szwarc [114, 117, 118] describe simple algorithmic rules to develop optimal schedules if the processing times satisfy certain conditions. For the general *M*-machine problems, Gupta [55], Khan [73], Nabeshima [85, 89], Panwalkar and Khan [94, 95, 96], and Smith et al. [108, 109] describe several algorithms to solve variety of special structure flowshops. The details of these developments and extensions will be covered in a separate paper.

23.3.4. Complexity of flowshop scheduling problems

The optimization techniques described thus far can efficiently solve flowshop scheduling problems containing a lesser number of jobs or machines. If the number of jobs increases beyond 12, economic considerations make the optimization techniques impractical unless special structural constraints are imposed. Several inherent complexities in scheduling and related combinational problems forbid the development of any efficient optimization technique (or algorithm) for the general *M*-machine flowshop scheduling problems [38]. Recent research in the theory of computational complexity of combinatorial problems [70, 71] and flowshop scheduling problems [26, 38] reveals that the existence of a polynomial-bounded algorithm even for the three-machine flowshop scheduling problem is highly unlikely. Thus, at present, the optimization algorithms are of limited applicability for practical situations. This does not, however, mean that the special structure flowshop scheduling problems cannot be solved in polynomial-bounded computational times. In fact, as indicated earlier, several special cases have been studied and efficiently solved. It does mean that for the general *M*-machine flowshops, heuristic or approximate procedures are appropriate and desirable [26, 38].

23.3.5. Heuristic approach

The heuristic approach to flowshop scheduling provides several solution procedures that generate an optimal or near-optimal with relatively little computational effort. Since these procedures do not depend on specific optimization theory, their optimality can not be assured. Nevertheless, in the absence of practical optimization techniques, the heuristic approach to flowshop scheduling provides better solutions than the trial and error procedures.

The heuristic solution procedures are based on acceptability rather than optimization criteria and are the result of several simplications and approximations of the combinatorial approach to flowshop scheduling. As a result of these simplifications and approximations, only a few schedules are generated, thereby obtaining a considerable saving in computational effort. We will describe the existing heuristic algorithms in three broad categories:

(a) Single-sort heuristic algorithms; (b) multi-sort heuristic algorithms; and (c) miscellaneous heuristic algorithms.

23.3.5.1. Single-sort heuristic algorithms: Approximate forms of the function $f(a) = f[t(a, 1), \ldots, t(a, M)]$ can be obtained to implement theorem 8 [91, 92]. Palmer's [83] slope index can be represented by an equivalent function as follows [40];

$$f(a) = \sum_{m=1}^{M} (M - 2m + 1)t(a, m) \tag{18}$$

Another function, proposed by Gupta [46], is similar to equation (16), and is defined by:

$$f(a) = \frac{\operatorname{sign}(t(a, 1) - t(a, M))}{\min\limits_{1 \leqq m \leqq M-1}(t(a, m) + t(a, m + 1))} \tag{19}$$

With any of the above two forms of function $f(a)$, the single-sort heuristic algorithm can be described as follows:

Step 1: Calculate $f(a)$ for each a. For Palmer's algorithm, use (18), otherwise employ equation (19).

Step 2: Arrange the jobs in ascending order of $f(a)$ values, breaking ties in favor of job with smallest sum of processing time on all machines.

Step 3: Calculate the cost of the schedule obtained in step 2. This is accepted as an optimal schedule.

When $M = 2$, the Palmer's heuristic algorithm generates the schedule in nondecreasing order of $[t(a, 1) - t(a, 2)]$ values. This does not minimize make-span. Use of equation (19) in algorithm 7, however, will optimize Johnson's [68] special three-machine problems.

The $f(a)$ values computed in equation (18) or (19) are independent of the sequence position of job a. It is possible to compute the functional values which depend on the partial schedule that precedes job a. Let $f_m(\sigma a)$ be the function value for job a if augmented to partial schedule σ and machine m is considered to be significant. Two heuristic algorithms are based on $f_m(\sigma a)$ values. Define:

$$f_m(\sigma a) = T(\sigma a, m) \tag{20}$$

and

$$f_m(\sigma a) = T(\sigma a, m) - t(a, m) \tag{21}$$

Collectively, equations (20) and (21) represent the foundations of MICOT and MINIT algorithms described by Gupta [42, 52]. The schedules obtained by employing equations (20) and (21) are of better quality than those obtained through equations (18) or (19). However, this increased quality is at the expense of computational time increase. Ashour [2, 3] Gupta [42, 52], and Gupta and Maykut [61], describe other single-sort algorithms.

23.3.5.2. Multi-sort heuristic algorithms: The effectiveness of the single-sort heuristic algorithms in producing an optimal flowshop schedule can be increased by generating more than one schedule. Encouraged by three-machine experience of Giglio and Wagner [41], Campbell, Dudek, and Smith [27] proposed generating $(M - 1)$ schedules. The function $f_k(a)$, used for generating the kth schedule is given by:

$$f_k(a) = \frac{\operatorname{sign}(\hat{t}_k(a, 1) - \hat{t}_k(a, 2))}{\min(t_k(k, 1); t_k(a, 2))}, \quad \forall\, k \leqq M - 1 \tag{22}$$

where:

$$\hat{t}_k(a, 1) = \sum_{m=1}^{k} t(a, m) \quad \forall\, k \leqq M - 1 \tag{23}$$

and:

$$\hat{t}_k(a, 2) = \sum_{m=M-m+1}^{M} t(a, m) \quad \forall\, k \leqq M - 1 \tag{24}$$

The equations (22) through (24) represent only one of several possible expressions for $f_k(a)$. Maintaining the equation (22), for example, $f_k(a)$ may be redefined by alternate expressions of $\hat{t}_k(a, 1)$ and $\hat{t}_k(a, 2)$ as follows [54, 67]:

$$\hat{t}_k(a, 1) = \sum_{m=k}^{M-1} t(a, m) \quad \forall\, k \leqq M - 1 \tag{25}$$

and

$$\hat{t}(a, 2) = \sum_{m=k+1}^{M} t(a, m) \;\; \forall\, k \leqq M - 1 \tag{26}$$

The multi-sort algorithms can be described as follows [49]:

Step 1: For each $k \leqq M - 1$ and each $a \leqq n$, calculate $f_k(a)$. The Campbell-Dudek-Smith algorithm requires equations (22) through (24), while Gupta's algorithm requires equations (22), (25), and (26).

Step 2: For each $k \leqq M - 1$, arrange the jobs in ascending order of $f_k(a)$ values, breaking ties in favor of a job with lesser values of $f_j(a)$, $j = k + 1, \ldots, M - 1$ or $j = k - 1, k - 2, \ldots, 1$. If the tie cannot be broken, choose any job arbitrarily.

Step 3: Among the $(M - 1)$ schedules generated in step 2, accept the lowest cost schedule as optimal.

Computationally, this algorithm will require more effort than single-sort algorithms. However, the quality of the schedule will be better in this algorithm.

Additional multi-sort algorithms, based on job merging and sorting, are discussed by Page [91, 92]. Spence and Dudek's network approach [112] can also be regarded as a multi-pass heuristic algorithm.

23.3.5.3. Miscellaneous heuristic algorithms: A decomposition approach to flowshop scheduling problems is suggested by Ashour [2, 3] and Gupta and Maykut [62]. The original problem with n jobs is decomposed into two problems with n_1 and n_2 jobs such that $n_1 + n_2 = n$. Each of these problems is solved by appropriate solution techniques determined by n_1 and n_2. Gupta and Maykut suggest $n_1 = 12$ and $n_2 = n - 12$. The problem with 12 jobs is solved by an optimization algorithm while a heuristic algorithm is utilized for the remaining $(n - 12)$ jobs. Results obtained through this method are encouraging and may provide practical solutions.

A variation of the Campbell-Dudek-Smith algorithm is considered by Aggarwal and Stafford [1]. Their approach consists of improving a known solution by exchange operations and improves the performance of the Campbell-Dudek-Smith algorithm.

Reddi [101] considers several heuristic algorithms to solve a flowshop scheduling problem when no intermediate space is available to store the partially completed jobs.

A Monte-Carlo simulation approach to scheduling is suggested by Heller [65]. In this approach, jobs are randomly selected to fill the sequence positions, and a complete schedule is then evaluated in terms of cost. The process is repeated for a large number of schedules, and among the sampled schedules, the one with minimum cost is accepted as optimal schedule. The number of schedules to be examined can be determined by the stopping rules proposed by Randolph et al. [100] and the effectiveness of Monte-Carlo simulation approach can be increased by using a refined chain Monte-Carlo technique [92] or neighborhood search techniques [100, 103]. If the assumptions for the flowshop scheduling problem, as outlined earlier, are satisfied, the cost of schedules obtained through heuristic algorithms is generally less than that of a schedule obtained through Monte-Carlo simulation [64]. However, if the assumptions are not satisfied, Monte-Carlo simulation may be the only approach available to seek approximate solutions to the practical problems.

23.4. Directions for future research

The reported progress in scheduling theory is not appreciable to solve flowshop scheduling problems optimally and efficiently. In spite of several developments in the last twenty-five years, even the theoretical flowshop scheduling problem remains largely unsolved. The future research directions suggested here are intended to bridge the gap between the development of theory and practical applications of theory. Three areas of research are identified: theoretical, computational, and empirical research.

23.4.1. Theoretical research

The development of flowshop scheduling techniques thus far are essentially curtailed enumeration schemes. The dominance conditions developed (in combinatorial and branch and bound procedures) depend on partial schedules that precede a job candidate. This situation makes the existence of a polynomial-bounded algorithm very unlikely. Theoretical research in flowshop scheduling should attempt to develop dominance conditions that are either independent of partial schedules that precede a job candidate or are such that a large number of partial schedules containing only a lesser number of jobs are rejected quickly. For the general *M*-machine problems, it is unlikely that dominance conditions independent of preceding and proceeding partial schedules can be developed since this would imply the existence of a polynomial-bounded algorithm – a result which contradicts the well established results on the complexity of scheduling and related combinatorial problems. The combinatorial analysis approach, however, can be specialized to develop polynomial-bounded algorithms for several special structure flowshop problems if there is enough justification for special cases. Smith [107] showed that the unidirectional nature of workload and restrictive assumptions outlined earlier do imply some structural relationships among the processing times of various jobs on different machines. It is reasonable to deduce that the restrictive flowshop scheduling problem will have well established structural relationships which are situation dependent. Therefore, theoretical research should consider as many special cases of flowshop scheduling as possible and develop efficient optimization techniques (with much less than polynomial bounds on computational effort) for their solution. Simultaneously, quick and reliable heuristic procedures should be developed. The slope matching approach of Bonney and Gundry [20] provides an excellent example of the approaches that can be taken for the development of heuristic procedures.

The measures of performance used in scheduling depend on such considerations as the interactions between scheduling, inventory, and plant layout. The theoretical research in scheduling theory should quantify these interactions and develop general purpose models of scheduling problems. These general purpose models could then provide an insight and perhaps the directions, for the development of solution techniques for only a narrow range of measures of performance.

23.4.2. Computational research

The past twenty-five years of flowshop scheduling research has provided a panorama of techniques that claim to find acceptable solutions. A practical schedule has difficulty in selecting an algorithm to solve the problem. The computational research should consider such aspects as comparative efficiency of various algorithms for specified problems. Thus, measures of computational effort required should be developed. The existing measures, average numbers of schedules and average computational time may be inappropriate measures for algorithm selection. Estimation of computational effort in terms of lower and upper bound on various types of computations, as described in Coffman et al. [26] would prove very useful. The mathematical programming approach to flowshop scheduling has been rejected because of excessive computational burden and heuristic solution procedures are being developed instead. Recent advances in solving large-scale mathematical programming problems and the availability of approximate solution procedures for the integer programming problem may show that the mathematical approach can, in fact, be used to find realistic schedules with less computational effort. A comparative computational investigation of the mathematical programming techniques and other flowshop scheduling procedures (exact and approximate) would be of immense value in indicating future research trends.

23.4.3. Empirical research

The mathematical theory of flowshop scheduling suffers from too much abstraction and too little application. The practical use of flowshop scheduling techniques is rare. This questions their suitability. In spite of twenty-three years of research, we know very little about the practical flowshop scheduling problem except that it is an often occurring problem. Perhaps we have over-emphasized the rigour in mathematical development at the cost of underemphasizing the realism of problem formulation. Future research in flowshop scheduling should be inspired more by real life problems rather than problems encountered in mathematical abstractions. For a realistic problem formulation, empirical research is necessary to understand the practical situations. The flowshop scheduling is only one of a few areas where no case histories are available. Empirical research should answer such questions as: What is the maximum problem size encountered in practice? What specific situations give rise to flowshop scheduling problems? What are the desired objectives of scheduling? What is the nature of processing times? How rigid (or flexible) are the operating policies? etc. Empirical research, therefore, needs to include a survey of industrial scheduling practices and situations. Without such a survey, we may in fact spend another twenty-five years in solving a problem that perhaps needs no solution, since it may be the wrong problem (from practical consideration).[1]

References

1. Aggarwal, S. C. and Stafford, E., 'A Heuristic Algorithm for the Flowshop Problem with a Common Sequence on All Machines', *Decision Sciences*, vol. 6 (1975), pp. 237–251.
2. Ashour S., 'A Decomposition Approach for the Machine Scheduling Problem', *The International Journal of Production Research*, vol. 6 (1967), pp. 109–122.
3. Ashour, S., 'A Modified Decomposition Algorithm for Scheduling Problems', *The International Journal of Production Research*, vol. 8 (1970), pp. 281–284.
4. Ashour, S., 'A Branch-and-Bound Algorithm for the Flowshop Scheduling Problems', *AIIE Transactions*, vol. 2 (1970), pp. 172–176.
5. Ashour, S., 'An Experimental Investigation and Comparative Evaluation of Flowshop Scheduling Techniques', *Operations Research*, vol. 18 (1970), pp. 541–549.
6. Ashour, A., 'A Statistical Analysis of Production Scheduling Systems', *Journal of Operations Research Society of Japan*, vol. 12 (1970), pp. 65–86.
7. Ashour, S., *Sequencing Theory*, Springer-Verlag, New York (1972).
8. Ashour, S. and Parker, R. G., 'A Precedence Graph Algorithm for the Flowshop Scheduling Problem', *Operational Research Quarterly*, vol. 22 (1971), pp. 165–175.
9. Ashour, S. and Hiremath, S. R., 'A Branch and Bound Approach to the Job-Shop Scheduling Problem', *The International Journal of Production Research*, vol. 11 (1973), pp. 47–58.
10. Ashour, S. and Quraishi, M. N., 'Investigation of Various Bounding Procedures for Production Scheduling Problem', *The International Journal of Production Research*, vol. 7 (1969), pp. 249–252.
11. Baker, K. R., *Introduction to Sequencing and Scheduling*, John Wiley and Sons, Inc., New York (1974).
12. Baker, K. R., 'A Comparative Study of Flowshop Algorithms', *Operations Research*, vol. 23 (1975), pp. 62–73.
13. Baker, K. R., 'An Elimination Method for the Flowshop Problem', *Operations Research*, vol. 23 (1975), pp. 159–162.
14. Bakshi, M. K. and Arora, S. R., 'The Sequencing Problem', *Management Science*, vol. 16 (1969), pp. B247–B263.
15. Balas, E., 'Discrete Programming by Filter Method', *Operations Research*, vol. 15 (1967), pp. 915–957.
16. Balas, E., 'Machine Sequencing Via Disjunctive Graphs: An Implicit Enumeration Algorithm', *Operations Research*, vol. 17 (1969), pp. 941–957.

1. *Acknowledgements*: The author is thankful to Dr. S. S. Panwalkar of Texas Tech. University, Lubbock, Texas and Dr. Paul H. Randolph of the Federal Energy Administration, Washington, D. C. for their valuable comments and suggestions on an earlier draft of this paper.

17. Bellman, R., 'Mathematical Aspects of Scheduling Theory', *Journal of SIAM*, vol. 4 (1956), pp. 168–205.
18. Bellman, R. and Gross, O., 'Some Combinatorial Problems Arising in the Theory of Multi-Stage Processes', *Journal of SIAM*, vol. 2 (1954), pp. 175–184.
19. Bestwick, P. F. and Hastings, N. A. J., 'A New Bound for Machine Scheduling', *Operational Research Quarterly*, vol. 27 (1976), pp. 479–487.
20. Bonney, M. C. and Gundry, S. W., 'Solution to the Constrained Flowshop Sequencing Problem', *Operational Research Quarterly*, vol. 27 (1976), pp. 869–883.
21. Bowman, E. H., 'The Schedule-Sequencing Problem', *Operations Research*, vol. 7 (1959), pp. 34–40.
22. Brooks, G. H. and White, C. R., 'An Algorithm for Finding Optimal or Near-Optimal Solutions to the Production Scheduling Problems', *Journal of Industrial Engineering*, vol. 16.
23. Brown, A. P. G. and Lomnicki, Z. A., 'Some Applications of the 'Branch and Bound' Algorithm to the Machine Scheduling Problem', *Operational Research Quarterly*, vol. 17 (1966), pp. 173–186.
24. Burns, F. and Rooker, J., 'A Special Case of $3 \times n$ Flowshop Problem', *Naval Research Logistics Quarterly*, vol. 22 (1975), pp. 811–817.
25. Burns, F. and Rooker, J., 'Johnson's Three-Machine Flowshop Conjecture', *Operations Research*, vol. 24 (1960), pp. 578–580.
26. Coffman, E. G. Jr., *Computer and Job-Shop Scheduling*, John Wiley and Sons, Inc., New York (1976).
27. Campbell, H. G., Dudek, R. A., and Smith, M. L., 'A Heuristic Algorithm for the *n* Job, *M* Machine Sequencing Problem', *Management Science*, vol. 16 (1970), pp. 630–637.
28. Conway, R. W., Maxwell, W. L., and Miller, L. W., *Theory of Scheduling*, Addison Wesley, Reading, Mass. (1967).
29. Day, J. E. and Hottenstein, M. P., 'Review of Job-Shop Scheduling', *Naval Research Logistics Quarterly*, vol. 17 (1970), pp. 11–39.
30. Dudek, R. A. and Ghare, P. M., 'Make-Span Sequencing on *M*-Machines', *Journal of Industrial Engineering*, vol. 18 (1967), pp. 131–134.
31. Dudek, R. A. and Teuton, O. F., Jr., 'Development of *M* Stage Decision Rule for Scheduling *n* Jobs through *M* Machines', *Operations Research*, vol. 12 (1964), pp. 471–497.
32. Eilon, S. and Chowdhury, I. G., 'Conditions for Optimal Scheduling for the Three-Machine Problems', *Journal of Institute of Mathematics and its Applications*, vol. 17 (1976), pp. 1–4.
33. Ellman, D. and Townsend, W., 'A Dynamic Programming Approach to the Three-Machine Scheduling Problem', *Journal of Institute of Mathematics and its Applications*, vol. 13 (1974), pp. 161–167.
34. Elmaghraby, S. E., 'The Machine Sequencing Problem – Review and Extensions', *Naval Research Logistics Quarterly*, vol. 15 (1968), pp. 205–232.
35. Fisher, M. L., 'Optimal Solution of Scheduling Problems Using Lagrange Multipliers Part I', *Operations Research*, vol. 21 (1973), pp. 1114–1127.
36. Fisher, M. L., 'Optimal Solution of Scheduling Problems Using Lagrange Multipliers Part II', pp. 294–318 in Elmaghraby, S. E. (ed.), *Symposium on the Theory of Scheduling and Its Applications*, Springer, New York (1973).
37. Florian, M., Trepant, P., and McMahon, G., 'An Implicit Enumeration Algorithm for the Machine Sequencing Problem', *Management Science*, vol. 17 (1971), pp. B782–B792.
38. Garey, M. R., Johnson, D. S., and Sethi, R., 'The Complexity of Flowshop and Jobshop Scheduling', *Mathematics of Operations Research*, vol. 1 (1976), pp. 117–129.
39. Giffler, B. and Thomson, G. L., 'Algorithms for Solving Production Scheduling Problems', *Operations Research*, vol. 8 (1960), pp. 487–503.
40. Gifler, B., Thompson, L., and Van Ness, V., 'Numerical Experience with Linear and Monte-Carlo Algorithms for Solving Production Scheduling Problems', Chapter 3 in reference [83] (1968), pp. 21–38.

41. Giglio, R. J. and Wagner, H. M. 'Approximate Solutions to the Three-Machine Scheduling Problem', *Operations Research*, vol. 12 (1964), pp. 305–324.
42. Gupta, J. N. D., 'Heuristic Rules for $n \times M$ Flowshop Scheduling Problem', *Opsearch* (India), vol. 5 (1968), pp. 165–170.
43. Gupta, J. N. D., 'Lexicographic Search Algorithm for Scheduling Problem', in *Advancing Frontiers in Operational Research*, Hindustan Publishing Corp., New Delhi, India (1969).
44. Gupta, J. N. D., 'A General Algorithm for the $n \times M$ Flowshop Scheduling Problem', *The International Journal of Production Research*, vol. 7 (1969), pp. 241–247.
45. Gupta, J. N. D., '*M* Stage Flowshop by Branch and Bound', *Opsearch* (1970), pp. 37–43.
46. Gupta, J. N. D., 'A Functional Heuristic Algorithm for the Flowship Scheduling Problem', *Operational Research Quarterly*, vol. 22 (1971), pp. 39–47.
47. Gupta, J. N. D., '*M* Stage Scheduling Problem – A Critical Appraisal', *The International Journal of Production Research*, vol. 9 (1971), pp. 267–281.
48. Gupta, J. N. D., 'Economic Aspects of Production Scheduling Systems', *The Journal of Operations Research Society of Japan*, vol. 13 (1971), pp. 167–193.
49. Gupta, J. N. D., 'The Generalized *n* Job, *M* Machine Scheduling Problem', *Opsearch*, vol. 8 (1971), pp. 173–185.
50. Gupta, J. N. D., 'An Improved Combinatorial Algorithm for the Flowshop Scheduling Problem', *Operations Research*, vol. 19 (1971), pp. 1753–1758.
51. Gupta, J. N. D., 'Optimal Flowshop Scheduling with Due Dates and Penalty Costs', *Journal of Operations Research Society of Japan*, vol. 14 (1971), pp. 35–46.
52. Gupta, J. N. D., 'Heuristic Algorithms for Multi-Stage Flowshop Scheduling Problem', *AIIE Transactions*, vol. 4 (1972), pp. 11–18.
53. Gupta, J. N. D., 'Optimal Scheduling in a Multi-Stage Flowshop', *AIIE Transactions*, vol. 4 (1972), pp. 238–243.
54. Gupta, J. N. D., 'Flowshop Scheduling via Sorting Analogy: Multi-sorting Heuristic Algorithm', paper presented at the Joint ORSA/TIMS meeting, San Juan, Puerto Rico (1974).
55. Gupta, J. N. D., 'Optimal Schedules for Special Structure Flowshops', *Naval Research Logistics Quarterly*, vol. 22 (1975), pp. 255–269.
56. Gupta, J. N. D., 'Analysis of a Combinatorial Approach to Flowshop Scheduling Problems', *Operational Research Quarterly*, vol. 26 (1975), pp. 431–440.
57. Gupta, J. N. D., 'A Search Algorithm for the Generalized Flowshop Scheduling Problem', *Computers and Operations Research*, vol. 2 (1975), pp. 83–90.
58. Gupta, J. N. D., 'Optimal Flowshop Scheduling with No Intermediate Storage Space', *Naval Research Logistics Quarterly*, vol. 23 (1976), pp. 235–243.
59. Gupta, J. N. D., 'A Heuristic Algorithm for the Flowshop Scheduling Problem', *Revue Francaise d'Automatique, Informatique, Recherche Operationelle*, vol. 10 (1976), pp. 63–73.
60. Gupta, J. N. D. and Dudek, R. A., 'Optimality Criteria for Flowshop Schedules', *AIIE Transactions*, vol. 3 (1971), pp. 199–205.
61. Gupta, J. N. D. and Maykut, A. R., 'Flowshop Scheduling by Heuristic Decomposition', *The International Journal of Production Research*, vol. 11 (1973), pp. 105–111.
62. Gupta, J. N. D. and Maykut, A. R., 'Heuristic Algorithms for Scheduling *n* Jobs in a Flowshop', *Journal of Operations Research Society of Japan*, vol. 16 (1973), pp. 131–150.
63. Gupta, J. N. D. and Reddi, S. S., 'Improved Dominance Conditions for the Three-Machine Flowshop Scheduling Problem', paper presented at the ORSA Conference on Theory of Scheduling, Orlando, Florida (1976), *Operations Research*, vol. 26 January–February 1978) pp. 200–203.
64. Gupta, J. N. D., Smith, M. L., Martz, H. F., and Dudek, R. A., 'Monte-Carlo Experimentation with Flowshop Scheduling Problem', *Sequencing Research Report, Qt 103–68*, Texas Technological College, Lubbock, Texas (1968).
65. Heller, J., 'Some Numerical Experiments for an $M \times J$ Flowshop and its Decision Theoretic Aspects', *Operations Research*, vol. 8 (1960), pp. 174–184.

66. Ignall, E. and Schrage, L., 'Application of the Branch and Bound Technique to Some Flowshop Scheduling Problems', *Operations Research*, vol. 13 (1965), pp. 400–412.
67. Ignizio, J. P. and Gupta, J. N. D., *Operations Research in Decision Making*, Crane, Russak and Co., New York (1975).
68. Johnson, S. M., 'Optimal Two- and Three-Stage Production Schedules with Setup Times Included', *Naval Research Logistics Quarterly*, vol. 1 (1954), pp. 61–68.
69. Johnson, S. M., 'Discussion Sequencing *n* Jobs on 2 Machines with Arbitrary Time Lags', *Management Science*, vol. 5 (1959), pp. 299–303.
70. Karp, R. M., 'Reducibility Among Combinatorial Problems', pp. 85–103 in: Miller, R. E. and Thatcher J. W. (eds.), *Complexity of Computer Computations*, Plenum Press, New York (1972).
71. Karp, R. M., 'On the Computational Complexity of Combinatorial Problems', *Networks*, vol. 5 (1975), pp. 45–68.
72. Karush, W., 'A Counter-Example to a Proposed Algorithm for Optimal Sequencing of Jobs', *Operations Research*, vol. 13 (1965), pp. 323–325.
73. Khan, A. W., 'On Sequencing Ordered Matrix Flowshop Problems', *Ph.D. Dissertation*, Texas Tech University, Lubbock, Texas (1974).
74. Lageweg, B. J., Lenstra, J. K., and Rinnooy Kan, A. H. G., 'A General Bounding Scheme for the Permutation Flowshop', Publication 227, Département d'informatique, Université de Montréal (1976), *Operations Research*, vol. 26 (January–February 1978), pp. 53–67.
75. Lomnicki, Z. A., 'A Branch and Bound Algorithm for the Exact Solution of the Three Machine Scheduling Problem', *Operational Research Quarterly*, vol. 16 (1965), pp. 89–100.
76. McMahon, G. B., 'Optimal Production Schedules for Flowshops', *Canadian Operational Research Society Journal*, vol. 7 (1969), pp. 141–151.
77. McMahon, G. B. 'A Study of Algorithms for Industrial Scheduling Problems', *Ph.D. Thesis*, University of New South Wales, Kensington (1971).
78. McMahon G. B. and Burton, P. G., 'Flowshop Scheduling with the Branch and Bound Method', *Operations Research*, vol. 15 (1967), pp. 473–481.
79. Manne, A., 'On the Job-Shop Scheduling Problem', *Operations Research*, vol. 8 (1960), pp. 219–223.
80. Makino, T., 'On a Scheduling Problem', *Journal of Operations Research Society of Japan*, vol. 8 (1965), pp. 32–44.
81. Mitten, L. G., 'Sequencing *n* Jobs on Two Machines with Arbitrary Time Lags', *Management Science*, vol. 5 (1959), pp. 293–298.
82. Mitten, L. G., 'A Scheduling Problem', *Journal of Industrial Engineering*, vol. 10 (1960), pp. 131–135.
83. Muth, J. and Thompson, G. L. (eds.), *Industrial Scheduling*, Prentice-Hall, Englewood Cliffs, N.J. (1963).
84. Nabeshima, I., 'The Order of *n* Items Processed on *m* Machines', *Journal of Operations Research Society*, vol. 3 (1961), pp. 170–175.
85. Nabeshima, I., 'The Order of *n* Items Processed on *m* Machines (Part 2)', *Journal of Operations Research Society of Japan*, vol. 4 (1961).
86. Nabeshima, I., 'Sequencing on Two Machines with Start and Stop Lags', *Journal of Operations Research Society of Japan*, vol. 5 (1963), pp. 97–101.
87. Nabeshima, I., 'On the Bounds of Make-Spans and Its Application in *M* Machine Scheduling Problems', *Journal of Operations Research of Japan*, vol. 9 (1967), pp. 98–136.
88. Nabeshima, I., 'Some Extensions of the *M* Machine Scheduling Problem', *Journal of Operations Research Society of Japan*, vol. 10 (1967), pp. 1–17.
89. Nabeshima, I., 'The Order of *n* Items Processed on *M* Machines, III', *Journal of Operations Research Society of Japan*, vol. 19 (1973).
90. Page, E. S., 'An Approach to the Scheduling of Jobs on Machines', *Journal of Royal Statistical Society*, vol. 23 (Series B), pp. 484–492.
91. Page, E. S., 'On the Scheduling of Jobs by Computers', *Computer Journal*, vol. 5 (1962), pp. 214–221.

92. Page, E. S., 'On the Monte-Carlo Methods in Congestion Problems I & II', *Operations Research*, vol. 13, pp. 291–305.
93. Palmer, D. S. 'Sequencing Jobs Through Multi-Stage Process in the Minimum Total Time – A Quick Method of Obtaining a Near Optimum', *Operational Research Quarterly*, vol. 16 (1965), pp. 101–107.
94. Panwalkar, S. S. and Khan, A. W., 'Ordered Flowshop Production Scheduling', Paper presented at the ORSA/TIMS Joint National Meeting, Chicago, Illinois (1974).
95. Panwalkar, S. S. and Khan, A. W., 'An Improved Branch and Bound Procedure for the $n \times m$ Flowshop Problems', *Naval Research Logistics Quarterly*, vol. 22 (1975), pp. 787–790.
96. Panwalkar, S. S. and Khan, A. W., 'An Ordered Flowshop Sequencing Problem with Mean Completion Time Criteria', *The International Journal of Production Research*, vol. 14 (1976), pp. 631–635.
97. Parsons, J. A., 'Easy Scheduling Rules for Certain Situations', *Systems and Procedures Journal*, vol. 19 (1968), pp. 28–33.
98. Piehler, J., 'Ein Beitrag Zum Reihenfolge Problem', *Untenehmensforchung*, vol. 4 (1960), pp. 138–142.
99. Pritsker, A. A. B., Watters, L. J., and Wolfe, P. M., 'Multi-Project Scheduling with Limited Resources: A Zero-one Programming Approach', *Management Science*, vol. 16 (1969), pp. 93–108.
100. Randolph, P. H., Swinson, G., and Ellingsen, C., 'Stopping Rules for Sequencing Problems', *Operations Research*, vol. 21 (1973), pp. 1309–1315.
101. Reddi, S. S., 'Sequencing Strategies in Pipline Computer Systems', *Ph.D. Dissertation*, The University of Texas at Austin, Texas (1972).
102. Reddi, S. S. and Ramanoorthy, C. V., 'On the Flowshop Sequencing Problem with No Wait in Process', *Operational Research Quarterly*, vol. 23 (1972), pp. 323–331.
103. Reiter, S. and Sherman, G., 'Discrete Programming', *Journal of SIAM*, vol. 13 (1965), pp. 864–889.
104. Roy, B., 'Cheminement et Connexité dans les Graphes – Applications aux Problèmes d'ordonnancement', *METRA Special Series no. 1*, Societé d'économie et de Mathématiques Appliquées, Paris (1962).
105. Roy, B. and Sussman, S., 'Les Problèmes d'ordonnancement avec Constraintes Disjonctives', Note DS no. 9 bis, *SEMA*, Montrougue (1964).
106. Sahney, V. K., 'Labor Assignments in a Single-Server Two-Machine Flowshop Problem with Switching Times', *AIIE Transactions*, vol. 3 (1971), pp. 264–270.
107. Smith, M. L., 'A Critical Analysis of Flowshop Sequencing', *Ph.D. Dissertation*, Texas Technological College, Lubbock, Texas (1968).
108. Smith, M. L., Panwalkar, S. S., and Dudek, R. A., 'Flowshop Sequencing Problem with Ordered Processing Time Matrices', *Management Science*, vol. 21 (1975), pp. 544–549.
109. Smith, M. L., Panwalkar, S. S., and Dudek, R. A., 'Flowshop Sequencing with Ordered Processing Time Matrice – A General Case', *Naval Research Logistics Quarterly*, vol. 23 (1976), pp. 431–486.
110. Smith, R. D. and Dudek, R. A., 'A General Algorithm for the Solution of the n Job, m Machine Sequencing Problem of the Flowshop', *Operations Research*, vol. 15 (1967), pp. 71–82. Also, see their 'Errata' *Operations Research*, vol. 17 (1969), p. 756.
111. Smith, W. E., 'Various Optimizers for Single-Stage Production', *Naval Research Logistics Quarterly*, vol. 3 (1956), pp. 59–66.
112. Spencer, D. L. and Dudek, R. A., 'The Dependent Shop Sequencing Algorithm. A general algorithm for solving flowshop, job-shop, and dependent shop sequencing problems', *The International Journal of Production Research*, vol. 11 (1973), pp. 325–340.
113. Story, A. E. and Wagner, H. M., 'Computational Experience with Integer Programming', Chapter 14 in reference [83] (1963), pp. 207–212.
114. Szwarc, W., 'On Some Sequencing Problems', *Naval Research Logistics* Quarterly, vol. 15 (1968), pp. 127–155. Also, see the note on this paper by Arthanari, T. S. and Mukhophadhyay, A. C., *Naval Research Logistics Quarterly*, vol. 18 (1971), pp. 135–138.

115. Szwarc, W., 'Elimination Methods in the $m \times n$ Sequencing Problem', *Naval Research Logistics Quarterly*, vol. 18 (1971), pp. 295–305.
116. Szwarc, W., 'Optimal Elimination Methods in the $m \times n$ Flowshop Scheduling Problem', *Operations Research*, vol. 21 (1973), pp. 1250–1259.
117. Szwarc, W., 'Mathematical Aspects of the $3 \times n$ Job Shop Sequencing Problem', *Naval Research Logistics Quarterly*, vol. 21 (1974), pp. 145–153.
118. Szwarc, W., 'A Note on Mathematical Aspects of the $3 \times n$ Job Shop Sequencing Problem', *Naval Research Logistics Quarterly*, vol. 21 (1974), pp. 725–726.
119. Talwar, P. P., 'A Note on Sequencing Problems in the Uncertain Job Times', *Journal of Operations Research Society of Japan*, vol. 9 (1967), pp. 93–97.
120. Van-Deman, J. M. and Baker, K. R., 'Minimizing Mean Flow-time in the Flowshop with No Intermediate Queue', *AIIE Transactions*, vol. 6 (1974), pp. 28–34.
121. Von-Lanzenaur, C. H. and Himes, R. C., 'A Linear Programming Solution to the General Sequencing Problem', *Canadian Operational Research Society Journal*, vol. 8 (1970), pp. 129–134.
122. Wagner, H. M., 'An Integer Linear Programming Model for Machine Scheduling', *Naval Research Logistics Quarterly*, vol. 6 (1959), pp. 131–140.
123. Wismer, D. A., 'Solution of the Flowshop Scheduling Problem with No Intermediate Queues', *Operations Research*, vol. 20 (1972), pp. 689–697.
124. Ming-I Yueh, 'On the n Job, m Machine Sequencing Problem of the Flowshop', in *Operational Research '75* (Haley, K. B., ed.), North Holland Publishing Company (1976).

24. An aggregate-disaggregate approach to the large scale multiple project scheduling problem

CHARLES M. JONES

Abstract

The current accepted method of solving the limited resource, multiple, large project scheduling problem is with a heuristic algorithm that was developed for the single project case. The projects are connected by dummy activities so that the algorithm sees only one very large project. The result of this procedure is a tendency to lengthen the duration of each project. A methodology is presented that aggregates the activities of each project into independent project resource profiles. A branch-and-bound algorithm is then used at the aggregate level to determine the optimal project resource profile schedule. This schedule is communicated back to the disaggregate level to be used in the detail activity scheduling heuristic algorithm. This procedure appears to be the first algorithm developed for the multiple large project scheduling problem. Test runs yielded an average twenty-four percent reduction in total scheduling costs over the method in common use today.

24.1. Introduction

A project can be defined as a contemplated major undertaking. The plan can be structured as a number of activities, some of which must be complete before others can start. Projects have a finite duration and generally involve considerable amounts of money, personnel, and equipment. Some organizations have a number of large projects in process simultaneously (i.e. a construction company).

Most of the project scheduling formulations that appear in the literature deal with the single project case [2], [3], [5]. The mathematical programming formulations, that give a guaranteed global optimal solution, include linear programming [4], integer programming [11], partial enumeration [12], and dynamic programming [1], [10]. Although formulated for the single project case, most of these models could be extended to the multiple project case.

Unfortunately, the state of the art of the computer and of the solution software for all the above approaches causes the large scale project (many thousands of activities) to be computationally infeasible. The only practical approach available is heuristic programming. A heuristic algorithm cannot guarantee a global optimal solution but it can generally be stated that a very good solution is obtained. The quality of the solution is dependent on the quality of the algorithm for the specific problem.

The algorithms that are available for the single project case [7], [9], [13], appear to give a relatively high quality solution for that case. However, no algorithms have been developed for the multiple project case. Mize [8] tested a number of activity sorting and conflict resolving decision rules for the multiple project case. The organizations that require a multiple project solution are forced to use a single project solution. The usual approach is to tie the projects together with dummy activities to give a common start and finish for the resulting conglomerate project. The implicit assumption is that the quality of the solution is not affected by this process. This paper will show the fallacy of this assumption and present a solution methodology developed for the multiple project case. The methodology, called the Resource Profile Procedure [6], consists of aggregating the activity information in a project profile. The fixed project profiles, at the aggregate level, are then scheduled subject to the total resource availability constraint, with an algorithm. The final step in the Resource Profile Procedure is to disaggregate the profiles with a heuristic algorithm that utilizes the information of project start and finish time from the aggregate optimization.

The assumptions of the large scale multiple project scheduling problem are:

1. A number, greater than one, of independent projects.
2. Standard CPM type precedence relationships exist between the deterministic activities of each project.
3. Activity durations may vary between three discrete levels (crash, normal, and slow) with corresponding resource assignments and costs.

4. One or more types of resources may be required by each activity.
5. Each resource type pool is fixed in size and available for assignment to activities in each of the projects.
6. The pertinent costs are:
   - Cost of project duration (overhead, etc.)
   - Cost of crashing activities (overtime, inefficiencies, etc.)
   - Cost of idle resources.
   - Late project completion penalties.
   - Incentives for early project completion (negative cost).

24.2. Aggregation methodology

The resource (for one resource only) profile of an activity for different levels of resource assignment is shown in Figure 1. If all the activities in a project were scheduled by some decision rule, the resource profile of the project could be determined. For example, if the decision rule was 'schedule all activities as early as possible at the normal level of resource assignment subject to an artificial resource constraint', then the project resource profile might resemble Figure 2.

A second decision rule, such as to assign the highest number of resources possible, would produce a second version of the same project. Each version contains the activity resource assignments and activity start/finish times relative to the start of the project.

The problem has now been reduced to the scheduling of the project resource profiles subject to the constraint that the total resources assigned to all projects, at any time, must be less than or

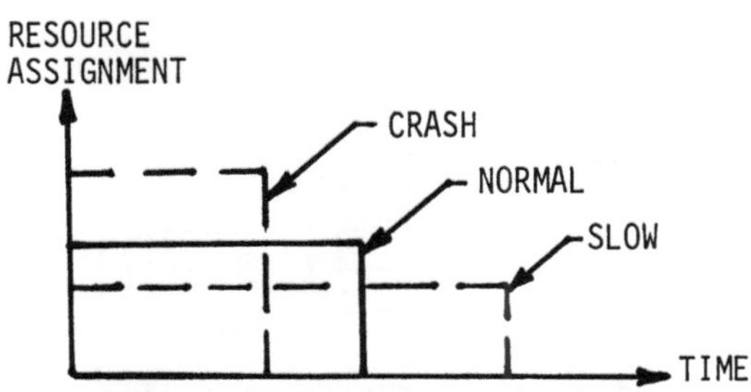

Figure 1. Activity resource profile.

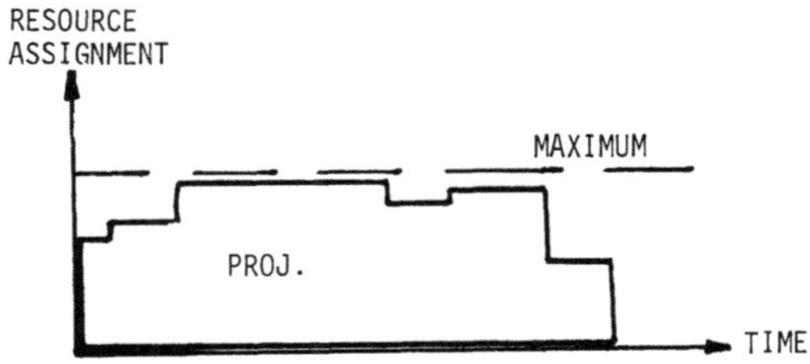

Figure 2. Sample project resource profile.

equal to the fixed resource pool size available. A second constraint is that only one version of each project may be scheduled. An analogy could be made to the task of fitting a number of large irregular shaped blocks into a container, on its side, as shown in Figure 3. There are also some similarities to the stock cutting problem.

24.3. Optimization at the aggregate level

Figure 3 shows one possible schedule for four projects. An aggregate level schedule is defined by the start time and version number of each project. A different schedule could have resulted by scheduling project 4 before project 1 in Figure 3. The maximum number of schedules that could exist are:

$$N! \prod_{p=1}^{N} V_p$$

where: N = the number of projects
V_p = the number of versions of project p

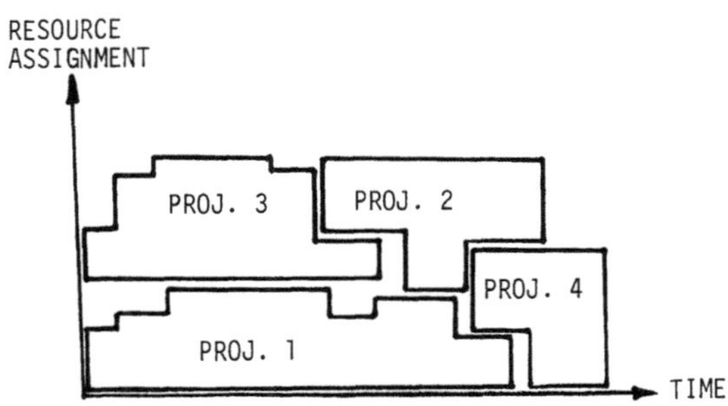

Figure 3. A typical project resource profile schedule

This represents the total number of permutations of N projects with V_p versions per project. However, some of the permutations may result in the same schedule. For example, the schedule in Figure 3 would result if project 3 were scheduled before project 1 or project 1 before project 3 (same versions). Theorems were developed to detect this situation and eliminate the need to generate the schedules that would not change. This was one of the primary bounds on a partial enumeration (branch and bound) algorithm that was developed to determine the optimal arrangement of projects and versions (blocks in a container).

A second, more obvious, bound is that if the cumulated cost of a partial schedule exceeds the cost of a previously scheduled sequence of projects and versions, then the partial schedule can be eliminated from further consideration.

The third bound is that if the finish time of any project in a partial schedule violates the absolute due date for that project, then that schedule is eliminated from further consideration.

The cost bound is very effective if the algorithm finds a low cost schedule early in the enumeration. To increase that probability, the first few sequences enumerated are the projects sorted by due date, project durations, and then by project completion costs.

The logic flow for the project profile scheduling algorithm is shown in Figure 4.

24.4. Disaggregation methodology

The results of the aggregate optimization are the optimal start times and version numbers for each project profile. Since each project profile contains the activity resource assignments and activity start times relative to the profile start time, the disaggregate detail schedule can be obtained by simply adding the project profile start times to the activity start times (relative to the profile) to get the detail activity start times (relative to absolute time) and resource assignments for each activity in every project. Although the solution would be feasible and relatively good, further improvement can be realized by smoothing the idle gaps between project profiles.

To reduce the size of these idle time gaps, a heuristic, very similar to the single project heuristic, was used. The main differ-

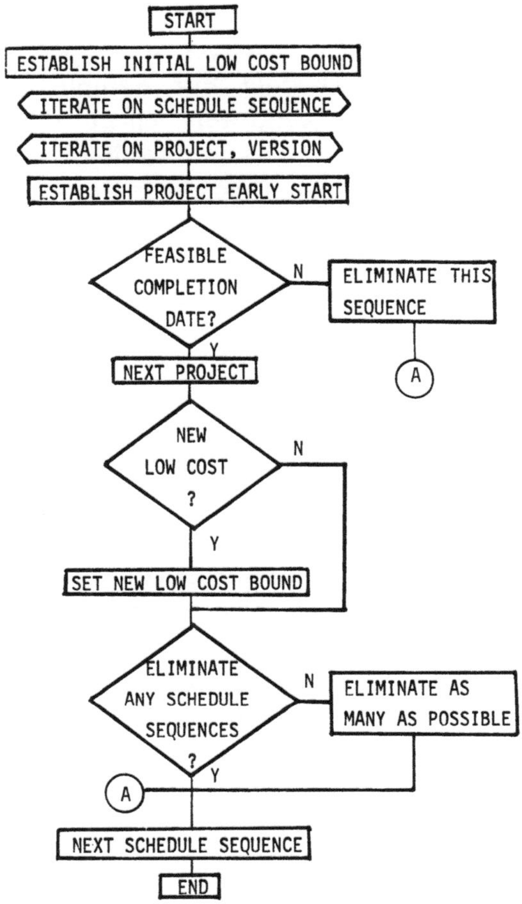

Figure 4. Project profile scheduling algorithm.

ence is that the activities of a project would not become available for scheduling until (or shortly before) the optimal profile start time for that project was reached.

24.5. Results

In order to test the partial enumeration algorithm, three types of cases were run. First, ten simple (rectangular resource profiles) project groups were scheduled. Each group had from three to eight projects. These are shown as test numbers one through ten in Figure

5. Then three groups consisting of five projects with more complex resource profiles, were scheduled. These are shown as test A_L, A_T, *B*, and *C* in Figure 5. Finally, test *D* consists of a group of five projects selected from the literature.

Test No.*	No. of Proj.	No. of Ver/proj.	No. of Resources	Resource Limits**
1	3	2	2	N
2	5	2	1	L
3	5	2	2	L
4	5	2	2	N
5	5	2	2	T
6	7	1	1	L
7	7	2	2	L
8	8	2	2	L
9	8	2	2	N
10	8	2	2	T
A_N	5	2	3	N
A_T	5	2	3	T
B	5	2	3	N
C	5	2	3	N
D	5	1	6	N

Test No.*	No. of Possible Sequences	No. of Seq. Evaluated	% Eliminated	No. of CPU Seconds
1	48	28	41	1.2
2	3840	2496	35	1.3
3	3840	36	99	1.5
4	3840	514	87	3.6
5	3840	3104	19	47.3
6	5040	1	99	1.5
7	645,120	820	99	5.7
8	10,321,920	256	99	2.8
9	10,321,920	21,220	99	148.8
10	10,321,920	***		over 300
A_N	3840	1092	72	80.
A_T	3840	2688	30	232.
B	3840	1920	50	95.
C	3840	1824	53	95.
D	120	86	28	10.

*Test numbers 1-10 are simple rectangular profiles. Tests A, B, and C were generated randomly. Test D projects were taken from the literature.

**Resource limits are classified as L=loose, N=normal, and T=tight.

***Computer time exceeded the maximum allowed of 300 CPU seconds.

Figure 5. Partial enumeration algorithm performance.

Project	Due period	Incentive per period	Late penalty per period	Project duration cost per period
1	50	110	110	1000
2	60	120	120	1000
3	70	130	130	1000
4	80	140	140	1000
5	90	150	150	1000

Figure 6. Test group costs.

The results of the partial enumeration at the aggregate level are shown in Figure 5. Included are the number of versions per project, the number of resources required by the projects, the total number of possible schedules, the number of schedules that had to be evaluated before a global optimal could be guaranteed, and the computer time required on a Univac 1108.

There is a large amount of variation in the computer time required for the partial enumeration algorithm. The causes of the variation are the tightness of the total resource availability constraint (more time is required as the constraint becomes tighter), the complexity of the project resource profiles, and the number of projects, resources, and versions.

		Start Period		Finish Period		Duration		No. Early Periods		No. Late Periods	
Group	Project	B/4	After	B/4	After	B/4	After	B/4	After	B/4	After
A_L	1	1	1	69	68	69	68			19	18
	2	1	19	69	63	69	45			9	3
	3	1	1	66	55	66	55	4	15		
	4	1	36	64	81	64	46	16			1
	5	1	10	77	79	77	70	13	11		
	Total							33	26	28	22
A_T	1	1	47	93	108	93	62			43	58
	2	1	76	103	124	103	49			43	64
	3	1	28	92	84	92	57			22	14
	4	1	1	104	47	104	47		33	24	
	5	1	1	114	56	114	56		34	24	
	Total								67	156	136
B	1	1	61	116	117	116	57			66	67
	2	1	11	97	55	97	55		5	37	
	3	1	1	106	64	106	64		6	36	
	4	1	84	104	136	104	53			24	56
	5	1	33	56	82	56	50	34	8		
	Total							34	19	163	123
C	1	1	66	108	116	108	51			58	66
	2	1	58	107	119	107	62			47	59
	3	1	1	92	58	92	58		12	22	
	4	1	1	118	93	118	93			38	13
	5	1	29	96	91	96	63			6	1
	Total								12	121	139
D	1	1	33	70	81	70	49			20	31
	2	1	57	60	102	60	46				42
	3	1	1	104	82	104	82			34	12
	4	1	85	72	130	72	46	8			50
	5	1	1	67	55	67	55	23	35		
	Total							31	35	54	135

Group	Project	Early Incentive B/4	Early Incentive After	Late Penalty B/4	Late Penalty After	Proj. Dur. Cost B/4	Proj. Dur. Cost After	Activity Crash Cost B/4	Activity Crash Cost After	Project Tot. Cost B/4	Project Tot. Cost After
A_L	1			2.1	2.0	69	68	3.9	3.8	75	74
	2			1.1	.4	69	45	3.5	3.6	74	49
	3	-.5	2.0			66	55	3.2	3.3	69	56
	4	-2.2			.1	64	46	3.4	3.6	65	50
	5	-2.0	-1.7			77	70	3.2	3.3	78	70
	Total	-4.7	-3.6	3.2	2.5	345	284	17.2	17.7	361	301
A_T	1			4.7	6.4	93	62	3.6	3.9	101	72
	2			5.2	7.7	103	49	3.4	3.6	112	60
	3			2.9	1.8	92	57	2.8	3.1	98	62
	4		-4.6	3.4		104	47	3.2	3.5	111	46
	5	-5.1	-1.2			56	50	1.6	1.7	52	51
	Total	-5.1	-2.6	19.7	15.2	479	279	13.6	15.3	507	307
C	1			6.4	7.3	108	51	2.8	3.0	117	61
	2			5.6	7.1	107	62	4.2	4.6	117	74
	3		-1.6	2.7		92	58	3.6	4.5	99	61
	4			5.3	1.8	118	93	3.2	3.6	126	98
	5			.9	.2	96	63	4.3	4.7	101	68
	Total		-1.6	21.1	16.3	521	327	18.1	20.4	560	362
D	1			2.2	3.4	70	49	44.9	43.5	117	96
	2				5.0	60	46	56.7	57.7	117	109
	3			4.4	1.6	104	82	88.4	88.4	197	172
	4	-1.1			7.0	72	46	0.	0.	71	53
	5	-3.5	-5.3			67	55	39.3	39.1	103	89
	Total	-4.6	-5.3	6.6	17.0	373	278	229.3	228.7	604	518

Group	Project	Idletime Cost B/4	Idletime Cost After	Total Schedule Cost B/4	Total Schedule Cost After	Percent Decrease
A_L	1					
	2					
	3					
	4					
	5					
	Total	88	98	449	398	11.2
A_L	1					
	2					
	3					
	4					
	5					
	Total	83	99	625	394	37.0
B	1					
	2					
	3					
	4					
	5					
	Total	71	98	578	405	30.0
C	1					
	2					
	3					
	4					
	5					
	Total	122	122	682	484	29.1
D	1					
	2					
	3					
	4					
	5					
	Total	60	74	654	692	9.4

Figure 7. Resource profile procedure results.

The costs and due dates used for all test groups are shown in Figure 6. In addition, there was a ten dollar cost associated with every idle resource period. The results of the Resource Profile Procedures (after) are compared to the results of the same groups using a single project heuristic (before) in Figure 7. The Resource Profile Procedure reduced costs in all cases. The cost reduction ranged from 9.4 percent to 37.0 percent. The average costs for all five groups are summarized by cost component in Figure 8.

As anticipated, the most significant improvement (35.5 percent) came from the reduction in project duration. This occurred because the single project heuristic (currently in common use) tends to increase project durations. Also anticipated was the increase in idle time costs (18.6 percent). This occurred because the single project heuristic can choose activities from all projects to fill idle time (at the cost of lengthening the projects). The dollar increase in idle time costs was much less than the dollar savings in project duration, however. There were insignificant changes in activity crashing costs and in late penalty costs. The largest percent change was a 58.3 percent improvement in early project completion incentives. However, the base is small so little significance should be attributed to this component.

The total average cost improvement from using the Resource Profile Procedure is 23.9 percent. It should be noted that each project profile could have represented thousands of activities with no significant increase in solution time to the approximation problem.

A comparison of the non-cost characteristics of the solution are shown in Figure 9. The percent changes are in proportion to the changes in cost components.

Cost component	Before	After	% Improvement
Early Incentives	-2.88	-4.56	58.3
Late Penalties	14.06	13.38	4.8
Project Duration	444.8	287.8	35.3
Crashing Activities	58.9	59.9	-1.7
Total Project	514.8	356.6	30.7
Idle Time	82.8	98.1	-18.6
Total Schedule	597.6	454.6	23.9

Figure 8. Cost improvement breakdown (in thousands of dollars).

Criteria	Before profile scheduling	After profile scheduling	% Chg.
Average duration per project in periods	89.0	57.6	-35.3
Average number of periods that projects were completed early per schedule	18.8	31.8	+69.1
Average number of periods that projects were completed late per schedule	108.4	111.0	+ 2.4
Average number of crashed activities per schedule	92.0	112.4	+22.1
Average number of idle resource periods per schedule	8254.0	9811.0	+18.9

Figure 9. Non-cost criteria improvement.

24.6. Job shop applications

The job shop problem consists of most of the attributes of the multiple project scheduling problem. There are a number of projects (jobs) that must be completed before a due date. Some have late penalty costs associated with the project. There are fixed size resource pools (over the short run) in the form of man-machine combinations. The job consists of a long narrow CPM type network where the operations are analogus to activities. The lot size could also be included as a decision variable by forming two or more versions of the project (job).

One strategy that could be used for the job shop problem is to schedule the large major jobs with Resource Profile Procedure and manually fill idle time gaps with small minor jobs.

It should be noted that the Resource Profile Procedure was developed for the large scale multiple project problem in which a large number of activities are aggregated into a relatively simple resource profile. The number of operations per job is generally not as great as the number of activities per project, so much of the advantage is lost. However, some of the concepts of the Resource Profile Procedure could be utilized in the development of a job shop oriented system.

24.7. Conclusions

The organizations that manage a number of large scale projects with limited resources generally use a heuristic algorithm that was developed for the single project case. These algorithms tend to lengthen the project durations and increase associated costs. A new approach, the Resource Profile Procedure, was developed that exploits the special structure of the limited resource multiple project scheduling problem. It is also feasible for very large scale project scheduling applications.

Tests on projects with high overhead costs (i.e. supervision, equipment, etc.) yielded approximately a 24 percent savings over the current method of scheduling multiple projects. The procedure consists of forming project resource profiles at the aggregate level, scheduling the profiles with a partial enumeration algorithm, and using the optimal aggregate schedule information in a heuristic algorithm to complete the disaggregate detail schedule of activity start times and resource assignments.

There is no realistic limit on the number of activities in each project. The implicit enumeration algorithm is limited only by the number of projects, the number of versions per project, and the number of resources types used. As the number of available resources of each type increases, the upper limit of projects, versions, and resource types also increases.

If the upper limit of projects, versions, and resource types is exceeded, the implicit enumeration algorithm, with its guaranteed global optimal solution at the aggregate level, could be eliminated and a heuristic algorithm could be used in its place. The global optimal solution could no longer be guaranteed but a very good solution could be assumed.

Regardless of the nature of algorithm applied at the aggregate level, the proposed Resource Profile Procedure offers significant cost savings over the current methods of solution of the limited resource, multiple project scheduling problem.

References

1. Carruthers, J. A. and Battersby, A., *Operational Research Quarterly*, vol. 17, no. 4 (1966), p. 359.

2. Davis, E. W., 'Resource Allocation in Project Network Models – A Survey', *Journal of Industrial Engineering*, vol. 17, no. 4 (April 1966), p. 177.
3. Davis, E. W. and Patterson, J. H., 'A Comparison of Heuristic and Optimal Solutions in Resource-Constrained Project Scheduling', *Management Science*, vol. 21, no. 8 (April 1975), p. 944.
4. Falkerson, D. R., 'A Network-Flow Computation for Project Cost Curve', *Management Science*, vol. 7, no. 2 (January 1961), p. 167.
5. Herroelen, W., 'Resource-Constrained Project Scheduling – The State of the Art', *Operations Research Quarterly*, vol. 23, no. 3 (1972), p. 261.
6. Jones, C. M., 'The Allocation of Limited Resources in Multi-Project Scheduling', Ph.D. thesis, Illinois Institute of Technology (1976).
7. Lambourn, S., 'Resource Allocation and Multiproject Scheduling (RAMPS) – A New Tool in Planning and Control', *The Computer Journal*, no. 5 (January 1963), p. 300.
8. Mize, J. H., 'A Heuristic Scheduling Model for Multi-Project Organizations', Ph.D. thesis, Purdue University (1964).
9. Pascoe, T. L., 'Heuristic Methods for Allocating Resources', Ph.D. thesis, University of Cambridge (1965).
10. Petrovic, R., 'Optimization of Resources Allocation in Project Planning', *Operations Research*, vol. 16, no. 3 (1968), p. 559.
11. Pritsker, A. B., Wallers, L., and Wolfe, P. M., 'Multi-project Scheduling with Limited Resources: A Zero-One Programming Approach', *Management Science*, vol. 16, no. 1 (September 1969), p. 93.
12. Schrage, L., 'Solving Resource-Constrained Network Problems by Implicit Enumeration – Preemptive Case', *Operations Research*, vol. 20, no. 3 (1972), p. 668.
13. Wiest, J. D., 'A Heuristic Model for Scheduling Large Projects with Limited Resources', *Management Science*, vol. 13, no. 6 (1967), p. 359.

Part C. Service

Section 7. Communication and transportation

25. Shift scheduling for telephone operators and service office employees

MICHAEL J. COSGROVE

Abstract

Telephone operator offices present a challenging scheduling problem because of the severe variation in demand for service, the stringent standards of service, and the round-the-clock operation.

Scheduling telephone service office employees is similar but complicated by the mixture of activities. Service offices answer incoming calls, process service and repair orders, and collect accounts. This paper describes an integrated operator scheduling system which has been implemented in several hundred GTE operator offices. The system forecasts demand, schedules shifts by a heuristic algorithm, and assigns individual operators to shifts.

Also described is a newly developed service office scheduling system. It measures actual demand and service level, forecasts demand, and heuristically draws shifts to meet demands in multiple activities, with the capability of shared tours.

25.1. Scheduling telephone operators and service office employees

25.1.1. Introduction

Telephone operator offices can be considered a service industry where the service offered is on-demand assistance by a telephone operator (directory assistance, coin-telephone toll calls; or toll call assistance). The demand for service is highly variable, the standards for service are stringently regulated, and the operation continues twenty-four hours a day. The scheduling problem emerging from this situation is to schedule operators to work shifts such that the demand is served uniformly at the response standard at all hours, with practical work shifts, satisfying legal, contractual, and human consideration.

Schedules must be created in advance; this leads to the further problem of forecasting the demand. Thus, the operator scheduling problem requires a forecast of demand, shift schedules to meet the demand, and assignment of individual operators to shifts. An integrated, computerized system to perform these tasks was developed and applied in GTE. It is described in [1] and will be briefly outlined here.

25.1.2. *Variability of demand*

The demand for service arrives in the form of telephone calls to operators. Generally, the standard of service is specified by public utility commissions in very specific form. Enough operators must be provided to answer calls within ten seconds, 90 percent of the time (85 percent for DA). Meeting this standard economically in

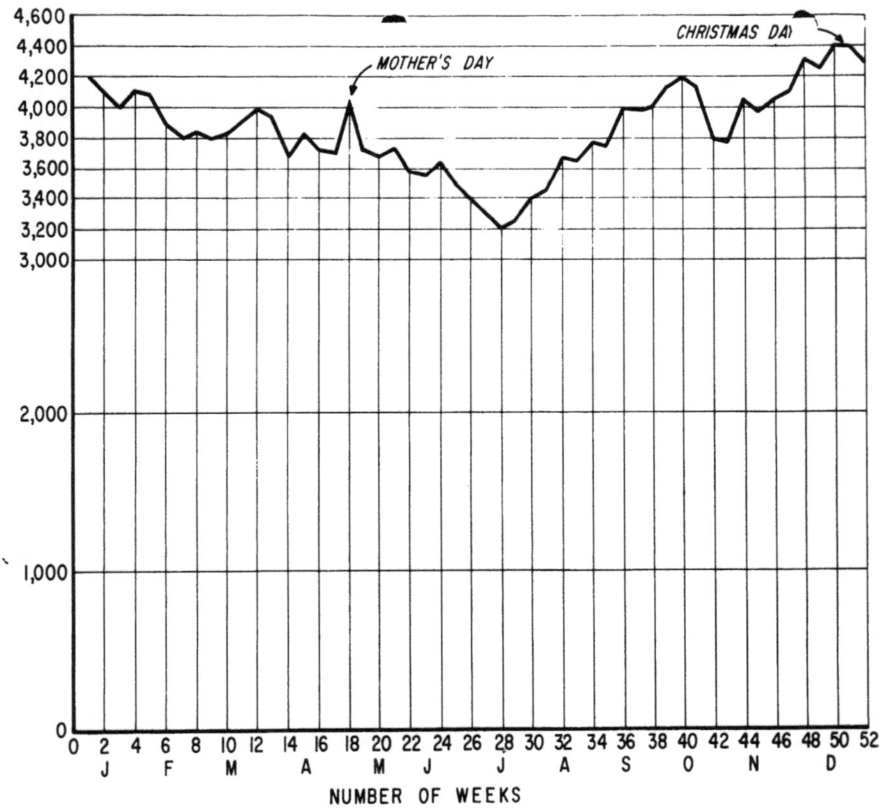

Figure 1. Number of calls originated during busiest hour each week.

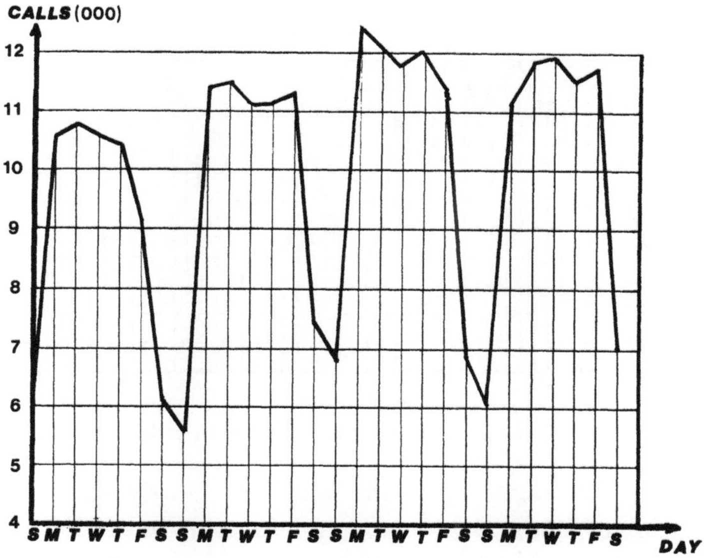

Figure 2. Daily toll call volume Long Beach toll 1/72.

the face of the extreme variation in call volume is the crux of the scheduling problem. The variations in call volume are illustrated in Figure 1 (annual), Figure 2 (daily), Figure 3 (half-hourly), and Figure 4 (by minute).

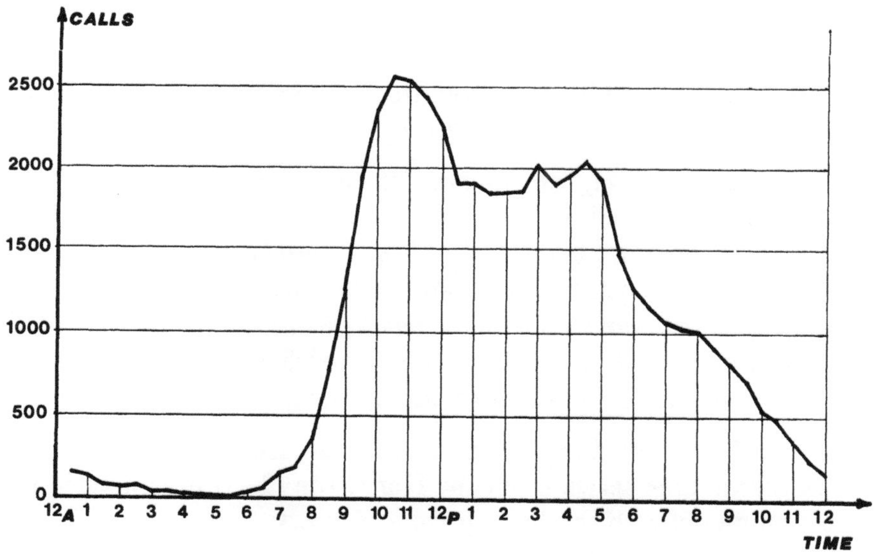

Figure 3. Half hourly call volume Bundy DA.

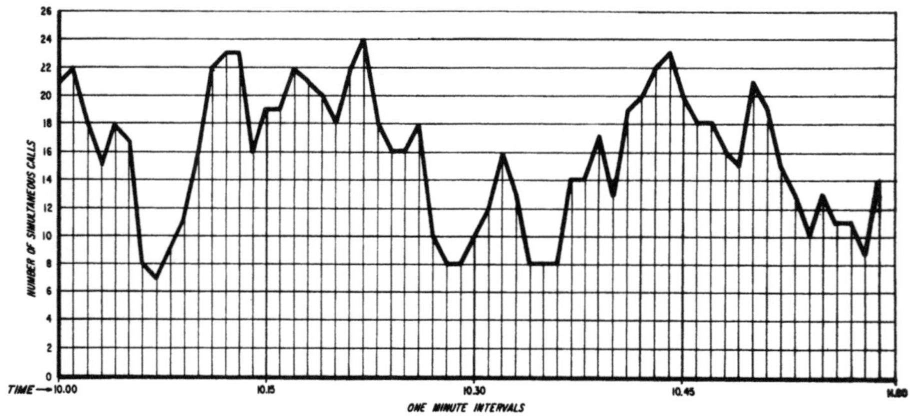

Figure 4. Intra-hour distribution of calls.

Typically, the seasonal, daily and half-hourly calls volumes, while variable, follow stable enough patterns to be predictable, and hence are forecasted and utilized in the scheduling process. In some larger operations, the basic forecasting/scheduling interval is 15 minutes. Call volume variation within the half-hour (or quarter hour) are found to be random (Poisson), hence not forecastable. Besides, it becomes impractical to try to schedule operators for any shorter intervals than quarter-hours.

25.1.3. Forecasting

Scheduling is a weekly operation. Its first component, the demand forecast, is produced in three steps:

1. Forecast *total daily call volume* for each day of the scheduling week, as described later.
2. Calculate required *total day board (productive) hours* using average call duration and productivity objectives.
3. Calculate *half-hourly operator requirements* by spreading total day hours by the exponentially smoothed percentages that each half-hour is of actual required hours.

25.1.3.1. Daily call forecasting: Daily calls are forecast useing a Box-Jenkins time series model by Harveston [2]. It is a univariate-seasonal model with the basic form as follows:

Calls next Monday = Calls last Monday

+ Weekly change last year
− Error last week × θ
− error 52 weeks ago × ϕ
+ Error 53 weeks ago × $\phi\theta$

where θ is a non-seasonal moving average parameter, and ϕ is a seasonal moving average parameter.

The same form of the model is used, but each location and each day of the week has its own parameter.

Figure 5 shows a sample of forecast versus actual calls. The average absolute percent error is 3.5 percent. The models are updated each week, and parameters re-estimated quarterly.

25.1.3.2 Calculation of half-hourly operator requirements: The daily call forecasts are then converted to half-hourly operator requirements using the model in Figure 6, with parameters:

- Average call duration
- Objective productivity

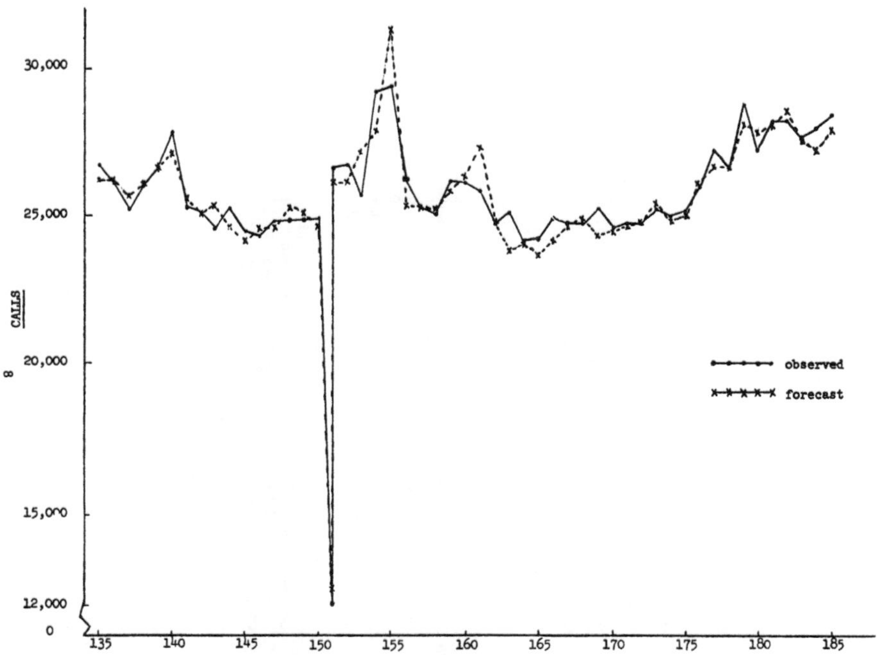

Figure 5. Forecast vs. observed Santa Monica DA: Thursday.

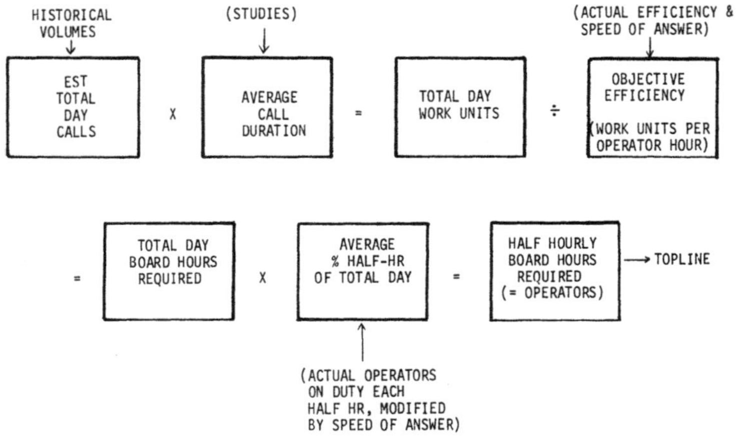

Figure 6. Calls to operators.

– Response standard
– Actual percentage half-hourly requirements.

The result of this conversion is a half-hourly profile of operator requirements, shown graphically in Figure 7.

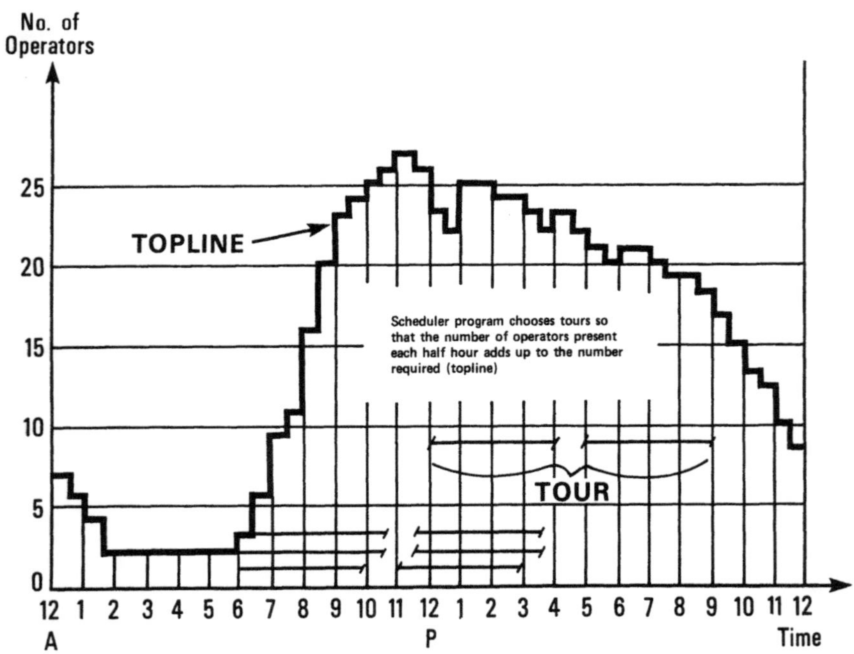

Figure 7. Topline profile and tour drawing.

25.1.3.3. Shift scheduling: Given the profile of requirements, the next stage is to choose a set of shifts so that the number of operators scheduled each half-hour add up as close as possible to the requirements. Shifts are chosen from a set of allowable shifts. The allowable shift set specifies the start, stop and lunch times of the shifts. Allowable shifts are determined by law, union contracts, company policy, and local management's judgment on desirability and practicality.

Shifts vary in length as well as in start-times and length of lunch. Shifts are grouped into types, such as:

1. Part time: 3 to 5 hours
2. Short: 6–7.5 hours
3. Regular: 8 hours
4. Splits: 7–8 hour tours with 3 to 4 hour non-work sessions in the middle.

This variety helps meet the variable requirements.

In building a schedule, shifts are chosen from the allowable shift schedule using a heuristic algorithm developed by Luce [3]. It is a building algorithm. The objective function is:

$$F = \sum |D_i - W_i| \tag{1}$$

where D = demand in period i.
W = number of workers provided in period i by the combinations of shifts chosen so far.

Let s be a shift in the allowable shift set S. In choosing a shift to include in the schedule, the objective function is calculated *for each shift* in the allowable shift set. The shift which *minimizes F* is chosen. This results in choosing the shift which minimizes the remaining area between the D and W step functions. This concept is illustrated in Figure 8. The criterion, minimize F, is applied in choosing each shift. This approach tends to favor the longer shifts since the longer a shift, the more intervals it contributes to. If this is not corrected for, distorted schedules can occur. For example, shifts ending after 9 p.m. must by contract be 7 hours long. These short shifts would tend to be avoided by the algorithm. The result would be schedules with very good fit during the middle part of the day, at the expense of poor fit in the evening.

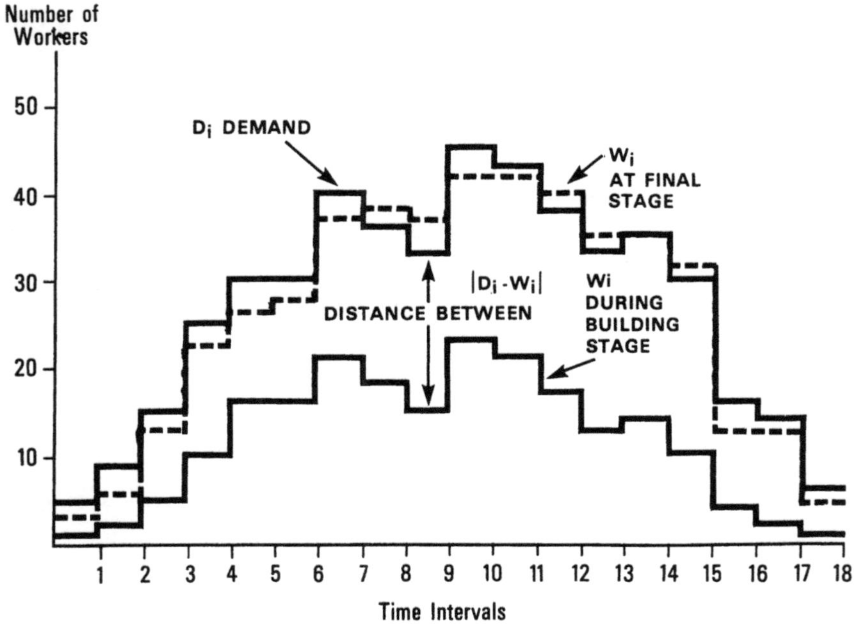

Figure 8. The schedule building process.

To correct this bias, shifts are weighted by the ratio of the length of the longest shift to their length. If the longest shift is 8 hours, then a 6.5 hour shift would be weighted by $8/6.5 = 1.23$.

Once the criterion F cannot be reduced by adding any shift, the process terminates. Relief periods are inserted in each session after the tour is picked. Reliefs are placed in the interval i inside that shift's 'relief window' which has minimum $|D_i - W_i|$.

The final result is a schedule of shifts which provide a sub-optimal fit to the predicted requirements.

Note that the concept of choosing from a predefined allowable shift set provides wide flexibility in applications, as well as making the computer program very resilient to changes in union contracts, legal requirements, etc.

25.1.4. Assignment of operators to shifts

After the shift schedules are developed for 7 days, operators must be assigned days off and work days as well as particular shifts.

This is a two stage process:

1. Day-off assignment
2. Shift assignment

Day-off assignment is done by an algorithm by Luce [4] which, given the number of operators available to work each day, and the number of shifts scheduled each day, assigns days off such that:

- All shifts are worked.
- Each operator gets at least one day off.
- Each operator gets at least 5 work days.
- Weekend days off are controlled by rotation.
- Consecutive days off (within a 7 day schedule) are maximized.
- If consecutive days off cannot be assigned, the days off are spread as far apart as possible.
- Overtime and extra days off are controlled by several methods.

Once days off are all assigned, there are the same number of operators working each day as there are shifts scheduled. The only remaining task is to assign a specific shift to an individual operator.

Shift assignment is controlled by seniority and preference. The most senior operator working that day gets his/her first preference of the shifts scheduled that day. To implement this, each operator makes up a list of shifts in preference order. The assignment algorithm proceeds down the list of working operators in decreasing seniority order, assigning each operator his/her highest preference of the remaining scheduled shifts.

25.2. Service office employee scheduling

25.2.1. Introduction

In GTE the service offices perform the following major functions:

1. Receive customer calls for:
   - New, changed, or terminated service.
   - Billing questions
   - Trouble reports (Repair)
2. Process the resulting transactions:
   - Service orders

- Billing adjustments
- Repair orders.

3. Account collections.
4. Dispatch and control the installation and repair force.

The scheduling problem in service offices is complicated by these multiple activities. In addition, the need for service representatives to have physical access to customer records, has dictated that teams of customer representatives be limited to 7. Thus, in larger offices, customer accounts are divided into two or more groups, each group assigned to a team of service representatives. Figure 9 shows the typical service office organization.

A simplifying condition is that service offices generally are open during normal business hours.

25.2.2. Demand for service

As in the case of operators, demand for service arrives in the form of customer calls. These calls vary strongly in volume by day of week (Figure 10) and by half-hour (Figure 11). As in the case of operator calls, there is a specific response standard: 90 percent of calls to service offices are to be answered within 20 seconds.

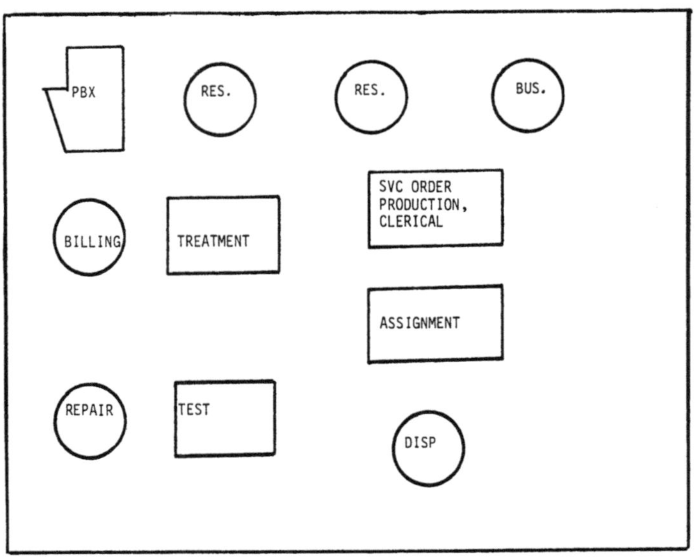

Figure 9. Typical GTE service office functional organization.

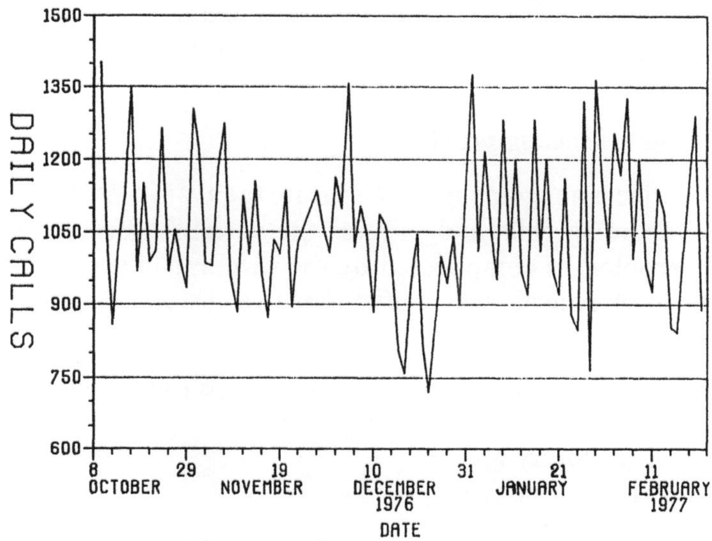

Figure 10. Daily call volume (Fort Wayne service office).

In addition, every billing cycle (three days) service offices receive copies of customer bills and delinquent account notices. Every three days, a different portion of the customers served by an office receive their bills. These 'bill days' generate an increase in billing inquiry calls. Likewise, bill days generate a new batch of filing and collec-

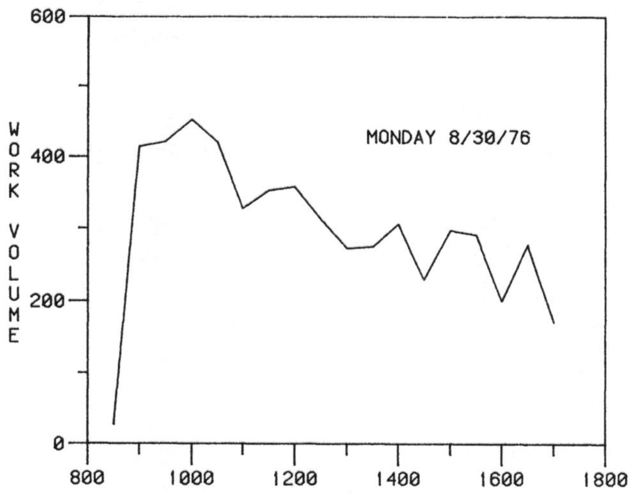

Figure 11. Half hourly work volume (Fort Wayne service office contact group).

tion work. The day after weekends or holidays usually brings a surge of incoming calls, from accumulated need.

25.2.3. The scheduling problem

Service office management must allocate the available work force to answer incoming calls and process the various transactions. The staffing problem is complicated by the various subgroups calls are directed to. A typical service office has five customer contact work groups:

- Two residential account service rep. groups (5 to 7 each).
- One business account service rep. group.
- One billing inquiry group.
- One repair contact group.

Managers need an effective procedure to allocate staff to each group and, within each group, to allocate staff time between the two competing tasks of answering calls and processing transactions. Each group is subject to the call response standard, as well as to objectives on processing service orders, repair orders, account collections, etc.

The need for effectively scheduling these employees is growing more important as the cost of labor increases. Service office labor expenses have been growing at a compounded rate of 12.2 percent per year while telephones in service have grown by only 5.3 percent annually as shown in Figure 12.

Customers and public utility commissions are increasingly expecting reasonably prompt answers to their calls to the service office.

Paper transactions and records are being replaced by data terminals and on-line data bases. These expensive resources must be efficiently utilized to be cost-effective.

These three factors led to the development of a system to improve the utilization of service office employees by improved scheduling.

25.2.4. The system

The system analysis of the service office scheduling problem identified the need for three components.

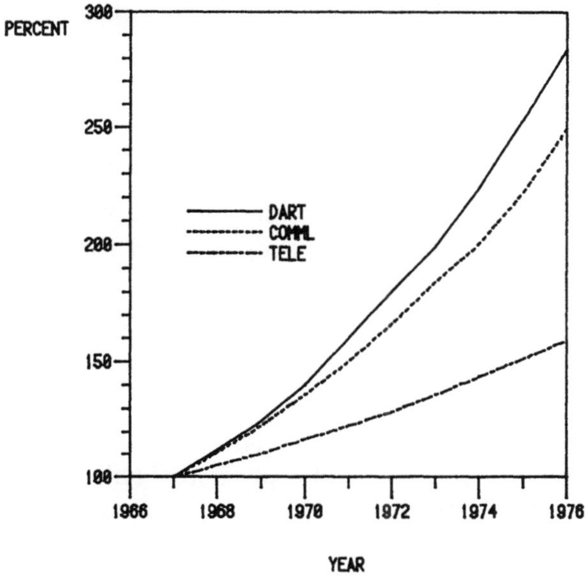

Figure 12. GTE telephone operations (service expense growth).

1. *Measurement* of call volumes, service levels, and workloads.
2. *Forecasting* of call workloads by group by half-hour, and transaction workloads by group by day.
3. *Scheduling* employee work shifts to meet the contact workload as well as the transaction work.

25.2.4.1. Measurement subsystem: The measurement system is comprised of standard electronic teletraffic measuring devices. Only the data measured is described here. The measurements include half-hourly counts, by work group, of:

- Incoming call volume
- Average call duration
- Average delay before answer
- Average time customers are placed on-hold
- Average number of positions available [open to or working on incoming calls].

These measurements are recorded automatically and, by use of a centralized polling minicomputer, are printed out within the next half-hour, at the service office.

This data is used by supervisors to evaluate actual workload and service levels and make necessary staffing adjustments within the day. It is input weekly into the forecasting system.

Daily transaction volumes are derived from various manual and automated sources.

25.2.4.2. The forecaster: The purpose of the Service Office Forecaster (SOFCAST) is to predict half-hourly staffing requirements for each contact work group, at lead times of one to five weeks.

The forecasted staffing requirements are determined by a three stage process:

- Forecast total day work volume.
- Distribute total day forecast to half-hours.
- Calculate staff size to handle predicted half-hourly work vol-
- ume at the desired service level using an Erlang-C (M/M/C) queuing model.

The daily forecasting model:

A review of the pertinent literature by Elton and Gruber [5], Berry, Maybert and Marcus [6], Hill and Maybert [7], Church [8], as well as experience with the effort and data needed to obtain and maintain a Box-Jenkins model, led to the trial of a model combining exponential smoothing with trend, and causal factors. Box-Jenkins models for each work group would have required storage of a large volume of data. Also, few if any service offices possessed the amount of historical data needed to identify a Box-Jenkins model for each group.

Two separate models are maintained for each day of the week: Non-Bill-Day and Bill Day models. The 3 day bill cycle causes bill days to hit on different days each week.

Other causal factors are introduced by use of Special Day Codes, based on judgment, due to the wide variety of local special conditions. Examples of special days are:

- Days after holidays
- Storm days
- Directory issue days

Output: A sample of SOFCAST output is shown in Figure 13.

UNIT: 01 CONTACT

OBJECTIVE AVERAGE SPEED OF ANSWER: 7 SECONDS
OBJECTIVE TOTAL DISPOSITION TIME: 205 SECONDS
ACTUAL AVERAGE DAILY HOLDING TIME: 157 SECONDS

TIME BEGIN	TIME END	WORK VOLUME	STAFF REQUIRED
730	800	69	7
800	830	146	12
830	900	177	14
900	930	189	15
930	1000	183	15
1000	1030	169	14
1030	1100	146	12
1100	1130	136	12
1130	1200	144	12
1200	1230	124	11
1230	100	149	12
100	130	150	13
130	200	159	13
200	230	145	12
230	300	150	13
300	330	138	12
330	400	134	11
400	415	57	10
DAY'S TOTAL:		2565	220 (107.50 HOURS)

Figure 13. Forecasted staffing requirements for: Wed 4/13/77.

Results: The initial trial of the forecasting model did not include trend or special day codes. Considering only day of week and bill days, it achieved a mean absolute error of 6 percent during the trial period. This accuracy has deteriorated somewhat since. The trend terms and special day codes are being developed for the next implementation.

25.2.4.3. Shift scheduling for multiple activities: The output of the forecaster is the half-hourly staffing requirements for the calling activity of each work group. These are input to the service office schedule (SOFSKED). Daily staffing requirements for the transaction (non-contact) workload are also required inputs. These are initially to be provided by management until an adequate model is developed.

The scheduler, which is still under development, has the purpose of drawing employee work schedules for each contact work group. It has the following features:

– Selects from a user-specified set of allowable shifts (tours).

- Attempts to optimize the fit between staff scheduled and forecasted requirements.
- Uses heuristic algorithms guided by an objective function which expresses an aversion for deficits and surpluses, a desire to meet constraints, and a preference toward assignments that tend to balance the deficits and surpluses among the units.
- The capability is provided to force certain tours to be assigned.
- Staff requirements may be specified either half-hourly, or as a daily total. However, for any work group, only one type of requirements may be entered for any given day.
- Off-line (non-contact) requirements may be specified, and staff scheduled accordingly. Two types of off-line time are considered. Type 1 off-line is for a special assignment which requires a certain number of people for a specified time interval. Type 2 off-line provides for periodic 'catch-up' work to be assigned within a specified window in each tour session.
- An initial assignment is developed by work group in a manner similar to that used in the shift scheduling algorithm for operator schedules discussed above.
- SOFSKED may be requested to consider a pre-defined set of shared tours (in which an employee from one unit is loaned for some length of time to another unit) in an effort to improve the performance of the service office as a whole. One shared session is allowed per tour. Provisions are made for the user to limit, by tour type and in total, the number of staff which each unit may loan on any day.
- Fifteen minute breaks are scheduled within the user-input break window in each tour session in such a manner as to least detract from the ability to meet the staffing requirements. However, the user may indicate that certain tour types are not to receive breaks.
- Regardless of requirements, only as many tours are drawn as there are employees available.

The scheduling algorithm [*9*]:

The Scheduler program operates on a daily basis to produce manpower schedules for each unit in the service office. The program operates as follows for each day to be scheduled:

1. The schedule date, daily unit parameters, and staff availability by unit and tour type are read.
2. Forced tours for the day are read, assigned, and the staff available by tour type and staff assigned by period are updated for the effected units.
3. Unit requirements are read. For units with a half-hourly requirement, the staff required by half-hour is converted into a quarter-hourly distribution.
4. Requirements and minimum staffing level are temporarily increased to adjust for the expected effect of break and off-line assignments.
5. The remaining staff for each unit is assigned tours in a manner which attempts to meet the specified requirements in an optimal fashion using the shift scheduling algorithm by Luce [3].
6. If the Shared Tour module is to be executed, the maximum shared staff availabilities are read, and the possibility of improving the assignment via tour sharing is examined.
7. The adjusted requirements are replaced by the original requirements.
8. An attempt is made to insure FIFO scheduling for lunches within each unit.
9. Type 1 off-line assignments are made.
10. FIFO breaks are assigned to each tour session for 5 which breaks are required.
11. Type 2 off-line time as required is assigned within the specified windows of each tour session.
12. All scheduler output reports are written to disk files.

The scheduling algorithms employed by SOFSKED are entirely heuristic. They will be tested in June–August, 1977 and the results reported thereafter.

25.3. Summary

The service office scheduling system is being developed to improve employee utilization, and customer service. It is designed for offices with multiple work groups each with contact and transaction workloads. It embodies the concept of flexible staffing to meet varying workloads. Varying staff levels are obtained with a constant employment level by timing the shift-start, reliefs, and lunch times; by use of part-time tours; and by shared tours among work groups.

References

1. Buffa, E. S., Cosgrove, M. J., and Luce, B. J., Jr., 'An Integrated Work Shift Scheduling System', *Decision Sciences*, vol. 7 (October 1976).
2. Harveston, M. F., Luce, B. J., and Smuczynski, T. A., 'Telephone Operator Management Systems – TOMS', ORSA/TIMS/AHE Joint National Meeting (November 1972).
3. Luce, B. J., Jr., 'A Shift Scheduling Algorithm', 44th National Meeting of the Operations Research Society of America, San Diego, Ca. (November 12–14, 1973).
4. Luce, B. J., Jr., 'Employee Assignment Systems', ORSA/TIMS Joint National Meeting (April 1974).
5. Elton, E. J. and Gruber, M. J., 'Earnings Estimates and the Accuracy of Expectational Data', *Management Sciences*, vol. 18, no. 8 (April 1972).
6. Berry, W. L., Mabert, V. A., and Marcus, M., 'Forecasting Teller Window Demand With Exponential Smoothing', Paper no. 536, Institute for Research in the Behavioral, Economic, and Management Sciences, Purdue University (November 1975).
7. Hill, A. V. and Mabert, V. A., 'A Combined Projection-Causal Approach for Short Range Forecasts', Paper no. 527, Purdue University, Krannert Graduate School of Industrial Administration, Institute for Research in the Behavioral, Economic, and Mangement Sciences (September 1975).
8. Church, J. G., 'Sure Staf: A Computerized Staff Scheduling System for Telephone Business Offices', *Management Sciences*, vol. 20, Part 2 (December 1973), pp. 708–720.
9. Cosgrove, M. J., Eckles, J. E., and Richards, J. E., 'Service Office Scheduler Specification and System Descriptions', unpublished documentation of General Telephone and Electronics Corporation (October 1976).

26. A complete control system for workforce management at a post office[1]

NORMAN W. CHLOSTA and ROBERT D'ALESSIO

Abstract

In the processing of mail, a post office functions as a hybrid of the service and manufacturing industry. From an input-output standpoint, mail is received in a given post office, processed (re-packaged), and dispatched as an output either to the consumer or to another post office for additional processing. In general, a postal facility handles two types of mail, priority and non-priority, with a commensurate rate structure for the consumer of each type. The priority mail must be expedited through the facility in a timely fashion, allowing for only temporary (hourly) inventory build-ups and back-logs. For the non-priority mail, decisions have to be made on the level and time-length in days of allowable inventory in order to smoothly integrate this mail into the production stream.

At post offices of any appreciable size the order of magnitude for the production workforce is in thousands, while the daily mail volume is in millions of pieces. The three aspects of the disaggregate decision-making process in a post office: general workforce level, tour workforce assignments, and tour scheduling are intimately interrelated due to a variety of factors. The most important of which are: (1) the hybrid nature of the production, (2) negotiated labor-management agreements which include a no-layoff clause, (3) the current state of implemented management information systems at local post offices, and (4) the human factors involved in local management acceptance of analytical solutions to their problems.

This paper reviews the current state of the art in disaggregation theory as it is being applied to postal problems. The major components of the system which are addressed are: the ability to establish the expected workload (mail volume forecast) for different planning horizons, and second, the optimization modeling of the workforce (level and placement) with respect to the forecasted demand.

1. The views expressed are those of the authors and should not be interpreted as necessarily reflecting those of the U.S. Postal Service.

26.1. Description of postal production

26.1.1. Introduction

The production system in a given post office is one which is essentially continuous in nature where the product is mail to be processed through the facility. In the larger-sized post offices, the product (mail) is measured in millions of pieces per day, while the resource (workforce) available to process the product is of the order of magnitude of thousands per day. The processing of mail, as shown in Figure 1, involves a network of interconnecting nodes, where the flow is generally in one direction (toward dispatch), with a limited amount of back flow allowed (not shown in the diagram). Mail arrives at a post office, where it is inventoried into N processing operations, subsequently sorted into various stages, and then dispatched either to a delivery unit or another post office for additional processing. Note that mail enters the inventory of a given operation via two possible paths: (1) directly after arrival in the post office, or (2) upon completion of prior handling at another operation within that post office. In addition, transit mail, which generally receives perfunctory handling as it is destined for another post office, is not considered here, although a small portion of the workforce must be committed to this function.

26.1.2. Planning decisions in a post office

Over a finite planning horizon, there are four primary decision areas with which local post office management is concerned. These areas are: (1) the quantity, and the associated time, of mail arriving for processing, (2) the workforce size, (3) the workforce schedule, i.e. tour and days-off assignments, and (4) tour starting times within a workday. Figure 2 shows the relationship of the decision areas to the production planning components in a post office. Items A through D enclosed in the dashed lines in Figure 2, spatially represent policy planning, where aggregate decisions are made, translated to disaggregated operational plans, and then applied to the actual production facility (item E) itself. Management's basic objective is to match the workforce (item B) with the workload (item C) under the constraints of union agreements, cost minimization, and achievement of delivery service standards.

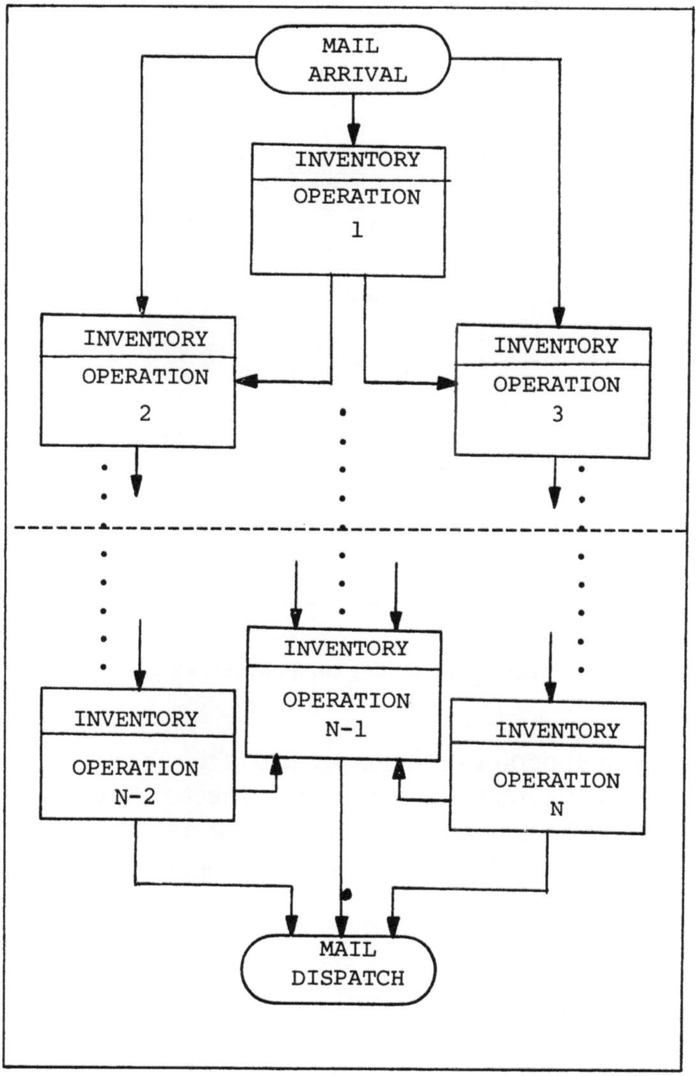

Figure 1. General schematic of mail processing in a post office.

Quantitative optimization methods, heuristics, and simulation models have been developed in [1], [3], [5], [6], [7], and [8] for the workforce, item B in Figure 2. All these methods, however, have implicitly assumed that an estimate of the quantity and arrival time of the mail to be processed is either known or obtainable, no matter

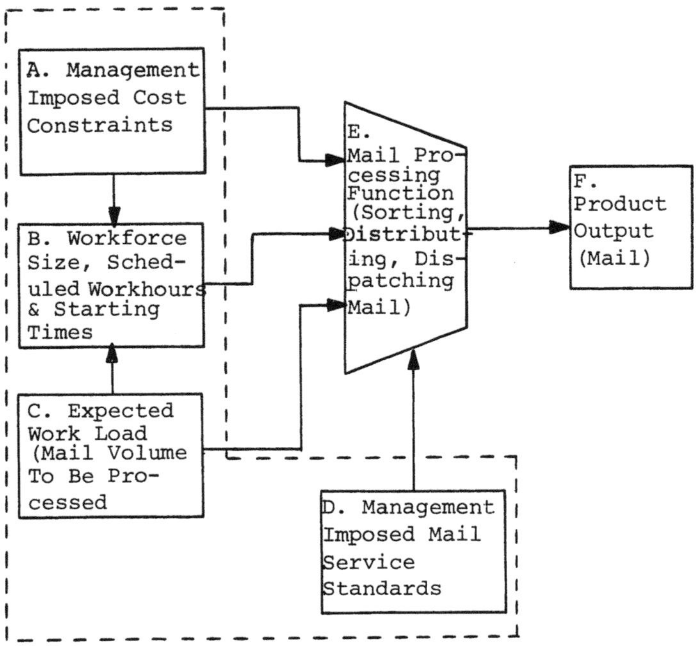

Figure 2. Production planning components in a post office.

whether the methodology is being applied to the aggregate planning situation or the disaggregate operational aspect of the problem. This information on the expected workload is important to the *implementation* of any proposed method of sizing, assigning, and scheduling the workforce.

26.2. Control system at a post office

26.2.1. Basic control system

Before describing the components, it is appropriate to establish boundaries for the control system. The proposed system is still concerned with two major planning components (Figure 2): the workforce, with its size, schedule, and starting time parameters, and the workload, i.e. mail volume with its quantity and time-of-arrival parameters. Further, it is assumed that the aggregate planning of general workforce size can be accomplished using already developed methodologies, such as the simulation briefly described in [1].

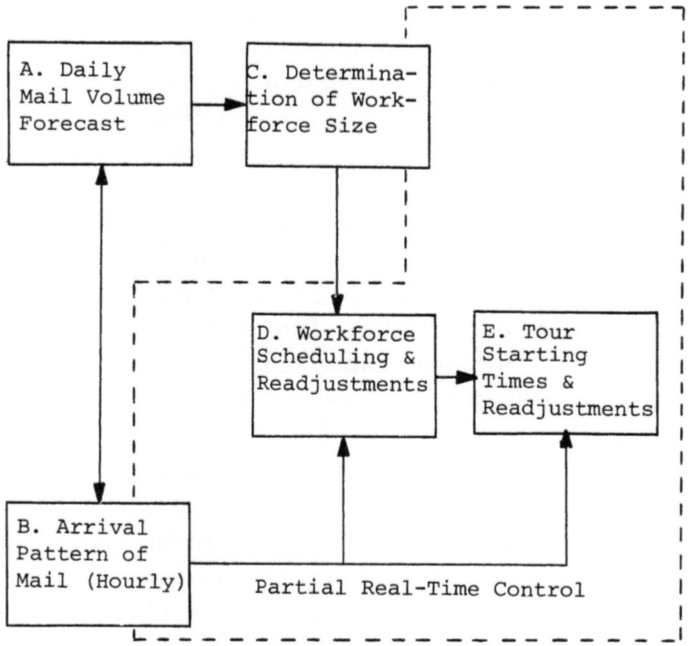

Figure 3. Control system components.

The basic components of the proposed control system are depicted in Figure 3. The dashed lines here indicate that some of the components have to be constructed as a hybrid of (a) planning decisions before operational implementation and (b) adjustments made on a real-time or near real-time basis. It is emphasized that the components are part of an integrated system in the sense that they are all interrelated, and successful implementation and local management acceptance dictate a complete development.

26.2.2. Volume forecast and arrival pattern of mail

For management planning, it is desirable to be able to forecast the time-dependent inventory levels (shown in Figure 1) on a daily, or fractional part of the day (hourly) basis. Knowledge of the expected inventory at this level of detail would provide flexibility and efficiency in scheduling the size of the workforce to match the workload. However, the mail which arrives for processing is not strictly a homogeneous product, containing letters, flats, parcels, etc. Even within the same type of mail, there are multiple flow paths available through the facility. The flow path which the mail takes is functionally dependent on a number of attributes. The most important of these are: (1) the amount of pre-sorting of the mail by customers or other post offices prior to its arrival at the stated post office, (2) local management subjectively, but not necessarily in an optimal way, selecting certain flow paths, and (3) policy changes such as a policy that would dictate that mail for sub-offices was to be processed by a main office in lieu of the sub. These attributes have a combinatorial impact on the inventory levels, which makes the development of a forecasting model conceptually feasible but with a minimal chance of empirical validation. As an alternative, the forecast aggregated one level to mail arrival at the post office on a daily basis is workable, and has a historical data base available in the Management Operating Data System (MODS) [4] for class 1 (large) post offices. MODS is a comprehensive management information system for the operational areas of a given post office. It is also possible to develop historical records for the arrival pattern of mail, so a model can be developed and evaluated in this area.

26.2.3. Workforce parameters

The workforce parameters of size, schedule, and start-time, items C, D, and E, respectively, in Figure 3, have been described in previous sections. The major task is to have them reside in some form of real-time system for control of them, where possible. They would then supply key information to the mail processing function for decision-making. In order to achieve respectability at the operating level in a given post office, the design of the workforce-control components has to have the following characteristics:

1. A data base which is responsive to the level of detail required to make, and readjust, operational decisions in the production system. This includes such things as: (a) advance knowledge of mail volume variations from major mailings, (b) a file of personnel by skill and/or training (scheme knowledge), (c) make-up of incoming mail to narrow its potential flow paths in the processing system, (d) historical productivity levels at each operation, and (e) historical flow percentages for mail from operation to

operation. The MOD System, with suitable modifications, has the capability to provide this kind of data base.
2. Acceptance of exception inputs from local management.
3. Monitor and report on actual volume and work-hour activity as it occurs.
4. Provide, as close as possible, a real-time feedback system to identify exception areas for corrective action by management. As indicated by King [2, pp. 10–11], the lowest levels of management in the hierarchical structure should receive highly detailed performance information, with the higher levels receiving summarized details of performance results achieved by their subordinate managers.

26.3. Summary and conclusions

The components of a complete control system for the management of production (mail processing) in a post office have been presented. The basic objective in the proposed design is to propose an integrated system which is both usable by local management, and provides an intrinsic analytical capability for decision-making at the planning stage and the operational implementation stage. With suitable modifications, the methods being developed and reported in the literature could be enhanced for use as components in the proposed control system. Currently, field experimentation is under way with two systems which incorporate major features of the one described in this paper. One has been installed at the San Diego, Ca., Post Office, and it essentially obtains data from the MODS information flow path between the data input terminal to the teleconcentrator site, and feeds this information into application programs which prepare performance reports which management can use to make adjustments in the production system. A second development is a Performance Feedback System currently being tested in the Rochester, N.Y., Post Office which also employs data from the MOD System to develop performance reports for the local management. It is expected that there will be increased utilization and development of such reporting systems, for their principal advantage for postal managers is the ability to have the feedback at the time when adjustments in prior production decisions can be accomplished.

References

1. Fox, Stewart B., 'The Mail Processing Simulation as a Teaching Aid', *Proceedings of the Fourth Annual Meeting of the American Institute for Decision Sciences* (November 1972).
2. King, J. R., *Production Planning and Control* (Oxford, England: Pergamon Press, Ltd., 1975).
3. Krajewski, Lee J., Henderson, John, and Showalter, Michael J., 'Selecting Optimal Empployee Complements in a Post Office: A Resolution of Multiple Objectives', Paper Presented at the Joint National Meeting of The Operations Research Society of America (ORSA)/The Institute of Management Sciences (TIMS) (November 1976).
4. 'Management Operating Data System', *Methods Handbooks M-32 and M-33*, U.S. Postal Service (Directives Control Division), Washington, D.C. (September 1975).
5. Ritzman, Larry P. and Krajewski, Lee J., 'Multiple Objectives in Linear Programming – An Example in Scheduling Postal Resources', *Decision Sciences*, vol. 4, no. 3 (July 1973), pp. 364–378.
6. Ritzman, Larry P., Krajewski, Lee J., and Showalter, Michael J., 'The Disaggregation of Aggregate Manpower Plans', *Management Science,* vol. 22, no. 11 (July 1976), pp. 1204–1214.
7. Showalter, Michael J., Krajewski, Lee J., and Ritzman, Larry P., 'A Methodology for Manpower Tour Assignment in Postal Sectional Center Facilities', Paper Presented at the Joint National Meeting of ORSA/TIMS (March–April 1976).
8. Stralberg, H. and Cappelli, A. P., 'Optimal Manpower Staffing in Mail Processing Facilities', Paper Presented at the Joint National Meeting of ORSA/TIMS (November 1976).

27. Decision making in the public sector: an application of goal interval programming for disaggregation in the post office

LEE J. KRAJEWSKI and JOHN HENDERSON

Abstract

Decision making in the public sector involves decision making with multiple objectives. The primary objectives are to minimize costs and maximize service. This paper presents a goal interval programming model for analyzing the selection of employee complement sizes in a large post office. Specification of the service goals requires the disaggregation of employee complements to tour assignments. The tradeoffs in complement size and service turn out to be nonlinear necessitating the interval goal approach. The model is used to analyze fixed versus variable complement size policies.

27.1. Introduction

27.1.1. Decision making in the public sector

Perhaps no other era in the history of this nation has put so much pressure on efficient and effective decision making in the public sector. For example, energy shortages and inflationary trends have created an environment where anything less than a sound, rational approach to decision making invites disaster. Unfortunately, most of the research into efficient decision making practices and aides has focused on the private sector which is not altogether the same thing as the public sector. In the first place, the set of alternatives to solve a problem may not be the same even if the problem itself is very similar. For example, one alternative for a manufacturing organization wishing to keep its facilities fully utilized while maintaining adequate customer service is to stockpile its finished goods during a 'slow period' in anticipation of increased requirements during the peak demand periods. However, an organization created for public service cannot stockpile its major product, service, in anticipation of future requirements. By virtue of the major outputs alone, the considerations to make in public sector decision making are unique.

Secondly, the public sector underscores the need to recognize multiple objectives. Perhaps the two most important ones, from the standpoint of efficiency and effectiveness, are minimizing costs and maximizing service. When operating at reasonably efficient levels, these objectives are conflicting and tradeoffs between them must be considered. Unfortunately, many decision makers in the public sector do not know how to estimate these tradeoffs. Information regarding these tradeoffs is an important input to the overall decision process. In this respect, optimizing models fall short of supplying all the relevant information because they only yield one of many feasible solutions, most often recognizing only one objective. Model building should strive to provide information to the decision maker in a format which is useful for the decision making process which necessarily must account for numerous considerations, many of which are not quantifiable. The purpose of this paper is to demonstrate how a goal interval programming model can be used to provide relevant information for determining the employee complement sizes (staff sizes) of a large post office.

27.1.2. Aggregate manpower planning in the post office

The specific problem we shall address is the aggregate manpower planning of postal clerks in a sectional center post office. This amounts to selecting optimal *employee complements* over a horizon of one year. An employee complement is the number of employees of a particular type employed at a post office for sorting the mail. Given a seasonal pattern of mail volumes, the problem is to determine the complement sizes of the various types of employees such that cost and service goals are met. However, if service is measured by the time mail spends in the postal facility (the lower the time, the better the service), these goals cannot be met simultaneously. Within the capacity limitations of the processing system, the greater the employee complements, the better the service and the higher the employee related costs. Obviously, the selection of employee complements involves tradeoffs in costs and service which have budgetary implications. Information which is useful in this context should include more than one solution, each one showing the effects of a given budget allocation on service [2].

In addition to the size of the employee complement, the employment *policies* also have an impact on costs and service. The U.S. Postal System usually utilizes a policy of *fixed* employee complements over the planning horizon. Whenever the complement falls below this level, new hires are authorized to return to the specified level. Although this policy might be administratively simple, a *variable* complement policy conceivably could result in the same level of service at less cost. The presentation in Section 4 will demonstrate the use of the goal model to analyze the tradeoffs made in these employment policies.

The next section describes the shift scheduling (or tour assignment) problem which must be analyzed to arrive at the service goals. Section 3 presents the interval goal programming model and Section 4 demonstrates the use of the model for the policies mentioned above.

27.2. Tour Assignment

Within the capacity limitations at the work centers (sorting stations), the greater the number of postal clerks, the better the service. However, there are a variety of mail classes, each with its own routing and hourly arrival pattern. For any given employee complement size, the resultant service can only be measured by actually assigning each employee in the complement to a work center and a tour of duty. Thus, we must disaggregate the employee complement decisions over the horizon to measure the attainment of service goals. Conversely, we could use the analysis of the tour assignment problem for a reasonable range of alternative employee complement sizes to generate information which could be used to *develop* the service goals. In this section we first describe the (simplified) postal system that is used in this study. Next, a tour assignment model which disaggregates the employee complement decisions is presented. The use of the model to develop service goals will be discussed in Section 3 when we present the goal model.[1]

1. See [3] for a review of the literature on disaggregation problems in manufacturing and service organizations.

27.2.1. The postal processing system

Mail arrives at the processing facility and, if it is machine processable, arrives at the mechanized primary or the manual primary. Mail can be classified as either *originating* mail, which is collected from the immediate area served by the facility, or *incoming* mail, which arrives from other facilities. Some pre-sorted mail goes directly to the secondary sorting stations. At the secondary stations the mail is sorted according to destination (local or outgoing) and by priority (preferential or non-preferential). The mail finally leaves the system according to the dispatch schedule. These three stages of mail processing are depicted in Figure 1.

The processing system can be formally described as a multi-chan-

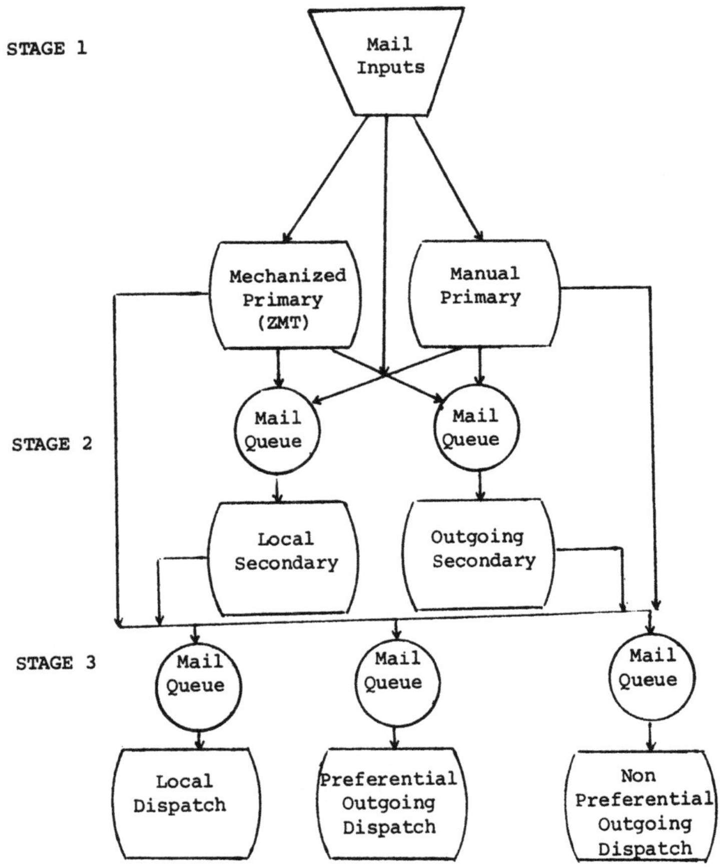

Figure 1. The postal processing system.

nel, multi-phase queuing system with non-stationary arrival rate distributions for each type of mail. The mean arrival rate of mail is time dependent, with significant hour-to-hour and day-to-day influences. Each classification of mail differs from the others in terms of its arrival pattern, priority and routing through the processing system. All of this makes for a difficult problem of assigning employees to the four work stations and to tours of duty such that service is maximized.

27.2.2. Tour assignment model

Because of the complexity of the problem, a heuristic model, TOURS, has been developed.[2] TOURS consists of heuristic assignment rules and a simulation component which computes the mail flows and inventory levels. It employs the construction method of heuristic programming whereby feasible manpower assignments are made iteratively using heuristic rules until the capacities set by the aggregate plan are exhausted.

The first function of TOURS is to make total manhour allocations to each of the four work centers shown in Figure 1. Given representative weekly data for mail arrivals, mail routings, and productivities, the total number of manhours required at each work center is calculated. Given these manhour requirements, the aggregate plan complements for career regulars, part-time employees and seasonal assistants are allocated to work centers in proportion to their relative need.[3]

The next step is to assign tours to the employees allocated to each work center. Each tour consists of eight hours a day, five consecutive days a week for career regulars and seasonal assistants; and four hours a day, five consecutive days a week for the part-time employees. Due to the uni-directional mail flows, assignments to tours can be made sequentially to the work centers. The first two work centers considered are the mechanized primary and the manual primary. Each day is divided into 12 two-hour time segments; thus there are 84 possible tour starting times for any

2. Because of space limitations, we cannot provide a detailed description of TOURS here. The interested reader is referred to [4] for a complete exposition.
3. The complement of seasonal assistants and part-time employees in any period are always assigned the manual primary work center.

employee. The assignments of employees are made iteratively to the tours which have the largest amount of mail yet to be processed. Of course, this is a function of the mail arrival patterns and the previous tour assignments.

Given the tour assignments at each primary work center, the mail flows into each secondary work center can be simulated for each day of the week. After doing this, TOURS initiates a series of assignment iterations for the secondary work centers.

After completing the assignments for the secondary operations, TOURS terminates with a deterministic simulation of the whole system over the entire week. Among other outputs, TOURS indicates the average work-in-process mail inventory at each work center per two-hour interval resulting from the tour assignment. It is the average work-in-process mail inventory that can be used as a surrogate for service. For a given mail arrival pattern and volume, the lower the work-in-process inventory, the greater the mail throughput per unit of time (service). In particular, the larger the work force complements, the lower will be the resultant work-in-process mail inventory. This relationship should continue until the capacities of the work centers are exceeded.

27.3. A goal interval programming model for aggregate manpower planning

This section describes the goal model that will be used to analyze cost and service tradeoffs for the hypothetical post office described in Section 4. We shall first present the 'technological' constraints followed by the 'goal' constraints and the objective function.

27.3.1. Technological constraints

The basic problem to be considered is the development of an annual employment program for mail processing clerks in a large post office. Major decisions in the development of an annual program include:

1. The size of each type of workforce (allowed complements) for career regulars, part-time employees and postal assistants,

2. The hiring/layoff schedule,
3. The planned overtime usage.

Annual employment programs and budgets are developed by the USPS on the basis of thirteen 4-week accounting periods. Thus, each of the three major types of decisions above must be made for each of the thirteen accounting periods. The decisions, of course are dependent upon the seasonal nature of the mail volumes forecasted for the postal facility.

The technological constraints in the goal model are those conditions which must be met to ensure a feasible solution. Policies which are 'non-negotiable' can also be a part of the technological constraint set.[4] The technological constraints are given below.

$$W_t = (1 - r)\, W_{t-1} + H_t^w \qquad t = 1, 2, \ldots, 13 \quad (1)$$

$$P_t = (1 - s)\, P_{t-1} + H_t^p - L_t^p \qquad t = 1, 2, \ldots, 13 \quad (2)$$

$$C_t = C_{t-1} + H_t^c - L_t^c \qquad t = 1, 2, \ldots, 13 \quad (3)$$

$$P_t \leqq \beta_t \qquad t = 1, 2, \ldots, 13 \quad (4)$$

$$C_t \leqq \gamma_t \qquad t = 1, 2, \ldots, 13 \quad (5)$$

$$O_t^w \leqq \theta^w W_t \qquad t = 1, 2, \ldots, 13 \quad (6)$$

$$O_t^p \leqq \theta^p P_t \qquad t = 1, 2, \ldots, 13 \quad (7)$$

$$O_t^c \leqq \theta^c C_t \qquad t = 1, 2, \ldots, 13 \quad (8)$$

$$\delta_t^p\, O_t^P + O_t^c \leqq O_t^w \qquad t = 1, 2, \ldots, 13 \quad (9)$$

$$O_t^c \leqq \delta_t^P O_t^P \qquad t = 1, 2, \ldots, 13 \quad (10)$$

where:

W_t = fulltime career regular employees in period t expressed in manperiods (140 hours per period).

P_t = part-time employees in period t expressed in manperiods. These employees work on a regular basis but less than 40 hours per week.

C_t = postal assistants in period t expressed in manperiods. These

4. In this study policies concerning the usage of part-time and postal assitant employees and the limitations on overtime usage are considered technological constraints and as such are non-negotiable. These policies could have been modeled in the goal constraint set, however.

employees are used on a short-term basis to supplement vacation schedules and peak seasonal demands.

H_t^k = new hires for employees of type k in period t.

L_t^k = planned releases of employees of type k in period t.

r, s = resignation rates expressed as a percentage of the workforce level for career regular and part-time employees respectively.

O_t^k = overtime for employee type k in period t expressed in manperiods.

θ_t^k = percentage of the regular time workforce capacity of employee type k which can be assigned to work overtime in period t.

δ_t^k = parameter, between zero and one, which transforms the planned capacity of type k employee to the equivalent capacity of a regular career employee. This parameter reflects shorter working hours as well as productivity differences.

β_t = maximum allowed complement of part-time employees in period t.

γ_t maximum allowed complement of casual employees in period t.

Several of these constraints need further elaboration. The first three constraints define the employee complements for each period. Since planned releases of full-time career employees are not allowed, the only way the career regular workforce can be depleted is by allowing attrition to take its toll. Policies on the maximum allowable complement sizes of the part-time and postal assistant workforces are reflected in (4) and (5). It is conceivable that more postal assistants may be employed in the Christmas season than other times of the year. Finally, (9) ensures that the overtime *hours* assigned to the regular time workforce are at least as great as the total *hours* assigned to part-time and postal assistant employees.[5] A similar relationship between part-time clerks and postal assistants is embodied in (10). These relationships enable an equitable distribution of overtime work according to the seniority of the workforce.

5. For the work that they perform, part-time employees are assumed to have the same productivity as career regular employees. Thus, δ_t^p only reflects a difference in the number of working hours. That is why δ_t^p appears in (9) and (10) and δ_t^c does not. Postal assistants are employed on a short-time basis but work full time.

27.3.2. Goal constraints

The goal constraint set specifies the various goals postal management may have relative to selecting optimal employee complement sizes. The goals to be considered in this model are:

1. Do not exceed a certain annual budget commitment,
2. Do not fall below certain stated service levels.

The first goal can be written as:

$$\sum_{t=1}^{13} \{c_w W_t + c_p P_t + c_c C_t + c_h^w H_t^w + c_h^p H_t^p + c_h^c H_t^c + c_L^p L_t^p + c_L L_t^c + c_o^w O_t^w + c_o^p O_t^p + c_o^c O_t^c\} + d_b^- - d_b^+ = B \quad (11)$$

where the lower-case c's correspond to the cost parameters and B is the annual budget commitment. The deviation variables d_b^- and d_b^+ measure the amount by which the budget is not exactly met. Of course, we would not be concerned if we did not use up the budget commitment, so we will be interested in minimizing d_b^+.

The determination of service goals requires information on the tradeoffs in service and employee complement sizes. The mail volume experienced by a post office is seasonal in nature. Figure 2 specifies the relationship between average work-in-process mail inventories and equivalent full-time manperiods generated from TOURS for each of four different mail volume levels. Curve 2 is defined as an 'average' level of mail volume whereas curve 1 is 80 percent of that volume and curves 3 and 4 are 120 percent and 140 percent respectively. These mail volumes are assigned to the thirteen accounting periods to give a seasonal requirements pattern. Even though TOURS determines *weekly* tour assignments, the same assignment would hold for each of the four weeks in an accounting period. The mail volume is the *average* weekly volume for that accounting period, thus the average work-in-process inventory is a measure of the service attainable during the entire accounting period.

The curves in Figure 2 indicate that service improves in a non-linear fashion as total equivalent full-time manperiods increase. Let the equivalent full-time manperiods be given by

$$M_t = W_t + \delta_t^p P_t + \delta_t^c C_t + O_t^w + \delta_t^p O_t^p + \delta_t^c O_t^c \qquad t = 1, 2, \ldots, 13 \quad (12)$$

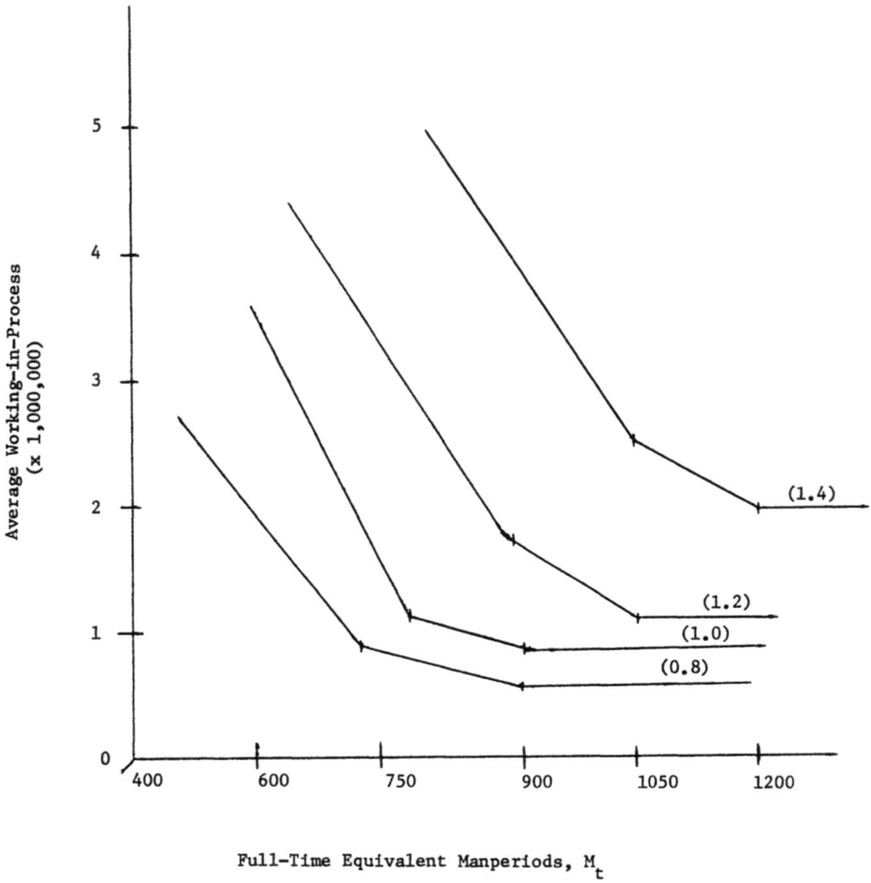

Figure 2. Average work-in-process inventory versus equivalent full-time manperiods for various weekly mail volumes.

Consider any one of the curves in Figure 2. Such a convex curve can be written as

$$f(t) = \sum_{j=1}^{n} \alpha_{jt} |M_t - g_{jt}| \beta_t M_t + \gamma_t \qquad (13)$$

where α_{jt}, g_{jt}, β_t, and γ_t are given constants for some period t and $\alpha_{jt} \geqq 0$ for all j.[6] In particular, we can choose the g_{jt} such that

6. See [1] for more details on this functional representation.

$g_{j-1,t} \leqq g_{jt}$. The other constants can be determined as follows:

$$\alpha_{jt} = \frac{k_{jt} - k_{j-1,t}}{2} \tag{14}$$

$$\beta = \frac{k_{n+1,t} + k_{1,t}}{2} \tag{15}$$

where k_{jt} is the slope of the line segment which runs from $g_{j-1,t}$ to g_{jt}. Since γ_t does not affect our choice of M_t we can ignore it. Thus each curve is represented in piece-wise linear form with $N + 1$ line segments.

We have chosen to approximate each curve in Figure 2 with 3 line segments. The values of g_{jt}, k_{jt}, α_{jt} and β_t for each of the thirteen periods can be found in Table 1. The g_{jt} values were chosen to be the natural break points in each curve. The slopes were taken from the graphs. The last line segment of each separated linear form has zero slope and is obviously the desired level of service for that mail volume. In particular, any value of M_t which falls in that interval is acceptable from the standpoint of service. Any value of M_t outside of that interval will represent a deviation from the goal and will be penalized according to the rate of increase in work-in-process inventories.

Given the values of g_{jt}, the following goal constraints can be written:

$$M_t + d_{1t}^- - d_{1t}^+ = g_{1t} \qquad t = 1, 2, \ldots, 13 \tag{16}$$

$$M_t + d_{2t}^- - d_{2t}^+ = g_{2t} \qquad t = 1, 2, \ldots, 13 \tag{17}$$

Table 1. Service goal constants derived from the Tour Assignment Analysis Accounting Period, *t*.

	1	2	3	4	5	6	7	8	9	10	11	12	13
g_{1t}	720	720	720	780	900	1050	900	780	720	900	780	780	720
g_{2t}	900	900	900	900	1050	1200	1050	900	900	1050	900	900	900
k_{1t}	-8333	-8333	-8333	-13888	-10000	-10000	-10000	-13888	-8333	-10000	-13888	-13888	-8333
k_{2t}	-1765	-1765	-1765	-2500	-3333	-3333	-3333	-2500	-1765	-3333	-2500	-2500	-1765
k_{3t}	0	0	0	0	0	0	0	0	0	0	0	0	0
α_{1t}	3284	3284	3284	5694	3333	3333	3333	5694	3284	3333	5694	5694	3284
α_{2t}	883	833	833	1250	1667	1667	1667	1250	883	1667	1250	1250	883
β_t	-4167	-4167	-4167	-6944	-5000	-5000	-5000	-6944	-4167	-5000	-6944	-6944	-4167

Since $|M_t - g_{jt}|$ is equivalent to $(d_{jt}^- + d_{jt}^+)$, the objective function can now be written:

$$\min Z = \omega_b d_b^+ + \sum_{t=1}^{13} \omega_t \left[\sum_{j=1}^{2} \alpha_{jt}(d_{jt}^- + d_{jt}^+) + \beta_t M_t \right] \tag{18}$$

where ω_b and ω_t are weights indicating the relative importance of the various goals. In this study $\omega_b \gg \omega_t$ for all t (to force achievement of the budget goal) and $\omega_t = 1$ for all t although the formulation is more general. The goal interval programming model consists of minimizing (18) subject to constraints (1)–(12), (16) and (17).

27.3.3. Cost and service tradeoffs

A cost/service relationship can be developed by solving a series of programs for increasing values of $B(11)$. The results illustrating this relationship are shown in Figure 3. The vertical axis measures the

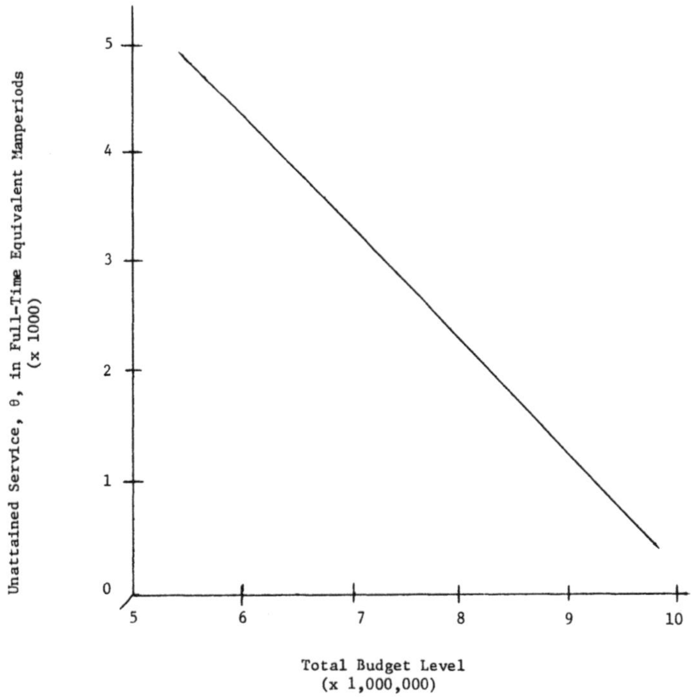

Figure 3. Unattained service, θ, versus service for model without full-time career complement size restrictions.

aggregate level of unattained service with respect to a particular goal. The service goal used corresponds to the desired maximum service goals, g_{2t}, in Table 1. Thus, the unattained service is given by

$$\theta = \sum_{t=1}^{13} d_{2t}^{-}$$

Thus, the vertical axis illustrates the extent to which the desired level of service is *not* achieved.

Figure 3 shows the trend towards full attainment of service as the budget is increased. For large changes in the budget, the relationship is linear. The slope provides the manager with an estimate of the marginal cost of increased service. For example, the slope of the curve in Figure 3 is approximately $-.001$, indicating that every additional thousand dollars allocated to the budget will result in achieving one full-time equivalent manperiod reduction in unattained service.

The model also provides a mechanism to evaluate the effect of management policies on both cost and service. For example, upper management may impose limits relative to the number of personnel a sectional or regional office may employ. This type of policy is particularly interesting if it involves limiting the number of full-time career personnel. Current policy holds that full-time career postal employees cannot be laid off. Moreover, sectional center postmasters normally maintain fixed complements for full-time career employees within the limits imposed by the regional headquarters. Given this situation, what would be a reasonable fixed full-time employee complement size and what are the effects of such a policy as opposed to a variable complement policy in light of the tradeoffs in costs and service? The next section illustrates how the goal model may be used to analyze such policy questions.

27.3.4. Manpower policy and service

The analysis of these policy questions requires the addition of a set of constraints of the form $w_t = w_{\max}$. $w_{\max}$ reflects the policy of imposing an upper limit on the full-time career complement size

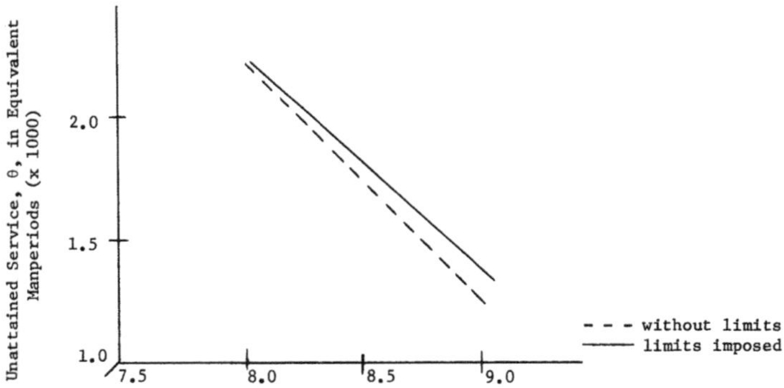

Figure 4. Unattained service, θ, versus total budget for models with and without full-time career complement size restriction.

while the equality sign reflects the policy of fixed complement sites.[7] A series of programs were solved for various budget levels so as to determine the impact of such a policy on both service and the optimal employment plan. For this analysis, $w_{\max}$ was chosen to be 750. While this selection is arbitrary, it is obvious that a series of programs for various limits could be solved so as to determine the sensitivity of the solution to $w_{\max}$.

It is apparent that this policy will have impact on a limited budgetary range. The necessity to maintain a fixed full-time complement size will result in a minimum feasible budget. Further, these constraints, in combination with the limiting policies for part-time and postal assistants (equations (4), (5)) establish a maximum level of service that is possible. For this analysis, feasible solutions to the problem are limited to annual budgets between $8 and $8 million.

The solid line in Figure 4 shows the cost/service relationship for the model incorporating the fixed full-time career complement size policy. The broken line is the cost/service relationship for the original model. The change in slope (−0.00103 (original) to −.000874 (limits imposed)) indicates the impact of the manpower policy. That is, if a limit of 750 is imposed, an additional allocation of $1000 (for budget levels between 8–9 million) will now only reduce unattained service by .87 full-time equivalent manperiods.

Figure 5 shows the proportion of the total equivalent man-

7. An alternative policy of $w_t \leqq w_{max}$ could also be analyzed.

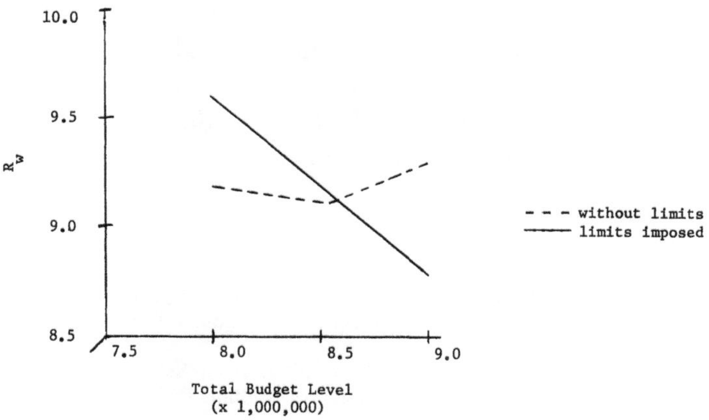

Figure 5. Ratio of full-time career manperiods to total manperiods versus budget level.

periods accounted for by full-time career employees at various budget levels. The vertical axis is given by $R = (\Sigma_{j=1}^{t} W_i)/(\Sigma_{j=1}^{t} M_i)$. Note that for the model incorporating full-time complement limits, as the budget levels decrease the mix of the various employee types becomes increasingly dominated by fulltime career employees. Since this category of employees is not subject to lay-off, this manpower policy reduces the flexibility of local managers to adjust for seasonal demand patterns.

Finally, the model could be solved for a series of upper limits. This sensitivity type analysis would provide useful information relative to the 'most appropriate' limit management should impose. Thus, the model offers a means to both determine cost/tradeoffs associated with a particular policy and to compare alternative policies.

27.4. Conclusions

There is a need for management to consider both cost and service in the formulation of policy. This paper demonstrates how the concept of disaggregation can be used to develop cost/service relationships. Further, having established these relationships, an interval goal programming model was developed to demonstrate how management might utilize this information in policy formulation. The example results illustrate that a policy of limiting the number of full-time career employees can have adverse impact on both cost and service. This analysis has shown that interval goal programming models are capable of providing relevant information for policy formulation and therefore should be considered as an important management tool in the Public Sector.

References

1. Charnes, A., Cooper W. W., Klingman, D., and Niehaus, R. J., 'Explicit Solutions in Convex Goal Programming', *Management Science*, vol. 22, no. 4 (December 1975), pp. 438–448.
2. Krajewski, L. J., Henderson, J. C., and Schowalter, M. J., 'Selecting Optimal Employee Complements in a Post Office: A Resolution of Multiple Objectives', WPS 76–66, The Ohio State University, Columbus, Ohio.
3. Krajewski, L. J. and Ritzman, L. P., 'Disaggregation in Manufacturing and Service Organizations: Survey of Problem Structures and Research Findings', Forthcoming *Decision Sciences* (January 1977).
4. Ritzman, L. P., Krajewski, L. J., and Showalter, M. J., 'The Disaggregation of Aggregate Manpower Plans', *Management Science*, vol. 22, no. 11 (July 1976), pp. 1204–1214.

28. Disaggregation of manpower in a service organization

MICHAEL J. SHOWALTER

Abstract

Disaggregation is an interfacing mechanism for the translation of aggregate plans into detailed schedules. This paper describes the general nature of the disaggregation problem in organizations and then formulates a disaggregation problem relating to a particular organization—sectional center facilities of the United States Postal Service. A methodology is described for solving this disaggregation problem and experimental results are presented.

28.1. Introduction

A recent article by Krajewski and Ritzman [3] suggests that an interfacing problem exists between aggregate planning and scheduling in organizations. Much of the research has focused upon either aggregate planning problems or scheduling problems. However, the authors conclude that the utility of these solution approaches is diminished when the problems are examined independently of each other.

An organization generally performs operational planning in a top-down, or sequential, manner. The aggregate plan is developed first and then a series of detailed schedules are generated based upon the resource allocations specified in the aggregate plan. The authors argue that inadequate information is provided by the aggregate plan and that an additional disaggregation (interface) problem must be solved before optimal detailed schedules can be developed.

Disaggregation is assumed to be a major problem in operational planning for manufacturing as well as for service organizations.

The primary difference is the kinds of resources that require disaggregation. Disaggregation for a manufacturing organization might well focus on the timing and sizing of component inventories, while in a service organization the disaggregation issue centers on the timing and sizing of the work force. Of course, the exact nature of the disaggregation problem in any organization will be a function of the particular operating environment.

This article explores the disaggregation problem existing in a service organization. Of particular interest is the operational planning process required by sectional center facilities (SCF's) of the United States Postal Service. These SCF's are the operations section of the postal system having responsibility for the collection, sorting, and delivery of mail to its final destination. There are approximately 600 SCF's in the United States with a work force complement averaging between 1000 to 2000 employees. Previous research [3], [5], [7] indicates that the proper planning and allocation of this manpower resource has a significant impact on the level of service provided by an SCF.

28.2. SCF processing system[1]

An SCF receives mail from a variety of external sources such as large business mailers, collection boxes, branch postal offices, rural postal offices, and other SCF's. The mean arrival rate of mail is time dependent, with variations occurring on a seasonal, daily, and hourly basis. Seasonal mail volume patterns reveal a peak during November and December and a slight trough during the summer months. Daily mail arrival volumes build up during the week to a peak on Friday and fall off on the weekend. On an hourly basis the mail arrival volume peaks during the early evening hours (4:00 p.m. to 10:00).[2] These patterns of demand for service (mail sorting and delivery) require different levels of operating capacity per month, week, day, and hour.

The SCF processing system can be characterized as a multi-stage system in which mail may flow through as many as six different

1. A more detailed description of the SCF processing system may be found in [7].
2. These patterns reflect the fact that 80 percent of all mail volume is generated by businesses which typically dispatch their mail at the end of each working day.

sorting operations. The exact sequence of sorting operations followed will depend on the characteristics of the mail.[3] All of the sorting operations performed in an SCF are manpower dependent. Although a few sorting operations are mechanized the lack of adequate manpower at any sorting operation will restrict the flow of mail through the system and delay delivery to its destination. Mail flow may also be restricted due to priority classification. For example, third-class mail must await sorting until all available airmail, first-class mail and second-class mail has been processed through the system.

Mail, once processed may not necessarily leave the SCF immediately. Processed mail leaves an SCF only at scheduled dispatch times each day. It is quite possible for mail to be rapidly processed through the system only to wait in a dispatch mail queue until the next scheduled dispatch. In this case, operating capacity could just as easily have been utilized in later time periods.

A measure of the service provided by an SCF is simply the time that mail spends in the system. A high level of service is achieved by dispatching mail from the system as quickly as possible. The key to providing such a high level of service is the proper timing and sizing of operating capacity, given the mail arrival pattern and dispatch schedule. Since SCF's are manpower limited systems, service level is more appropriately a function of the proper timing and sizing of the work force complement.

28.3. Disaggregation problem

Operational planning in an SCF must give special attention to the allocation of the manpower resource. Figure 1 shows the hierarchical structure of operational manpower planning needed to effectively allocate the work force complement. At the aggregate level, the work force complement size, necessary hires and fires, overtime and undertime levels, and vacation levels are specified for each 4-week period over the fiscal year. Disaggregate manpower planning determines the weekly work schedule, processing center

3. These characteristics include the priority classification, destination, and physical dimensions.

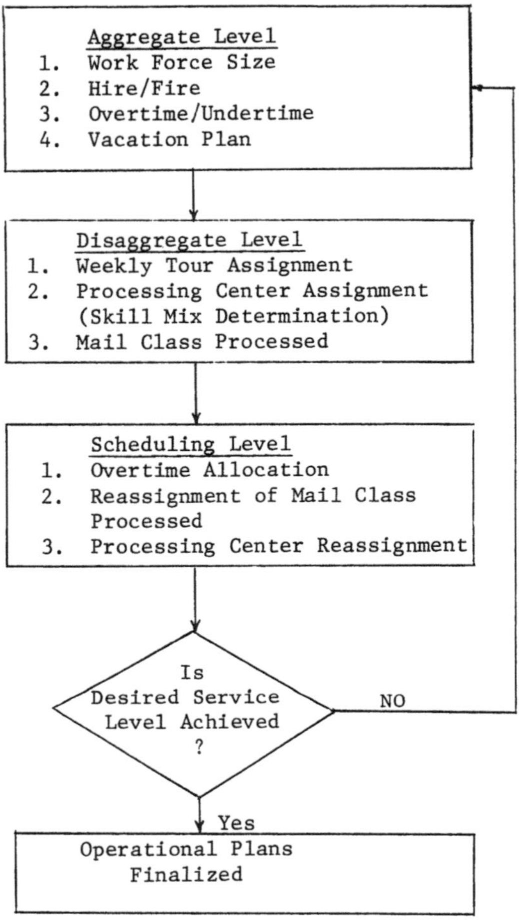

Figure 1. Hierarchy of operational planning for the manpower resource.

assignment, and class of mail to process for each employee in the work force complement.[4] Detailed scheduling then modifies these mail class processing assignments and processing work center assignments for employees, given their skill flexibility, in order to meet daily and hourly mail volume variations. If these short-term variations in demand for service cannot be satisfied through employee reassignment, it then becomes necessary to plan overtime allocations. Upon completion of these planning phases the

4. The decision to assign employees to specific processing centers also determines the appropriate skill mix since most processing centers require unique sorting skills.

manpower assignments are evaluated to measure their ability to achieve the desired service level. If unsatisfied, the operational manpower planning must recycle with adjustments made to the objective function and/or constraints of the aggregate planning model until the desired service level is attained.

Operational manpower planning in an SCF necessitates some degree of disaggregate planning. Knowledge of the work force complement size is clearly an inadequate resource constraint specification from which to generate hourly, or even daily, work assignments. The disaggregation problem, as described above, presents a clear illustration of the interfacing nature of disaggregate planning between the aggregate and detailed planning levels. However, it should be recalled that disaggregate planning is situational in nature and the disaggregation problem would be defined differently for any other service or manufacturing organization.

28.4. Disaggregation methodology

Formulation of the disaggregation problem associated with operational manpower planning in a SCF immediately raises the question of how to solve this problem. Since the disaggregation problem is unique to each organization, it is expected that any solution methodology will be unique to the disaggregation problem under consideration. Therefore, not only must the disaggregation problem be carefully reformulated for each new situation, but a new solution procedure must be developed for each disaggregation problem formulation.

To simplify the development of a solution methodology, it was decided to assume that optimal algorithms exist for generating the aggregate plan and detailed schedules. This assumption allows the development of a disaggregation algorithm independently of the other planning phases. It is expected that the disaggregation methodology would be capable of translating the work force complement size into:

1. A weekly work schedule for each employee.
2. An assignment of each employee to a specific processing work center.

3. A specification of the class of mail to be processed by each employee in a processing work center.

It is theoretically possible to formulate this disaggregation solution methodology as a mixed integer programming problem. However, the overwhelming size and lack of efficient computer codes makes such an approach impractical. It was finally decided to resort to a non-optimal approach, in particular, heuristic programming. The heuristic approach is advantageous because of its ability to handle large ill-structured problems and the potential ease of programming. However, these advantages are weighed against the fact that good, not necessarily optimal, solutions are generated.

The solution methodology proposed employs a building, or construction, heuristic procedure.[5] Feasible employee assignments are made in an iterative manner using heuristic decision rules uniquely suited to this disaggregation problem. Employee assignments are made to work centers which process airmail first. Next, employees are assigned to work centers which process first-class mail, and so on, until all priority classes of mail have been assigned manpower processing capacity and the work force complement, as specified by the aggregate plan, is fully allocated.

The heuristic decision rules used to assign employees are linked to the arrival pattern of mail. For a work center which processes a specific class of mail, an employee allocation is made to the weekly tour schedule with the *largest* volume of unprocessed mail.[6] The actual number of employees allocated in each iteration is a function of:

1. The volume of unprocessed mail available divided by the weekly tour productivity per employee at the particular work center.
2. The number of employees remaining in the work force complement who are not yet assigned.
3. The number of work stations within the work center which have not been assigned an employee during the relevant weekly tour.

5. A more detailed explanation of this heuristic methodology can be found in [8].
6. A weekly tour (work) schedule of an 8-hour shift for 5 consecutive days with the daily shift starting at the same time each day.

28.5. Simulation model

In order to analyze the capability of the heuristic methodology to generate acceptable work force allocation solutions a deterministic simulation model was developed. The simulation model is structured to represent the processing system of a SCF. It is generalized in the sense that any SCF can be depicted by modifying a few parameter inputs.

Any work force tour assignment generated by the heuristic program can be entered into the deterministic simulation model to measure its impact on the level of service. The simulation model is deterministic in the sense that only one week of arrival mail volume is being processed. The mail arrival pattern used in the simulation model is expressed as an average of the mail volume received in bi-hourly intervals over the week.[7] A simulation period longer than one week is considered redundant since the work force tour assignment is identical from one week to the next.[8]

To measure the impact of a work force tour assignment on processing system performance a surrogate measure of service is used. The mean level of work-in-process inventory per scheduled dispatch over the week accurately reflects the service level achieved by a particular work force tour assignment. When the timing and sizing of the work force complement is correct, mail will be rapidly processed through the SCF and dispatched for final delivery. However, if the timing and sizing of the work force complement is incorrect mail will queue (at various sorting operations) in the system and when a scheduled dispatch occurs it will not be available for shipment. Obviously, an optimal service level is achieved when the mean work-in-process inventory per scheduled dispatch is minimized.

28.6. Experimental results

A hypothetical SCF was constructed to study the capability of the heuristic methodology to allocate the work force complement. It is

7. Although we would never expect the actual mail arrival volumes to exactly match this pattern, any deviations must be considered at the scheduling level of operational manpower planning.
8. Actually, a two-week simulation period was used. The first week was used to initialize system inventory levels and the second week was used to measure system performance.

modeled from data collected at a large SCF located in a metropolitan area. Although much of the data used reflected actual measurement of system characteristics, a portion of the data was estimated because it was not available in the form required by this study.

Experimentation was limited to an examination of how the heuristic methodology responds to a variety of operational manpower planning levels. Referring back to Figure 1 it is possible for almost any work force complement size to be defined at the aggregate planning level. It is expected that the heuristic methodology should generate a work force tour assignment solution yielding a higher level of service for an incremental increase in the size of the work force complement. Figure 2 shows the effect on mean work-in-process inventory level over a range of work force complement sizes. The graph indicates that improved service is achieved by increasing work force complement size, however, service improves at a decreasing rate. In fact, expansion of the work force complement beyond 1000 employees yields only minor improvement in service. Thus, it would appear that for any SCF there exists some

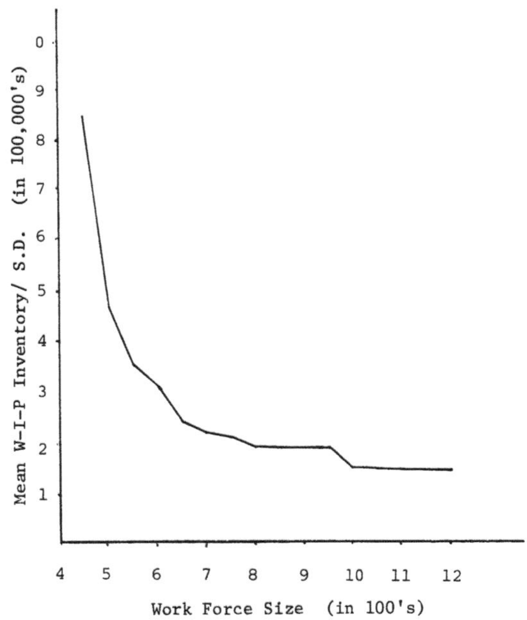

Figure 2. Effect of work force size on service level.

maximum level of work force which can be effectively disaggregated with this heuristic methodology.

Figure 3 presents the relationship between work force complement size and service level by priority level of mail. The heuristic methodology should provide maximum service to the highest priority mail first. This appears to be correct since the mean work-in-process inventory per scheduled dispatch is minimized for airmail at the lowest work force complement size (600 employees). However, second- and third-class mail does attain maximum service levels at lower work force sizes than first-class mail. This contradiction appears to be due to their relative proportions of total mail volume. First-class mail constitutes approximately 80 percent of total mail volume while second- and third-class mail constitutes only 15 percent. The heuristic methodology allocates increases in work force size over all mail classes with the greatest improvements in service accruing to the priority mail with the largest volume.

Experimentation also reveals that the heuristic methodology does

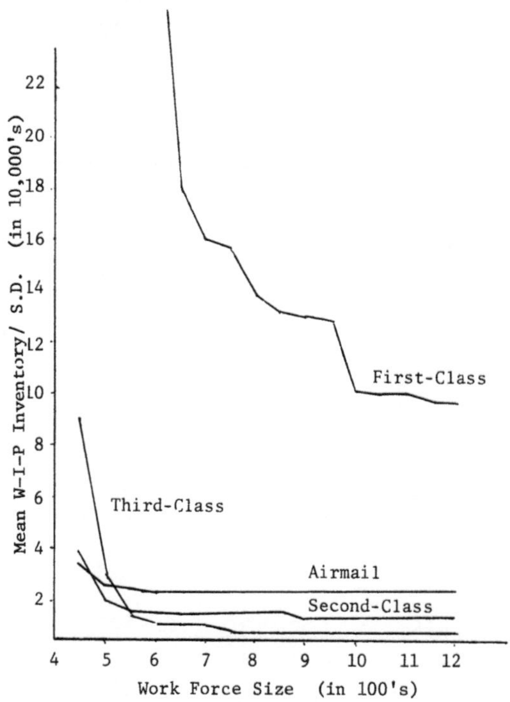

Figure 3. Effect of work force size on service level by mail class.

not always generate a work force tour assignment solution which is capable of processing all arriving mail volume over the week. Figure 4 shows the total volume of mail processed by a work force tour assignment, given a specific work force complement size. Only at work force complement sizes of 750 employees or more is the heuristic methodology capable of generating *feasible* work force tour assignments. Any work force tour assignment which cannot process all the total weekly mail volume is infeasible because it implies the build-up of infinite inventories of unprocessed mail over time.

28.7. Conclusions

The disaggregation problem is clearly a viable issue for consideration in operational manpower planning in service organizations. The heuristic methodology suggested for resolving the disaggregation problem in sectional center facilities of the United States Postal Service does provide a good, though not necessarily optimal, work force tour assignment solution. The experimental results indicate

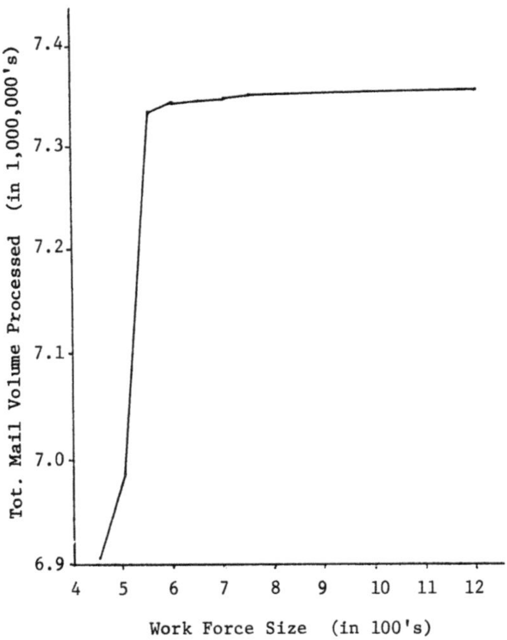

Figure 4. Mail volume processed, by work force complement.

that there exists some minimum (at which total weekly mail arrival volume is processed) and maximum (at which service does not significantly improve) work force complement sizes which could provide a lower and upper bound on the aggregate planning work force complement decision.

References

1. Abernathy, W. J., Baloff, N., Hershey, J. C., and Wandel, S., 'A Three-Stage Manpower Planning and Scheduling Model: A Service Sector Example', *Operations Research*, vol. 21, no. 3 (May–June 1973), pp. 693–711.
2. Krajewski, L. J., Henderson, J. R., and Showalter, M. J., 'Aggregate Manpower Planning in the Post Office', Presentation at Joint ORSA/TIMS Conference, Miami Beach (November 1976).
3. Krajewski, L. J. and Ritzman, L. P., 'Disaggregation in Manufacturing and Service Organizations: Survey of Problems and Research', *Journal of Decision Sciences* (forthcoming issue).
4. Krajewski, L. J. and Ritzman, L. P., 'Tour Assignments in a Service Organization', Working Paper Series, Division of Research, The Ohio State University (1974).
5. Mabert, Vincent A., 'A Methodology for Work Scheduling and Labor Assignment Within a Single Postal Facility', Unpublished doctoral dissertation, The Ohio State University (1973).
6. Ritzman, L. P., Krajewski, L. J., and Showalter, M. J., 'The Disaggregation of Aggregate Manpower Plans', *Management Science*, vol. 19, no. 11 (July 1976), pp. 1204–1214.
7. Showalter, M. J., 'A Methodology for Manpower Tour Assignment within a U.S. Postal Center Facility', Unpublished doctoral dissertation, The Ohio State University (1976).
8. Showalter, M. J., Krajewski, L. J., and Ritzman, L. P., 'A Methodology for Manpower Tour Assignment in Postal Sectional Center Facilities', Presentation at Joint ORSA/TIMS Conference, Philadelphia, Pa. (March 1976).

29. Facilities planning in the railroad industry: the need for disaggregation

SUFI M. NAZEM and LARRY C. PEPPERS

Abstract

The United States is served by sixty-eight Class I railroads which are simultaneously competitive and mutually dependent. Each year the rail industry spends billions of dollars to maintain and expand the rail network, but it does so in a highly fragmented process which assures massive inefficiency in rail freight transport. This paper isolates four levels of disaggregation in the rail planning process, focuses on the interdependence of the rail industry, investigates the sources of the traditional aversion to strategic planning, and suggests an alternative rail planning system.

29.1. Introduction

Facilities planning in the railroad industry is a diverse area encompassing both very aggregative expenditure decisions – the total budget for new freight cars, locomotives, and classification yards can easily top $100 million per year for an individual railroad – and disaggregative decisions related to the utilization of these resources across the entire rail network – for example, intrarailroad and interrailroad actions which must be coordinated in distributing the fleet of cars and locomotives on a regional and national basis.

This paper disentangles the levels of disaggregation (both actual and potential) which exist in the rail industry, analyzes their interrelationships and develops a methodology for facilities planning which can be adopted by the individual railroad. In particular, the paper focuses on four levels of disaggregation. Level I (the universal level) involves macro-economic analysis of national freight transport demand, intermodal freight transportation, and the capacity of the railroads, vis-a-vis demand. In particular, the decision process at this level centers on the ability (in terms of actual and planned facilities) of the entire rail industry to handle aggregate freight demand over a one-to-five year planning horizon. Level II (global analysis by each railroad) includes the translation of the aggregate rail demand in level I into a detailed set of individual rail unit projections for commodity freight demand, locomotive and car requirements, and maintenance and manpower needs; a one-to-three year time horizon is most suitable. Level III (the strategic level) incorporates the simultaneous coordination of intracompany actions with interrailroad operational activities. Starting from global estimates of the demand for and supply of rail services constructed in level II, the strategic level focuses on input-output decisions related to the distribution of freight cars and locomotives (both internally and in conjunction with 'foreign' railroads), the service levels (speed and handling) provided to various shippers, and the expediting of traffic received from or forwarded to other railroads. For level III, the time horizon is from one month to one year. Finally, level IV (the tactical level) deals with the day-to-day operations of the individual railroad – shipper scheduling, demand for cars, quality of customer service, and the carrying out of level III decisions. Here, the time horizon stretches from one day up to one month.

29.2. Rail Balkanization

Facilities planning is a monumental task and has traditionally been the subject of rather pragmatic problem solving. This pragmatism can be traced to the interdependent structure of the rail industry, a characteristic which permeates the entire decision making process. The final report of the task force on railroad productivity, *Improving Railroad Productivity*, noted that the railroad industry in the United States is a victim of geographic Balkanization; that is, there are sixty-eight class I railroads which are simultaneously competitive and mutually dependent [2]. While the aggregate demand for rail service is derived from the concomitant demand for final goods and services in the economy, the individual railroad which originates a shipment for a particular commodity is also dependent upon the planning or lack of planning, of other connecting carriers.

While interdependence is a feature of many other industries, the typical manufacturing or service company can increase output, expand into new markets, augment capacity, and alter prices without being highly dependent upon the simultaneous cooperation of other companies in the industry. A manufacturer, for example, can estimate with reasonable accuracy its capacity to produce widgets. For the individual railroad, however, capacity is an ambiguous concept. Rail freight cars owned by a single railroad move over the entire national rail network. While one railroad may be able to handle trains composed of mammoth one hundred and twenty-five ton cars, it may be constrained by the antiquated roadbed of a connecting carrier. While price leadership is a well-known phenomenon in oligopolistic industries, rail rate bureaus (formal rail associations which make collective price recommendations to the Interstate Commerce Commission) may block innovative pricing changes, thereby negating the ability of the individual rail competitor to fashion a complete marketing package for the shipper.

29.3. Planning in a vacuum: the rail dilemma

On the one hand, the railroad industry attempts to function as a fully integrated rail transport network. On the other, it can be described as sixty-eight separate fiefdoms, each vying to increase its share of transport pie at the expense of other rail competitors.

At the most aggregative tier (level I), the rail planning system is a victim of benign neglect. In the absence of an active trade association or government agency which can produce a universal (level I) outlook for national rail freight demand, the industry has adopted a completely decentralized process which forces each individual railroad to vacillate between the role of monopolist and competitor.

In trying to evaluate next year's likely business volume, each railroad generates a detailed forecast of the steel, coal, grain, chemical, food, automotive, consumer, iron ore, lumber, and other traffic which will be moving over its system [5]. This, in essence, is disaggregation at its worst. Each railroad pays lip service to the concept of rail network integration, but, in reality, the fundamental building block – the commodity forecast – is generated in a highly secretive procedure designed to minimize intercompany information flows. The unknown planning parameters for each railroad are (1) the collective interpretation of future business conditions by all other railroads and (2) the impact of the resulting decisions on system capacity and service quality. In other words, level II (global analysis by the individual railroad) is carried out without the benefit of level I (the macroanalysis of a national freight demand). As each railroad tries to develop a 'quick and dirty' macro picture, it generates greater uncertainty for other railroads whose macro scenarios are likely to differ. In essence, it is impossible to produce an efficient plan in level II when each railroad is making a different starting point – its own level I.

Decentralized commodity forecasts are, truly, the bane of the railroad industry. As will be discussed below, the potential for national and regional coordination on such basic topics as location and size of classification yards, fleet acquisition, freight car utilization, rail network flow patterns – in other words, total facilities planning – is directly tied to the industry's success in achieving a unified outlook in level I. Suppose, for example, three railroads, *X*, *Y*, and *Z*, provide a regular transcontinental movement of consumer goods from New York to California. Railroad *X* originates the shipment in New York and forwards it to *Y* in Chicago. *Y*, in turn, transfers the load to *Z*, which finally terminates the shipment in California. Based on past precedent, each railroad has provided one-third of total equipment needed to accomplish this transcontinental movement. Assume that railroad *X* correctly forecasted 1977 freight growth for this commodity, while neither *Y* nor *Z* foresaw any increase in 1977 traffic over that experienced in 1976. As a result, the shipper now determines that aggregate rail capacity is inadequate; part, or maybe all, of the business may be switched to alternative transport modes. Railroad *X*, and potentially *Y* and *Z*, is left with surplus equipment, the railroad share of consumer goods' business has fallen, and consumers are probably paying more for the delivered product. At the other extreme, if railroads overestimate demand, the traffic will not be lost, but the industry will suffer from poor freight car utilization and reduced profitability.

29.4. Facilities planning: a top-down approach

In addition to a myriad of other jobs, the rail industry is confronted (at level III or the strategic tier) with the task of allocating a stock of freight cars and locomotives to meet the perennial supply-demand problem. The optimum solution for national rail car distribution conflicts with the disaggregated solutions of the individual railroads. That is, each individual railroad is attempting to maximize its freight car utilization rate (the ratio of loaded to total car miles). These individual allocation decisions do not, however, maximize national freight car utilization. To increase the efficiency of this dimension of facilities planning in the railroad industry, therefore, a structural change must occur.

In order to break new ground, we have ignored three of the more frequently mentioned structural rail alterations, namely, nationalization of the railroad industry, revitalization (or abolition) of the Interstate Commerce Commission (ICC), and formation of a small number of transcontinental railroads. Any short-term improvements in facilities planning will have to take place in the current mixed environment of quasi-nationalization (especially in the East), heavy regulatory control, and regionally oriented railroads. It is the thesis of this paper that facilities planning in the railroad industry is being frustrated by a 'bottom-up' approach which focuses on locomotive and freight car purchases by individual railroads rather than industry requirements, which attempts to reduce empty car miles for each railroad or a regional clustering of railroads rather than minimize wastage of national transport resources, and which looks at the freight commodity demand of individual railroads rather than projecting national freight demand for all transport modes and 'splitting out' national, regional, and company freight demand.

As opposed to this bottom-up approach, we envision a 'top-down' disaggregation process. Starting with a macroeconometric model of the economy, estimates of final demand (consumption, investment, government expenditures, and net exports) and industrial production (steel, rubber, glass, etc.) would be generated. In turn, these projections would be translated into sector forecasts of aggregate freight demand. For example, there would be individual forecasts of freight demand generated by the steel, automotive, chemical, rubber, and appliance industries. These projections would serve as the basis for a series of intermodal 'split' models which would estimate the respective portions of the total freight 'pie' to be transported via rail, truck, pipeline, barge, or air. It is critical to the success of facilities planning in the rail industry that complete and timely forecasts flow downward to the member railroads. Together with aggregate tonnage projections, a top-down framework would analyze the aggregate supply-demand situation for boxcars, flat cars, gondolas, refrigerator cars, open hoppers, covered hoppers, and the multitude of highly specialized cars which comprise the present rail fleet. Moving down the disaggregation ladder, this national information would be translated into equivalent regional information. For example, there would be tonnage estimates of steel originations in each section of the country, as well as the concomitant supply-demand picture for locomotives and cars at the regional level. Each member railroad would have at its disposal a complete assessment of national business conditions, intermodal freight demand patterns, and national and regional rail demand to input into its facilities planning system. By way of contrast, under the present system, each railroad has a fragmented view of its position vis-a-vis the total rail network and very little, if any, perspective on its role in the total intermodal freight system.

29.5. Empty car haul: a potential application

In recent years, the rail industry has faced the strange dichotomy of an increasing number of empty cars and a rising incidence of car shortages. While car shortages generate an outpouring of protests from shippers, consumers, and legislators, the empty car haul problem is generally ignored by the public.

Although the rail industry has significantly improved (via the introduction of sophisticated computer systems) its car information and monitoring system, empty car miles have actually increased from thirty-four percent of total car miles in 1950 to over forty-four percent in 1974 [1]. The source of this growth can be traced to the increasingly uneven geographical distribution of freight transportation demand, highly specialized cars for particular commodities (general purpose cars have a greater likelihood of securing traffic on the return trip), the appearance of unit trains (entire trains carrying one commodity in a continuous process), shipper-owned cars assigned for their own use, and railroad-owned cars assigned to specific shippers, all of which have been forced upon the industry by changing patterns in demand for transportation. It is widely recognized, however, that the rail industry has compounded this problem by its sluggishness, that is, by its inability to perceive and react to changing market forces [2 and 4]. This lack of responsiveness is, we believe, a structural characteristic which is largely explained by the interdependent nature of the rail industry and its 'bottom-up' approach to facilities planning. In trying to decode its own part of the freight transport puzzle, each railroad has been unable to clearly discern the trends which have buffeted the industry during the postwar period.

Leaving aside 'unavoidable' empties resulting from service oriented responses to the rail market (for example, unit coal trains to power companies), a substantial number of 'avoidable' empties can be traced to regulatory restrictions and car flow patterns in this Balkanized industry. Once member railroads have an adequate top-down system detailing demand-supply relationships at the national and regional levels, the industry would be in the position to organize a car clearing house (CCH), with clearing houses to be situated at critical junction points in each geographical region. Since the flow of cars is not restricted to an individual railroad's network, it follows that each CCH needs to have the representation of numerous roads, not just the particular road operating in that region. While the CCH concept has been tried by particular pairs of railroads, it has not been adopted on a system-wide basis due, at least in part, to the lack of forecast information.

To work properly, all cars would have to be assigned to a particular CCH. Each CCH would be responsible for the allocation of cars within a particular region and for any interregional transfers that would prove necessary. The obvious economic advantage of such a system would be the ability to provide total rail transport service with a smaller number of cars. In other words, transportation efficiency would arise from the ability to predict more accurately shifting rail freight flows and the capability of allocating the rail fleet to meet this demand.

29.6. Rail management and market responsiveness

The performance of each rail unit is linked to its ability to respond to the competitive market environment. While the above analysis has concentrated on facilities planning constraints generated by an interdependent rail network of sixty-eight class I railroads, the capacity of an individual railroad to utilize the 'top-down' facilities planning schema is also checked by the failure of individual railroads to articulate and carry out an integrated company strategy – the third level of disaggregation.

Functionalism, or what has been labeled the 'Chinese Walls of Management,' has resulted from a nineteenth century preoccupation with the operating function and an attitude of benign neglect toward the commercial or marketing function. This, in turn, was a by-product of both a monopolistic mentality and the systemic nature of a railroad. One hundred years ago the railroad industry was not faced with intermodal competition from trucks, barges, and pipelines. The operating department ran the railroad while the marketing department had only to 'charge what the traffic would bear.' The rail industry in 1977 has very few, if any, substantial havens from competition. The systemic nature of each railroad – failure of any operating activity will paralyze a railroad's entire transport system – has led, however, to the continued dominance of the operating function vis-a-vis marketing and to a myopic concern with day-to-day operation (level IV) rather than formulation of strategic responses (level III) to cyclical and secular shifts in intermodal freight patterns [6].

When one looks at the organizational hierarchy of the typical railroad company in 1977 and analyzes its ability to formulate and carry out a detailed facilities planning strategy (level III), the overriding defect is the absence of effective functional integration [3]. Whereas the interrailroad facilities planning process (levels I and II) is overly decentralized and fragmented, intrarailroad decisions (levels III and IV) concerning freight car and locomotive acquisitions, construction and location of freight classification yards and maintenance programs are overly concentrated in the hands of individuals concerned with the minimization of operating difficulties (level IV problems) rather than the maximization of rail profit and competitiveness. While the two strategems are not necessarily in complete opposition, overpreoccupation with either extreme may produce disasterous results – for example, introduction of longer freight trains (a level IV decision to improve operating efficiency) at a time when the presence of intense truck competition would call for shorter trains and more frequent departures.

The micro-systemic operating solution for an individual railroad overlooks, however, the macro-systemic nature of the entire transport system, namely, the total dependence of the individual railroad on its commercial environment. The analysis which follows outlines some changes in the regulatory environment which could serve to prod the industry toward an alternative planning structure.

29.7. Potential for implementation

From a purely technological standpoint, the regional rail freight planning system and the CCH concept are totally achievable. A substantial amount of relevant information, even at disaggregated levels, is obtainable from sources such as the Interstate Commerce Commission (ICC) and the American Association of Railroads; the capability of linking disaggregated projections to an aggregate forecast has already been demonstrated in other industrial sectors. The real pitfalls are institutional. First, the railroad industry fears that such coordination may, in fact, be utilized by the ICC to achieve even tighter control of the industry. Second, it is only recently that railroads have begun to become marketing oriented [5]. If strategic planning is a new phenomenon within the individual rail unit, it is totally alien across company boundaries. For example, the thought of surrendering partial control of one's car fleet to the CCH is particularly distasteful. Not to be overlooked, however, is the prime mover of recalcitrance in the rail industry – the ICC. To develop the expanded sense of car ownership and control alluded to above, changes in ICC regulatory restrictions will be necessary. Most crucial of these is the method of per diem payments (charges levied against a railroad which borrows a foreign car) which, at present, penalize car owners and work against full utilization of the existing fleet of cars. The existing system of per diem charges must be revamped so that car ownership becomes a worthwhile investment, even though the car may, in fact, be under the control of other roads a substantial percentage of the time.

Given the lack of initiative by the rail industry and the apparent indifference of the American Association of Railroads, the logical candidate to supply the missing link – level I – is the Department of Transportation (DOT). This agency is already in existence, has a high-powered staff, and has been heavily involved in national transportation planning. Taxpayers (via their indirect 'ownership' of Con Rail) have an obvious interest in the quality of rail forecast information. A DOT publication could, for example, entail a monthly review sent to all railroads; it would analyze the domestic and international environment and translate this into rail scenarios for important commodity categories.

Only after this information is available and the rail industry conducts an aggregate study at level I on the size and composition of the national car fleet, the scope of the CCH, and the accompanying work rules can the global planning (level II) of individual railroads be carried out in an effective manner. This need not imply totalitarian control of one railroad by a central planning group. Rather, the individual railroad will, of its own volition, develop a different plan for freight car acquisition and marketing strategy when there exists a top-down information flow from level I to level II. Similarly, such an information system will help to delineate strategic planning (level III) from tactical planning (level IV). The latter is analogous to production scheduling in a manufacturing operation where detailed input-output decisions are made. While the making up of trains, train schedules, and the weekly allocation of cars to various shippers is an important function, it must remain subordinate to and flow from the strategic planning carried out in level III.

The Rail Revitalization and Regulatory Reform Act of 1976 (Quad-R Act) has injected a new sense of urgency into the facilities planning process. Among its many provisions, the Quad-R Act has given the ICC a mandate to develop a seasonal or peak-pricing framework applicable to the rail industry. Just as telephone companies have developed peak and off-peak telephone rates, the rail industry has divergent peaks for its commodities and for various types of cars. Under the present facilities planning process, each individual railroad will begin a separate and, probably, futile attempt to determine the optimum peak pricing policy. This type of problem obviously lends itself to the four-level facilities planning process outlined above. It is, in reality, just the 'flip side' of the empty car haul problem. A higher freight rate at particular traffic junctions may serve to move the peak and allow better utilization of equipment. To engage in sophisticated attempts to manipulate demand peaks, the rail industry must have the technical competence to assess regional and national car supply patterns.

Although the disaggregation process outlined above for the rail industry assumed no fundamental structural alterations, it is also clear that any long-run changes will also profit from the existence of this planning system. If rail mergers should produce transcontinental railroads, if the harsh regulatory environment of the industry should be modified, or if the industry is nationalized, the industry will benefit from a top-down planning system. The greatest obstacle to integrated rail planning is the present Balkanized structure which diverts railroads from their joint task.

References

1. Interstate Commerce Commission, *Annual Report on Transport Statistics* (Washington, D.C.: U.S. Government Printing Office, 1974).
2. Meyer, John R. and Morton, A. L., *Improving Railroad Productivity: Final Report of the Task Force on Railroad Productivity* (Washington, D.C.: National Commission on Productivity and Council of Economic Advisors, 1973).
3. Morris, Stuart, 'Stalled Professionalism: The Recruitment of Railway Officials in the United States, 1885–1940', *Business History Review* (Autumn 1973), pp. 318–334.
4. Nazem, Sufi M., 'Empty Car Haul in Rail Freight Transportation', unpublished paper presented at the Fourth Intersociety Conference on Transportation (Los Angeles: July, 1976).
5. Peppers, Larry C., 'Transportation Planning: A New Look at the Role of Railroad Forecasting', *Transportation Journal* (Summer 1975), pp. 18–25.
6. Wyckoff, D. Daryl, *Railroad Management* (Lexington, Massachusetts: Lexington Books, 1976).

30. Vehicle dispatching – Sweep algorithm and extensions

BILLY E. GILLET, LELAND E. MILLER and JERRY G. JOHNSON

Abstract

This paper surveys the original Sweep Algorithm for the vehicle dispatch problem along with several modifications and applications. The original Sweep Algorithm was developed by Gillett and Miller [5]. It divides the single terminal vehicle dispatch problem into two subproblems; one of assigning locations to routes and the other of minimizing the length of each route using a traveling salesman algorithm. A number of people have applied modified versions of the Sweep Algorithm to various applications [1], [11], [12]. Others have improved the original version and have extended it to the multi-terminal problem [6], [8].

30.1. Sweep Algorithm

The original Sweep Algorithm addresses the problem of supplying customers at different locations with a desired quantity of a single type of product from a single terminal in such a way that the total distance traveled in supplying all demands is minimized. Each vehicle which supplies the product to the locations has the same load and distance constraints.

Basically, the Sweep Algorithm divides the problem into two subproblems; one of assigning locations to routes and the other of minimizing the length of each route using a traveling salesman algorithm.

More specifically, the forward Sweep Algorithm orders the locations in ascending order according to the size of their polar coordinate angle with respect to the terminal and then starts forming routes by collecting locations while moving around the terminal in a sweeping fashion. The first route consists of the location with the smallest angle, the location with the second smallest angle, etc. up through the location added just before the maximum load of the vehicle is exceeded. At this point a traveling salesman algorithm (Lin's 3-opt) is used to determine the optimal path to visit the locations in the first route. If the maximum distance capacity of the vehicle is exceeded, the last location added is removed and the traveling salesman algorithm is executed again. This process is repeated until a feasible route is found. At this point, the procedure tries to replace one location in the current route with one or more locations in the next route to be formed. Specifically, a location, say p, nearest the last location added to the current route is considered for inclusion. In addition, the location not in the current route that is closest to location p is considered for inclusion. The location considered for deletion from the current route is close to the terminal and also close to the next route to be formed. An actual replacement is made only if the next few locations after the current route indicate that the total distance traveled will probably be reduced if the replacement is made.

This process of forming routes is continued until all locations are assigned to a route. The x and y axes are then rotated counterclockwise so the first location becomes last, the second becomes first and so forth. The above procedure is then repeated. The process of rotating the x and y axes is continued with a minimum distance calculated each time, until all possibilities have been exhausted. The smallest of the minimum distances is taken to be a good approximation of the true minimum distance.

A second algorithm, called the backward-sweep algorithm, is exactly like the forward-sweep algorithm except it forms the routes in reverse order. Many times the backward-sweep gives a better solution than the forward-sweep. The Sweep Algorithm is ideally suited for problems of any size with a small number of locations per route. More specifically, if the number of locations per route remains relatively constant, the computer time increases linearly. However, the computer time increases quadratically with the average number of locations per route if the total number of locations remains relatively constant. It is practical timewise even up to 1000 locations if the average number of locations per route is less than 6, but may not solve a 60 location problem with 30 locations per route. For large problems from the literature, it proved better than the best known algorithms in 1970 but required slightly more computer time.

30.2. Modified Sweep Algorithm

A modified version of the Sweep Algorithm was developed by Gillett and Johnson [6] in 1975. It reduces the number of sweeps around the terminal, eliminates unnecessary computations by considering distance constraints as well as load constraints in building routes, and avoids resolving many traveling salesman problems. In addition, the algorithm uses the Lin 3-opt method to solve each traveling salesman problem consisting of less than 15 locations and uses a modified version of the Lin-Kernighan method in all other cases. These modifications reduce the computation time significantly and generally obtain better solutions.

The original Sweep Algorithm actually employs four variations of the basic step – two versions while scanning in a counterclockwise direction and two similar versions while scanning in a clockwise direction. The difference between these two versions lies in the manner in which the decision to end each route is made. Version one terminates the growth of a route when the next location to be added would cause the load constraint to be exceeded and when the interchange of a location results in no overall improvement in the total distance traveled. Version two always attempts to add the location after the next one to the route before it attempts the interchange of two locations. The second version sometimes produces a better solution than the first version, but its use accounts for fifty percent of the computation time. Therefore the Sweep Algorithm has been modified in an attempt to combine the contributions of the two original versions into a single version which is executed only once in each direction.

The apparent purpose of requiring that the second version examine at least two candidates for assignment to the route before attempting the interchange of locations is to try to utilize the load capacity of each route to its fullest extent. This tends to minimize the number of routes required and is frequently influential in minimizing the overall distance. The proposed modification to the Sweep Algorithm attempts to obtain the same effect through a slight change in the procedure for interchanging locations. In the original procedure, a nearby location to enter the route and a likely location to be deleted from the route are both chosen. In the modified procedure the location to be added to the current route is chosen first. If it can be added without violating the load constraint, no location is deleted, and the effect of the addition on the overall distance is used to determine whether the new assignment will take place or whether the current route will be declared complete. However, one other factor must be taken into account. If the addition of a new location without any deletions causes the distance constraint to be violated, then the interchange procedure must be done as it is in the original Sweep Algorithm. Although these additional steps require extra time to perform, the fifty percent savings in required computation time obtained by omitting the two applications of the second version produces a significant overall savings.

A second modification to the Sweep Algorithm has been introduced to eliminate unnecessary computations which had been required when the lengths of routes are determined by the distance constraint rather than the load constraint. In the original approach, a violation of the distance constraint is not discovered until the load limit is also exceeded. When this occurs, the Sweep Algorithm literally backs up, deleting locations from the route and solving traveling salesman problems until a route of feasible length is obtained. When distance is the binding constraint, much efficiency could be gained by maintaining a rough estimate of the length of the current route as it is formed, so that the formation of the route could be halted when its length is closer to the distance limit. One relatively simple way of doing this is to assume that the route is arranged in the order that the locations were added to it. This is not too unreasonable, since the locations are added in the order of their bearing angles. The distance estimate thus obtained will usually exceed the actual minimum length distance of the route, and will usually signal a violation of the distance constraint sooner than it actually occurs instead of later. The traveling salesman problem must then be solved. If the distance constraint has actually been exceeded, the deletion procedure of the original algorithm is followed, although fewer locations are deleted because the condition is detected earlier. If the true minimal length of the route is within the distance limit, the true value replaces the estimated length and is used as a basis for further estimation of route length. This updating should minimize the number of 'false alarms' and reduce the number of traveling salesman problems that have to be solved before the distance limit is reached.

A third modification to the Sweep Algorithm involves a technique which may reduce computation times for large vehicle-dispatch problems. The clockwise and counter-clockwise phases of the algorithm each involve several solutions to the vehicle-dispatch problem. Each new solution obtained follows a rotation of coordinate axes so that a different location is chosen to start the first route each time. The best solution in this sequence is the final answer obtained by the Sweep Algorithm. Sometimes a rotation of axes results in a change in only the first few routes. When there are many routes or a large number of locations per route, as is the case for large problems, the new set of routes often contains a significant number that are the same as the routes before the rotation of axes. It is possible to avoid the repeated solution of the traveling salesman problem for these routes by saving as many of the solutions of the previous set of routes as possible. Since only enough computer memory is required to store the tours examined in the current sweep and the previous sweep, the additional storage requirements will be small in comparison with the memory requirements of the rest of the program. This technique requires a certain amount of time for checking the table of solutions, so that when few routes are repeated, the problem may actually take longer to solve. Reductions in execution time from 3 percent to 47 percent were observed, while some smaller problems took 12 percent to 21 percent longer to solve. Since the smaller problems do not take very long to solve anyway, this modification makes an overall contribution to the efficiency of the algorithm.

A fourth modification to the Sweep Algorithm involves using the Lin 3-opt method for solving traveling salesman problems with less than 15 locations and a modified Lin-Kernighan method otherwise. Three modifications to the Lin-Kernighan method are used. Since the initial arrangement of the locations in the order of their bearing angles is often a good starting arrangement, only one iteration of the Lin-Kernighan method is used. A second modification allows additional backtracking. The third modification involves choosing the links to add and delete in forming tours.

30.3. Comparison of vehicle dispatch algorithms

The vehicle-dispatch problems in Table 1 were solved on an IBM 370/168 computer using both the original Sweep Algorithm and the

Table 1. List of problems.

Prob. No.	Source	No. Loc. (a)	Max. Load	Max. Dist.
1	[4]	21	6000	200
2	[4]	22	4500	240
3	[4]	29	4500	240
4	[4]	32	8000	240
5	[2]	50	160	Unlim
6	New Prob	75	100	Unlim
7	[2]	75	140	Unlim
8	New Prob	75	180	Unlim
9	New Prob	75	220	Unlim
10	New Prob	100	112	Unlim
11	[2]	100	200	Unlim
12	New Prob	100	300	Unlim
13	New Prob	100	400	Unlim
14	New Prob	249	500	Unlim
15	New Prob	249	800	Unlim
16	New Prob	249	1000	Unlim
17	New Prob	249	1200	Unlim

(a) Excludes terminal

Modified Sweep Algorithm. The solutions are shown in Table 2 along with Gaskell's [4] and Christofides and Eilon's [2] solutions to some of the problems. The computation time using the original and modified algorithms is given in Table 3. The computation times using Gaskell's as well as Christofides and Eilon's methods are not shown since an IBM 7090 was used. In general their computation times are slightly better than those using the original Sweep Algorithm.

The Modified Sweep Algorithm is generally faster than the original Sweep Algorithm and almost always gives a better solution value. This is particularly true with large problems (more than 50 locations). For example, problem 11, with 100 locations and an average of 12.5 locations per route was solved in half the time it took the original Sweep Algorithm and the solution was 1.4 percent better. Problem

Table 2. Comparison of vehicle dispatch algorithms

No. Loc	Max. Load	SOLUTIONS [4]	[2]	[5]	[6]
21	6000	598	*585	591	589
22	4500	955	*949	956	956
29	4500	963	*875	*875	883
32	8000	839	*810	*810	813
50	160	585	556	531	*524
75	100			1127	*1096
75	140	900	876	*865	*865
75	180			754	*752
75	220			714	*704
100	112			1170	*1146
100	200	887	863	863	*851
100	300			743	*740
100	400			712	*700
249	500			*5815	5831
249	800			*4079	4086
249	1000			3614	*3609
249	1200			3326	*3182

* Best solution

17, with 249 locations and an average of 24.9 locations per route, was solved in one-fourth the time it took the original Sweep Algorithm, the solution was 4 percent better and one less route was required. The solutions for problems 5–13 and 16–17 using the modified version are better than the best known solutions.

The Modified Sweep Algorithm has the following attributes:

1. It is approximately 2 times faster than the original Sweep Algorithm when the average number of locations per route is less than 15 and is approximately two to four times faster otherwise.
2. For small problems (less than 50 locations) it generally does not find the best solution; however, the solutions are within 1 or 2 percent of the optimal. For most problems with 50 or more locations, it finds better solutions than other methods in considerably less time.

Table 3. Comparison of vehicle dispatch algorithms

			COMPUTATION TIME	
No. Loc	Max Load	Ave No. Per Pt.	Orig. Sweep (sec)	Mod Sweep (sec)
21	6000	5.25	1.08	.92
22	4500	4.40	7.24	1.39
29	4500	*7.25	16.62	2.77
32	8000	8.00	10.83	4.25
50	160	10.00	9.56	5.14
75	100	5.00	4.32	4.56
75	140	7.50	8.58	6.11
75	180	9.38	21.66	12.17
75	220	10.71	31.30	15.33
100	112	7.14	12.68	9.85
100	200	12.50	53.40	24.53
100	300	20.00	195.22	67.18
100	400	25.00	436.51	96.46
249	500	9.96	72.00	51.46
249	800	15.56	280.27	168.57
249	1000	19.15	583.30	237.44
249	1200	*22.65	1022.97 (17+min)	255.86

* Modified Sweep has slightly larger values due to one less route required.

3. The computer time increases linearly with the total number of locations if the number of locations per route remains relatively constant.
4. The computer time increases quadratically with the average number of locations per route when all other parameters remain constant.

5. Large problems with an average of 10 to 25 locations per route can be solved in a reasonable amount of time. For example, a problem with 1000 locations and an average of 10 locations per route can be solved in approximately 3.5 minutes on the IBM 370/168.

30.4. Multi-terminal Sweep Algorithm

The Modified Sweep Algorithm was extended to the multi-terminal program by Gillett and Johnson [6], [7]. Their algorithm, the Multi-Terminal Sweep Algorithm, partitions the multi-terminal problem into a collection of subproblems which are solved as single-terminal problems using the Modified Sweep Algorithm.

The Multi-terminal Sweep Algorithm uses an ordering function initially to form partial clusters of locations around each terminal. Clusters are then built up by inserting unassigned locations, one at a time, into the partially formed clusters. The algorithm takes into consideration the distance between clusters by minimizing, for each location, the extra distance a vehicle would have to travel to include that location in the cluster about the selected terminal. If j is a location to be considered for assignment, the algorithm determines the unassigned location k which is nearest to it. An estimate of the extra distance required to assign both locations j and k to each of the two nearest clusters is then calculated. If the terminal with the minimum insertion distance for j alone also has the smallest estimated insertion distance for the two points, then j is assigned to that terminal. Otherwise, the assignment of location j is deferred until after location k has again been considered for assignment. During this cluster forming process, the distance constraint must be checked so that no location will be assigned to a terminal too distant to serve it.

After all locations have initially been assigned to terminals, each terminal acts as an attracting terminal which attempts to draw locations away from adjacent terminals. Locations on the periphery between the attracting terminal and an adjacent terminal are declared unassigned and the cluster forming process begins again. After the assignment procedure is completed, two single-terminal vehicle-dispatch problems are solved. If an overall improved solu-

Table 4. List of problems.

Prob No.	Source	No. of Term	No. of Demand Pt.	Max Load	Max Dist
1	[2]	4	50	80	Unlim
2	[2]	4	50	160	Unlim
3	[2]	5	75	140	Unlim
4	[2]	2	100	100	Unlim
5	[2]	2	100	200	Unlim
6	[2]	3	100	100	Unlim
7	[2]	4	100	100	Unlim
8	[5]	2	249	500	310
9	[5]	3	249	500	310
10	[5]	4	249	500	310
11	[5]	5	249	500	310

Table 5. Solutions obtained by the multi-terminal sweep algorithm.

Prob. No.	Aver No. of Loc/ RT (a)	No. Iter (b)	Sol.	CPU Sec. IBM 370/168
1	5.17	1	593.16	9.34
2	9.33	12	486.19	13.23
3	7.82	24	652.38	20.43
4	7.19	8	1066.65	51.24
5	13.50	10	778.87	227.67
6	7.25	21	912.22	53.05
7	7.25	25	939.45	52.48
8	10.58	17	4832.03	457.61
9	10.58	26	4219.69	444.33
10	10.58	41	3821.98	344.04
11	10.22	48	3754.14	306.85

(a) Includes terminal.
(b) The initial solution and any refinement which utilized the Sweep Algorithm count as an iteration.

tion results, the change becomes part of the current best solution, and this becomes the basis for further refinement.

This process is then repeated for each terminal which is adjacent to the attracting terminal. The solution which results after all terminals have served as attracting terminals is a near-optimal solution.

The Multi-terminal Sweep Algorithm is capable of solving problems with many terminals and hundreds of locations in a reasonable amount of computer time. In fact, for large problems with relatively constant average number of locations per route and total number of locations, the computation time usually decreases as the number of terminals increase from two. The computation time increases quadratically with the average number of locations per route as long as the other parameters remain constant. In addition, if the number of terminals and the average number of locations per route remain constant, the computation time increases in proportion to the square of the total number of locations. In view of these comments, the Multi-terminal Sweep Algorithm is ideally suited for large problems with many terminals and a small number of locations per route.

30.5. Applications of the Sweep Algorithm

Buddhiraju and Viswanathan [1] modified the original Sweep Algorithm to solve several problems related to the transportation of checks and paper for the Federal Reserve Bank of Philadelphia. Their algorithm differs from the Sweep Algorithm in the rule used to include a new location in an existing route, in the rule used to exchange locations between consecutive routes, and in the rule used to choose starting points for renumbering locations. It appears from the limited amount of data presented that their algorithm gave results almost as good as the Sweep Algorithm in much less time.

Robbins and Turner [11] used a modified version of the Sweep Algorithm to manually route school buses in a rural environment. They reported a savings of 15.3 percent over existing routes.

Russell [12] used a modified version to route trucks for industrial refuse collection. His algorithm reduced the travel time approximately two hours for each truck. He basically approximated many route distances without solving traveling salesman problems each time a location was reassigned to a new route and also eliminated half of the sweeps which the Sweep Algorithm executes. He reported results that were about the same but were obtained in only one-half to one-tenth of the time taken by the Sweep Algorithm.

30.6. Future directions in vehicle dispatching

Efficient algorithms by Gillett and Johnson [6] in 1974 and by Golden, Magnanti and Nguyen [8] in 1975 are capable of giving good solutions to many fairly large (up to 1000 locations) multi-terminal, single product problems. Golden et al. [8] indicate that their algorithm obtains results comparable to the results of Gillett and Johnson [6] and is considerably faster. This is generally true since they use data structuring features in their computer code. Although Golden et al. [8] reported solving a 600 location problem with two terminals, it appears that their algorithm, which is based on the savings approach of Clark and Wright [3] is dependent on the number of terminals used, both computer time wise and storage wise. This is not the case with the Sweep Algorithm. On the other hand, the Golden et al. [8] algorithm is not highly dependent on the average number of locations per route as is the Sweep Algorithm.

It appears that the efforts to solve large-scale multi-terminal problems should concentrate on combining sequential clustering of locations with the best features of the Modified Sweep Algorithm, the Golden et al. [8] algorithm and the approaches used by Russell [12] and Buddhiraju and Viswanathan [1].

References

1. Buddhiraju, K. and Viswanathan, P., 'A Heuristic Approach for Vehicle Dispatching with Some Side Conditions', ORSA/TIMS National Meeting, Las Vegas (Fall 1975).
2. Christofides, N. and Eilon, S., 'An Algorithm for the Vehicle-Dispatch Problem', *Operational Research Quarterly*, vol. 20 (1969), pp. 309–318.
3. Clark, G. and Wright, J. W., 'Scheduling of Vehicles from a Central Depot to a Number of Delivery Points', *Operations Research*, vol. 11 (1963), pp. 568–581.
4. Gaskell, T. J., 'Bases for Vehicle Fleet Scheduling', *Operational Research Quarterly*, vol. 18 (1967), pp. 281–295.
5. Gillett, B. E. and Miller, L. E., 'A Heuristic Algorithm for the Venicle-Dispatch Problem, *Operations Research*, vol. 22, (1974), pp. 340–349.
6. Gillett, B. E. and Johnson, J. G., 'Sweep Algorithm for the Multiple Depot Vehicle-

Dispatch Problem', ORSA/TIMS National Meeting, San Juan, Puerto Rico (Fall 1974)
7. Gillett, B. E. and Johnson, J. G., 'Multi-Terminal Vehicle Dispatch Algorithm', *OMEGA, The International Journal of Management Science*, vol. 4, no. 6 (November–December 1976).
8. Golden, B. L., Magnanti, T. L., and Ngyuen, H. Q., 'Implementing Vehicle Routing Algorithms', Tech. Report no. 115, Operations Research Center, MIT (1975).
9. Lin, Shen, 'Computer Solutions for the Traveling Salesman Problem', Bell Systems Tech. Journal, vol. 44 (1965); pp. 2245–2269.
10. Lin, Shen and Kernighan, B. W., 'A Heuristic Algorithm for the Traveling Salesman Problem', Computer Science Tech. Report no. 1, Bell Labs., (1972).
11. Robbins, J. A. and Turner, W. C., 'A Manual Method for Routing School Buses', ORSA/TIMS National Meeting, Las Vegas (Fall 1975).
12. Russell, Robert A., 'Efficient Truck Routing of Industrial Refuse Collection', ORSA/TIMS National Meeting, San Juan, Puerto Rico (Fall 1974).

Section 8. Defense and public policy

31. | Navy enlisted manpower planning

ABDUL W. HAMMOOD and ROBERT K. LEHTO

Abstract

The Advancement, Strength and Training Planning (ADSTAP) system has been introduced, to coordinate and to develop Navy enlisted planning and research for force analysis and management. Some of its objectives and modes are described.

An important characteristic of this system is that it seeks to be both an operational research system and an integral part of management (i.e. Authorization Management). The argument of this dual role is based upon the experience of Bureau of Naval Personnel.

31.1. Introduction

The general objective of this paper is to present an overview of the practical as well as the theoretical levels of disaggregation which characterize the Navy enlisted force management system. The scope of the paper includes an examination of the development of computer-based models and the integrated methodology for applying these models to the Navy manpower planning management system. ADSTAP (or Advancement, Strength and Training Planning System) has the operational capability for both regular planning processes and special analyses. Ideally, ADSTAP should accommodate most organizational changes and personnel plans as they result from uncertain future goals and constraints in addition to supporting development of management policies, in the Navy's long range goal setting, policy analysis and economic planning for enlisted personnel.

31.2. History

It was argued at length in an earlier paper by Smith [23], [24] that manpower planning is a necessary element of any personnel management system. Without it, for instance, there is great risk of imbalance in resources and abortive expenditure. In fact, the general aim is to minimize the risk of either surplus or shortage; since any imbalance between manpower and other resources will involve waste; that planning should aim to avoid both numerical and qualitative imbalance. In addition, the basic planning task is to forecast the manpower likely to be needed, forecast the numbers likely to be available, and take action to increase the likelihood that supply and demand is in balance. The literature of manpower and personnel modelling which is directly related to the current system (known as ADSTAP) is not lacking in either techniques or applications which address problems of manpower planning management [1], [2], [3], [9], [19], [13], [20].

In the following sections examples will be given of 'micro-scale approach' planning models in a very satisfactory level of disaggregation.

Before turning to these models, however, it is probably worthwhile to repeat one of the conclusions which may be drawn from the Bureau of Naval Personnel experience; and that is both the solution to any specific short-range management problems and the carrying out of research aimed at less specific long-range forecasting. In fact, the level of disaggregation of the present ADSTAP System is quite efficient both mathematically and conceptually, and hence can become a part of the Manpower Personnel management system, and be assigned line-management responsibilities (i.e. Authorization Management). In short Navy Personnel experience suggests that there is a considerable benefit to having this level of disaggregation both in research and in line-management. Such a dual role certainly will provide the decision maker with the best possible information.

31.3. Structure of enlisted force management: ADSTAP system

The ADSTAP system functionally integrates the objectives of enlisted personnel strength, training, and advancement planning. In its final form, this system would enable personnel managers to accomodate rapidly to modifications in requirements, to identify significant problem areas, and to test alternative enlisted plans and policies prior to their establishment. The present form of ADSTAP would also provide the capability to generate relatively accurate projections of personnel strength for long-range planning purposes such as budget forecasting or policy planning. Although the ADSTAP system is a fairly complex arrangement of massive data files and varied computer programs tied together in detailed interrelationships, the basic structure of the system is relatively straightforward, consisting of three essential components: (1) planning data base, (2) projection model, and (3) planning programs and models. These components operate in a series of input-output relationships reflecting the process of enlisted personnel planning. For instance, the Planning Data base provides input to the Projection Model in the form of starting inventories and rates of change. The Projection Model acts on these inventories by calculating the major input-output flows in the personnel system, and producing a projection of the enlisted force, by size and composition, at specified times in the future. This output then becomes input for programs which produce plans for career development, enlisted advancement, strength management, training input, and personnel policy evaluation. The execution of such plans triggers recruitment, promotion, separation, and training actions throughout the system. These actions are consequently recorded by the personnel system and become new input for the data base.

The foundation is the Planning Data Base which contains both historic and current data. An historical Change Data Bank furnishes the raw material not only for the development of ADSTAP models and programs, but also for the development of rates of change which are applied in the Projection Model to predict variables affecting the force structure – such as attrition, retirement, and demotions. Inventory Files extracted from the most recent Enlisted Master Tape provide the starting personnel inventory for the Projection Model. These are tabulated for each rating in a pay grade and length of service table. Other data files such as the Advancement Exam Data Bank furnishes historical test taker and passer information. From this, rates are developed for the purpose of predicting advancement eligibles in the Projection Model for each rating and pay grade.

Another component, the Projection Model, calculates the major input-output flows in the personnel system to produce projections of the enlisted force by size and composition at specified times in the future – typically, at the end of a fiscal year. Gains and losses are computed and applied to each rating population. The resulting vacancies are then used to compute the advancements necessary to meet requirements. An output routine in the Projection Model processes this data for subsequent input to various computer programs used to assist in the development of specific plans.

During the year 1972–1973, the Enlisted Force Management Program was operating in a management environment in transition from manual to computerized operation, utilizing non-integrated models in various stages from development to fully operational [5]. The vehicle for the integration is called MAD (Monitored ADSTAP System). The objective of the MAD system is to provide a flexible tool for use of personnel planners such that a heuristic planning process can become a reality. Finally, the ADSTAP System has essentially three modes of operations, the development of quantified plans, or implementing directives, which provide the guidance within which the remainder of the personnel system operates, the development of career management goals to guide policy, and the performance of policy analysis.

During FY73, goal specification and goal setting for the enlisted force were introduced. The essential elements of goal setting entail the specification of some idealized distribution of the force along specified dimensions and the demonstration that such an idealized distribution is, by some measure, better than the force which will result from current 'free-flow' policies.

The Navy has developed a specification of an 'ideal' force along the dimensions of rating, pay grade, and length of service using a static or stable force model [2].

31.4. Billet Cost Model

The development and the use of the military personnel Billet Cost Model for the Navy has been a continuing effort for almost a decade. Substantial data gathering and statistical analysis were required to determine the manpower resource costs on the basis of the characteristics of Navy personnel. The Billet Cost Model is a mathematical model which includes Navy manpower costs from initial recruitment to develop a set of computer programs. Based on these programs, analysis determined the cost of obtaining a man in an aggregate form. These models were further extended to determine personnel life-cycle billet costs. Analyses of the costs were performed within the guide lines of the Navy enlisted manpower requirements and other constraints. In meeting these requirements for life-cycle costs, the manpower process is viewed as a dynamic one, moving through procurement, training, reenlistment, to retirement, death or other attrition factors. In essence, this cost model views each rating as a flow of men through a pipeline which is divided into year-long intervals with all costs incurred by the rating in each interval being observed. In fact, the cost that is developed by the model results in an 'operational billet cost per year' for all except E-1 enlisted billets.

The main feature of the Billet Cost Model is that the distribution of the cost is flexible with respect to the length of service, ratings and paygrades. For instance, a hypothetical rating or group of ratings can be created and the statistical profile of its cost presented. In particular, the current cost estimates for the average enlisted man include base pay, hazard pay, constant cost, training cost, retirement contributions among other things. Finally, all of these elements can be estimated using different discount rates [4].

31.5. Per Capita Model

The Per Capita Costing Management Subsystem is designed to compute the average cost of an average enlistee in a given rating for each grade and each length of service, and is used to determine the impact of policy on the cost of maintaining a specified force distribution. The model works as an integrated part of the ADSTAP system so that the cost impact on planning decisions may be evaluated concurrently with the impact of strength (rating structure).

The cost data base of the PCM Subsystem utilizes cost parameters that can be defined into two basic groupings as follows:

1. General costs (base personnel costs)
   - Base pay and hazardous duty pay

  - Costs that apply to all personnel regardless of grade or rating and are best defined as general proratable costs in each year of service.
  - Costs that differ by grade regardless of rating that apply only when the grade is achieved.
2. Specific rating related costs.
  - Costs that apply to a particular rating and are best defined as occurring in particular years of service.
  - Costs that can be defined by grade and depend only on when the grade is achieved.

The statistical data used in conjunction with the cost elements are extracted from the various subsystems of the ADSTAP system.

The Per Capita Costing subsystem is embedded within the ADSTAP system so that policy and planning decisions impacting on the strength structure of a rating also change the statistical profile that is used to determine the annual cost. Accordingly, a realistic cost appraisal of policy and planning changes can be made before implementation in the active force.

Recently, the statistics of the billet cost model have been updated and a new probabilistic model derived from the actual continuation rate for each rating has been introduced. The model has the capability of redistributing the training cost over the length of service for the average enlisted man, thus serving as a planning guideline for effective and accurate cost allocation in the area of training.

31.6. The Ideal Force Model

The Ideal Force Model is an equilibrium or steady-state inventory model which operates iteratively under control of a goal directed search routine. Some of these goals and objectives are (1) the size of the total inventory of the Navy, (2) the size of the proportion of the TOPSIX relative to all Navy, (3) the distribution of personnel within each skill group (rating and paygrades). These three goal statements, among others, are basically derived from the Enlisted Requirements Plan as modified by the End Strength authorizations for specified years. To satisfy these goals and objectives, the model employs several parameters (e.g. continuance rates, advancement parameters, promotions zone, careerists proportions) jointly or otherwise [11], [12].

31.7. Clustering methodology for rating management

A key factor in the Navy Enlisted Force Management System (ADSTAP) is the integration of goals implementation. The desired force composition (goal development) results from the process of the ideal force development. Ideally, the quantified specification of an objective force distribution is insufficient, however, for a complete control of the system. The policies necessary to shape the force distribution toward the desired goals must also be developed and implemented. Successful implementation is totally dependent on feasibility testing using the simulation models of the ADSTAP system. The principal information available for shaping the ideal force distribution is: loss management, accession control, expanding and contracting training pipelines, controlling advancement flows, and application of bonuses.

A number of clustering methodologies for grouping ratings into logical categories have been developed for the Navy. Several of these clustering schemes have been investigated, one of the most likely being the medical syndrone structure for use in the operational system.

In this case, similar individual ratings are clustered based on the direction and magnitude of the deviation from a given norm (the objective rating distribution). On the basis of current experience, it is expected that such clustering will reduce the number of policy sets required, perhaps to ten or twelve. At present the Navy has some 100 broad skills and therefore 100 policy sets. Thus far the model has not succeeded in clustering these skills into categories based upon common characteristics and requisite policies [25].

31.8. Optimization Model overview

The development of the enlisted force optimization methodology discussed in this section will be very brief. The models were developed to enable the Bureau of Naval Personnel to define long-range management goals for each major Navy personnel category. Specifically, these goals are defined in terms of an objective optimum force distribution with respect to skill, length of service and pay grade. The objective functions (conceptually) were formulated in such a way that the cost per utile per man-year is minimum in a fully normative sense. In addition, many functional evaluations were performed through the use of four major models: the per capita cost model, the stable strength model, the utility model and the reenlistment elasticity model. In building these models and performing the research, several problem areas have been uncovered. In this section, key issues will be reviewed and more practical assessments will be briefly discussed.

The block diagram of the optimization methodology, shown in Figure 1, depicts the relationship between its major components:

1. Steady State Inventory Model
2. Per Capita Cost Model
3. Utility Model
4. Reenlistment Elasticity Model
5. Optimization Algorithm

Prior to its inclusion as part of the optimization methodology, each model was designed to be implemented as a stand-alone policy evaluation tool [5], [7], [10].

An explanation of the function of each model follows.

The *Steady State Inventory Projection Model* calculates the inventory distribution which will be attained at equilibrium as a function of the number of jobs to be done, the expected continuance behavior, advancement parameters, and the input service contract mix. Outputs include begin inventory, losses, net inventory and advancements.

The *Per Capita Cost Model* computes the economic costs (including retirement costs) of personnel by rating, paygrade and LOS as a function of force parameters developed by the inventory projection models. The per capita costs are the monies that are being, or will be, expended on an average man in all grades and in all years of service for all general ratings and apprenticeships.

The *Utility Model* is a function which expresses quantitatively on a

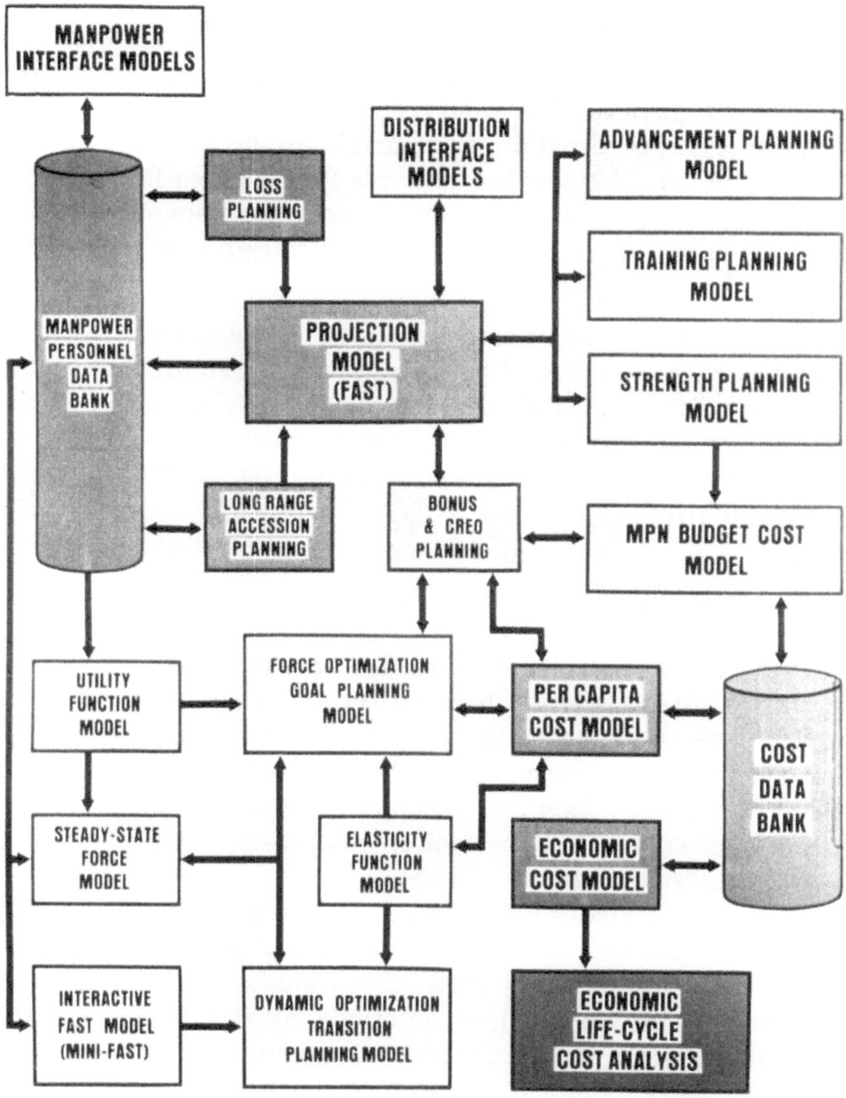

Figure 1. Enlisted force management system: ADSTAP.

scale of numerical value from 0 to 100 the accrual of value to the Navy of the average enlisted man serving at a given paygrade and LOS [17].

The *Reenlistment Elasticity Model* estimates the cost to the Navy of changing the prevailing reenlistment rates of the enlisted force. The

Elasticity Model was developed in recognition of the fact that changes in continuance or reenlistment behavior of the enlisted personnel are not free. One would expect that an attempt to increase reenlistments would require some action on the part of the Navy, for example, increases in the Selective Reenlistment Bonus. Costs also would be taken into account in considering means of decreasing the propensity of enlisted men in certain categories to continue in service.

The last of the five major components, the *Optimization Algorithm*, searches over the range of policy variables for enlisted personnel inventory distributions for the purpose of satisfying personnel and cost constraints with the least cost per unit per man-utile. Presently a variable metric algorithm of the Davidon-Fletcher-Powell type is being employed [10].

31.9. Force Analysis Simulation Technique

Administrative systems with multiple externalities pose special problems for managers. Characteristically, such systems operate under uncertain organizational conditions and are influenced in irregular ways by external social [6] and economic [18] factors. Because of these influences, the operative goals of the system tend to be more variable than constant. In many ways, the Navy's enlisted personnel system is a case in point.

The model called FAST, described briefly in this paper, has structural aspects which in some ways parallel personnel models of the stochastic variety [14]. FAST also contains features amenable to many of the applications described by the Navy's enlisted personnel system which classifies all personnel into some 100 occupational skills known as ratings, 31 length-of-service categories representing years of service, and 9 pay grades which establish a hierarchy of skills.

The behavior of the enlisted personnel system is also characterized by flows to and from the force structure. The most important in this system is the requirement for manpower. Periodically, the military authority issues an official specification, sometimes with sudden changes, of its manpower requirement; according to needs by grades and ratings. As a result of this and other limitations, the Navy must be able to adjust its current requirements. With or without adjustment, the statement of manpower needs for each rating and grade constitute the goals of the personnel system. The personnel force structure at some point represents the initial condition. Then, the flow of personnel into, through, and out of the active duty force represents the attempt by personnel management to achieve the goals. Of course, the entire process occurs within the limits of budget, administrative rules, availability of resources and other constraints.

A comprehensive formulation of the structure of the FAST Model at a very detailed level of disaggregation is given by Silverman [21]. Although the initial versions of the FAST model were introduced and used experimentally in the Bureau of Naval Personnel as early as 1970, the operational version of the model in regular planning and analysis was not implemented until 1975. As noted above, the model became the focus of a fairly elaborate computer-based planning system known as ADSTAP. Figure 1 shows the major component and linkage of the ADSTAP system in its current form, and its relationship to FAST. Typically, the FAST Model is set up for periodical planning runs by introducing a set of goals and constraints as well as modifications to a case line forecast. Given an input, the modifications and run parameters, the FAST model will deliver an extensive array of planning data. The output can be retrieved in terms of various expectations and on several levels of management.

31.10. Concluding remarks

In summary, the ADSTAP System will eventually stand or fall depending on its truth as an important idealization of actual manpower planning systems, or as a set of models with values of fair distributions of efficient cost allocation and of utilization of resources. As a normative system (to describe what ought to be) we find great merit in its disaggregation features (Schumacher's popular book, *Small is Beautiful* [16], Danies [7] and Grisnold [9] express some of our sentiments on disaggregation). In fact, these features can be seen and understood especially clearly due to the 'micro-scale' approach of the ADSTAP System, and one can use this approach as a tool in developing alternative models. To us it would seem overly difficult to construct and communicate successfully any alternate without having first studied very thoroughly the failings in the aggregation theory which are well-presented in recent economic literature [15], [22]. Also, we would like to give reasons why we feel that the disaggregation approach of the ADSTAP System is very satisfactory in working on cost/benefit analysis, optimum force management, and refinement of management indicators. Recognizing that the specification of true manpower requirements, the needs of the individuals, the need of the Navy, and the budgetary constraints may separately indicate policies which are at cross purposes, the challenge is to determine the mix of policy which reaches a desirable compromise between these countervailing components.

References

1. Bartholomew, D. J., *Models for Social Processes* (New York: Wiley, 1967).
2. Bartholomew, D. J., 'The Statistical Approach to Manpower Planning', *Statistician*, vol. 20 (1971), pp. 3–26.
3. Bartholomew, D. J., Hopes, R. F. A., and Smith, A. R., 'Manpower Planning' in the Face of Uncertainty', *Personnel Review*, vol. 5 (1976), pp. 5–17.
4. B-K Dynamics, Inc., 'Billet Cost Model: Users Manual, TR-3-159' (September 1970). 1970).
5. Clark, R. W., 'Computerized Assisted Management of a Personnel Planning System, MAD (Monitored ADSTAP System)', Washington, D.C.: Bureau of Naval Personnel (June 1972).
6. Conrath, D. W., 'Organization Decision Making Behavior under Varying Conditions of Uncertainty', *Management Science*, vol. 13, no. 8 (April 1967), pp. 487–500.
7. Davies, G. S., 'Structural Control in a Gradual Manpower System', *Management Science*, vol. 20, no. 1 (1973), pp. 76–84.
8. Gani, J., 'Formulae for Projecting Enrollments and Degrees Awarded in Universities', *Journal of the Royal Statistical Society*, Series A, vol. 126 (1963), pp. 400–409.
9. Grinold, R. I., 'Manpower Planning with Uncertain Requirements', *Operations Research*, vol. 24, no. 3 (May–June 1976), pp. 387–399.
10. Hovey, Richard K. and Schmid, J. R., 'Utility Theory and Optimization in Military Personnel Management, TR-3-138', B-K Dynamics, Inc. (15 January 1975).
11. Lehto, R. K., 'Enlisted Personnel Planning through Computerized Integrated Systems', Paper presented to ONR-Naval Postgraduate School Conference on Manpower Planning and Personnel Management, Washington, D.C. (April 1972).
12. Lehto, R. K., 'STAPLAN Guide', Washington, D.C.: Bureau of Naval Personnel (1966).
13. Linsert, H., 'The Navy Rating Structure and the Self Renewing Occupational Field (SROP) Concept: An Analysis', Washington, D.C.: Naval Personnel Research and Development Laboratory (1970).
14. Marshall, K. T., 'A Comparison of Two Personnel Prediction Models', *Operations Research*, vol. 21, no. 3 (May–June 1973), pp. 810–822.
15. Mills, E. S., 'An Aggregation Model of Resource Allocation in a Metropolitan Area', *American Economic Review*, vol. 57, no. 2 (1967).

16. Schumacher, E. F., *Small is Beautiful: Economics as if People Mattered* (New York: Harper and Row, 1973).
17. Schmid, J. R., 'Development of a Utility Measure for Manpower Planning, TR-3-177', B-K Dynamics (28 February 1973).
18. Shackle, G. L. S., *The Nature of Economic Thought* (London: Cambridge University Press, 1966).
19. Silverman, J., 'Operations Guide for the ADSTAP System: An Integrated Computerized Enlisted Personnel Planning System', San Diego: Naval Personnel Training Research Laboratory (October 1970).
20. Silverman, J., 'New Concepts in Enlisted Personnel Planning. Introduction to the ADSTAP System, SRR 71-28', San Diego: Naval Personnel and Training Research Laboratory (May 1971).
21. Silverman, J., Boller, R. L., Offir, J., and Lehto, R. K., 'Design and Use of a Force Structure Simulation Model', San Diego: Naval Personnel and Training Research Laboratory.
22. Smale, S., "Global Analysis and Economics IIA', *Journal of Mathematical Economics*, vol. 1 (1974), pp. 1–14.
23. Smith, A. R., 'Defense Manpower Studies', *Operational Research Quarterly*, vol. 19, no. 3 (1966).
24. Smith, A. R., 'Manpower Planning in the Management of the Royal Navy', *Journal of Management Studies*, vol. 4 (1967), p. 124.
25. Spencer, W. Franklin, 'The Application of Clustering Techniques to Enlisted Force Management, TR-3-199', B-K Dynamics, Inc. (July 1975).

32. A public policy optimization model with simulation of disaggregation aspects: formulation of energy R and D policy

WILPEN L. GORR

Abstract[1]

In the public sector, aggregate policy makers often lose control over disaggregate solutions which are the result of bargaining by competing interests. The problem of this paper is to optimize policy (selection of product type and levels, resource type and levels, production technologies etc.) in a multiple objective framework where disaggregation (resource allocation in the aggregate framework) is viewed as a chance event. A general formulation is provided in which the practical approach through policy 'scenarios' is established. Scenario design and selection is carried out in a man-machine process aided by a simulation and a goal programming model. Specific models are developed and illustrated for industrial fuels policy by a state-level ERDA.

32.1 Introduction

Krajewski and Ritzman [16] have recently drawn attention to the 'disaggregation' problem in production and the service industries: '... an intermediate step between aggregate planning at the top level and the more detailed decision areas of inventory control and scheduling at the bottom level ... [with] a sequential or top-down approach to problem solving.' This paper provides a general framework for the public sector counterpart where public officials design aggregate policy which is later disaggregated by other individuals or organizations in multiobjective bargaining settings (de Neufville and Marks [7] or other forums such as 'science court' (Hammond and Adelman [14].

1. This research was supported in part by a Deans' Research Professorship from the Ohio State University, College of Administrative Science.

In the stage 1 aggregate problem, officials are to optimally choose product types, production technologies, resource supply types and levels etc. for several facilities from the 'policy space' of feasible alternatives. A specific policy results in a 'solution space' of alternative disaggregations that is viewed as deterministic in stage 2, but as a sample space of experimental outcomes during the stage 1 decision process.

Section 2 develops the general optimization framework for the stage 1 problem with linkages established to stage 2 via simulation of the disaggregation process, which in this case has a transportation model structure. In Section 3, specific models are developed and illustrated (from materials related to [22] for a state-level energy R and D policy problem on industrial fuels. Finally, Section 4 suggests future work.

32.2. General formulation

32.2.1. Mixed integer policy space

The disaggregation problem of this paper has a constraint set with transportation model structure. There are m types of substitutable production rescources measured in a common unit (e.g. MMBTU/hour of input fuel) to be allocated to n production facilities. At most S_i units of resource i are available and facility j requires at least D_i units of resources. The S_i and D_j are fixed (in part by aggregate policy) in reference to a stated time interval.

The mathematical description of the transportation type constraints is

$$\sum_{j=1}^{n} x_{ij} \leqq S_i \quad \text{for } i = 1, \dots, m \text{ (supply)} \tag{1}$$

$$\sum_{i=1}^{m} -x_{ij} \leqq -D_j \quad \text{for } j = 1, \dots, n \text{ (demand)} \tag{2}$$

$$x_{ij} \leqq 0 \quad \text{for all } i \text{ and } j. \tag{3}$$

Associated notation is

$A = \{a_{i'j'}\}$, an $(m + n)$ x $(m \cdot n)$ matrix of transportation technological coefficients

$$a_{i'j'} = \begin{cases} 1 & \text{for } i' = 1, \ldots, m \\ & \quad j' = (i'-1)n+1, (i'-1)n+2, \ldots, i'n \\ -1 & \text{for } i' = m+1, \ldots, m+n \\ & \quad j' = i'-m, i'-m+n, \ldots, i'-m+ \\ & \qquad +(m-1)n \\ 0 & \text{otherwise} \end{cases}$$

$$X' = [x'_1, x'_2, \ldots, x'_{j'}, \ldots, x'_{m \cdot n}]$$

$$x'_{(i-1)n+j} = x_{ij}$$

$$b' = [s_1, s_2, \ldots, s_m; -D_1, -D_2, \ldots, -D_n)$$

so that constraints (1) and (2) can be written as $AX < b$. (Note that here and hereafter, primes are deleted from variables where the context allows without confusion.)

In the stage 1 aggregate problem, officials determine policy by choosing the dimensions of A and b and by calculating values for A and b. Policy defines a collection of disaggregate solutions,

$$\underline{\bar{X}} = \{(x_1, \ldots, x_{m \cdot n}) \mid AX < b\},$$

that is viewed as a sample space with joint p.d.f. $p_{\bar{X}}(x_1, \ldots, x_{m \cdot n})$ during stage 1 and as a deterministic solution space during stage 2 disaggregation. Stage 1 multiple goals are denoted as:

Aggregate $U_k = f_k(A, b)$ for $k = 1, \ldots, p$

Disaggregate $v_l = g_l(x_1, \ldots, x_{m \cdot n})$ for $l = 1, \ldots, q$.

In this paper 'acceptable intervals' are stated for disaggregate goals via known bounds $v_l^0 \leqq V_l \leqq v_l^1$ so that the probability of acceptance at the disaggregate stage is calculated from $p_{\underline{\bar{X}}}$ as

$$P_{\underline{\bar{X}}}(v_1^0 \leqq V_1 \leqq v_1^1, \ldots, v_q^0 \leqq V_q \leqq v_q^1).$$

Futhermore, bounds b^0 and b^1 are stated for b and deterministic 'mock-x variables,' $y_{j'}$, are defined analogous to the $x_{j'}$ variables in an $(m+n)$-vector Y. The stage 1 program is now written as:

Program (I) – Policy Design

Calculate A (technologies), b (resources and demands), and Y to

$$\text{maximize } U_1, \ldots, U_p, P_{\underline{X}}(v_1^0 \leqq V_1 \leqq v_1^1, \ldots, v_q^0 \leqq V_q \leqq v_q^1) \tag{4}$$

subject to

$$AY - b \leqq 0 \tag{5}$$

$$-b \leqq -b^0 \tag{6}$$

$$b \leqq b^1 \tag{7}$$

$$a_{i'j'} = \begin{cases} 0,1 & \text{for } i' = 1, \ldots, m \\ & \quad j' = (i'-1)n+1, (i'-1)n+2, \ldots, i'n \\ 0,1 & \text{for } i' = m+1, \ldots, m+n \\ & \quad j' = i'-m, i'-m+n, \ldots, i'-m+ \\ & \qquad + (m-1)n \\ 0 & \text{otherwise} \end{cases} \tag{8}$$

$$b_{i'} \geqq 0 \quad i' = 1, \ldots, m+n \tag{9}$$

$$y_{j'} \geqq 0 \quad j' = 1, \ldots, m \cdot n \tag{10}$$

The set of feasible values for constraints (5) through (10) is termed the 'policy space,' which is of a mixed integer nature in this section. The optimal solution to program (I) is denoted (A^*, b^*) and this leads to a non-empty solution space $\underline{\bar{X}}$ for stage 2 due to nonlinear constraint set (5).

Program (I) is a compact statement of the stage 1 policy design problem; however, this program is not computationally solvable as stated due to nonlinearities and nonconvexities in (5), and inability to theoretically determine $P_{\underline{\bar{X}}}$. Section 2.2 provides a solvable program by restricting attention to a finite number of points or 'scenarios' from the policy space. Program (I) does bear some resemblance to stochastic programs such as studied by Sengupta et al. [23]; however, one notable exception is that the V_l random variables are not generally statistically independent. This is because they are defined over the space $\underline{\bar{X}}$ which highlights a 'finite resources' philosophy: even though x_{ij} allocations are random, only fixed S_i units of resource are available. With allocation viewed as a sequential process, this implies that the probability of an i, j pairing conditionally depends on previous allocations (e.g., is any resource i yet available?). In fact, the only readily available means to evaluate $P_{\underline{X}}$ is via simulation of the allocation process as illustrated in the next section.

32.2.2. Discrete policy space

'Scenarios' are a set of feasible solutions to Program (I):

$$(A^s, b^s) \quad s = 1, \ldots, r$$

determined exogenously by expert opinion, output of economic equilibrium models, technological forecasting, etc. in combina-

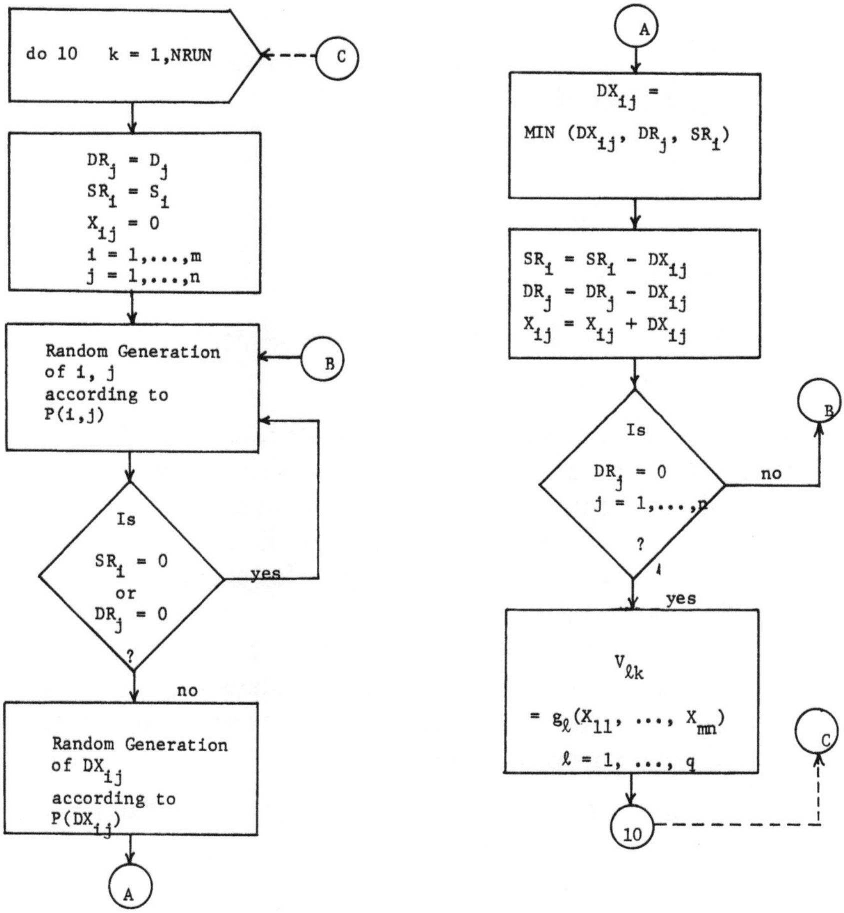

Figure 1. Subroutine for sampling multiple objectives over sample space X.

tion with heuristic procedures such as the goal programming model, program (II). Scenario (A^s, b^s) yields sample space $\underline{\bar{X}}^s$. Figure 1 is a flow chart for a simulation to determine $P_{\underline{\bar{X}}}$. Subjective probabilities of i, j matches and X_{ij} allocations are used to simulate the process of allocation within $\underline{\bar{X}}^s$. Limited experimental results show reasonable convergence in marginal distributions of $P_{\underline{\bar{X}}}$ for 1000 runs.

Of importance to the current energy/environmental policy problems is to choose policies that are acceptable for disaggregation. Goal programming (Charnes and Cooper [3]) has proven to be a useful approach (Gorr [10], Massey et al. [14], and Gorr [11] – all using the Chebyshev metric):

Program (II)

Calculate X, d^+, and d^-

$$\text{to minimize} \sum_{l=1}^{q} (w_l^+ d_l^+ + w_l^- d_l^-)$$

subject to

$$A^s X \leqq b^s$$

$$g_l(x_1, \ldots, x_{m \cdot n}) + d_l^- + d_l^+ = \hat{v}_l \quad l = 1, \ldots, q$$

$$x_{j'}, d_l^+, d_l^- \geqq 0$$

Here $\hat{v}_l \in [v_l^0, v_l^1]$ is a specified value. Note that interval goal programming (Charnes et al. [5]) is also a desirable approach here. Program (II) can be used in a man-machine mode by employing the dual variables for b^s to suggest policy modifications leading to a solution space with an acceptable region for stage 2. In the case study of Section 4, the duals are also used to suggest modifications in regulations on the disaggregation goals after it was judged that the other aspects of the policy space were exhausted. The counterpart of program (I) for the discrete policy space problem is merely a multiple objective decision problem:

Choose a scenario, (A^*, b^*), from $\{(A^s, b^s)\}s^r = 1$ that optimizes

$$U_1^s, \ldots, U_p^s, P_{\underline{\bar{X}}^s}(v_1^0 \leqq V_1 \leqq v_1^1, \ldots, v_q^0 \leqq V_1 \leqq N_q^1). \quad (11)$$

Any one of several approaches may be used, such as summarized by MacCrimmon [17].

32.3. Models for industrial fuels policy

Current energy policy models such as the Stanford PILOT model Dantzig and Parikh [6] and the Wisconsin WISE model Foell et al. [9]) interact the energy sector with other sectors in the economy and project aggregate energy supply and demand balances or shortfalls. They tend to make less contact, however, with disaggregation aspects of the policy problem which are, however, now dominating considerations. For example, the environmental acceptability of a given industrial fuels supply policy depends on fuel allocation patterns because of congestion phenomena of air pollution; thus, it is not wise to distribute dirty-burning fuels to centers of cities and clean fuels to outlying areas. Dunlap et al. [8] and Gorr [11] established that the air resource (for waste disposal) is sensitive to disaggregation on a scale of regions 10 km in radius.

Let $i = 1, \ldots, m$ be the set of fuel types under consideration and $j = 1, \ldots, n$ be the set of facilities assumed to be operating and using fuels. For a future point in time, we represent a fuel supply and demand scenario by vectors S and D where

$S_i =$ regional supply level of fuel i (MMBTU/hour)
$D_i =$ average fuel input demand of facility j (MMBTU/hour).

A subscript t may be added to follow a series of points of time, and this is a focus of Dantzig and Parikh [6]. An S and D scenario is disaggregated by fuel allocations:

$x_{ij} =$ fuel allocation of fuel i to facility j (MMBTU/hour).

Substitutability of fuel types and qualities is already common due to multiple-fuel firing boilers, multiple boilers of various fuel types at a facility, and relative ease of converting boilers. Impossible i, j combinations are assumed to have $x_{ij} = 0$; alternatively, policy may require new technology. Thus an S and D scenario gives rise to the transportation-like constraints of Section 2.1, $AX \leq b$, where $b = [S, D]$; and the solution space $\bar{X}$ of the disaggregate problem.

There is an extensive literature dealing with the disaggregation problem of fuel allocations, related resource allocations and environmental problems; e.g., Kohn [15], Gorr et al. [12], Massey et al. [18], Gorr [11], Panagitakopoulos [19], Hamlen and Hamlen [13], Reiquam [21], and Charnes et al. [4]. For the most part, this literature does not directly interact with the aggregate policy problem as formulated in this paper.

32.3.1. Goal programming model

Whereas much of the aggregate level assessment relates to price systems, the disaggregate assessment here is by a non-price system of performance measures and standards legislated by law. The Ohio Energy Research and Development Agency (OERDA) policy problem of industrial fuels is heavily constrained by SO_2 regulations and standards, and it is believed by many that no aggregate S and D-policy exists to satisfy these SO_2 requirements. Thus the goal programming approach of Section 2.2 including deviations from these requirements is especially suitable.

Fuel i is characterized by its pollution content (SO_2, total suspended particulates, or other pollutants)

c_i = pollution content of fuel type i (pounds pollutant/MMBTU),

so that air pollution emission rates can be estimated by:

$Q_j = \sum_i c_i x_{ij}$ = pollutant emission rate of facility j (pounds pollutant/hour),

and compared with emission regulations:

E_j = maximum allowable pollution content for facility j (pounds pollutant/MMBTU)

$E_j D_j$ = maximum allowable emission rate (pounds pollutant/hour).

Corresponding to each facility and averaging time (e.g. 24 hours or a year) there exist atmospheric diffusion coefficients relating Q_j to pollutant concentration at receptor point $k = 1, \ldots, n_k$:

u_{ijk} = diffusion coefficient relating fuel use i by facility j to receptor k ($\mu g/m^3$ pollutant ÷ MMBTU/hour)

$\sum_i c_i u_{ijk} x_{ij}$ = contribution of facility j to ambient pollutant concentration at k ($\mu g/m^3$ pollutant).

The u_{ijk} coefficients are calculated by standard atmospheric diffusion models. The influx of pollutant into a region is

B_k = background concentration of pollutant at receptor k

which can be estimated via 'background monitors' (see Carbone and Gorr [1]).

Thus ambient concentration, such as can be monitored at k, is estimated by

$$\sum_i \sum_j c_j u_{ijk} x_{ij} + B_k$$

and is regulated by federal law to be less than the national ambient air quality standard

δ_k = maximum allowable concentration of pollutant at receptor k for a stated averaging time ($\mu g/m^3$).

Now we can write the specific version of Program (II):

Program (IIa)

minimize

$$\sum_{j=1}^{n} w_{1j} d_{1j}^{+} + \sum_{k=1}^{n_k} w_{2k} d_{2k}^{+}$$

subject to

$$\sum_{j=1}^{n} x_{ij} \leqq S_i \quad i = 1, \ldots, m \tag{11}$$

$$\sum_{i=1}^{m} - x_{ij} \leqq -D_j \quad j = 1, \ldots, n \tag{12}$$

$$\sum_{i=1}^{m} \bar{c}_i x_{ij} + d_{1j}^{-} - d_{1j}^{+} = 100 \quad j = 1, \ldots, n \tag{13}$$

$$\sum_{i=1}^{m} \sum_{j=1}^{n} c_i \bar{u}_{ijk} x_{ij} + \bar{B}_k x_0 - d_{2k}^{-} - d_{2k}^{+} = 100 \tag{14}$$

$$k = 1, \ldots, n_k$$
$$x_0 = 1$$

$$x_{ij}, d_{1j}^{-}, d_{1j}^{+}, d_{2k}^{-}, d_{2k}^{+} \geqq 0 \tag{15}$$

where

$\bar{u}_{ijk} = 100\, u_{ijk}/\delta_k$
$\bar{B}_k = 100\, B_k/\delta_k$
$\bar{c}_i = 100\, c_i/E_j D_j$

Because of the normalized coefficients and right hand sides, deviational variables represent the percentage of violation (d^+) or overkill (d^-) of an emission regulation or air quality standard.

In model runs thus far 'equitable weights' have been used for deviations as follows:

$$w_{1j} = W_1 D_j / \sum_{i=1}^{m} D_j$$

$w_{2k} = W_2 \cdot$ geographic area of grid element k/total area in grid system

$W_1, W_2 =$ scale factors to differentially weight emissions versus air quality standards goals.

32.3.2. *Policy evaluation simulation*

Random variables based on the simulation as in Section 2.2 are defined as follows (where x_{ij} is a random variable and all other quantities on the right hand side are constants):

$$d_{2k}^+ = \max\{\sum_{i=1}^{m} \sum_{j=1}^{n} c_i \bar{u}_{ijk} x_{ij} + \bar{B}_k - 100, 0\}$$

$$d_{1j}^+ = \max\{\sum_{i=1}^{m} \bar{c}_i x_{ij} - 100, 0\}$$

$$V_1 = \sum_{j=1}^{n} w_{1j} d_{1j}^+ \tag{16}$$

$$V_2 = \sum_{k=1}^{n_k} w_{2k} d_{2k}^+ \tag{17}$$

To illustrate, Figure 2 contains the marginal distributions of V_2 for three simple S and D scenarios from a case study of Franklin County, Ohio [22]. These scenarios are based on data as follows:

$i = 1, 2$
$j = 1, 2, \ldots, 33$
$c_1 = 0 \quad c_2 = 5.5$ pounds SO_2/MMBTU
$\sum_{j=1}^{33} D_j = 3300$ MMBTU/hour

Scenario 1: $S_1 = 500$ MMBTU/hour, $\quad S_2 = \infty$

Scenario 2: $S_1 = 1500, \quad S_2 = \infty$

Scenario 3: $S_1 = 2000, \quad S_2 = \infty$

Fuel 1 is a sulfur-free fuel such as synthetic natural gas, and fuel 2 is a typical Ohio coal. All i, j matches were assumed to be equally likely, and the probability density functions for allocation size were assumed to be uniform over D_j. Figure 2 shows that an S and D scenario can be remarkably sensitive to disaggregation by the wide ranges of V_2. Also shown in this Figure are the corresponding optimal values of program (IIa) with V_2 being weighted preemptively over V_1. Note that the random variables (16) and (17) relate to chance constrained goal programming concepts independently being developed by Cooper and Karwan [20]. Here, how-

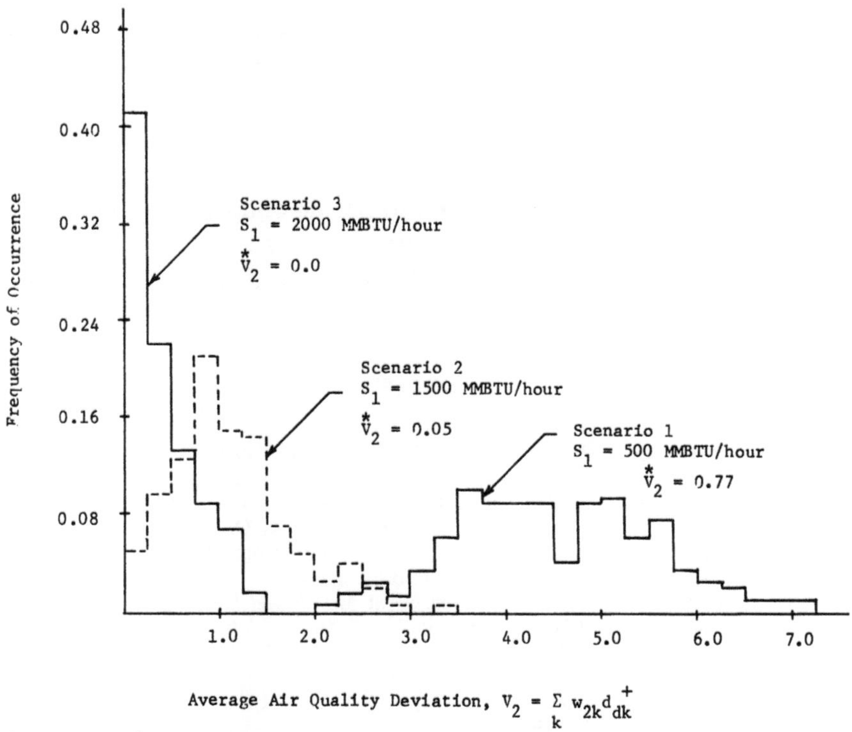

$^{+}$ Values for $\overset{*}{V}_2$ were calculated in program (II-a) with $W_1 = 1$, $W_2 = 50$. Also NRUN = 1000 and $\sum_j D_j = 3300$.

Figure 2. Sample distributions of goal V_2 for three scenarios .

ever, the 'decision variables' themselves are random variables with the technical coefficients and right hand sides being deterministic; whereas, the opposite is true in [20].

32.4. Future work

A forthcoming paper will relate an extensive case study using the concepts and models of this paper. Scenarios have been designed and evaluated with OERDA officials with implications on the desirability of redesigning air pollution regulations in Ohio. Part of a general policy problem is that regulatory agencies, such as the United States EPA or state-level EPA's, tend to attempt to design regulations in a closet. Many interests then do not get represented, including OERDA's, so that regulations are not optimal or acceptable. An open forum and bargaining process are required, such as suggested by Carbone et al. [2] for an equity versus efficiency problem.

One area requiring additional work at the policy level is in the selection of case studies and relation of results back to the total aggregate problem. For example, Ohio has 88 counties and OERDA has the possibility of maintaining detailed case studies of perhaps three counties for a test bed of policy vis-a-vis disaggregate effects. These counties must in some way span the variety of interest.

References

1. Carbone, R. and Gorr, W. L., 'Adaptive Forecasting of Background Concentrations Using Feedback Control and Pattern Recognition Techniques', in Ott, W. R., (ed.). *Environmental Modeling and Simulation*, (USEPA, EPA 600/9-76-016, 1976).
2. Carbone, R., Gorr, W. L., Gustafson, S., Kortanek, K. O., and Sweigart, J., 'A Bargaining Resolution of the Efficiency Versus Equity Conflict in Energy and Air Pollution Regulation', *Management Science* (forthcoming).
3. Charnes, A. and Cooper, W. W., *Management Models and Industrial Applications of Linear Programming*, vol. I (Wiley, 1961, pp. 215–223).
4. Charnes, A., Cooper, W. W., Harrold, J., Karwan, K. R., and Wallace, W. A., 'A Goal Interval Programming Model for Resource Allocation in a Marine Environmental Protection Program', Working Paper, School of Urban and Public Affairs, Carnegie-Mellon University (1975).
5. Charnes, A., Cooper, W. W., Klingman, D., and Niehaus, R. J., 'Explicit Solutions in Convex Goal Programming', *Management Science*, vol. 22 (1976), pp. 438–448.
6. Dantzig, G. B. and Parikh, S. C., 'On a Pilot Linear Programming Model for Assessing Physical Impact on the Economy of a Changing Energy Picture', Technical Report SOL 75-14R, Stanford University (August 1975).

7. de Neufville, R. and Marks, D. H., *Systems Planning and Design – Case Studies in Modeling, Optimization and Evaluation* (Englewood Cliffs, New Jersey: Prentice-Hall, Inc., 1974), pp. 291–302.
8. Dunlap, R. W., Gorr, W. L., and Massey, M. J., 'The Desulfurization of Coke Oven Gas: Technology, Economics and Regulatory Activity', in Szekely, J., (ed.). *The Steel Industry and the Environment*, (Marcel Dekker, 1973).
9. Foell, W. K., Mitchell, J. W., and Pappas, J. L., 'The Wisconsin Regional Energy Model: A Systems Approach to Regional Energy Analysis', Institute for Environmental Studies Report 56, University of Wisconsin-Madison (September 1975).
10. Gorr, W. L., *A Theoretical and Empirical Investigation of the Design of Optimal Air Pollution Regulations*, unpublished Ph.D. dissertation, Carnegie-Mellon University (1973), pp. 187, 188.
11. Gorr, W. L., 'Strategic Allocation of Clean Fuels to Industry: Case Study of Franklin County, Ohio', *Proceedings of the 32nd Annual Meeting of the East Central Section of the Air Pollution Control Association*, Dayton, Ohio (1975).
12. Gorr, W. L., Gustafson, S., Kortanek, K. O., 'Optimal Control Strategies for Air Quality Standards and Regulatory Policy', *Environment and Planning*, vol. 4 (1972), pp. 183–192.
13. Hamlen, S. and Hamlen, W., 'The Use of Goal Programming in Evaluating Air Pollution Control Strategies', Working Paper, School of Management, SUNY at Buffalo, (1976).
14. Hammond, K. R. and Adelman, L., 'Science, Values, and Human Judgment', *Science*, vol. 194 (October 22, 1976), pp. 389–396.
15. Kohn, R. E., 'Application of Linear Programming to a Controversy on Air Pollution Control', *Management Science*, vol. 17 (1971), pp. B609–B621.
16. Krajewski, L. J. and Ritzman, L. P., 'Disaggregation in Manufacturing and Service Organizations: Survey of Problem Structures and Research Findings', Administrative Science Working Paper, The Ohio State University.
17. MacCrimmon, K. R., 'An Overview of Multiple Objective Decision Making', in Cochrane, J. L. and Zeleny, M., (ed.). *Multiple Criteria Decision Making* (Columbia, S. Carolina, 1973).
18. Massey, M. J., Gorr, W. L., and Dunlap, R. W., 'Methodology for Defining Industrial Fuel Policy', *Proceedings, 36th Annual American Power Conference*, Chicago (1974).
19. Panagiotakopoulas, D., 'A Multiobjective Framework for Environmental Management Using Goal Programming', *J. Environmental Systems*, vol. 5 (1975), pp. 133–147.
20. Private Communication.
21. Reiquam, H., 'A Method of Optimizing Pollutant Emissions in an Air Shed', *Atmospheric Environment*, vol. 5 (1971), pp. 57–64.
22. Ryan, R. S., 'An Evaluation of the Impact of the Proposed USEPA Standards for Ohio', Technical Report, Ohio Energy and Resource Development Agency, Columbus, Ohio (January 1977).
23. Sengupta, J. K., Tinter, G., and Millham, C., 'On Some Theorems of Stochastic Linear Programming with Applications', *Management Science*, vol. 10 (1963), pp. 143–159.

33. Costs and benefits of a computer based regional blood inventory system

KENNETH E. KENDALL, C. CARL PEGELS and JOHN P. SEAGLE

Abstract

As part of a study of the operations management problems of regional blood supply centers, a computer-based blood inventory information and planning system was designed, developed and implemented. The system was designed and developed in six stages. The six design and development stages are: (A) maintenance and listing of blood inventory in largest blood banks, (B) summary reporting by blood bank location, (C) reporting of blood inventory by age and type, (D) expansion to include smaller blood banks, (E) reporting on a greater variety of transactions, and (F) forecasting of short term blood inventory levels. All six stages have been implemented and are still operational. The development and operating costs of each stage are reported, and compared with estimated benefits, both potential and attained. Estimated benefits of the system substantially exceed costs. The final version of the system consists of several modules, some of which are optional.

33.1. Introduction

Management of a regional blood supply center (center), which collects blood and supplies it to participating hospital blood banks (blood banks) is generally charged with meeting four objectives. These are: blood must be of high quality; enough blood must be available to meet demands; costs must be kept low; and waste of blood must be minimized. These objectives are in partial conflict (e.g., ample inventory to satisfy demand usually leads to waste through outdating of blood). Some of these objectives can be measured in terms of dollars, but measurements of others, such as quality and availability, must be partially value judgements.

An inventory information and planning system (system) for the center was designed, developed, and implemented in order to test the feasibility of using such a system to aid blood center management in reaching and evaluating their objectives, and to determine how to best present the information to the individual decision makers within the management organization. The system is described by Pegels and Wallace [6].

The analysis reported here is an ex-post analysis using the cost-benefit approach described by McRae [4]. The authors are not primarily concerned with questions of cost-effectiveness of the hardware-software computer configuration: good computer men can, and are now trying to, produce the outputs of the system at lower cost. What is established here is that a certain flow of information provides benefits to a loose organization of blood banks and a blood center, and that these benefits far exceed the costs.

Seven specific goals were identified. These goals are observable management activities that are directly supported by the system. Attainment of these goals in turn assures attainment of the four management objectives mentioned above. The specific goals are: 1. reduction in administrative costs; 2. plan distribution to avoid shortages; 3. transfer blood to fill acute needs; 4. transfer blood to reduce outdating; 5. know location of blood; 6. reduce long cross-matches; and 7. forecast inventory levels.

The system was developed in six stages, each of which led toward the attainment of, or improvement upon, one or more of the seven goals. The degree to which each stage contributed information relevant to the seven goals is shown in Table 1. Entries in the table show that the early stages contributed to the goals considered most essential by the designers. Later stages served both to improve upon earlier achievements, and to serve additional goals. The six stages are: A. supplying lists of units in largest blood banks; B. preparation of management summary reports; C. breakdown of inventory by age and type; D. expansion of the system to include smaller blood banks; E. expansion of the system to report more types of transactions; F. addition of short-term inventory level forecast.

The attainment of goals, however, required management to accept and act upon the information presented. The degree to which this acceptance and action was achieved is summarized in Table 2. The payoffs of all the effort are presented in Table 3, where costs are compared with estimated benefits for each of the six stages. Costs for design, development, and implementation are shown. Operating costs and benefits are presented on an annual basis for a

Table 1. Achievement of goals by supplying necessary information.

Goal / Development Stage	1	2	3	4	5	6	7
A	1	1	1	1	1	1	
B			2	2	2		
C			2	2	2		
D	2		3	3	3		
E	2						
F				4			3

Achievement measures
1. Partial achievement of goal.
2. Improvement, but insufficient for minimum goal.
4. Improvement after goal achieved.

center that draws and distributes 64,000 units (one unit equals approximately 1 pint) of blood each year. The potential benefits for each stage are estimated under the assumption of full development and acceptance. The degree of development and acceptance, as indicated in Tables 1 and 2, is estimated, and the range of attained benefits is also displayed in Table 3.

Table 2. Acceptance and use by management.

Goal / Development Stage	1	2	3	4	5	6	7
A	2		2	2	2	1	
B		1	2	2	2		
C		1	1	1	1		
D	2		2	2	2		
E	2						
F		2		2			2

Acceptance measures
1. Partial acceptance
2. acceptance and use

Table 3. Cost-benefit table.

Development Stage	Development Cost $	Annual Oper. Cost $	Maximum Annual Benefits $	Realized Annual Benefits $
A	9500	19,850	74,200	40,810
B	3300	500	14,800	12,580
C	1450	50	8,200	4,510
D) E)	10600	3,500	35,000	29,750
F	7750	400	52,800	29,040

We have listed all costs and benefits in dollar terms. The reader should be aware, as Mishan [5] has pointed out, that these costs and benefits are not incurred by and accrued to one agency, the regional blood center. If they were, this paper would simply be an investment analysis of the implemented information system here presented. In cost-benefit analysis we are concerned with the economy (or society) as a whole. We are concerned with the welfare of a defined society and not with one of its components. Therefore, costs incurred by one agency, the blood center, may under certain circumstances exceed the benefits attained by the blood center. Benefits accrued by other agencies or organizations may be virtually costless to them. For example, elimination of delays in surgical operations because of blood shortages offers substantial monetary and other benefits to the hospitals, surgeons and patients involved. These benefits come at no cost to the affected parties because the costs of operating the information system are borne by the blood center.

A detailed description of the costs and benefits for each of the developmental stages is presented in the following sections. A summary of the authors' conclusions about the costs, benefits, and lessons learned from the study is given in the final section.

33.2. Developmental stages

33.2.1. Supplying lists of units in largest blood banks

The first stage was planned to produce inventory lists for major blood banks after a short development time, and to permit experimentation in the presentation of information to management and the acquisition of data from blood banks. The resulting system consisted of a file containing data about every unit of blood in the larger blood banks, along with computer programs to maintain the files and generate reports. Listings showing the status of each unit in a blood bank were sent to the blood bank daily, and were used for internal control. A copy was kept at the center to use as a work sheet for recording changes reported by the blood banks over the telephone, these changes were then used in updating the respective blood bank files. The center manager also received a copy for use in filling routine and emergency requests, controlling excessively long crossmatches, and identifying units that were approaching expiration (outdating).

These inventory listings were quite detailed, each unit of blood was identified by its unique number, and grouped by type for each blood bank. The status of the unit ('crossmatched' if reserved for a particular patient and 'free' if not) was included. The purpose of the status identification was to reduce the number of outdates caused by allowing blood to remain on crossmatch status longer than necessary. The date the unit was shipped to the blood bank was provided to help blood banks keep their own required records. The number of days of usable life of each unit (blood outdates in 21 days) was included in the listings to identify old units that could possibly be transferred to blood banks were likelihood of usage was greater.

Acceptance of this initial computer-based system by the center was greater than expected, and blood banks became eager to cooperate when they saw that they would receive a report they could use for internal inventory control. In effect, the inventory listings served as a tangible reward for supplying data. The number of participating blood banks rose from two to seven in one month's time, and other blood banks asked to join the system.

Certain features distinguish this system from others in use. The short development time necessarily led to a high operation cost, but enabled the researchers to observe the use of the information at an early date. Flexibility was another important characteristic. Programming was in a simple language (BASIC), and computer operations were on a commercial time-sharing service. These features permitted a rapid turn-around in the development of computer programs. Changes were easily made as various users were observed and given the opportunity to criticise the system. In addition, the time-sharing mode placed control of the system at the center, and in the hands of a secretary. Management did not have to deal with 'experts' at some distant service center. Errors in data could be corrected as they were observed, further reinforcing the attitude that center management was in control of the system.

In addition to the computer related features, the system is unusual in that partial implementation is allowed. Individual blood banks can participate or not as they wish, an important factor where, as in many regions, the blood supplier has little jurisdiction over the blood banks. Several other inventory information systems require every unit of blood to be entered in the files.

Although information regarding blood distribution of major blood banks was now available at the center, it was not easy to use this information to transfer old blood or to identify excessively long crossmatches. Many separate reports had to be examined in detail to accomplish this, and summarization of these reports was the next step to delegate to a computer. A summary of the state of the blood system inventory, discussed further in the following stage, was needed for reference by center management. Details on a particular unit would then be found in the blood bank listings.

Other changes of the system became necessary when operational

	Incremental costs	
Developmental costs	Personnel – 6 man months	$ 8,400
	Computer time, storage, etc.	1,100
Total developmental costs		$ 9,500
Annual operational costs	Personnel – 1 person full-time	$ 5,200
	Teletype – 1 terminal (10 char/sec)	950
	Computer time, storage, etc.	13,700
Total operational costs		$19,850
	Incremental benefits	
Maximum	Reduce outdating 2,700 units at $26	$70,200
Potential	Avoid 5 deferred operations at $400	2,000
Annual benefits	Reduce record keeping costs in blood banks	2,000
Total maximum potential benefits		$74,200
Percentage attainment: 50–60%		

costs jumped to 73c per unit of blood after the system was enlarged to include seven blood banks. This was an expected consequence of the earlier decision to limit development time, and enough had been learned about data acquisition and reporting to reduce the need for flexibility. A major revision, described later in this article, allowed the system to include the remainder of the 46 blood banks in the region.

33.2.2. Preparation of management summary reports

The second stage involved the preparation of a report of aggregate blood inventory by blood bank and by blood type. These summary reports were developed to facilitate the transferring of blood to fill acute needs, and to prevent outdating. Lack of a clear-cut methodology for applying the information prevented full anticipated achievement of goals in the reduction of outdating and the prevention of shortages. However, management of the center was given a clearer picture of the location of the blood in the region; the detailed information provided in the previous stage did not lend itself to the quick identification of shortages and oversupplies. While such problems were not prevented, the system aided in their resolution. The report was accepted and used by center management only after the output was redesigned to resemble tables from the center's earlier attempt to implement a blood inventory tracking system.

	Incremental costs	
Developmental costs	Personnel – 2 man months	$ 2,800
	Computer time, storage, etc.	500
Total developmental costs		$ 3,300
Annual operational costs	Computer time, storage, etc.	$ 500
Total added operational costs		$ 500
	Incremental benefits	
Maximum	Reduce outdating 500 units at $26	$13,000
Potential	Avoid 2 deferred operations at $400	800
Annual benefits	Reduce supplementary shipments	1,000
Total maximum potential benefits		$14,800
Percentage attainment: 80–90%		

33.2.3. Breakdown of inventory by age and type

Reporting the distribution of blood by age and type was planned to enable center management to identify impending shortages and oversupplies in time to avoid the need for emergency action. Lack of methodology for making decisions from this information, however, limited usefulness to the recognition of severe imbalances only. For example, the information enabled center management to pinpoint the critical days of a holiday season long noted for shortage conditions. Intensive recruiting alleviated shortage conditions on the most critical days.

	Incremental costs	
Developmental costs	Personnel – 1 man month	$ 1,400
	Computer time, storage, etc.	50
Total developmental costs		$ 1,450
Annual operational costs tional Costs	Computer time, storage, etc.	50
Total added operational costs		$ 50
	Incremental benefits	
Maximum potential Potential	Reducing outdating 300 units at $26	$ 7,800
Annual benefits Benefits	Avoid 1 deferred operation at $400	400
Total maximum potential benefits		$ 8,200
Percentage attainment: 50–60%		

33.2.4. Expanding the system to include smaller blood banks and to report more types of transactions

The pilot version of the system had enabled the research group and center management to establish the information requirements and means for obtaining data. However, expansion of that version would have led to ever increasing unit costs. In order to prevent costs per unit of blood from rising, a complete redesign and reprogramming effort was decided upon, although reports and input procedures were to be changed but slightly.

The basic logic of the redesign was to merge transactions related to blood units into the appropriate blood bank files. In addition to the desired cost reduction, this method removed existing limitations on the variety of transactions that could be processed. Thus, simultaneously with the expansion to all blood banks, the system was expanded in scope to process transactions reflecting all possible actions that could be taken with respect to a unit of blood. New transactions included transfers between blood banks, packing of red cells, and returns of both usable and outdated blood to the center. By maintaining records of all transactions, the system contained all necessary information for the center to bill the blood banks. Automation of billing has not been implemented, but is now possible and would lead to substantial saving in administrative costs.

The expansion of the system to cover all blood banks followed the redesign. Management at the center knew the status of every blood bank supplied by the center, as well as every blood unit. Requests of the smaller blood banks could be evaluated against their inventory levels as well as the degree of excess or shortage in the entire region. Transfers could be suggested among geographically close blood banks to fill emergency needs. The system also made it possible to recall older blood from smaller blood banks in time to use it at the larger city blood banks.

	Incremental costs	
Developmental costs	Personnel – 6 man months	$ 8,400
	Computer time, storage, etc.	2,200
Total developmental costs		$10,600
Annual operational costs	Personnel – an additional 1/2 person	$ 2,600
	Teletype – 1 high speed terminal (30 char/sec) price difference	4,150
	Computer time, storage,	– 1,250*
Total added operational costs		$ 3,500
	Incremental benefits	
Maximum potential	Reduce outdating 900 units at $26	$23,400
Annual benefits	Avoid 4 deferred operations at $400	1,600
	Reduce record keeping work in blood banks	10,000
Total maximum potential benefits		$35,000
Percentage attainment: 80–90%		

*Redesigning decreased computer costs even though blood banks were added.

Additional features added at this time improved the reliability and simplified restarting after communication or computer system breakdowns, permitted on-line corrections, and facilitated extension of the system by the addition of modules. Storage was divided into separate files in order to allow each blood bank to query its file at any time. Use of individual blood bank files also kept the cost of updating down when only a few blood banks were affected.

Costs of operating the system came down to 37c per unit of blood collected, even though all 46 blood banks served by the blood center were being served. This cost included an additional half-time person to handle the transactions of the additional blood banks, and rental of faster teletype to handle the increased volume of reports. Savings were entirely due to program redesign. This improved version replaced the previous development stages, and became the basic blood inventory tracking system as reported by Frankfurter, et al. [2].

33.2.5. Addition of a short-term inventory level forecast

The dynamic short-term inventory forecast module (forecast module), as was reported by Frankfurter, et al. [3], was developed to determine future shortages or oversupply periods for the region in order to plan the collection and distribution of blood. This module uses exponential smoothing methods to forecast demand

	Incremental costs	
Developmental costs	Personnel – 5 man months	$ 7,000
	Computer time, storage, etc.	750
Total developmental costs		$ 7,750
Annual operational costs	Computer time, storage, etc.	$ 400
Total added operational costs		$ 400
	Incremental benefits	
Maximum potential	Reduce outdating 2000 units at $26	$52,000
Annual benefits	Avoid 2 deferred surgical operations at $400	800
Total maximum potential benefits		$52,800
Percentage attainment: 50–60%		

and committee forecasts to estimate collections. The forecast module had extremely low operating cost and significantly aided management in smoothing inventory levels. Collections were cut back if high inventory levels were forecast, and attempts were made to increase collections when shortage periods were predicted. A more responsive system for planning blood collections would be needed to take full advantage of the forecasts.

33.3. Conclusion

The cost benefit study described in this paper is only one element in a larger research effort aimed at determining the extent to which modern management techniques such as cost benefit analysis, operations research, computer technology, organization analysis, and behavioral science can be used to solve partly or wholly the operations management problems of regional blood banks.

The computer-based information system, which formed the subject of this cost-benefit study, has been designed to provide information support for a majority of the decision-making tasks relating to short-term regional planning of blood collections and distribution. The study demonstrates that benefits exceed costs by far.

The information system was designed, developed and implemented in stages. The first stage consisted of the core and subsequent stages were added to or built around this core. This approach provided rapid feed-back of the cost and effectiveness of each module that was added. Hence, decisions to stop or proceed to the next stage could be made at the completion of each stage. This type of development is quite unlike the conventional approach of designing an entire project and then developing and implementing it as one system.

This study is a cost-benefit study following the virtual completion, including implementation, of the entire project. Most cost-benefit studies are made prior to the actual design and development of a project. We decided to do an *a posteriori* study to evaluate in detail the costs and especially the benefits that have been attained and potential benefits that may still be attained.

The difficulty of makiing *a priori* estimates of costs and benefits has been aptly pointed out by Turvey [8]. In our study we found benefits were also difficult to measure ex-post, largely because we were dealing with an ongoing operation that was undergoing many changes besides the ones we instigated, and which had no regular measures of performance. Perhaps this is not unusual; McRae reported that ex-post justifications are rare [4].

Prest and Turvey provide extensive guidelines for *a priori* cost-benefit analysis [7]. Particular applications reviewed by them included water projects, transportation, land-usage schemes, health, education, research and development, and defense. Our objective of providing improved information flow to improve blood system management was quite different from the above studies. Reported problems in evaluating benefits were not encountered in the information system discussed here. Externalities were not a problem in the closed structure of the regional blood system. Political changes, natural disasters, and uncertainty in general have little to do with the continuance of the actual regional blood system or its management information system. Finally, choosing an appropriate discount rate was not a problem because of the relative low cost of designing, developing, and initially implementing the system. The specific problems encountered all involved attempts to quantify benefits associated with reduction of outdating, reduction of administrative work, and avoidance of deferred surgical operations.

References

1. Boyd, D. F. and Krasnow, H. J., 'Economic Evaluation of Management Information Systems', *IBM Systems Journal*, vol. 2 (1963), pp. 2–23.
2. Frankfurter, G. M., Jelmert, A. E., Pegels, C. C., Seagle, J. P., and Wallace, E. L., 'A Regional Computer-Based Blood Inventory Information System', *Transfusion*, vol. 10, no. 4 (July–August 1970).
3. Frankfurter, E. M., Kendall, K. E., and Pegels, C. C., 'Management Control of Blood Through a Short Term Supply Demand Forecast System', *Management Science*, vol. 21, no. 4 (December 1974), pp. 444–452.
4. McRae, T. W., 'The Evaluation of Investment in Computers', *Abacus*, vol. 6 (1970), pp. 56–70.
5. Mishan, E. J., *Cost-Benefit Analysis* (New York: Praeger Publishers, 1971).
6. Pegels, C. C. and Wallace, E. L., 'A Computerized Management Information System for Human Blood Utilization', *Information Processing 71*, North Holland Publishing Company, Amsterdam (1972).
7. Prest, A. R. and Turvey, A., 'Cost Benefit Analysis: A Survey', *The Economic Journal*, vol. LXXV, no. 300 (December 1965).
8. Turvey, Ralph, 'On the Development of Cost Benefit Analysis', *Cost Benefit Analysis*, edited by Kendall, M. G. (American Elsevier Publishing Company, Inc., New York, 1971).

Section 9. Emergency and health services

34. Multi-level police patrol planning

LAWRENCE D. VITT

Abstract

This paper presents an introduction to critical system design elements in each major planning level. The multi-level development of patrol planning is of considerable importance because the relationships between levels are highly interactive. Modifications of district boundaries or cruiser beats interact with the allocation of patrol resources and patrol scheduling. The 'level two' programs provide the major constraints for 'level three' manpower planning. Some 'level three' dispatching policies, such as the encouragement or discouragement of intersector travel, will affect the district/location programming. Decision making at all levels will have an impact on the levels of patrol service provided.

One of the characteristics of police patrol planning is that the patrol programs can be easily changed. The primary resources, vehicles and officers, are small sized and highly mobile. Patrol programs are readily modified on a temporal and spacial basis. Even a transfer involving one or two vehicles can have a significant impact on the patrol performance measures. Patrol planning has been facilitated in recent years by the availability of an excellent data base. The comprehensive calls for service reporting provide detailed data that are not available in most organizations. U.S. Department of Justice support has led to extensive use of automated data processing. One of the ironies of modern patrol planning is that the information processing induces a reluctance to modify patrol programs. If temporal and spacial changes are made in patrol programs, then the historical patrol data are less relevant for current managerial decision making.

34.1. Level one: district and beat design

This patrol design problem has two major components: (1) the partitioning of a region into areas of primary responsibility (districts) and (2) the location of patrol units when they are not responding to calls for service. The number of districts will be influenced by the organization structure and procedures for patrol supervision. The size of each district will be affected by the department's policies governing cross-district dispatching. Larger districts tend to encourage dispatching between cruiser beats but may lead to reduced cross-district dispatching. The districts are then subdivided into beats or cruiser districts which provide a basis for locating vehicles when not responding to calls for service. These beat assignments can vary from a general assignment to very rigid and specific patrol areas for each vehicle. In the latter case, patrol officers establish a sector identity and are responsible for patrol performance within the beat.

With highly mobile resources and radio dispatching of vehicles, a question could be raised concerning the importance of the district/location design problem. Districts could be viewed as reporting areas for data processing. Some cities have adopted less rigid district structures and emphasize city-wide dispatching of vehicles. To develop this question consider vehicle *X* which has been assigned a cruiser district that is too large. This leads to the positioning of other vehicles further from vehicle *X*. With automated car location equipment, the radio dispatcher identifies vehicle *X* as the nearest vehicle for more of the calls for service. All of the major performance measures are adversely affected by this location decision. The major objectives for the 'level one' problem are: to provide balanced workloads, to provide minimum response times, and to minimize intersector travel. Thus, even the city with flexible city-wide dispatching would find the location decision an important design problem.

34.1.1. The hypercube queuing model

The Hypercube Model was developed as an aid in designing response districts for ambulances, police patrol vehicles, and fire-fighting units [2], [12], [13]. It is considered to be the best available model for the district/location design problem. More than 10 percent of the units should be busy at one time, thus, the model was primarily developed for the design of police patrol areas.

The model does not develop or suggest the best district design. It simply helps the user evaluate alternative plans that have been identified by the user. The predicted performance for each plan is computed in terms of: mean travel time, workload imbalance, and fractions of dispatches that are interdistrict. The major model inputs are: calls for service data for each 'block,' travel related data, and the patrol configuration (level two) for each district.

A current evaluation of the model indicates considerable interest in the program and identifies a number of user implementation problems [7]. The program is currently being revised to facilitate implementation. The model operates in an exact mode for 15 vehicles or an 'approximate' mode for more than 15 vehicles. The evaluation study suggests that future policy users will want to use the approximate model exclusively.

34.1.2. Interaction with level two

The primary difficulty encountered with the Hypercube Model is in the development of the patrol configuration for each proposed district plan. The Hypercube Model must be given the number of patrol vehicles on a temporal and spacial basis. The development of good 'level two' resource allocations and vehicle schedules is extremely difficult for even the existing police districts. The development of patrol configurations for proposed districts can become rather complex and subject to considerable error. Furthermore, the resultant change in patrol performance predicted by the Hypercube Model could be more related to the patrol configuration than the district plan.

The model evaluation study [7] notes that several cities plan to use the Patrol Car Allocation Model (PCAM) to generate the proposed patrol configuration. This is a rather intriguing strategy but it may require an inordinate amount of time and effort. The PCAM model requires considerable effort to generate one patrol configuration for each shift and day-of-week.

An alternative approach is to use the PCAM model as the evaluation tool for the district/location problem.[1] The PCAM model output is rather similar to that provided by the Hypercube Model. The evaluation study states that 'PCAM appears to be hypercube's most formidable competitor' [7, p. 30]. This is an interesting development because the PCAM manuals warn the prospective user that PCAM is not designed for aid in district

1. The author is currently developing a research project to evaluate this method of analysis. A large U.S. urban police department will assist in this evaluation.

design. It certainly illustrates the importance of interaction between levels one and two for this design problem.

The location plan for cruiser beats will have to be modified on a shift basis if the number of vehicles varies by shift. The best 'level two' shift programs often call for unequal-sized shifts. The easiest approach is to assign fractional beats to these vehicles. The Dayton Police Department has undertaken a rather challenging project to develop a different beat 'map' for each shift. This illustrates the existence of an undesirable built-in rigidity against possible changes in a city's 'level two' shift schedules.

34.2. Level two: patrol allocation and scheduling

The allocation and scheduling of police patrol resources are important and critical decision areas for police management. These resource management decisions are a major determinant of both the cost of the patrol activity and the level of service provided. An oversimplified statement of the objective of efficient resource allocation would be to have the right number of vehicles, of the right type, available at the right place and time. The achievement of this objective becomes an exceedingly difficult task due to: (1) the demand uncertainty, (2) the considerable variation in the number of calls for service by hour, by day, and by season, and (3) the relatively fixed assignment of resources to districts and shifts throughout the planning period.

For several decades leaders in the field of patrol research, such as O. W. Wilson [19], have advocated the proportional allocation of patrol resources to the demand for service. The typical urban police department will allocate manpower equally among the shifts for each district. The principal reason for this practice appears to be that it is easier to rotate shift assignments with equal-sized shifts. A significant interaction with a 'level three' program can be observed with this relationship. Another important factor is that patrol vehicles are assigned to beats or cruiser districts; thus, unequal-sized shifts require more complex vehicle area assignments, a 'level one' interaction. The equal shift concept generally leads to wide variations in resource utilization and the amount of preventive patrol tends to be inversely proportional to the calls for service workload. It should be noted that even with equal-sized manpower shifts the number of vehicles available can vary by modifying the proportion of two-person vehicles scheduled during each shift.

34.2.1. The author's research

The nature of the police patrol resource planning problem suggests that the principal means of synchronizing the available resources with the demands for service should be considered in the allocation and scheduling decision process. These synchronization alternatives include: (1) the assignment of officers and vehicles to districts and shifts in proportion to the demands for service, (2) providing sufficient 'slack' in the workload schedules to allow for the stochastic variation in the arrival rates, the prompt processing of high priority calls for service, and to provide some desired level of preventive service, (3) varying the percentage of one-person and two-person vehicles by district and shift, (4) scheduling off-duty days, (5) vacation programming, (6) using overlapping shifts, (7) timing of shift changes, and (8) seasonal timing of changes in the resource levels.

A four-quarter linear programming model was developed by the author for the specific evaluation of all the major synchronization alternatives [17]. The major parameters in the model for each district/shift were the desired utilization ratios and the proportion of two-person vehicles. Research with this model indicated that the planning model was viable but additional research was needed in order to obtain adequate estimates of the parameters. The two sets of parameters and the workload data determined the patrol configuration for each district/shift.

A major patrol allocation research project was completed with the cooperation of the Columbus Police Department [18]. This research led to the implementation of a new city-wide patrol allocation with selective use of unequal-sized shifts and 8-day vehicles. The proportion of two-person vehicles scheduled for each shift was significantly modified. This research focused on the analysis of the utilization ratios and the requirements for two-person vehicles. A diagnostic intersector travel model assisted the development of new patrol allocations and the implementation of the new program. Interaction with 'level one' location decisions resulted in the redesign of several cruiser districts.

This research project provided the framework for the development of a computerized patrol allocation and scheduling algorithm. The allocation algorithm and a diagnostic program form the basis for a new method of patrol planning. This program is now in the test and evaluation stage.

Patrol allocation and scheduling decision making would be rather simple if resource levels were directly proportional to the calls for service workloads. Most urban areas have these workload data. For example, if the desired utilization ratio for every police cruiser in the city was thirty-five percent the resources required could easily de determined. But utilization ratios may vary from ten percent in outlying districts during a Tuesday night shift to sixty percent in center-city districts during a Friday early evening shift. The investigation of desired utilization ratios is an important area for future patrol research.

A research project is being developed by the author and Brooke A. Saladin to investigate the factors that lead to variations in the desired utilization ratios. Previous research indicated that the nonlinear relationships can be related to: (1) the workload per citizen by district, (2) the 'preventive' requirements of the area, (3) the population density, and (4) the square miles per patrol unit. The results of this research will be used to further refine the computerized allocation algorithm.

34.2.2. The patrol car allocation model

The need for new allocation techniques was recognized by the National Institute of Law Enforcement and Criminal Justice, L.E.A.A., U.S. Department of Justice. This organization sponsored the development of new planning techniques which could be used by all urban police departments. One significant improvement was the Patrol Car Allocation Model (PCAM) developed by the RAND Corporation [4]. The PCAM program was available in 1975 and is being used by several urban areas. PCAM has the potential to be widely used by police departments in the future.

In a descriptive mode, the PCAM program allows the user to evaluate proposed district/shift allocations for each day-of-week by displaying the resultant performance measures. The user must evaluate the predicted performance and can try other patrol configurations. In the prescriptive mode, the user can specify minimum levels of performance or 'weight' certain performance measures. The program can estimate the number of vehicles required to satisfy patrol requirements or it can assist in getting the best allocation of a given number of vehicles. The model can provide a very comprehensive evaluation of the major patrol design strategies. For example, an overlapping shift structure and various shift starting times can be evaluated.

The display of predicted performance measures is an outstanding feature of this program. For each district/shift/day vehicle configuration the user is provided the following data: average vehicle utilization, average travel time, average patrol frequency, average service delays, and the probability of service delays for each of the three priority call classifications.

A major performance measure used to evaluate these patrol configurations is the average utilization ratio. A problem posed for the PCAM user is the selection of a desirable utilization ratio. The previously cited utilization ratio research by the author and Saladin will be beneficial to future PCAM users. With a more specific utilization ratio objective in mind for each district/shift, the PCAM user should obtain better results from the program.

34.2.3. Interaction with level three

The interaction of level two decisions with the development of detailed manpower schedules is rather obvious. The patrol configuration and the number of recreation days in the schedule specify the major constraints for level three manpower programming. To some extent level three requirements influence patrol configurations, but the level two design problem is rather dominant.

The level two decisions have a significant impact on the patrol response time and the level of service provided. A multi-level analysis is provided by a recent queuing-linear programming approach to patrol scheduling [9]. In this research a highly iterative three-stage approach is developed with the primary objective being to satisfy a specified level of service with the minimum number of patrol vehicles. Shift timing and mealtime schedules are important design elements.

In stage one of this program a queuing model is used to estimate patrol vehicle requirements. For a given set of vehicle utilization ratios, hourly call rates, and service rates, the model computes the minimum number of vehicles per hour so that the probability of a call waiting is less than .1. No priority structure is provided for the calls for service. In stage two a mixed integer linear programming model (MPSX-MIP) generates patrol schedules using the stage one vehicle requirements. The model will minimize the number of vehicles required per time period while satisfying mealtime and demand constraints. The solution identifies the best mealtime schedules and shift start times. A time-dependent M/M/n queuing model is proposed for the stage three program evaluation. This analysis includes such patrol characteristics as the probability distribution of busy vehicles and the number of calls queued.

34.3. Level three: manpower programming and dispatching

The activities at this level include the scheduling of work days, days off, court days, vacation days, and patterns of shift rotation for the patrol officers. These schedules are a disaggregation of the 'level two' patrol configuration with the number of available officers matching the daily district/shift requirements. These manpower programs also seek a 'fair' schedule in terms of providing each officer a desirable set of working/recreation schedules. However, officer seniority may affect these schedules. Officers are then assigned to vehicles or teams and some departments attempt to develop close supervisory relationships. Another design problem at this level involves the staggering of shift change assignments for contiguous cruiser districts.

A computerized program is available for the development of desirable days off and shift schedules [6]. The user can specify the features that constitute a desirable schedule, such as the maximum number of consecutive working days and recreation weekends. This program also has an interesting interactive structure with 'level two' programming. The first program component uses an integer programming procedure to determine the optimum allocation of available manpower to on-duty days for each shift and week. The second program component designs recreation schedules of the appropriate length for each shift. An implicit enumeration technique constructs all feasible recreation schedules and a lexicographic scheme is used to develop an aggregate rating for each schedule. The final component in the program merges one-shift schedules to form multi-shift schedules.

A major 'level three' activity is the design of dispatching policies, priority call structures, and the dispatching communications system. Simulation models provide the only viable method of analysis for these design problems. The more comprehensive simulation models can analyze design problems for all three 'levels' [1], [8], [10], [15]. One important use of the comprehensive simulation model has been to evaluate the proposed 'level two' patrol configurations.

34.4. Conclusion

The entire realm of patrol planning has obviously been subjected to considerable analysis and model building during the past decade. Financial support from the U.S. Department of Justice has had an impact on these design activities. But the primary motivational forces may be the rapidly increasing rates of police patrol activity and the budget constraints of each city. The decision making at each level has a significant influence on the patrol service provided and the cost of providing this service. The cost of providing continuous annual service is over $100,000 for a one-person vehicle and over $200,000 for a two-person vehicle. These cost data provide some insight into the current concern for the one-person versus two-person vehicle decision. The author's research and the simulation models have considered this important design element.

With the exception of 'level three' programming, the methods of patrol planning have not considered offficer morale as a direct performance measure. The objectives for performance measures, such as utilization ratios and workload imbalances, are obviously related to officer morale. The morale issue is becoming increasingly significant and may lead to different 'weighting' of the patrol performance measures. The two-person vehicle decision is influenced by: (1) the workload for two-person calls and (2) the safety and morale factors.

New methodologies are constantly appearing in this dynamic field and provide opportunities for innovative research and implementation. The PREWARNS program [21] presents a new framework for patrol planning. PREWARNS is based on the assumption that the phenomenon of crime is functionally related to the social characteristics in the community. The program seeks to provide relevant information to police departments, monitor the results of existing programs, identify causes of calls for servcie, and assist in the development of effective patrol beats and patrol patterns.

References

1. Adams, R. T. and Barnard, S. R., 'Simulation of Police Field Forces for Decision Making in Resource Allocation', *Third National Symposium on Law Enforcement Science and Technology*, Chicago (April 1970).
2. Chaiken, J. M., *Hypercube Queuing Model: Executive Summary*, R-1688/1-HUD, The RAND Corporation, Santa Monica, California (July 1975).
3. Chaiken, J. M., *Patrol Allocation Methodology for Police Departments*, R-1852-HUD, The RAND Corporation, Santa Monica, California (September 1975).
4. Chaiken, J. M. and Dormont, P., *Patrol Car Allocation Model: Executive Summary*, R-1786/1-HUD/DOJ, *Patrol Car Allocation Model: User's Manual*, R-1786/2-HUD/DOJ, *Patrol Car Allocation Model: Program Description*, R-1786/3-HUD/DOJ, The RAND Corporation, Santa Monica, California (September 1975).
5. Chaiken, J. M. and Larson, R. C., 'Methods for Allocating Urban Emergency Units: A Survey', *Management Science*, vol. 19, no. 4 (December, Part 2) (1972), pp. 110–130.
6. Heller, N. B., McEwen, J. T., and Stenzel, W. W., *Computerized Scheduling of Police Manpower, Vol. 1: Methods and Conclusions*, PB-232-071, *Vol. 2: Evaluations and Program User's Manual*, PB-232-072, National Technical Information Service, U.S. Department of Commerce, Washington, D.C. (1973).
7. Heller, N. B., Stenzel, W. W., Kolde, R. A., and Gill, A. D., *Field Testing the NSF/MIT Hypercube Patrol Sector Design Methods – Progress Report*, The Institute for Public Program Analysis, St. Louis, Missouri (September 1976).
8. Knoppers, B. A., 'Simulation of Police Patrol and Dispatch', *Proceedings of the 7th Annual Simulation Symposium*, Tampa, Florida (1974).
9. Kolesar, P. J., Rider, K. L., Crabill, T. B., and Walker, W. E., *A Queuing-Linear Programming Approach to Scheduling Police Patrol Cars*, P-5260-1, The RAND Corporation, Santa Monica, California (March 1975).
10. Kolesar, P. J. and Walker, W. E., *A Simulation Model of Police Patrol Operations: Executive Summary*, R-1625/1-HUD, The RAND Corporation, Santa Monica, California (March 1975).
11. Larson, R. C., *Urban Police Patrol Analysis* (The MIT Press, Cambridge, Massachusetts, 1972).
12. Larson, R. C., *Hypercube Queuing Model: User's Manual*, R-1688/2-HUD, The RAND Corporation, Santa Monica, California (1975).
13. Larson, R. C., 'Approximating the Performance of Urban Emergency Service Systems', *Operations Research*, vol. 23, no. 5 (September–October 1975), pp. 845–868.
14. Larson, R. C. and Williamson, J. C., *On-Line Simulation of Urban Police Patrol and Dispatching*, Urban Sciences, Inc., Wellesley, Massachusetts (1972).
15. Lipsett, F. R. and Arnold, J. G., 'Computer Simulation of Patrol Operations of a Semi-Rural Police Force', *Journal of Police Science and Administration*, vol. 2, no. 2 (1974), pp. 190–207.
16. Sohn, R. L. and Kennedy, R. D., *Patrol Force Allocation for Law Enforcement*, National Criminal Justice Information and Statistics Service, U.S. Department of Justice, Washington, D.C. (February 1976).

17. Vitt, L. D., 'Aggregate Programming for Police Patrol', *Proceedings of the Midwest Conference American Institute for Decision Sciences*, Indianapolis, Indiana (April 1975).
18. Vitt, L. D. and the Planning and Research Bureau of the Colombus, Ohio Division of Police, *A Proposal for the Allocation and Distribution of Patrol Bureau Personnel on a Permanent Watch Basis*, Columbus, Ohio (May 1975).
19. Wilson, O. W., *Distribution of Police Patrol Force*, Publication no. 74, Public Administration Service, Chicago, Illinois (1941).
20. Wilson, O. W. and McLaren, R. C., *Police Patrol Administration*, Third Edition (McGraw-Hill Book Company, 1963).
21. *Police Response Early Warning System (PREWARNS) – Project Summary*, Department of Police, City of University City, Missouri.

35. Disaggregation of the decisions to allocate patrol resources to police precincts

DUNDAR F. KOCAOGLU

Abstract

The patrol division is the largest division in police departments and is responsible for the performance of all primary police tasks. Patrol officers respond to both criminal and non-criminal service calls ranging from homicide to damaged sidewalks. The police executives have to decide on the type and quantity of resources to be allocated to each geographic area within the jurisdiction of the Police Department. The allocation has to be made such that the effectiveness value of a given type of police coverage in a given precinct is maximized with respect to the need in that area evaluated according to public priorities. The allocation decisions reflect the judgment of the police executives in conjunction with the quantitative data available on the distribution of calls in the city. They should also conform to the value structure of the public during the relevant time span.

The quantitative calls-for-service data are usually available in the Police Department's files. However, the subjective factors that are implicit in the decision process are not clearly defined, nor easily quantifiable.

This paper describes a decision process through which the resource allocation decisions are disaggregated by introducing intermediate levels into the decision hierarchy and obtaining the functional relationships at each level from the police executives.

35.1. Introduction

The Police System is an integral part of the overall social structure of the society. Its objectives, strategies and outputs both strongly affect and are strongly affected by the other subsystems within the Urban System. Unlike organizations motivated by economic rewards, the Police System does not have any simple, straightforward measures to define its objectives and to control its operations.

Because of the highly multidimensional nature of the public issues that it deals with, there is no universal agreement concerning the objectives of the Police System, nor is there an agreement on the relative importance of the elements of its objective vector. The performance criteria and the measurement methods vary greatly and they are primarily directed toward operational policies rather than strategic decisions. The 'police effectiveness' is not a clear concept. The relative effectiveness of a certain police action is extremely difficult to measure. The strategic alternatives are not easy to identify nor to evaluate.

The police executives are faced with many strategic decisions in the allocation of manpower and financial resources to provide the public with maximum service. They have to decide on the type and the amount of patrol coverage in each police precinct. The criterion would be to optimize the city-wide effectiveness of their effort. Several patrol alternatives can be used for this purpose.

The police information systems typically contain data about the type, time and location of a call for police services and the duration of the service. However, the transfer of system inputs into outputs represents a highly complex set of interrelationships and there is a general lack of knowledge in the area of system interactions. Because of this lack, the transfer functions to predict the system outputs from a given set of inputs cannot be developed from the available data alone.

The patrol force performs a wide spectrum of duties every day handling a variety of cases ranging from 'murder' to 'damaged sidewalk'. Some of these duties are directed toward the apprehension of criminals while some can be categorized as non-criminal service. Fast response, personal contact, etc., have different relative values with respect to each of these categories. None of these internal relationships is available in explicit form but experienced police executives can provide subjective values for them. Such judgmental measures reflect the value structures of the police executives and the decision rules implicit in their actions.

It is necessary to obtain the effectiveness values subjectively from the police decision makers and combine them with statistical data in analyzing the resource allocation decisions.

35.2. Hierarchical decision elements

The mission of the police departments is defined by the society as providing security for its citizens. In order to achieve this overall goal, the police serve the society by responding to public needs in both criminal and non-criminal cases. The services of the police department are interrelated with the services performed by other public organizations, which constitute the Urban System and the Criminal Justice System. It is a subsystem of these higher systems and it competes with similar subsystems for public resources to perform its tasks. Internally, it is also made up of subsystems interacting with each other and competing for the total resources allocated to the police department. The typical subsystems within the police department are the patrol division, the communications division, the traffic division, etc.

The public wants to receive maximum service for the funds it allocates to each of the public service organizations. Thus, when receiving resources from the public and allocating them to its subsystems, the police department operates to optimize the total police effectiveness with respect to public demands and priorities.

The boundary of the system is defined at the patrol subsystem level in this paper. The issues within the patrol subsystem include the restrictions on patrol resources, the selection of patrol alternatives, their equitable distribution to specific areas in the city, the preventive patrol activities, the calls received from the public and the effectiveness of the patrol subsystem in terms of its contribution to the overall police objectives.

The resource allocation decisions are made at several levels. At the highest level in the decision hierarchy is the allocation to precincts. This paper is addressed to the decisions at that level. Subsequently, the resources allocated to each precinct will have to be distributed to shifts and beats within that precinct.

Patrol officers and cars are allocated to precincts in various combinations. The police executives could decide to use several patrol alternatives, such as foot patrol, one-man cars, two-man cars, etc. Each patrol alternative contributes to the effectiveness of the patrol system in a different way. A car unit can reduce the response time, while a foot patrol unit contributes to the overall effectiveness by maintaining personal contact with the citizens. The effectiveness of the patrol forces should be considered in a multi-dimensional space.

The police service categories (objectives) are also multidimensional. Typical dimensions are the apprehension of criminals, the deterrence of criminal activity, the service for non-criminal calls, etc. Each effectiveness dimension has a different value with respect to each service category.

The interface between the patrol system and the public is defined by the service calls received from the public. A police department typically receives over a hundred types of calls, which are grouped together into several call categories. A response to each type of call has a different value along each of the service categories.

The resource allocation decisions in police patrol can therefore be disaggregated into a series of cascaded relationships between patrol alternatives, effectiveness dimensions, service categories, call categories and public priorities.

35.3. The decision process

The critical part of this approach is the identification of the intermediate decision levels and the evaluation of their interrelationships. This was done through a series of task force meetings in the Buffalo Police Department. Members of the task force were selected from all the divisions to assure that the interfaces among the internal subsystems were accounted for. Weekly meetings were held for open discussions on the issues. The task force was made up of the Police Commissioner, the Deputy Commissioners, the Inspectors, and a Captain in charge of planning. Discussions were held in the meetings until the task force agreed on the decision elements at each level of the decision hierarcy.

The internal relationships between patrol alternatives, effectiveness dimensions, service categories and call categories were obtained from the police executives by quantifying their subjective judgmental values in the task force meetings. This was done by presenting them with pairs of attributes and asking for comparisons. The responses were evaluated by using the constant-sum technique [3] and further refined in the discussion of the subsequent task force meetings.

After combining these subjective values, the relative effectiveness of sending a certain type of patrol unit to any call category was evaluated. The results were combined with the calls-for-service statistics in each precinct and weighed with public priorities to obtain the coefficients for the optimization model for resource allocation. The public priorities were measured using a questionnaire for pairwise comparison of call categories. The ordinary citizens were asked to indicate their judgment for the relative importance of police response to calls in each of the call categories. The results were again evaluated by the constant-sum method.

The constraints of the system were also defined in the task force meetings. Seven types of constraints were considered:

1. Resource limitations.
2. Equity policies.
3. Non-response patrol policies.
4. Call restrictions.
5. Consistency constraints.
6. Upper and lower bounds on patrol resources.
7. Integer constraints.

The policies of the police department, the inputs from the political system received through the city council and the demands of the Police Benevolent Association were all expressed in terms of resources and incorporated into the constraints.

The changes in the budget, in the number of officers and/or cars, the officers' salaries and benefits can be reflected in resource limitations. Internal equity can be established in terms of workload, population distribution, or tax base as mandated by the political system. The minimum desired preventive patrol activity is defined by the police executives as a proportion of total patrol services. The calls that should be limited to a certain type of patrol unit, such as a two-man car are defined in each precinct if desired. If the city council wants the police department to change the number of precincts or the boundary of any precinct, such changes can also be reflected in the decision model.

The coefficients of the objective function include the relative effectiveness measures of the patrol alternatives, the demand for patrol services in each precinct and the public value structure in terms of the priorities assigned to the various patrol activities. A change in any of these elements can be incorporated into the resource allocation decisions by appropriate changes in the coefficients.

Three patrol alternatives are considered in the following decision model. They are foot patrol units, one-man car units and two-man car units.

35.4. The model

35.4.1. Objective function:

Let

I = number of patrol alternatives
L = number of effectiveness dimensions
M = number of service categories
K = number of call categories
J = number of precincts
γ_{il} = relative value of patrol alternative (i) with respect to effectiveness dimension (l)
δ_{lm} = relative contribution of effectiveness dimension (l) with respect to service category (m)
θ_{mk} = relative weight of service category (m) with respect to call category (k);

Then;

$$\epsilon_{ik} = \sum_{m=1}^{M} \sum_{l=1}^{L} \gamma_{il} \delta_{lm} \theta_{mk} \tag{1}$$

is the relative effectiveness of patrol alternative (i) with respect to call category (k).

Define

b_{h_j} = number of h-type calls in precinct (j)
k = call categories ($k = 1, \ldots, K$)
b_{k_j} = number of k-category calls in precinct (j)
α_k = relative weight assigned to call category (k) by the public,
r_{k_j} = relative value of responding to the k-category calls in precinct j from public's point of view

$$b_{k_j} = \sum_{h \text{ in } k} b_{hj} \quad \text{for } k = 1, \ldots, K \tag{2}$$

$$r_{k_j} = \alpha_k \cdot b_{k_j} \tag{3}$$

$$e_{ij} = \sum_{k=1}^{K} \epsilon_{ik} \cdot r_{k_j} \tag{4}$$

where e_{ij} is the relative effectiveness of an (i) type patrol unit allocated to precinct (j).

Using d_i as the annual cost of an (i) type patrol unit;

define

$$C_{ij} = e_{ij}/d_i \tag{5}$$

as the measure of effectiveness of a type (i) patrol unit allocated to precinct (j). C_{ij} is essentially a measure of 'productivity' as defined by the subjective values obtained from the police executives and the public.

Let

X_i = number of patrol units of alternative (i)
X_{ij} = number of patrol units of alternative (i) in precinct (j)
Y_i = $\Pi_i x_i$ = number of officers used in alternative (i)

$$Y_{ij} = \sum_{i=1}^{L} x_{ij} \cdot \Pi_i \tag{6}$$

where Π_i = 1 for one-man units
= 2 for two-man units.

Formulate the objective function as

$$\text{Max } Z = \sum_{j=1}^{J} \sum_{i=1}^{I} C_{ij} X_{ij} + C^*_{ij} X^*_{ij} \tag{7}$$

where X^*_{ij} is the number of cars used by the patrol alternative (i) in precinct (j) and C^*_{ij} is the productivity measure of the car assigned to patrol alternative (i) in precinct (j).

The X^*_{ij}'s are included in the objective function as dummy variables to satisfy the consistency constraints. Since the effectiveness of the cars is already included in the productivity measures of the one-man and two-man car units, the C^*_{ij}'s are assigned zero values.

35.4.2. Constraints

The constraints will be described in this paper but the mathematical formulation will not be given. The detailed model development can be found in reference 5, pp. 75–109.

Resource limitations:

1.1. Number of cars cannot be exceeded. (1 constraint)
1.2. Number of patrol officers cannot be exceeded. (1 constraint)
1.3. The patrol budget cannot be exceeded. (1 constraint)

Equity (one of the following):

2.1. The number of officers assigned to each precinct should be at least equal to the ratio of the service time needed in that precinct to the total service time in the city. (J constraints)
2.2. Same as (2.1.) but with police priorities assigned to each type of service call. (J constraints)
2.3. Similar to (2.1.) but equity based on number of calls instead of service time. (J constraints)
2.4. Similar to (2.2.) but based on number of calls instead of service time. (J constraints)
2.5. Same as (2.1.) but based on population distribution in the city. (J constraints)
2.6. Same as (2.1.) but based on tax distribution in the city. (J constraints)
2.7. Same as (2.1.) but based on geographic area of each precinct. (J constraints)

The decision system developed in this study can be based on any of the above equity policies but the recommended policy is (2.2.) as decided by the task force. However, additional capability was built-in to test the other policies if needed.

Non-response patrol:

3. The model is based on calls-for-service of criminal and non-criminal nature. However, patrol officers also spend time on other activities in addition to responding to these calls. The relative importance of such activities is left to the user of the model. He specifies a proportional figure to define the mini-

mum non-response activity representing preventive patrol, court duty, etc. (J constraints)

Call restrictions:

4.1. The proportion of the foot patrol units in a precinct cannot exceed the proportion of the service time required to respond to calls that can be handled by foot patrol units in that precinct. (J constraints)
4.2. The proportion of 'one-officer' patrol units (foot patrol and one-man car) should not exceed the proportion of the service time required to respond to calls that can be handled by one-officer units in each precinct. (J constraints)

The types of calls that can be handled by foot patrol units and one-officer units are identified in one of the task force meetings.

Consistency constraints:

5.1. The number of cars assigned to one-man car units should be consistent with the number of one-man car units in each precinct. (J constraints)
5.2. Same as (5.1.) for two-man cars. (J constraints)

Upper/lower bounds (if desired):

6.1. Upper limit for the number of officers per precinct. (J constraints)
6.2. Lower limit for the number of officers per precinct. (J constraints)
6.3. Minimum number of foot patrol units per precinct. (J constraints)

Integer constraints:

All decision variables are integers.

35.5. Solution

For the three patrol alternatives considered in this paper, the model presented in the preceding section has $5 \times J$ integer non-zero decision variables and up to $(9J + 3)$ constraints for a police department with J precincts.

The model was tested with the data obtained at the Buffalo Police Department for $J = 14$. There were several computational problems caused by the size of the problem and the tightness of the constraints. An algorithm was developed to solve the problem by decomposing it into several subproblems, testing for consistency and equity conditions after each cycle and repeating the process until either a near optimum was reached or the problem became infeasible. Eighty one cases were studied under different policies and assumptions [5, 6]. The results indicate that the over all cost effectiveness of the present system can be improved up to 70 percent.

35.6. Implementation

The decision process described in this paper is a participatory approach to the decision making process in a complex organization. The primary thrust is in bringing the decision makers to a continuous dialogue among themselves and with the analyst. The model itself enables the user to test various policy decisions and assumptions under different scenarios. It is not a 'black box' model.

Introduction of the task force idea to discuss the subjective values of police executives was a difficult proposition. However, after the first three of four meetings the task force members became very enthusiastic. The process resulted in the model described in this paper. At present, it is being tested under anticipated external conditions. The police values and priorities evaluated during the process have already been used by the Buffalo police executives in several planning decisions.

References

1. Bottoms, A. M., Nilsson, E. K., and Olson, D. G., *Allocations of Resources in the Chicago Police Department*, Report of the O. R. Task Force (1972).
2. Gass, S. I. and Dawson, J. M., *An Evaluation of Policy Related Research: Reviews and Critical Discussions of Policy-related Research in the Field of Police Protection*, Report prepared by Mathematica, Inc. (1974).
3. Guilford, J. P., *Psychometric Methods*, 2nd edn., New York, McGraw Hill (1954).
4. Heller, N. B., *Operations Research at the St. Louis Metropolitan Police Department*, Paper presented at the 39th National Meeting of ORSA (1971).
5. Kocaoglu, D. F., *A Systems Approach to the Resource Allocation Process in Police Patrol.* Unpublished Ph.D. Dissertation, University of Pittsburgh (1976).

6. Kocaoglu, D. F., *Allocation of Patrol Resources to Police Precincts: A Systems Approach*, Paper presented at the ORSA/TIMS National Meeting in Miami Beach, Florida (November 1976).
7. Larson, R. C., *Urban Police Patrol Analysis*, Cambridge, Mass., The MIT Press (1975).

36. Economically optimal quantity and mix of fire department services

SAMUEL M. SEWARD

Abstract

Aggregate planning for municipal fire departments is the process of determining the amount of funds to be budgeted for that activity. In determining the amount of fire protection a municipality should provide, there is an important trade-off between the public costs of a fire department and the private costs of fire insurance. An economically optimal quantity can be found by finding the point at which the sum of the public and private costs is minimized. Level one disaggregation consists of determining the mix of services at the least cost point. This paper illustrates a use of mathematical programming which enables the municipal decision-maker to find both the economically optimal quantity and mix of fire services. The application of this procedure in Boulder, Colorado is described.

36.1. Aggregate planning

All organizations are faced with the difficult task of resource allocation. For business organizations, this difficulty is reduced by analysis procedures that allow comparison of alternatives by some measure of profitability. This procedure forces the decision-maker to consider both revenue and cost structures of each alternative. In municipal decision-making, the allocation problem is often complicated by the lack of revenue streams which can be tied directly to a given service. Since returns for municipal investments are usually not measured in dollars but in service to the community, the municipal decision-maker usually has measurable costs but no directly measurable benefits.

In examining municipal expenditures for fire protection, the cost structure is usually all that is needed to determine the minimum acceptable expenditures for fire department services. Fire protection is provided by fire department services financed through tax dollars (public expenditures) and also by fire insurance (private expenditures). Thus, the total fire protection cost for residents and organizations of a municipality is the sum of the cost of fire services and fire insurance. Since fire insurance costs are a function of the amount and quality of the municipal fire services, there is a trade-off between dollars spent on fire department services and dollars spent on fire insurance.

36.1.1. Methodology

Fire insurance rates are a function of the level of fire protection as defined by the Insurance Services Office, or a similar organization. The Insurance Services Office (ISO) renders a wide range of advisory, actuarial, rating, statistical, research, and other types of services. In most states, the ISO provides the rate-making function for the insurance companies. Most insurance companies subscribe to the service because an individual company usually does not have the statistical base to provide the actuarial work needed to develop a rate schedule.

Every municipality of the United States is graded by the ISO and classified according to the quality of its fire protection. There are ten possible classes that represent degrees of fire protection. Cities with a high degree of protection, as perceived by the ISO, receive a low numbered class; those with little or no protection receive a high numbered class. Since fire insurance rates are a function of the level of fire protection as perceived by this and similar organizations, cities which they assess as having better fire protection benefit from lower insurance rates. The property owners in a municipality that spends more money on fire service, thereby raising the quality of fire protection, will have to spend less on fire insurance premiums.

A total cost function can be developed which is the sum of fire service cost and insurance cost. Figure 1 demonstrates the cost relationships. In moving from class 10 to the minimum cost (economically optimal) class the savings in insurance cost are greater than the additional cost of the fire services needed to achieve the least cost class. Any moves beyond the least cost class must be partially justified in benefits from fire protection not recognized by insurance savings, such as increased personal safety.

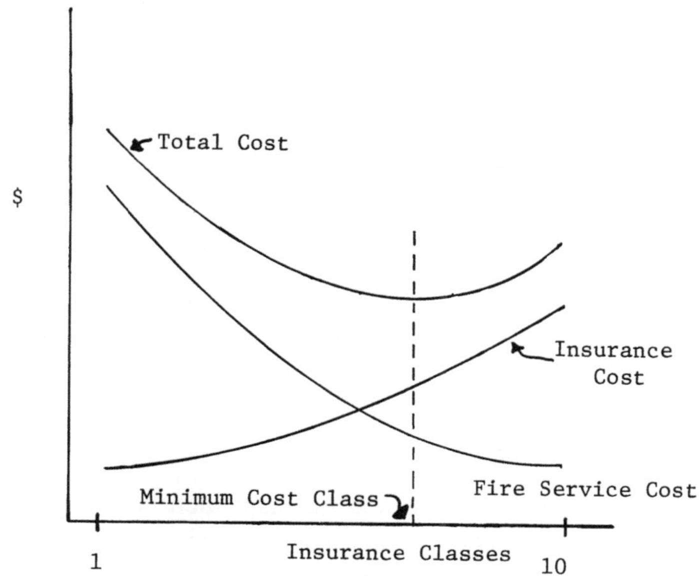

Figure 1

36.1.2. Determining fire service costs

The first component in Figure 1 is the cost and mix of fire department services needed to achieve each insurance class. The insurance class for a city is determined through the application of a grading schedule by the Insurance Service Office. The set of services provided by a municipality is evaluated and a class assigned. For any given insurance class, it is possible that many different sets of fire services could satisfy the requirements for that class. The schedule defines five areas to be rated: (1) water supply, (2) fire department, (3) fire service communications, (4) fire safety control, and (5) miscellaneous additional deficiencies. Fire services in each area are graded on the basis of the percentage a given city is deficient with respect to the standard. These percentages are converted to points and a city's insurance class is determined by the total number of deficiency points.

A zero-one integer linear programming model can be used to identify the least cost set of fire services for any specified number of deficiency points. This formulation will be further explored in the level one disaggregation.

Class	Points of deficiency
1	0 – 500
2	501 – 1,000
3	1,001 – 1,500
4	1,501 – 2,000
5	2,001 – 2,500
6	2,501 – 3,000
7	3,001 – 3,500
8	3,501 – 4,000
9	4,001 – 4,500
10	More than – 4,500

36.1.3. Determining fire insurance costs

The second component is the total insurance cost for residents and businesses under each of the insurance classes. The survey of premiums is segmented into three strata:

1. One- and two-family dwellings.
2. Apartments.
3. Businesses.

A random sample of buildings is taken in each of the three strata of the population. Insurance premiums for these buildings are then determined under the rate schedules for each of the ten insurance classes. This provides the basis for inferences about the insurance costs for the population of buildings in a city. To get the total insurance costs for the population of buildings, the average premium costs must be multiplied by the number of units in each group.

The premiums can be calculated using the Insurance Services Office advisory schedules. These schedules are standards to be followed by all member insurance companies unless they specifically apply to the Insurance Commission for an exception.

36.2. Level one disaggregation

Level one disagregation is the selection of the mix of fire services for each insurance class. The mix of services is a byproduct of the determination of the least cost quantity needed in developing the fire service cost curve in Figure 1.

36.2.1. The model

A zero-one integer linear programming model can be used to identify the least cost mix of fire services for any specified number of deficiency points.

The model is:

$$\text{Min } Z = \sum_{j=1}^{n} c_j x_j$$

Subject to $\sum d_j(1 - X_j) \leqq D$

Where:

x_j = 0, 1 to indicate whether project j should be undertaken.
c_j = cost of project j
D = desired upper bound on deficiency points
d_j = number of deficiency points incurred if project j is not undertaken

In the model formulation, the variables X_j are the fire service projects affecting the level of fire protection as outlined in the ISO grading schedule. The coefficients c_j are the cost for the fire service. The use of $1 - X_j$ in the first constraint forces the model to count the deficiency points, d_j, only when that variable is not in solution. The first constraint defines the allowable number of deficiency points D. It is possible to evaluate the entire fire service cost curve by varying the value of D.

In addition, other constraints may be imposed by the physical nature of the projects. For example, in the Boulder project no. 8 was a fire marshall, no. 9, no. 10, and no. 11 were the three assistants. Each assistant has a unique cost and deficiency point benefit so that they must be hired in a prescribed order:

$$X_9 \leqq X_8$$
$$X_{10} \leqq X_9$$
$$X_{11} \leqq X_{10}$$

Similar constraints insure that the fire companies are added in a prescribed order as determined by the fire chief. Lastly, constraints were included to correctly deal with replacement vehicles for various companies.

36.2.2. Application

The fire service allocation model is a cost minimization model that includes both expense items such as fire marshals and capital items such as fire trucks. The capital and expense items are the decision variable for the model, and together form a set of fire services. For each decision variable, an equivalent annual cost was calculated, and the number of deficiency points avoided by its implementation was determined. This information gathering task was undertaken in a two-phase approach. A current rating of the city was necessary for this approach. The first phase was to examine the rating to determine what fire services could be added to eliminate deficiencies that currently existed. The second phase was an examination of all present fire services to determine their value in deficiency points and their cost. This yielded a set of fire services that included all present services and all possible additions that would have an impact on the city's grading. It was then possible to select the least cost set of services for a specified number of deficiency points.

36.2.3. Results

The model was run on an IBM 360 Model 67 using an integer programming code based on the Balas method [3]. The results were the least cost mix of capital and expense items (fire services) at selected deficiency point levels, and the total cost for the mix at that point. Sensitivity was investigated by looking at the possible shift in the minimum total cost for fire service integer programming solutions ranging from the upper end of the class to the lower end of the class. Since it is difficult to use every point in the range of the class, two points were selected to provide insights into the sensitivity of the model. On the basis of a subjective judgment, it was decided that an optimistic solution would be one that was about one-fourth of the way into the point range for the insurance class, and a pessimistic solution would be one that was three-fourths of the way into the class. The results from the application of the model in Boulder are presented below.

Allocation model – data points by class.

Class	Pessimistic	
	Points	Cost
1	125	No Solution
2	625	$1,207,953
3	1,125	897,955
4	1,650	622,438
5	2,125	414,828
6	2,625	269,017
7	3,125	197,851
8	3,625	185,000
9	4,125	185,000
10	4,625	185,000

Class	Optimistic	
	Points	Cost
1	375	No Solution
2	875	$1,061,809
3	1,375	771,605
4	1,875	570,743
5	2,375	324,192
6	2,875	236,104
7	3,375	185,000
8	3,875	185,000
9	4,375	185,000
10	4,875	185,000

The mix of fire services represented by each cost figure is the least cost mix. Some fire services came into an out of solution with no particular pattern. Other variables entered the solution and remained in solution as the upper bound on deficiency points was decreased. The variables that entered the solution and remained represented the variables that are most important in fire department planning. The number of key fire services that must be implemented is dependent, of course, on the insurance class desired by the city.

36.3. Summary and conclusions

36.3.1. Results for Boulder Colorado

In order to determine the least cost insurance class, considering only the public costs of fire protection and the private insurance costs, the two components must be combined. There are several possible ways of combining these two elements:

1. If it is assumed that only savings to residences should be included, (perhaps under the argument that consumers pay the majority of municipal taxes) the total of insurance costs and fire service costs indicates that class 6 is the least cost class for Boulder.
2. If it is assumed that savings to both residences and business should be included, the total cost for each class changes; but the least cost class remains class 6.

In either case, the least cost class is class 6, regardless of whether the optimistic or pessimistic number of deficiency points for a class is used.

A further sensitivity study was undertaken to investigate the importance of sampling error in evaluating insurance costs. Using either the upper or lower 95 percent confidence limit on insurance costs, class 6 is still the least cost class for Boulder, Colorado.

36.3.2. Incorporating political considerations into the model

The discussion combining excess insurance costs and fire service costs suggests that Boulder (which is currently a class 5 city) could save money by regressing to a class 6 city. However, this discussion has made an assumption whose validity is questionable. That assumption is that the decision on the amount of fire protection is based only upon the insurance benefits that accrue to property owners. The benefits of fire protection also include additional personal safety to the residents of the city which, among other things, includes the strategic location of fire companies. For example, see [7, 8]. Hence, a complete analysis might include the imputed values for reduction in loss of life and personal injury. Such an imputation was beyond the scope of this research. However, a much simpler way of incorporating these benefits was through constraints.

In Boulder's political environment, there has been no pressure to reduce the level of fire protection in any part of the city. From these political realities, it is reasonable to constrain the model so that all currently-provided fire services must be provided. The addition of this constraint indicates that Boulder should become a class 3 city by using its current fire companies, its current fire marshals, and by completing the training facility (already under construction) and the communications center.

36.3.3. Application to other municipalities

It is important for other municipalities to recognize that the results derived from the Boulder data base cannot be generalized to their communities. The ISO has indicated that due to the quality of the gravity feed water supply, Boulder would be able to achieve class 6 with few fire department services. This situation and all cost structures are unique to Boulder. The methodology, however, can be applied to any municipality. It must be recognized that the level and mix of services resulting from the model are only optimal with respect to the grading schedule. If this schedule places incorrect deficiency point values on individual grading items, then the quantity and mix derived from its application may not be the best for the community.

References

1. Hendrick, Thomas E. and Plane, Donald R., *An Application of Operations Management for Municipal Fire Station Locations*. Business Research Division, University of Colorado, Denver (1974).
2. Henrick, Thomas E., *An Analysis of the Deployment of Fire-Fighting Resources in Denver, Colorado*. The New York City-Rand Institute, R-1566/3-HUD (May 1975).
3. Plane, Donald R. and McMillan, Claude, Jr., *Discrete Optimization: Integer Programming and Network Analysis for Management Decisions*. Englewood Cliffs, N.J.: Prentice-Hall (1971).

4. Seward, Samuel M., *Minimizing Fire Department and Fire Insurance Costs: A Case Study.* Unpublished doctoral dissertation, Graduate School of Business Administration, University of Colorado (1976).

37. Disaggregation planning, scheduling, and allocation of nursing staff

HARRY B. WOLFE

Abstract

Nursing salaries make up the largest single element of hospital costs. Thus the effective planning, scheduling, and allocation of available nursing staff to patient care requirements is perhaps the most important tool available to control hospital health care delivery costs. This paper presents the requirements and constraints for nursing staff and describes procedures for more effective utilization of nursing staff, utilizing disaggregation principles. The three levels of disaggregation are:

1. Forecasting and planning. This involves forecasting overall nursing staff requirements over a year, taking into account such considerations as seasonality of patient census, staff vacation requirements, and new patient care programs.
2. Scheduling. This refers to the preparation of staff schedules, shift by shift, taking into account staff requirements and nursing unit constraints. These schedules are typically developed for a period two to eight weeks ahead.
3. Allocation. This is a process of reallocation of nursing staff on a day-to-day and shift-to-shift basis, to take into account short-time fluctuations in patient requirements, unforeseen staff absences, and availability of supplementary nursing staff.

37.1. Introduction

Unprecedented increases in medical care costs over the past two years, have seen health expenditures increase to become 8.6 percent of gross national product this year, totaling some 140 billion dollars for fiscal 1976. Hospital costs account for about half of overall health expenditures. Within hospitals, the largest single factor in the hospital budget, typically representing 35 to 40 percent of the total, is the salaries of the nursing staff. Thus, if we are to make any inroads in the current escalation of hospital costs, we must consider the most effective and efficient possible utilization of nursing staff.

We can identify three levels of disaggregation, [1], in determining the utilization of nursing staff:

1. *Forecasting and planning.* By this, we mean the forecasting of overall nursing staff requirements over an extended period (a year or more), taking into account such considerations as seasonality of patients, staff vacation requirements, and new patient care programs.
2. *Scheduling.* This refers to the preparation of staff schedules, shift-by-shift, taking into account staffing requirements and individual constraints. These schedules are typically developed for periods two to eight weeks ahead.
3. *Allocation.* This is the process of allocating and reallocating nursing staff on a day-to-day and shift-to-shift basis, making minor adjustments to the schedule to take into account short-term fluctuations in patients requirements and staff deviations from the schedule.

Thus, the disaggregation decisions that must be made are similar to those that must be made in other service sectors and many of the techniques developed for planning and scheduling in other sectors do have some applicability [4]. However, hospitals and nursing departments have special problems, and, although a number of systems have been developed to facilitate planning, scheduling, and allocation of nursing staff, very few have won acceptance and been successfully implemented, and the vast majority of hospitals still schedule and allocate nurses on an informal basis.

We first describe the overall problem of scheduling of nursing staff in the hospital. We then discuss approaches for each of the three levels of disaggregation planning, scheduling, and allocation, and then make some comments on the problems of implementing such systems in hospitals and how these might be overcome.

37.2. The disaggregation planning, scheduling and allocation problem

The basic problem of scheduling is to provide patient care every day, 24 hours a day, with nursing staff who generally work five days a week, one shift per day, and prefer to have weekends off. Scheduling is usually done by nursing supervisors for the units of floors for which they are responsible. They estimate patient care requirements and allocate the available nursing staff to the days of the week so that these requirements are approximately satisfied and hospital personnel regulations observed. They try to schedule the nursing staff so that each nurse gets her share of weekends off and none of the nurses is rotated to evenings or night shifts for an unduly long time, and they also try to accommodate individual nurses' requests for specific days off. A schedule is typically prepared every other week, specifying work days and days off for each member of the nursing staff over the ensuing two weeks.

The overall level and budget for nursing personnel is typically determined once a year through the joint efforts of nursing supervision and the hospital administrators. Permanent nursing staff positions are reviewed and new ones approved based on estimates of average daily census for the following year and estimated appropriate levels of service, typically expressed as nursing hours per patient day. The average daily patient census is estimated by projecting the historic trends of patient census, refined by other related information such as proposed openings or closings of nursing units.

Preparation of the schedule is a time-consuming task for the nursing supervisor. In addition, most hospitals seem to feel some dissatisfaction with the results:

1. Coverage tends to fluctuate widely, particularly in the case of RN's; the number of RN's assigned to a given unit on a given shift may vary from day to day by a factor of two or more.
2. In their position of total authority over schedules, supervising nurses are apt to be suspected of favoritism, particularly when they try – as is often necessary and desirable – to take into account the desires and constraints of individual nurses.
3. The attempt to resolve scheduling and allocation problems can result in excessive use of overtime.
4. Nurses often feel that there is excessive rotation.
5. Schedules frequently have to be changed on short notice because of changes in patient care requirements, illness of a nurse, etc.

Most of these problems result from the complexity of the scheduling decision and the difficulty of taking all relevant factors into account. The following are the most important factors in the decision [5].

1. The different levels of nursing staff – registered nurses, licensed practical nurses, and nurses' aides – have different capabilities; LPN's and aides are legally allowed to perform only certain functions. Even within these categories, individuals can be classified by degree of experience and by the amount of responsibility they are able to assume.
2. Nursing coverage must, of course, be provided 24 hours a day, 7 days a week. Nursing requirements are typically lower during the evening and night shifts than during the day shift. Saturday and Sunday requirements tend to be 20–30 percent lower than weekday requirements, depending on the medical service, due to a lower patient census, fewer new physicians' orders, or both.
3. Vacations and time off for holidays must be staggered to ensure continued patient coverage and equitable treatment for nurses.
4. Weekend days off are highly prized by the nursing staff, preferably both days in a row. Next in preference is two or more days off in a row in the middle of the week.
5. Long stretches of consecutive working days (usually defined as more than five in a row) are undesirable.
6. Despite a salary differential, the evening and night shifts are more difficult to staff than the day shift. As a result, schedules must often provide for 'rotation'; daytime staff must work on the other two shifts from time to time. Also, staff on evening and night shifts may sometimes have to work on the day shift in order to attend special programs, training courses, etc.
7. Most nurses prefer to remain on one nursing unit, rather than being 'floated' or shifted from one unit to another, partly because of the competence and expertise they are able to develop in a particular unit, and partly because of the camaraderie of continued association with the same group. However, there are some nurses who do not mind, and in fact prefer, floating because of the variety of experience it gives them.

The objectives of a scheduling and allocation procedure are to assign working days and days off to individual members of the nursing staff so that:

1. Adequate patient care is assured while overstaffing is avoided.
2. A desirable distribution of days off is achieved.
3. Individual members of the nursing staff are treated fairly.
4. Individuals know well in advance what their schedules are.

As described below, there exists a fairly considerable amount of work on the scheduling and allocation problems (levels 2 and 3). Least effort has been devoted to level 1 planning – the longer-term determination of nursing staff requirements related to seasonal patient census patterns.

37.3. Level 1: the annual planning problem

Figure 1 shows the average daily census for a major teaching, research-oriented hospital, averaged by week, for fiscal years 1974 and 1975. Patient census patterns are very similar for the two years,

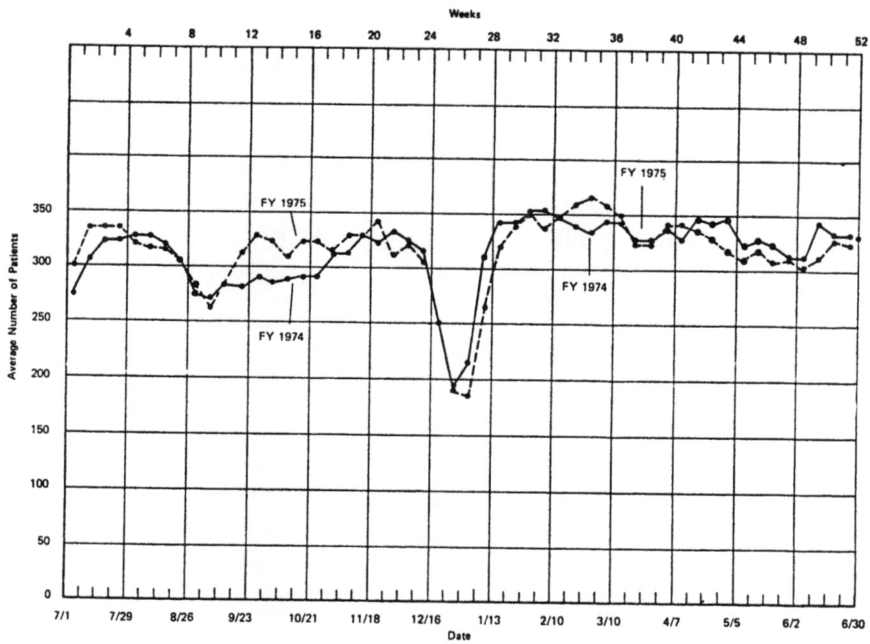

Figure 1. University hospital: average daily census, FY 1974 and FY 1975.

with reductions in census during the Christmas season, late August and early September, and May and early June, being consistent from year to year (the latter dips in census represent periods when professional medical society meetings result in postponing of elective admissions). The maximum average census was about 350, achieved in February; the lowest was during the two-week Christmas period, when census dipped to about half of normal. Thus, there may be considerable seasonality in patient census and in resulting nursing staff requirements, and this seasonality can be reasonably consistent from year to year. Obviously, if average staffing is based on peak seasonal requirements, then there will be periods when the hospital will be overstaffed, unless adequate attention is taken to adjust nursing staff to such seasonal requirements. Such efforts might include, for example:

1. Encouraging nursing staff to take vacation during periods of lower census;
2. Attempting to maintain a pool of 'on-call' nursing staff who can be hired for short-term assignments during peak census periods.

The overall staff planning problem is complicated, however, by the following:

1. There is normally a fair amount of turnover throughout the year, which may be accentuated at certain periods (such as at the end of the school year when nurses' husbands, for example, move to another location). A staff turnover of 35 percent per year, is not unusual.
2. A large number of nurses 'come on the market' at the close of nursing schools' years.

Very little work has been done on development of formal methods of planning, hiring, and overall utilization of nursing staff, taking into account the above requirements and constraints. Certainly, the techniques developed for disaggregation forecasting of seasonal requirements in other industries could be applicable to the census forecasting problem. The overall planning and hiring of nursing staff in response to such requirements is considerably more difficult.

37.4. Level 2: the principle of cyclical scheduling

A number of systems have been developed to create cyclical schedules for nursing staff, taking into account the requirements and constraints described above.

Table 1. A 5-week cyclical schedule.

S	M	T	W	T	F	S	S	M	T	W	T	F	S	S	M	T	W	T	F	S	S	M	T	W	T	F	S	S	M	T	W	T	F	S	S	M	T	W	T	F	S
D				*D*					*D*	*D*					*D*					*D*	*D*					*D*				*D*				*D*	*D*				*D*		
		D				*D*	*D*				*D*					*D*	*D*					*D*					*D*	*D*					*D*				*D*				*D*
D					*D*				*D*				*D*	*D*				*D*					*D*	*D*					*D*					*D*	*D*					*D*	
	D					*D*	*D*					*D*				*D*				*D*	*D*				*D*					*D*	*D*					*D*					*D*
		D	*D*					*D*					*D*	*D*					*D*				*D*				*D*	*D*				*D*					*D*	*D*			

Table 1 shows a simple cyclical schedule. There are five nurses and the cycle length of the schedule is five weeks. Days off are denoted by *D*. The first line indicates working days and days off for the first nurse, the second line for the second nurse and so forth. The first nurse has the first Sunday off, then a Thursday, then she has a Tuesday and Wednesday off, and so on untill the five weeks are up, at which point the entire pattern of working days and days off begins again. The overall pattern of working days and days off is exactly the same for all of the nurses; the only difference is that it begins in a different week for each nurse. Thus, the schedule followed by the first nurse in the first week is followed by the second nurse the following week, the third the week after, and so on. The weeks start with Sunday and end with Saturday. Each nurse works five days a week, works at most four days in a row, and has two out of five weekends off. Four of the five nurses are always present except on Tuesdays and on weekends, when only three are present.

Let a pattern of working days and days off be described by a sequence of variables y_i where

$$y_i = \begin{matrix} 1 \\ 0 \end{matrix} \quad \begin{matrix} \text{if day } i \text{ is off} \quad i = 1, 2, \ldots 7n \\ \text{otherwise} \end{matrix} \tag{1}$$

and n is the number of weeks covered by the pattern. Suppose now that a cyclical schedule is constructed for N individuals such that individual j starts the given pattern $r_j (1 \leq r_{j_2} \leq n)$ weeks after day 1. For instance, if r_3 is equal to 2, individual 3 starts the pattern on day 15. The total number of individuals absent on day i is then simply

$$D_i = \sum_{j=1}^{N} y_{i-7rj} \tag{2}$$

where r_1 is equal to zero and for any integer k

$$y_{i+7kn} = y_i \tag{3}$$

The requirement that the total number of inidividuals absent on a given day of a week be the same for all weeks means that

$$D_{i+7k} = D_i \tag{4}$$

for any integers i and k. The pattern given by expression (1) is defined such that it cannot be broken down into two or more patterns that repeat themselves. Now, it we assume for simplicity that

$$r_{j+1} = r_j + 1 \tag{5}$$

then requirement (4) becomes

$$\sum_{j=1}^{N} y_{i+7(k+1-j)} = \sum_{j=1}^{N} y_{i-7(j-1)}. \tag{6}$$

By leaving out the terms common to both sides, this can be reduced to

$$\sum_{j=0}^{K-1} y_{i-7j+7K} = \sum_{j=N-k}^{N-1} y_{i-7j}. \tag{7}$$

Requirement (7) is true for arbitrary integers i and k only if N is an integer multiple of n. In this case, expression (3) can be used to reduce the condition to an identity.

In the example of Table 1, we did not distinguish between charge nurses, registered nurses, licensed practical nurses, and aides. Since there must always be a nurse present who can take charge of the unit and since there must always be present a certain number of registered nurses and licensed nurses regardless of the number of aides, the assignment of individual nurses to the cycles of a schedule must be planned with care.

A number of scheduling techniques have been developed for building cyclical schedules that provide for an even distribution of weekends off; provide at least the minimum anticipated staffing requirements for charge nurses, registered nurses, LPNs, and aides; and are sufficiently flexible to accommodate vacations, holidays, and changes in individual's plans and preferences. These are primarily heuristic algorithmic methods [3], [5], [6], [8], [9], [13], [14], although, in principle, optimizing approaches, such as integer programming or mathematical programming [7], [10], [11], could be utilized. The techniques include computer-generated, as well as manual scheduling procedures.

These techniques have been aimed at improving the traditional three eight-hour shift assignment. However, a few hospitals have experimented with 10-hour shift, 4-day work weeks [12], and even 12-hour shift schedules with seven days on, seven days off work weeks [2]. These newer schedules appear to have some desirable features and advantages in some instances, but it is unlikely that they will be universally accepted or adopted.

37.5. Allocation procedure

Patient care requirements change from day to day and even from one hour to the next. The cyclical schedule guarantees a certain minimum coverage but does not take into account fluctuations in patient care requirements. It is evident that the relative fluctuations on one floor are larger than those of an entire division consisting of several floors. Thus, these fluctuations can be accommodated by short-term assignment of nurses from a 'float pool' to those floors that need them most. This is the only way to provide extra coverage without permanent overstaffing. In special situations when peaks of patient care requirements on one or several floors cannot be accommodated from the float pool, individuals may be temporarily shifted from floors with lighter requirements to those with heavy requirements. However, this should be considered only as a last resort since it reduces coverage below desirable levels on the floors from which the extra staff are obtained; also, nurses generally dislike being 'pulled'.

Since these adjustments in schedule are based on patient-care requirements, a method of assessing these requirements is needed. Considerable effort has been devoted to assessing nursing care requirements on the basis of patient medical status. In practice, however, a simple classification scheme for patient assessment is sufficiently accurate to provide the appropriate level of detail required for nursing reallocation [5]. Table 2 shows such a classification. According to this scheme, patients are classified into four categories: acute care, complete care, partial care, and, ambulatory care.

Table 2. Patient classification form.

Classification	No. of patients	Specials*	Rel. value	Total value
Acute			4	
Complete			3	
Partial			2	
Ambulatory			1	
Expected discharges			0.5	

* For patients with specials subtract half the relative value from the total.

The differences in patient care requirements among categories are quantified by assigning relative values: 4, 3, 2 and 1 for acute, complete, partial, and ambulatory care, respectively. If a private duty nurse is assigned to a patient, it is assumed that only half the normally required care is provided by the regular staff. In addition, discharges are given a relative value of 0.5. The total relative value per floor is then calculated by multiplying the number of patients in each category by the relative value of the category and adding the resulting products.

The system operates as follows. Patients are classified twice a day, at 6 a.m. and 2 p.m., to provide guidance for the day and evening staffing respectively. Patient classification forms are filled out by the unit floor supervisor (it typically takes only a few minutes to fill them out) and forwarded to the nursing supervisor for all medical units. The nursing supervisor or her secretary or assistant copies the relative patient values for each unit onto a form, notes the number of available staff (number of assigned staff per unit minus no-shows), totals these, and adds the sum to the float staff available to get total available staff. She then divides total relative values by total available staff to find the workload index: the number of relative value points per staff member. By then dividing the total relative value for each floor by the workload index, she determines how many nurses should be assigned to each floor to equalize the index. The staffing supervisors then assign the float staff to the individual floors, taking into account their knowledge of the type and quality of assigned staff on each floor and of the float pool. If further adjustment is necessary, nursing staff may be 'pulled' from one floor and assigned to another. If interactive computer terminals are available, the calculation may be computerized rather than manual.

In order to provide the desirable flexibility while minimizing the amount of 'pulling' from one floor to another, it is desirable to build up a large float pool. Part-time staff can be automatically assigned to the float pool, nurses who enjoy floating should be encouraged to remain in the pool, and new nursing staff should whenever possible be hired for the pool rather than for specific floor assignments.

37.6. Comments

One of the major considerations that has obviated against utilization of disaggregation planning, scheduling, and allocation procedures, is the belief that nursing staff scheduling and allocation is relatively inflexible. For example, it is commonly assumed that nurses cannot be transferred from one unit to another; that nurses must be hired for full eight-hour shifts; that it is difficult to hire nurses on a short-term basis, etc. In actuality, however, nursing departments frequently can achieve greater flexibility, and greater efforts should be made to take advantage of this flexibility. For example, there are nurses who do not mind working on more than one unit and, in fact, welcome the diversity of such nursing experience. There frequently are nurses in the community who would be willing to work on a part-time basis – not necessarily a full eight-hour shift. One major indirect benefit resulting from the studies and systems described in this paper has been to point out and quantify the economic benefits that can accrue from taking greater advantage of such flexibility. When sufficient effort is taken to do so, then application of formal disaggregation procedures, together with more flexibility in staffing, can improve nursing utilization in hospitals.

Where such systems have been implemented, they have enabled nursing staff to improve staffing allocation and utilization, resulting in, typically, small reductions in nursing staff, reductions in overtime, and improved relationship between patient requirements in available nursing staff and (presumably) quality of nursing care.

As we have mentioned, however, the vast majority of hospitals still schedule and allocate nurses on an informal basis. The rejection of more systematic methods appears to result, at least in part, from a set of beliefs:

1. Nursing as a profession is not amenable to formal scheduling and allocation procedures, being more oriented to individualizing both patient requirements and nurses' interest and capabilities;
2. Most nurses are non-quantitatively oriented and, therefore, resist any system involving computers;
3. At least in part, the failure of previous efforts to take into account variables that were important to nursing staff;
4. Most hospitals are, by standards normally under consideration by manufacturing and other enterprises, comparatively small concerns. The average hospital community has about 160 beds, and annual revenues of $5,000,000. The administration of the typical hospital feels that it cannot afford to devote the level of effort or funds for development of such formal systems, particularly under the current stringent fiscal situation.

As a result, in order to achieve successful implementation of more formal, improved systems, considerable effort must be devoted to understanding and taking into account, not only the problems and special restraints of hospitals and nursing departments generally, but the special requirements, and mores of each individual hospital and its nursing staff. Thus, the age distribution of the nursing staff, geographical location of the hospital, availability of nurses in the area, all will have an impact on development of the most appropriate procedures.

References

1. Abernathy, William J., Baloff, Nicholas, Hershey, John C., and Wandel, Sten, 'A Three-Stage Manpower Planning and Scheduling Model – A Service Sector Example', *Operations Research*, vol. 21 (1973), pp. 693–711.
2. Ganong, Warren L., Ganong, Joan M., and Harrison, Edwin T., 'The 12-Hour Shift: Better Quality, Lower Cost', *Journal of Nursing Administration* (February 1976), pp. 17–29.
3. Howell, John P., 'Cyclical Scheduling of Nursing Personnel', *Hospitals*, vol. 40, (16 January 1966), pp. 77–85.
4. Krajewski, LeRoy J. and Ritzman, Larry P., 'Disaggregation in Manufacturing and Service Organizations: Survey of Problems and Research'.

5. Maier-Rothe, Christoph and Wolfe, Harry B., 'Cyclical Scheduling and Allocation of Nursing Staff', *Socio-Economic Planning Sciences*, vol. 7 (1973), pp. 471–487.
6. McCartney, Richard A., McKee, Barbara, and Cady, Lee D., 'Nurse Staffing Systems', *Hospitals*, vol. 44, pp. 102–105.
7. Miller Holmes P., Pierskalla, William P., and Rath, Gustave J., 'Nurse Scheduling Using Mathematical Programming', *Operations Research*, vol. 24, no. 5 (September–October 1976), pp. 857–870.
8. Moorish, Arthur R. and O'Connor, Anna R., 'Cyclical Scheduling', *Hospitals*, vol. 44, (16 February 1970), pp. 66–71.
9. Smith, L. Douglas, 'The Application of an Interactive Algorithm to Develop Cyclical Rotational Schedules for Nursing Personnel', *INFOR*, vol. 14, no. 1 (February 1976), pp. 53–70.
10. Warner, D. Michael, 'Scheduling Nursing Personnel According to Nursing Preference: A Mathematical Programming Approach', *Operations Research*, vol. 24, no. 5 (September–October 1976).
11. Warner, D. Michael and Prawda, Juan, 'A Mathematical Programming Model for Scheduling Nursing Personnel in a Hospital', *Management Science*, vol. 19, no. 4 (December, Part I, 1972), pp. 411–422.
12. Wittman, John, Ph.D., and Johnson, William C., 'Four-Day Workweek Anyone?', *Hospitals, J.A.H.A.*, vol. 44 (July 16, 1973), pp. 60–63.
13. Wolfe, Harvey and Young, John P., 'Staffing the Nursing Unit. Part I., Controlled Variable Staffing', *Nursing Res.*, vol. 14, no. 3 (1965), pp. 236–243.
14. Wolfe, Harvey and Young, John P., 'Staffing the Nursing Unit', Part II., The Multiple Assignment Technique. *Nursing Res.*, vol. 14, (1965), pp. 299–303.

38. Disaggregate mathematical models for optimal hospital bed management[1]

AUGUSTINE O. ESOGBUE and AMAR J. SINGH

Abstract

Efficient bed distribution and management may enhance quality and cost containment goals of the modern hospital administrator.

The problem of the design of optimal bed management strategies for a total hospital system is decomposed into the following interrelated subproblems: optimal allocation amongst the various distinctive patient facilities (wards), optimal priority bed allocation between patient classes in a given ward, and the optimal transfer policies for transfers in the buffer (improper) accommodation case. Concentrating on the first two level problems in this paper, we model the resultant problems via the tools of stochastic processes and dynamic programming.

38.1. Introduction

The three major prescriptions for our ailing health care delivery system are i) the provision of equity of access, ii) the improvement of quality of care provided and iii) the containment of costs of delivery. Focussing on the hospital as an important delivery mode, we examine how hospital management could exercise with effectiveness one important leverage at their disposal namely – optimal bed management. Beds are unquestionably an important resource central to the existence of most hospitals both in terms of service and revenue generation.

The major issues connected with the design of optimal bed management strategies in a hospital with bed complement N, and

1. Reprinted from Proceedings of Conference on The Problems of Disaggregation in Manufacturing and Service Organizations, The Ohio State University, Columbus, Ohio. March 1977, pp. 37–42.

K distinctive patient facilities (DPF), nursing stations, wards may be disaggregated into the following three level problems: i) allocation of beds to the various DPFs in the total hospital system, ii) within a given DPF, the design of priority or allocation discipline to be employed in assigning beds to patients, and iii) assuming that under certain exigencies, management admits patients into improper wards or DPFs (buffer accommodation problem) the design of optimal policies with regards to inpatient transfers. Our primary concern in this paper is with the first two level problems. The first level problem is treated for the first time in this paper while much of the second level problem was discussed at length in a recent paper [2]. We also develop mathematical models for describing the state of the system in the buffer accommodation case but must refer the interested reader to Rabinowitz et al. [3] for a detailed treatment of transfer policies appropriate for the third level problem.

38.2. First level problem: mathematical bed allocation model

Consider a hospital with a total bed complement N to be allocated among K distinctive patient facilities or services such as pediatrics, obstetrics, general medicine, dermatology etc. determined primarily on the basis of type of diseases treated in the hospital. Not considered therefore, are exceptional situations where the service to which a patient is admitted is determined primarily by the admitting privileges of his physician. Two models are discussed.

38.2.1. Case 1: deterministic demand

Assuming that the demand for each category of disease is known then the following deterministic model could be constructed:

Let

$\bar{\nu}_k$ = average number of patients in facility k, $k \in K$ (average daily census)
m_k = number of beds to be allocated in the k-th facility.
N = total number of beds in the whole hospital.
C_k^h = cost per unit time of keeping a bed empty or unused; since

some diseases may require special equipment, it is assumed such a cost is different for different wards.

C_k^s = cost of not providing a bed for a patient belonging to category k; this cost may vary according to the background of the patient and other factors; in this model, however, C_k^s is assumed to be constant.

We assume linear costs, i.e., the holding and shortage costs are proportional to the difference between the beds actually allocated and the average demand. Linear costs will be a good approximation to any possible non-linear costs, because we will be dealing with DPFS with a limited number of beds, and the average number of beds held empty (or fallen short of demand) will be small.

The holding cost C_k^h per unit bed may consist of:

a) floor space occupied, b) overhead costs (heating, lighting, air-conditioning, cleaning, etc.) c) paramedical staff (nurses, maids, etc.) usually assigned based on bed complement, and d) other indirect costs.

In the above we observe that if there is enough floor space available in a *DPF*, and one extra bed is added, it is possible that with this extra bed additional paramedical staff will have to be added. This situation could arise if the existing load on the present staff is sufficiently large so that they could not assume the burden of an extra patient. Under such conditions, the cost of maintaining an empty bed may become a variable. However, for our analysis of this problem, C_k^h is assumed constant for each bed. We can write the following costs for each of the k facilities:

1. Fixed Cost: $A_k \delta_k \quad \delta_k = \begin{cases} 0, \text{ if } m_k = 0 \\ 1, \text{ otherwise} \end{cases}$

2. Holding Cost: $C_k^h(\bar{v}_k - m_{\bar{k}})^-$

3. Shortage Cost: $C_k^s(v_k^- - m_k)^+$

where $X^- = -\min(0, X)$ and $X^+ = \max(0, X)$

Thus the total operating cost for facility K when m_k beds are allocated to it is given by

$$\Omega'(m_k > \bar{v}_k)$$

where

$$\Omega'(m_k\bar{v}_k) = A_k\delta_k + C_k^h(\bar{v}_k - m_k)^- + C_k^s(\bar{v}_k - m_k)^+ \tag{1}$$

The total system cost Ω' may thus be represented by

$$\Omega' = \sum_{k=1}^{K} \Omega'(m_k, \bar{v}_k) = \sum_{k=1}^{K} \Big\{ A_k\delta_k + C_k^h\bar{v}_k - m_k)^- + + C_k^s(\bar{v}_k - m_k)^+ \Big\} \tag{2}$$

The resultant optimization problem is then

Minimize

$$\Omega'$$

Subject to

$$\sum_{k=1}^{K} m_k \leqq N \tag{3}$$

The above is a fixed-charge problem. The values A_k are called fixed charges, since A_k is only incurred if $m_k > 0$. However, if $A_k = 0$, then it could be solved by linear programming. Because of the possibility of local optima, it may be difficult to solve it via linear programming. Although algorithms exist for solving such integer programming problems, it seems that the time needed to solve such problems is too high. This is directly attributable to the computational inefficiencies of such algorithms.

By solving the problem via dynamic programming we are able to decompose the problem involving functions of two or more variables into many problems involving functions of only one variable. This helps to reduce the computer memory requirement. Moreover, by using dynamic programming it is also possible to determine explicitly the ith best solution along with the global optimum. Also, dynamic programming techniques can easily handle the problems involving any of the following types of functions:

1. discontinuous; defined only at discrete points,
2. with local and global optimum,
3. non-linear.

Define

$\xi_k(N)$ as the minimum cost of providing beds to k facilities, given that the total number of available beds is N, and that an optimal policy is adopted.

For $k = 1, 2, \ldots K$, we have

$$\xi_k(N) = \min \{\Omega'(m_k, \bar{v}_k) + \xi_{k-1}(N - m_k)\} \quad 0 \leqq m_k \leqq N \quad (4)$$

and

$$\delta_k = \begin{cases} 1, \text{ if } m_k > 0 \\ 0, \text{ if } m_k = 0 \end{cases}$$

with boundary conditions

$$\xi_o(N) = 0 \text{ and } \xi_o(0) = 0$$

The problem is solved when $\xi_k(N)$ has been calculated.

Sometimes teaching hospitals or some insurance companies require that there should at least be a minimum number (M_k) of beds for facility k, $k \in K$. To take into account such a constraint, we have:

$$m_k \geqq M_k.$$

Our recursive equation (4) then becomes

$$\xi_k(N) = \min \{\Omega'(m_k, \bar{v}_k) + \xi_{k-1}(N - m_k)\}. \quad M_k \leqq m_k < N \quad (5)$$

38.2.2. Case 2: stochastic demand

The deterministic case discussed above is unrealistic in certain cases where demand for beds is clearly a random variable. Previous studies particularly [6] indicate that demand follows some well known distribution such as the Poisson or CENSA. Thus, considering demand to be a random variable with a given probability distribution, we develop the following more realistic stochastic allocation model.

Let v_k be a random variable representing the total demand of beds in facility k. Since the demand will be finite, we assume it has an upper bound Ψ_k.

Let $p(v_k)$ be probability that there is a demand of v_k beds for facility k. Since the problem is concerned with integer solutions, $p(\cdot)$ are discrete probabilities. Let m_k be the number of beds to be allocated for disease k, with $k = 1, 2, \ldots, K$.

Then the expected cost of providing m_k beds to the k-th facility is given by, $\Omega(m_k, v_k)$.

$$\Omega(m_k, v_k) = A_k\delta_k + C_k^h \sum_{v_k=0}^{m_k} (m_k - v_k)\, p(v_k)$$

$$+ C_k^s \sum_{v_k=m_k+1}^{\Psi_k} (v_k - m_k)\, p(v_k) \tag{6}$$

Let the expected cost for K facilities with total capacity of N beds be $\Lambda(N, K)$. Thus

$$\Lambda(N, K) = \sum_{k=1}^{K} \Omega(m_k, v_k). \tag{7}$$

Define

$\xi_k(N)$ as the minimum expected cost of providing beds to k distinctive patient facilities in an optimal manner, given that the total available beds are N.

Then invoking the principle of optimality [1], we can write the following recursive equations for $k = 2, 3, \ldots, K$

$$\xi_k(N) = \min_{\substack{m_k \leqq N \\ m_k,\ \text{integer}}} \{\Omega(m_k, v_k) + \xi_{k-1}(N - m_k)\} \tag{8}$$

and for $k = 1$,

$$\xi_1(N) = \min_{m_1,\ \text{integer}} \{A_1\delta_1 + C_k^h \sum_{v_1=0}^{m_1} (m_1 - v_1)\, p(v_1) \tag{9}$$

$$+ C_k^s \sum_{v_1=m_1+1}^{\Psi_1} (v_1 - m_1)\, p(v_1)\}$$

with boundary conditions

$$\xi_0(N) = 0 \text{ and } \xi_0(0) = 0$$

Thus, the problem of finding an optimal allocation solution to the K category facilities is reduced to that of solving K problems taking one facility at a time. Therefore, there are only K complete iterations necessary to obtain the optimal values.

We note that in the foregoing, if $\Omega(m, v)$ of equation (7) is convex, then $\xi_k(N)$ is also convex. Since the problem is to be solved for integer values only, it follows that the minimum of the right hand side of equation (8) must be found for all feasible values of m_k. However, if $\xi_k(\cdot)$ is convex then one of the efficient search techniques could be employed to find this minimum. That $\Omega(m_k, v_k)$ is convex and thus the functional $\xi_k(\cdot)$ is established in [1]. Thus, the derivation of the optimum is essentially routine and consequently not of particular interest to us here.

38.3. Second level problem: patient priority allocation models[2]

In order of beds in a specific DPF to be utilized efficiently, one of the many requirements is that admitting procedures be designed so that the total or average time a bed remains empty is minimized. If we assume that all patients waiting to be admitted to the ward could benefit equally from a bed day and that delays do not seriously inhibit the outcome of inpatient treatment, the admitting schedule can be relatively simply designed to achieve a high level of average per cent occupancy or bed usage. In a more complex system however, where waiting time prior to admission is an important determinant of treatment outcome for some cases but not for others, it might be necessary to tolerate a reduced occupancy to ensure that, with an acceptable probability, a bed will be available for randomly arriving urgent or more interesting cases. At this level, we present mathematical models useful in devising an admission policy for patients with different levels of severity or appeal in a ward and optimize it with respect to an objective function that is a hybrid of the traditional measure of efficiency, occupancy maximization, and a new one, the minimization of unsatisfied needs.

Specifically, the objective of the model is to provide a quantitative, rational, and operational basis for establishing a priority 'cut-off occupancy' which will maximize the medical benefits that can be provided by a given set of beds in a ward where differentiation by case types is possible. Such a 'cut-off' priority (or occu-

2. Portions of this section reprinted by permission of Augustine O. Esogbue and Amar J. Singh, 'Optimal Hospital Bed Distribution', *Operations Research*, vol. 24, pp. 884–898. Copyright (1976), Operations Research Society of America.

pancy) sets the number of beds beyond which a certain class of casesis not scheduled or admitted. We assume that in a ward, the patients can be classified into two categories, namely, type 1 (serious) and type 2 (non-serious). Other categories, classifications, and interpretations can be considered. For example, in a surgical ward, where beds are normally assigned to various classes of surgery in a rather less sophisticated way, type 1 may be the most frequent case (general surgery) while type 2 may refer to all other classes. Thus, if there are N beds in the ward, one seeks an optimal value of 'cut-off' priority, m, such that if the number of occupied beds is more than or equal to m, then patients of type 2 are not admitted. This is in contrast to existing practice or arbitrarily setting aside a fixed number of beds for certain cases and exercising limited control on this 'quota'. Problems akin to this and closely related to space management issues are encountered in other hospital sectors.

38.3.1. Mathematical model for selection of cut-off priority

For the two types of patients considered in this model, let,

λ_i = arrival rate for type i patients and μ_i = service (discharge) rate for type i patients, $i = 1, 2$.

Assuming that the number of arrivals in each category is a random variable with Poisson distribution, and the length of stay follows a negative exponential distribution, and admissions and discharges can occur independently of each other, it is possible to develop the birth and death equations describing the state of the system. The validity of these assumptions has been borne out by several empirical studies of the hospital in patient census.

38.3.2. Structure of the model

Computational considerations motivate the adoption of the following notation:

Let $P_{n,n_2}(t)$ = probability that at time t, in a ward containing n patients, n_2 beds are occupied by type 2 patients.
m = cut-off occupancy, expressed in number of beds.

Thus, out of a total on N beds in the ward, $(N - m)$ are reserved only for type 1 patients. Relating the probabilities at time $(t + \Delta t)$ with those at time t, (for a discrete system), we develop a system of equations for computing the probabilities associated with various values of the total number of occupied beds n, and later for numerical determination of m, the cut-off occupancy. Since these equations may be generated by slight modifications of the familiar 'birth-death process' formulations, we omit their derivations here. It is instructive to present the equations for calculating the final limiting probabilities for the various conceivable scenarios. However, we will exhibit only the first two cases here and refer the interested reader to [3] where they are given in greater detail.

Define $\tau_{n,n_2} = \lim_{t\to 0} P_{n,n_2}(t)$. Assuming that these limiting probabilities τ_{n,n_2} exist independently of the initial state of the system, it can readily be shown that the resultant set of equations are satisfied by τ_{n,n_2} with $P'_{n,n_2}(t) = 0$. The corresponding system of linear-difference equations for the two cases discussed explicitly here may thus be written as:

Case 1: For $n = 0$, $n_2 = 0$

$$0 = -(\lambda_1 + \lambda_2)\tau_{0,0} + \mu_1\tau_{1,0} + \mu_2\tau_{1,1} \tag{10}$$

Case 2(a): For $1 \leqq n < m$, $n_2 < n$

$$\begin{aligned}0 = &-[\lambda_1 + \lambda_2) + n_2\mu_2 + (n - n_2)\mu_1]\tau_{n,n_2}\\ &(n + 1 - n_2)\mu_1\tau_{n+1,n_2} + (n_2 + 1)\mu_2\tau_{n+1,n_2+1} + \lambda_1\tau_{n-1,n_2} +\\ &+ \lambda_2\tau_{n-1,n_{2-1}}\end{aligned} \tag{11}$$

Case 2(b): For $1 \leqq n < m$, $n_2 = n$

$$\begin{aligned}0 = &-[(\lambda_1 + \lambda_2) + n\mu_2]\tau_{n,n} + \mu_1\tau_{n+1,\mathrm{n}} +\\ &+ (n + 1)\mu_2\tau_{n+1,n+1} + \lambda_2\tau_{n-1,n-1}\end{aligned} \tag{12}$$

To be fully and completely described one must proceed along the preceeding scheme and develop linear difference equations for the following remaining cases.

Case 3(a): $n = m$, $n_2 < m$
Case 3(b): $n_2 = n = m$
Case 4(a): $m < n < N$, $n_2 < m$

Case 4(b): $m < n < N, n = m$
Case 5: $n = N, n_2 \leqq m, m \neq N$

The total number of equations generated by the above system is given by π where

$$\pi = m(m + 1)/2 + (m + 1)(N - m + 1) \tag{13}$$

For example, suppose $N = 3$, and $m = 2$ i.e., a situation where the total number of beds in the ward is 3 and the cut-off priority is set at 2, one gets a coefficient matrix $\vec{A}$ whose form is displayed below in equation (14).

$$\vec{A} = \left|\begin{array}{ccccccccc}
-(\lambda_1+\lambda_2) & \mu_1 & \mu_2 & & & & & & \\
\lambda_1 & -[\lambda_1+\lambda_2+\mu_1] & & 2\mu_1 & \mu_2 & & & & \\
\lambda_2 & \lambda_1 & -[\lambda_1+\mu_2+\mu_2] & & \mu_1 & & & & \\
 & \lambda_2 & \lambda_1 & -[\lambda_1+2\mu_1] & & 2\mu_2 & 3\mu_1 & \mu_2 & \\
 & & & & -[\lambda_1+\mu_2+\mu_1] & & & 2\mu_1 & 2\mu_2 \\
 & & \lambda_2 & & & -[\lambda_1+2\mu_2] & & & \\
 & & & & \lambda_1 & & -[\lambda_1+3\mu_1] & & \mu_1 \\
 & & & & & \lambda_1 & & -[\lambda_1+\mu_2+2\mu_1] & \\
 & & & & & & \lambda_1 & & -[\lambda_1+2\mu_2+\mu_1]
\end{array}\right| \tag{14}$$

This matrix which is approximately tridiagonal has a probability vector (column) τ given by

$$\tau = [\tau_{00}\tau_{10}\tau_{11}\tau_{21}\tau_{22}\tau_{30}\tau_{31}\tau_{32}] \tag{15}$$

Solution of the foregoing set of equations is best accomplished by recourse to numerical procedures of the sort followed in [3].

38.3.3. Shortage probabilities

In the system described before, if the number of beds occupied (n) is equal to or greater than m, the cut-off occupancy level, then patients of type 2 are not admitted in the ward. Thus, if $n \geqq m$, and n_2, the number of beds occupied by type 2 patients, assumes any value from 0 to m, then the steady state probability that a patient of type 2 is turned away is given by

$$\phi_2 = \sum_{n=m}^{N} \sum_{n_2=0}^{m} \tau_{n,n_2} \tag{16}$$

However, if all the beds are occupied, then type 1 patients are also refused admission. The steady state probability of type 1 patients being turned away is given by

$$\phi_1 = \sum_{n_2=0}^{m} \tau_{N,n_2} \tag{17}$$

38.3.4. Optimizing the value of cut-off point

Let c_2^i be the cost of not supplying a bed per unit time to a patient of type i when a request is made and c_1 be the cost of maintaining an empty bed per unit time. Also, let v_i be expected number of patients of type i who will be turned away in a unit time period. Thus

$v_i = \phi_{i\lambda i}$. From (16) and (17), we have

$$v_1 = \lambda_1 \sum_{n_2=0}^{m} \tau_{N,n_2} \text{ and } v_2 = \lambda_2 \sum_{n=m}^{N} \sum_{n_2=0}^{m} \tau_{n,n_2}$$

The costs involved in the model are the expected penalty cost per unit period,

$$\Psi_p = c_2^1 v_1 + c_2^2 v_2$$

and the expected holding cost per unit period $\Psi_h =$

$$c_l \sum_{n=m+1}^{N} \sum_{n_2=0}^{m} (N - n)\tau_{n,n_2}, \text{ if } n > m$$

$$c_1 \sum_{n=0}^{m} \sum_{n_2=0}^{n} (N - n)\tau_{n,n_2}, \text{ if } n \leqq m \tag{18}$$

The equation for expected cost may then be written as

$$c(m, N) = \Psi_p + \Psi_h = c_2^1 v_1 + c_2^2 v_2 +$$

$$c_1 \left\{ \sum_{n=m+1}^{N} \sum_{n_2=0}^{m} (N - n)\tau_{n,n_2} + \sum_{n=0}^{m} \sum_{n_2=0}^{n} (N - n)\tau_{n,n_2} \right\} \tag{19}$$

The total cost $c(m, N)$ is the sum of two components, the holding cost (c_1), the cost incurred when a maintained bed is empty in a given period, and the short-age cost (c_2), the cost of being unable to provide a bed in a given period. As the number of beds increases the expected number of shortages and the shortage cost reduce while the expected number of empty beds and the holding cost increase. Thus, total cost will tend to decrease as the number of beds increases until a minimum is reached and the holding cost becomes dominant. The actual number of beds which minimizes cost is dependent on the form of the holding and shortage cost functions. The particular form of these functions does not pose any problem to our model and computational schema, however.

The objective therefore, is to minimize $c(m, N)$ as a function of m which is the cut-off point. Note that m, n, n_2 and N are all integers. This means that $c(m, N)$ is not a continuous function of m and hence does not possess derivatives. Thus, it is not possible to accomplish the minimization of (19) with respect to m via the usual calculus procedures.

38.3.5. Valuation of model costs

Basically, three types of costs are considered in this model:

1. Holding costs (cost per unit time of maintaining an empty bed).
2. Shortage cost (cost of refusing, or being unable to provide a patient a bed in a unit time period).
3. Fixed operating cost (initial set up including maintenance).

The holding cost, c_1 per bed per unit time may consist of the following: Floor space occupied; overhead costs such as heating, lighting, air conditioning, cleaning, etc.; paramedical staff such as nurses, nursing aids, maids, etc. usually assigned a ward on the basis of bed complement; other indirect costs. The holding cost could be a variable in certain situations but in the present model, we consider it reasonably constant for each bed in the ward. Evaluation of this cost as well as the fixed costs is relatively easy to accomplish via established hospital accounting procedures.

The other important cost element considered in this model is shortage cost. In industry such a shortage cost would be evaluated by considering lost sales, loss of good will, and/or any penalties attached to inability to meet demands. Some difficulty with its evaluation in the hospital setting is anticipated but we can compute it by evaluating the expected cost of the various alternatives available to a patient who is refused admission for whatever nonmedical reason. Details of this approach may be found in [3].

38.3.6. Implementation of model

The foregoing model was validated for a pediatric ward consisting of 15 beds in a university teaching hospital in Cleveland, Ohio. Data on average number of requests for admissions per day, average length of stay in days and the average daily census for both staff and private patients were collected and utilized. The data for costs were obtained by questioning a group of hospital personnel in a manner akin to the Delphi process of eliciting concensus opinion on otherwise elusive issues. The difficulty associated with obtaining values for c_2^i was minimized in this case by normalizing it with respect to c_1. Hospital staff were found more able to relate to this ratio than to the absolute values of c_2^i for all i. The assumption of a linear relationship was justified on the basis that the ward sizes are not unusually large and, further, that the average number of beds held empty would be small.

Solution of the model for various cases showed that minimum operating cost is obtained by a delicate balance between the shortage costs and holding costs as was conjectured. Thus bed assignment strategies which fail to explicitly consider these variables and relationships may prove to be considerably inefficient. The benefit of this model is that it allows management to parameterize on these costs as their relative values change to determine the optimal number of beds to reserve for the different classes thus providing for dynamic control.

38.4. Buffer accommodation

Let us turn our attention to a variation of the foregoing models by considering a leverage sometimes employed by hospital management. In certain exigencies, excess arrivals (overflows) are not or cannot be turned away but are either accommodated in a temporary, usually inappropriate facility, or taken care of via the use of the so-called 'center beds.' This possibility sometimes leads hospital management to erroneously consider their resource so elastic as to downplay the role of scheduling or optimization. The buffer accommodation model is actually more realistic since it considers a situation where a patient might be rejected in the appropriate ward (for the purposes of our priority decision model) but in fact is satisfied (psychologically) with being accepted in another ward in the hospital. In the sequel, we show how the models developed earlier can be adapted to treat the new situation.

38.4.1. Systems equations

Suppose patients of type 1 are not turned away but are temporarily accommodated in a buffer ward. Since it is a temporary accommodation we assume it is not equipped with all the elaborate facilities which are available in a proper ward. For this reason, it is reasonable to believe that the maintenance cost of a bed in buffer (c_1^b) is less than that of a proper ward, i.e.,

$$c_1^b < c_1.$$

Redefining the probabilities to include the patients in the buffer, we say

$P_{n,n_2}(t)$ = probability that at time t, out of n patients (including those in the buffer) in the system, n_2 are of type 2. ($n_2 \leqq m$).

Under this assumption only the steady state equation for case 5 will change as follows:

$$0 = -[\lambda_1 + (N - n_2)\mu_1 + n_2\mu_2]\tau_{n,n_2} + (N - n_2)\mu_1\tau_{n+1,n_2}$$
$$+ n_2\mu_2\tau_{n+1,n_2+1} + \lambda_1\tau_{n-1,n_2},\ n \geqq N,\ n_2 < m \qquad (20)$$

In the above we assume patients of type 1 are discharged only from the proper ward and not from the buffer. Suppose we had an upper limit of N_b on the number of beds available in the buffer. Then the equation describing the system when all beds, i.e., $(N + N_b)$ are full is as follows:

$$0 = -[\lambda_1 + (N - n_2)\mu_1 + n_2\mu_2]\tau_{(N+N_b),n_2} + \lambda_1\tau_{(N+N_b-1)\,n_2}$$
$$n = N_b + N \qquad (21)$$

Accordingly the changes in the cost function are given by:

$$c^b(m, (N + N_b)) = c_2^1\lambda_1 \sum_{n_2=0}^{m} \tau_{(N+N_b),n_2} + c_2^2\lambda_2 \sum_{n=m}^{(N+N_b)} \sum_{n_2=0}^{m} \tau_{n,n_2}$$

$$+ c_1^b \sum_{n=N+1}^{N+N_b} \sum_{n_2=0}^{m} (N + N_b - n)\tau_{n,n_2}$$

$$+c_1 \sum_{n=m+1}^{n} \sum_{n_2=0}^{m} \tau_{n,n_2} + c_1 \sum_{n=0}^{m} \sum_{n_2=0}^{n} \tau_{n,n_2} \tag{22}$$

38.4.2. Analysis

The buffer accommodation problem is central to the misplacement problem treated by Rabinowitz et al. [4]. This problem is most critical in hospitals of large size (≧500 beds) and high occupancy (≧90 percent) where usually 10–15 percent of the hospital daily census is attributed to inappropriate beds. Generally, such misplaced patients are subsequently transferred back to their appropriate wards as vacancies occur by some simple but demonstratively suboptimal strategies. The central mathematical problem could be solved as a general linear program employing a generalized upperbound algorithm as done by Dantzig in a hospital admission problem discussed in [2]. The practical model proposed by Rabinowitz however is a two stage general linear program in which at the first stage 'an aggregated service transfer model', a capacitated transshipment problem is solved and in the second stage, 'a disaggregated algorithm' is employed to convert the first stage solution and retrieve the information needed by the hospital in reaching the necessary transfers in an optimal manner. When compared with actual hospital operations, this model resulted in higher inpatient transfers than the simple policies thereto employed by the hospital. It is further shown that this will in general be the case. Their model however, differs from ours in that it does not explicitly consider costs as introduced in this paper.

References

1. Bellman, Richard and Dreyfus, Stuart, *Applied Dynamic Programming* (New Jersey, Princeton University Press, 1962).

2. Dantzig, George, 'A Hospital Admission Problem', Technical Report 69–15 (Operations Research House, Stanford University, Stanford, California 1969).
3. Esogbue, Augustine and Singh, Amar Jit, 'A Stochastic Model for an Optimal Priority Bed Distribution Problem in a Hospital Ward', *Operations Research*, vol. 24, no. 5 (September–October 1976), pp. 884–898.
4. Rabinowitz, Manus, Dumas, Barry, and Valinsky, David, 'A Two-Stage Optimization Model for In-Patient Transfers', *Operations Research*, vol. 24, no. 5 (September–October 1976), pp. 871–883.
5. Singh, Amar J., 'Optimal Strategies for Bed Allocation and Patient Treatment in a Hospital', (Ph.D. Dissertation, The Department of Operations Research, Case Western Reserve University, Cleveland, Ohio, 1972).
6. Young, John, P., 'A Queuing Theory Approach to the Control of Hospital Inpatient Census', Ph.D. Dissertation, School of Engineering, The John Hopkins University, Baltimore (1962).

39. Recursive modeling of outpatient health care settings

DEAN H. KROPP and ROBERT C. CARLSON

Abstract

Previous work dealing with the planning of outpatient health care has primarily used either linear programming or simulation. Linear programs are rather severe abstractions of reality. Simulation models are more realistic, but are very expensive and do not necessarily identify optimal solutions. A recursive optimization-simulation approach takes advantage of the best features of both methods while minimizing the disadvantages of each method used alone. A mixed integer program generates staffing and facility plans, thus reducing the number of alternatives requiring analysis via simulation. The simulation model then evaluates the feasibility of alternative plans, considering detailed information and complex relationship omitted from the optimization model.

39.1. Introduction

The existence of a national health care crisis has been widely publicized in recent years. Due to this crisis, researchers have started to search for more effective methods of providing health care. Thus, alternatives to the traditional physician-hospital mode of care are now being examined to determine their value. One alternative that has gained growing acceptance involves the use of outpatient facilites to relieve the strain on the system of inpatient health care. Increasing costs of hospitalization will continue to shift diagnosis and treatment of patients from inpatient to out-patient facilities wherever feasible. This shift will occur because the clinic represents less of a commitment in terms of plant and equipment, and thus allows greater flexibility in planning and location, leading to greater accessibility and utilization.

The management problem in an outpatient setting has several dimensions – personnel, plant, patients, and processes – each requiring long-term, intermediate-term, and short-term decisions. The long-run time horizon gives rise to the simultaneous problems of demand and capacity. Prior to opening an outpatient clinic, planners must set certain parameters that will remain more or less constant throughout its lifetime. Examples are the number of examination rooms, the size of the waiting room, the laboratory capacity, and the number of providers.

The intermediate-term horizon involves operational policy decisions for the clinic – those decisions that cannot feasibly be changed every day, but which do not entail substantial structural changes. The intermediate-term management decisions are of two types – personnel and patient flow. While the physical plant sets some limits on the number of providers the clinic can employ, it does not necessarily determine the type of provider. It is still necessary to determine whether to use physicians, nurse practitioners, medical students, or nurses as providers.

The short-run decisions are, in an operational sense, the most important of all because they supply key inputs to the longer-term decision environment. As in the intermediate-term environment, this area involves personnel and patient flow decisions. In the short-term environment, however, the decisions also depend on the dynamic state of the clinic, represented by considerations such a patient arrival rates, the pace of work, queue sizes, and waiting time.

The management problem in an outpatient setting has been made even more complicated by the recent introduction of physician's assistants. The physician's assistant is trained both to relieve the physician of certain routine duties and to extend and enhance the quality of services offered by the physician. Recent years have seen the introduction of physician's assistants into outpatient health care settings, primarily because they appear to represent a more efficient way of providing routine health care. With such new personnel, management must now decide whether physician's assistants are to be used, and if so, in what manner.

The objective of this work is to discuss a method which can help improve the utilization of outpatient health care resources. This method, which can deal with the entire range of time horizons faced by management, also is flexible enough to permit detailed analysis of many alternative policies. Before presenting this new method and an example of its use, we will first discuss the existing work dealing with modeling of health care settings and the limitations of such work.

39.2. Modeling of health care settings

Several studies concerning management of outpatient health care settings have been performed. These studies can be classified into two groups, descriptive and analytical. The descriptive studies use verbal or tabular presentations and are usually based upon personal observations, experience, or structured surveys. The analytical studies are based on mathematical models which often use information from the descriptive studies.

39.2.1. Descriptive studies

Descriptive studies provide a description of the health care process and help identify important variables affecting its delivery. Riddick, et al. [21] develop information on the nature of tasks currently being delegated by internists to other health care professionals. They also identify the types of tasks that can be delegated, assuming that appropriately trained personnel are available and that no legal constraints are imposed. Yankauer, et al. [33] examine the relationship between the manpower composition and task delegation policy of a pediatric practice. Their primary interest is in the productivity of the practice in terms of number of patient visits and the length of time per visit. Lairson, et al. [14] document the nature of duties assumed by a physician's assistant. This work provides some insights into attitudes towards physician's assistants, both before and after their introduction into a clinic practice.

More recent descriptive studies include an examination of the manner in which the physician's assistants are actually being used. They also characterize the types of people entering the physician's assistant training programs [22].

39.2.2. Analytical studies

Analytical studies using mathematical models enable the investigator to go beyond descriptive studies to examine alternative hypotheses concerning a health care setting and to make predictions about the setting. The models used have been based primarily on either continuous production functions, linear programs, or computer simulations.

39.2.3. Models using continuous production functions

Empirical estimates of continuous production functions have been made by fitting predetermined algebraic functional forms to data from a cross section of medical practices. Production input variables are represented by data on health manpower, supplies, and capital. Production output is represented by one variable, such as patient visits. The continuous production function is most appropriate where it is desirable to analyze large numbers of observations, or where limitations on available data make a more detailed approach infeasible.

Studies using the continuous production function provide useful information about the average rate of output for a given set of inputs for the cross section of medical practices under study. For example, Reinhardt [19], [20] shows that auxiliary personnel in a medical practice can have a substantial positive impact on average physician productivity. Zeckhauser and Eliastram [34], [35] predict that a physician's assistant could replace one half of a full-time physician within an urban health center.

39.2.4. Models using linear programming

Linear programming models characterize the primary care practice as a multiproduct firm which transforms inputs of labor, equipment, and materials into specific medical service outputs. These models assume a linear relationship between the inputs and the outputs. One of the most important contributions to come from these studies is the careful attention which has been paid to the problems of classifying the medical service inputs and outputs. Pondy et al. [18]; Golladay, et al. [5], [6], [7], and Schneider and Kilpatrick

[23], [24] closely examine the equivalence of case types and inputs in the categorization of service outputs. Recent work by Smith, et al. [27] which is based on a large-scale analysis of several health care settings, has gone even further in this area.

Early work in linear programming assumes an infinite divisibility of productive inputs, thus producing optimal solutions requiring fractional manpower inputs. This result is inconsistent with many health care settings, which hire personnel on a full-time, or nearly full-time, basis. Accordingly, recent linear programming studies use mixed-integer programming models which place full-time constraints on manpower inputs. One of the most detailed of these models is that formulated by Schneider and Kilpatrick [23], [24]. Their model includes indirect manpower requirements (such as supervisory time), utilization of technology, facility requirements, and capital limitations. This model is now being used to identify manpower and facility needs for new health care organizations. Other work using linear programming models has been done by Willemain and Moore [32] and Shuman, et al. [25].

39.2.5. Models using computer simulation

Computer simulation models, such as those of Fetter and Thompson [1], [2]; Horvitz, et al. [9]; and Kilpatrick, et al. [10], provide a more realistic representation of the complexity and variability in health care settings. Recent work has examined the use of physician's assistants. For example, in his model of a pediatric clinic, Uyeno [30], [31] incorporates a stochastic demand function and provides for varying team compositions and facility levels. The objective of this work is to develop a methodology for the analysis of the effect of reallocation of tasks and for the determination of optimal team compositions. Accordingly, emphasis is placed on the identification and analysis of inputs in terms of delegable tasks. Lazarus, et al. [15] address certain management concerns in the use of allied health manpower, such as decision rules for task delegation and patient scheduling. Their model is designed to demonstrate to the physician the effects of alternative delegation decision rules.

A recent simulation model of a general medical practice reported by Kilpatrick [11] evaluates the effects of a small set of alternative physical configurations, patient input mixes, and skill levels of physician's assistants in an attempt to derive a production function of the medical practice. This work is based on Freeman's [3] use of simulation to analyze a medical practice and on simulation techniques developed by Kilpatrick, et al. [10] to examine the use of expanded function auxiliary personnel in a dental practice. Glenn and Roberts [4] have done work that is similar to that of Kilpatrick concerning alternatives for a medical clinic. Their work, however, did not focus on the effect of using physician's assistants.

39.2.6. Limitations of existing work

Most analytical studies have concluded that there are significant advantages to be gained in the use of the physician's assistant in outpatient health care [5], [19], [20]. Yet the physician's assistant is not being utilized to the extent that is apparently technically feasible and profitable [27]. Some explanation for this apparent discrepancy may be found through careful examination of the models used in the analytical studies. Since these models are abstractions from reality, conclusions drawn from them are limited in their applicability by the extent to which the models depart from reality.

Considering the work that has been done to date, there appear to be four areas in which improvements to the analytical process can be made. These areas are: (1) the scope of the performance measures used in the analyses, (2) the scope of the alternative policies examined, (3) the accuracy of the models in describing the health care process, and (4) the long-term focus of the studies.

39.2.6.1. Performance measures: To date, only a limited number of performance measures have been used. In the linear programming models, the major measures are costs, number of patients served, and time requirements placed upon the health care providers. For the simulation models a broader range of measures has been examined, including costs, provider service times, provider utilization, resource utilization, patient waiting time, and number of patients served. Such expanded performance measures permit a more detailed analysis.

The problem with existing work is that a study which considers only a few performance measures may result in a misleading recommendation, because a gain in any one measure is most likely achieved at some cost in another measure that is not examined. For example, a study of alternative practice sizes and personnel configurations that examines only number of patients seen, direct provider-patient contact time, and net income may result in a recommendation for a particular personnel mix and practice size. The actual implementation of the recommendation, however, may be infeasible due to the impact upon other variables not considered by the study. These variables may include patient waiting time, overtime demands upon support staff, outside office hour demands upon the physician or physician's assistant for hospital calls and emergencies, indirect manpower requirements for support activities, and the capacity of the examination rooms and waiting areas to handle the patient load.

To emphasize this problem, Hershey, et al. [8] found that a linear programming model predicted that a 100 percent increase in patient load would occur when a physician's assistant was added to a one-physician office. When a more realistic simulation model was used to analyze the effects of such a change in the same office, they found that total waiting time for the patients more than doubled and that the office would have had to stay open 90 minutes longer every day in order to accommodate the increased load. On the other hand, if the office times and queuing statistics were not changed, the addition of a physician's assistant to the office resulted in a maximum increase in patient load of only 50 percent.

39.2.6.2. Alternative policies examined: The second area in which the existing studies are limited concerns the set of alternative policies examined by the model. The linear programs are essentially restricted to the examination of one policy at a time, and optimal solutions are provided based upon a given set of constraints. Simulation studies have examined larger sets of policies; however the overall set of policy alternatives examined has been small. Further, where these studies have investigated alternative numbers of personnel, types of personnel, and numbers of rooms, only a few values of each variable have been used.

39.2.6.3. Accuracy of the models: The model used in an analytical study represents an abstraction from reality and includes only the variables that are thought to affect the process under study.

If important features are omitted, conclusions about the likely effects of alternative decisions are limited in their applicability. The studies performed to date have significant weaknesses in this area.

The continuous production function requires that a precise algebraic equation be derived to represent the underlying technology of the health care setting. This derivation can be extremely difficult when the technology itself has not been well defined. Additionally, a single output measure makes it difficult to incorporate complexities of case mix or services provided into the model.

The existing linear programming models also have limited capability for characterizing the complexities of the medical care setting. Service time is assumed to be deterministic and each patient is assumed to require a linear combination of all medical services. Patient scheduling is ignored; patients are always made available when needed. Sequencing of medical tasks performed by the health care providers during a patient's visit is ignored. Work breaks and other non-patient care activities are not considered. Given these shortcomings, it is difficult to use a linear programming model to study alternative management policies such as appointment scheduling, service priorities, daily office hours, or continuity of care. Modifications to the model could be accomplished to deal with some of these concerns, but the resulting model would be extremely cumbersome.

Although simulation provides a better representation of the complexities of the medical care setting, improvements are needed for a better representation of the setting being modeled. Specifically, the characterization of input requirements for medical services has not been well defined. Also, only a limited set of patient characteristics – such as age, sex, and type of visit – have been used as model inputs. Additionally, the working relationships of the medical providers have not been defined clearly. The models have assumed a serial performance of multiple service tasks, even when such assumptions violate common sense and actual practice.

39.2.6.4. Long-range focus: Most analytical studies have addressed long-term policies such as personnel structure, but have paid little attention to potential implementation barriers and to such alternative day-to-day decision rules as appointment scheduling and patient dispatching. Given the predictions of the analytical studies, it is the day-to-day working policies and ease of implementation that are key factors in determining the extent to which the predictions are realized. Therefore, it is necessary that future studies examine both the long-range and the short-range concerns of the health care setting.

Given these limitations of the existing work, it is evident that a new analytical technique could prove useful. One attractive possibility, the recursive optimization-simulation method, is described below.

39.3. The recursive optimization-simulation approach to system modeling

Researchers often reject optimizing methods because of their lack of realism (such as linearity restrictions) or because the desired 'richness of detail' is not available. In such cases, computer simulation may be used because it can handle complex relationships and can provide sufficient detail. However, the costs of simulation are very high. In addition, because simulation is not an optimizing method, the investigators discover that they will have to examine many alternatives without any assurance that they are approaching an optimal solution.

An alternative approach to modeling with only an optimizing method or a computer simulation alone uses a recursive optimization-simulation algorithm, such as that described by Nolan and Sovereign [17] or used in modified form by Kolesar, et al. [12]. With such a method, an optimization technique is used to analyze the system at an aggregate level. The results are then used in a simulation model of the *same* system, which identifies other information which can be passed back to the optimization model. The reason for employing both an optimization model and a simulation model is that optimization methods can answer most questions asked by the analyst, whereas simulation cannot. Simulation is largely a descriptive tool. Unless a complete experimental design is used, simulation can answer little more than questions concerning the feasibility of a given alternative.

In the recursive method, the optimization and simulation techniques can be used to complement each other. The optimization model permits the analyst to reduce the number of variables (and the resultant number of alternatives) to be examined by simulation. The simulation model is then used to handle the system's complex relationships (such as nonlinearities, queuing, and discreteness) which are too cumbersome for the optimization model. Thus, the recursive method attempts to capitalize on the advantages of both approaches while attempting to reduce the disadvantages of either method used by itself.

To demonstrate the use of the recursive optimization-simulation approach in health care settings, the method will now be applied to the problem of planning of an office-based medical practice. The optimization model will be used to generate staffing and facility plans for the practice, thus reducing the number of alternatives requiring analysis by the simulation. Then, the simulation model will evaluate the feasibility of these plans by considering more detailed information (such as possible delegation policies, and scheduling algorithms) omitted from the optimization model. If the plans prove to be infeasible, the simulation will identify new parameters and relationships which should be included in the optimization model.

39.4. Optimization model

The optimization model used to examine the health care setting is a mixed integer program based on the work of Schneider [23] and of Schneider and Kilpatrick [24]. Given a fixed capitation rate (revenue per person per period of time) and a specified subscriber base, the model's objective is to find the personnel to be hired, the services to be offered, the delegation of services from the physicians to physician's assistants, and the facilities required to minimize total annual cost. The constraints on the problem include meeting annual demand, meeting budget and capital limits, meeting limits on numbers of personnel and on their use, and insuring that a minimum number of examination rooms is provided.

As noted previously, most analytical models of health care

have been used for long-range studies. The mixed integer program discussed here is no exception, with the basic unit of time of one year. Critical variables such as the number and types of personnel assigned to services and the number and types of personnel employed have units of man-years. Clearly, the model is not directed at predicting day-to-day performance. It assumes that the utilization of medical services occurs at a constant level and ignores the variation in time for personnel to perform medical services.

In spite of these limitations, the mixed integer program has been found to be of sufficient accuracy to be used in aggregate planning for health care organizations. In particular, Schneider found that the model closely approximated the operation of a prepaid group practice in Central Florida, and that many of the model's results were parallel to those of the clinics of the Kaiser system of hospitals in Southern California. Since 1973 the models have been used to plan health care organizations in at least five other areas.

39.5. Computer simulation model

The computer simulation model used to evaluate the setting on a day-to-day basis is based on work performed at Stanford University [8], [13], [29]; and at the University of Florida [3], [11]. This model has three major sections – one determining the patient characteristics, one describing the diagnosis and treatment process, and one determining the office and provider availabilities.

39.5.1. Patient characteristics

Patient input consists of patient mix, interarrival time, 'no-show' rates, emergency visit rates, and 'preference for provider' rates. All of these characteristics may be stochastic in nature. The patient characteristics section can be run independently of the other model sections so that the same patient input stream can be passed through alternative system configurations. This technique insures that any differences between the results of different configurations are caused only by the configurations themselves.

39.5.2. Diagnosis and treatment process

The logical network of the diagnosis and treatment process controls the flow of patients through the facility and specifies the type and amount of resources required at each step in the process. Input parameters determine personnel staffing patterns and working relationships, capabilities of the physician's assistants, number of patient examination rooms, physical configuration of the facility, and patient management decision rules.

A patient is randomly assigned a reason for visit based on the frequency distribution of visits used as input data for the mixed integer program. Depending on the branch probabilities assigned for the visit type, laboratory tests, x-ray examination, and other procedures may be ordered. Each procedure has associated with it a probability distribution for the procedure time. The choice of the person to perform a procedure depends on the optimal task assignments identified by the mixed integer program and on the dynamic state of the system (e.g., whether the lowest level person capable of performing the task is currently available).

39.5.3. Office and provider availability

This section regulates the functioning of the office with respect to its normal opening time, closure for lunch and coffee breaks, and closure at the end of the day. It also provides for provider lateness or absence, telephone calls for the providers, and patient record-keeping.

39.6. Integration of optimization and simulation models in the recursive approach

The recursive approach involves use of the optimization model to provide input information to the simulation model; and then use of the simulation model to provide information to the optimization model. In the first step the optimization model identifies the optimal facility characteristics (such as the number of examination rooms) and the staffing patterns (including both the numbers of each type of personnel and the assignments of personnel to tasks) for the aggregate problem. Then the simulation model is used to evaluate the day-to-day feasibility of this optimal aggregate solution. In this application, for instance, the simulation model views patient waiting time as the day-to-day variable of interest.

The aggregate solution may not be feasible on a day-to-day basis because, for example, the patient waiting times may be excessive. In such an event, other possible solutions will have to be examined and the recursive method used in an iterative fashion until the resulting aggregate solution is also feasible on a day-to-day basis. Thus, the recursive method proceeds as follows:

1. Identify resources to be used.
2. Given estimated resource productivities and other assumed parameters, solve the optimization model.
3. Run the simulation model using the optimal plan generated in step 2.
4. Based on several simulation runs, identify a range of values of the variables which is expected to produce average patient waiting times which are acceptable.
5. Incorporate the information of step 4 into the optimization model.
6. Return to step 2.
7. Repeat the process until the optimization model identifies an aggregate solution which has acceptable patient waiting times.

39.7. An example of use of the recursive method

The application of the recursive optimization simulation approach to the planning of a hypothetical setting for outpatient health care will now be described. The setting is an outpatient clinic providing adult medical care to approximately 30,000 patients for a total of about 50,000 patient visits per year. The clinic has a staff consisting of physicians, physician's assistants, registered nurses, and licensed practical nurses. In this clinic, each provider spends no more than 35 hours per week in direct contact with patients. Patient services can be performed by alternative sets of manpower technologies which involve one or more providers. For example, a physical examination may be performed by the physician alone or by the physician with the help of one of the support personnel.

The mixed integer program is formulated to minimize the facility's total annual cost for a specified number of subscribers. Necessary additional inputs to the model include the types of services available, the distribution of service requirements, the alternative manpower technologies, the average time required for each service, the salary of each type of provider, the annual number of visits per subscriber, and the amount of equipment and floor space required per provider. The number of providers and the manpower technologies that will minimize total annual cost are obtained as the solution of the model.

The simulation model includes more detailed information including daily operating hours, schedules of patient appointment, varied arrivals of walk-in and non-emergency patients, variability in patient arrivals, required services and service times, and sequencing of tasks performed to meet patient service requirements. Based on this information, the following is a more detailed description of the practice.

The practice is open five days a week, with regular hours from 8:00 a.m. to 5:00 p.m., a lunch break from 12:00 Noon to 1:00 p.m., and ten minute coffee breaks at 10:30 a.m. and 3:00 p.m. Appointment patients are scheduled at 15 minute intervals from 9:00 a.m. to 12:00 noon and from 1:00 p.m. to 4:00 p.m. Although equal numbers of patients are scheduled for each of the appointment intervals, approximately ten percent of them are 'no shows'. The actual arrival time of these appointment patients is considered to be normally distributed with the average arrival time being 2.5 minutes early. In addition, walk-in patients and acutely ill near-emergency patients come to the clinic, with their mean inter-arrival times depending on the time of day. The days examined are those in which the clinic is fully loaded; the number of patients seen on these days is about 25 percent higher than the annual average number of patients seen per day.

Patient service requirements are randomly determined based on the frequency distribution of the different services. Once the patient's medical needs are known, the optimal manpower technology identified by the mixed integer program is used to identify which provider or providers the patient will see. Service time is considered to be gamma distributed, with the mean time equal to the time requirements used in the mixed integer program. For services associated with the assessment of the patient's condition, the tasks are performed serially. For services associated with a treatment, the providers must see the patient concurrently.

The simulation model incorporating the foregoing characteristics provides for the collection of data used to calculate such performance measures as direct patient contact time for each provider, number of patients seen by each provider, utilization of facilities, delays in lunch periods and coffee breaks, the time at which the office closes every day, total waiting time for each patient, and size of queues for providers and facilities.

To demonstrate the use of the recursive method, the operational goal of the clinic was assumed to be achieving an average waiting time per patient no greater than 35 minutes, approximately half of the total time the patient is busy. Table 1 summarizes the data for the five iterations it took for the recursive approach to achieve the facility's desired 35 minute waiting time. In Table 1 the waiting time figure is averaged over five days of simulated operation of the clinic.

The average four hour patient waiting time of iteration 0 clearly reveals the day-to-day problems that would occur from blind implementation of the optimal aggregate solution. Based on the simulated results of this solution, it is evident that the practice would not be attractive either to patients or providers. In addition to not meeting the facility's own criterion, the excessive patient

Table 1. Solutions from recursive method.

Iteration	Annual Cost of Solution	Average Patient Waiting Time	MDs	PAs	RNs	LPNs	Rooms
0	$1,453,366	253.3 min	9	6	6	1	15
1	2,426,133	68.7	25	6	18	4	31
2	2,534,013	41.9	25	6	14	17	45
3	2,456,172	39.1	24	6	22	6	40
4	2,553,865	36.7	26	6	22	6	40
5	2,486,365	34.0	23	6	25	9	50

MDs: Physicians
PAs: Physician's Assistants
RNs: Registered Nurses
LPNs: Licensed Practical Nurses

waiting times would affect the physicians' availability for patient care activities outside the clinic, as well as the morale of the clinic staff. Further, the patient waiting time and the resulting congestion would likely cause patients to go to other practices involving less waiting. Thus, even before use of the recursive method, the simulation has revealed important implications about the feasibility of the optimal aggregate solution.

The data in Table 1 demonstrate the rapid convergence of the recursive approach to the 'new' optimal solution, the one in which cost is minimized subject to the additional constraint that patient waiting time be acceptable. The great differences between this 'new' solution and the initial aggregate solution indicate the value of the recursive method compared to a method specifying 'across-the-board' increases in all personnel and facilities. One by-product of the recursive method is the cost increase associated with the reduction in waiting time. In this case, for example, the annual cost of approximately $5.50 for each one hour reduction in patient waiting time could be extremely useful to the facility in any cost-sharing discussions with its patients.

39.8. Discussions and conclusions

The primary objective of this paper has been to discuss how planning of health care facilities can be improved through use of a recursive modeling approach. The example was used only to demonstrate this point. It is important, therefore, to recognize that the medical practice analyzed in the example is hypothetical and based on data from a variety of sources. Parameter values were chosen to be representative of a typical practice, not to dramatize the limitations of aggregate planning techniques. Similarly, the reader is cautioned from drawing *general* conclusions based on the above example. The results for any given facility will depend on the specific characteristics of the facility. Nevertheless, it is clear that a new approach, such as the recursive one, can be of great value to health care planners because of its focus on the entire time horizon faced by management.[1]

1. This project was supported by Grant Number 1 RO3 HS 02398–01 from the National Center for Health Services Research, HRA. The authors would also like to thank Mr. David Lawton of Stanford University for his valuable research assistance.

References

1. Fetter, R. B. and Thompson, J. D., 'The Simulation of Hospital Systems', *Operations Research*, vol. 13 (September/October 1965), pp. 689–711.
2. Fetter, R. B. and Thompson, J. D., 'Patient's Waiting Time and Doctor's Idle Time in the Outpatient Setting', *Health Services Research*, vol. 1, no. 2 (Summer 1966), pp. 66–90.
3. Freeman, John R., 'Manpower Analysis for General Medical Practice', Health Systems Research Division, University of Florida (1970).
4. Glenn, J. K. and Roberts, S. D., 'The Relationships Between Resource and Utilization Factors in an Outpatient Care System', *AIIE Transactions*, vol. 5, no. 1 (March 1973), pp. 24–32.
5. Golladay, F. L., Miller, M., and Smith, K. R., 'Allied Health Manpower Strategies: Estimates of the Potential Gains from Efficient Task Delegation', *Medical Care*, vol. 11, no. 6 (November/December 1973), pp. 457–469.
6. Golladay, F. L. and K. R. Smith, 'Policy Planning for the Mid-Level Health Worker: Economic Potentials and Barriers to Change', Health Economics Research Center, University of Wisconsin (May 1974).
7. Golladay, F. L., Manser, M. E., and Smith, K. R. 'Scale Economics in the Delivery of Medical Care: A Mixed Integer Programming Analysis of Efficient Manpower Utilization', *The Journal of Human Resources*, vol. 9, no. 1 (Winter 1974), pp. 50–62.
8. Hershey, John C., Kropp, D. H., and Kuhn, I. M. 'Physician's Assistants in Ambulatory Health Care Settings: Need for Improved Analysis', Research Paper Series, Health Services Administration, Stanford University School of Medicine (February 1976).
9. Horvitz, D. G., Kennedy, F. D., Shah, B. V., and Jones, D. C., 'Methods for Building a Health Manpower Simulation Model', Proceedings and Report of Conference on a Health Manpower Simulation Model, vol. 2, Bureau of Health Manpower Education (December 1970).
10. Kilpatrick, K. E., Mackenzie, R. S., and Delaney, A. G., 'Expanded Function Auxiliaries in General Dentistry: A Computer Simulation', *Health Services Research*, vol. 7, no. 4 (Winter 1972), pp. 288–300.
11. Kilpatrick, Kerry E., 'Implications of New Manpower Technology for Medical and Dental Practice: A Computer Simulation Analysis,' Technical Report no. 20, Health Services Research Division, J. Hillis Miller Health Center, University of Florida (1974).
12. Kolesar, P. J., Rider, K. L., Crabill, T. B., and Walker, W. E., 'A Queuing-Linear Programming Approach to Scheduling Police Patrol Cars', *Operations Research*, vol. 23, no. 6 (November/December 1975), pp. 1045–1062.
13. Kropp, D. H. and Kuhn, I. M., 'The Introduction of a Physician's Assistant into an Ambulatory Primary Health Care Setting: A Simulation Analysis', Department of Industrial Engineering, Stanford University (June 1975).
14. Lairson, P. D., Record, J. C., and James, J. C., 'Physician Assistants at Kaiser: Distinctive Patterns of Practice', Paper presented at the American Public Health Association Meeting (November 1972).
15. Lazarus, S. S., Wilhoite, D. H., Johnson, K. G., Jacobs, A. R., and Lynn, W. R., 'The Use of a Simulation Model for Investigating the Delegation of Ambulatory Patient Care to Physician's Assistants', Paper presented at the 45th ORSA/TIMS National Meetings, Boston, Massachusetts (April 1974).
16. Nolan, L. C. and Nolan, G. R., 'Status of the New Health Care Providers: The Physician's Assistant', *Medical Care Review*, vol. 32, no. 4 (April 1975), pp. 430–449.
17. Nolan, R. L. and Sovereign, M. G., 'A Recursive Optimization and Simulation Approach to Analysis With an Application to Transportation Systems', *Management Science*, vol. 18, no. 12 (August 1972), pp. B676–B690.
18. Pondy, L., Jones, J., and Braun, J., 'Utilization and Productivity of the Duke Phy-

sician's Associate', *Socio-Economic Planning Sciences*, vol. 7, no. 4 (August 1973), pp. 327–352.

19. Reinhardt, U. E., 'A Production Function for Physician Services', *Review of Economics and Statistics*, vol. 54, no. 1 (February 1972), pp. 55–66.
20. Reinhardt, U. E., 'Manpower Substitution and Productivity in Medical Practice: A Review of Research', *Health Services Research*, vol. 8, no. 3 (Fall 1973), pp. 200–227.
21. Riddick, F. A., Byran, J. B., Gershenson, M. I. and Costello, A. C., 'Use of Allied Health Professionals in Internist's Offices', *Archives of Internal Medicine*, vol. 127, no. 5 (May 1971), pp. 924–931.
22. Scheffler, R. M. and Stinson, O. D., 'Characteristics of Physician's Assistants: A Focus on Specialty', *Medical Care*, vol. 12, no. 12 (December 1974), pp. 1019–1030.
23. Schneider, D. P., 'A Systems Analysis of Optimal Manpower Utilization in Health Maintenance Organizations', Unpublished Ph.D. Dissertation, University of Florida (1973).
24. Schneider, D. P. and Kilpatrick, K. E., 'An Optimum Manpower Utilization Model for Health Maintenance Organizations', *Operations Research*, vol. 23, no. 5 (September/October 1975), pp. 869–889.
25. Shuman, L. J., Young, J. P., and Naddor, E., 'Manpower Mix for Health Services: A Prescriptive Regional Planning Model', *Health Services Research*, vol. 6, no. 2 (Summer 1971), pp. 103–119.
26. Smith, K. R., Over, A. M., Hanson, J. F., Golladay, F. L., and Davenport, E. J., 'An Analytic Framework and Measurement Strategy for Investigating the Production of Ambulatory Medical Care Services', Health Economics Research Center, University of Wisconsin (April 1975).
27. Social Security Administration, Office of Research and Statistics, Physician Extender Literature, Review, by Policy Analysis, Incorporated, Boston, Massachusetts (1974).
28. Stimson, D. H. and Charles, G. 'The Study of Physician Extendors in Primary Care', *Health Services Research*, vol. 10, no. 1 (Spring 1975), pp. 6–19.
29. Sulat, J. R. and Hershey, J. C., 'An Outpatient Clinic Simulation Model', Research Paper Series, Health Services Administration, Stanford University School of Medicine (May 1974).
30. Uyeno, D. H., 'Health Manpower Systems: An Application of the Management Sciences to the Design of Primary Health Care Teams', Unpublished Ph.D.Dissertation, Northwestern University (1971).
31. Uyeno, D. H., 'Health Manpower Systems: An Application of Simulation to the Design of Primary Health Care Teams', *Management Science*, vol. 20, no. 6 (February 1974), pp. 981–989.
32. Willemain, T. R. and Moore, G. T., 'Planning a Medical Practice Using Paramedic Personnel', *Health Services Research*, vol. 9, no. 1 (Spring 1974), pp. 53–61.
33. Yankauer, A., Schneider J., Jones, S. J., Hellman, L. M. and Feldman, J. J., 'Physician Output and Task Delegation in Obstetric-Gynecological Practices in the U.S.', *Obstetrics and Gynecology*, vol. 31 (January 1972), pp. 151–165.
34. Zeckhauser, R. and Eliastam, M., 'The Physician Assistant', Report no. 8, Teaching and Research Materials, Public Policy Program, Kennedy School of Government, Harvard University (April 1972).
35. Zeckhauser, R. and Eliastam, M., 'The Productivity Potential of the Physician Assistant', *Journal of Human Resources*, vol. 9, no. 1 (Winter 1974), pp. 95–116.

40. Nurse scheduling: a case of disaggregation in the public sector

HOLMES E. MILLER and WILLIAM P. PIERSKALLA

Abstract

This paper deals with the problem of generating day on-day off patterns for nurses during a two to six week period. The formulation implies selecting a configuration of nurse schedules that minimizes an objective function balancing the trade-off between staffing coverage and schedule preferences of individual nurses, subject to certain feasibility constraints on the nurse schedules. The problem is solved by a cyclic coordinate descent algorithm. Results are presented pertaining to a six month application in a hospital setting.

40.1. Introduction

Because of demands for service seven days a week and around the clock, generating work schedules for nurses in a manner satisfactory to both employer and employee is a difficult task. From the hospital's point of view, the schedules should contain staffing levels satisfying requirements for various nursing classes on the days and shifts in question. The nurses, on the other hand, would like to receive schedules that assure as favorable day on-day off and shift rotation patterns as possible. Unfortunately, neither's desires can be totally satisfied. The hospital must work with a configuration of nurses greater than a hypothetical minimum and the nurses must be willing to accept schedules somewhat less than the 'ideal'.

In this paper, we shall present a mathematical programming based procedure that has generated favorable nurse schedules and has been implemented at a number of hospitals in the United States and Canada. The model is one stage in a disaggregated solution process encompassing three different levels where scheduling occurs.

The highest level involves allocation of nurses to departments over the long term. The output from this phase is often an employee roster. For example, it may specify that three RN's, five LPN's and four Nursing Aides are assigned to a nursing station for the first half of the year.

The employee roster is then used as the input for the second level determining patterns of days on and days off for employees. This phase will be discussed at length in this paper where the final schedules are the solution to a model which trades off employer and employee preferences. The output of this phase, in the case of nursing, is a work schedule for the coming two to six weeks, specifying working and recreation days and, when applicable, shift rotation.

By their nature, day on-day off schedules are made in advance. The requirements on which the schedules are based are forecasts. Moreover it is implicitly assumed all employees scheduled to work on a particular day will actually be working. Reality often does not conform to these assumptions. For example, when the nurse schedules are generated minimum requirements may have specified three LPN's but when the day in question actually arrives the requirements may have risen to four. The number of RN's scheduled to work on a day may be three but one may be sick and only two actually report for work.

To adjust to these realities, the lowest level of the disaggregated solution procedure involves short term personnel allocation. Allocation policies differ in different situations. One common method of short term allocation in nursing involves utilizing a pool of 'float' nurses. They are assigned to various departments to adjust to the changed supply and/or demand conditions.

In Section 2, we shall present the model and solution procedure to a nurse scheduling problem where individual preferences are considered and where the output is a set of personalized nurse schedules. It is an example of intermediate level disaggregation.

Section 3 will discuss how one may use results from lower level disaggregation to examine higher level problems.

40.2. Generating a roster of days on and off

40.2.1. The model

The mathematical programming model to be presented schedules days on and days off for nurses assigned to a given working unit for a two, four, six, or eight week scheduling horizon subject to certain hospital policy and nurse preference constraints. Because of the large number of constraints, no feasible solutions to the scheduling problem would exist if all constraints were binding. We thus divide these constraints into two classes: Feasibility set constraints, which define the sets of feasible nurse schedules, and non-binding nurse and hospital constraints, whose violation incurs a penalty cost which appears in the objective function of the math programming problem. The definition regarding which constraints constitute these classes may change depending upon where the model is being applied.

40.2.2. Constraints: the feasibility set

Because of the possibility of special requests by nurses, no constraints are binding in the sense that they hold under all circumstances except those constraints emanating from the special requests. We do, however, distinguish between constraints we would *like to hold* in the absence of special requests, and those which we shall always allow to be violated while incurring a penalty cost.

The former constraints define what we call the *feasibility set* Π_i, i.e., $\Pi_i =$ the set of feasible schedule patterns for nurse *i*.

In the *absence* of special requests, this set might include all schedules satisfying:

- A nurse works ten days every pay period (i.e., 14 day scheduling period)
- No work stretches (i.e., stretches of consecutive days on) are allowed in excess of σ days (e.g., $\sigma = 7$).* No work stretches of τ or fewer days are allowed (e.g., $\tau = 1$).* Hence one schedule in an Π_i satisfying these might be (with $\sigma = 7, \tau = 1, 1 =$ day on, $0 =$

* These are calculated within a scheduling period and also at the interface of a scheduling period and past and future scheduling periods.

day off)

1 1 1 1 1 1 1 0 0 1 1 1 0 0

Now suppose a nurse has special requests. For example, suppose the nurse requests the schedule:

1 1 1 1 1 1 1 1 0 1 0 0 0 B

where the *B* indicates a birthday off. In this case *all* of the above constraints would be violated and Π_i would consist of only the schedule just given. Thus in the general case, Π_i is the set of schedules which:

1. Satisfies a nurse's special requests.
2. Satisfies as many of the constraints we *would like* to see binding as possible, given the nurse's special requests.

The constraints we would like to hold are a function of the situation in which the model is applied. For example, we could easily specify five out of seven days working as ten out of fourteen or specify additional constraints we would like to see satisfied such as no split days off, i.e., schedules containing 101 patterns.

40.2.3. *Constraints: non-binding*

Each schedule pattern $x^i \in \Pi_i$ may violate a number of *non-binding schedule pattern constraints* while incurring a penalty cost.

Define

N_i = The index set of the non-binding schedule pattern constraints for nurse *i*.

For example, if the site in which the model was being implemented deemed them as non-binding, the following constraints might define N_i:

- No work stretches longer than S_i days (where $S_i \leqq \sigma$);*
- No work stretches shorter than T_i days (where $T_i \geqq \tau$);*
- No day on, day off, day on patterns (1 0 1 pattern);*
- No more than κ consecutive 1 0 1 patterns,*
- Q_i weekends off every scheduling period (e.g., 4 or 6 weeks);
- No more than W_i week ends working each scheduling period;

- No patterns containing four consecutive days off;
- No patterns containing split weekends on (i.e., a Saturday on – Sunday off – pattern, or vice versa).

In addition to non-binding schedule pattern constraints, we also have *non-binding staffing level constraints*. Define:

d_k = The desired staffing level for day k; and m_k = the minimum staffing level for day k. Then we have: a) The number of nurses scheduled to work on day k is greater than or equal to m_k and b) The number of nurses scheduled to work on day k is equal to d_k.

40.2.4. *Objective function*

As was mentioned, the objective function is composed of the sum of two classes of penalty costs; penalty costs due to violation on non-binding schedule pattern constraints and staffing level constraints.

40.2.4.1. Staffing level costs: Define the *group* to be scheduled as the set of all nurses in the unit who are to be scheduled by one application of the solution algorithm. Further define a *subgroup* as a subset of the group. For example, the group to be scheduled may be all those nurses assigned to a nursing unit and the subgroups may be registered nurses, licensed practical nurses, and nursing aides. Alternatively, the group may be defined as all registered nurses and a subgroup might be those capable of performing as head nurses.

Then, for each day $k = 1, \ldots, 14$ (where there are I nurses), the group staffing level costs are given by:

$$f_k\left(\sum_{i=1}^{I} x_k^i\right)$$

where $x^i = (x_1^i, \ldots, x_{14}^i)$. For example, this function might appear as seen in the following page.

Now define:

B_j = The index set of nurse subgroups j, where
J = The index set of all subgroups.

If m_k^j and d_k^j are the minimum and desired number of nurses re-

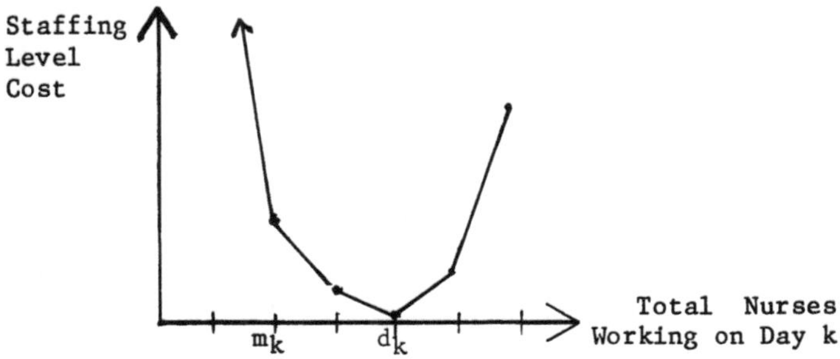

quired on day k for subgroup j, we define the staffing cost for violating those constraints on day k for subgroup j as: $h_{jk}\,(\Sigma\, x_k^i)$ where $h_k(\cdot)$ is defined similarly to $f_k(\cdot)$ $i \in B_j$

Then the total staffing level costs for all 14 days of the pay period are:

$$\sum_{k=1}^{14} f_k\left(\sum_{i=1}^{I} x_k^i\right) + \sum_{k=1}^{14} \sum_{j\in J} h_{jk}\left(\sum_{j\in B_j} x_k^i\right)$$

40.2.4.2. Schedule pattern costs: For each nurse $i = 1, \ldots, I$, the schedule pattern costs for a particular pattern x^i measure:

1. The costs inherent in that pattern in relation to which constraints in N_i are violated.
2. How nurse i perceives these costs in light of that nurse's schedule preferences.
3. How this cost is weighed in light of the nurse's schedule history.

For example, for (1) the pattern,

1 1 1 1 1 0 0 1 1 1 0 0 1 1

may incur a cost for nurse i whose minimum desired work stretch is 4 days. This is a cost inherent in the pattern. Considering (2), we next ask how nurse i perceives violations of the minimum desired stretch constraints, i.e., how severely are violations of this non-binding constraint viewed vis-a-vis others in N_i. Finally (3), gives us some indication of how we should weigh this revised schedule pattern cost in light of the schedule employee i has received in the past. Intuitively, if nurse i has been receiving bad schedules, we would want the cost to he higher to cause a good schedule to be accepted when the solution algorithm is applied and vice versa.

Thus, we define:

$g_{in}(x^i)$ = the cost of violating non-binding constraint $n \in N_i$ of schedule x^i.

a_{in} = the 'weight' nurse i gives a violation of non-binding constraint $n \in N_i$, which we shall call the *aversion coefficient*.

A_i = the *aversion index* of nurse i; i.e., a measure of how good or bad nurse i's schedules have been historically vis-a-vis nurse i's preferences.

Then the total schedule pattern cost to nurse i for a schedule pattern x^i is: $A_i \sum_{n \in N} \alpha_{in} g_{in}(x^i)$, and the sum of these costs for all nurses $i = 1, \ldots, I$ is the total schedule pattern cost.

40.2.5. Problem formulation

The nurse scheduling problem may now be formulated as: (where $0 < \lambda < 1$ weighs staffing level and schedule pattern costs). Find $x^1, x^2, \ldots, x^I$ which minimize:

$$\lambda \left[\sum_{k=1}^{14} f_k\left(\sum_{i=1}^{I} x_k^i \right) + \sum_{k=1}^{14} \sum_{j \in J} h_{jk}\left(\sum_{i \in B_j} x_k^i \right) \right] +$$

$$(1 - \lambda) \sum_{i=1}^{I} A_i \sum_{n \in N_i} a_{in} g_{in}(x^i) \quad \text{s.t.} \quad x^i \in \Pi_i, \, i = 1, \ldots, I.$$

40.2.5.1. Description of the solution procedure: The solution procedure used is a near-optimal algorithm. It starts with an initial configuration of schedules, one for each nurse. Fixing the schedules of all nurses but one, say nurse i, it searches Π_i. The lowest present cost and best schedule configuration are updated if, when searching Π_i, a schedule is found which results in a lower schedule configuration cost than the lowest cost to date. When all the schedules in Π_i have been tested either 1) A lower cost configuration has been found or 2) No lower cost configuration has been found. The process cycles among the I nurses and terminates when no lower cost configuration has been found in I consecutive tests.

The algorithm is:

1. Determine the set of feasible schedules for each nurse's Π_i. Let $|\Pi_i|$ denote the number of schedules in Π_i.

2. Calculate the schedule pattern costs for each schedule $x^{ik} \in \Pi_i$, for $i = 1, \ldots, I$.
3. Get initial schedule configuration and let BEST = its cost (e.g., choose the lowest cost schedule from each Π_i).
4. Let $i = 1$, $K = |\Pi_i|$, $k = 1$, and CYCLE = 0.
5. Insert schedule x^{ik} in schedule mix and let TEST = the cost of this configuration.
6. If TEST < BEST go to step. 8.
7. Let $k = k + 1$. If $k = K + 1$ go to step 9. Otherwise go to step 5.
8. Let CYCLE = 0 and BEST = TEST. Insert x^{ik} in complement of 'best schedules to date'. Go to step 7.
9. If CYCLE = I stop. Otherwise let $i = i + 1$ (if $i > I$, let $i = 1$) and let $K = |\Pi_i|$, $k = 1$, and CYCLE = CYCLE + 1. Go to step 5.

If we view the feasibility region as $\Pi_1 x \ldots x\Pi_I$ the algorithm is simply a cyclic coordinate descent algorithm along the coordinate directions Π_i. Each Π_i contains all feasible schedules for employee i. When 4 days are given off every 14 day pay period, Π_i contains at most $\binom{14}{4} = 1001$ schedules. This number is reduced considerably when previous schedules, special requests, and other feasibility set constraints are considered. The convergence of the algorithm is assured since $\Pi_{1x} \ldots x\Pi_I$ contains a finite number of points, namely, $\Pi_{i=1}^{I} |\Pi_i|$.

40.2.5.2. Results: Preliminary tests were conducted for scheduling nurses on a small sample problem comparing the algorithm presented above with a branch and bound algorithm which yielded the optimal solution. These tests showed the algorithm generated schedules almost as good as the optimal ones in far less computer time. For example, in one run on a 4 nurse, 20 schedule problem the cost of the algorithm generated schedule was 12.3 while the optimal cost was 7.55 (the initial cost of the algorithm solution was 239.45). The CPU time for the algorithm on a CDC 6400 was .367 seconds vs. 10.509 for the branch and bound. Moreover, this was when the initial upper bound in the branch and bound was the final solution generated by the algorithm. Arbitrarily large upper bounds yielded running times on the order of 30 seconds.

More extensive tests were run for the day shift of a unit in a large 800 bed hospital. The hospital had collected historical data regarding nurse schedule preferences and minimum and desired staffing levels. This data was used in the application of the algorithm. Because the algorithm schedules and the hospital schedules were generated from the same base data, it enabled us to compare the algorithm schedules and hospital schedules.

40.2.6. Algorithm generated schedules

Figure 1 presents some schedules generated by the algorithm for 4 weeks of the 6 month trial period: October 22 to November 18. Note that on 14 of the 28 days the actual staffing levels were identical

Group 1

RN's	M	T	W	T	F	S	S	M	T	W	T	F	S	S	M	T	W	T	F	S	S	M	T	W	T	F	S	S
1A	V	V	R	1	1	1	1	R	M	1	1	1	0	0	0	1	M	1	1	1	1	0	M	1	1	1	0	0
1B	1	1	1	1	1	0	0	1	1	1	1	1	0	0	1	1	1	0	1	1	1	1	M	1	1	0	0	0
1C	1	1	1	1	0	0	0	1	1	1	1	0	1	1	1	1	0	1	1	1	1	1	0	1	1	1	0	0
1D	1	0	0	1	1	0	0	1	1	1	1	1	1	1	0	1	1	1	1	0	0	1	1	1	0	1	1	1
1E	1	1	1	1	1	1	1	0	0	1	1	1	0	0	1	1	1	1	0	B	0	1	1	1	0	0	1	1
1F	1	1	1	0	1	1	1	1	1	1	1	0	0	0	1	1	1	1	0	0	0	1	1	0	1	1	1	1
1G	V	V	1	1	1	0	0	1	1	0	0	1	1	1	1	0	1	1	1	0	0	1	1	0	1	1	1	1

Group 2

LPN																												
2A	1	1	1	0	0	1	1	1	1	1	0	0	1	1	1	1	1	1	1	R	R	R	1	1	1	R	1	1
2B	1	1	0	B	1	1	1	1	0	1	1	1	0	0	1	1	1	0	1	1	1	1	1	1	1	0	0	0
2C	1	1	1	C	0	0	0	1	1	0	C	1	1	1	1	1	0	C	1	1	1	1	0	1	C	1	0	0
2D	0	1	1	1	1	1	1	V	V	1	1	0	0	0	1	1	1	1	0	0	0	1	1	1	0	1	1	1
2E	0	1	1	1	1	0	0	1	1	1	0	1	1	1	0	0	1	1	1	0	0	1	1	1	1	1	1	1
Total Desired	9	9	9	9	9	5	6	9	9	9	8	8	6	5	9	9	9	9	9	5	6	9	9	9	8	8	7	6
Total Actual	8	9	9	9	9	6	6	9	9	10	9	8	6	6	9	10	10	10	9	5	5	10	10	10	9	8	7	7

Legend:

1 = Day Scheduled On
0 = Day Scheduled Off
M = Day on for Meeting
V = Vacation Day Off
R = Requested Day Off
B = Birthday Off
C = Day on for Class

Figure 1. A two-week set of nurse schedules generated by the solution algorithm.

with the desired staffing levels. The unit is understaffed by 1 nurse on 2 days and overstaffed by 1 nurse on 12 days.

When the schedule pattern costs for the schedule in Figure 1 were examined, we found that in all cases but one the nurses were given a schedule better than 90 percent or more of those in the feasible pattern set. Moreover, over half the time the number of feasible patterns in the sets Π_i were well in excess of 200 so there were many schedules to choose from.

When the entire 6 month period was considered, it was found that in 90 percent of the days the deviation from the desired staffing level was 0 or +1. This was unadjusted for aggregate unit under or overstaffing which would necessitate some deviations. These same algorithm generated schedule configurations yielded the lowest cost schedule in a nurse's feasible schedule pattern almost 44 percent of the time and/or schedules with a cost less than or equal to 90 percent of the schedules in the nurse's feasible schedule set almost 88 percent of the time. The algorithm generated schedules compared favorably to those actually used by the hospital according to schedule patterns as well as staffing level inturn. See [1] for more extensive results.

40.2.7. *Extensions*

The model may be extended to include shift rotation and part-time nurses by redefining the feasibility sets Π_i in an appropriate manner. For example, if we consider shift rotation, we:

1. Schedule night and evening shifts first.
2. If the staffing level patterns require shift rotation to reduce staffing costs, and if the day shift has nurses available to be rotated, select nurses from those available to rotate and have them rotate to the night and evening shifts. The exact rotation patterns selected must conform with various rotation constraints and must result in reduction of staffing costs on the shifts rotated to.
3. Schedule the day shift treating these rotation patterns as fixed conditions.

The problem of part-time nurses is handled in a way analogous to full-time nurses. Feasibility sets Π_i are constructed for part-time nurses depending on appropriately defined constraints (e.g., a nurse must work four days out of every fourteen). Then the schedules are listed according to how they meet a set of appropriately defined non-binding constraints. Then we proceed in the same manner as with full-time nurses choosing schedules from the sets Π_i where now some of these sets contain part-time nurses schedules and some contain full-time nurses schedules.

40.3. Discussion

The nurse scheduling procedure just presented is an example of intermediate level scheduling in a three level disaggregated scheduling process. The natural flow of things indicates one solves the long range, intermediate range, and short term problems in sequential order. This pertains to the operational mode. This natural order may be reversed when one considers the planning mode, where the planning may be carried out in concert with a simulation experiment.

For example, suppose a hospital is interested in determining the effects of a long-term nurse allocation policy. Using the lower levels of the disaggregation procedure, day on-day off schedules as well as short-term allocation needs may be simulated indicating the effects of the long-term procedure.

We see the presence of a higher to lower level flow in the operational modes and lower to higher level flows in the planning mode.

In both cases a large complex problem has been broken up into smaller, solvable components. The preceding has discussed how one of those components may be defined in the case of nurse scheduling. Because of its generality, the model may also be applied to other situations where tradeoffs between employer and employee preferences must be made.

References

1. Miller, H. E., Pierskalla, W. P., and Rath, G. J., 'Nurse Scheduling Using Mathematical Programming', *Operations Research*, vol. 24, no. 5 (September–October 1976), pp. 857–870.

41. Computerized scheduling of hospital nursing personnel: disaggregation to accommodate individual preferences and nonroutine constraints

L. DOUGLAS SMITH, DAVID A. BIRD and A. WIGGINS

Abstract

In generating monthly shift schedules for hospital nursing personnel numerous policy constraints are imposed to ensure that work stretches are reasonable in length, sufficient rest is provided between consecutive shifts worked by an individual, weekends-off occur with sufficient frequency and regularity, and sufficient coverage is provided to meet demands for service. In addition to these constraints of an institutional nature, supervisors often consider preferences of individual nurses for particular shift assignments and days off. At the same time, a desire for efficient utilization of resources encourages centralized staff planning, scheduling and control. This paper describes a computer based system designed to support centralized scheduling, while incorporating individual preferences and allowing considerable flexibility to include nonroutine constraints in the production of monthly shift schedules.

41.1. Introduction

Managing a hospital nursing unit is a complicated exercise. Personnel from several skill categories (e.g., Registered Nurses, Licensed Practical Nurses, Nurses' Aides, and Unit Secretaries) provide the blend of talents required on three shifts, seven days each week. The mix of talents required will vary from shift to shift, and from unit to unit, depending upon the specific medical treatments to be rendered. In order to obtain acceptable staffing levels on all three shifts at reasonable cost, some nurses are required to rotate among the three daily shifts (e.g., work 8 a.m. to 4 p.m. some days, and 4 p.m. to midnight, or midnight to 8 a.m. other days). In addition, float staff (who can be assigned to whatever work team requires assistance on a particular day) and part-time personnel (who work less than the usual 5 shifts per week) are often utilized. Some constraints reflecting general staffing policies are derived from labor contracts; others are derived considering potential decline in quality of patient care and increased likelihood of absenteeism if nurses are exposed to unfavorable schedules. Each nurse is entitled to a particular number of days off each week (usually 2), must obtain weekends off with a specified minimum frequency, must receive work tours (consecutive working days) which are of reasonable length, and must receive sufficient rest between consecutive shifts worked. Further constraints are imposed by vacations, holidays, staff vacancies, and reluctance of many employees to accept irregular shift assignments.

Individual preferences and nonroutine constraints must also be accommodated. One employee may have to attend classes on a particular night. Another may have to be home with young children every evening. Nursing supervisors frequently make special efforts to recruit personnel whose shift preferences and day-off preferences are complementary, thus minimizing personal disruption when covering unpopular shifts.

Management of nursing personnel is typically structured at the following levels (in order of decreasing aggregation):

1. determination of the average number of staff from each skill category which would be desired on each shift, each day of the week. This is accomplished by predicting patient census, and analysing type of care required for patients typically assigned to the unit.
2. staffing the unit by assigning a group of permanent staff from various skill categories to the unit. Some individuals may be part-time. Some may rotate among all three shifts; others may be assigned straight shifts or rotate between two shifts.
3. generation of monthly shift schedules for the unit perhaps augmenting the permanent staff by dedicating some 'float' staff to cover predicted deficiencies.
4. daily monitoring of staffing levels in light of patient census and staff absences due to illness, etc. Float staff are assigned to the units with greatest need, and occasionally some transfers occur among similar units to equalize workload.

5. assignment of specific patients and/or tasks to individual nurses.

The focus of this paper is upon the third level mentioned above. To be discussed is the disaggregation of the scheduling problem to the extent that individual preferences and nonroutine constraints are considered in addition to the more general policy constraints when generating shift schedules automatically on a monthly basis. Alternative approaches to this exercise will be acknowledged, and a computer-based system currently implemented in a large St. Louis hospital will be described.

41.2. Organizational considerations in the disaggregation of the scheduling problem

A supportive organizational structure (formal and informal) and system of information flows are essential if a proper allocation of resources is to be maintained among the different nursing units. Flexibility must be maintained to adjust allocations when the tentative assignment of personnel in the monthly schedule becomes inappropriate for current circumstances. In order to achieve this flexibility, the Jewish Hospital of St. Louis has operated a central staffing office which generates monthly staff schedules for a number of nursing units, monitors staffing requirements in light of changes in patient census, manages a central float pool of nurses who are assigned as needed on short notice, and maintains staffing records for payroll and general administration. This system has been extremely effective in relieving nursing supervisors of the burden of scheduling their staff, and has facilitated rational allocation of resources among different nursing units. Each day, calls reporting absenteeism are processed in the central office by scheduling clerks who, being aware of the staffing status on each unit, can respond quickly to reallocate available resources as necessary.

Each month the staffing clerks collect special requests from individuals on the different units, and attempt to incorporate them into the schedules. Unfortunately, considerable time is required to generate the monthly schedules manually, and individual preferences of a large staff become obscured in the process. The scheduling clerks found themselves working many overtime hours to meet deadlines for posting schedules, necessitating some units to continue to be scheduled independently.

We therefore undertook a project to develop a computer-based system which would help the scheduling clerks in the central staffing office to produce more timely schedules, incorporating vacations, holidays, special requests, personal preferences for shifts and days-off, and individual specification of weekend-off frequencies, work tour limits, etc. Our objective was to achieve the advantages of managing the nursing staff with a centralized perspective, but not to lose the capability to consider individual factors more commonly associated with decentralized planning and scheduling.

41.3. Development of the computer-based scheduling system

There are two basic approaches to handling individual preferences, each reflecting a different managerial bias. One alternative is to post tentative schedules which satisfy the basic institutional constraints, incorporating vacations and holidays as necessary, but leaving individuals to negotiate trades when their personal circumstances make it difficult to cover their shifts. An extreme application of this approach is the use of cyclical schedules which are rotated among employees, producing predictable work patterns and an equal sharing of all work assignments. Howell [9], Frances [5], Monroe [13], Baker [4], Maier-Rothe and Wolfe [12] and Smith [15] describe procedures for developing cyclical scheduling patterns. The latter references [4, 12, 15] deal with problems of providing desired coverage when institutional constraints are imposed upon the scheduling exercise, and when the schedules are required to exhibit various attributes with respect to weekend-off frequency, work tour limits, and day-off patterns. We tried initially to approach the scheduling problem by superimposing vacations, holidays, restricted rotation, and special requests upon a tentative cyclical schedule, but found that the adjustments absorbed nearly as much effort as producing the entire schedule by hand. Modifying the algorithms and computer programs to construct schedules which were cyclical in terms of weekly days-off, but which assigned employees to specific shifts on a monthly basis [16] did help somewhat, but not enough to make the approach seem practical for our environment. The supervisors felt (not unreasonably) that individual preferences for shifts and days-off, assignments for part-time employees, vacations, holidays, and special requests should all be considered while generating the basic monthly schedule.

Rather than focusing upon the regular aspects of the problem, and then adjusting a basic schedule to incorporate irregularities, an alternative approach is to take account of the irregularities, incorporate them into a schedule, and then build the remainder of the schedule around them. This is the approach which had been assumed by the scheduling clerks when generating schedules manually, and which we finally adopted in our computer-based system. Warner [19] and Warner and Prawda [20] report the implementation of an integer programming system which also approaches the problem from this perspective. They minimize the sum of penalty costs in connection with the discomfort which individual employees experience from their schedules and penalty costs attached to deviations from desired staffing coverage. Conceptually, an integer programming model can incorporate virtually any constraint which one wishes to impose upon the problem. The technique was very appealing to us because it enabled simultaneous consideration of all constraints while attempting to balance costs of violating constraints against costs of employee discomfort with schedules. Upon closer examination of this alternative however, we encountered problems which motivated us to concentrate upon developing an efficient means of supplementing the human judgment of staffing clerks and/or nursing supervisors, rather than laboriously computing an 'optimal' schedule which they seemed bound to change anyway. Two factors influenced our thinking. First, we had modest computational capacity available in the form of an IBM 370/125 computer. Secondly, the mathematical structure became cumbersome when we attempted to impose constraints involving specific individuals across traditional skill categories (e.g., a particular LPN who could perform most functions normally restricted to an RN) and when discretionary use of float staff and student nurses could supplement staff to avoid an unfavorable aspect in the schedule of a particular nurse. In other words, the scheduling clerks made use of so many options which could not conveniently be included in the mathematical programming formulation that it seemed better to produce a tentative (rough) schedule which incorporated relevant details about nurses' preferences and special requests, and then let them prescribe remedial action in the context of the tentative schedule. Initial schedules are generated by a heuristic which utilizes list processing and performs operations directly upon problem-oriented data structures. The heuristic has been described in a previous paper by Smith and Wiggins [17]. Discussion in the remainder of this paper will concentrate upon information used in the computer-based scheduling system, thus illustrating the extent of disaggregation deemed necessary for the scheduling exercise. Note that it is deemed *inappropriate* to try to generate sets of open schedules for staff of various skill categories in order to satisfy general institutional constraints and then try to *assign* people to fill vacant slots in the schedule. The schedules themselves are generated considering *detailed* information about the personnel on the unit.

41.3.1. Schedule generation

Schedule generation consists of two basic functions: (1) file maintenance and (2) processing to generate schedules. Figure 1 portrays the files utilized and steps performed in producing schedules. A discussion of each function follows immediately.

41.3.2. File maintenance

The data base employed by the system consists of seven master files. Two files are maintained for EMPLOYEE DATA. One file contains data used to generate a schedule. The other file (UPDATED EMPLOYEE DATA) is used to generate a modified schedule. The EMPLOYEE DATA files contain, for each nurse: name, employee number, skill classification, number of shifts to be assigned weekly, number of weekends worked between weekends off, maximum and minimum length of work tour, preferred shifts, measures of aversion to alternative shifts, preferred day-off assignments, cumulative number of assignments to each shift, a cumulative measure of aversion to shifts assigned, a cumulative measure of days-off assigned, and additional information required to ensure acceptable linkage with next month's schedule. Figure 2 illustrates the form used when initializing an employee's records in the EMPLOYEE DATA files. The STAFF REQUIREMENTS file con-

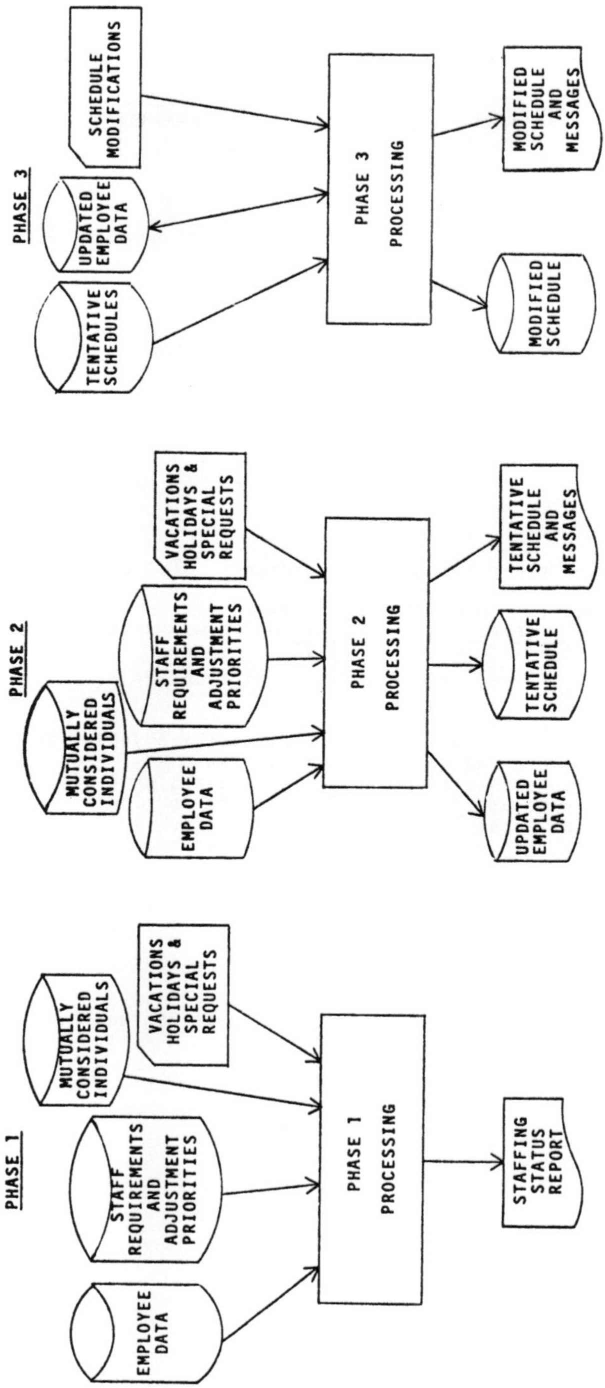

Figure 1. Files utilized in monthly processing.

Record

1
B

1. Unit No.

2	3	4	5	6	7
				6	3

2. Employee No.

8	9	10	11	12	13
	8	2	8	5	0

3. Employee Name

14	15	16	17	18	19	20	21	22	23	24	25	26	27	28	29
F	O	X	X	,	F	.									

4. Classification [30: 5] (1-head nurse, 2-assistant head, 3-RN, 4-LPN, 5-NA/ORD, 6-Sec.)

5. Number of shifts to be assigned weekly: Minimum [31: 5] Desired [32: 5] Maximum [33: 5]

6. No. of weekends can work between weekends off. [34: 2]

7. Length of work stretch (consecutive days): Minimum [35: 2] Maximum [36: 6]

8. Shift Rankings (1: 7p.m. to 3 p.m. (days); 2: 3 p.m. to 11 p.m. (eves.); 3: 11 p.m. to 7 a.m. (nights))

   First Choice [37: 1] Second Choice [38: 2] Third Choice [39: 3]

9. Shift aversion points:
   a) If assigned to straight shifts, assign 9999.0 to first choice, and leave 2nd and 3rd choices blank.
   b) If can rotate among three shifts, assign 0.0 to first choice, and allocate 10 points between 2nd and 3rd choices.
   c) If can rotate only between two shifts, assign 0.0 to 1st choice and assign 5.0 points to 2nd and 3rd choices.

First Choice Aversion

40	41	42	43	44	45
			0	.	0

Second Choice Aversion

46	47	48
1	.	0

Third Choice Aversion

49	50	51
9	.	0

10. State the pair of days to comprise your "weekend" (usually (7,1)).

   First day of weekend [52: 7] Second day of weekend [53: 1]

Figure 2. Employee data.

Record

1
C

Unit No. (as before)

2	3	4	5	6	7
				6	3

Employee No. (as before)

8	9	10	11	12	13
	8	2	8	5	0

11. Indicate preference for the first day off in a week prior to a weekend off. (2=Mon.; 3=Tues.; 4=Wed.; 5=Thur.; 6=Fri.)

First Choice	Second Choice	Third Choice	Fourth Choice	Fifth Choice
14	15	16	17	18
2	3	4	6	5

12. Indicate preference for the second day off in a week following a weekend off.

First Choice	Second Choice	Third Choice	Fourth Choice	Fifth Choice
19	20	21	22	23
6	5	4	2	3

13. Indicate preference for day off pairs midweek. (Usual alternatives are (2,3), (3,4), (4,5), (5,6), (2,5), (2,6), (3,6).

	Columns	Pair
First choice pair	24, 25	4, 5
Second Choice	26, 27	5, 6
Third Choice	28, 29	3, 4
Fourth Choice	30, 31	2, 3
Fifth Choice	32, 33	2, 6
Sixth Choice	34, 35	2, 5
Seventh Choice	36, 37	3, 6

14. Current value of shift aversion index (9999.0 for straight shifts), (if not on straight shifts, then 5.0 for new employees)

38	39	40	41	42	43	44	45	46	47
			5	.	0				

15. Current value of day off aversion index (2.0 for new employee)

48	49	50	51	52	53	54	55	56	57
			2	.	0				

16. Number of times shifts worked to date:

Shift 1

58	59	60
		0

Shift 2

61	62	63
		0

Shift 3

64	65	66
		0

17. Shift worked on last day of previous month

67
0

18. Number of weekends worked since last weekend off

68
0

19. Last day off previous week

69
7

20. Remarks (eg. mutually considered individual information)

tains for each nursing unit, desired and minimum staffing levels for each skill category on each day of the week. Minima are also stated for skill categories in combination. The STAFF ADJUSTMENT PRIORITIES file contains directions for adjusting scheduling objectives on specific shifts in event of a staff shortage or surplus.

The MUTUALLY CONSIDERED INIDIVIDUALS file contains groups of people to be given special mutual consideration in generating schedules. The maximum number of employees on each list who can be off simultaneously, and the minimum number who must be assigned to each shift are specified. This feature can be used to impose constraints on subsets of individuals which may or may not coincide with the formal skill categories. For example, a particular RN may be able to substitute for a supervisor (HN or AHN). If either a supervisor or the particular RN must be present on the day shift, the supervisor and the RN can be specified on a list for special mutual consideration. The minimum number to be assigned shift 2 would be specified as 1 for that list. The 'special mutual consideration' lists can also be used to impose constraints upon a member of a staff category who is hired to rotate to evening shifts when a particular evening person receives a day-off. One can avoid the problem of assigning both individuals the same day-off by setting 'maximum number to be off same day' equal to 1. Finally, the lists can be used to impose redundant constraints (useful in assigning days off) to prevent individuals assigned to straight evening and night shifts from receiving the same days off. This prevents unnecessary rotation to unpopular shifts for the rotating personnel. These options allow considerable power to the user to determine the shape of the final schedules.

The VACATIONS, HOLIDAYS, AND SPECIAL REQUESTS (inputs) file contains individuals' vacation schedules, holiday assignments, and special requests for days off or shift assignments. These requests are treated by the computer as inviolable during the generation of schedules. In addition, a RUN LOG is maintained on disk to control file allocations for the scheduling program, and a COMPACT SCHEDULES file contains the most recent schedules generated.

File maintenance if performed on demand, and usually prior to the generation of schedules for the next four week period.

Special programs perform additions, deletions, and alterations to the files, and also check for valid records. The files are organized sequentially on disk. Tape back-up is taken following each scheduling run.

41.3.3. Processing to generate schedules

Scheduling is initiated by submitting the Vacations, Holidays, and Special Requests form illustrated in Figure 3. The data are imposed directly upon the schedule, and are unaltered during the scheduling exercise. This form also provides the mechanism whereby an individual's phase in his weekend off cycle can be shifted. One simply overrides the automatic scheduler by superceding it with a special request. Such shifts are frequently necessary around vacations, and it may take several periods to reestablish weekend-off cycles to provide sufficiently uniform coverage among weekends. Figure 4 contains an excerpt from a computer run of SCHEDULE. We encourage the staffing clerks to distinguish between requests which must be granted and requests which may be granted only if they do not seriously disrupt the schedules. Then they can perform a preliminary run including the essential requests, and examine alterations which would be necessary to grant the discretionary requests. If substantial revisions are prescribed, the clerks may decide to request the revisions and return SCHEDULE before proceeding to phase 3 (MODIFY). The latter option is usually selected when shifts in the phases of several individuals' weekend-off cycles are required. Finally, MODIFY is executed to incorporate any adjustments to the monthly schedules.

41.3.4. Computer job structure

Computer processing is structured so that the scheduling clerks simply fill in the relevant forms and submit them to keypunching service for punching, verification, and forwarding to the computer operator. A record code on each card enables automatic extraction of relevant data for each job step. Each maintenance program performs a comprehensive edit of the file contents and prints a report of invalid entries.

Instructions: For each employee who is to be assigned a vacation, holiday, or special request during the next four weeks, partially complete his schedule using the following codes for each daily insertion:

X - regular day off

V - vacation day
H - holiday
U - unavailable
D - day shift (7 a.m.)
E - evening shift (3 p.m.)
N - night shift (11 p.m.)
- (blank space) daily assignment to be made by computer

Header Card: 1 W

Unit No. (2–7): 83

Schedule Beginning: 5 / 15 / 77 (Mo. / Day / Year; columns 8–13)

Run Type (column 14): 2
1. For Summary
2. For Schedule

1	Unit Number (2–7)	Name	Employee Number (8–13)	S 14	M 15	T 16	W 17	T 18	F 19	S 20	S 21	M 22	T 23	W 24	T 25	F 26	S 27	S 28	M 29	T 30	W 31	T 32	F 33	S 34	S 35	M 36	T 37	W 38	T 39	F 40	S 41
X	83	HOWELL	173302	X	V	V	V	V	V	X	X	V	V	V	V	V	X	X	D	D	D	X	X	X	X	X	X	E	E	X	D
X	83	HARTER	161240						H	X	X	V	V	V	V	V	X	X	V	V	V	V	V	X	X	H					
X	83	GRIFFIN	165076											X	X	X				X				X	X	V	V	V	V	V	X
X	83	SHARPE	178319																												X
X																															
X																															
X																															
X																															
X																															
X																															
X																															
X																															
X																															
X																															

Figure 3. Vacations, holidays, special requests.

```
              1 1 1 1 1 2 2  2 2 2 2 2 2 2  2 3 3 0 0 0 0  0 0 0 0 0 1 1
              5 6 7 8 9 0 1  2 3 4 5 6 7 8  9 0 1 1 2 3 4  5 6 7 8 9 0 1
            S S M T W T F S  S M T W T F S  S M T W T F S  S M T W T F S

LEWIS.L.         (LP)
(     83)
50336       E E X D D D D X  X D D D D X D  D D D X X D D  D X D D D D X

-----------------------------------------------------------------------
HOWELL.G.        (LP)
(     83)       R R R R R R R  R R R R R R R  R R R R R R R  R R R R R R R
173302      X X V V V V V X  X V V V V V X  X D D D X X X  X X X E E X D

-----------------------------------------------------------------------
COCHRAN.S.       (LP)
(     83)
175299      D D D X D D D X  X D D D X D D  D D X D D X D  D D X D D D X

-----------------------------------------------------------------------
LUEDERS.B.       (LP)
(     83)
183194      X X D D D X D D  D X X D D D N  N X D D D D X  X D D D X D D

-----------------------------------------------------------------------
HARRIS.M.        (LP)
(     83)
11547       N N N N X X N N  N N N X N N X  X N N N X N N  N N N X X N N

-----------------------------------------------------------------------
HARTER.J.        (LP)
(     83)               R R  R R R R R R R  R R R R R R R  R R
161240      N N X N N N H X  X V V V V V X  X V V V V V X  X H N N X N N

-----------------------------------------------------------------------
GRIFFIN.L.       (LP)
(     83)                          R R R          R     R  R R R R R R R
165076      X X E X X E X E  E X E X X X E  E X X X E E X  X V V V V V X

-----------------------------------------------------------------------
SHARPE.L.        (LP)
(     83)                                                              R
178319      X X E E E X E E  E X X E E E E  E X E E E E X  E E X E E E X

-----------------------------------------------------------------------
```

Figure 4. Portion of a tentative (rough) schedule.

41.3.5. Performance of the scheduling system

Substantial reductions have been observed in the time required to produce acceptable monthly schedules. The scheduling procedure seems to be a natural extension of manual methods, and the staffing clerks seem to find it simple to adopt. Fortunately, the basic scheduling algorithm requires only about one minute of CPU time per schedule on the IBM 370/125 (approximately two seconds per schedule on a 370/168), enabling processing of schedules to be undertaken during transition between larger batch jobs, or in background while data processing operations proceed. Indeed, the main consumer of computer time is overhead for file maintenance.

Approximately 11 percent of the individual entries seem currently to be modified in the third phase (MODIFY). The manual review and adjustments seem to take between 25 and 60 minutes for units employing about 40 people. The longer times occur in months when significant staffing shortages exist, where several alterations of weekend-off cycles are required because of vacations, and where numerous holidays have to be assigned.

A smoothing routine is being incorporated to reduce manual effort in adjusting schedules during the MODIFY phase. Its purpose is to achieve a better balance of coverage, at the expense of granting lower priority choices for days-off and shift assignments. This should enable further time reductions of approximately 10 to 20 minutes per unit.

41.4. Conclusion

Too frequently the impression is conveyed that one may generate "schedules" which satisfy basic institutional constraints, and simply assign individuals to positions in the "schedules", making minor adjustments as necessary to accomodate individual factors. In implementing a computer-based scheduling system, we found that individual factors were extremely important to consider from the start. This paper illustrates the extent of disaggregation found necessary in generating monthly schedules for hospital nursing units.

References

1. Abernathy, W. J., Baloff, N., Hershey, J. C., and Wandel, S., "A Three-stage Manpower Planning, and Scheduling Model – A Service Sector Example", *Operations Research*, vol. 22, no. 3 (May–June 1973), pp. 693–711.
2. Ahuja, H. and Sheppard, R., "Computerized Nurse Scheduling", *Industrial Engineering*, vol. 7 (October 1975).
3. Aydelotte, M. K., 'Nurse Staffing Methodology, A. Review and Critique of Selected Literature', DHEW Publication no. (NIH) 73-433 (January 1973).
4. Baker, K. L., "Scheduling Full-time and Part-time Staff to Meet Cyclical Requirements", *Operational Research Quarterly*, vol. 25 (March 1974).

5. Sister Frances, M. A., "Implementing a Program of Cyclical Scheduling of Nursing Personnel", *Hospitals, Journal of the American Hospital Association*, vol. 40 (July 1966).
6. Healy, W. C. "Shift Scheduling Made Easy", *Factory*, vol. 117, no. 10 (October 1969).
7. Heller, N. B., *Proportional Rotating Schedules*, unpublished Ph.D. dissertation, University of Pennsylvania (1969).
8. Heller, N. B., McEwen, J. T., and Stenzel, W. W., *Police Manpower Scheduling*, Board of Police Commissioners, St. Louis Police Department, St. Louis, Missouri (1972).
9. Howell, J. P., "Cyclical Scheduling of Nursing Personnel", *Hospitals, Journal of the American Hospital Association*, vol. 40 (January 1966), pp. 71–85.
10. Luce, B. J., Jr., "Employee Assignment System", Paper delivered to the Joint National Meeting of the Operations Research Society of America and The Institute of Management Science, Boston, Massachusetts (1974).
11. Mack, H. L. and Smith, L. D., "An Example of the Utility of List Processing and Problem Oriented Data Structures to Facilitate the Development of Computerized Scheduling Algorithms", paper presented to the Annual Conference of the Canadian Operational Research Society, Waterloo, Canada (1975).
12. Maier-Rothe C. and Wolfe, H. B., "Cyclical Scheduling and Allocation of Nursing Staff", *Socio-Economic Planning Sciences*, vol. 7 (1973), pp. 471–487.
13. Monroe, G., "Scheduling Manpower for Service Operations", *Industrial Engineering*, vol. 2, no. 28 (August 1970), pp. 10–17.
14. Rothstein, M., "Hospital Manpower Staff Scheduling by Mathematical Programming", *Health Services Research*, vol. 8 (Spring 1973), pp. 60–66.
15. Smith, L. D., "The Application of an Interactive Algorithm to Develop Cyclical Rotational Schedules for Nursing Personnel", INFOR, *The Canadian Journal of Operational Research and Information Processing*, vol. 14, no. 1 (February 1976). pp. 53–70.
16. Smith, L. D., "Integrated Algorithms for Analyzing Staff Requirements and Scheduling Hospital Nursing Personnel", *PROCEEDINGS of the Annual Conference of the Canadian Association of Administrative Sciences*, Edmonton, Canada (1975).
17. Smith, L. D. and Wiggins, A., "A Computer-Based Nurse Scheduling System", *Computers and Operations Research* to appear.
18. Tebrawala, R., Philippe, D., and Brown, J., "Optimal Scheduling of Two Consecutive Idle Periods", *Management Science*, vol. 19, no. 1 (September 1972), pp. 17–75.
19. Warner, D. M., "Scheduling: Nursing Personnel According to Nursing Preference: A Mathematical Programming Approach", *Operations Research*, vol. 24, no. 5, pp. 842–856.
20. Warner, D. M. and Prawda, J., "A Mathematical Programming Model for Scheduling Nursing Personnel in a Hospital", *Management Science*, vol. 19, no. 4 (December 1972), pp. 411–422.

42. Disaggregating health utilization data for planning

J. WILLIAM GAVETT

Abstract

The purpose of this paper is to provide a structure for disaggregating health utilization data that will explain how resources are used to service a particular population, that is easy to understand, and that relates to an information system. For a particular population, that is easy to understand, and that relates to an information system. For a particular health service, resource consumption can be related to population serviced by either an *analytical* model that is based upon a functional relationship between the resource level and various explanatory variables or a *synthetic model* that aggregates an estimate by adding together independently derived estimates of elements of the system. Combinations of the two methods are possible. This paper delas with a synthetic model that classifies the population-resource system and uses compounded ratios for estimating resource needs.

42.1. Utilization ratios

42.1.1. Elementary structure

For purposes of example, consider the home health care system for a community of 710,000 persons. We are interested in determining the quantity of professional home-care nursing required to serve the community and how these services are being used. A simple estimating model is a linear relationship between the population and the nursing service. Assume that this relationship is empirically derived and is 48.32 nursing hours per 1,000 population gained by dividing the nurse hours consumed in 1976 by the population in 1000's (34,307 hours ÷ 710). This type of simple model is frequently used for planning, such as physician per 1000 population. Critics of such models have voiced the need for models and systems that more accurately represent the complex reality of medical or health care [4].

42.1.2. Model refinement – full tree

The purpose of refining the model is to derive more accurate estimates of resource requirements, provide more detailed knowledge for better management and control, or to determine the effect of anticipated or unanticipated changes in the structure of the system.

One obvious approach to specificity is to disaggregate by introducing sub-classes of the population and to relate these sub-classes to the resource by specific linear rates. These relations, involving some degree of cross classification of basic data, may be modeled in the form of a tree, the branches of which interconnect population and resource(s). Figure 1 shows such a tree where the population has been classified into two categories, namely Male and Female. Their utilization of nursing hours is disaggregated in terms of Visit Type (First Visit-Type 1, Revisit-Type 2). The nodes of the tree represent levels or quantities and the arcs connecting the nodes are appropriate linear rates. The disaggregation takes place in two dimensions. The first is the introduction of stages, each stage representing a classification of some phenomenon that helps to explain

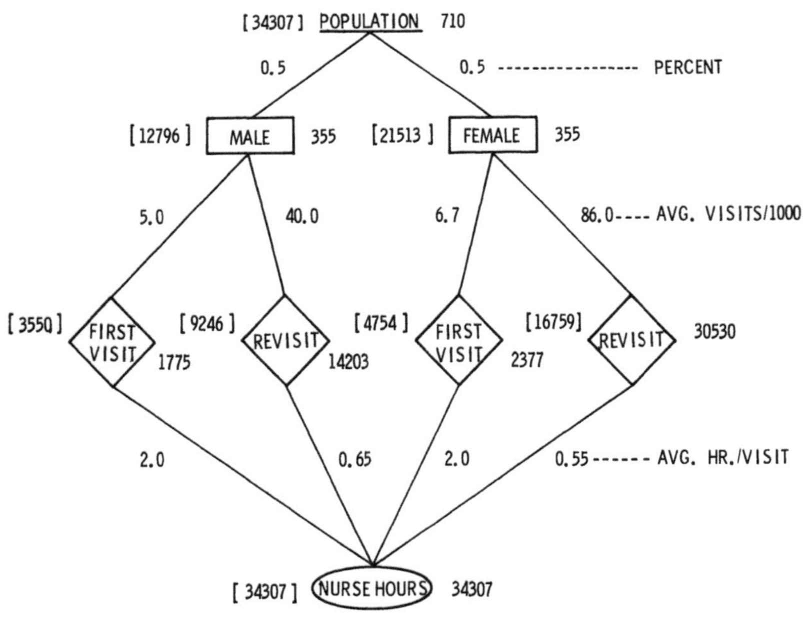

Figure 1.

the consumption of the resource(s). The second is the number of classes in each stage. Figure 2 shows a five-stage model that interrelates population, region, episodes of morbidity, visit type, and resource.

These trees are designated as full trees to distinguish them from other kinds of trees described later on. In general, for the full tree, let:

s = index of stage not including the source node. $s = 1, 2, \ldots, S$.

The index number also denotes an ordering of the stages in the tree.

(s, i) = index of a node in stage s. $i = 1, 2, \ldots, I_s$

$(r(s, i)\ (s + 1, i))$ = a rate arc connecting a node (s, i) at stage s with a node $s + 1, i$ at stage $s + 1$.

The total number of rates in the system is

$$R(S) = \sum_{s=1}^{S} I_s$$

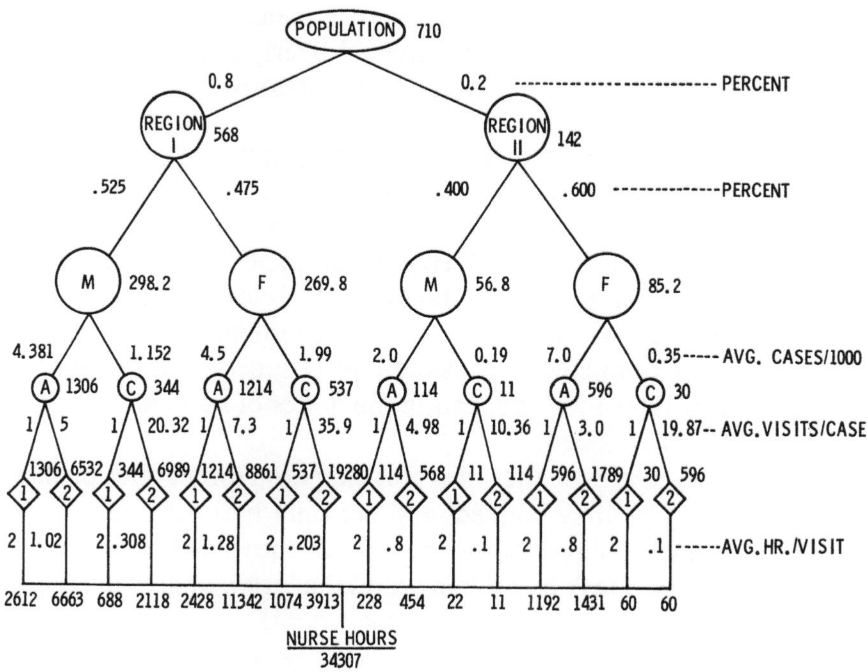

Figure 2.

including the $I(1)$ rates connecting the source node (population) with the first-stage nodes (classes).

At each stage, a node will represent a level or value $w(s, i)$

$$w(s, i) = [w(s - 1, i)][r(s - 1, i)(s, i)].$$

The value of the terminal node will be

$$W(S) = \sum_{i \in s-1} [w(S - 1, i)][r(S - 1, i)(S, i)].$$

Note that the rates can come from independent sources either within the organization or without the organization, representing averages for probabilistic variables. The variance of the node value, $w(s, i)$, is a function of the variances of the rates in the arcs of the path leading to node (s, i).

42.1.3. Model refinement – folded three

Pragmatically, time and cost constraints frequently limit the manager's use of derived data. Conceptually, the uncertainty over the planning time horizon in concert with measurement problems obviates any advantages of sophisticated overly precise rates. For these reasons, often more aggregate linear rates are used in planning models.

In order to avoid the data detail embodied in the full cross classification tree, an alternative arrangement is to construct a simplified network representation of the full tree. This is referred to as a folded tree. Figure 3 is a folded representation of the full tree shown in Figure 2. If a full three has S stages and $I(s)$ classes at each stage, s, the folded tree will also have the same dimensions. However, the number of branches is considerably reduced, and therefore, the number of rates interconnecting the nodes of successive stages will be similarly reduced.

It is important to note that the rates express a direct relationship between the nodes they connect and are only indirectly related to the nodes in earlier stages of the tree.[1] Thus, the folded tree reduces the data collection task by utilizing rates that are weighted averages

1. Those familiar with the industrial science may recognize the similarity between the folded tree and product explosion. Neither the terms patient explosion nor population explosion seemed appropriate to designate our activity.

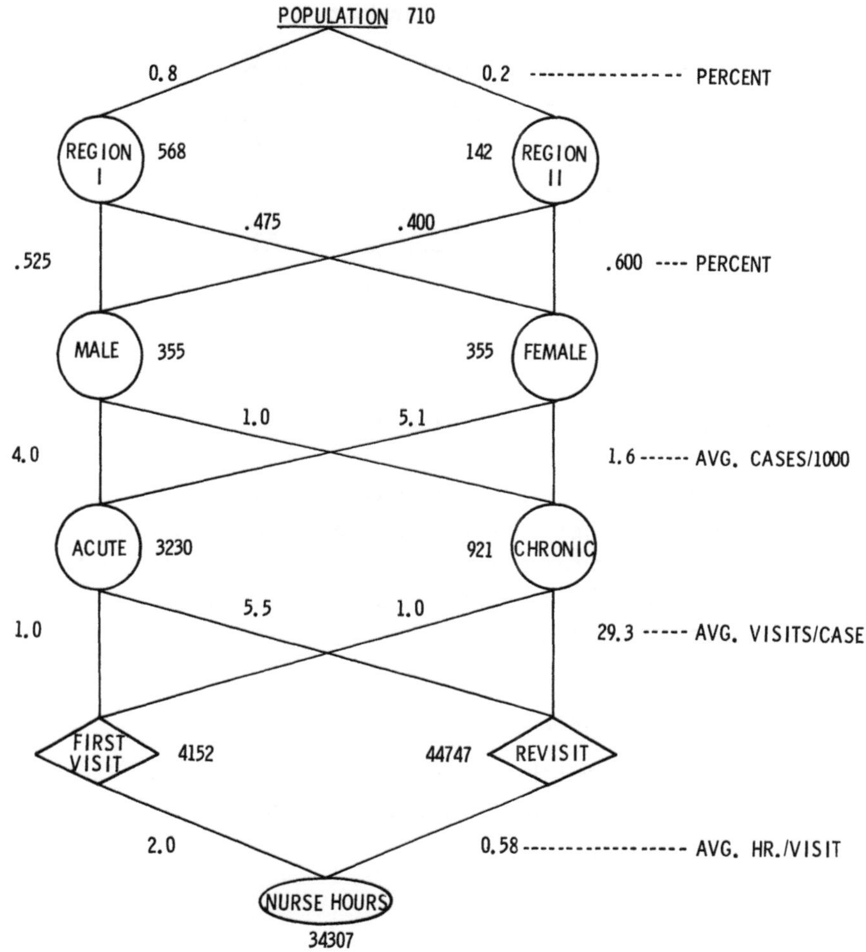

Figure 3.

of the full tree rates, but it introduces an error due to aggregation. For example, Table 1 compares the two kinds of trees for different numbers of stages assuming two classes at each stage except the last stage which has one node for a single resource and assuming the source node is not included. In general, for the folded tree the total number of paths, consisting of some unique combination of rates, will be the same for a corresponding full tree. However, the total number of rates in the system is a function of the number of classes at each stage.

If we let $c(s)$ be the number of classes at each stage, then the

Table 1. Size comparison of full and folded trees.

No. of Stages	Full Tree		Folded Tree	
	No. of Nodes	No. of Rates	No. of Nodes	No. of Rates
2	3	4	3	4
3	7	10	5	8
5	31	46	9	16
10	1,023	1,534	19	36

number of rates is

$$R'(S) = c(1) + \sum_{s=1}^{S-1} c(s)c(s+1)$$

One can recommend a variety of tree styles including: partially folded trees, where any two or more stages are folded; non-symmetrical trees, where the number of successor nodes is not necessarily the same for all predecessor nodes at a given stage; or various combinations of the two.

42.1.4. *Linear programming format*

We may note that given the values of the source node(s), $w(\text{source}, i)$, all $w(s, i)$ can be determined by linear programming where:

Objective is: Minimize $W(S)$

Subject to:

$$W(\text{source}, i) = K(i) \text{ for all source nodes}$$

$$w(s, j) = \sum_{i \in (s-1)} w(s-1, i) + r((s-1, i)(s, j)),$$

$$s = 1, 2, \ldots, S$$

The LP yields the values $w(s, i)$ in the solution basis. In addition, each equality on the value of the node i, will have an artificial variable whose shadow prices, in the final solution, equal the ratio of $x(s, i)$ to $w(s, i)$ where $x(s, i)$ is the amount of the resource consumed by each node (i.e. bracketed number in Figure 1). For example, the tree shown in Figure 1 has original and final tableaus shown below.

42.2. Discussion

42.2.1. Analytical versus synthetic model

One can reasonably question this kind of a model in contrast to the use of more analytical ones such as multiple regression related to demand and production functions. The obvious advantage of the latter would be a more unbiased explanatory model of demand and production than provided by the synthetic model. The proposed advantages of the synthetic model are:

1. There are real problems in deriving the sample space for the analytical model. The alternatives are a longitudinal series of the history for a particular system being studied or a cross sectional study of different populations or systems. The former is often impossible because of the lack of consistent historical data. The latter presents the problem of defining the sample points in the cross section. The study of a set of organizations (e.g., home health care agencies in different geographic locations) may yield a 'global' explanation that lacks specificity about the organization in question. Or, for example, a cross section of the given organization's population of users requires some geographic clustering, such as by census tract. In either event, data about independent variables may be lacking or difficult to obtain.
2. Changes in the system's indogenous variables (policy decisions) such as visit times, or visit rates, for different population classes can be altered in the synthetic model but cannot be evaluated by the analytical model. In this sense, the synthetic model offers more opportunity to calculate the consequences of possible changes whereas the analytical model assumes a system of correlation parameters.
3. It is hypothesized that the working manager is more likely to understand the structure of his system with the synthetic rather than the analytical model. The manifold outputs of computerized regression analyses are not easy to understand by the uninitiated.
4. The model fits the data system of many health care agencies where data about population and resources are not interrelated but maintained in separate files. The degree of cross classification possible depends on the data system. Furthermore, the

model sets the stage for introducing linear programming into the planning process. While the demonstrated model consists solely of equalities it is very easy to introduce constraints or objectives related to the node values ($w(s, i)$).

5. The model can also produce simple aggregated ratios of $w(s, i)$ to $s(s - k, i)$, where $K \geqq 2$; and $w(s, i)$ to $w(j, s)$ as they become meaningful to the manager.

42.2.2. *Other issues*

Disaggregation costs money and a fundamental question is how much disaggregation is required in terms of numbers of stages (variables to be included) and how many classes per stage? The answer to this question requires some research in which alternative tree designs are used for a specific estimate. While our examples have used deterministic rates, the stochastic nature of rates should be included in order to provide a variance on the node levels. Furthermore, the research needs to be linked to specific management issues and problems. The degree of estimation refinement due to disaggregation can only be evaluated in terms of the expected losses due to the consequence of error, or to lack of specific information.

Obviously one would want to include stages (variables) that influence the expenditure of the resource(s) being considered. At this point analytical techniques may be useful. For example, the

FIRST TABLEAU

	Pop	M	F	M-1	M-2	F-1	F-2	N	A_{pop}	A_M	A_F	A_{M-1}	A_{M-2}	A_{F-1}	A_{F-2}	A_N	=	Z
	0	0	0	0	0	0	0	1	0	0	0	0	0	0	0	0	=	Z
A_{pop}	1.0	0	0	0	0	0	0	0	1	0	0	0	0	0	0	0		710.0
A_M	0.5	-1.0	0	0	0	0	0	0	0	1	0	0	0	0	0	0		0
A_F	0.5	0	-1.0	0	0	0	0	0	0	0	1	0	0	0	0	0		0
A_{M-1}	0	5.0	0	-1.0	0	0	0	0	0	0	0	1	0	0	0	0		0
A_{M-2}	0	40.0	0	0	-1.0	0	0	0	0	0	0	0	1	0	0	0		0
A_{F-1}	0	0	6.7	0	0	-1.0	0	0	0	0	0	0	0	1	0	0		0
A_{F-2}	0	0	86.6	0	0	0	0	0	0	0	0	0	0	0	1	0		0
N	0	0	0	2.0	0.65	2	0.55	-1.0	0	0	0	0	0	0	0	1		0

SOLUTION TABLEAU

	0	0	0	0	0	0	0	0	-48.35	-36	-60.7	-2.0	-0.65	-2.0	-.55	-1.0	
Pop	1	0	0	0	0	0	0	1	0	0	0	0	0	0	0	0	710
M	0	1	0	0	0	0	0	0	.5	-1.0	0	0	0	0	0	0	355
F	0	0	1	0	0	0	0	0	.5	0	-1.0	0	0	0	0	0	355
M-1	0	0	0	1	0	0	0	0	2.5	-5.0	0	-1.0	0	0	0	0	1775
M-2	0	0	0	0	1	0	0	0	20.0	-40.0	0	0	-1.0	0	0	0	14203
F-1	0	0	0	0	0	1	0	0	3.25	0	-6.7	0	0	-1.0	0	0	2377
F-2	0	0	0	0	0	0	1	0	43.0	0	-86.0	0	0	0	-1.0	0	30530
N	0	0	0	0	0	0	0	1	48.35	-36.0	-60.7	-2.0	-0.65	-2.0	-0.55	-1.0	34307

Automatic Interaction Detection System (AIDS) offers a method of constructing a tree since it derives a set of independent variables (corresponding to the stages in the tree) that best explain the nature of variance in a dependent variable (e.g. resource utilization) among the individuals of a population. However, it is limited to the use of dichotomous classes.

42.2.3. An empirical study

We have recently modeled the home care system of the Rochester-Monroe County N.Y. community in which the population was related to net professional nursing hours in terms of a synthetic model. Professional home care is a relatively homogeneous service rendered by only two public agencies for which data were available. The system was disaggregated into five stages not including the source, or population node. The classification scheme is as shown in Table 2.

The computation of the total net hours (travel and home contact time) using the disaggregated system resulted in an annual requirement of 87,000 hours for 1973. The actual hours used by the agencies in 1973 was 85,000 hours. Thus, the number of hours derived by synthesizing independent estimates was within 3 percent of the actual hours reported by the agencies.

The current effort includes duplicating the disaggregation for the year 1975. A ten class stage is being added that classifies patient cases in terms of their intensity of resource utilization for five categories of human services. Criterion for class boundaries include the

Table 2.

Stage	Description	Classes	Source of Data
Source	Population of Monroe County	-	1970 Census
1	Population of Monroe County by Age Class	0 - 4 years 5 - 19 20 - 44 45 - 64 65 and over	1970 Census
2	Admissions by Visit Class	Cases with only one nurse visit Cases with multiple nurse visits	Agency Data Base
3	Annual admissions by general purpose of admission	Cases for well health guidance Cases for maternal care Cases for mental health Cases for morbidity care	Agency Data Base
4	Number of Nurse Visits	Number of first visits Number of revisits	Sample of Patient Discharge Records
5	Number of Nurse Hours	Number of hours for first visit Number of hours for revisits	Sample of Nurse Daily Reporting Records

duration of the case (uninterrupted time record is active), the total cost per case, and the ratio of the duration to total cost.

While our efforts are research oriented, a practical result is that we know more than anyone else in the community about the dimensions of the *community* home care system and are in a position to answer questions of what might happen if certain parameters of the system are changed. It's just a matter of getting the right people to ask those questions!

References

1. Armstrong, J. Scott and Andress, James G., 'Exploratory Analysis of Marketing Data: Tree vs Regression', *Journal of Marketing Research*, vol. VII, (November 1970).
2. Elnicki, Richard A., 'Hospital Productivity, Service Intensity, and Costs', *Health Services Research*, (Winter 1974).
3. Fahs, I., Choi, T., Barcas, K., and Zakariasen, P., 'Indicators of Need for Health Care Personnel', *Medical Care*, vol. IX:144 (March–April 1971).
4. Falk, I., Schonfeld, H., Harris, B., Landau, S., and Milles, S., "The Development of Standards for the Audit and Planning of Medical Care I', *A.J.P.H.*, vol. 57:118 (July 1967).
5. Halpern, Jonathan, 'Ratios in Planning Budgeting and Bounds on Resource Requirements', *Operations Research*, vol. 20 (September–October 1972).
6. Johnson, W. and Rosenfield, L. 'Indices of Performance in Ambulatory Care Service', *Medical Care*, vol. VIII(3):250 (May–June 1969).
7. Mills, Ronald et al., 'AUTOGRP: An Interactive Computer System for the Analysis of Health Care Data', *Medical Care*, vol. XIV, no. 7 (July 1976).
8. Schonfeld, Hyman K., Henston, J. F. and Falk, I. S., 'Numbers of Physicians Required for Primary Medical Care', *New England Journal of Medicine*, vol. 286, no. 11 (March 1972).
9. Solon, J., Feeney, J., Jones, S., Rigg, R., and Sheps, C. 'Delineating Episodes of Medical Care', *A.J.P.H.*, vol. 57:401 (March 1967).
10. Wennberg, John and Alan Gittelsohn, 'Small Area Variations in Health Care Delivery', *Science*, vol. 182 (December 14, 1973).
11. Wirick, Grover C. Jr., 'Multiple Equation of Demand for Health Care', *Health Services Research*, vol. 1 (Winter 1966).
12. Zemach, R., 'A Model of Health Service Utilization and Resource Allocation', *Operations Research*, vol. 18 (November–December 1970).

Section 10. Personnel shift scheduling

43. Scheduling workers in situations having highly variable manpower requirements

SING-CHOI CHONG and RICHARD J. GIGLIO

Abstract

Many service industries face the problem of scheduling employees to meet a work load which can change from day to day and from hour to hour. This paper describes an improvement to existing heuristic algorithms. The improvement is based on a two-phase integer programming formulation which exploits the structure of the scheduling problem to efficiently produce schedules which meet manpower demands at minimum costs. The algorithm also includes restrictions on 'days-off' patterns and on working-hour patterns of both part-and full-time employees. An extension of the algorithm to include shifts of arbitrary lengths is also discussed. Results from an application in the food service industry are given.

43.1. Introduction

Manpower Scheduling is the process of converting daily or hourly workforce requirements into precise scheduling assignments by specifying both the days and the shift patterns each employee works. Manpower scheduling is important in all business operations, and is especially critical in the case of service operations because services often cannot be inventoried or deferred, and because minimum manpower requirements vary from hour to hour, shift to shift, and day to day. Examples of service operations are telephone directory assistance, turnpike toll collection, airline reservation booking, and food service operations – the application which prompted this research.

The scheduling of workers has become more important lately because of the rapid increase in labor costs in both government and private firms. A recent study [11], showed that labor costs can be as much as 55 percent of the total annual cost of food service operations while another [1], stated that in restaurant operations, as much as 33 percent of the available labor is wasted through lack of proper scheduling.

The objective of this research is to provide a manager with an automated (computerized) program for scheduling manpower. At the present time, the scheduling of food service workers at a military installation is accomplished manually by each of the dining hall stewards. The number of workers to be scheduled at a given dining facility ranges from 12 to 125 depending upon the number of customers and hours of operation.

Some of the benefits to be realized by implementation of an automated scheduling system are expected to include:

1. saving of time spent by the manager to create a schedule,
2. saving in labor cost due to a more efficient schedule,
3. improved employee morale due to a fairer and more efficient schedule,
4. better customer service because employees are working in the right place at the right time.

43.2. Review of manpower scheduling in service operations

There are several types of manpower scheduling problems. The literature reveals three general types of manpower scheduling problems in service operations. The first type [2], [5], [8], [9], [13], involves allocating employees to fluctuating daily manpower requirements such that each employee has a certain days-off pattern, e.g. two consecutive days off each week. Although these problems can be formulated as integer programs, Tibrawala, et al. [13] and Baker [2] have both developed other algorithms which exploit the special structure of the problem.

A second type of problem [6], [10], concerns the allocation of employees to different shift patterns (that is, different patterns of working hours) to meet manpower requirements which change throughout a working day. The mathematical formulation is similar to problems of the first type, except that shift patterns are generally quite different from days-off patterns. Problems where the shift patterns consist of only continuous periods can be formulated as a transshipment problem [4]. However, for problems involving shift patterns which are split shifts (non-contiguous working periods), an integer program approach is required unless the number of workers is so large that fractional answers can be rounded up or down with no appreciable loss of accuracy.

Segal [10] used a transshipment algorithm as a first approximation to his problem of scheduling telephone operators to ideal shift patterns (which are split shifts) so as to satisfy minimum quarter-hourly manpower requirements throughout the working day. Fitting his approximate solution to the ideal shift patterns, he then moved excess workers to deficient periods. This he accomplished by means of another network formulation. His method is reported to provide good, but not necessarily the optimal, schedules.

The problem which is the focus of this paper is essentially a combination of the previous two situations. Here the task is to allocate employees to different shift and days-off patterns such that the fluctuating manpower requirement for each period of each day of the week is satisfied. For any realistic problem, the integer programming formulation is relatively straightforward. However, even the most skillful formulation results in a problem involving hundreds of constraints and variables. Consequently some researchers [7], [11], have developed heuristic algorithms. Since we are concerned with an application where the algorithm would have to be run at numerous locations on moderate-sized computers, we also did not wish to rely on the standard integer programming approach. As a result, we have developed a two-phase algorithm which gives optimal solutions to a large class of problems and near-optimal solutions to many others.

The first phase of the algorithm consists of an integer program which assigns workers to work shifts for each day of the week singly. The resulting seven small integer programs are of course solved much more quickly than one large program. The second phase relies on an integer program and assignment rules to combine the single day schedules into a weekly schedule which insures that workers have the desired days off patterns.

The operation of the algorithm is best described by demonstrating its operation on a particularly well structured problem we refer to as "Case A". The applicability of the algorithm to less well ordered problems will be subsequently described.

43.3. Description of base problem: case A

The assumptions for Case A are:

A1. The objective is to minimize the cost of employee working hours.

A2. The hour-by-hour manpower requirements for each day of the week cycle must be met.

A3. Each employee works five consecutive days and is given two consecutive days off per week.

A4. An employee can work one shift one day and another shift on another day.

A5. The number of hours in each working day is no longer than sixteen hours, so that every employee is given at least eight hours of break before working again.

A6. A full time shift is a shift of eight consecutive hours work.

A7. A part time shift is a shift of four consecutive hours work.

A8. A full time employee is one who works only in full time shifts. Similarly, a part time employee is one who works only in part time shifts.

A9. Except for the last seven hours of any working day, there exists one full time shift beginning at every hour. Similarly, except for the last three hours of any working day, there exists one part time shift beginning at every hour.

A10. The cost of an employee depends on whether s/he is a full time or a part time employee and does not depend on the shifts s/he is assigned to on each day. The cost of each full time employee is the same and the cost of each part time employee is also the same. The cost of one full time employee can be greater or less than the cost of two part time employees.

A11. Each hour has at least one full time employee on duty.

Relaxations or modifications to the above assumptions will be discussed in Section 5.

43.4. The algorithm

43.4.1. Phase 1

In phase 1, the optimal solution for every day of the week is obtained using the integer program below, (one problem for each day, 7 problems altogether). If two consecutive part time (PT) shifts appear in the optimal solution, it is desired that they appear as one corresponding full time (FT) shift. This can be done by costing PT shifts slightly more than $\frac{1}{2}$ the cost of a FT shift, i.e., ($C^P = \frac{1}{2}C^F + \epsilon$) where ϵ is an arbitrarily small number. By moving all consecutive PT shifts to their corresponding FT shift in phase 1, it becomes only necessary to consider replacing one FT shift with two consecutive PT shifts in phase 2. If some part time employees cost less than half of a full time employee (who works twice as long), the phase 1 costing will not affect optimality because it is in phase 2 where the total cost of manpower is minimized. The phase 1 formulation for day i is shown below:

Minimize

$$C^F \sum_{f=1}^{qF} S_f^F + C^P \sum_{g=1}^{qP} S_g^P \tag{1}$$

Subject to

(1a) $$\sum_{f=1}^{qF} \delta_{kf}^E S_f^F + \sum_{g=1}^{qP} \delta_{kg}^P S_g^P \geqq R_k \quad \text{for } k = 1, \ldots m_i$$

(1b) $$S_1^F \geqq 1$$
$$S_{qF}^F \geqq 1$$

(1c) $$S_f^F \geqq 0 \text{ integers for } f = 1, \ldots q^F$$
$$S_g^P \geqq 0 \text{ and integers for } f = 1, \ldots q^P$$

where

C^F = cost of one FT shift.
S_f^F = number of FT shift pattern f.
C^P = cost of one PT shift.
S_q^P = number of PT shift pattern g.
q^F = number of FT shift patterns.
q^P = number of PT shift patterns.

$$\delta^F_{kf} = \begin{cases} 1 \text{ if FT employee works during period } k \text{ in shift pattern } f. \\ 0 \text{ otherwise.} \end{cases}$$

$$\delta^P_{kg} = \begin{cases} 1 \text{ if PT employee works during period } k \text{ in PT shift pattern } g. \\ 0 \text{ otherwise.} \end{cases}$$

$$R_k = \text{Minimum number of employees required during period } k.$$

$$m_i = \text{number of periods in working day } i.$$

Constraint Set (1a) ensures that the minimum manpower requirements for each hour are satisfied.

Constraint Set (1b) ensures that during any period of the day, there is at least one full time employee on duty.

Constraint Set (1c) ensures that all variables are nonnegative and integers. Since the shift patterns are contiguous, (1) can be formulated as a transshipment problem as discussed in Section 2. If the shift patterns were not continguous, (1) would have to be solved using integer programming. Let us assume that the solution obtained is as follows:

$$\sum_{f=1}^{qF} S_f^{F*} = \alpha_i$$

$$\sum_{g=1}^{qP} S_g^{P*} = \beta_i$$

Since the length of the FT shift is twice that of a PT shift,

$$\begin{aligned} \text{Solution} &= \alpha_i \text{ FT} + \beta_i \text{ PT} \\ &= (2\alpha_i + \beta_i) \text{ PT equivalents} \end{aligned}$$

We know that this is the best (i.e., least cost) schedule we can obtain for each particular day i.

43.4.2. Phase 2

In phase 2, the seven optimal solutions for each day of the week are connected by another integer program. In this formulation we have to make sure that each employee is given two consecutive days off per week. Also, two replacement possibilities have to be represented in the formulation: replacing one FT with two consecutive PT shifts and replacing one PT by one FT shift. The other possibility, that of replacing two consecutive PT shifts by one FT shift does not need to be considered because by costing PT employees slightly more than ½ the cost of a FT employee in phase 1, all consecutive PT shifts are moved to their corresponding FT shift.

Minimize

$$C^F \sum_{j=1}^{7} x_j + C^P \sum_{j=1}^{7} y_j$$

Subject to

$$\text{(2a)} \qquad \sum_{j=1}^{7} A_j x_j - F - Q = 0$$

$$\text{(2b)} \qquad \sum_{j=1}^{7} A_j y_j - P + Q = 0 \qquad (2)$$

$$\text{(2c)} \qquad 2F + P \geqq 2\alpha + \beta$$

$$\text{(2d)} \qquad \gamma \leqq F \leqq \alpha$$

(2e) $X \geqq 0$, $Y \geqq 0$, $F \geqq 0$, $P \geqq 0$, $Q \geqq 0$ are integer vectors.

where,

- C^F = cost of one FT employee.
- C^P = cost of one PT employee.
- X = column vector whose elements are x_j, $j = 1, \ldots 7$ where x_j is the number of FT employees whose days off pattern is j.
- Y = column vector whose elements are y_i, $j = 1, \ldots 7$ where y_j is the number of PT employees whose days off pattern is j.
- F = column vector whose elements are F_i, $i = 1, \ldots 7$ where F_i is the number of FT shifts required on day i, not counting those created from PT.
- P = column vector whose elements are P_i, $i = 1, \ldots 7$ where P_i is the number of PT shifts required on day i, not counting those converted to FT.
- Q = column vector whose elements are Q_i, $i = 1, \ldots 7$ where Q_i is the number of FT shifts required on day i, which are created from equal number of PT shifts. (Where one PT shift is replaced by one FT shift).

α = column vector whose elements are α_i, $i = 1, \ldots 7$
β = column vector whose elements are β_i, $i = 1, \ldots 7$
γ = column vector whose element γ_i, $i = 1, \ldots 7$ is the minimum number of FT employees for any day i.

For $m_i < 8$, $\gamma_i = 1$; for $8 < m_i < 16$, $\gamma_i = 2$ to ensure that a FT employee is working every hour of the day.

A_j = column vector representing the days-off patterns of employees and is consistent with the columns of the following matrix:

$$\begin{bmatrix} 1 & 0 & 0 & 1 & 1 & 1 & 1 \\ 1 & 1 & 0 & 0 & 1 & 1 & 1 \\ 1 & 1 & 1 & 0 & 0 & 1 & 1 \\ 1 & 1 & 1 & 1 & 0 & 0 & 1 \\ 1 & 1 & 1 & 1 & 1 & 0 & 0 \\ 0 & 1 & 1 & 1 & 1 & 1 & 0 \\ 0 & 0 & 1 & 1 & 1 & 1 & 1 \end{bmatrix} \tag{3}$$

Constraint (2c) shows that $(2\alpha_i + \beta_i)$ PT equivalents is the best schedule we can ever hope to produce for the ith day.

Constraints (2a) and (2b) specify the days-off patterns. Also, constraint (2b) allows a PT shift to become a FT shift and so is removed from (2b) and added on to (2a). This flexibility to allow a PT shift to become a FT shift is built in to allow some PT shifts to join up with FT shifts if that creates a better schedule. Constraint (2d) ensures that for any day i, the number of FT shifts must be greater than γ_i but not greater than α_i.

43.4.3. Obtaining the final schedule

The x_j's and y_j's are the optimal number of FT and PT employees. They will cover the daily requirements as indicated by the schedule obtained in phase 1. Obtaining actual manpower assignments is a straight forward but cumbersome process which is best explained by a flow chart as shown in Figure 1.

43.4.4. Problem sizes

The 2-phase algorithm exploits the structure of the scheduling problem by breaking the problem up into two phases. For a problem in-

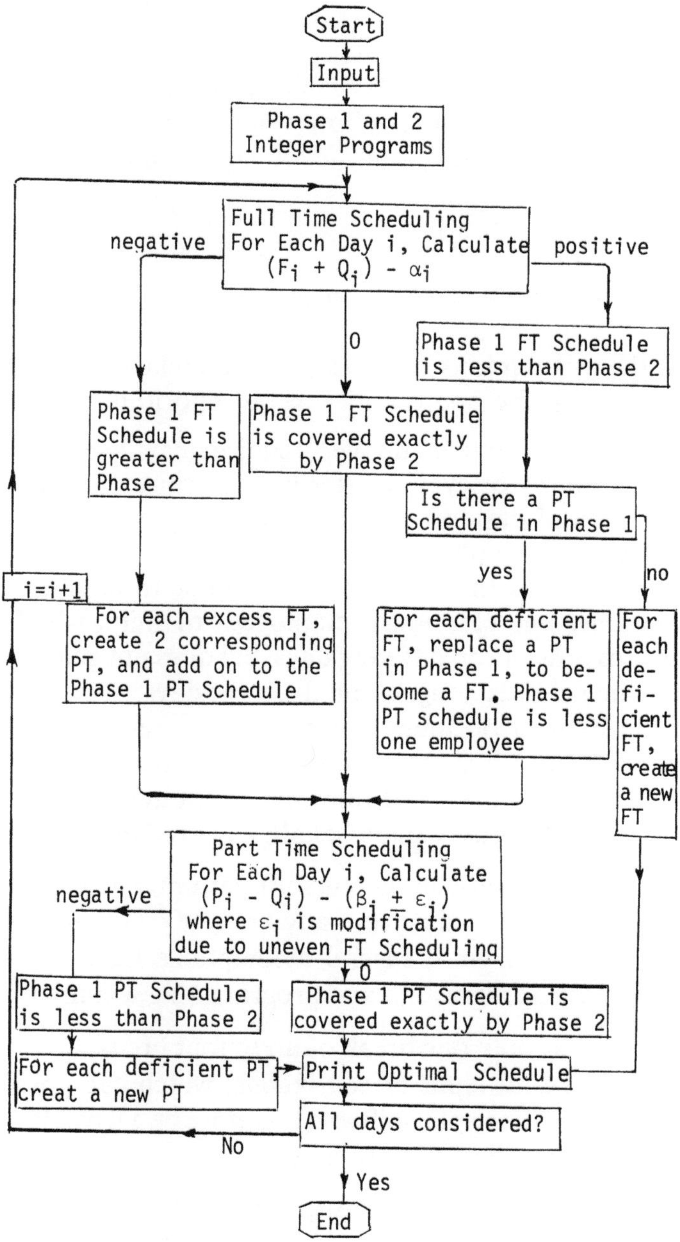

Figure 1. Macro-flow chart showing how final optimal schedule is created from phase 1 and 2 solutions.

volving 7 days, 16 working hours a day, phase 1 consists of seven integer programs (1), each having 22 variables and 18 constraints. Phase 2 consists of problem (2) which has 35 variables and 35 constraints for which 14 are upper/lower bounds on variables. Notice that all the problems are small, involving not more than 35 constraints.

43.5. Relaxation of assumptions on case A

Many of the assumptions on Case A can be relaxed without significantly changing the applicability of the algorithm.

A2. The hour-by-hour manpower requirements can be modified to half hourly or even quarter hourly requirements.

A3. Any kind of days-off patterns can be represented in the formulation of the phase 2 problem.

A4. When creating the final optimal schedule from phase 1 and 2 solutions, one can assign employees to shifts which are as close as possible on different days, but does not guarantee that the same shift is assigned on different days.

A5. If the number of hours in each working day is greater than sixteen hours, then the condition that a break of at least eight hours before working again is not guaranteed.

A6. and A7. Split shifts can be handled by the 2-phase algorithm.

A split-shift is any non-contiguous shift pattern. Since the number of split shifts is large and since many are not reasonable from an employee's point of view, several assumptions have to be made when developing an algorithm and programming a computer code:

- A split-shift has only one break of up to four hours
- Any full time shift (split or contiguous) which can possibly encompass a part time split shift and therefore be a feasible replacement for it, is a valid full time shift.

When a full time shift is not an integral multiple of a part time shift the 2-phase algorithm can be modified as shown in Section 6. When multiple shifts, i.e. three or more types of shifts of different lengths are involved, the 2-phase algorithm becomes complicated as shown in Section 7.

A9. If certain shift patterns are undesirable, one could cost these shift patterns many times more than the cost of the desirable shift patterns. However, the phase 2 problem is blind to the fact that certain shift patterns are undesirable, and so may produce an 'optimal' schedule involving undesirable shifts if using them utilizes less manpower. Undesirable shift patterns will not be in the solution if full time shifts and their corresponding part time shifts are removed simultaneously. Also, the algorithm can search among existing shift patterns and choose only the desirable shift patterns to be included in the final schedule. This can happen in three instances:

- Phase 2 requires some of the FT shifts to become two PT shifts. We assume that all the FT shifts in phase 1 solution are desirable shifts (this assumption is reasonable unless user specified too many shifts as undesirable, so that a feasible solution must consist of an undesirable shift). The algorithm has to search for those FT shifts in phase 1 solution which can be broken up into two desirable PT shifts. Although unlikely, the search may not be successful, in which case, an undesirable shift has to appear in the final schedule. The user should be notified with an appropriate message.
- Phase 2 requires some of the PT shifts to become FT shifts. Again we assume that all the PT shifts in phase 1 solution are desirable shifts. The algorithm has to search for a PT shift which can be replaced by a desirable FT shift. Although unlikely, the search may not be successful, in which case an undesirable shift has to appear in the final schedule. The user should be notified with an appropriate message.
- Phase 2 requires a FT or PT shift to be created. The algorithm has to choose among the desirable shift patterns.

A11. The condition to have at least one full time employee on duty at each hour of the working day can be removed. Additional constraints like having a desired ratio of full time employees to part time employees can also be incorporated.

When part time and full time shifts are not integral multiples of each other, the replacement alternatives become more complicated.

Consequently, we introduce two more cases:

Case B: Same as Case A except a part time shift consists of five consecutive hours.

Case C: Same as Case A except there are three or more shifts of arbitrary lengths.

43.6. Case B algorithm

Case B provides an example of how the solution approach is complicated when a full time shift is not an integer multiple of a part time shift. In the current formulation, we have allowed five-hour part time shifts.

43.6.1. Phase 1

First, we need to establish the replacement relationships between FT and PT shifts.

i. 1 FT can be replaced by 2 PT.
ii. 1 PT can be replaced by 1 FT; 2 consecutive PT can be replaced by 2 FT.
iii. 3 consecutive PT can be replaced by 2 FT.

For a 16 hour workday, only 3 basic replacement relationships are found. (i) and (ii) are similar to that of case A, so we only need to handle (iii).

One way to handle (iii) is to include in the formulation of phase 1 shift patterns of three PT shifts totaling 15 working hours. For a 16 hour workday, there are only 4 such shifts:

a. Break, 3 consecutive PT
b. 1 PT, Break, 2 consecutive PT
c. 2 consecutive PT, Break, 1 PT
d. 3 consecutive PT, Break.

The cost of these shifts would be slightly less than the cost of 3 PT employees, so that,

C^P = cost of one PT shift
C^Z = cost of one 15 hour shift patterns $= 3C^P - \epsilon$.
C^F = cost of one FT shift $= 8/5\ C^P$.

Formulate the phase 1 problem as in (1). Let the solution on day i be as follows:

The number of FT shifts equals α_i
The number of PT shifts equals β_i
The number of 15 hour shift patterns equals ξ_i

43.6.2. *Phase 2*

Formulate the phase 1 problem as in (1). Let the solution on day i fications:

Minimize

$$C^F \sum_{j=1}^{7} x_j + C^P \sum_{j=1}^{7} y_j$$

Subject to

$$\text{(4a)} \qquad \sum_{j=1}^{7} A_j x_j - F - Q - 2Z = 0$$

$$\text{(4b)} \qquad \sum_{j=1}^{7} A_j y_j - P + Q + 3Z = 0 \qquad (4)$$

$$\text{(4c)} \qquad 2F + P \geqq 2\alpha + \beta + 3\xi$$

$$\text{(4d)} \qquad \gamma \leqq F \leqq \alpha$$

$$\text{(4e)} \qquad Z \leqq \xi$$

(4f) $X \geqq 0, Y \geqq 0, F \geqq 0, P \geqq 0, Q \geqq 0, Z \geqq 0,$ are integer vectors.

Where,

ξ = column vector whose elements are ξ_i, $i = 1, \ldots, 7$
Z = column vector whose element Z_i, $i = 1, \ldots, 7$.
z_i is the number of 15 hour shift patterns required on day i.

Note that if $\xi_i = 0$ from phase 1, then $Z_i = 0$. All other notations are consistent with those used in (2).

43.7. Case C algorithm

An attempt is made here to devise a more general 2-phase algorithm based on case A conditions, except that multiple contiguous shift patterns of arbitrary lengths are allowed instead of just full time and part time shifts. The problem is difficult because a large number of possibilities exist for replacing one shift or combination of shifts by other shifts or combination of shifts which can satisfy demand for a span of time. When only full time and half time shifts are considered, two half time shifts can be replaced uniquely by a full time shift, or a full time shift can be replaced by two half time shifts. When multiple shifts of arbitrary lengths are involved, the number of replacement relationships can be large.

Some definitions of the terms to be used will be explained below.

43.7.1. Efficient replacement relationships

When multiple shift patterns are allowed, many replacement relationships are possible. For example, any shift or combination of shifts can be replaced by another shift or combination of shifts in any instance when the span of working hours of the latter is longer than the former. However, in any replacement relationship, there exist at least one which performs the replacement in the most efficient way (i.e. with least excessive man-hours). Such replacement relationships are termed 'efficient'. In general, there can be several efficient replacement relationships in a given situation and it would be wasteful to include equivalent relationships in a mathematical model. Also, it would be redundant to include complex sets of relationships as individual alternatives in the model, when the model itself could construct the replacement relationships by combinations of simple relationships. We define these replacement relationships, which cannot be formed by a combination of other efficient replacements as being 'basic'.

43.7.2. Determining efficient replacement relationships

An approach for determining a set of basic efficient replacement relationships is given for a problem involving three different shifts. This approach can be generalized to handle any number of shifts but the process becomes tedious and requires an exhaustive computer search.

Given shift S_1 is h_1 hours and shift S_2 is h_2 hours, $h_1 > h_2$. Let r be the smallest integer greater than h_1/h_2. Then a basic efficient replacement relationship of S_1 by S_2 exists where r of S_2 can replace S_1; or

*R1. $1(S_1) \Rightarrow r(S_2)$ where $\Rightarrow$ means 'can be replaced by' and * means 'basic replacement relationship.'

R2. If $2(S_1) \Rightarrow 2r(S_2)$, this replacement relationship is not basic because it can be established by two cases of (R1), which is $1(S_1) \Rightarrow r(S_2)$.

*R3. If $2(S_1) \Rightarrow p(S_2)$ where $p < 2r$, then the replacement relationship is basic because it cannot be established through (R1).

R4. If $3(S_1) \Rightarrow p(S_2) + r(S_2)$, or $3(S_1) \Rightarrow p(S_2), r(S_2)$ this replacement relationship is not basic because it can be established through (R3), which is $2(S_1) \Rightarrow p(S_2)$ and (R1), which is $1(S_1) \Rightarrow r(S_2)$.

*R5. If $3(S_1) \Rightarrow q(S_2)$ where $q < p + r$, then this replacement relationship is basic because it cannot be established through (R1) and/or (R3).

*R6. Consider another shift S_3 such that $1(S_3) \Rightarrow 1(S_1)$.

*R7. Since shift S_2 is shorter than S_1, $1(S_2) \Rightarrow 1(S_1)$.

*R8. Let us assume that $2(S_2) \Rightarrow 1(S_1)$.

*R9. If $1(S_2), 1(S_3) \Rightarrow 1(S_1)$, the replacement relationship is basic because it cannot be established through previously established basic relationships.

*R10. If $2(S_2), 1(S_3) \Rightarrow 1(S_1)$, the replacement relationship is also basic because it cannot be established through previously established basic relationships.

R11. If $2(S_2), 2(S_3) \Rightarrow 2(S_1)$, that replacement relationship is not basic because the replacement can be established through 2 cases of (R9), which is $1(S_2), 1(S_3) \Rightarrow 1(S_1)$.

*R12. If $1(S_2), 2(S_3) \Rightarrow 1(S_1)$, the replacement relationship is basic because it cannot be established through previously established basic relationships.

R13. If $1(S_2), 2(S_3) \Rightarrow 2(S_1)$, that replacement relationship is not basic because the replacement could be established through

(R9), which is $1(S_2)$, $1(S_3) \Rightarrow 1(S_1)$ and (R6), which is $1(S_3) \Rightarrow 1(S_1)$.

To summarize, if an efficient replacement relationship is such that it cannot be established through a combination of previously established basic replacement relationships, then it is basic and has to be represented in the mathematical model.

43.7.3. Joint shifts

A joint shift is a combination of shifts. Examples of joint shifts are $2(S_1)$, or $1(S_2)$, $1(S_3)$ or $2(S_1)$, $3(S_2)$. The shifts forming the joint shift are always non-overlapping.

A statement of the algorithm is given below:

Step 1. Establish all basic efficient replacement relationships between shifts or joint shifts. If a basic replacement relationship involves replacing joint shifts, the latter have to appear as column vectors in phase 1.

Step 2. Phase 1 costs are ordered and longer shifts or joint shifts are costed proportionately higher.

Step 3. Convert all phase 1 solutions in terms of the shortest shift type.

Step 4. Except for the shortest shift, phase 1 solutions provide the upper bound to all other shifts or joint shifts, to be used in phase 2.

Step 5. In phase 2, all basic replacement relationships between shifts or joint shifts (except for direct replacement of basic shift by the shortest shift), will have to be represented as variables in the formulation, thus, allowing shifts or joint shifts to move from one type to another.

We now apply the preceding algorithm to a simple problem involving 3 different shifts – S_1, an 8 hour shift, S_2, a 5 hour shift, and S_3, a 3 hour shift, and a working day of 10 hours.

Step 1:

$S_1 \Rightarrow S_3$	*Ratio*	*Phase 2 variables*
$1(8) \Rightarrow 3(3)$	3:1* (Basic replacement)	Not applicable because all S_1 shifts are converted to S_3 shift equivalents.

$S_2 \Rightarrow S_3$		
$1(5) \Rightarrow 2(3)$	$2:1^*$	Not applicable because all S_2 shifts are converted to S_3 shift equivalents.
$S_1 \Rightarrow S_2$		
$1(8) \Rightarrow 2(5)$	$2:1^*$	P^1
$S_2 \Rightarrow S_1$		
$1(5) \Rightarrow 1(8)$	$1:1^*$	P^2
$S_3 \Rightarrow S_1$		
$1(3) \Rightarrow 1(8)$	$1:1^*$	P^3
$2(3) \Rightarrow 1(8)$	$1:2^*$ joint shift	P^4
$3(3) \Rightarrow 2(8)$	$J_1 = 2(3)$	
$S_3 \Rightarrow S_2$	$2:3 = (1:1) + (1:2)$	
$1(3) \Rightarrow 1(5)$	$1:1^*$	P^5
$2(3) \Rightarrow 2(5)$	$1:1$	
$3(3) \Rightarrow 2(5)$	$2:3^*$ joint shift $J_2 = 3(3)$	P^6
$(S_2, S_3) \Rightarrow S_1$		
$1(5), 1(3) \Rightarrow 1(8)$	$1:1,1^*$ joint shift $J_3 = 1(5), 1(3)$	Replacement not represented because J_3 has total working length of 8 hours which is S_1 itself.
$2(5), 1(3) \Rightarrow 2(8)$	$2:2,1 = (1:1, 1) + (1:1, 0)$	
$S_1 \Rightarrow (S_2, S_3)$		
$1(8) \Rightarrow 1(5), 1(3)$	$1,1:1^*$	P^7

Joint shift J_1 has to be represented as column vector in phase 1.

e.g. $S_3, S_3, 4B$ Where B = break for an hour $S_3, 2B, S_3, 2B$ and so on

Similarly, joint shift J_2 has to be represented as column vector in phase 1.

e.g. S_3, S_3, S_3, B

B, S_3, S_3, S_3
S_3, B, S_3, B

Joint shift J_3 has a total working length of 8 hours which is S_1 itself. Therefore, it is already considered in phase 1.

Step 2: Essentially, we have 3 basic shifts (S_1, S_2, S_3) and 2 joint shifts (J_1, J_2). Order them in descending order: J_2, S_1, J_1, S_2, S_3. The longer shifts are cost proportionately higher. Phase 1 problem is formulated as in (1).

Step 3: Let us assume that phase 1 solution for any day would consist of the following, converted to the shortest shift S_3.

The number of S_1 shift $= \alpha^1 \Rightarrow 3\alpha^1 S_3$
The number of S_2 shift $= \alpha^2 \Rightarrow 2\alpha^2 S_3$
The number of S_3 shift $= \alpha^3$
The number of J_1 shift $= \alpha^4 \Rightarrow 2\alpha^4 S_3$
The number of J_2 shift $= \alpha^5 \Rightarrow 3\alpha^5 S_3$

Step 4:

α^4 is upper bound for P^4
α^5 is upper bound for P^6
α^1 is upper bound for F^1
α^2 is upper bound for F^2

Step 5: The phase 2 problem becomes:

Min

$$C(X, Y, Z)^T$$

Subject to

(5a) $\sum A_j x_j - F^1 + P^1 - P^2 - P^3 - P^4 \quad + P^7 = 0$

(5b) $\sum A_j y_j - F^2 - 2P^1 + P^2 \quad - P^5 - 2P^6 - P^7 = 0$

(5c) $\sum A_j z_j - F^3 \quad + P^3 + 2P^4 + P^5 + 3P^6 - P^7 = 0$

(5d) $3F^1 + 2F^2 + F^2 \geqq 3\alpha^1 + 2\alpha^2 + \alpha^3 + 2\alpha^4 + 3\alpha^5$

(5e) $\gamma \leqq F^1 \leqq \alpha^1 \quad P^4 \leqq \alpha^4$ (5)
$F^2 \leqq \alpha^2 \quad P^6 \leqq \alpha^5$

(5f) $X \geqq 0, Y \geqq 0, Z \geqq 0, F^i \geqq 0, P^i \geqq 0$ and integer vectors, α^i are also integer vectors for all i.

where

C = row vector whose elements represent the cost of an employee with the corresponding shift and days off pattern.

Z = column vector whose element $Z_j, j = 1, \ldots, 7$ is the number of S_3 shift employees whose days off pattern is j.

F^1 = column vector whose elements are F_i^1, $i = 1, \ldots, 7$ where F_i^1 is the number of S_1 shifts required on day i, not counting those created from other shifts or joint shifts.

F^2 = column vector whose elements are F_i^2, $i = 1, \ldots, 7$ where F_i^2 is the number of S_2 shifts required on day i, not counting those created from other shifts or joint shifts.

$P^j(j = 1, \ldots, 7)$ = column vector whose ith element is defined in step 1 for the ith day.

$\alpha^j(j = 1, \ldots 5)$ = column vector whose ith element is defined in step 3 for the ith day.

All other notations are consistent with those used in (2).

43.8. Results and conclusion

Randomly selected problems were run using the two-phase algorithm based on case A conditions including split shifts. Exhibit 1 shows some of the results. The algorithm was shown to be extremely efficient. The maximum running times for the few selected problems do not exceed 14 seconds on a CDC 6600. The integer program subroutine used was a branch and bound code based on linear program with DKW/Tomlin's penalties [3], [14]. When part time shift is not a 4 hour shift, the two-phase algorithm can be modified to handle the new problem. However, because the replacement re-

Exhibit 1. Type III problems.

Sample Problem Numbers	Number of Working Hours for Day Number 1	2	3	4	5	6	7	Computer Running Times on CDC 6600
1	10	10	10	10	10	12	12	11.7 sec.
2	12	12	12	12	12	12	12	13.1 sec.
3	9	10	13	10	10	12	12	12.2 sec.
4	16	16	16	16	16	12	12	14.0 sec.

lationship between the full time and part time shifts is not as simple as the 8 hour PT and 4 hour PT problem before, the problem formulation sizes in both phase 1 and phase 2 are increased appreciably as shown for case B.

When multiple shifts are involved, the two-phase algorithm becomes even more complicated. Replacement relationships between shifts/joint shifts become more complex. For a problem involving 3 different shift patterns (case C), phase 1 problem can have as many as a hundred variables, although the number of constraints remains the same. However, in phase 2, the number of variables is as many as 91 and the number of constraints is 63 for which 35 are upper/lower bounds on the variables. It appears from the problem sizes, that the two-phase algorithm is quite efficient even for a problem involving 3 different shift patterns.

References

1. Armatas, J. P. and Lundbert, D. E., 'The Management of People in Hotels, Restaurants, and Clubs', Wm. C. Brown C., Dubuqueo Iowa.
2. Baker, K. R., 'Scheduling a Full Time Work Force to Meet Cyclic Staffing Requirements', *Management Science* (August 1974).
3. Davis, R. E., Kendrick, D. A., and Weitzman, J., 'A Branch and Bound Algorithm for 0-1 Mixed Integer Programming Problems', Development Economic Report no. 69, Center for International Affairs, Harvard University.
4. Ford, L. R., Jr. and Fulkerson, D. R., 'Flows in Networks', Princeton University Press (1962).
5. Healy, W. C., 'Shift Scheduling Made Easy', *Factory* (October 1957).
6. Luce, W. J., 'A Shift Scheduling Algorithm', Technical paper presented at the 44th National Meeting of ORSA, San Diego, California (November 1973).
7. Luce, W. J., 'Employee Assignment System', Technical paper presented at Joint National Meeting of ORSA/TIMS, Boston, Mass. (April 1974).
8. Monroe, G., 'Scheduling Manpower for Service Operations', *Industrial Engineering* (August 1970).
9. Rothstein, J., 'Scheduling Manpower by Mathematical Programming', *Industrial Engineering* (April 1972).
10. Segal, M., 'The Operator Scheduling Problem: A Network Flow Approach', *Journal of ORSA* (July 1974).
11. Smith, R. S., 'Two-Phase Employee Scheduling Algorithm for Operations Having Variable Manpower Requirements with Applications Involving Single and Composite Planning Cycles', Doctoral Dissertation, University of Massachusetts (February 1975).
12. Smith, R. S., et al., 'A Systems Evaluation of Army Garrison Feeding at Fort Lewis, Washington', Tech. Report no. 72–37, OR/SA (January 1972). U.S. Army Natick Labs.
13. Tibrawala, R., et al., "Optimal Scheduling of Two Consecutive Idle Periods", *Management Science*, vol. 19, no. 1 (September 1972).
14. Tomlin, J. A., 'Branch and Bound Methods for Integer and Non-Linear Programming', edited by Abadie, Amsterdam, North Holland Publishing Co. (1970).

44. Optimal scheduling of two consecutive work periods

RAJEN TIBREWALA, JAMES BROWNE and BHARAT DOSHI

Abstract

In many manpower scheduling problems it is necessary to meet fluctuating, but cyclical, staffing needs. This paper deals with the case when the cycle consists of 'n' periods and each worker works for two consecutive periods. A heuristic algorithm is proposed and its convergence to an optimal solution is established.

44.1. Introduction

For service facilities which operate continuously, it is frequently the case that the staffing requirements vary with time, but are cyclic in nature. Toll collectors, policemen, and firemen are some examples of this situation. Scheduling of manpower in these situations means assigning working hours to each individual in such a way that the staffing requirements are satisfied and the total manpower is minimized. Normally, we have a cycle consisting of 'n' periods, and each worker works for 'p' consecutive periods. Here scheduling a worker is equivalent to deciding his beginning period.

This problem can be readily formulated as a linear integer programming problem. Let $r_i (i = 1, 2, \ldots, n)$ denote the requirement for ith period. We define the following variables of interest.

$W_i (i = 1, 2, \ldots, n - p + 1)$: the number of workers starting in period i and working for periods $i, i + 1, \ldots, i + p - 1$.

$W_i (i = n - p + 2, \ldots, n)$: the number of workers starting in period i and working for periods $i, i + 1, \ldots, n, 1, 2, \ldots, i + p - 1 - n$.

$X_i (i = 1, 2, \ldots, n)$: the number of employees working in period i.

Then the scheduling problem is to minimize $W = \Sigma_{i=1}^{n} W_i$ subject to the constraints:

$$W_{n-p+2} + W_{n-p+3} \cdots\cdots + W_n + W_1 \geqq r_1$$
$$W_{n-p+3} + W_{n-p+4} \cdots\cdots + W_1 + W_2 \geqq r_2$$
$$\vdots$$
$$W_n + W_1 \cdots\cdots\cdots\cdots + W_{p-1} \geqq r_{p-1}$$
$$W_1 + W_2 \cdots\cdots\cdots\cdots + W_p \geqq r_p$$
$$\vdots$$
$$W_{n-p+1} + W_{n-p+2} \cdots\cdots + W_n \geqq r_n$$

where all W_i are non-negative integers. This formulation is an old one [4] [6] [11], and various methods are available for its solution. Most general techniques available for the solution of linear integer programming problems are not economically feasible when 'n' and 'p' are large. This necessitates a search for simple algorithms specialized for this class of problem. Such algorithms can exploit the special structure of the problem, and thus solve fairly large-scale problems economically.

Tibrewala, et al. [10] considered the case when 'n' is any positive integer and $p = n - 2$. They described and established the optimality of a simple algorithm requiring essentially hand calculations. A very important practical example of this situation is scheduling five consecutive working days for each worker when the number of workers needed varies from day to day, repeating every week.

In this paper we consider another special case where 'n' is any positive integer and $p = 2$. We present a pleasantly simple algorithm and show the optimality property of the same. Another algorithm to solve this problem ($p = 2$) has been proposed by Baker, Crabill and Magazine [1]. The algorithm presented here is simpler to apply. It is also of theoretical interest, because a proposed generalization to the case $p > 2$[5] uses the algorithm in this paper as a first step.

In the following section we present the algorithm. Some examples and the proof of optimality will be presented in the subsequent sections.

44.2. The algorithm

We denote the jth trial solution by $W^j = \{W_i^j; i = 1, 2, \ldots, n\}$. The algorithm inductively obtains W^j, $j = 1, 2, \ldots$ until an optimal solution is reached.

Step 1. Let $W_1^1 = r_1$.

Step 2. Let $W_i^1 = \max\{0, r_i - W_{i-1}^1\}$, $i = 1, \ldots, n$.

Step 3. If $W_1^1 = 0$ or $W_n^1 = 0$, then stop. The first solution is optimal. Otherwise proceed to step 4 with $j = 1$.

Step 4. In the following, skip steps (a) and (d) if $j = 1$.

(a) If $W_1^j + W_n^j < r_1$, then W^j is infeasible. Stop. W^{j-1} is an optimal solution. If $W_1^j + W_n^j \geqq r_1$, then W^j is feasible. Proceed to (b).
(b) If $W_1^j + W_n^j = r_1$, then stop. W^j is optimal. Otherwise proceed to (c).
(c) If there exists an i such that $W_i^j = 0$, and if the smallest i is odd, then stop. W^j is an optimal solution. Otherwise proceed to (d).
(d) If $W_n^j > W_n^{j-1}$, then stop. W^{j-1} is an optimal solution. If $W_n^j \leqq W_n^{j-1}$, proceed to (e).
(e) If n is even and $W_i^j > 0$ for all i, then W^j is optimal. Otherwise go to step 5 and calculate W^{j+1}.

Step 5. W^{j+1} is calculated by

$$W_1^{j+1} = r_1 - 1$$
$$W_i^{j+1} = \max\{0, r_i - W_{i-1}^{j+1}\} \quad i = 2, 3, \ldots n.$$

Go back to step 4 with $j + 1$.

Remark: Since r_1 is finite the algorithm terminates in a finite number of iterations. In fact, the algorithm will terminate before j exceeds

$$\min\left\{W_1^1,\ W_n^1,\left[\Sigma W_i^1 - \frac{\Sigma r_i}{2}\right]\right\},\ \text{where } [X] \text{ is the largest}$$

integer smaller than or equal to X.

44.3. Proof of optimality

Theorem 1: The first feasible solution is optimal if $W_n^1 = 0$ or $W_1^1 = 0$.

Proof: Consider $\{W_i^1;\ i = 1, 2, \ldots, n\}$ obtained in steps 1 and 2. If $W_i^1 = 0$, then it cannot be reduced. If $i \geqq 2$ and $W_i^1 > 0$, then by step 2, $W_{i-1}^1 + W_i^1 = r_i$. Any reduction in W_i^1 will have to be accompanied by an equal increase in W_{i-1}^1.

This holds for $i = 2, 3, \ldots, n$ and so for the sum $\Sigma_2^n W_i$. If $W_1^1 = 0$, then it cannot be reduced further. If $W_n^1 = 0$, then $W_1^1 \geqq r_1 - 0 = r_1$. So when W_1^1 or W_n^1 is 0, we cannot reduce W_1^1. Thus in this case $W = \Sigma_{i=1}^n W_i^1$ is minimized over all feasible solutions.

Theorem 2: If the algorithm terminates in step 4a, then W^{j-1} is an optimal solution.

Proof: The constraints may be written as:

$$\begin{aligned} &W_n + W_1 \geqq r_1 \\ &W_1 + W_2 \geqq r_2 \\ &\quad\vdots \\ &W_{n-1} + W_n \geqq r_n \end{aligned} \tag{1}$$

and W_i's are non-negative integers.

Adding the constraints we get

$$2(W_1 \ldots + W_n) \geqq r_1 + r_2 \ldots + r_n$$

and

$$W = \Sigma W_i \geqq \frac{\Sigma r_i}{2}.$$

so

$$W \geqq \langle \frac{\Sigma r_i}{2} \rangle \tag{2}$$

where $< X >$ is the smallest integer greater than or equal to X. Now if $W_1^{j-1} + W_n^{j-1} > r_1$ and $W_1^j + W_n^j < r_1$, then $W_1^{j-1} + W_n^{j-1} = r_1 + 1$ and

$$W_1^{j-1} + W_2^{j-1} = r_2$$
$$W_2^{j-1} + W_3^{j-1} = r_3$$
$$\vdots$$
$$W_{n-1}^{j-1} + W_n^{j-1} = r_n.$$

Adding the above n equations we get

$$2(W_1^{j-l} + W_2^{j-1} \ldots + W_n^{j-1}) = \Sigma r_i + 1$$
$$\Sigma W_i^{j-1} = \frac{\Sigma r_i}{2} + \tfrac{1}{2}.$$

Thus W^{j-l} is feasible and achieves the lower bound in (2). So W^{j-1} is optimal.

Theorem 3: If the algorithm terminates in step 4b, then W^j is optimal.

Proof: Since $W_1^j + W_n^j = r_1$, W^j is a feasible solution. As in the proof of theorem 1, $W_i^j(i = 2, \ldots, n)$ cannot be reduced further without an equal increase in W_{i-1}^j. Also, since $W_n^j + W_1^j = r_1$, W_1^j cannot be reduced without an equal increase in W_n^j. It follows that the sum $\Sigma\ W_i^j$ is the minimum over all feasible solutions and so W_i^j is optimal.

Theorem 4: If for some feasible solution W^j there exists an i^* such that $W_i^j = 0$ and the smallest such i^* is odd, then W^j is an optimal solution.

Proof: As in the proof of theorem 1, $W_i^j(i = 2, \ldots, n)$ cannot be reduced without an equal increase in W_{i-1}^j. In particular the sum $\Sigma_{i^*}^n W_i^j$ cannot be reduced further. Also, since i^* is the smallest index with $W^j_{i^*} = 0$, we have:

$$W^j_1 + W^j_2 = r_2$$
$$W^j_3 + W^j_4 = r_4$$
$$\vdots$$
$$W^j_{i^*-2} + W^j_{i^*-1} = r_{i^*-1}$$
$$\sum_1^{i^*-1} W^j_i = r_2 + r_4 + \cdots + r_{i^*-1}$$

But, the right hand side is a lower bound on the sum $\Sigma_1^{i^*-1} W^j_i$ for any feasible solution W. Thus $\Sigma_1^{i^*-1} W^j_i$ cannot be reduced further. It follows that $\Sigma_1^n W^j_i$ is minimum over all feasible solutions and so W^j is optimal.

Theorem 5: If at any stage in the algorithm $W^j_n > W^{j-1}_n$, then W^{j-1} is optimal.

Proof: It is clear that this can arise only when n is even. Also $W^j_n > W^{j-1}_n$ implies that

$$W^{j-1}_1 + W^{j-1}_2 = r_2$$
$$W^{j-1}_3 + W^{j-1}_4 = r_4$$
$$\vdots$$
$$W^{j-1}_{n-1} + W^{j-1}_n = r_n$$

Adding the above $n/2$ equations

$$\sum_{i=1}^{n} W^{j-1}_i = r_2 + r_4 \ldots + r_n.$$

But the right hand side is a lower bound on the number of workers required to satisfy the requirements. So W^{j-1} is an optimal solution.

Theorem 6: If n is even and at any stage $W^j_i > 0$ for all i, then W^j is optimal.

Proof: $W_i^j > 0$ for all i imples that

$$W_1^j + W_2^j = r_2$$
$$W_3^j + W_4^j = r_4$$
$$\vdots$$
$$W_{n-1}^j + W_n^j = r_n$$

so, as in the proof of theorem 5, W^j is optimal.

44.3.1. Examples

1. Optimal

r	W^1	W^2	W^3	
5	5	4	3	Termination at 4a $W_1^3 + W_5^3 < r_1$.
8	3	4	5	
7	4	3	2	
5	1	2	3	
4	3	2	1	W^2 is optimal because W^3 is infeasible.
	16	15	14	

2. Optimal

r	W^1	W^2	W^3	W^4	
5	5	4	3	2	Termination at 4b $W_1^4 + W_5^4 = r_1$.
3	0	0	0	1	
7	7	7	7	6	
5	0	0	0	0	
3	3	3	3	3	W^4 is optimal.
	15	14	13	12	

3. Optimal

r	W^1	
3	3	Termination at 4c
5	2	
2	0	W^1 is optimal.
6	6	
	11	

4. Optimal

r	W^1	W^2	
3	3	2	Termination at 4d
3	0	1	
5	5	4	$W_4^2 > W_4^1$.
7	2	3	
	10	10	W^2 is optimal.

5. Optimal

r	W^1	
3	3	Termination at 4e
4	1	
5	4	n even and $W_i^1 > 0$ for all i.
7	3	
	11	W^1 is optimal.

References

1. Baker, K. R., Crabill, T. B., and Magazine, M. J., 'An Optimal Procedure for Allocating Manpower with Cyclic Requirements', *A.I.I.E. Transactions*, vol. 5, no. 2 (1973).
2. Bennett, B. and Potts, R., 'Rotating for a Transit System', *Transportation Science*, vol. 2 no. 1 (1968), pp. 14–34.
3. Bodin, L., 'Towards a General Model for Manpower Scheduling – Part 2', *Journal of Urban Analysis*, vol. 1, no. 2 (1973).
4. Dantzig, G. B., 'A comment on Edie's "Traffic Delays at Toll Booths"', *Operations Research*, vol. 2, no. 3 (1954), pp. 339–341.
5. Guha, D. K., 'An Optimal Procedure for Allocating Manpower with Cyclic Requirements: General Case', ORSA/TIMS Conference, San Juan (October 1974).
6. Hadley, G., *Nonlinear and Dynamic Programming*. Addison-Wesley (1964).
7. Heller, N., 'Proportional Rotating Schedule', Ph.D. Thesis, University of Pennsylvania (1969).
8. Monroe, G., 'Scheduling Manpower for Service Operations', *Industrial Engineering*, vol. 4, no. 8 (1970).
9. Rothstein, M., "Scheduling Manpower by Mathematical Programming', *Industrial Engineering*, vol. 4, no. 4 (1972), pp. 29–33.
10. Tibrewala, R., Phillipe, D., and Browne, J., 'Optimal Scheduling of Two Consecutive Idle Periods', *Management Science*, vol. 10, no. 1 (1972).
11. Wagner, H. M., *Principles of Operations Research with Applications to Management Decisions*. Prentice Hall (1969).

45. A simple method for obtaining cyclic employee schedules

JAMES J. BROWNE and RAJEN TIBREWALA

Abstract

This paper describes newly developed and greatly simplified methods for obtaining cyclic employee tour schedules. Procedures for obtaining an intial solution, improvement methods, and conditions for optimality are given and illustrated for the general problem of minimizing the number of tours of p consecutive periods each to cover a set of cyclic requirements for n periods per cycle. Particular attention is given to the problems of developing optimal schedules for 8 hours tours per cycle of 24 hours.

45.1. Introduction

Many services must be provided continuously, 24 hours every day. Typically, the demand for services varies by the hour of the day, and there are often weekly demand cycles as well. Employees must be scheduled for tours of work to meet the varying requirements as efficiently as possible. In this paper, tours are sets of consecutive work periods which occur in each cycle. Practical examples would be 7, 8 or 9 hour tours per 24 hours, or 5 days worked per cycle of 7 days.

The simple method described here is easily programmed and understood. It provides solutions believed optimal for consecutive work periods per cycle and has been tested on more than 50 problems. A typical solution of 8 hour tours per 24 hour cycle with random two digit requirements took less than 15 minutes by hand calculations.

The related problem of integrating daily tour assignments and days off to obtain a total weekly job, or set of tours, per employee, is treated in reference [5].

45.2. The problem

Consider a set of requirements R_i representing the number of employees needed for each of n periods (hours or days e.g.) per cycle (day or week e.g.). The problem is to find the minimum number of employees and their tour assignments (specified starting periods) when each employee works p ($p \leqq n$) periods per cycle.

45.3. Existing solution methods

It is well known that this problem can be formulated and solved by integer programming [4], [7], [10]. Segal [8] and Chong [3] have shown that the problem can be formulated and solved as a transshipment problem. Such solution methods are not readily accessible to many potential users. Algorithms suitable for manual arithmetic calculation and providing optimal solutions, are available for the special cases of two work periods ($p = 2$) per cycle [2], [9], and two idle periods ($p = n - 2$) per cycle [1], [10]. A general, but complex, solution algorithm has been proposed by Guha [4]. The method presented here is simple to understand, is easily programmed, and is believed to provide optimal solutions in all cases although final details of the formal proof are still being worked out. It is also expected that the new method which extends and generalizes the method of Tiberwala et al. [9], will itself be useful as a basis for solving more difficult problems (specifically those which include meal and/or relief breaks between work tours).

45.4. Outline of the method

A specific procedure is provided for ordering the requirements and obtaining a first feasible solution in which at most, one of the products X_iS_i (for $i = 1, 2, \ldots, n$) is greater than zero, where X_i is the number of employees starting work in period i, and S_i is the slack in period i, $S_i = \Sigma_{j=i-p+1}^{i} X_j - R_i$. If all are zero, i.e. $\Sigma_{i=1}^{n} X_iS_i = 0$, the first solution is optimal [4]. If not, methods of reducing the X_i for which $X_iS_i > 0$ are explored in three ways: (1) direct reduction of X_i without other solution adjustment; (2) direct reduction of X_i

with other adjustments; and (3) indirect reduction through development of alternate solutions which shift the slack and make possible a subsequent reduction in X_i. Each time an improved solution is obtained, it is tested for optimality. It is also shown that in the case of n, a multiple of p, slack can only be shifted within the X_i's which are equal modulo p. This leads to an additional optimality test for this case. Examples will be given to illustrate each of the procedures involved in the method. Finally, sample results for the important practical case of scheduling 8 hour work tours per 24 hour cycles will be used to illustrate the method for problems based on random and smoothed requirements.

45.4.1. Obtaining the initial solution

To obtain the first solution, rearrange the problem so that the first requirement R_1 is the largest of all requirements. This will ensure that $X_2, X_3, \ldots, X_p$ can be set equal to zero since the X_1 employees starting in period 1 will work until period p. The remaining $X_i (p < i \leqq n)$ are set to zero if R_i is met by the preceding $(p - 1)$ values of X, or are set so that R_i is met exactly (i.e. no slack). The initial assignment will assure that $\Sigma_{i=2}^{n}, X_i S_i = 0$, while X_1 and S_1 may both be non-zero. Note that since S_1 through S_5 are all equal to 1, X_1 can be reduced by 1 to obtain an improved feasible solution.

45.4.2. Direct reduction

Whenever, as in example 1, the first p slacks (S_i's) are non-zero, then X_1 can be directly reduced by the minimum of these values. In the resulting next solution, each of the first p slacks will be reduced by

n=7 p=5

i	R_i	X_i	S_i
1	3	3	1
2	3	0	1
3	3	0	1
4	2	0	1
5	2	0	1
6	1	1	0
7	1	0	0

Example 1

n=7 p=5

i	R_i	Initial Solution X_i	Initial Solution S_i	Second Solution X_i	Second Solution S_i
1	10	10	2	8	0
2	9	0	3	0	1
3	9	0	3	0	1
4	7	0	3	0	1
5	8	0	2	0	0
6	2	2	0	2	0
7	2	0	0	0	0

Example 2

min (S_i, 1, 2, 3, ..., p). Note that in the second solution the sum of the products $X_iS_i = 0$, i.e. either $X_i = 0$ or $S_i = 0$ for all i. This indicates that an optimal solution has been reached. ($\Sigma X_iS_i = 0$) is sufficient condition for optimality by the Theorem of Complimentary Slack [11].

Even when all of the first p slacks are not greater than zero, direct reductions in X_1 may be possible in conjunction with other changes in the solution. Consider example 3 as shown below. In the initial solution, only four slacks are positive. We can still try to reduce the work force by entering a -1 alongside X_1 (-1 indicates a planned reduction). Recall that all other $X_iS_i = 0$ and any net reduction in work force must include a reduction in X_1. This reduction is feasible for periods 2, 3, and 4, because S_i's for these periods are greater than zero. $S_5 = 0$, however, and in order to maintain a feasible solution, X_5 must be increased. A tentative increase of $+1$ for X_5 is therefore indicated. This will, of course, add to the slack in the next

n=7 p=5

i	R_i	Initial Solution X_i	Initial Solution S_i	Changes in Solution			Second Solution X_i	Second Solution S_i
1	10	10	2	-1	+1	-1	8	0
2	9	0	3	-1	+1	-1	0	1
3	8	0	4	-1		-1	0	0
4	7	0	3	-1			0	1
5	10	0	0	-1	+1		2	0
6	2	2	0		+1	-1	0	0
7	0	0	2		+1	-1	0	2

Example 3

$(p - 1) = 4$ periods. Since, in the trial solution $X_6 > 0$ (from the initial solution) and S_6 has been increased from 0 to 1, a reduction in X_6 can be attempted. Since there is a positive slack in the next $(p - 1) = 4$ periods (i.e. periods 7, 1, 2, and 3), we do not need to add anything. Therefore, a direct reduction in X_1 can be made in conjunction with an increase in X_5 and a decrease in X_6.

The direct reduction need not be limited to one unit. It cannot exceed X_1 or X_6 which are to be reduced, nor can it exceed $S_3/2$ (since S_3 is reduced 2 units for each one unit change in X_1), or S_4. The maximum feasible reduction is therefore $[\min(10, 2, 2, 7)] = 2$, where $[X]$ is the largest integer equal to or less than X.

The second solution thus reduces total manpower from 12 to 10 and is optimal since $\Sigma_{i=1}^{n}, X_i S_i = 0$. To generalize the procedure, one develops a trial solution by reducing X_1 by 1, increasing any X_i as necessary to maintain a feasible solution, and decreasing any $X_i > 0$ for which $X_i S_i > 0$. Then one makes the changes by the largest integer less than the least of the X_i being reduced, while maintaining non-negative slack for all S_i.

45.4.3. Indirect reduction

When no direct reduction is possible, we may still be able to shift slack advantageously so that a reduction can be made at the succeeding step. Consider Example 4. In this case, there is no net reduction, only a rearrangement of slack. The net result is simple – the first pair of changes ($X_1 - 1$ and $X_2 + 1$) moves one unit of slack form S_1 to S_5; the second pair of changes ($X_5 - 1$ and $X_6 + 1$) moves the slack from S_5 to S_2. Thus, the net result is to move slack from S_1 to S_2. There is no point in moving the full 4 units from S_1. It is more useful to move only 2 units, thus maintaining $S_1 = 2$ so that a net reduction in X_1 can be made. The third solution is optimal.

45.5. Special Case – n a multiple of p

Suppose n, the number of periods per cycle, is a multiple of p, the number of periods per tour. Two integers a and b are said to be in a congruent relationship modulo p if they have the same remainder when divided by p. Under a congruence relation modulo p, the set

$n=7 \quad p=4$

		Initial Solution		Changes in Solution			
i	R_i	X_i	S_i				
1	10	10	4	-1		-1	+1
2	10	0	0	-1	+1		+1
3	8	0	2	-1	+1		
4	8	0	2	-1	+1		
5	4	4	0		+1	-1	
6	4	0	0			-1	+1
7	3	0	1			-1	+1

i	R_i	X_i	S_i	X_i	S_i
1	10	8	2	6	0
2	10	2	2	2	0
3	8	0	2	0	0
4	8	0	2	0	0
5	4	2	0	2	0
6	4	2	0	2	0
7	3	0	1	0	1

Example 4

of periods n is partitioned into p distinct sets, or equivalence classes, i.e. each period belongs to one of the p equivalence classes depending on its remainder when divided by p. (See [6], p. 87 for details).

Any direct reduction of a solution involves removal of an equal amount of slack from each of the p equivalence classes and any shifting of slack can only be accomplished within equivalence classes. To see this, first suppose that any changes do not overlap, i.e. affect the same period. It is clear that each reduction removes 1 from each equivalence class (since it affects p consecutive periods) and each addition adds 1 to each equivalence class. Thus a direct reduction of Y units will reduce the slack in each equivalence class by Y units. Similarly, a slack shift will reassign slacks but maintain the total slack per equivalence class to be the same as before.

Now suppose any reductions and additions do overlap. The periods of overlap are obviously in the same equivalence class for both the reduction and addition. When these equal cancellations per equivalence class, are subtracted from the basically equal reductions and additions, the result is still an equal change in each equivalence class, i.e. a reduction of all by a single amount (which is positive for a direct reduction, and zero for a slack shift). No net reduction can ever be effected without a reduction in each equivalence class. Thus, it is clear that if the total slack in any equivalence class is zero, no improvement can be made. Thus we have an additional sufficient condition for optimality $\Sigma S_k = 0$ where S_k are the members of the same equivalence class modulo p.

The application of the method will be illustrated for the important practical case of scheduling 8 hour tours per cycle of 24 hours.

Example 5 *Example 6*

n=24 p=8

i	R_i	X_i^1	X_i^2	X_i^3	S_i^3	R_i	X_i^1	X_i^2	S_i^2	
1	99	99	77	53	0	77	77	39	21	
2	47	0	0	0	52	74	0	0	6	
3	8	0	0	0	91	57	0	0	12	
4	76	0	0	0	23	39	0	0	0	*
5	21	0	0	0	78	32	0	0	7	
6	57	0	0	0	37	36	0	0	3	
7	77	0	0	24	0	34	0	0	5	
8	54	0	0	0	23	27	0	0	12	
9	96	96	96	72	0	37	37	37	0	
10	2	0	0	0	94	54	17	17	0	
11	73	0	0	0	23	54	0	0	0	
12	76	0	0	0	20	71	17	17	0	*
13	56	0	0	0	40	57	0	0	14	
14	98	2	2	2	0	51	0	0	20	
15	68	0	0	0	6	44	0	0	27	
16	5	0	0	0	69	35	0	0	36	
17	45	43	43	43	0	51	17	17	0	
18	45	0	0	0	0	52	18	18	0	
19	19	0	0	0	26	63	11	11	0	
20	37	0	0	0	8	76	30	30	0	*
21	25	0	0	0	20	51	0	0	25	
22	48	5	5	5	0	57	0	0	19	
23	89	41	41	41	0	50	0	0	26	
24	25	0	0	0	64	68	0	0	8	

* Total slack in the same equivalence class is zero.

45.5.1. Solutions for 8 hour tours per 24 hour cycle

To illustrate this procedure, two examples constructed from two digit random numbers are given below. Note that example 5 required two iterations to reach the optimality criteria ($\Sigma_{i=1}^{n} X_i S_i = 0$) and example 6 required one iteration to reach the alternate optimality condition that the sum of the slacks in one of the equivalence classes is zero. Example 5 was picked from a set of six problems with random requirements, and example 6 is based on the requirements of example 5 when smoothed by using a three point moving average. The average number of iterations required for optimality was five for the problems with random requirements, and 1.2 for the smoothed ones. The examples with smoothed requirements seem closer to practical problems than the random value example.

45.5.2. Why the procedure works

The insight that slack can be shifted only within equivalence classes provides a means of understanding why the procedures of direct reduction and slack shifting will lead to improvements in the solution. The trial reduction in X_1 reduces slack in modulo class 1 and in succeeding classes up to k, (k being the period for which slack is already zero and for which an addition to X_k must be made in order to maintain a feasible solution). This addition provides the opportunity for a reduction at X_9 (which has been increased by one net unit of slack) or a succeeding X_i. This reduction will affect period $k + 8$ but the addition at X_k will not.

Suppose $S_{k+8} > 0$. Then the slack in modulo class k can be removed (if a direct reduction is possible) or shifted to S_{k+16} and then to S_k by adding to $X_r (10 < r \leqq 17)$ as necessary, and reducing X_{17} or a succeeding value and adding to $X_m (18 < m \leqq 24)$ as necessary. Next suppose $S_{k+8} = 0$. Now, if $S_{16} = 0$, then the previous solution was optimal since all three periods in modulo class k were zero. If $S_{k+16} > 0$, then its slack can be shifted to S_k. Thus, wherever there is an $S_i > 0$ in the modulo class for which $S_k = 0$, the procedure will shift the slack to S_k. Recall that when all $S_i (i = 1 \text{ to } 8)$ are greater than zero, a direct reduction in X can be made while maintaining a feasible solution.

45.6. A conjecture

When p and n have a common factor, slack can only be shifted within modulo classes. Therefore, it seems that schedules with p and n relatively prime, are inherently more efficient. When p and n are relatively prime, all periods are in the same equivalence class and slack can potentially be shifted from any period to any other period. Although not all of this potential is realizable (since possible shifts depend on the pattern of non-zero X_i and S_i) there is more flexibility than in the situation where p and n have a common factor q and the periods fall into q equivalence classes. In theory, at least, a greater efficiency could be capitalized upon by scheduling employees to work for 480 consecutive minutes per tour and specifying requirements per minute for 1439 (a prime number) minutes leaving one minute, e.g. 2:00 a.m. to 2:01 a.m., per day uncovered.

Examples 7 and 8 illustrate the principle conjectured above. In example 7 the optimal solution has 166 tours to cover requirements for 6 periods with each tour two periods long. This is restructured into example 8 where each period in example 7 is split into four parts and one part with the lowest requirement is dropped to obtain a 23 period cycle with each tour 8 periods long. The optimal solution requires only 158 tours, a reduction of about 5 percent, although requirements were only reduced by about 3 percent (32 out of 1260).

n=6 p=2

i	R_i	X_i	S_i
		Optimal Solution	
1	77	73	0
2	74	1	0
3	57	56	0
4	39	0	17
5	32	32	0
6	36	4	0
		166	

Example 7

n=23 p=8

i	R_i	X_i (Optimal Solution)	S_i (Optimal Solution)
1	77	41	0
2	77	8	0
3	77	8	0
4	77	8	0
5	74	9	0
6	74	0	0
7	74	0	0
8	74	0	0
9	57	24	0
10	57	8	0
11	57	8	0
12	57	8	0
13	39	0	9
14	39	0	9
15	39	0	9
16	39	0	9
17	32	8	0
18	32	8	0
19	32	8	0
20	36	12	0
21	36	0	0
22	36	0	0
23	36	0	0
		158	

References

1. Baker, K. R., 'Scheduling a Full Time Workforce to Meet Cyclic Staffing Requirements', *Management Science*, vol. 20, no. 12 (1974), pp. 1561–1568.
2. Baker, K. R., Crabill, T. B., and Magazine, M. J., 'An Optimal Procedure for Allocating Manpower with Cyclic Requirements', *A.I.I.E. Transactions*, vol. 5, no. 2 (1973).
3. Chong, S. C. and Giglio, R. J., 'Manpower Scheduling Models in Service Operations', *ORSA/TIMS*, Miami (November 1976).
4. Guha, D. K., 'An Optimal Procedure for Allocating Manpower with Cyclic Requirements: General Case', *ORSA*, San Juan (October 1974).
5. Guha, D. K. and Browne, J., 'Optimal Scheduling of Tours and Days Off', *ORSA/TSS Workshop on Automated Techniques for Scheduling of Vehicle Operators for Urban Public Transportation Services*, Chicago (April 1975).
6. Pettofrezzo, A. J. and Byrkit, D. R., *Elements of Number Theory*, Prentice Hall (1970).
7. Rothstein, M., 'Scheduling Manpower by Mathematical Programming', *Industrial Engineering*, vol. 4, no. 4 (1972), pp. 29–33.
8. Segal, M., 'The Operator Scheduling Problem: A Network Flow Approach', *Operations Research*, vol. 22, no. 4 (July 1974).
9. Tibrewala, R., Doshi, B., and Browne, J., 'Optimal Scheduling of Two Consecutive Work Periods', *Conference on the Disaggregation Problem*, Columbus (1977).
10. Tibrewala, R., Phillipe, D., and Browne, J., 'Optimal Scheduling of Two Consecutive Idle Periods', *Management Science*, vol. 10, no. 1 (1972), pp. 71–75.
11. Wagner, H. M., *Principles of Operations Research*, Prentice Hall (1969).

46. Heuristic work force scheduling with variable shift lengths and labor productivity differences: a case study of encoder staffing

VINCENT A. MABERT

Abstract

This paper illustrates heuristic work shift scheduling procedures to schedule the proof and encoder work force in a commercial bank to handle daily check loads. The scheduling and check processing problem is described in detail, indicating the factors that contribute to this complex problem. Seven linear program heuristics are described that provide solutions to the shift scheduling decision. The results of the study show that the heuristic procedures provide good solutions. Also, there is a statistically significant difference in performance of the heuristics under different operating conditions.

46.1. Introduction

This paper investigates the use of heuristic procedures for shift scheduling of check proof and encoder machine operators in commercial banks. Scheduling this work force presents a complex problem to management that is characterized by (1) work loads that vary over the course of the day, day of week, and seasonally; (2) the available time to process checks is restricted to a few hours before opportunity costs are incurred; (3) overlapping work shift schedules are present; (4) full and part-time personnel are utilized; (5) wage and productivity differentials are present for various work force categories; (6) different shift schedule patterns are possible that involve various lengths, start times, and rest periods; and (7) equipment restrictions are present, limiting the number of workers that could be effectively scheduled. The importance of this problem is highlighted by the number of people involved, since many banks in larger metropolitan areas employ over a hundred workers just for this task. For example, banking giants like First National City

Bank have over two hundred encoder machines, while Chemical Bank utilizes over one hundred and fifty. Even moderate size banks like Cleveland Trust and Indiana National employ between forty to eighty encoders in their check processing department.

Check processing in commercial banking is an important operation where the number of checks and the cost to handle checks should increase in the future. Gambs [2] estimates a cost of $.30 per check for commercial banking costs for the writing, mailing, receiving, and processing of checks. This cost should increase in the future due to increasing work force costs that all banks are experiencing. Departments processing checks shall also increase in size. The number of checks written from 1970 to 1974 increased at an annual rate of 7 percent [11]. If this rate continues, check volumes should double in ten years. Even with an increasing use of Electronic Funds Transfer Systems (EFTS), work loads on the traditional check processing departments should remain heavy. Thus, effective scheduling of the work force is important in maintaining good service and keeping costs under control.

The development of daily work schedules involves three stages. Stage One requires the forecasting of daily and within day work loads. Stage Two requires the converting of the expected work loads to the appropriate number of operators, their shift starting times, and their work schedules to meet the forecasts. Stage Three requires the assigning of individual operators to particular work shifts in the schedule.

This paper deals with Stage Two, determining appropriate shift schedules. Prior work has been done in Stage One. Boyd and Mabert [1] discuss one approach for forecasting daily proof and encoding work while Hill and Mabert [3] suggest a different approach for individual branch work. Svestka [12] illustrates how daily forecasts can be converted to within day work load profiles. This load profile is controlled by the courier routes. Shorter routes provide a more constant flow of work but are less efficient, while longer routes cause work to arrive in large volume but at discrete points. The assignment of individuals to particular work shifts is discussed by Luce [6] and Miller [7].

Moondra [8] models the Stage Two decision using a linear programming formulation allowing for fractional assignments. His goal is to minimize labor costs subject to meeting all the work load requirements in each period. Therefore, the work force capacity in any period must be greater than or equal to the work available. Such an assumption misrepresents the true situation. Work available in a period does not need to be processed in that period. Rather, it may be inventoried to a later period and processed then. This paper presents an alternate formulation that provides feasible integer solutions where the sum of operating and opportunity costs are minimized.

We shall initiate our discussion by describing the key elements that comprise the scheduling of encoder operators. Then, a mixed integer linear programming formulation is presented based upon the problem structure. Next, heuristic procedures are described that select the appropriate set of work schedules from a set of feasible schedules. Finally, a comparison of the heuristic methods is made for different work load levels, arrival patterns, and available process time.

46.2. Shift scheduling

The arrival of work requiring encoding a central bank operations is not uniform over the day. On the contrary, most work arrives at

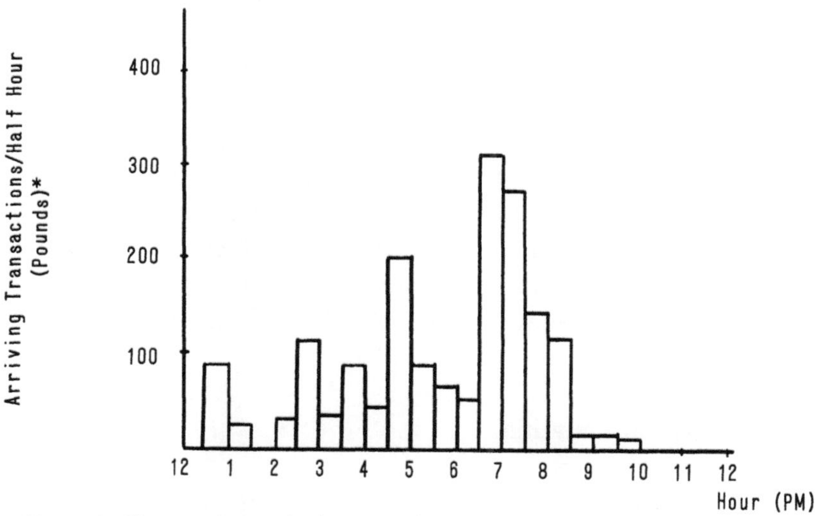

Figure 1. Transaction arrival pattern for Chemical Bank for April 4, 1976.

*There are 300 to 375 transactions per pound.

the end of the day. Figure 1 illustrates a typical day for Chemical Bank where over 50 percent of their work arrives after 6 p.m. This late arrival creates tremendous pressure on the system to process this work quickly, since dispatch deadlines are just a few hours away. For example, Chemical Bank has dispatches occurring between 6 and 11 p.m., while smaller banks like Lafayette National Bank have one dispatch occurring at 9 p.m. However, whether one or multiple dispatches are present, they both require quick processing of transactions since they only have a limited time to process this work.

Unprocessed transit checks represent opportunity costs for the bank. For example, checks drawn against one bank and cashed at another must be processed before the cashing bank can receive these funds from the other bank. At Citibank the holdover has been as high as $30 million on some days [9]. This represents a $3 million annualized opportunity cost when money can be loaned at 10 percent. The sooner the checks are processed, the quicker the funds are put to use to earn a return.

Of course, the processing of checks involves efficient management of the work force and equipment to keep operating and opportunity costs low. This requires effective daily shift scheduling of the work force. Many banks use both full and part-time workers to process checks, allowing management the option of only employing individuals for a fraction of a normal shift, since there is a four to five hour peak load period. Generally, full-time shifts are for eight hours with half hour lunch and one or two fifteen minute rest breaks. Part-time encoders' shifts range from as little as three hours up to five to six hours. Shorter shift workers receive one break while longer shifts, such as six hours, get two rest breaks. Determining the shift schedules for individual operators to meet work load requirements in Figure 1 involves establishing the starting and ending time for individuals as well as breaks throughout the shift.

46.3. Problem formulation

The determination of the number of workers to employ at different times during the day can be stated as a mixed integer problem. The objective function requires the minimization of the wage and opportunity costs, subject to the work load and encoding machine availability. The model is:

$$\text{Min } Z = \sum_{jk} C_{jk}X_{jk} + \sum_{t} C'_t Y_t \tag{1}$$

subject to:

$$\sum_{jk} a_{tjk}X_{jk} + \sum_{t}(Y_t - Y_{t-1}) \geqq b_t \quad t = 1, 2, \ldots, T \tag{2}$$

$$Y_T = 0 \tag{3}$$

$$\sum_{jk} a'_{tjk}X_{jk} \leqq M_t \quad t = 1, 2, \ldots, T \tag{4}$$

$$X_{jk} = \text{integer} \tag{5}$$

$$Y_t \geqq 0 \tag{6}$$

where:

X_{jk} = the number of j type workers assigned to work shift k.
Y_t = the number of unprocessed items at the end of period t.
C_{jk} = the cost per worker j to work shift k.
C'_t = the opportunity cost of an unprocessed item missing its deadline at time t.
a_{tjk} = the process rate (in items/period) for worker j assigned to shift k for period t.
a'_{tjk} = a zero/one element in the matrix, indicating the absence (zero) or presence (one) in period t of worker j assigned to shift k.
b_t = the number of items arriving in period t and available for processing.
M_t = the number of available encoding machines in period t.
T = the number of periods in the work horizon.

Equation (1) represents the combined wage cost ($C_{jk}X_{jk}$) and opportunity cost ($C'_t Y_t$) to be minimized. The variable X_{jk} indicates the k available work shifts for the j labor classes. A shift is defined by the start and finish times of a worker, as well as the break times. For example, X_{11} would indicate class one could work from 11 a.m. to 7 p.m., while X_{12} would indicate a noon to 8 p.m. shift for full-time encoders. On the other hand, X_{21} and X_{22} could mean work shifts of 11 a.m. to 3 p.m. and noon to 4 p.m. respectively for part-timers.

The number of assigned workers to each shift is multiplied by the appropriate shift wage to obtain the total wage cost.

The opportunity cost is represented by the number of uncoded items missing the clearance time, multiplied by the opportunity cost. Now, C_t' equals zero in all periods except the cut-off period(s), since work held over between periods does not result in an opportunity cost until it misses the clearance period. For example, if period 10 is the deadline time, then all unprocessed work available at the end of period 10 is charged the opportunity cost of foregone interest.

Equation (2) indicates the inventory identity relationship of beginning inventory, plus new arrivals, minus process capacity equals ending inventory. Now, a_{tjk} is the process rate (items/period) in period t for one worker j assigned to shift k, where Σ_{jk}, $a_{tjk}X_{jk}$ represents the total capacity available in period t to process the newly arrived work b_t and the prior period's holdover volume (Y_{t-1}).

Equation (3) requires that all work be done by the end of the planning period, even though the availability deadline has passed. Banks update their customer's accounts each night, thus requiring all items be encoded and available for processing before the next operating day. All work processed after the deadline is assigned a cost of $C_t' = 0$.

Finally, equation (4) ensures that the number of workers scheduled in a period t does not exceed the available encoding equipment. Each encoding machine requires one worker to operate it.

46.4. Problem setting

Each bank has its own employment, organization and institutional policies, and customers. This fact prevents one from defining a single environment that is representative of all banks throughout the country. Therefore, we shall describe one medium size bank's encoding operation. The following characteristics are present.

1. The manager finds it convenient to plan for eight, six, four and three hour shift lengths.
2. Full-time personnel working the six to eight hour schedules

receive a higher wage package and are more productive than part-time workers yielding the following data:[1]

Shift length	Capacity (items/shift)	Wage/ hours	Wage/ shift	Cost/ item
8 hours	6750	$5.25	$42.00	.00622
6 hours	4950	$5.25	$31.50	.00636
4 hours	2625	$4.25	$17.00	.00647
3 hours	1925	$4.25	$12.75	.00662

3. The expected opportunity cost for an item missing a deadline is $.01748. This is based upon the number of transit checks, interest rate, and transit value.
4. Even though multiple dispatches are present, one time (9:30 p.m.) represents the main time where 95 percent of all work must be done. Since sorting, microfilming, and bundling must be done by dispatch time, thus the encoding department's cut-off time is 7 p.m.
5. One hour time intervals for estimating work loads and determining the beginning and ending times of shifts for staffing are used.
6. Rest breaks last fifteen minutes and dinner breaks are half an hour. The exact timing of these breaks is controlled by the floor supervisor. The breaks are reflected in productivity reductions of the work force.
7. Work loads range from 100,000 to 200,000 items per day, arriving between the first and tenth hour.
8. Thirty-five encoding machines are present, providing an upper bound on the number of individuals that can be assigned.
9. The work day for the encoding department runs from 11 a.m. to midnight, or thirteen hours in length. This allows for 35 potential overlapping work schedules for the thirteen hour work interval. There are six different eight-hour shift start times, eight different six-hour shifts, ten different four-hour, and eleven different three-hour shift times that comprise the complete set of available schedules, from which a feasible subset will be selected.

1. Moondra [8] suggests that part-timers may be more economical on a wage basis, but absenteeism, scheduling, and turnover problems should also be considered that reduce their productivity.

46.5. Scheduling heuristics

With a work load forecast developed, an encoding shift schedule can be prepared. Henderson and Berry [3] indicate that linear programming heuristics are feasible methods for work force shift scheduling, using 30 to 50 shift schedules. Therefore, we can use a linear programming formulation of equations (1) through (4) to initiate one's search for satisfactory and feasible work shift schedules. When using this formulation, the theoretical minimum cost (C^*) can be determined. However, fractional assignments are made under this approach. Seven heuristics are presented that transform the linear program solution into an integer one. These heuristics involve the use of construction and exchange procedures. In all cases, the final solution must be within the inventory and machine limits of equations (3) and (4) to be feasible.

1. Truncate + Add Heuristic (TADD):
The TADD heuristic transforms the linear programming solution into a feasible solution in two steps. Step one truncates or rounds down all fractional solutions. Then one worker is added sequentially to each work shift schedule (X_{jk}). Any addition violating the machine constraint is given a large penalty cost. The addition that provides the best improvement that is feasible is incorporated into the Solution Work Schedule (SWS). This procedure is repeated until no cost reduction is obtained. Ending inventory conditions are checked and additional workers are sequentially assigned until the ending position reaches zero. Again, only the lowest cost solution is incorporated into SWS.

2. Truncation + Add + Swap One Heuristic (TAS1):
This heuristic begins with the solution produced by the TADD heuristic and attempts to improve it. One-for-one swaps or exchanges are made between work shift schedules to obtain improvement. The heuristic evaluates all one-for-one swaps. The feasible exchange with the greatest improvement is incorporated in the SWS. Then all one-for-one swaps are again evaluated. This sequence continues until no improvement has been found.

3. Truncation + Add + Swap Two Heuristic (TAS2):
This heuristic starts with the solution produced by the TADD. This

heuristic then considers all one-for-one feasible exchanges and incorporates all improvements. When no improvement occurs then two-for-one swaps are considered. Since the economics of the operators bias the linear program solution to employing longer shifts, we systematically removed one worker from one schedule and added two to another. When improvement was obtained, this swap was added to SWS. Then, one-for-one and two-for-one exchanges are repeated in sequence until no improvements are obtained.

4. Truncation + Add + Swap Three Heuristic (TAS3):
This is similar to the TAS2 heuristic, except that it now considers feasible three-for-one swaps between shifts. It cycles between one-for-one, two-for-one, three-for-one exchanges until no improvement has been obtained over the current SWS.

5. Truncation + Swap One (TS1):
This heuristic starts by truncating or rounding down the linear program solution. The one-for-one feasible exchanges are evaluated for improvement. TS1 repeats the swap cycle each time it improves SWS until no improvement is attained. Ending inventory requirements of zero are maintained. If they are greater than zero, the TADD heuristic is employed until zero inventories are attained.

6. Truncation + Swap Two (TS2):
This heuristic is similar to the TS1 heuristic. It considers swaps where one worker is removed and two are added to another schedule. It follows the same cycle sequence of the TAS2 heuristic. Again, only feasible solutions are incorporated.

7. Truncation + Swap Three (TS3):
The TS3 heuristic considers feasible three-for-one swaps between shifts schedules. This rule checks for improvement at each stage like the TAS3 heuristic. If improvement is obtained, it returns to one-for-one exchanges. Again, the evaluation terminates when no improvement has been recorded at any stage.

46.6. Experimental comparisons

An experimental analysis was conducted to determine both the solution quality and computational performance of the scheduling heuristics over a wide range of problem parameters. The experimental design consisted of changes in three problem characteristics: (1) the work load (three levels), (2) the work load arrival rate as definite by the slope (three levels), and (3) the work horizon length (2 levels). Each combination of factor settings in the design had four randomly generated hour to hour variations. This provided a design (3 × 3 × 2 × 4) containing 72 observations for each heuristic. The solution quality was measured by dividing the heuristic scheduling cost solution by the linear program scheduling cost. This provides a measure of percent cost above theoretical minimum. The computational efficiency of the various heuristics is measured in terms of computer time (CDC 6500 CPU times in seconds).

Factor Setting:

Factor 1: Three levels of work loads are set in this analysis: 100,000; 150,000; and 200,000 items per day. This provided a measure of performance as more 'strain' was placed on the department.

Factor 2: Three arrival rates were set as a function of the slope. A positive, zero and negative arrival rate were posed. The positive and negative slopes changed at a rate of 10 percent per hour, where work could start arriving in the first hour, but could not arrive after the tenth hour. Since these slopes are at constant rates, four within-day profiles were randomly generated, with coefficients of variation ranging from .25 to 1.25.

Factor 3: Two cut-off times were set, one in the seventh hour and the other in the ninth, providing a two hour difference in available time to complete work without incurring the foregone opportunity cost.

46.7. Experimental results

Table 1 presents a comparison of the heuristics cost performance. Each cell entry represents the average percent penalty cost above the theoretical linear programming minimum (C^*). A quick glance shows that the average heuristic solution is within two percent of the minimum for each day solved. In absolute terms, this represents

Table 1. The average penalty cost above theoretical mininum*.

Demand level	Slope	TADD	TAS1	TAS2	TAS3	TS1	TS2	TS3
				Work horizon 1				
	1	1.29%	1.29%	1.29%	.84%	1.29%	1.18%	.73%
100000	2	1.92	1.92	1.92	1.45	1.92	1.07	.52
	3	1.33	1.33	1.18	1.18	1.33	.97	.68
	1	.35	.35	.35	.35	.35	.37	.38
150000	2	.86	.86	.86	.60	1.05	.44	.44
	3	1.16	1.16	.55	.45	1.21	.55	.38
	1	.51	.34	.34	.34	.64	.55	.40
200000	2	1.06	1.06	1.06	1.06	1.06	.13	.13
	3	.57	.57	.57	.57	.57	.83	.83
Average		1.01	.99	.90	.76	1.05	.68	.50
				Work horizon 2				
	1	1.61	1.61	1.61	1.01	1.61	1.25	.65
100000	2	1.57	1.48	1.57	.88	1.57	1.14	.60
	3	1.22	1.22	1.22	.77	1.29	1.02	.72
	1	.36	.36	.36	.36	.36	.37	.39
150000	2	.56	.28	.28	.28	.66	.36	.36
	3	.57	.57	.30	.30	.57	.47	.40
	1	.40	.40	.40	.40	.40	.40	.40
200000	2	.48	.44	.48	.36	.48	.44	.36
	3	.43	.43	.43	.43	.43	.26	.26
Average		.80	.76	.74	.53	.82	.63	.46

*The average percent penalty cost is calculated as

$$\text{Cost} = \frac{(100)\text{ Heuristic Solution}}{\text{LP Solution}} - 100$$

Four observations were used to calculate each cell entry.

between \$12 and \$30, since daily solution costs ranged between \$600 and \$1500.

Table 2 lists the standard deviation of the percent above C^*. Again, note that all values are less than one percent. Thus, we see that all solutions are clustered close together.

An analysis of variance was conducted on the results of this study. Listed in Table 3 are the main and two-way interaction results. All factors in the experimental design were significant for main effects, with most two-way effects being important. The three and four-way effects were insignificant in this study.

Table 2. The standard deviation of percent penalty cost above theoretical minimum.

Demand level	Slope	TADD	TAS1	TAS2	TAS3	TS1	TS2	TS3
				Work horizon 1				
	1	.62%	.62%	.62%	.32%	.62%	.12%	.17%
100000	2	.30	.30	.30	.85	.30	.92	.18
	3	.39	.39	.72	.72	.39	.63	.36
	1	.01	.01	.01	.01	.01	.01	.02
150000	2	.40	.40	.40	.41	.36	.28	.28
	3	.54	.54	.29	.27	.47	.47	.22
	1	.14	.21	.21	.21	.39	.38	.38
200000	2	.63	.66	.66	.66	.66	.12	.12
	3	.30	.30	.30	.30	.30	.35	.35
				Work horizon 2				
	1	.00	.00	.00	.00	.00	.00	.00
100000	2	.08	.25	.08	.25	.08	.48	.09
	3	.65	.65	.65	.36	.51	.34	.20
	1	.00	.00	.00	.00	.00	.00	.01
150000	2	.50	.09	.09	.09	.70	.11	.11
	3	.45	.45	.10	.10	.45	.24	.03
	1	.00	.00	.00	.00	.00	.00	.00
200000	2	.15	.06	.15	.08	.15	.06	.08
	3	.23	.23	.23	.23	.23	.19	.19

Marginal analyses of factors two, three and four provide interesting insight into performance. First, the presence of a longer work horizon provided for solutions that were closer to the theoretical minimum. This result can be seen in Table 1 by comparing average heuristic performance for horizon one and two. Second, heavier work loads provides solution closer to C^* than lower demand rates. This results from the integerization of the schedule. Low demand results in lower utilization of personnel, as compared to higher work loads. And third, the rate of arrivals showed that negative slope rates provided the lowest cost, while zero slope yielded the highest penalty.

The heuristic rule performance showed that the exchange procedure provided improvement over the TADD heuristic. To test the significance of performance, a Duncan LSD test [4] was conducted on the results. Table 4 shows the grouping of the rules. The values in parentheses indicate overall performance. The results

Table 3. Analysis of variance of heuristic rule performance on percent penalty.

Source of variation	DF	F-value	Significance
Main effects	11	56.5	.001
Heuristic	6	16.2	.001
Work Horizon	1	26.1	.001
Demand Level	2	237.8	.001
Slope	2	11.5	.001
Two-way interaction	38	3.6	.001
Heuristic-work horizon	6	1.0	.387
Heuristic-demand level	12	4.4	.001
Heuristic-slope	12	2.2	.011
Work horizon-demand level	2	3.2	.040
Work horizon-slope	2	12.5	.001
Demand level-slope	4	5.0	.001
Three-way interaction	52	.8	.999
Four-way interaction	24	.6	.999
Residual	378		
Total	503		

illustrate that the three-for-one swapping procedure makes a significant difference in results. We can also see a decrease in performance as the swap ratio decreases to one-for-one. At this point there is no difference between the TADD and one-for-one exchanges.

Table 4. Heuristic rule grouping Duncan LSD procedure.

Group	Grouping
1	TS3 (.483)* TAS3 (.650)
2	TAS3 (.650) TS2 (.660)
3	TS2 (.660) TAS2 (.825)
4	TAS2 (.825) TAS1 (.870) TADD (.908) TS1 (.938)

*Average percent penalty for all observations in study.

Table 5. Computer time requirement of heuristics*

Heuristic Procedure	Lowest Time	Average Time	Highest Time
TADD	4.3	5.5	6.6
TAS1	10.2	11.2	13.6
TAS2	13.6	15.2	17.2
TAS3	10.6	17.3	24.9
TS1	11.4	12.0	14.8
TS2	14.9	17.6	23.1
TS3	14.2	19.7	36.4

2. Attempts to solve this problem using branch-and-bound procedures required between 300 to 400 seconds of computer CPU time for a single problem.

Table 5 shows the computer time requirements for each heuristic, which includes the time used to solve the linear program formulation. As one would expect, the TADD heuristic required the least time. When exchanges between schedules are made, the time increases as the exchange ratio increases. In this case, the TS3 heuristic required the most time to solve problems, requiring about 20 seconds on the average. We noted that computer time increases are matched with improved performance in the heuristic procedure.

46.8. Conclusions

This paper has presented a comparison of heuristic procedures for shift scheduling in the presence of variable shift lengths and productivity differences. The heuristics illustrated here were based upon an improvement procedure, where a linear program formulation of the problem was solved to obtain an initial integer feasible

*All computer times are in seconds, using a CDC 6500. The linear program solution and heuristic time are represented. All programs required 32,000 words of core storage to execute.

2. Attempts to solve this problem using branch-and-bound procedures required between 300 and 400 seconds of computer CPU time for a single problem.

solution. Then different rules were applied to find improved feasible solutions.

Since obtaining optimal integer solutions would require substantial amounts of computer time, the linear program solution (C^*) was used as a basis for comparison.[2] It represented the theoretical minimum or lower bound that could be attained. We see that all heuristic solutions were within two percent of the C^*, implying that the optimal feasible integer solution must lie between C^* and the heuristic. Therefore, linear program based heuristics appear to be excellent solution procedures to solve work force scheduling problems with the seven characteristics outlined in the introduction.

References

1. Boyd, K. and Mabert, V. A., 'A Two Stage Forecasting Model for Check Processing', *Journal of Bank Research* (forthcoming).
2. Gambs, C. M., 'The Cost of the U.S. Payments System', *Journal of Bank Research* (Winter 1976), pp. 240–244.
3. Henderson, W. and Berry, W. L., 'Heuristic Methods for Telephone Operator Shift Scheduling: An Experimental Analysis', *Management Science*, vol. 22 (August 1976), pp. 1372–1380.
4. Mabert, V. A. and Hill, A. V., 'A Combined Causal-Projection Approach for Short Range Forecasts', *International Journal of Production Research* (Forthcoming).
5. Kirk, R., *Experimental Design Procedures for the Behavioral Sciences*, Belmont, California: Brooks/Cole Publishing Co. (1967).
6. Luce, Bill, 'Employee Assignment System', Joint National Meeting of ORSA/TIMS (April 1974).
7. Miller, Holmes E., 'A Personnel Scheduling and Work Assignment Problem', Working Paper, Rensselear Polytechnical Institute, Troy, New York (May 1976).
8. Moondra, S. L., 'An LP Model for Work Force Scheduling for Banks', *Journal of Bank Research* (Winter 1976), pp. 299–301.
9. Newman, Barry, 'Moving Money', *The Wall Street Journal*, vol. 55, no. 165 (June 6, 1975), p. 1.
10. Plaxton, Arthur, 'A Linear Programming Model to Optimally Schedule Check Processing Activities', Presented at the ORSA/TIMS Joint National Meeting (April 1976).
11. Powers, R. W., 'A Survey of Bank Check Volumes', *Journal of Bank Research*, (Winter 1976), pp. 245–256.
12. Svestka, Joseph, 'A System Model for Controlling the Operations of Check Processing in a Branch Bank Network', *Interfaces*, vol. 7, no. 1 (November 1976), pp. 69–79.

GPSR Compliance
The European Union's (EU) General Product Safety Regulation (GPSR) is a set of rules that requires consumer products to be safe and our obligations to ensure this.

If you have any concerns about our products, you can contact us on

ProductSafety@springernature.com

In case Publisher is established outside the EU, the EU authorized representative is:

Springer Nature Customer Service Center GmbH
Europaplatz 3
69115 Heidelberg, Germany

www.ingramcontent.com/pod-product-compliance
Ingram Content Group UK Ltd.
Pitfield, Milton Keynes, MK11 3LW, UK
UKHW041141300926
15471UKWH00011B/85
* 9 7 8 9 4 0 1 5 7 6 3 7 6 *